KEY CASES, COMMENTS, AND QUESTIONS ON

SUBSTANTIVE CRIMINAL LAW

KEY CASES, COMMENTS, AND QUESTIONS ON

SUBSTANTIVE CRIMINAL LAW

HENRY F. FRADELLA, J.D., PhD
The College of New Jersey

Australia • Canada • Denmark • Japan • Mexico • New Zealand • Philippines
Puerto Rico • Singapore • South Africa • Spain • United Kingdom • United States

TABLE OF CONTENTS

INTRODUCTION: SOURCES OF LAW AND THEIR RELEVANCE TO CRIMINAL LAW 1

CHAPTER 1 - AN INTRODUCTION TO CRIME AND PUNISHMENT 2

    A. An Overview of The Principle of Legality 2
        Shaw v. Director of Public Prosecutions, 1962 A.C. 220 2

    B. Punishment and The Principle of Proportionality 4
        Harmelin v. Michigan, 501 U.S. 957 (1991) 6

    C. What to Punish? 13
        Commonwealth v. Bonadio, 415 A.2d 47 (Pa. 1980). 15
        Bowers v. Hardwick, 478 U.S. 186 (1986) 18

CHAPTER 2 - BASIC CONCEPTS OF CRIMINAL LAW 30

    A. The Starting Point for Criminal Law 30
        1. Presumptions 30
        2. Types of Evidence 30
        3. Direct and Circumstantial Evidence 31
        4. Burdens of Proof 32
            Victor v. Nebraska/Sandoval v. California, 511 U.S. 1 (1994) 34

    B. Essential Elements of a Crime: Actus Reus 40
        1. Requirement of a Voluntary Act 40
            People v. Decina, 138 N.E.2d 799 (1956). 41
        2. An Omission as an Actus Reus 44
            State v. Miranda, 715 A.2d 680 (1998) 45

    C. Essential Elements of a Crime: Mens Rea 49
        1. Specific and General Intent Crimes 50
            Thacker v. Commonwealth, 114 S.E. 504 (Va. 1922) 50
            State v. Rocker, 475 P.2d 684 (1970) 52
        2. Mens Rea Under the Model Penal Code 54
            Wetzler v. State, 455 So.2d 511 (Fla. 1984) 55
            State v. Brooks, 658 A.2d 22 (Vt. 1995) 57
            State v. Magby, 969 P.2d 965 (N.M. 1998) 61
            State v. Pittera, 651 A.2d 931 (N.H. 1994) 63
        3. Strict Liability and Vicarious Liability 64
            Commonwealth v. Olshefski, 64 Pa. D. & C. 343 (1948) 65
            People v. Stuart, 302 P.2d 5 (Cal. 1956) 66
            Furek v. The University of Delaware, 594 A.2d 506 (Del. 1991) 69
        4. Transferred Intent 77
            Smith v. State, 419 S.E.2d 74 (Ga. Ct. App. 1992) 78
            State v. Bryant, 447 S.E.2d 852 (S.C. 1994) 79
        5. Causation 80
            People v. Schmies, 44 Cal. App. 4th 38, 51 Cal. Rptr. 2d 185 (1996) 81

CHAPTER 3 THEORIES OF INCHOATE CRIMINAL LIABILITY 86

    A. Attempt 86
        1. Mens Rea for Attempt 86
            Commonwealth v. Dunne, 474 N.E.2d 538 (Mass. 1985) 87

        2. Actus Reus for Attempt 88
             People v Rizzo, 158 N.E. 888 (N.Y. 1927) 89
             Walters v. Maass, 45 F.3d 1355 (9th Cir. 1995) 90
        3. The Defense of Impossibility for the Crime of Attempt 93
             People v. Dlugash, 363 N.E.2d 1155 (N.Y. 1977) 93
        4. The Defense of Abandonment for the Crime of Attempt 99
             People v. Taylor, 598 N.E.2d 693 (N.Y. 1992) 99

   B. Solicitation 101
      State v. Lee, 804 P.2d 1208 (Or. Ct. App. 1991) 101

   C. Facilitation 103

   D. Complicity: Group Criminality, Accomplice Liability, and Post-Offense Charges 103
        1. Actus Reus for Accessorial Liability 104
             Hicks v. United States, 150 U.S. 442 (1893) 104
        2. Mens Rea for Accessorial Liability 108
             People v. Abbott, 84 A.D.2d 11 (N.Y. Sup. Ct. App. Div. 1981) 108
        3. Guilt and Grading Difference Between Principal and Accomplice 110
             United States v. Edmund, 924 F.2d 261 (D.C. Cir. 1991) 111
        4. The Defense of Abandonment 113
        5. Accessories After-the-Fact and Obstruction of Justice 113
             Commonwealth v. Neckerauer, 617 A.2d 1281 (Pa. Ct. App. 1992) 115

   E. Conspiracy 119
        1. Actus Reus for Conspiracy: Bilateral v. Unilateral Agreements 119
             Garcia v. State, 394 N.E.2d 106 (Ind. 1979) 120
        2. Actus Reus for Conspiracy: Necessary Parties and the Wharton Rule 122
             Iannelli v. United States, 420 U.S. 770 (1975) 123
        3. Distinguishing The Number and Types of Conspiracies 129
             United States v. Rosnow, 977 F.2d 399 (8th Cir. 1992) 130
        4. Mens Rea for Conspiracy and Problems with Inferred Intent 133
             People v. Lauria, 251 Cal. App. 2d 471, 59 Cal. Rptr. 628 (1967) 134
        5. Scope of Conspiracy 139
             Pinkerton v. United States, 328 U.S. 640 (1946) 140
        6. Defense of Abandonment 143

CHAPTER 4 - DEFENSES OF EXCUSE I: DEFENSES THAT NEGATE MENS REA 144

   A. Ignorance and Mistake 144
        1. Mistake of Fact 144
             State v. Pelleteri, 683 A.2d 555 (N.J. Super. Ct. App. Div. 1996) 144
        2. Mistake of Law 146
             Cox v. Louisiana, 379 U.S. 559 (1965) 147

   B. Duress, Coercion, and Necessity 149
      Regina v. Dudley & Stephens, 14 QB.D. 273 (1884) 149

   C. Intoxication 153
        1. Voluntary Intoxication: Specific v. General Intent Crimes 154
             People v. Hood, 1 Cal.3d 444, 462 P.2d 370, 82 Cal. Rptr. 618 (1969) 154
        2. Involuntary Intoxication 157
        3. Due Process Considerations 158

CHAPTER 5 - DEFENSES OF EXCUSE II: MENTAL CAPACITY 159

A. Infancy 159
    State v. Linares, 880 P.2d 550 (Wash. Ct. App. 1994) 159

B. Competency to Stand Trial 162
    1. Timing 162
    2. Burdens of Proof 163
    3. Constitutional Implications of Denial of a Hearing 163
        United States v. Loyola-Dominguez, 125 F.3d 1315 (9th Cir. 1997) 163
    4. The Competency Hearing 166
        United States v. Mason, 56 F.3d 403 (2d Cir. 1995) 167
    5. After a Competency Determination 174

C. Insanity 174
    1. Overview 174
    2. Justifications for the Insanity Defense 174
    3. Common Misperceptions Regarding the Insanity Defense 175
    4. The Wild Beast Defense 175
    5. The M'Naghten Rule 176
    6. The Short-Lived Durham Rule 177
    7. The ALI/MPC Affective Test 177
    8. The Modern Federal Formulation of the Insanity Defense 178
    9. Guilty But Mentally Ill & Guilty Except Insane 180
    10. What Is a Mental Disease or Defect? 182
        People v. Bieber, 856 P.2d 811 (Colo. 1993) 183
    11. What is "Wrong"? 189
        State v. Crenshaw, 659 P.2d 488 (Wash. 1983) 189
    12. Abolition of the Insanity Defense: The Mens Rea Approach 194
        State v. Korell, 690 P.2d 992 (Mont. 1984) 194
    13. After an Insanity Verdict 201

D. Diminished Capacity 202
    1. Overview 202
        State v. Galloway, 628 A.2d 735 (N.J. 1993) 203
    2. Beyond Diminished Capacity 207

CHAPTER 6 - DEFENSES OF JUSTIFICATION 210

A. Self-Defense 210
    1. The General Rule on Use of Physical Force in Self-Defense 210
    2. When Self-Defense Is Not Available as a Criminal Defense 211
    3. Special Rules for Use of Deadly Force 211
        People v. Goetz, 68 N.Y.2d 96, 506 N.Y.S.2d, 497 N.E.2d 41 (1986) 212

B. Defense of Others 218
    People v. Young, 11 N.Y.2d 274, 299 N.Y.S.2d 1, 183 N.E.2d 319 (1962). 219

C. Defense of Property 221
    People v. Ceballos, 12 Cal.3d 470, 526 P.2d 241, 116 Cal. Rptr. 233 (1974) 221

D. Law Enforcement and the Use of Force 224
    Tennessee v. Garner, 471 U.S. 1 (1985) 225

E. Battered Women's Syndrome 233
    1. The Cycle of Violence 233
        State v. Kelly, 478 A.2d 364 (N.J. 1984). 233
    2. The Problem with the "Imminent Danger" Requirement 242
        State v. Stewart, 763 P.2d 572 (Kan. 1988) 242

CHAPTER 7 - HOMICIDE 252

A. The Killing of a Person 252
    1. A Life in Being 252
        People v. Greer, 402 N.E.2d 203 (Ill. 1980) 252
    2. Corpus Delicti 255
        People v. Lipsky, 443 N.E.2d 925, 457 N.Y.S.2d 451 (1982) 255

B. Murder 259
    1. Premeditation and Murder in the First Degree 259
        Green v. State, 450 S.W.2d 27 (Tenn. Ct. Crim. App. 1969) 260
    2. Murder in the Second Degree 263
        Brown v. Commonwealth, 975 S.W.2d 922 (Ky. 1998) 263
    3. Felony Murder 265
        State v. Noren, 371 N.W.2d 381 (Wis. Ct. App. 1985) 265
        State v. Lee, 969 S.W.2d 414 (Tenn. Ct. Crim. App. 1997). 268

C. Manslaughter 270
    1. Voluntary Manslaughter 270
        People v. Simpson, 473 N.E.2d 350 (Ill. Ct. App. 1984) 270
    2. Involuntary Manslaughter and Criminally Negligent Homicide 273
        Commonwealth v. Twitchell, 617 N.E.2d 609 (Mass. 1993) 274
    3. Unlawful Act Manslaughter 279

D. Suicide, Assisting Suicide, and Euthanasia 279
    Vacco v. Quill/Washington v. Gluckesberg, 117 S. Ct. 2293 (1997) 280

CHAPTER 8 - RAPE AND SEX-RELATED CRIMES 294

A. Rape and Sexual Assault 294
    1. The Elements of Rape 294
        State v. Smith, 554 A.2d 713 (Conn. 1989). 294
    2. Issues of Proof and Rape Shield Laws 299
        Williams v. State, 681 N.E.2d 195 (Ind. 1997) 300
    3. Modern Sexual Assault/Sexual Battery Laws 303

B. Sodomy 304
    Bowers v. Hardwick, 478 U.S. 186 (1986) 18

C. Fornication and Adultery 305

D. Statutory Rape 305
    Michael M. v. Superior Court of Sonoma County, Cal., 450 U.S. 464 (1981) 305

E. Miscellaneous Sex Offenses 310
    1. Child Molestation 310
    2. Incest 310
    3. Lewd and Lascivious Conduct 310
    4. Prostitution 311

F. Sexually Dangerous Person Laws 311
    Kansas v. Hendricks, 117 S. Ct. 2072 (1997) 311

G. Obscenity, Pornography, and Indecency 317
    Reno v. American Civil Liberties Union, 521 U.S. 844 (1997) 318

CHAPTER 9 - CRIMES AGAINST THE PERSON 328

A. Assault and Battery 328
    United States v. Moore, 846 F.2d 1163 (8th Cir. 1988) 328

B. Child Abuse and Neglect and their Relationship to Other Crimes 331
    1. Child Abuse 331
        State v. Taylor, 701 A.2d 389 (Md. 1997) 332
    2. Child Neglect 336
        Commonwealth v. Twitchell, 617 N.E.2d 609 (Mass. 1993) 274

C. Kidnaping and False Imprisonment 336
    State v. Fulcher, 243 S.E.2d 338 (N.C. 1978) 337

CHAPTER 10 - CRIMES AGAINST PROPERTY AND HABITATION 341

A. Larceny and Embezzlement 341
    Gwaltney v. Commonwealth, 452 S.E.2d 687 (Va. 1995) 342

B. Burglary, Criminal Trespass, and Robbery 344
    Kinsey v. State, 716 S.W.2d 188 (Ark. 1986) 345

C. Arson 346
    Lawrence v. State, 453 S.E.2d 733 (Ga. 1995) 347

INDEX 349

ABOUT THE AUTHOR 350

DEDICATION

For Dr. Robert L.K. Richardson and Dr. SunHee Kim Gertz –
my inspirations at Clark University to have entered the professoriate.

For Brian McIntyre, Adam Shelton, and Jennifer Gifford –
my former students while I was in graduate school who inspired me to stick with it.

And for my criminal law students at TCNJ who continually motivate me to teach with passion.

ACKNOWLEDGEMENTS

I wish to acknowledge the assistance of: Brian McIntyre, J.D., who helped research and write the section of this text on the defense of diminished capacity; Paul Sperco and Michael Kuchma who both assisted in proofreading this book; and Michelle Indoe and Dave DeOliveira who consistently helped me balance its writing with the other demands in life while still making time for fun.

INTRODUCTION: SOURCES OF LAW AND THEIR RELEVANCE TO CRIMINAL LAW

The nearly all of criminal law applicable in the United States has its roots in what is known as English *Common Law*. Accordingly, it is often referred to as Anglos-Saxon or Anglo-American law. Common Law is really nothing more than judge-made law. It first started to appear in feudal England in the eleventh century as means of settling disputes between the estates of Lords. By the time of the reign of King Henry II (1154-1189), the royal court system was established. One of its primary purposes was to insure that the law applied in one part of England was not different from the law applied in another part of the kingdom. Hence, a set of "common" laws would prevail throughout the country.

As the common law developed, judges were called upon to interpret the law as it existed in prior precedent and then apply it in each case that came before them. The method of reasoning they used, based in logical and analytic reasoning, is still used in the courts of England and the United States today. The decisions handed down by judges add to the prior body of judge-made law and subsequently serve as *precedent* for the next dispute. The collective body of judge-made law is "common law."

There are three other main sources of law. *Statutory law* are those laws enacted by a legislative body, such as the U.S. Congress or a state assembly. Today, these laws are *codified* into statutory compilations. U.S. federal laws are codified in the various titles of the United States Code. State laws are similarly codified into state codes.

Both statutory law enacted by legislative bodies and common law made by judges are subject to limitations. The primary limitations on the creation of common and statutory law comes from the U.S. Constitution. *Constitutional law* is, therefore, that body of law which is set forth in the constitution of a government. It sets forth the structure of government and the laws limiting the power to be exercised by that government. In short, constitutional law governs the government.

Finally, there is *administrative law*. Administrative law consists primarily of regulations issued by administrative agencies given the power to enact regulations that carry the force of law by an act of a legislative body. For example, Congress empowers the Federal Trade Commission to make administrative law by issues regulations that govern trade and commerce.

The study of criminal law is a complex mixture of statutory and common law, subject to the limitations of constitutional law. For example, the legislature of your state could not pass a law making it a crime to criticize the governor because the First Amendment of the United States Constitution (via the application of the Fourteenth Amendment for reasons that are beyond the scope of the current discussion) guarantees your right to do so under the "freedom of speech" clause. Keeping in mind such constitutional constraints as the freedom of speech, the right to free association, the right to privacy, the right to be free from unreasonable searches and seizures, and similar constitutional rights, the criminal law sets the outer parameters of acceptable conduct in society. It does so by setting forth that conduct which shall be criminally punishable because it is deemed unacceptable by the body creating the law.

Today, criminal law is codified into the statutory law of the federal government and the code of each U.S. state. These criminal statutes are referred to by various names, but are often called *penal codes* or *criminal codes*. Throughout your study of criminal law, you will most likely focus on the elements of various criminal offenses and the applicable defenses to such crimes. While it is possible to study criminal law by simply examining the penal code of your jurisdiction, criminal law is much more complex. Rarely is law black or white, but it is nuanced into various shades of gray. By exploring the written decisions of trial and appellate court judges, you will begin to see these shades of gray and, therefore, begin to have a deeper understanding of the criminal law in all of its complexities. The goal of this book is to give you sufficient exposure to judicial opinions so that you may reason through the logic (and, perhaps, illogic) of the criminal law as you encounter it in the future as a professional in the justice system.

Henry F. Fradella, J.D., Ph.D.
Author and Professor of Law and Justice

CHAPTER 1
AN INTRODUCTION TO CRIME AND PUNISHMENT

A. An Overview of The Principle of Legality

As discussed in the introduction, modern criminal laws are set forth in penal codes, the codifications of laws setting forth the criminally proscribed acts of a jurisdiction. There are various reasons for this.

Before the late 1800's when the codification of criminal laws became widespread, the common law set forth the criminal law of the land. Under the doctrine of common law crimes which that existed at English common law and in the United States for much of its history, courts were able to impose criminal liability on someone for an act that injured society in some way even though there was no statute expressly prohibiting the conduct in effect at the time the actor engaged in the relevant conduct. While the remnants of the doctrine surface from time to time, the doctrine has all but been abolished in the United States under what is known in philosophical terms as the *principle of legality*.

Under the principle of legality, no one can be punished for an act that is not expressly designated a criminal act by a penal code. In fact, most states' penal codes have explicitly abolished all common law crimes, effectively limiting the imposition of criminal punishment only to those acts expressly deemed illegal in the penal code.

The principle of legality is expressed in the ancient Latin phrase "nulla poena sine lege," meaning no punishment without law. In the United States, the principle of legality has become constitutionally enmeshed with the concept of due process; we must give fair warning to people as to the nature of conduct that will be punished. Accordingly, under the Fourteenth Amendment, states may not constitutionally punish someone under their respective criminal laws if the laws do not clearly set forth that conduct which is proscribed. Laws that fail to give citizens fair notice of what conduct will be deemed criminal are often struck down as "unconstitutionally vague."

Consider the case of *Shaw v. Director of Public Prosecutions.* While reading it, keep in mind the question, "Is this fair?"

SHAW
v.
DIRECTOR OF PUBLIC PROSECUTIONS

House of Lords
[1962] A.C. 220

Issue: Legality

[Appellant Shaw was convicted, among other things, of the offense "conspiracy to corrupt public morals." He appealed his conviction arguing that there was no such offense known to the common law. The House of Lords, the highest tribunal in Great Britain, affirmed his conviction as follows.]

Viscount Simonds

When the Street Offenses Act of 1959 came into operation if it was no longer possible for *took place* prostitutes to ply their trade by soliciting in the streets, and it became necessary for them to find some other means of advertising the service that they were prepared to render. It occurred to the appellant that he could, with advantage to himself, assist them to this end. The device that he adopted was to publish . . . a magazine or booklet which was called "Ladies' Directory." Is contained the names, addresses, and telephone numbers of prostitutes with photographs of nude female figures, and in some

2

cases, details which conveyed to initiates willingness to indulge not only in ordinary sexual intercourse, but also in various perverse practices.

* * *

I am concerned only to assert what was vigorously denied by counsel for the appellant, that such an offence is known to the common law, and that it was open to the jury to find on the facts of this case that the appellant was guilty of such an offense. I must say categorically that, if it were not so, Her Majesty's courts would strangely have failed in their duty as servants and guardians of the common law. . . . I am no advocate of the right of the judges to create new criminal offenses . . . [b]ut I am at a loss to understand how it can be said either that the law does not recogni[z]e a conspiracy to corrupt public morals or that, though there may not be an exact precedent for such a conspiracy as this case reveals, it does not fall fairly within the general words by which it is described.

In the sphere of criminal law, I entertain no doubt that there remains in the courts of law a residual power to enforce the supreme and fundamental purpose of the law, to conserve not only the safety and order but also the moral welfare of the State, and that it is their duty to guard it against attacks which may be the more insidious because they are novel and unprepared for. . . . Such occasions will be rare, for Parliament has not been slow to legislate when attention has been sufficiently aroused. But gaps remain and will always remain since no one can foresee every way the wickedness of man may disrupt the order of society.

Lord Morris

It is said that there is a measure of vagueness in a charge of conspiracy to corrupt public morals, and also that there might be peril of the launching of prosecutions in order to suppress unpopular or unorthodox views. My Lords, I entertain no anxiety on these lines. Even if accepted public standards may to some extent vary from generation to generation, current standards are in the keeping of juries, who can be trusted to maintain the corporate good sense of the community and to discern attacks upon values that must be preserved. If there were prosecutions which were not genuinely and fairly warranted juries would be quick to perceive this. There could be no conviction unless 12 jurors were unanimous in thinking that the accused person or persons had combined to do acts which were calculated to corrupt public morals.

Lord Reid

In my opinion there is no such general offense known to the law as conspiracy to corrupt public morals. I agree with R.S. Wright, J., when he says . . . "there appear to be great theoretical objections to any general rule that agreement may make punishable that which ought not to be punished in the absence of agreement." And I think, or at least I hope, that it is now established, that the courts cannot create new offences by individuals. . . . [Doing so would have the effect of leaving] it to the judges to declare new crimes and enable them to hold anything which they considered prejudicial to the community to be a misdemeanor. However beneficial that might have been in days when Parliament met seldom or at least only at long intervals it surely is now the province of the legislature and not of the judiciary to create new criminal offenses.

Even if there is still a vestigial power of this kind, it ought not, in my view, to be used unless there appears to be general agreement that the offence to which it is applied ought to be criminal if committed by an individual. Notoriously, there are wide differences of opinion today as to how far the law ought to punish immoral acts which are not done in the face of the public. Some think that the law already goes too far, some that it does not go far enough. Parliament is the [only] proper place to settle that. When there is sufficient support from public opinion, Parliament does not hesitate to intervene. Where Parliament fears to tread it is not for the courts to rush in.

Finally I must advert to the consequences of holding that this very general offence exists. It has always been thought to be of primary importance that our law, and particularly our criminal law, should be certain: that a man should be able to know what conduct is and what is not criminal, particularly when heavy penalties are involved. Some suggestion was made that it does not matter if this offence is very wide: no one would ever prosecute and if they did, no jury would ever convict if the breach was venial. Indeed, the suggestion goes even further: that the meaning and application of the words "deprave" and "corrupt" (the traditional words in obscene libel now enacted in the 1959 Act) or the words "debauch" and "corrupt" in this indictment ought to be entirely for the jury, so that any conduct of this kind is criminal if in the end a jury think it so. In other words, you cannot tell what is criminal except by guessing what view a jury will take, and juries' views may vary and may change with the passing of time.

[But] normally, the meaning of words is a question of law for the court. For example, it is not left to a jury to determine the meaning of negligence: they have to consider on evidence and on their own knowledge a much more specific question – Would a reasonable man have done what this man did? . . . If the trial judge's charge in the present case was right, if a jury is entitled to water down the strong words "deprave," "corrupt," or "debauch" show as merely to mean lead astray morally, than it seems to me that the court has transferred to the jury the whole of its function as a sensor morum, the law will be whatever any jury may happen to think it ought to be, and this branch of the law will have lost all of the certainty which we rightly prize in other branches of our law.

QUESTIONS

1.   The issue in this case, in essence, was whether the passage of a statute making it illegal for prostitutes to solicit on the public streets of England could reasonably be construed to include the conduct with which Shaw was charged. Viscount Simonds and Lord Morris both believed the statute enacted by Parliament was sufficient to allow Shaw's conviction for "conspiracy to corrupt public morals" to be upheld. Lord Reid, on the other hand, disagreed. It was his feeling that if Parliament wanted the crime of conspiracy to corrupt public morals to be criminally punishable, then it should have passed a law proscribing such conduct. With whom do you agree? Why?

2.   Do you think the result in *Shaw* is in accord with the principle of legality, or a departure from it? Why? If the *Shaw* case had occurred in the United States, do you think the outcome would have been different? Why or why not?

B. Punishment and The Principle of Proportionality

What do you think of when you hear the term "***criminal punishment***"? There are many forms it can take. The formal punishments most closely associated with criminal law include fines, restitution, probation, community service, intensive monitoring, home arrest, imprisonment, and even death. There are also informal forms of punishment that go along with the formal criminal sanction such as the social stigma of having been labeled a criminal. This label might not only hold one out for scorn, shape, or other form of disapproval, but also might be a barrier to future employment, result in the loss of voting privileges, and subject the actor to the risk of enhanced punishments for a future offense.

Regardless of the form punishment takes, there are two threshold questions that are largely matters of philosophy, sociology, and psychology that we should be concerned with. First, why punish? What are the purposes we serve in punishing a criminal wrongdoer? Second, what should be punished? The next few cases in this book should serve as springboards for consideration of both questions. Before considering the case law dealing with these questions, there are some important pieces of background information that will be helpful to you. Let's start by considering the main theoretical views on criminal punishment.

There are four main approaches to criminal punishment. The first is ***retribution*** theory. It holds that the criminal justice system should exact retribution – deserved punishment – on the wrongdoer. The approach is one of "just desserts" that is justifiable from both the standpoint of revenge and from the viewpoint of expatiation – suffering helps the wrongdoer atone for sin.

4

The second major approach to criminal punishment is deterrence theory. Classical deterrence theory rejects the notion of retributive justice on the grounds that punishment as an end in and of itself cannot be justified. Instead, deterrence theory is predicated on the utilitarian notion that the criminal law should be used as a tool to control rational decision-making. Thus, it seeks to deter the prohibited conduct by threatening punishment. A rational decision-maker, who theoretically would not like the criminal punishment that would be inflicted upon the actor if he or she committed the crime, would therefore conclude it was in his or her best interests *not* to do the crime, thereby avoiding the unpleasant consequences that would come with criminal punishment.

Deterrence theory suggests that the criminal justice system can effectuate two types of deterrence: general and specific. The *general deterrent* goal of criminal law presumes that the threat of punishment will prevent the general population from engaging in the proscribed conduct. The *specific deterrent* goal of criminal law postulates that those for whom the general deterrent of law was insufficient to prevent them from having engaged in the proscribed conduct should be subjected to punishment so that they are likely to be discouraged from engaging in the proscribed conduct again.

Much scholarly research has demonstrated that the effectiveness of law as a deterrent is dependent upon three factors: severity, certainty, and celerity. The first, *severity*, is concerned with how severe the punishment is. The theory postulates that the more severe the punishment, the less likely the actor is to engage in the proscribed conduct. The second factor, *certainty*, is concerned with how likely the actor is to get away with the crime as opposed to being caught. According to deterrence theory, the more likely the actor is going to be caught, the less likely he or she is to engage in the conduct. Finally, *celerity* is the factor that looks at the swiftness of punishment. The theory suggests that the faster the punishment is inflicted after the offense, the less likely the person is to engage in the proscribed conduct. Conversely, the later or further off the punishment, the more likely the person is likely not to be deterred. Scholars continue to argue which of the three is the most important for criminal law to be an effective deterrent, but legislatures have seized on severity as key, perhaps improperly from a theoretical standpoint. After all, even if the punishment were quite severe, if you had a near perfect chance of not being caught, might you not risk it?

The third major approach to criminal punishment is *rehabilitation* theory. It advocates that the proper aim of the criminal justice system should be to reform the criminal so that he or she can become part of the general social order. The very notion of criminal "corrections" connotes "correcting" the criminal wrongdoer along the lines of rehabilitation theory. While popular in the 1960's and 1970's, and arguably still an important consideration from the viewpoint of correctional system personnel, rehabilitation as justification for imposing criminal punishment fell out of favor with legislators and much of the public-at-large in the 1980's when the "get tough on crime" attitude became prevalent. This punitive attitude toward criminal punishment embraces retribution and deterrence, and, arguably, the fourth main approach to punishment: incapacitation.

Incapacitation theory rejects the ideals of retribution, deterrence, and rehabilitation as either illegitimate or unworkable. Instead, it holds that we simply incapacitate criminals – usually by getting them off the streets – in order to protect society from evil-doers.

The four main theories on punishment help us to answer the question, "Why punish?" But they only go so far in helping us decide how to punish, and they are woefully inadequate in addressing the important question of what should be punished. There are three principles that limit the imposition of punishment. Through your reading of *Shaw v. Director of Public Prosecutions*, you have already been exposed to one of them, the *principle of legality*, closely associated with the notions of due process and fairness. Later in this book (and presumably in your study of criminal law), you will likely spend significant time on the second principle, that of *culpability*. According to this principle, we should punish only those who are responsible for their conduct. Conversely we do not punish those persons who commit an act when they are without legal fault for their conduct. At the heart of this concept are the notions of "free will" and "autonomy." While these constructs are open to attack both philosophically and psychologically, the criminal law accepts these as givens, not necessarily because the law takes them as being "true," but rather because the law operates better if they are accepted as if they were true. Accordingly, as you will learn, the law does not seek to criminally punish involuntary acts or even the deliberate actions of those who are not culpable due to mental illness.

The third limiting principle is referred to as the principle of *proportionality*. The notion that punishment be roughly proportional to the offense has been one of the limiting principles of punishment for hundreds of years. Indeed, *lex talionis*, the very embodiment of the doctrine of proportionality in the phrase "an eye for an eye, a tooth for a tooth," dates back to the Code of Hammurabi.

There is no magic formula to judging the proportionality of crime or punishment. We differentiate what is more severe as compared to what is less severe often using nothing more than common sense. The exercise of reasoned judgment, however, can be guided by certain moral principles.

Consistent with his utilitarian beliefs that the moral thing to do is that which promotes the greatest good for the greatest number of people, Jeremy Bentham argued that the law must be effective in order to be justifiable. Accordingly, he asserts that the law should punish, and can only effectively punish, when three main criteria are met. First, closely related to the principles of legality and culpability, there must be *grounds* for punishment. Where there is no mischief for the law to punish, why punish at all? Second, the punishment must be *effective*. Why bother to punish when punishment will not be effective in stopping the mischievous conduct? Finally the punishment must be *profitable*. Why bother to punish when the results of punishment produce greater harm that the act being punished itself? Using Bentham's three criteria for legal effectiveness is one way that we can attempt to reason through questions of proportionality.

In short, the principle of proportionality is the embodiment of the notion that the punishment should "fit the crime." Doing so not only serves the retributive notion of revenge, but also serves to safeguard the offender from excessive or arbitrary punishment. Toward these ends, some states have specifically provided for the notion of proportionality as part of their penal codes. However, the extent to which, if any, the doctrine of proportionality is embedded in U.S. constitutional and criminal law is open to debate. The following case illustrates the fact that the Justices on the U.S. Supreme Court cannot even agree about the proper role of the doctrine in modern American jurisprudence. Read the case of *Harmelin v. Michigan* and see where you stand on the issue.

Allen HARMELIN, Petitioner v. The State of MICHIGAN, Respondent
501 U.S. 957 (1991).

Justice Scalia

Petitioner was convicted of possessing 672 grams of cocaine [more than 1.5 pounds] and sentenced to a mandatory term of life in prison without possibility of parole. The Michigan Court of Appeals initially reversed his conviction because evidence supporting it had been obtained in violation of the Michigan Constitution. On petition for rehearing, the Court of Appeals vacated its prior decision and affirmed petitioner's sentence, rejecting his argument that the sentence was "cruel and unusual" within the meaning of the Eighth Amendment. The Michigan Supreme Court denied leave to appeal, and we granted certiorari.

The Eighth Amendment, which applies against the States by virtue of the Fourteenth Amendment, provides: "Excessive bail shall not be required, nor excessive fines imposed, nor cruel and unusual punishments inflicted." [T]o use the phrase "cruel and unusual punishment" to describe a requirement of proportionality would have been an exceedingly vague and oblique way of saying what Americans were well accustomed to saying more directly. The notion of "proportionality" was not a novelty (though then as now there was little agreement over what it entailed). In 1778, for example, the Virginia Legislature narrowly rejected a comprehensive "Bill for Proportioning Punishments" introduced by Thomas Jefferson. Proportionality provisions had been included in several state constitutions. There is little doubt that those who framed, proposed, and ratified the Bill of Rights were aware of such provisions, yet chose not to replicate them.

We think it enough that those who framed and approved the Federal Constitution chose, for whatever reason, not to include within it the guarantee against disproportionate sentences that some State Constitutions contained. It is worth noting, however, that there was good reason for that choice. While there are relatively clear historical guidelines and accepted practices that enable judges to determine which modes of punishment are "cruel and unusual," proportionality does not lend itself to such analysis. Neither Congress nor any state legislature has ever set out with the objective of crafting a penalty that is "disproportionate," yet as some of the examples mentioned above indicate, many enacted dispositions seem to be so – because they were made for other times or other places, with different social attitudes, different criminal epidemics, different public fears, and different prevailing theories of penology. This is not to say that there are no absolutes; one can imagine extreme examples that no rational person, in no time or place, could accept. But for the same reason these examples are easy to decide, they are certain never to occur. The real function of a constitutional proportionality principle, if it exists, is to enable judges to evaluate a penalty that some assemblage of men and women has considered proportionate – and to say that it is not. For that real-world enterprise, the standards seem so inadequate that the proportionality principle becomes an invitation to imposition of subjective values.

[First,], the difficulty of assessing gravity is demonstrated in the very context of the present case: Petitioner acknowledges that a mandatory life sentence might not be grossly excessive for possession of cocaine with intent to distribute. But surely whether it is a "grave" offense merely to possess a significant quantity of drugs – thereby facilitating distribution, subjecting the holder to the temptation of distribution, and raising the possibility of theft by others who might distribute – depends entirely upon how odious and socially threatening one believes drug use to be. Would it be "grossly excessive" to provide life imprisonment for "mere possession" of a certain quantity of heavy weaponry? If not, then the only issue is whether the possible dissemination of drugs can be as "grave" as the possible dissemination of heavy weapons. Who are we to say no? The Members of the Michigan Legislature, and not we, know the situation on the streets of Detroit.

[Second,] one cannot compare the sentences imposed by the jurisdiction for "similarly grave" offenses if there is no objective standard of gravity. Judges will be comparing what they consider comparable. Or, to put the same point differently: when it happens that two offenses judicially determined to be "similarly grave" receive significantly dissimilar penalties, what follows is not that the harsher penalty is unconstitutional, but merely that the legislature does not share the judges' view that the offenses are similarly grave. Moreover, even if "similarly grave" crimes could be identified, the penalties for them would not necessarily be comparable, since there are many other justifications for a difference. For example, since deterrent effect depends not only upon the amount of the penalty but upon its certainty, crimes that are less grave but significantly more difficult to detect may warrant substantially higher penalties. Grave crimes of the sort that will not be deterred by penalty may warrant substantially lower penalties, as may grave crimes of the sort that are normally committed once-in-a-lifetime by otherwise law-abiding citizens who will not profit from rehabilitation. Whether these differences will occur, and to what extent, depends, of course, upon the weight the society accords to deterrence and rehabilitation, rather than retribution, as the objective of criminal punishment (which is an eminently legislative judgment). In fact, it becomes difficult even to speak intelligently of "proportionality," once deterrence and rehabilitation are given significant weight. Proportionality is inherently a retributive concept, and perfect proportionality is the talionic law.

[Finally, as for] the character of the sentences imposed by other States for the same crime – it must be acknowledged that that can be applied with clarity and ease. The only difficulty is that it has no conceivable relevance to the Eighth Amendment. That a State is entitled to treat with stern disapproval an act that other States punish with the mildest of sanctions follows a fortiori from the undoubted fact that a State may criminalize an act that other States do not criminalize at all. Indeed, a State may criminalize an act that other States choose to reward – punishing, for example, the killing of endangered wild

7

animals for which other States are offering a bounty. What greater disproportion could there be than that? "Absent a constitutionally imposed uniformity inimical to traditional notions of federalism, some State will always bear the distinction of treating particular offenders more severely than any other State." *Rummel*, 445 U. S., at 282. Diversity not only in policy, but in the means of implementing policy, is the very raison d'etre of our federal system. Though the different needs and concerns of other States may induce them to treat simple possession of 672 grams of cocaine as a relatively minor offense, [Wyoming and West Virginia punish it at six months], nothing in the Constitution requires Michigan to follow suit. The Eighth Amendment is not a ratchet, whereby a temporary consensus on leniency for a particular crime fixes a permanent constitutional maximum, disabling the States from giving effect to altered beliefs and responding to changed social conditions.

The judgment of the Michigan Court of Appeals is affirmed.

Justice Kennedy, with whom Justice O'Connor and Justice Souter join, concurring in part:

I write this separate opinion because my approach to the Eighth Amendment proportionality analysis differs from Justice Scalia's. Regardless of whether Justice Scalia or the dissent has the best of the historical argument, stare decisis counsels our adherence to the narrow proportionality principle that has existed in our Eighth Amendment jurisprudence for 80 years. Although our proportionality decisions have not been clear or consistent in all respects, they can be reconciled, and they require us to uphold petitioner's sentence.

Our decisions recognize that the Cruel and Unusual Punishments Clause encompasses a narrow proportionality principle. We first interpreted the Eighth Amendment to prohibit "greatly disproportioned" sentences in *Weems v. United States*, 217 U.S. 349, 371 (1910). Since *Weems*, we have applied the principle in different Eighth Amendment contexts. Its most extensive application has been in death penalty cases. In *Coker v. Georgia*, 433 U.S. 584, 592 (1977), we held that "a sentence of death is grossly disproportionate and excessive punishment for the crime of rape and is therefore forbidden by the Eighth Amendment as cruel and unusual punishment." We applied like reasoning in *Enmund v. Florida*, 458 U.S. 782 (1982), to strike down a capital sentence imposed for a felony murder conviction in which the defendant had not committed the actual murder and lacked intent to kill.

The Eighth Amendment proportionality principle also applies to noncapital sentences. In *Rummel v. Estelle*, 445 U.S. 263 (1980), we acknowledged the existence of the proportionality rule for both capital and noncapital cases, but we refused to strike down a sentence of life imprisonment, with possibility of parole, for recidivism based on three underlying felonies. In *Hutto v. Davis*, 454 U.S. 370 (1982), we recognized the possibility of proportionality review but held it inapplicable to a 40-year prison sentence for possession with intent to distribute nine ounces of marijuana. Our most recent decision discussing the subject is *Solem v. Helm*, 463 U.S. 277 (1983). There we held that a sentence of life imprisonment without possibility of parole violated the Eighth Amendment because it was "grossly disproportionate" to the crime of recidivism based on seven underlying nonviolent felonies. The dissent in *Solem* disagreed with the Court's application of the proportionality principle but observed that in extreme cases it could apply to invalidate a punishment for a term of years.

Though our decisions recognize a proportionality principle, its precise contours are unclear. This is so in part because we have applied the rule in few cases and even then to sentences of different types. . . . [C]lose analysis of our decisions yields some common principles that give content to the uses and limits of proportionality review.

The first of these principles is that the fixing of prison terms for specific crimes involves a substantive penological judgment that, as a general matter, is properly within the province of legislatures, not courts. Determinations about the nature and purposes of punishment for criminal acts implicate difficult and enduring questions respecting the sanctity of the individual, the nature of law, and the relation between law and the social order. The efficacy of any sentencing system cannot be assessed absent agreement on the purposes and objectives of the penal system. And the responsibility for making these fundamental choices and implementing them lies with the legislature.

The second principle is that the Eighth Amendment does not mandate adoption of any one penological theory. "The principles which have guided criminal sentencing . . . have varied with the times." The federal and state criminal systems have accorded different weights at different times to the penological goals of retribution, deterrence, incapacitation, and rehabilitation. And competing theories of mandatory and discretionary sentencing have been in varying degrees of ascendancy or decline since the beginning of the Republic.

Third, marked divergences both in underlying theories of sentencing and in the length of prescribed prison terms are the inevitable, often beneficial, result of the federal structure. Our federal system recognizes the independent power of a State to articulate societal norms through criminal law. State sentencing schemes may embody different penological assumptions, making interstate comparison of sentences a difficult and imperfect enterprise. And even assuming identical philosophies, differing attitudes and perceptions of local conditions may yield different, yet rational, conclusions regarding the appropriate length of prison terms for particular crimes. Thus, the circumstance that a State has the most severe punishment for a particular crime does not by itself render the punishment grossly disproportionate.

The fourth principle at work in our cases is that proportionality review by federal courts should be informed by objective factors to the maximum possible extent. The most prominent objective factor is the type of punishment imposed. In *Weems*, "the Court could differentiate in an objective fashion between the highly unusual cadena temporal and more traditional forms of imprisonment imposed under the Anglo-Saxon system." In a similar fashion, because the penalty of death differs from all other forms of criminal punishment, the objective line between capital punishment and imprisonment for a term of years finds frequent mention in our Eighth Amendment jurisprudence. By contrast, our decisions recognize that we lack clear objective standards to distinguish between sentences for different terms of years. Although no penalty is per se constitutional, the relative lack of objective standards concerning terms of imprisonment has meant that outside the context of capital punishment, successful challenges to the proportionality of particular sentences are exceedingly rare.

All of these principles – the primacy of the legislature, the variety of legitimate penological schemes, the nature of our federal system, and the requirement that proportionality review be guided by objective factors – inform the final one: the Eighth Amendment does not require strict proportionality between crime and sentence. Rather, it forbids only extreme sentences that are "grossly disproportionate" to the crime.

With these considerations stated, it is necessary to examine the challenged aspects of petitioner's sentence. . . . Petitioner's life sentence without parole is the second most severe penalty permitted by law. It is the same sentence received by the petitioner in *Solem*. Petitioner's crime, however, was far more grave than the crime at issue in *Solem*. The crime of uttering a no account check at issue in *Solem* was one of the most passive felonies a person could commit. It involved neither violence nor threat of violence to any person, and was viewed by society as among the less serious offenses. The felonies underlying the defendant's recidivism conviction, moreover, were "all relatively minor."

Petitioner was convicted of possession of more than 650 grams of cocaine. This amount of pure cocaine has a potential yield of between 32,500 and 65,000 doses. From any standpoint, this crime falls in a different category from the relatively minor, nonviolent crime at issue in *Solem*. Possession, use, and distribution of illegal drugs represents one of the greatest problems affecting the health and welfare of our population. Petitioner's suggestion that his crime was nonviolent and victimless, echoed by the dissent, is false to the point of absurdity. To the contrary, petitioner's crime threatened to cause grave harm to society.

Quite apart from the pernicious effects on the individual who consumes illegal drugs, such drugs relate to crime in at least three ways: (1) A drug user may commit crime because of drug-induced changes in physiological functions, cognitive ability, and mood; (2) A drug user may commit crime in order to obtain money to buy drugs; and (3) A violent crime may occur as part of the drug business or culture. Studies bear out these possibilities, and demonstrate a direct nexus between illegal drugs and crimes of violence. . . . These and other facts and reports detailing the pernicious effects of the drug epidemic in this country do not establish that Michigan's penalty scheme is correct or the most just in any abstract sense. But they do demonstrate that the Michigan Legislature could with reason conclude that the threat posed to the individual and society by possession of this large an amount of cocaine – in terms of violence, crime, and social displacement – is momentous enough to warrant the deterrence and retribution of a life sentence without parole. . . . The severity of petitioner's crime brings his sentence within the constitutional boundaries established by our prior decisions.

Justice White, with whom Justice Blackmun and Justice Stevens join, dissenting:

Justice Scalia concludes that "the Eighth Amendment contains no proportionality guarantee." Accordingly, he says *Solem v. Helm,* 463 U.S. 277 (1983), "was simply wrong" in holding otherwise, as would be the Court's other cases interpreting the Amendment to contain a proportionality principle. Justice Kennedy, on the other hand, asserts that the Eighth Amendment's proportionality principle is so "narrow," that *Solem*'s analysis should be reduced from three factors to one. With all due respect, I dissent.

The language of the Amendment does not refer to proportionality in so many words, but it does forbid "excessive" fines, a restraint that suggests that a determination of excessiveness should be based at least in part on whether the fine imposed is disproportionate to the crime committed. Nor would it be unreasonable to conclude that it would be both cruel and unusual to punish overtime parking by life imprisonment, or, more generally, to impose any punishment that is grossly disproportionate to the offense.

Justice Scalia concedes that the language of the Amendment bears such a construction. His reasons for claiming that it should not be so construed are weak. [He] asserts that if proportionality was an aspect of the restraint, it could have been said more clearly – as plain-talking Americans would have expressed themselves (as for instance, I suppose, in the Fifth Amendment's Due Process Clause or the Fourth Amendment's prohibition against unreasonable searches and seizures).

Justice Scalia argues that all of the available evidence of the day indicated that those who drafted and approved the Amendment "chose . . . not to include within it the guarantee against disproportionate sentences that some State Constitutions contained." Even if one were to accept the argument that the First Congress did not have in mind the proportionality issue, the evidence would hardly be strong enough to come close to proving an affirmative decision against the proportionality component. Had there been an intention to exclude it from the reach of the words that otherwise could reasonably be construed to include it, perhaps as plain-speaking Americans, the Members of the First Congress would have said so. And who can say with confidence what the members of the state ratifying conventions had in mind when they voted in favor of the Amendment? Surely, subsequent state court decisions do not answer that question. . . . In any event, the Amendment as ratified contained the words "cruel and unusual," and there can be no doubt that prior decisions of this Court have construed these words to include a proportionality principle.

Contrary to Justice Scalia's suggestion, the *Solem* analysis has worked well in practice. Courts appear to have had little difficulty applying the analysis to a given sentence, and application of the test by numerous state and federal appellate courts has resulted in a mere handful of sentences being declared unconstitutional. Thus, it is clear that reviewing courts have not baldly substituted their own subjective moral values for those of the legislature. Instead, courts have demonstrated that they are capable of applying the Eighth Amendment to disproportionate noncapital sentences with a high degree of sensitivity to principles of federalism and state autonomy. *Solem* is wholly consistent with this approach, and when properly applied, its analysis affords substantial deference to the broad authority that legislatures necessarily possess in determining the types and limits of punishments for crimes, as well as to the discretion that trial courts possess in sentencing convicted criminals, and will only rarely result in a sentence failing constitutional muster. The fact that this is one of those rare instances is no reason to abandon the analysis.

Two dangers lurk in Justice Scalia's analysis. First, he provides no mechanism for addressing a situation such as that proposed in *Rummel*, in which a legislature makes over-time parking a felony punishable by life imprisonment. He concedes that "one can imagine extreme examples . . . that no rational person, in no time or place, could accept," but attempts to offer reassurance by claiming that "for the same reason these examples are easy to decide, they are certain never to occur." This is cold comfort indeed, for absent a proportionality guarantee, there would be no basis for deciding such cases should they arise.

Second, as I have indicated, Justice Scalia's position that the Eighth Amendment addresses only modes or methods of punishment is quite inconsistent with our capital punishment cases, which do not outlaw death as a mode or method of punishment, but instead put limits on its application. If the concept of proportionality is downgraded in the Eighth Amendment calculus, much of this Court's capital penalty jurisprudence will rest on quicksand.

Justice Kennedy's abandonment of the second and third factors set forth in *Solem* makes any attempt at an objective proportionality analysis futile. The first prong of *Solem* requires a court to consider two discrete factors – the gravity of the offense and the severity of the punishment. A court is not expected to consider the interaction of these two elements and determine whether "the sentence imposed was grossly excessive punishment for the crime committed." Were a court to attempt such an assessment, it would have no basis for its determination that a sentence was – or was not – disproportionate, other than the subjective views of individual judges, which is the very sort of analysis our Eighth Amendment jurisprudence has shunned. Justice Kennedy asserts that "our decisions recognize that we lack clear objective standards to distinguish between sentences for different terms of years," citing *Rummel* and *Solem* as support. But *Solem* recognized that "for sentences of imprisonment, the problem is not so much one of ordering, but one of line-drawing. It is clear that a 25-year sentence generally is more severe than a 15-year sentence, but in most cases it would be difficult to decide that the former violates the Eighth Amendment while the latter does not.

Because there is no justification for overruling or limiting *Solem*, it remains to apply that case's proportionality analysis to the sentence imposed on petitioner. Application of the *Solem* factors to the statutorily mandated punishment at issue here reveals that the punishment fails muster under *Solem* and, consequently, under the Eighth Amendment to the Constitution.

Petitioner, a first-time offender, was convicted of possession of 672 grams of cocaine. The statute under which he was convicted provides that a person who knowingly or intentionally possesses any of various narcotics, including cocaine, "which is in an amount of 650 grams or more of any mixture containing that substance is guilty of a felony and shall be imprisoned for life." No particular degree of drug purity is required for a conviction. Other statutes make clear that an individual convicted of possessing this quantity of drugs is not eligible for parole. . . . There is no room for judicial discretion in the imposition of the life sentence upon conviction. The asserted purpose of the legislative enactment of these statutes was to "stem drug traffic" and reach "drug dealers."

The first *Solem* factor requires a reviewing court to assess the gravity of the offense and the harshness of the penalty. The mandatory sentence of life imprisonment without possibility of parole is the most severe punishment that the State could have imposed on any criminal for any crime, for Michigan has no death penalty. Although these factors are by no means exhaustive, in evaluating the gravity of the offense, it is appropriate to consider the harm caused or threatened to the victim or society, based on such things as the degree of violence involved in the crime and the absolute magnitude of the crime, and the culpability of the offender, including the degree of requisite intent and the offender's motive in committing the crime.

Drugs are without doubt a serious societal problem. To justify such a harsh mandatory penalty as that imposed here, however, the offense should be one which will always warrant that punishment. Mere possession of drugs – even in such a large quantity – is not so serious an offense that it will always warrant, much less mandate, life imprisonment without possibility of parole. Unlike crimes directed against the persons and property of others, possession of drugs affects the criminal who uses the drugs most directly. The ripple effect on society caused by possession of drugs, through related crimes, lost productivity, health problems, and the like, is often not the direct consequence of possession, but of the resulting addiction, something which this Court held in *Robinson v. California*, cannot be made a crime.

To be constitutionally proportionate, punishment must be tailored to a defendant's personal responsibility and moral guilt. Justice Kennedy attempts to justify the harsh mandatory sentence imposed on petitioner by focusing on the subsidiary effects of drug use, and thereby ignores this aspect of our Eighth Amendment jurisprudence. While the collateral consequences of drugs such as cocaine are indisputably severe, they are not unlike those which flow from the misuse of other, [even] legal substances. The "absolute magnitude" of petitioner's crime is not exceptionally serious. Because possession is necessarily a lesser included offense of possession with intent to distribute, it is odd to punish the former as severely as the latter. Nor is the requisite intent for the crime sufficient to render it particularly grave. To convict someone under the possession statute, it is only necessary to prove that the defendant knowingly possessed a mixture containing narcotics which weighs at least 650 grams. There is no mens rea requirement of intent to distribute the drugs, as there is in the parallel statute. Indeed, the presence of a separate statute which reaches manufacture, delivery, or possession with intent to do either, undermines the State's position that the purpose of the possession statute was to reach drug dealers.

The second prong of the *Solem* analysis is an examination of "the sentences imposed on other criminals in the same jurisdiction." Life without parole, the punishment mandated here, is the harshest penalty available [in Michigan]. It is reserved for first-degree murder, manufacture, distribution, or possession with intent to manufacture or distribute 650 grams or more of narcotics; and possession of 650 grams or more of narcotics. Crimes such as second-degree murder, rape, and armed robbery, do not carry such a harsh mandatory sentence. It is clear that petitioner has been treated in the same manner as, or more severely than, criminals who have committed far more serious crimes.

The third factor set forth in *Solem* examines "the sentences imposed for commission of the same crime in other jurisdictions." No other jurisdiction imposes a punishment nearly as severe as Michigan's for possession of the amount of drugs at issue here. Of the remaining 49 States, only Alabama provides for a mandatory sentence of life imprisonment without possibility of parole for a first-time drug offender, and then only when a defendant possesses ten kilograms or more of cocaine. Possession of the amount of cocaine at issue here would subject an Alabama defendant to a mandatory minimum sentence of only five years in prison. Even under the Federal Sentencing Guidelines, with all relevant enhancements, petitioner's sentence would barely exceed ten years. Thus, it appears that petitioner was treated more severely than he would have been in any other State. Indeed, the fact that no other jurisdiction provides such a severe, mandatory penalty for possession of this quantity of drugs is enough to establish "the degree of national consensus this Court has previously thought sufficient to label a particular punishment cruel and unusual."

Application of *Solem*'s proportionality analysis leaves no doubt that the Michigan statute at issue fails constitutional muster. The statutorily mandated penalty of life without possibility of parole for possession of narcotics is unconstitutionally disproportionate in that it violates the Eighth Amendment's prohibition against cruel and unusual punishment. Consequently, I would reverse the decision of the Michigan Court of Appeals.

QUESTIONS

1.   As the *Harmelin* case evidences, whether the principle of proportionality is embodied in some way, shape, or form in the Eighth Amendment's Cruel and Unusual Punishment Clause is unclear. Justice Scalia said no; Justices Kennedy, O'Connor, and Souter said a qualified yes; and Justices White, Blackmun, and Stevens said yes. Whose arguments/analyses do you find most persuasive? Why?

2.   The introduction to this case explained the four main approaches to criminal punishment, all four of which were mentioned by the Justices in the case. Consider the following questions regarding the four main approaches:

(a)   Retribution - Do you agree that criminal punishment should serve a retributive function? Why or why not? Can you justify your position using theoretical material from philosophy and political science?

(b)   Deterrence - Do you feel that criminal law can effectively deter conduct that society deems, via a legislative enactment, to be socially undesirable? Can you think of an example of a criminal law that has effectively deterred you from engaging in conduct in which you might otherwise have engaged? How about one that has *not* been a successful *general deterrent* for you? Are there any that have not even been a successful *specific deterrent* for you? Can you think of an assumption of deterrence theory that, if untrue (or, perhaps when untrue) might undercut the law's ability to serve any deterrent effect?

(c)   Rehabilitation - Do you think that criminal law, via sentencing, can serve to rehabilitate criminal offenders? If so, what are the barriers to effective rehabilitation? If not, why not; and what could be changed to alter your opinion, if anything?

(d)   Incapacitation - Do you feel that the "lock 'em up and throw away the key" approach to the criminal sanction is justifiable? Can you reconcile your answer to that question with the result in *Harmelin*?

3.   Do you agree with the ultimate result in *Harmelin*? Beyond the specifics of the case, should the law contain some guarantee of proportionality? Why or why not? Does the argument raised about federalism – the fact that the United States is comprised of 50 sovereign states – have any influence on your answer to the question? Research the laws of any two U.S. jurisdictions of your choosing in which an act is considered a minor offense in one state and a serious felony in the other. Should it make a difference in terms of the punishment imposed on you where you did the act?

4.   Several years ago, a teenage by the name of Michael Fay was arrested and convicted of an act of vandalizing a car in Singapore. He was sentenced to a term of incarceration and to "caning" – a form of corporal punishment inflicted by a martial arts expert using a rattan cane to the bare buttocks of the person being caned. Do you think Fay's sentence was proportional to his crime? After reading the *Harmelin* decision, do you think such a sentence would be permissible in the United States under the Eighth Amendment? Why or why not? Separate and apart from the issue of whether it would be constitutionally permissible in the U.S., *should* it be? Reason through your response using the four main theories on criminal punishment discussed above as well as the doctrine of proportionality.

C. What to Punish?

Up to this point, we have explored the questions "why punish" and "how severely should be punish?" Whether you come from the perspective of retribution, deterrence, rehabilitation, incapacitation, or some blend of the four main theories regarding the role of criminal punishment, the question we have not yet considered is, arguably, the most practical of the socio-philosophical questions with which the criminal law must deal: what should be criminally punished?

13

The question of what ought to be a crime has been debated in scholarship and around the meal table for decades, if not centuries. Most people would argue that conduct proscribed by the criminal law is "bad," "evil," "immoral," or otherwise "wrong" in some way. But these terms are descriptive of conduct that necessarily depends upon some normative, shared definitions. Take, for example, the commandment "thou shalt not kill." Most of us would agree it is wrong – in a morally normative sense – to kill another human being in cold blood. But what about in war? How about in self-defense? Like it or not, morality, a concept often tied to religious beliefs, plays a big role in deciding what ought to be illegal.

The degree to which the law, the criminal law in particular, ought to be related to conceptualizations of morality is the central focus of what scholars have termed the Hart-Devlin debate. H.L.A. Hart, who advocates a separation of law and morality, asks us to consider three questions: (1) Has society the right to pass judgment at all on matters of morals? In other words, should there be a public morality, or are morals better left to be a matter for private judgment? (2) If society has a right to pass judgment, has it also the right to use the weapon of law to enforce it? (3) If so, ought it use that weapon in all cases, or only in some; and if only in some, on what principles should it be distinguished?

Lord Patrick Devlin, who believes law and morality ought to be closely linked, responds to Hart's three questions as follows: (1) Without such a thing as public morality . . . "without shared ideas on politics, morals, and ethics, no society can ever exist." (2) Accordingly, he asserts, society is entitled, by means of its laws, to protect itself from dangers. Just as society may punish treason to protect itself, it should protect violation of common morality to prevent societal decay. (3) Nothing should be punished by the law that does not lie "beyond the limits of tolerance." But not everything ought to be "tolerated." Devlin cites homosexuality as an example — "the vice is so abominable that its mere presence is an offence." Do you agree?

While an oversimplification, Hart's answers to these questions illustrate that questions of morality invite relativistic answers which are vulnerable to charges of hypocrisy. Accordingly, they are self-defeating, the logical consequence of which is that people lose respect for the law. In turn, this loss of respect for law breeds cynicism and indifference to the criminal law, resulting in both increased violations of law and discriminatory enforcement of law. Given these problems, Hart advocates that society ought only concern itself with breaches of morality when the resultant harm affects someone other than the actor — not the limits of tolerance as advocated by Devlin.

Another problem with criminalizing conduct that lies "beyond the limits of tolerance" is the fact that people have very different tolerance levels! What is acceptable in Los Angeles and New York might not play well in many parts of the mid-western United States. And socio-geography aside, what ought not be tolerated would likely get very different responses from Jesse Jackson and Louis Farrakhan, both of whom are African-American men of the cloth. Ask Jerry Falwell and Larry Flint what lies beyond the limits of tolerance and, for sure, you'll get diametrically opposed viewpoints. It is no different in legislatures, as Newt Gingrich and Barney Frank, two long-time members of the U.S. House of Representatives, have very different viewpoints on the what the law ought to be. So if we use morality as a baseline to set the prescriptions and proscriptions of law, the question becomes, then the question becomes "whose morality?" Hart seeks to avoid this question, to the extent possible, by divorcing law and morality up to the point that one's conduct causes harm to another.

Hart's reference to harm as the gauge by which the criminal law ought to be set is based upon the harm principle, a notion found in the writings of John Stuart Mill, Jeremy Bentham, and other utilitarian philosophers. The harm principle asserts that if no harm is caused to another's autonomy – his right to life, liberty, property, and to pursue happiness – then the law ought not to interfere with the conduct, even if the conduct is undesirable in the eyes of most people.

The Hart-Devlin debate, and therefore questions surrounding the legislation of morality, should become more clear to you after reading the next two cases in this book: *Commonwealth v. Bonadio* and *Bowers v. Hardwick.* Both cases deal with the crime of *sodomy*, a crime that statutes have referred to as "deviate sexual intercourse" and "the infamous crime against nature." Sodomy is a generic term that usually encompasses oral sex and anal sex, although some states also include bestiality (sexual contact with an animal) in their sodomy statutes.

Sodomy, originally an ecclesiastical offense, was made a crime at common law under the reign of King Henry VIII. It was a criminal offense in colonial America and was a crime in nearly every U.S. jurisdiction for many years. In the 1960s, some jurisdictions began to decriminalize consensual sodomy. As of the time of this writing, it remains a criminal offense in twenty-one U.S. jurisdictions ranging in seriousness to a low misdemeanor punishable by a fine and/or a short jail sentence (e.g., Arizona) to being a high felony, punishable by up to twenty years in prison (e.g., Georgia).

When reading *Commonwealth v. Bonadio* and *Bowers v. Hardwick*, keep the central points of both Hart and Devlin in mind. See with whose position you find yourself more aligned when the legislation or morality debate is taken out of the abstract world of philosophy and applied under the facts of these two real-world cases.

COMMONWEALTH of Pennsylvania, Appellant v. Michael BONADIO, et al., Appellees
415 A.2d 47 (Pa. 1980).

[The defendants in this case were with sodomy (termed "deviate sexual intercourse" at the time in Pennsylvania) and/or conspiracy to commit deviate sexual intercourse. The statute under which they were charged provided, in relevant part, "A person who engages in deviate sexual intercourse under circumstances not covered by section 3123 of this title (related to involuntary deviate sexual intercourse) is guilty of a misdemeanor of the second degree. . . . 'Deviate sexual intercourse' [is] a sexual intercourse per os or per anus between human beings who are not husband and wife, and any form of sexual intercourse with an animal."]

Justice Flaherty delivered the opinion of the majority:

This is an appeal from an Order of the Court of Common Pleas of Allegheny County granting appellees' Motion to Quash an Information on the ground that the Voluntary Deviate Sexual Intercourse Statute is unconstitutional. Appellees were arrested at an "adult" pornographic theater on charges of voluntary deviate sexual intercourse and/or conspiracy to perform the same.

The Commonwealth's position is that the statute in question is a valid exercise of the police power pursuant the authority of states to regulate public health, safety, welfare, and morals. Yet, the police power is not unlimited. . . . The threshold question in determining whether the statute in question is a valid exercise of the police power is to decide whether it benefits the public generally. The state clearly has a proper role to perform in protecting the public from inadvertent offensive displays of sexual behavior, in preventing people from being forced against their will to submit to sexual contact, in protecting minors from being sexually used by adults, and in eliminating cruelty to animals. To assure these protections, a broad range of criminal statutes constitute valid police power exercises, including proscriptions of indecent exposure, open lewdness, rape, *involuntary* deviate sexual intercourse, indecent assault, statutory rape, corruption of minors, and cruelty to animals. The statute in question serves none of the foregoing purposes and it is nugatory to suggest that it promotes a state interest in the institution of marriage. The Voluntary Deviate Sexual Intercourse Statute has only one possible purpose: to regulate the private conduct of consenting adults. Such a purpose, we believe, exceeds the valid bounds of the police power while infringing the right to equal protection of the laws guaranteed by the Constitution of the United States and of this

With respect to regulation of morals, the police power should properly be exercised to protect each individual's right to be free from interference in defining and pursuing his own morality but not to enforce a majority morality on persons whose conduct *does not harm others*. "No harm to the secular interests of the community is involved in atypical sex practice in private between consenting adult partners." Model Penal Code § 207.5 – Sodomy & Related Offenses. Comment (Tent. Draft No. 4, 1955).

Many issues that are considered to be matters of morals are subject to debate, and no sufficient state interest justifies legislation of norms simply because a particular belief is followed by a number of people, or even a majority. Indeed, what is considered to be "moral" changes with the times and is dependent upon societal background. Spiritual leadership, not the government, has the responsibility for striving to improve the morality of individuals. Enactment of the Voluntary Deviate Sexual Intercourse Statute, despite the fact that it provides punishment for what many believe to be abhorrent crimes against nature and perceived sins against God, is not properly in the realm of the temporal police power.

The concepts underlying our view of the police power in the case before us were once summarized as follows by the great philosopher, John Stuart Mill, in his eminent and apposite work, On Liberty (1859):

> [T]he sole end for which mankind are warranted, individually or collectively, in interfering with the liberty of action of any of their number, is self-protection . . . [T]he only purpose for which power can be rightfully exercised over any member of a civili[z]ed community, against his will, is to prevent harm to others. His own good, either physical or moral is not a sufficient warrant. He cannot rightfully be compelled to do or forbear because it will be better for him to do so, because it will make him happier, because, in the opinions of others, to do so would be wise, or even right. These are good reasons for remonstrating with him, or reasoning with him, or persuading him, or entreating him, but not for compelling him, or visiting him with any evil in case he do otherwise. To justify that, the conduct from which it is desired to deter him must be calculated to produce evil to some one else. *The only part of the conduct of any one, for which he is amenable to society, is that which concerns others. In the part which merely concerns himself, his independence is, of right, absolute. Over himself, over his own body and mind, the individual is sovereign.*

The Harm principle

> * * *
>
> This, then, is the appropriate region of human liberty. It comprises, first, the inward domain of consciousness; demanding liberty of conscience, in the most comprehensive sense; liberty of thought and feeling; absolute freedom of opinion and sentiment on all subjects, practical or speculative, scientific, *moral, or theological* . . . . Secondly, the principle requires liberty of tastes and pursuits; of framing the plan of our life to suit our own character; of doing as we like, subject to such consequences as may follow: without impediment from our fellow-creatures, *so long as what we do does not harm them, even though they should think our conduct foolish, perverse, or wrong.* Thirdly, from this liberty of each individual, follows the liberty, within the same limits of combination among individuals; freedom to unite, for any purpose not involving harm to others: the persons combining being supposed to be of full age, and not forced or deceived. [Emphasis supplied by the Court].

This philosophy, as applied to the issue of regulation of sexual morality presently before the Court, or employed to delimit the police power generally, properly circumscribes state power over the individual. Not only does the statute in question exceed the proper bounds of the police power, but, in addition, it offends the Constitution by creating a classification based on marital status (making deviate acts criminal only when performed between unmarried persons) where such differential treatment is not supported by a sufficient state interest and thereby denies equal protection of the laws. Assuming, without deciding, that no fundamental interest is at stake (i.e., the right of privacy), so that strict scrutiny of the classification is not required, the classification still denies equal protection . . . .

The Commonwealth submits that the classification is justified on the ground that the legislature intended to forbid, generally, voluntary "deviate" sexual intercourse, but created an exception for persons whose exclusion is claimed to further a state interest in promoting the privacy inherent in the marital relationship. We do not find such a justification for the classification to be reasonable or to have a fair and substantial relation to the object of the legislation. Viewing the statute as exceeding the proper bounds of the police power, however, since none of the previously discussed valid legislative interests in regulating sexual conduct are promoted by the statute, the classification itself could not bear a substantial relation to a valid legislative objective. Furthermore, even if the subject of the statute's regulation were properly within the police power, the marital status of voluntarily participating adults would bear no rational relationship to whether a sexual act should be legal or criminal.

In *Eisenstadt v. Baird*, 405 U.S. 438 (1972), the Supreme Court of the United States stated: "[T]he State could not, consistently with the Equal Protection Clause, outlaw distribution [of contraceptives] to unmarried but not to married persons. In each case the evil, as perceived by the State, would be identical, and the underinclusion would be invidious." Similarly, to suggest that deviate acts are heinous if performed by unmarried persons but acceptable when done by married persons lacks even a rational basis, for requiring less moral behavior of married persons than is expected of unmarried persons is without basis in logic. If the statute regulated sexual acts so affecting others that proscription by law would be justified, then they should be proscribed for all people, not just the unmarried. Affirmed.

Roberts, Justice, dissenting.

The record plainly demonstrates that these appellants engaged in the proscribed conduct on a stage before a public audience and in plain view of the arresting officers. Thus there is no basis, constitutional or otherwise, for the majority's hasty invalidation of our Legislature's Crimes Code. Accordingly, I would reverse the order of the Court of Common Pleas of Allegheny County and allow the prosecution to proceed.

Nix, Justice, dissenting.

The majority tries to justify its novel and shocking ruling by suggesting that they are defending the individual from state intervention on questions of morality and personal conscience. Regrettably this theory ignores the facts of the case before the court. This is not a case of private, intimate conduct between consenting adults.

Appellees, Mildred Kannitz, known on the stage as "Dawn Delight" and Shanne Wimbel are "exotic" dancers. Appellees, Patrick Gagliano and Michael Bonadio are employees of the Penthouse Theater in downtown Pittsburgh, in which Ms. Delight and Ms. Wimbel perform. In March of last year, plainclothes police officers went to the Penthouse Theater, paid an admission fee, entered the theater, and viewed the performances of Ms. Delight and Ms. Wimbel. During the course of these performances Ms. Delight and Ms. Wimbel engaged in sexual acts with members of the audience. The police officers arrested the two performers, the patrons who participated in the sexual acts, as well as the theater's cashier, Bonadio, and the theater's manager, Gagliano. Ms. Delight and Ms. Wimbel were each charged by information with one count each of voluntary deviate sexual intercourse. . . . Bonadio and Gagliano were charged with one count each of criminal conspiracy.

The majority attempts to avoid the privacy issue by reasoning that there was not a valid exercise of the state's police power in the prohibition of this type of conduct. The absurdity of such a position does not require demonstration. Here we have a public display of the most depraved type of sexual behavior for pay. Any member of the public who pays the fee can witness and participate in this conduct. That the majority would suggest that this is beyond the state's power to regulate public health, safety, welfare, and morals is incredible. I assume that regulation of prostitution and hard core pornography are also now prohibited by today's ruling.

Finally, the majority's conclusion that the statute violates equal protection presents a "red herring." Concern over the marital exception contained within the voluntary deviate sexual intercourse statute, is misplaced, for the heart of this exception is the intimacy and warmth of a *private* marital sexual relationship. Here the sexual acts were performed in *public* and in return for monetary compensation. It is therefore clear that the marital status of the participants in this conduct would not have affected their culpability. To suggest that the marital exception was intended to insulate a marital couple who performed deviate sexual acts for public display for pay would distort the obvious legislative objective in providing for this exception. The marital exception was designed to protect the intimacy and privacy of the marital unit. It did not give married couples the license to publicly engage in lewd and lascivious public acts.

QUESTIONS

1. In invalidating Pennsylvania's sodomy statute, the court relied, in part, on the harm principle. Do you feel that the criminal law ought to be guided by the harm principle – in other words, *should* the law regulate consensual conduct that does not harm anyone? Do you think the harm principle should apply to sodomy between consenting adults? Why or why not?

2. Had the defendants been charged with the crime of "public sexual indecency," the result may have been quite different. Even if you feel that private, sexual conduct between consenting adults should be beyond the police power of the state, do you feel different rules should apply when the conduct is public? Does your answer depend on the definition of "public" used? For example, should oral sex performed out in the open in a public park be treated the same as the oral sex at issue in this case – a performance on stage at an adult theater?

3. As the dissent points out, the majority based its decision partially on the right to privacy and partially on the Equal Protection Clause of the Fourteenth Amendment. As the majority pointed out, the statute at issue in this case criminalized sodomy between unmarried persons, but allowed sodomy between married persons. Do you think marriage is an appropriate benchmark by which to gage the criminality of conduct between consenting adults? Why or why not? Does the Supreme Court's decision in *Eisenstadt v. Baird*, discussed in the majority's opinion, have any influence on your answer?

4. As you will see in the next case, *Bowers v. Hardwick*, the Supreme Court decided the right to privacy did not encompass the right for two homosexual men to engage in consensual oral sex in the privacy of one of the men's own home. The issue of the homosexual nature of the sodomy in *Bowers* was central to the Supreme Court's handing of the privacy issue. *Bonadio* thus differs from *Bowers* on two grounds: *Bonadio* involved sodomy in public, rather than in the privacy of one's own home, and it involved heterosexual sodomy rather than homosexual sodomy. Do you think sexual orientation is an appropriate category upon which to differentiate the criminality of oral or anal sex? Why or why not? If so, why do you feel that consensual oral sex between a man and a woman should be legally permissible, but consensual oral sex between two men or between two women should be criminally punishable? What role, if any, do you think the Equal Protection Clause of the Fourteenth Amendment should play in determining the constitutionality of a sodomy law that differentiates on the basis of sexual orientation? Why?

Michael J. BOWERS, Attorney General of Georgia, Petitioner, v. Michael HARDWICK, Respondent.
478 U.S. 186 (1986).

Justice White delivered the opinion of the Court.

In August 1982, respondent Hardwick [hereinafter respondent] was charged with violating the Georgia statute criminalizing sodomy by committing that act with another adult male in the bedroom of respondent's home.[1] After a preliminary hearing, the District Attorney decided not to present the matter to the grand jury unless further evidence developed.

---

[1] Georgia Code Ann. § 16-6-2 (1984) provides, in pertinent part, as follows:

(a) A person commits the offense of sodomy when he performs or submits to any sexual act involving the sex organs of one person and the mouth or anus of another . . . .

(b) A person convicted of the offense of sodomy shall be punished by imprisonment for not less than one nor more than 20 years . . . .

Respondent then brought suit in the Federal District Court, challenging the constitutionality of the statute insofar as it criminalized consensual sodomy. He asserted that he was a practicing homosexual, that the Georgia sodomy statute, as administered by the defendants, placed him in imminent danger of arrest, and that the statute for several reasons violates the Federal Constitution. The District Court granted the defendants' motion to dismiss for failure to state a claim, relying on *Doe v. Commonwealth's Attorney for the City of Richmond*, 403 F. Supp. 1199 (E.D. Va.1975), which this Court summarily affirmed, 425 U.S. 901 (1976).

A divided panel of the Court of Appeals for the Eleventh Circuit reversed. The court first held that, because *Doe* was distinguishable and in any event had been undermined by later decisions, our summary affirmance in that case did not require affirmance of the District Court. Relying on our decisions in *Griswold v. Connecticut*, 381 U.S. 479 (1965); *Eisenstadt v. Baird*, 405 U.S. 438 (1972); *Stanley v. Georgia*, 394 U.S. 557 (1969); and *Roe v. Wade*, 410 U.S. 113 (1973), the court went on to hold that the Georgia statute violated respondent's fundamental rights because his homosexual activity is a private and intimate association that is beyond the reach of state regulation by reason of the Ninth Amendment and the Due Process Clause of the Fourteenth Amendment. . . . Because other Courts of Appeals have arrived at judgments contrary to that of the Eleventh Circuit in this case, we granted the Attorney General's petition for certiorari questioning the holding that the sodomy statute violates the fundamental rights of homosexuals. We agree with petitioner that the Court of Appeals erred, and hence reverse its judgment.

This case does not require a judgment on whether laws against sodomy between consenting adults in general, or between homosexuals in particular, are wise or desirable. It raises no question about the right or propriety of state legislative decisions to repeal their laws that criminalize homosexual sodomy, or of state-court decisions invalidating those laws on state constitutional grounds. The issue presented is whether the Federal Constitution confers a fundamental right upon homosexuals to engage in sodomy, and hence invalidates the laws of the many States that still make such conduct illegal and have done so for a very long time. The case also calls for some judgment about the limits of the Court's role in carrying out its constitutional mandate.

We first register our disagreement with the Court of Appeals and with respondent that the Court's prior cases have construed the Constitution to confer a right of privacy that extends to homosexual sodomy and, for all intents and purposes, have decided this case. The reach of this line of cases was sketched in *Carey v. Population Services International*, 431 U.S. 678 , 685 (1977). *Pierce v. Society of Sisters*, 268 U.S. 510 (1925), and *Meyer v. Nebraska*, 262 U.S. 390 (1923), were described as dealing with childrearing and education; *Loving v. Virginia*, 388 U.S. 1 (1967), with marriage; *Griswold v. Connecticut, supra*, and *Eisenstadt v. Baird, supra*, with contraception; and *Roe v. Wade*, 410 U.S. 113 (1973), with abortion. The latter three cases were interpreted [in *Carey*] as construing the Due Process Clause of the Fourteenth Amendment to confer a fundamental individual right to decide whether or not to beget or bear a child.

Accepting the decisions in these cases and the above description of them, we think it evident that none of the rights announced in those cases bears any resemblance to the claimed constitutional right of homosexuals to engage in acts of sodomy that is asserted in this case. No connection between family, marriage, or procreation on the one hand and homosexual activity on the other has been demonstrated, either by the Court of Appeals or by respondent. Moreover, any claim that these cases nevertheless stand for the proposition that any kind of private sexual conduct between consenting adults is constitutionally insulated from state proscription is [i]nsupportable. Indeed, the Court's opinion in *Carey* twice asserted that the privacy right, which the *Griswold* line of cases found to be one of the protections provided by the Due Process Clause, did not reach so far.

Precedent aside, however, respondent would have us announce, as the Court of Appeals did, a fundamental right to engage in homosexual sodomy. This we are quite unwilling to do. It is true that despite the language of the Due Process Clauses of the Fifth and Fourteenth Amendments, which appears to focus only on the processes by which life, liberty, or property is taken, the cases are legion in which those Clauses have been interpreted to have substantive content, subsuming rights that to a great extent are immune from federal or state regulation or proscription. Among such cases are those recognizing rights that have little or no textual support in the constitutional language.

Striving to assure itself and the public that announcing rights not readily identifiable in the Constitution's text involves much more than the imposition of the Justices' own choice of values on the States and the Federal Government, the Court has sought to identify the nature of the rights qualifying for heightened judicial protection. In *Palko v. Connecticut*, 302 U.S. 319 , 325 , 326 (1937), it was said that this category includes those fundamental liberties that are "implicit in the concept of ordered liberty," such that "neither liberty nor justice would exist if [they] were sacrificed." A different description of fundamental liberties appeared in *Moore v. East Cleveland*, 31 U.S. 494, 503 (1977), where they are characterized as those liberties that are "deeply rooted in this Nation's history and tradition." It is obvious to us that neither of these formulations would extend a fundamental right to homosexuals to engage in acts of consensual sodomy. Proscriptions against that conduct have ancient roots. Sodomy was a criminal offense at common law and was forbidden by the laws of the original thirteen States when they ratified the Bill of Rights. In 1868, when the Fourteenth Amendment was ratified, all but 5 of the 37 States in the Union had criminal sodomy laws. In fact, until 1961, all 50 States outlawed sodomy, and today, 24 States and the District of Columbia continue to provide criminal penalties for sodomy performed in private and between consenting adults. Against this background, to claim that a right to engage in such conduct is "deeply rooted in this Nation's history and tradition" or "implicit in the concept of ordered liberty" is, at best, facetious.

Respondent, however, asserts that the result should be different where the homosexual conduct occurs in the privacy of the home. He relies on *Stanley v. Georgia,* 394 U.S. 557 (1969), where the Court held that the First Amendment prevents conviction for possessing and reading obscene material in the privacy of one's home: "If the First Amendment means anything, it means that a State has no business telling a man, sitting alone in his house, what books he may read or what films he may watch."

Stanley did protect conduct that would not have been protected outside the home, and it partially prevented the enforcement of state obscenity laws; but the decision was firmly grounded in the First Amendment. The right pressed upon us here has no similar support in the text of the Constitution, and it does not qualify for recognition under the prevailing principles for construing the Fourteenth Amendment. Its limits are also difficult to discern. Plainly enough, otherwise illegal conduct is not always immunized whenever it occurs in the home. Victimless crimes, such as the possession and use of illegal drugs, do not escape the law where they are committed at home. *Stanley* itself recognized that its holding offered no protection for the possession in the home of drugs, firearms, or stolen goods. And if respondent's submission is limited to the voluntary sexual conduct between consenting adults, it would be difficult, except by fiat, to limit the claimed right to homosexual conduct while leaving exposed to prosecution adultery, incest, and other sexual crimes even though they are committed in the home. We are unwilling to start down that road.

Even if the conduct at issue here is not a fundamental right, respondent asserts that there must be a rational basis for the law and that there is none in this case other than the presumed belief of a majority of the electorate in Georgia that homosexual sodomy is immoral and unacceptable. This is said to be an inadequate rationale to support the law. The law, however, is constantly based on notions of morality, and if all laws representing essentially moral choices are to be invalidated under the Due Process Clause, the courts will be very busy indeed. Even respondent makes no such claim, but insists that majority sentiments about the morality of homosexuality should be declared inadequate. We do not agree, and are unpersuaded that the sodomy laws of some 25 States should be invalidated on this basis.[2] Accordingly, the judgment of the Court of Appeals is reversed.

---

[2]   Respondent does not defend the judgment below based on the Ninth Amendment, the Equal Protection Clause, or the Eighth Amendment.

● Chief Justice Burger, concurring.

I join the Court's opinion, but I write separately to underscore my view that in constitutional terms there is no such thing as a fundamental right to commit homosexual sodomy. As the Court notes, the proscriptions against sodomy have very "ancient roots." Decisions of individuals relating to homosexual conduct have been subject to state intervention throughout the history of Western civilization. Condemnation of those practices is firmly rooted in Judeo-Christian moral and ethical standards.

no fundam. right

Homosexual sodomy was a capital crime under Roman law. During the English Reformation when powers of the ecclesiastical courts were transferred to the King's Courts, the first English statute criminalizing sodomy was passed. Blackstone described "the infamous crime against nature" as an offense of "deeper malignity" than rape, a heinous act "the very mention of which is a disgrace to human nature," and "a crime not fit to be named." The common law of England, including its prohibition of sodomy, became the received law of Georgia and the other Colonies. In 1816, the Georgia Legislature passed the statute at issue here, and that statute has been continuously in force in one form or another since that time. To hold that the act of homosexual sodomy is somehow protected as a fundamental right would be to cast aside millennia of moral teaching. This is essentially not a question of personal "preferences" but rather of the legislative authority of the State. I find nothing in the Constitution depriving a State of the power to enact the statute challenged here.

● Justice Powell, concurring.

I join the opinion of the Court. I agree with the Court that there is no fundamental right – i.e., no substantive right under the Due Process Clause – such as that claimed by respondent Hardwick, and found to exist by the Court of Appeals. This is not to suggest, however, that respondent may not be protected by the Eighth Amendment of the Constitution. The Georgia statute at issue in this case authorizes a court to imprison a person for up to 20 years for a single private, consensual act of sodomy. In my view, a prison sentence for such conduct – certainly a sentence of long duration – would create a serious Eighth Amendment issue. Under the Georgia statute, a single act of sodomy, even in the private setting of a home, is a felony comparable in terms of the possible sentence imposed to serious felonies such as aggravated battery, first-degree arson, and robbery.

In this case, however, respondent has not been tried, much less convicted and sentenced. Moreover, respondent has not raised the Eighth Amendment issue below. For these reasons, this constitutional argument is not before us.

Justice Blackmun, with whom Justice Brennan, Justice Marshall, and Justice Stevens join, dissenting.

This case is no more about "a fundamental right to engage in homosexual sodomy," as the Court purports to declare than *Stanley v. Georgia*, was about a fundamental right to watch obscene movies. Rather, this case is about "the most comprehensive of rights and the right most valued by civilized men," namely, "the right to be let alone." *Olmstead v. United States*, 277 U.S. 438, 478 (1928) (Brandeis, J., dissenting, 1928). The statute at issue, denies individuals the right to decide for themselves whether to engage in particular forms of private, consensual sexual activity. The Court concludes that [the statute] is valid essentially because "the laws of . . . many States . . . still make such conduct illegal and have done so for a very long time." But the fact that the moral judgments expressed by statutes like [the present one] may be " 'natural and familiar . . . ought not to conclude our judgment upon the question whether statutes embodying them conflict with the Constitution of the United States.'" *Roe v. Wade*. Like Justice Holmes [as he wrote in 1897], I believe that "it is revolting to have no better reason for a rule of law than that so it was laid down in the time of Henry IV. It is still more revolting if the grounds upon which it was laid down have vanished long since, and the rule simply persists from blind imitation of the past." I believe we must analyze Hardwick's claim in the light of the values that underlie the constitutional right to privacy. If that right means anything, it means that, before Georgia can prosecute its citizens for making choices about the most intimate aspects of their lives, it must do more than assert that the choice they have made is an "'abominable crime not fit to be named among Christians.'"

21

I

In its haste to reverse the Court of Appeals and hold that the Constitution does not "confer a fundamental right upon homosexuals to engage in sodomy," the Court relegates the actual statute being challenged to a footnote and ignores the procedural posture of the case before it. A fair reading of the statute and of the complaint clearly reveals that the majority has distorted the question this case presents.

First, the Court's almost obsessive focus on homosexual activity is particularly hard to justify in light of the broad language Georgia has used. Unlike the Court, the Georgia Legislature has not proceeded on the assumption that homosexuals are so different from other citizens that their lives may be controlled in a way that would not be tolerated if it limited the choices of those other citizens. Rather, Georgia has provided that "a person commits the offense of sodomy when he performs or submits to any sexual act involving the sex organs of one person and the mouth or anus of another." The sex or status of the persons who engage in the act is irrelevant as a matter of state law. In fact, to the extent I can discern a legislative purpose for Georgia's 1968 enactment of [the statute], that purpose seems to have been to broaden the coverage of the law to reach heterosexual as well as homosexual activity. I therefore see no basis for the Court's decision to treat this case as an "as applied" challenge to [the statute] or for Georgia's attempt, both in its brief and at oral argument, to defend [it] solely on the grounds that it prohibits homosexual activity. Michael Hardwick's standing may rest in significant part on Georgia's apparent willingness to enforce against homosexuals a law it seems not to have any desire to enforce against heterosexuals. But his claim that [the statute] involves an unconstitutional intrusion into his privacy and his right of intimate association does not depend in any way on his sexual orientation.[3]

Second, I disagree with the Court's refusal to consider whether [the statute] runs afoul of the Eighth or Ninth Amendments or the Equal Protection Clause of the Fourteenth Amendment. Respondent's complaint expressly invoked the Ninth Amendment, and he relied heavily before this Court on *Griswold v. Connecticut*, which identifies that Amendment as one of the specific constitutional provisions giving "life and substance" to our understanding of privacy. More importantly, the procedural posture of the case requires that we affirm the Court of Appeals' judgment if there is any ground on which respondent may be entitled to relief. This case is before us on petitioner's motion to dismiss for failure to state a claim. It is a well-settled principle of law that "a complaint should not be dismissed merely because a plaintiff's allegations do not support the particular legal theory he advances, for the court is under a duty to examine the complaint to determine if the allegations provide for relief on any possible theory." Thus, even if respondent did not advance claims based on the Eighth or Ninth Amendments, or on the Equal Protection Clause, his complaint should not be dismissed if any of those provisions could entitle him to relief. I need not reach either the Eighth Amendment or the Equal Protection Clause issues because I believe that Hardwick has stated a cognizable claim that [the statute] interferes with constitutionally protected interests in privacy and freedom of intimate association. But neither the Eighth Amendment nor the Equal Protection Clause is so clearly irrelevant that a claim resting on either provision should be peremptorily dismissed. The Court's cramped reading of the issue before it makes for a short opinion, but it does little to make for a persuasive one.

Despite historical views of homosexuality, it is no longer viewed by mental health professionals as a "disease" or disorder. But, obviously, neither is it simply a matter of deliberate personal election. Homosexual orientation may well form part of the very fiber of an individual's personality. Consequently, under Justice White's analysis in *Powell*, the Eighth Amendment may pose a constitutional barrier to sending an individual to prison for acting on that attraction regardless of the circumstances. An

---

[3] Until 1968, Georgia defined sodomy as "the carnal knowledge and connection against the order of nature, by man with man, or in the same unnatural manner with woman." In *Thompson v. Aldredge*, the Georgia Supreme Court held that [this older version of the statute] did not prohibit lesbian activity. And in *Riley v. Garrett*, the Georgia Supreme Court held that it did not prohibit heterosexual cunnilingus. Georgia passed the act-specific statute currently in force perhaps in response to the restrictive court decisions such as *Riley*.

individual's ability to make constitutionally protected decisions concerning sexual relations, is rendered empty indeed if he or she is given no real choice but a life without any physical intimacy.

With respect to the Equal Protection Clause's applicability to [the statute], I note that Georgia's exclusive stress before this Court on its interest in prosecuting homosexual activity despite the gender-neutral terms of the statute may raise serious questions of discriminatory enforcement, a question that cannot be disposed of before this Court on a motion to dismiss. The legislature having decided that the sex of the participants is irrelevant to the legality of the acts, I do not see why the State can defend [the statute] on the ground that individuals singled out for prosecution are of the same sex as their partners. Thus, under the circumstances of this case, a claim under the Equal Protection Clause may well be available without having to reach the more controversial question whether homosexuals are a suspect class.

II

Our cases long have recognized that the Constitution embodies a promise that a certain private sphere of individual liberty will be kept largely beyond the reach of government. In construing the right to privacy, the Court has proceeded along two somewhat distinct, albeit complementary, lines. First, it has recognized a privacy interest with reference to certain decisions that are properly for the individual to make. Second, it has recognized a privacy interest with reference to certain places without regard for the particular activities in which the individuals who occupy them are engaged. The case before us implicates both the decisional and the spatial aspects of the right to privacy.

A.   The Court concludes today that none of our prior cases dealing with various decisions that individuals are entitled to make free of governmental interference "bears any resemblance to the claimed constitutional right of homosexuals to engage in acts of sodomy that is asserted in this case." While it is true that these cases may be characterized by their connection to protection of the family, the Court's conclusion that they extend no further than this boundary ignores the warning in *Moore v. East Cleveland*, against "closing our eyes to the basic reasons why certain rights associated with the family have been accorded shelter under the Fourteenth Amendment's Due Process Clause." We protect those rights not because they contribute, in some direct and material way, to the general public welfare, but because they form so central a part of an individual's life. "[T]he concept of privacy embodies the 'moral fact that a person belongs to himself and not others nor to society as a whole.'" And so we protect the decision whether to marry precisely because marriage "is an association that promotes a way of life, not causes; a harmony in living, not political faiths; a bilateral loyalty, not commercial or social projects." *Griswold v. Connecticut*.

We protect the decision whether to have a child because parenthood alters so dramatically an individual's self-definition, not because of demographic considerations or the Bible's command to be fruitful and multiply. And we protect the family because it contributes so powerfully to the happiness of individuals, not because of a preference for stereotypical households. The Court recognized in *Roberts v. United States Jaycees,* 468 U.S. 609, 619 (1984), that the "ability independently to define one's identity that is central to any concept of liberty" cannot truly be exercised in a vacuum; we all depend on the "emotional enrichment from close ties with others." Only the most willful blindness could obscure the fact that sexual intimacy is "a sensitive, key relationship of human existence, central to family life, community welfare, and the development of human personality," *Paris Adult Theatre I v. Slaton*, 413 U.S. 49, 63 (1973). The fact that individuals define themselves in a significant way through their intimate sexual relationships with others suggests, in a Nation as diverse as ours, that there may be many "right" ways of conducting those relationships, and that much of the richness of a relationship will come from the freedom an individual has to choose the form and nature of these intensely personal bonds.

In a variety of circumstances we have recognized that a necessary corollary of giving individuals freedom to choose how to conduct their lives is acceptance of the fact that different individuals will make different choices. For example, in holding that the clearly important state interest in public education should give way to a competing claim by the Amish to the effect that extended formal schooling threatened their way of life, the Court declared: "There can be no assumption that today's majority is 'right' and the Amish and others like them are 'wrong.' A way of life that is odd or even erratic but interferes with no rights or interests of others is not to be condemned because it is different." *Wisconsin v. Yoder*, 406 U.S. 205, 223-224 (1972). The Court claims that its decision today merely refuses to recognize a fundamental right to engage in homosexual sodomy; what the Court really has refused to recognize is the fundamental interest all individuals have in controlling the nature of their intimate associations with others.

B.   The behavior for which Hardwick faces prosecution occurred in his own home, a place to which the Fourth Amendment attaches special significance. The Court's treatment of this aspect of the case is symptomatic of its overall refusal to consider the broad principles that have informed our treatment of privacy in specific cases. Just as the right to privacy is more than the mere aggregation of a number of entitlements to engage in specific behavior, so too, protecting the physical integrity of the home is more than merely a means of protecting specific activities that often take place there. Even when our understanding of the contours of the right to privacy depends on reference to a 'place,' the essence of a Fourth Amendment violation is not the breaking of a person's doors, and the rummaging of his drawers, but rather is the invasion of his indefeasible right of personal security, personal liberty and private property.

The Court's interpretation of the pivotal case of *Stanley v. Georgia*, is entirely unconvincing. *Stanley* held that Georgia's undoubted power to punish the public distribution of constitutionally unprotected, obscene material did not permit the State to punish the private possession of such material. According to the majority here, *Stanley* relied entirely on the First Amendment, and thus, it is claimed, sheds no light on cases not involving printed materials. But that is not what *Stanley* said. Rather, the *Stanley* Court anchored its holding in the Fourth Amendment's special protection for the individual in his home:

> The makers of our Constitution undertook to secure conditions favorable to the pursuit of happiness. They recognized the significance of man's spiritual nature, of his feelings and of his intellect. They knew that only a part of the pain, pleasure and satisfactions of life are to be found in material things. They sought to protect Americans in their beliefs, their thoughts, their emotions and their sensations.

* * *

> These are the rights that appellant is asserting in the case before us. He is asserting the right to read or observe what he pleases – the right to satisfy his intellectual and emotional needs in the privacy of his own home.

The central place that *Stanley* gives Justice Brandeis' dissent in *Olmstead*, a case raising no First Amendment claim, shows that *Stanley* rested as much on the Court's understanding of the Fourth Amendment as it did on the First. Indeed, in *Paris Adult Theatre I v. Slaton*, the Court suggested that reliance on the Fourth Amendment not only supported the Court's outcome in *Stanley*, but actually was necessary to it: "If obscene material unprotected by the First Amendment in itself carried with it a 'penumbra' of constitutionally protected privacy, this Court would not have found it necessary to decide *Stanley* on the narrow basis of the 'privacy of the home,' which was hardly more than a reaffirmation that 'a man's home is his castle.'" The right of the people to be secure in their . . . houses, expressly guaranteed by the Fourth Amendment, is perhaps the most "textual" of the various constitutional provisions that inform our understanding of the right to privacy, and thus I cannot agree with the Court's statement that "the right pressed upon us here has no . . . support in the text of the Constitution. Indeed, the right of an individual to conduct intimate relationships in the intimacy of his or her own home seems to me to be the heart of the Constitution's protection of privacy.

III

The Court's failure to comprehend the magnitude of the liberty interests at stake in this case leads it to slight the question whether petitioner, on behalf of the State, has justified Georgia's infringement on these interests. I believe that neither of the two general justifications for [the statute] that petitioner has advanced warrants dismissing respondent's challenge for failure to state a claim.

First, petitioner asserts that the acts made criminal by the statute may have serious adverse consequences for "the general public health and welfare," such as spreading communicable diseases or fostering other criminal activity. Inasmuch as this case was dismissed by the District Court on the pleadings, it is not surprising that the record before us is barren of any evidence to support petitioner's claim. In light of the state of the record, I see no justification for the Court's attempt to equate the private, consensual sexual activity at issue here with the "possession in the home of drugs, firearms, or stolen goods," to which *Stanley* refused to extend its protection. None of the behavior so mentioned in *Stanley* can properly be viewed as "victimless," [as the majority stated above]. Drugs and weapons are inherently dangerous, and for property to be "stolen," someone must have been wrongfully deprived of it. Nothing in the record before the Court provides any justification for finding the activity forbidden by [the statute] to be physically dangerous, either to the persons engaged in it or to others.

The core of petitioner's defense of [the statute], however, is that respondent and others who engage in the conduct prohibited by it interfere with Georgia's exercise of the "right of the Nation and of the States to maintain a decent society." *Paris Adult Theatre I v. Slaton.* Essentially, petitioner argues, and the Court agrees, that the fact that the acts described in [the statute] "for hundreds of years, if not thousands, have been uniformly condemned as immoral" is a sufficient reason to permit a State to ban them today. I cannot agree that either the length of time a majority has held its convictions or the passions with which it defends them can withdraw legislation from this Court's scrutiny. *See, e.g., Roe v. Wade; Loving v. Virginia;* 388 U.S. 1 (1967);[4] *Brown v. Board of Education,* 347 U.S. 483 (1954). As Justice Jackson wrote so eloquently for the Court in *West Virginia Board of Education v. Barnette,* 319 U.S. 624, 641-42 (1943),"we apply the limitations of the Constitution with no fear that freedom to be intellectually and spiritually diverse or even contrary will disintegrate the social organization . . . . Freedom to differ is not limited to things that do not matter much. That would be a mere shadow of freedom. The test of its substance is the right to differ as to things that touch the heart of the existing order." It is precisely because the issue raised by this case touches the heart of what makes individuals what they are that we should be especially sensitive to the rights of those whose choices upset the majority.

The assertion that "traditional Judeo-Christian values proscribe" the conduct involved, cannot provide an adequate justification for [the statute]. That certain, but by no means all, religious groups condemn the behavior at issue gives the State no license to impose their judgments on the entire citizenry. The legitimacy of secular legislation depends instead on whether the State can advance some justification for its law beyond its conformity to religious doctrine. Thus, far from buttressing his case, petitioner's invocation of Leviticus, Romans, St. Thomas Aquinas, and sodomy's heretical status during the Middle Ages undermines his suggestion that [the statute] represents a legitimate use of secular coercive power. A State can no more punish private behavior because of religious intolerance than it can punish such behavior because of racial animus. "The Constitution cannot control such prejudices, but neither can it tolerate them. Private biases may be outside the reach of the law, but the law cannot, directly or indirectly, give them effect." *Palmore v. Sidoti,* 466 U.S. 429, 433 (1984). No matter how uncomfortable a certain group may make the majority of this Court, we have held that "mere public intolerance or animosity cannot constitutionally justify the deprivation of a person's physical liberty."

---

[4]   The parallel between *Loving* and this case is almost uncanny. There, too, the State relied on a religious justification for its law. <u>Compare</u> the decision of the Trial Court in *Loving*: "Almighty God created the races white, black, yellow, malay and red, and he placed them on separate continents . . . ." The fact that he separated the races shows that he did not intend for the races to mix", <u>with</u> Brief for Petitioner 20-21 (relying on the Old and New Testaments and the writings of St. Thomas Aquinas to show that "traditional Judeo-Christian values proscribe such conduct." There, too, defenders of the challenged statute relied heavily on the fact that when the Fourteenth Amendment was ratified, most of the States had similar prohibitions. There, too, at the time the case came before the Court, many of the States still had criminal statutes concerning the conduct at issue. Yet the Court held, not only that the invidious racism of Virginia's law violated the Equal Protection Clause, but also that the law deprived the Lovings of due process by denying them the "freedom of choice to marry" that had "long been recognized as one of the vital personal rights essential to the orderly pursuit of happiness by free men."

Nor can [the statute] be justified as a "morally neutral" exercise of Georgia's power to protect the public environment. Certainly, some private behavior can affect the fabric of society as a whole. Reasonable people may differ about whether particular sexual acts are moral or immoral, but "we have ample evidence for believing that people will not abandon morality, will not think any better of murder, cruelty and dishonesty, merely because some private sexual practice which they abominate is not punished by the law." H.L.A. Hart, *Immorality and Treason*, reprinted in The Law as Literature 220, 225 (L. Blom-Cooper ed. 1961). Petitioner and the Court fail to see the difference between laws that protect public sensibilities and those that enforce private morality. Statutes banning public sexual activity are entirely consistent with protecting the individual's liberty interest in decisions concerning sexual relations: the same recognition that those decisions are intensely private which justifies protecting them from governmental interference can justify protecting individuals from unwilling exposure to the sexual activities of others. But the mere fact that intimate behavior may be punished when it takes place in public cannot dictate how States can regulate intimate behavior that occurs in intimate places.[5]

This case involves no real interference with the rights of others, for the mere knowledge that other individuals do not adhere to one's value system cannot be a legally cognizable interest, let alone an interest that can justify invading the houses, hearts, and minds of citizens who choose to live their lives differently.

IV

It took but three years for the Court to see the error in its analysis in *Minersville School District v. Gobitis*, 310 U.S. 586 (1940), and to recognize that the threat to national cohesion posed by a refusal to salute the flag was vastly outweighed by the threat to those same values posed by compelling such a salute. I can only hope that here, too, the Court soon will reconsider its analysis and conclude that depriving individuals of the right to choose for themselves how to conduct their intimate relationships poses a far greater threat to the values most deeply rooted in our Nation's history than tolerance of nonconformity could ever do. Because I think the Court today betrays those values, I dissent.

Justice Stevens, with whom Justice Brennan and Justice Marshall join, dissenting.

Like the statute that is challenged in this case, the rationale of the Court's opinion applies equally to the prohibited conduct regardless of whether the parties who engage in it are married or unmarried, or are of the same or different sexes. Sodomy was condemned as an odious and sinful type of behavior during the formative period of the common law. That condemnation was equally damning for heterosexual and homosexual sodomy. Moreover, it provided no special exemption for married couples. The license to cohabit and to produce legitimate offspring simply did not include any permission to engage in sexual conduct that was considered a "crime against nature."

The history of the Georgia statute before us clearly reveals this traditional prohibition of heterosexual, as well as homosexual, sodomy. Indeed, at one point in the 20th century, Georgia's law was construed to permit certain sexual conduct between homosexual women even though such conduct was prohibited between heterosexuals. The history of the statutes cited by the majority as proof for the proposition that sodomy is not constitutionally protected, similarly reveals a prohibition on heterosexual, as well as homosexual, sodomy.

---

[5]   At oral argument, a suggestion appeared that, while the Fourth Amendment's special protection of the home might prevent the State from enforcing [the statute] against individuals who engage in consensual sexual activity there, that protection would not make the statute invalid. The suggestion misses the point entirely. If the law is not invalid, then the police can invade the home to enforce it, provided, of course, that they obtain a determination of probable cause from a neutral magistrate. One of the reasons for the Court's holding in *Griswold v. Connecticut*, was precisely the possibility, and repugnancy, of permitting searches to obtain evidence regarding the use of contraceptives. Permitting the kinds of searches that might be necessary to obtain evidence of the sexual activity banned by [the statute] seems no less intrusive, or repugnant.

Because the Georgia statute expresses the traditional view that sodomy is an immoral kind of conduct regardless of the identity of the persons who engage in it, I believe that a proper analysis of its constitutionality requires consideration of two questions: First, may a State totally prohibit the described conduct by means of a neutral law applying without exception to all persons subject to its jurisdiction? If not, may the State save the statute by announcing that it will only enforce the law against homosexuals? The two questions merit separate discussion.

I

Our prior cases make two propositions abundantly clear. First, the fact that the governing majority in a State has traditionally viewed a particular practice as immoral is not a sufficient reason for upholding a law prohibiting the practice; neither history nor tradition could save a law prohibiting miscegenation from constitutional attack. *Loving v. Virginia.* Second, individual decisions by married persons, concerning the intimacies of their physical relationship, even when not intended to produce offspring, are a form of "liberty" protected by the Due Process Clause of the Fourteenth Amendment. *Griswold v. Connecticut.* Moreover, this protection extends to intimate choices by unmarried as well as married persons. *Eisenstadt v. Baird.*

In consideration of claims of this kind, the Court has emphasized the individual interest in privacy, but its decisions have actually been animated by an even more fundamental concern. As I wrote some years ago: "These cases do not deal with the individual's interest in protection from unwarranted public attention, comment, or exploitation. They deal, rather, with the individual's right to make certain unusually important decisions that will affect his own, or his family's, destiny. The Court has referred to such decisions as implicating 'basic values,' as being 'fundamental,' and as being dignified by history and tradition. The character of the Court's language in these cases brings to mind the origins of the American heritage of freedom – the abiding interest in individual liberty that makes certain state intrusions on the citizen's right to decide how he will live his own life intolerable. Guided by history, our tradition of respect for the dignity of individual choice in matters of conscience and the restraints implicit in the federal system, federal judges have accepted the responsibility for recognition and protection of these rights in appropriate cases."

Society has every right to encourage its individual members to follow particular traditions in expressing affection for one another and in gratifying their personal desires. It, of course, may prohibit an individual from imposing his will on another to satisfy his own selfish interests. It also may prevent an individual from interfering with, or violating, a legally sanctioned and protected relationship, such as marriage. And it may explain the relative advantages and disadvantages of different forms of intimate expression. But when individual married couples are isolated from observation by others, the way in which they voluntarily choose to conduct their intimate relations is a matter for them – not the State – to decide. The essential "liberty" that animated the development of the law in cases like *Griswold* and *Eisenstadt* surely embraces the right to engage in non-reproductive, sexual conduct that others may consider offensive or immoral.[6]

II

If the Georgia statute cannot be enforced as it is written – if the conduct it seeks to prohibit is a protected form of liberty for the vast majority of Georgia's citizens – the State must assume the burden of justifying a selective application of its law. Either the persons to whom Georgia seeks to apply its statute do not have the same interest in "liberty" that others have, or there must be a reason why the State may be permitted to apply a generally applicable law to certain persons that it does not apply to others.

The first possibility is plainly unacceptable. Although the meaning of the principle that "all men are created equal" is not always clear, it surely must mean that every free citizen has the same interest

---

[6]   Indeed, the Georgia Attorney General concedes that Georgia's statute would be unconstitutional if applied to a married couple.

in "liberty" that the members of the majority share. From the standpoint of the individual, the homosexual and the heterosexual have the same interest in deciding how he will live his own life, and, more narrowly, how he will conduct himself in his personal and voluntary associations with his companions. State intrusion into the private conduct of either is equally burdensome.

The second possibility is similarly unacceptable. A policy of selective application must be supported by a neutral and legitimate interest – something more substantial than a habitual dislike for, or ignorance about, the disfavored group. Neither the State nor the Court has identified any such interest in this case. The Court has posited as a justification for the Georgia statute "the presumed belief of a majority of the electorate in Georgia that homosexual sodomy is immoral and unacceptable." But the Georgia electorate has expressed no such belief – instead, its representatives enacted a law that presumably reflects the belief that all sodomy is immoral and unacceptable. Unless the Court is prepared to conclude that such a law is constitutional, it may not rely on the work product of the Georgia Legislature to support its holding. For the Georgia statute does not single out homosexuals as a separate class meriting special disfavored treatment. Nor, indeed, does the Georgia prosecutor even believe that all homosexuals who violate this statute should be punished. This conclusion is evident from the fact that the respondent in this very case has formally acknowledged in his complaint and in court that he has engaged, and intends to continue to engage, in the prohibited conduct, yet the State has elected not to process criminal charges against him. As Justice Powell points out, moreover, Georgia's prohibition on private, consensual sodomy has not been enforced for decades. The record of nonenforcement, in this case and in the last several decades, belies the Attorney General's representations about the importance of the State's selective application of its generally applicable law.

Both the Georgia statute and the Georgia prosecutor thus completely fail to provide the Court with any support for the conclusion that homosexual sodomy, simpliciter, is considered unacceptable conduct in that State, and that the burden of justifying a selective application of the generally applicable law has been met.

III

The Court orders the dismissal of respondent's complaint even though the State's statute prohibits all sodomy; even though that prohibition is concededly unconstitutional with respect to heterosexuals; and even though the State's post hoc explanations for selective application are belied by the State's own actions. At the very least, I think it clear at this early stage of the litigation that respondent has alleged a constitutional claim sufficient to withstand a motion to dismiss. Indeed, at this stage, it appears that the statute indiscriminately authorizes a policy of selective prosecution that is neither limited to the class of homosexual persons nor embraces all persons in that class, but rather applies to those who may be arbitrarily selected by the prosecutor for reasons that are not revealed either in the record of this case or in the text of the statute. If that is true, although the text of the statute is clear enough, its true meaning may be "so intolerably vague that evenhanded enforcement of the law is a virtual impossibility."

I respectfully dissent.

QUESTIONS

1.   *Bowers v. Hardwick* is among the most criticized Supreme Court decisions of all time. While that is so, it remains "the law" as of the time of this writing that the right to privacy does not encompass the right to engage in private, consensual homosexual sodomy. Although there has been no ruling on whether the right to privacy would encompass the right to engage in private, consensual heterosexual sodomy, a matter not at issue in *Bowers* given the way the majority framed the issue in the case, do you think the Court would have held differently if a heterosexual couple had brought suit to challenge the constitutionality of the Georgia sodomy statute? Why or why not? Would it make a difference if the heterosexual couple was married? Why?

2.	*Bowers* raises the issue of the link between law and morality. Do you think oral and/or anal sex between consenting adults in the privacy of one's own home is immoral? Does your answer depend on the sexual orientation of the participants? Defend your position keeping in mind the mandate of the Equal Protection Clause of the Fourteenth Amendment that similarly situated people be treated by the law in a similar manner. Regardless of your feelings regarding the morality of the act of sodomy, whether heterosexual or homosexual, do you think the criminal law ought to punish such conduct? Why or why not?

3.	In the context of sodomy laws, the alleged biblical condemnation of sodomy contained in the Book of Leviticus is often cited as the justification for morally condemning sodomy. Whether this interpretation of the Bible is a proper one is subject to debate in the scholarly literature, but to the extent that views on the immorality of sodomy have their origins in theology, what role do you think the separation of church and state should play, if any, in determining whether the religious nature of the condemnation of sodomy ought to be codified into criminal law? Explain.

4.	Earlier in this text, the four main theories of punishment were briefly described (retribution, deterrence, rehabilitation, and incapacitation). Evaluate the applicability of each of these theories when applied to laws punishing private acts of oral or anal sex between consenting adults.

5.	Recall Jeremy Bentham's three criteria for justifying punishment: there must be grounds for punishment, the punishment must be effective, and it must be profitable. Are laws against sodomy justifiable using Bentham's three criteria? Explain your answer.

CHAPTER 2
BASIC CONCEPTS OF CRIMINAL LAW

A. The Starting Point for Criminal Law

1. Presumptions

Criminal trials all begin at the same point: the defendant is presumed innocent until proven guilty in court. The presumption of innocence is just one type of presumptions. A **presumption** is a conclusion (or deduction) which the law requires the trier of fact to make (the trier-of-fact is usually a jury in a criminal case, but some criminal cases, called **bench trials**, are tried only before a judge who must render a verdict). The purpose of a presumption is to give the trier of fact a starting point for evaluating the case. True presumptions deal with deductions made from some fact actually proved (the basic fact) to some other critical fact (the presumed fact).

There are two main types of presumptions. The first type of presumption is known as a **conclusive or mandatory presumption**. If the law makes the presumption conclusive, then the finder of fact must accept the fact as presumed regardless of the evidence presented. There are very few mandatory presumptions today. One that comes to mind is the presumption of incapacity for a child under the age of seven to commit a crime. While theoretically possible to have six-year-old genius who could plot and carry out a crime with criminal intent, the law would conclusively presume a child of that age incapable of doing so. No evidence regarding the uniqueness of that particular child to show the presumption did not apply in that particular case would be admissible because the presumption is mandatory.

Conclusive presumptions played a larger role in the past than they do today. For example, at common law, it was conclusively presumed that a husband could not rape his wife. Today, nearly all U.S. jurisdictions penal codes recognize marital rape as a crime. Another example of a conclusive presumption that is no longer with us is the presumption of paternity. At common law, any child born to a married women was conclusively presumed to be the child of that woman's husband. Evidence to show that the husband was infertile was inadmissible because the presumption was mandatory. Today, that presumption has either been abolished, or has been converted to the second type of presumption, known as a rebuttable or permissive presumption.

Most presumptions today are **rebuttable presumptions**. That is, the trier of fact must presume a certain fact to be the case unless the presumption is overcome or "rebutted" by other evidence. An example is the presumption of innocence. All criminal defendants are presumed innocent unless proven guilty beyond a reasonable doubt. The way the presumption is overcome is by introducing evidence to prove the presumption of innocence is not correct when applied to a particular defendant, given the evidence in the case against him or her.

2. Types of Evidence

Evidence is anything that tends to prove the truth or untruth of any fact which is alleged. There are five main types of evidence.

Testimonial evidence is the evidence with which most people are most familiar. It is the term that refers to the testimony of a witness in court, is under oath, and is subject to cross-examination. The victim telling his or her version of the events constituting the crime; an eyewitness relaying his or her recollection of the events he or she perceived; a police offer's summary of what she discovered upon arrival at a scene; even an account of the allegedly peaceful/non-violent nature of the defendant by his or her best friend are all examples of testimonial evidence.

Physical evidence, sometimes called "real" evidence, refers to objects that have evidentiary value in and of themselves. Examples of physical evidence include weapons, drugs, clothing, and documents. Finding the murder weapon at the defendant's apartment, for example, would be the recovery of physical evidence.

Physical evidence is often confused with **scientific evidence**. Scientific evidence are the results of forensic investigatory techniques such as crime lab reports, autopsy findings, firearm matches, etc. The forensic procedures that are performed on physical evidence yield results that are scientific evidence. Thus, while blood found at a crime scene is physical evidence, once the blood is serologically analyzed, the results of the laboratory analysis of the blood are considered to be scientific evidence. Usually, the person performing the scientific test of the physical evidence is required to come to court and give testimonial evidence regarding his or her scientific findings. This illustrates well how proving (or disproving) a fact using "evidence" often involves the use of several types of evidence.

Evidence that is produced for use at trial to demonstrate certain things to a trier of fact such as diagrams, charts, maps, photographs, etc. are called **demonstrative evidence**. Unlike physical evidence, demonstrative evidence has no value in and of itself. Rather, demonstrative evidence is created for use at trial in order to illustrate certain points to the jury and/or judge.

Finally, there is a fifth type of evidence called **judicial notice**. Judicial notice does not involve evidence per se, but rather is a process that excuses a party from having to introduce evidence in order to prove something. In other words, judicial notice is the process whereby the trier of fact accepts certain facts as true without the necessity of formal proof. It's a short cut which excuses a party from the burden of having to prove certain facts through testimonial, physical, or other means when the matter is commonly known in the community by judges and jurors without further proof. For example, a court would take judicial notice of the fact that Halloween falls on October 31st or that Christmas falls on the December 25th without the requirement of having a calendar introduced into evidence. This would be appropriate since the dates of these holidays are within the common knowledge of the jury and the community at large. The meaning of certain words and phrases might be another example of something which a court might take judicial notice, such as "turning a trick" or "getting a fix."

3. Direct and Circumstantial Evidence

Evidence can be either direct or circumstantial. **Direct evidence** is that which proves a fact in issue directly without any reasoning or inferences needing to be drawn. Eyewitness testimony is a good example of direct evidence. If an eyewitness testifies that she saw the defendant stab the victim using a butcher's knife, that is direct evidence that the defendant did, in fact, stab the victim. See, however, that direct evidence does not necessarily mean the evidence is "true." The eyewitness may be lying. Alternatively, the eyewitness may be testifying truthfully to the best of his or her recollection, but the eyewitnesses' perceptions of the events may have been inaccurate.

In contrast to direct evidence, **circumstantial evidence** is that which indirectly proves a fact in issue. In other words, given whatever the circumstantial evidence is, the trier of fact would have to reason through it and infer the existence of some fact in dispute. Circumstantial evidence is very important since in many criminal cases, the perpetrator of the crime does not leave a trail of direct evidence. Take, for example, a homicide investigation where a husband is thought to have killed his wife.

Presume there is no direct evidence that he did it. The fact that the husband cannot account for his whereabouts during the time period the medical examiner has determined to be the time of death is circumstantial evidence of his guilt. Certainly, though, that fact alone would not be sufficient evidence to obtain a conviction. But if more circumstantial evidence were uncovered, the case would get stronger. Suppose that the husband stood to inherit a million dollars in life insurance proceeds upon her death. What if you also learned she was very unhappy in the marriage and planned to divorce the husband, thereby terminating his right to inherit her estate? See how you begin to feel more and more confident that these facts, if proven, go a long way toward confirming the husband's guilt. That is the importance of circumstantial evidence.

The distinction between direct and circumstantial evidence depends on the context of the question being examined. Suppose your fingerprints are found on a gun that forensic firearm testing reveals was the weapon used to kill the victim. Are you fingerprints direct or circumstantial evidence? It depends. They are direct evidence that you came in contact with the gun, but that doesn't mean you are the who fired it and killed the victim. Thus, your fingerprints are only circumstantial evidence of your being guilty of a homicide. An inference needs to resolve the question of your guilt.

Inferences are related to presumptions, but they differ in an important way. Inferences are conclusions that the trier of fact may deduce from the evidence presented, but is not required to deduce. They are permissive in nature. And they can be wrong. Go back to the example discussed above about the husband suspected of killing his wife. Given circumstantial evidence of her intent to divorce him, the money he stood to inherit if she dies while married to him, and his inability to account for his whereabouts at the time it is thought she was killed, you might *infer* his guilt, but you need not do so just from that evidence. And, in fact, you might be wrong.

In order to insure inferences that are made do not result in the innocent being convicted, the criminal law requires that there be a sufficient amount of evidence to convince the trier of fact of the defendant's guilt "beyond a reasonable doubt." Beyond a reasonable doubt is just one of several levels of proof used in courts of law.

4. Burdens of Proof

The term "burden of proof" is often erroneously referred to being the level of proof necessary to obtain a verdict in a case. It is not. Technically, the "burden of proof" has two distinct sub-components, the burden of production and the burden of persuasion.

The *burden of production* is also known as the burden of coming forward. It is called because the party who bears this burden must "come forward" with enough evidence to put a certain fact in issue. This burden does not belong to one party or the other. Rather, it shifts between prosecution or defense depending on the issue. For example, the defense bears the burden of coming forward with certain defenses, like insanity. The purpose of the defense bearing the burden of production on certain defenses is to give both the court and the prosecution notice that something (such as, in the case of insanity, the defendant's state of mind) will be an issue in the case. That is the primary purpose of the burden – to give notice so that a case may be properly litigated on the relevant issues. It is usually satisfied either simply giving notice or by introducing some evidence that need not rise to the level of any particular level of proof.

What most people think of as the burden of proof is technically called the *burden of persuasion*. The burden of persuasion is the responsibility of convincing the trier of fact (usually a jury in criminal cases, but it could also be a judge) that something is or is not the case. The party who bears the burden of persuasion must convince the trier of fact that whatever facts are at issue in a case ought to be resolved in its favor. In criminal cases, the prosecution bears the burden of persuasion to prove all of the necessary elements of a criminal offense beyond a reasonable doubt. There are times, however, when the defense will bear the burden of persuasion to prove the existence of facts which support a particular defense (for example, a defendant might be required to prove his or her insanity, or the existence of some provocation to mintage a murder down to the lesser crime of manslaughter). When the defense does bear such a burden, the defense raised is referred to as an *affirmative defense*. And there are even times, usually with respect to elements of crimes that are not central to the criminality at issue (often referred to as "attendant circumstances," a concept we will explore later), when the prosecution will bear the burden of persuasion at some lessor level of proof than beyond a reasonable doubt.

There are several different levels of burdens of persuasions. At the low extreme end, there would be no proof at all. Just above that, there is what is called *mere suspicion*. You have experienced this before. Think back to a time when you had no real information, nothing you could point to and explain it objectively to someone else. Yet, somehow, you knew something was true or that something had occurred. Call it intuition, a hunch, or a gut-instinct. That is mere suspicion. That level of proof will get you no where in the a court of law. No matter what phase in the criminal judicial process, something more than mere suspicion will be required.

To keep the metaphor running, presume that you have more than mere suspicion that is telling you something. Presume you have a reason beyond your intuition, hunch, or gut-instinct – a reason you can explain to another person and have that person understand why you were feeling suspicious. That level of proof is called *reasonable, articulable suspicion*. It is called that because at this level of proof, you can articulate your reasons for being suspicious. Reasonable, articulable suspicion is required to conduct a limited investigatory detention known as a "stop and frisk" or "Terry Stop" (based on the case *Terry v. Ohio* that established this level of proof).

Next up the scale is the level of proof known as *probable cause*. It is difficult to define what probably cause is. And the truth is that it not only often means different things to different people, but also varies from situation to situation. In general, the term means "reasonable to believe under the facts and circumstances known." It has also been defined as "a fair probability, given the totality of the facts and circumstances known, to believe that criminal activity is afoot." Key to establishing probable case is the existence of <u>facts</u> that can be objectively evaluated by some third person, such as a judge. Probable cause is the level of proof necessary to make an arrest, issue a warrant, or to hold a person in custody. Keep in mind that probable cause does not mean "more likely than not," but rather means there is a fair probability given what is known.

The next higher level of proof is called *preponderance of the evidence*. This standard means that something is more likely than not. Unlike the other levels of proof which are qualitative in nature and therefore defy quantification, this level of proof can be quantified. More likely than not means just over the 50% mark. Thus, 50.01% would be a preponderance of the evidence, even though just slightly so. This is the burden of persuasion most plaintiffs bear in civil cases. It is also the level of proof that the defense must meet in order to prevail on certain affirmative defenses, as you will learn later in this book.

As one goes further toward the certainly of the existence of in issue in dispute, the next level is called *clear and convincing evidence*. This level of proof requires the party bearing the burden to produce evidence that clearly establishes something. The trier of fact can still be left with doubts, but in spite of the doubts that exist, still feels relatively convinced. This level of proof is required for the plaintiff to meet its burden of persuasion in a small number of civil cases and for the defense to prove in a handful of affirmative defenses in criminal cases.

Finally, the highest of the burdens of persuasion is that required to convict a person of a crime. It is known as proof *beyond a reasonable doubt*. Defining this standard has proven to be problematic for the courts even after centuries of use. Generally, a doubt for which a reason can be given after there has been a fair and rational consideration of the evidence is a reasonable doubt. The doubt must be one that would cause a reasonable person of ordinary prudence to hesitate or pause before concluding that the defendant was guilty. It should be clearly understood that the concept of "reasonable doubt" is an inherently *qualitative* one. It cannot be quantified, and any attempt to do so for a jury is likely to result in reversible error. *See, e.g., McCullough v. State*, 657 P.2d 1157 (Nev. 1983).

This high level of proof in criminal cases serves several important functions. First, it reduces the risk of factual error. The philosophy of the criminal justice system has long been that it is better to let a guilty person go free than to deprive an innocent person of life, liberty, or property unjustly. Second, the beyond a reasonable doubt standard helps to ensure the presumption of innocence is honored. And finally, it helps to instills confidence in the application of criminal law.

The following case illustrates the problems associated with this level of proof.

Clarence VICTOR, Petitioner, v. State of NEBRASKA, Respondent;
and the companion case of
Alfred Arthur SANDOVAL, Petitioner, v. State of CALIFORNIA, Respondent.
511 U.S. 1 (1994).

Justice O'Connor delivered the opinion of the Court.

I

The government must prove beyond a reasonable doubt every element of a charged offense. *In re Winship*, 397 U.S. 358 (1970). Although this standard is an ancient and honored aspect of our criminal justice system, it defies easy explication. In these cases, we consider the constitutionality of two attempts to define "reasonable doubt."

The beyond a reasonable doubt standard is a requirement of due process, but the Constitution neither prohibits trial courts from defining reasonable doubt nor requires them to do so as a matter of course. Indeed, so long as the court instructs the jury on the necessity that the defendant's guilt be proved beyond a reasonable doubt, the Constitution does not require that any particular form of words be used in advising the jury of the government's burden of proof. Rather, "taken as a whole, the instructions [must] correctly conve[y] the concept of reasonable doubt to the jury." *Holland v. United States*, 348 U.S. 121, 140 (1954).

In only one case have we held that a definition of reasonable doubt violated the Due Process Clause. *Cage v. Louisiana*, 498 U.S. 39 (1990).). There, the jurors were told:

> [A reasonable doubt] is one that is founded upon a real tangible substantial basis and not upon mere caprice and conjecture. It must be such doubt as would give rise to a grave uncertainty, raised in your mind by reasons of the unsatisfactory character of the evidence or lack thereof. A reasonable doubt is not a mere possible doubt. It is an actual substantial doubt. It is a doubt that a reasonable man can seriously entertain. What is required is not an absolute or mathematical certainty, but a moral certainty.

We held that . . . the words "substantial" and "grave," as they are commonly understood, suggest a higher degree of doubt than is required for acquittal under the reasonable doubt standard. When those statements are then considered with the reference to "moral certainty," rather than evidentiary certainty, it becomes clear that a reasonable juror could have interpreted the instruction to allow a finding of guilt based on a degree of proof below that required by the Due Process Clause.

II

On October 14, 1984, petitioner Sandoval shot three men, two of them fatally, in a gang-related incident in Los Angeles. About two weeks later, he entered the home of a man who had given information to the police about the murders and shot him dead; Sandoval then killed the man's wife because she had seen him murder her husband. Sandoval was convicted on four counts of first degree murder. The jury found that Sandoval personally used a firearm in the commission of each offense, and found the special circumstance of multiple murder. He was sentenced to death for murdering the woman and to life in prison without possibility of parole for the other three murders. The California Supreme Court affirmed the convictions and sentences.

The jury in Sandoval's case was given the following instruction on the government's burden of proof:

> A defendant in a criminal action is presumed to be innocent until the contrary is proved, and in case of a reasonable doubt whether his guilt is satisfactorily shown, he is entitled to a verdict of not guilty. This presumption places upon the State the burden of proving him guilty beyond a reasonable doubt. "Reasonable doubt" is defined as follows: It is not a mere possible doubt; because everything relating to human affairs, and depending on moral evidence, is open to some possible or imaginary doubt. It is that

34

state of the case which, after the entire comparison and consideration of all the evidence, leaves the minds of the jurors in that condition that they cannot say they feel an abiding conviction, to a moral certainty, of the truth of the charge.

Sandoval's primary objection is to the use of the phrases "moral evidence" and "moral certainty" in the instruction. . . . We recognize that the phrase "moral evidence" is not a mainstay of the modern lexicon, though we do not think it means anything different today than it did in the 19th century. The few contemporary dictionaries that define moral evidence do so consistently with its original meaning.

Moreover, the instruction itself gives a definition of the phrase. The jury was told that "everything relating to human affairs, and depending on moral evidence, is open to some possible or imaginary doubt" – in other words, that absolute certainty is unattainable in matters relating to human affairs. Moral evidence, in this sentence, can only mean empirical evidence offered to prove such matters – the proof introduced at trial.

This conclusion is reinforced by other instructions given in Sandoval's case. The judge informed the jurors that their duty was "to determine the facts of the case from the evidence received in the trial and not from any other source." The judge continued: "Evidence consists of testimony of witnesses, writings, material objects, or anything presented to the senses and offered to prove the existence or non-existence of a fact." The judge also told the jurors that "you must not be influenced by pity for a defendant or by prejudice against him," and that "[y]ou must not be swayed by mere sentiment, conjecture, sympathy, passion, prejudice, public opinion or public feeling." These instructions correctly pointed the jurors' attention to the facts of the case before them, not (as Sandoval contends) the ethics or morality of Sandoval's criminal acts. Accordingly, we find the reference to moral evidence unproblematic.

We are somewhat more concerned with Sandoval's argument that the phrase "moral certainty" has lost its historical meaning, and that a modern jury would understand it to allow conviction on proof that does not meet the beyond a reasonable doubt standard. Words and phrases can change meaning over time: A passage generally understood in 1850 may be incomprehensible or confusing to a modern juror. [W]e are willing to accept Sandoval's premise that "moral certainty," standing alone, might not be recognized by modern jurors as a synonym for "proof beyond a reasonable doubt." But it does not necessarily follow that the California instruction is unconstitutional.

Sandoval first argues that moral certainty would be understood by modern jurors to mean a standard of proof lower than beyond a reasonable doubt. In support of this proposition, Sandoval points to contemporary dictionaries that define moral certainty in terms of probability. E.g., Webster's New Twentieth Century Dictionary, supra, at 1168 ("based on strong probability"); Random House Dictionary of the English Language 1249 (2d ed. 1983) ("resting upon convincing grounds of probability"). But the beyond a reasonable doubt standard is itself probabilistic. "[I]n a judicial proceeding in which there is a dispute about the facts of some earlier event, the factfinder cannot acquire unassailably accurate knowledge of what happened. Instead, all the factfinder can acquire is a belief of what probably happened." *In re Winship*, 397 U.S., at 370. The problem is not that moral certainty may be understood in terms of probability, but that a jury might understand the phrase to mean something less than the very high level of probability required by the Constitution in criminal cases.

Although in this respect moral certainty is ambiguous in the abstract, the rest of the instruction given in Sandoval's case lends content to the phrase. The jurors were told that they must have "an abiding conviction, to a moral certainty, of the truth of the charge." An instruction cast in terms of an abiding conviction as to guilt, without reference to moral certainty, correctly states the government's burden of proof. As used in this instruction, therefore, we are satisfied that the reference to moral certainty, in conjunction with the abiding conviction language, "impress[ed] upon the factfinder the need to reach a subjective state of near certitude of the guilt of the accused." *Jackson v. Virginia*, 443 U.S. at 315. Accordingly, we reject Sandoval's contention that the moral certainty element of the California instruction invited the jury to convict him on proof below that required by the Due Process Clause.

Sandoval's second argument is a variant of the first. Accepting that the instruction requires a high level of confidence in the defendant's guilt, Sandoval argues that a juror might be convinced to a moral certainty that the defendant is guilty even though the government has failed to prove his guilt beyond a reasonable doubt. A definition of moral certainty in a widely used modern dictionary lends support to this argument, see American Heritage Dictionary 1173 (3d ed. 1992) ("Based on strong likelihood or firm conviction, rather than on the actual evidence"), and we do not gainsay its force.

But the moral certainty language cannot be sequestered from its surroundings. In the *Cage* instruction, the jurors were simply told that they had to be morally certain of the defendant's guilt; there was nothing else in the instruction to lend meaning to the phrase. Not so here. The jury in Sandoval's case was told that a reasonable doubt is "that state of the case which, after the entire comparison and consideration of all the evidence, leaves the minds of the jurors in that condition that they cannot say they feel an abiding conviction, to a moral certainty, of the truth of the charge." The instruction thus explicitly told the jurors that their conclusion had to be based on the evidence in the case. Other instructions reinforced this message. The jury was told "to determine the facts of the case from the evidence received in the trial and not from any other source." The judge continued that "you must not be influenced by pity for a defendant or by prejudice against him.... You must not be swayed by mere sentiment, conjecture, sympathy, passion, prejudice, public opinion or public feeling." Id., at 39. Accordingly, there is no reasonable likelihood that the jury would have understood moral certainty to be disassociated from the evidence in the case.

We do not think it reasonably likely that the jury understood the words "moral certainty" either as suggesting a standard of proof lower than due process requires or as allowing conviction on factors other than the government's proof. At the same time, however, we do not condone the use of the phrase. As modern dictionary definitions of moral certainty attest, the common meaning of the phrase has changed since it was used in the Webster instruction, and it may continue to do so to the point that it conflicts with the Winship standard. Indeed, the definitions of reasonable doubt most widely used in the federal courts do not contain any reference to moral certainty. See Federal Judicial Center, Pattern Criminal Jury Instructions 28 (1988); 1 E. DEVITT & C. BLACKMAR, Federal Jury Practice and Instructions § 11.14 (3d ed. 1977). But we have no supervisory power over the state courts, and in the context of the instructions as a whole we cannot say that the use of the phrase rendered the instruction given in Sandoval's case unconstitutional.

III

On December 26, 1987, petitioner Victor went to the Omaha home of an 82-year-old woman for whom he occasionally did gardening work. Once inside, he beat her with a pipe and cut her throat with a knife, killing her. Victor was convicted of first degree murder. A three-judge panel found the statutory aggravating circumstances that Victor had previously been convicted of murder, and that the murder in this case was especially heinous, atrocious, and cruel. Finding none of the statutory mitigating circumstances, the panel sentenced Victor to death. The Nebraska Supreme Court affirmed the conviction and sentence.

At Victor's trial, the judge instructed the jury that "[t]he burden is always on the State to prove beyond a reasonable doubt all of the material elements of the crime charged, and this burden never shifts." The charge continued:

"Reasonable doubt" is such a doubt as would cause a reasonable and prudent person, in one of the graver and more important transactions of life, to pause and hesitate before taking the represented facts as true and relying and acting thereon. It is such a doubt as will not permit you, after full, fair, and impartial consideration of all the evidence, to have an abiding conviction, to a moral certainty, of the guilt of the accused. At the same time, absolute or mathematical certainty is not required. You may be convinced of the truth of a fact beyond a reasonable doubt and yet be fully aware that possibly you may be mistaken. You may find an accused guilty upon the strong probabilities of the case, provided such probabilities are strong enough to exclude any doubt of his guilt that is reasonable. A reasonable doubt is an actual and substantial doubt reasonably arising from the evidence, from the facts or circumstances shown by the evidence, or from the lack of evidence on the part of the State, as distinguished from a doubt arising from mere possibility, from bare imagination, or from fanciful conjecture.

Victor's primary argument is that equating a reasonable doubt with a "substantial doubt" overstated the degree of doubt necessary for acquittal. We agree that this construction is somewhat problematic. On the one hand, "substantial" means "not seeming or imaginary"; on the other, it means "that specified to a large degree." The former is unexceptionable, as it informs the jury only that a reasonable doubt is something more than a speculative one; but the latter could imply a doubt greater than required for acquittal under *Winship*. Any ambiguity, however, is removed by reading the phrase in the context of the sentence in which it appears: "A reasonable doubt is an actual and substantial doubt . . . as distinguished from a doubt arising from mere possibility, from bare imagination, or from fanciful conjecture."

This explicit distinction between a substantial doubt and a fanciful conjecture was not present in the *Cage* instruction. We did say in that case that "the words 'substantial' and 'grave,' as they are commonly understood, suggest a higher degree of doubt than is required for acquittal under the reasonable doubt standard." *Cage*, 498 U.S. at 41. But we did not hold that the reference to substantial doubt alone was sufficient to render the instruction unconstitutional. Rather, we were concerned that the jury would interpret the term "substantial doubt" in parallel with the preceding reference to "grave uncertainty," leading to an overstatement of the doubt necessary to acquit. In the instruction given in Victor's case, the context makes clear that "substantial" is used in the sense of existence rather than magnitude of the doubt, so the same concern is not present.

In any event, the instruction provided an alternative definition of reasonable doubt: a doubt that would cause a reasonable person to hesitate to act. This is a formulation we have repeatedly approved, and to the extent the word "substantial" denotes the quantum of doubt necessary for acquittal, the hesitate to act standard gives a common sense benchmark for just how substantial such a doubt must be. We therefore do not think it reasonably likely that the jury would have interpreted this instruction to indicate that the doubt must be anything other than a reasonable one.

IV

The Due Process Clause requires the government to prove a criminal defendant's guilt beyond a reasonable doubt, and trial courts must avoid defining reasonable doubt so as to lead the jury to convict on a lesser showing than due process requires. In these cases, however, we conclude that taken as a whole, the instructions correctly conveyed the concept of reasonable doubt to the jury. There is no reasonable likelihood that the jurors who determined petitioners' guilt applied the instructions in a way that violated the Constitution. The judgments in both cases are accordingly affirmed.

Justice Ginsburg, concurring in part and concurring in the judgment.

I agree with the Court that the reasonable doubt instructions given in these cases, read as a whole, satisfy the Constitution's due process requirement. As the Court observes, the instructions adequately conveyed to the jurors that they should focus exclusively upon the evidence, and that they should convict only if they had an "abiding conviction" of the defendant's guilt. I agree, further, with the Court's suggestion that the term "moral certainty," while not in itself so misleading as to render the instructions unconstitutional, should be avoided as an unhelpful way of explaining what reasonable doubt means.

Similarly unhelpful, in my view, are two other features of the instruction given in Victor's case. That instruction begins by defining reasonable doubt as "such a doubt as would cause a reasonable and prudent person, in one of the graver and more important transactions of life, to pause and hesitate before taking the represented facts as true and relying and acting thereon." A committee of distinguished federal judges, reporting to the Judicial Conference of the United States, has criticized this "hesitate to act" formulation because the analogy it uses seems misplaced. In the decisions people make in the most important of their own affairs, resolution of conflicts about past events does not usually play a major role. Indeed, decisions we make in the most important affairs of our lives – choosing a spouse, a job, a place to live, and the like – generally involve a very heavy element of uncertainty and risk-taking. They are wholly unlike the decisions jurors ought to make in criminal cases.

Federal Judicial Center, Pattern Criminal Jury Instructions 18-19 (1987) (commentary on instruction 21).

More recently, Second Circuit Chief Judge Jon O. Newman observed:

Although, as a district judge, I dutifully repeated [the 'hesitate to act' standard] to juries in scores of criminal trials, I was always bemused by its ambiguity. If the jurors encounter a doubt that would cause them to 'hesitate to act in a matter of importance,' what are they to do then? Should they decline to convict because they have reached a point of hesitation, or should they simply hesitate, then ask themselves whether, in their own private matters, they would resolve the doubt in favor of action, and, if so, continue on to convict?"

Beyond "Reasonable Doubt," 68 N.Y.U. L. Rev. 201, 204 (1994) (James Madison Lecture, delivered at New York University Law School, Nov. 9, 1993).

These and similar difficulties have led some courts to question the efficacy of any reasonable doubt instruction. At least two of the Federal Courts of Appeals have admonished their District Judges not to attempt a definition. This Court, too, has suggested on occasion that prevailing definitions of "reasonable doubt" afford no real aid. But we have never held that the concept of reasonable doubt is undefinable, or that trial courts should not, as a matter of course, provide a definition. Nor, contrary to the Court's suggestion, have we ever held that the Constitution does not require trial courts to define reasonable doubt.

Because the trial judges in fact defined reasonable doubt in both jury charges we review, we need not decide whether the Constitution required them to do so. Whether or not the Constitution so requires, however, the argument for defining the concept is strong. While judges and lawyers are familiar with the reasonable doubt standard, the words "beyond a reasonable doubt" are not self-defining for jurors. Several studies of jury behavior have concluded that "jurors are often confused about the meaning of reasonable doubt" when that term is left undefined. Thus, even if definitions of reasonable doubt are necessarily imperfect, the alternative – refusing to define the concept at all – is not obviously preferable.

Fortunately, the choice need not be one between two kinds of potential juror confusion – on one hand, the confusion that may be caused by leaving "reasonable doubt" undefined, and on the other, the confusion that might be induced by the anachronism of "moral certainty," the misplaced analogy of "hesitation to act," or the circularity of "doubt that is reasonable." The Federal Judicial Center has proposed a definition of reasonable doubt that is clear, straightforward, and accurate. That instruction reads:

[T]he government has the burden of proving the defendant guilty beyond a reasonable doubt. Some of you may have served as jurors in civil cases, where you were told that it is only necessary to prove that a fact is more likely true than not true. In criminal cases, the government's proof must be more powerful than that. It must be beyond a reasonable doubt.

Proof beyond a reasonable doubt is proof that leaves you firmly convinced of the defendant's guilt. There are very few things in this world that we know with absolute certainty, and in criminal cases the law does not require proof that overcomes every possible doubt. If, based on your consideration of the evidence, you are firmly convinced that the defendant is guilty of the crime charged, you must find him guilty. If on the other hand, you think there is a real possibility that he is not guilty, you must give him the benefit of the doubt and find him not guilty.

Federal Judicial Center, Pattern Criminal Jury Instructions, at 17-18 (instruction 21).

This instruction plainly informs the jurors that the prosecution must prove its case by more than a mere preponderance of the evidence, yet not necessarily to an absolute certainty. The "firmly convinced" standard for conviction, repeated for emphasis, is further enhanced by the juxtaposed prescription that the jury must acquit if there is a "real possibility" that the defendant is innocent. This model instruction surpasses others I have seen in stating the reasonable doubt standard succinctly and comprehensibly.

Justice Blackmun, with whom Justice Souter joins, concurring in part and dissenting in part.

The majority today purports to uphold and follow *Cage*, but plainly falters in its application of that case. There is no meaningful difference between the jury instruction delivered at Victor's trial and the jury instruction issued in *Cage*, save the fact that the jury instruction in Victor's case did not contain the two words "grave uncertainty." But the mere absence of these two words can be of no help to the State, since there is other language in the instruction that is equally offensive to due process. I therefore dissent from the Court's opinion and judgment in No. 92-8894, Victor v. Nebraska.

The majority's attempt to distinguish [the] instruction[s in this case] from the one employed in *Cage* is wholly unpersuasive. Both instructions equate "substantial doubt" with reasonable doubt, and refer to "moral certainty" rather than "evidentiary certainty." And although Victor's instruction does not contain the phrase "grave uncertainty," the instruction contains language that has an equal potential to mislead, including the invitation to the jury to convict based on the "strong probabilities" of the case and the overt effort to dissuade jurors from acquitting when they are "fully aware that possibly they may be mistaken." Nonetheless, the majority argues that "substantial doubt" has a meaning in Victor's instruction different from that in *Cage's* instruction, and that the "moral certainty" language is sanitized by its context. The majority's approach seems to me to fail under its own logic.

First, the majority concedes, as it must, that equating reasonable doubt with substantial doubt is "somewhat problematic" since one of the common definitions of "substantial" is "that specified to a large degree." But the majority insists that the jury did not likely interpret the word "substantial" in this manner because Victor's instruction, unlike Cage's instruction, used the phrase "substantial doubt" as a means of distinguishing reasonable doubt from mere conjecture. According to the majority, "[t]his explicit distinction between a substantial doubt and a fanciful conjecture was not present in the *Cage* instruction," and thus, read in context, the use of "substantial doubt" in Victor's instruction is less problematic.

A casual reading of the *Cage* instruction reveals the majority's false premise. The *Cage* instruction plainly states that a reasonable doubt is a doubt "founded upon a real tangible substantial basis and not upon mere caprice and conjecture." The *Cage* instruction also used the "substantial doubt" language to distinguish a reasonable doubt from "a mere possible doubt." Thus, the reason the Court condemned the "substantial doubt" language in *Cage* had nothing to do with the absence of appropriate contrasting language; rather, the Court condemned the language for precisely the reason it gave: "[T]he words 'substantial' and 'grave,' as they are commonly understood, suggest a higher degree of doubt than is required for acquittal under the reasonable doubt standard." Id. at 41. In short, the majority's speculation that the jury in Victor's case interpreted "substantial" to mean something other than "that specified to a large degree" simply because the word "substantial" is used at one point to distinguish mere conjecture is unfounded and is foreclosed by *Cage* itself.

QUESTIONS

1.   What do you think of the Court's decision? Do you have a better conceptualization of what "beyond a reasonable doubt" is after having read the case, or does it seem more complicated now? Why?

2.   The Court found the phrase "proof to a moral certainty" to be "problematic." Why? What does this phrase mean to you? What are the drawbacks of referring a standard of proof that is concededly qualitative in terms of morality? Explain your position.

3.   Of the various definitions of proof beyond a reasonable doubt discussed in the majority and dissenting opinions, which do you find to be the most helpful? Can you define this standard in your own words?

B. Essential Elements of a Crime: Actus Reus

Crimes generally consist of four components: actus reus, mens rea, attendant circumstances, and result. Every crime, by definition, sets forth some physical act or conduct that is prohibited – the "thing" you are not allowed to do under the criminal law. Such proscribed conduct is called the **actus reus** (Latin for the "evil act"). For example, taking the personal property of another (if couple with the mental state of intent to steal) is the crime of theft. The actus reus is the actual taking of the property.

Most crimes, however, do not impose a criminal sanction for doing an actus reus unless it is coupled with some culpable state of mind referred to as the **mens rea** (Latin for "evil mind"). Mens rea is concerned with the level of intentionality with which the actus reus occurred. For example, was the actus reus done on purpose? Perhaps it was done negligently, or totally innocently. Take the theft example again. If you accidental take someone else's property, that is not the crime of theft. But if you purposely take it, then a theft may have occurred. The level of mens rea entertained by a person often is what differentiates and accident from a crime, or a serious crimes from a petty one. It should be noted, though, there is a narrow class of crimes that are exceptions to this general requirement of a union of actus reus and mens rea. These offenses that are punished without regard to the actor's state of mind are referred to as crimes of **strict liability**. We will cover strict liability crimes later in this chapter.

The third major component to crimes is the **result** – that which actually occurred due to the commission of the actus reus. As stated above, all crimes, save strict liability offenses, require some union of actus reus and mens rea, making both actus reus and mens rea necessary components to nearly all criminal offense. The same cannot be said for result component or the fourth component, attendant circumstances. Only certain crimes require that a particular result occur. All homicide crimes are good examples. One cannot be convicted of any type of homicide unless one's act caused a particular result, namely, the death of another human being.

The fourth and last of the major components of crimes is known as **attendant circumstances**. Attendant circumstances are those circumstances which must surround the occurrence of the actus reus for the crime to have occurred, or for it to be graded in a particular manner. For example, the crime of speeding does not take place unless one is traveling on a public roadway. Hence, it is not a crime to race in the Indianapolis 500 because the attendant circumstance of being a public roadway is not present.

1. Requirement of a Voluntary Act

For an actus reus to be deemed to have occurred, it must be the result of either a voluntary act (even state of possession), or a qualifying omission. A "**voluntary act**" means a bodily movement performed consciously and as a result of effort and determination. For example, punching someone is a voluntary act that would qualify as the actus reus for the crime of battery. Similarly, shooting someone is a voluntary act that would qualify as the actus reus for a homicide if the victim died. Even speaking certain words may be a voluntary acts upon which a criminal prosecution may be based if the words spoken are prohibited, as in the crime of a criminal solicitation, or in the use of fighting words which incite a riot.

Involuntary acts, defined as any bodily movements that are not a product of the effort or determination of the actor (whether conscious or habitual), do *not* qualify as an actus reus for the criminal law. Accordingly, acts that are a product of automatism (e.g., innate reflexes, spasms, spontaneous convulsions, and other muscular actions that occur without the conscious control of the mind) are not considered to be voluntary acts, and thus, are not crimes. But an act is not considered involuntary merely because (a) the actor does not remember it; (b) the actor could not control his/her impulses to do the act; (c) the act was unintentional or its consequences were unforseen; or (d) it was habitual.

Similarly, because voluntariness presupposes consciousness, any act that occurs while the actor is unconscious will not qualify as an actus reus so long as the unconscious state was not self-induced. While this is a seemingly clear rule, there are situations in which a defendant may be held criminally liable even though the action immediately causing the harm was clearly involuntary. Consider the following case.

The PEOPLE of the State of New York, Appellant-Respondent, v. Emil DECINA, Respondent-Appellant. 138 N.E.2d 799, 157 N.Y.S.2d 558 (1956).

Froessel, Judge

At about 3:30 p.m. on March 14, 1955, a bright, sunny day, defendant was driving, alone in his car, in a northerly direction on Delaware Avenue in the city of Buffalo. The portion of Delaware Avenue here involved is 60 feet wide. At a point south of an overhead viaduct of the Erie Railroad, defendant's car swerved to the left, across the center line in the street, so that it was completely in the south lane, traveling 35 to 40 miles per hour. In then veered sharply to the right, crossing Delaware Avenue and mounting the easterly curb . . . at a speed estimated to have been about 50 or 60 miles per hour or more. During this latter swerve, a pedestrian testified that he saw defendant's hand above his head; another witness said he saw defendant's left arm bent over the wheel, and his right hand extended towards the right door.

A group of six schoolgirls were walking north on the easterly sidewalk of Delaware Avenue, two in front and four slightly in the rear, when defendant's car struck them from behind. One of the girls escaped injury by jumping against the wall of the viaduct. Three of the children, 6 to 12 years old, were found dead on arrival by the medical examiner, and a fourth child, 7 years old, died in a hospital two days later as a result of injuries sustained in the accident.

After striking the children, defendant's car continued on the easterly sidewalk, and then swerved back onto Delaware Avenue once more. It continued in a northerly direction, passing under a second viaduct before it again veered to the right and remounted the easterly curb, striking and breaking a metal lamppost. With its horn blowing steadily apparently because defendant was stopped over the steering wheel the car proceeded on the sidewalk until if finally crashed through a 7 ¼-inch brick wall of a grocery store, injuring at least one customer and causing considerable property damage.

When the car came to a halt in the store, with its horn still blowing, several fires had been ignited. Defendant was stooped over in the car and was "bobbing a little." To one witness he appeared dazed, to another unconscious, lying back with his hands off the wheel. Various people present shouted to defendant to turn off the ignition of his car, and "within a matter of seconds the horn stopped blowing and the car did shut off."

Defendant was pulled out of the car by a number of bystanders and laid down on the sidewalk. To a policeman who came on the scene shortly he appeared "injured, dazed"; another witness said that "he looked as though he was knocked out, and his arm seemed to be bleeding." An injured customer in the store, after receiving first aid, pressed defendant for an explanation of the accident and he told her: "I blacked out from the bridge."

When the police arrived, defendant attempted to rise, staggered and appeared dazed and unsteady. When informed that he was under arrest, and would have to accompany the police to the station house, he resisted and, when he tried to get away, was handcuffed. The foregoing evidence was adduced by the People, and is virtually undisputed defendant did not take the stand nor did he produce any witnesses.

From the police station defendant was taken to the E.J. Meyer Memorial Hospital, a county institution, arriving at 5:30 p.m. . . . On the evening of that day, after an intern had visited and treated defendant and given orders for therapy, Dr. Wechter, a resident physician in the hospital and a member of its staff, came to his room. . . . Defendant then proceeded to relate to Dr. Wechter his past medical history, namely, that at the age of 7 he was struck by an auto and suffered a marked loss of hearing. In 1946 he was treated in this same hospital for an illness during which he had some convulsions. Several burr holes were made in his skull and a brain abscess was drained. Following this operation defendant had no convulsions from 1946 through 1950. In 1950 he had four convulsions, caused by scar tissue on the brain. From 1950 to 1954 he experienced about 10 or 20 seizures a year, in which his right hand would jump although he remained fully conscious. In 1954, he had 4 or 5 generalized seizures with loss of consciousness, the last being in September, 1954, a few months before the accident. Thereafter he had more hospitalization, a spinal tap, consultation with a neurologist, and took medication daily to help prevent seizures.

On the basis of this medical history, Dr. Wechter made a diagnosis of Jacksonian epilepsy, and was of the opinion that defendant had a seizure at the time of the accident. Other members of the hospital staff performed blood tests and took an electroencephalogram during defendant's three-day stay there. The testimony of Dr. Wechter is the only testimony before the trial court showing that defendant had epilepsy, suffered an attack at the time of the accident, and had knowledge of his susceptibility to such attacks.

Defendant was indicted and charged with violating section 1053-a of the Penal Law. That section provides that any person who operates or drives any vehicle of any kind in a reckless or culpable negligent manner, whereby a human being is killed, is guilty of criminal negligence in the operation of a vehicle resulting in death. A person so convicted may be punished by a term of imprisonment up to 5 years, or a fine up to $1,000, or both.

We turn first to the subject of defendant's cross appeal, namely, that his demurrer should have been sustained, since the indictment here does not charge a crime. The indictment states essentially that defendant, knowing "that he was subject to epileptic attacks or other disorder rendering him likely to lose consciousness for a considerable period of time," was culpably negligent "in that he consciously undertook to and did operate his Buick sedan on a public highway" and "while so doing" suffered such an attack which caused said automobile "to travel at a fast and reckless rate of speed, jumping the curb and driving over the sidewalk" causing the death of 4 persons. In our opinion, this clearly states a violation of section 1053-a of the Penal Law. The statute does not require that a defendant must deliberately intend to kill a human being, for that would be murder. Nor does the statute require that he knowingly and consciously follow the precise path that leads to death and destruction. It is sufficient when his conduct manifests a disregard of the consequences which may ensue from the act, and indifference to the rights of others. No clearer definition, applicable to the hundreds of varying circumstances that may arise, can be given. *Actus Reaus → operating the vehicle* *Mens Rea → unconscious*

Assuming the truth of the indictment, this defendant knew he was subject to epileptic attacks and seizures that might strike at any time. He also knew that a moving motor vehicle uncontrolled on public highway is a highly dangerous instrumentality capable of unrestrained destruction. With this knowledge, and without anyone accompanying him, he deliberately took a chance by making a conscious choice of a course of action, in disregard of the consequences which he knew might follow from his conscious act, and which in this case did ensue. How can we say as a matter of law that this did not amount to culpable negligence within the meaning of section 1053-a? To hold otherwise would be to say that a man may freely indulge himself in liquor in the same hope that it will not affect his driving, and if it later develops that ensuing intoxication causes dangerous and reckless driving resulting in death, his unconsciousness or involuntariness at that time relieve him from prosecution under the statute. His awareness of a condition which he knows may produce such consequences as here, and his disregard of the

42

consequences, renders him liable for culpable negligence, as the courts below have properly held. To have a sudden sleeping spell, an unexpected heart or other disabling attack, without any prior knowledge or warning thereof, is an altogether different situation, and there is simply no basis for comparing such cases with the flagrant disregard manifested here.

Desmond, Judge (concurring in part and dissenting in part).

I think the indictment should be dismissed because it alleges no crime. The indictment charges that defendant knowing that "he was subject to epileptic attacks or other disorder rendering him likely to lose consciousness" suffered "an attack and loss of consciousness which caused the said automobile operated by the said defendant to travel at a fast and reckless rate of speed" and to jump a curb and run onto the sidewalk "thereby striking and causing the death" of 4 children. Horrible as this occurrence was and whatever necessity it may show for new licensing and driving laws, nevertheless this indictment charges no crime known to the New York statutes. Our duty is to dismiss it.

Section 1053-a of the Penal Law describes the crime of "criminal negligence in the operation of a vehicle resulting in death." Declared to be guilty of that crime is "a person who operates or drives any vehicle of any kind in a reckless or culpably negligent manner, whereby a human being is killed." The essentials of the crime are, therefore, first, vehicle operation in a culpably negligent manner, and, second, the resulting death of a person. This indictment asserts that defendant violated section 1053-a, but it then proceeds in the language quoted in the next-above paragraph of this opinion to describe the way in which defendant is supposed to have offended against that statute. That descriptive matter shows that defendant did not violate section 1053-a. No operation of an automobile in a reckless manner is charged against defendant. The excessive speed of the car and its jumping the curb were "caused," says the indictment itself, by defendant's prior "attack and loss of consciousness." Therefore, what defendant is accused of is not reckless or culpably negligent driving, which necessarily connotes and involves consciousness and volition. The fatal assault by this car was after and because of defendant's failure of consciousness. To say that one drove a car in a reckless manner in that his unconscious condition caused the car to travel recklessly is to make two mutually contradictory assertions. One cannot be "reckless" while unconscious. One cannot while unconscious "operate" a car in a culpably negligent manner or in any other "manner." The statute makes criminal a particular kind of knowing, voluntary, immediate operation. It does not touch at all the involuntary presence of an unconscious person at the wheel of an uncontrolled vehicle. To negative the possibility of applying section 1053-a to these alleged facts we do not even have to resort to the rule that all criminal statutes are closely and strictly construed in favor of the citizen and that no act or omission is criminal unless specifically and in terms so labeled by a clearly worded statute.

No motorist suffering from any serious malady or infirmity can with impunity drive any automobile at any time or place, since no one can know what physical conditions make it "reckless" or "culpably negligent" to drive an automobile. Such a construction of a criminal statute offends against due process and against justice and fairness. The courts are bound to reject such conclusions when, as here, it is clearly possible to ascribe a different but reasonable meaning. A whole new approach may be necessary to the problem of issuing or refusing drivers' licenses to epileptics and persons similarly afflicted. But the absence of adequate licensing controls cannot in law or in justice be supplied by criminal prosecutions of drivers who have violated neither the language nor the intendment of any criminal law.

Entirely without pertinence here is any consideration of driving while intoxicated or while sleepy, since those are conditions presently known to the driver, not mere future possibilities or probabilities. The demurrer should be sustained and the indictment dismissed.

QUESTIONS

1. What is the actus reus at issue in *Decina*? What mens rea is necessary for conviction?

2. As the case makes clear, acts that someone commits while unconscious are not "voluntary acts" that will qualify as an actus reus so long as the unconscious state was not self-induced. Why do you think there is an exception for unconscious states that are self-induced? Given the general requirement of consciousness, how do you think the criminal law would deal with an act committed while the actor was sleepwalking?

3. Putting aside the issue of qualifying omissions for the moment, given the requirement of a conscious, voluntary act, 2, how could the court have deemed a qualifying actus reus to have occurred in *Decina* since he was not conscious at the time the car went out of control and killed the children? Do you agree with the court? Why or why not?

2. An Omission as an Actus Reus

An *omission*, defined as a failure to act, can qualify as an actus reus in limited circumstances. Liability for the commission of an offense may not be based on an omission unaccompanied by any other action unless: (a) the omission is expressly made sufficient by the law defining the offense (such as the failure to pay income taxes or the failure to yield when traffic laws requires it); or (b) a duty to perform the omitted act is otherwise imposed by law. The "imposed by law" part is important since only legal duties to act, not moral ones, can serve as the basis of an omission qualifying as an actus reus.

Legal duties to act normally come about in one of four ways. The first way a legal duty to act may be imposed is by the nature of a special relationship. A parent owes a legal duty to care for his or her child; a physician owes a legal duty to care for his or her patient. A failure to live up to the duties imposed by the nature of such a special relationship can be an omission that qualifies as an actus reus for criminal law purposes.

The second way a legal duty to act might be imposed is by statute. For example, there are laws in most U.S. jurisdictions that require a driver to stop and render aid at the scene of an accident in which he or she was involved. Failing to do so can be deemed an actus reus by omission. A fairly controversial duty to act statute in effect in a handful of U.S. jurisdictions are mandatory "Good Samaritan" laws. Minnesota was the first state to mandate Good Samaritan rescue efforts under penalty of a criminal fine. Vermont, Rhode Island, and Wisconsin followed suit. And some local jurisdictions have ordinances that require someone to come to the aid of another person if they can do so safely. This was the premise of the final episode of "Seinfeld" in which the four main characters were tried, convicted, and sentenced to a year in jail for failing to assist someone else in need. Most European countries require one to aid another as well. Even in those states that do not require Good Samaritan aid to be rendered, most states make it a crime to refuse to obey the lawful order of a police officer who commands a bystander to assist them.

As an aside, when one who acts to help someone does so out of a moral duty, as opposed to a legal one, he or she may be subject to a civil suit if the person acts negligently in assisting the person in need. To prevent this, nearly every U.S. jurisdiction has enacted civil Good Samaritan Laws that absolve bystanders from civil liability when they help persons in need. These are different from criminal Good Samaritan Law which, as described in the preceding paragraph, require someone to render aid to someone in need when they are capable of doing so without harm to themselves.

Before leaving the category of a statutory duty to act, the common law crime of "misprision of felony" should be addressed. Misprision of felony was an omission that qualified as an actus reus at common law and even today in most of Europe. It made it a felony to fail to report a known felony to legal authorities. Today, however, there is no such legal duty to disclose a felony to authorities in the United States. Thus, simply keeping one's mouth shut about a crime the person knows to have taken place will not normally subject someone to criminal liability absent some other legal duty to act. However, any affirmative act of concealing a crime can subject a person to complicity or accessory liability and/or obstruction of justice charges.

The third way a legal duty to act is imposed is by contract. People take on contractual obligations all the time. So of these contractual obligations require one of the parties to act when they otherwise may not have had a duty to act. For example, a lifeguard contractually agrees to act when witnessing a drowning. In contrast, a civilian on the beach, even if an Olympic gold-medalist swimmer, has no legal duty to act to save the life of that same drowning victim. Similarly, a police officer contractually agrees to act when witnessing a felony in progress, while the ordinary citizen normally has no such legal duty to act.

The fourth and final way in which a legal obligation to act can be imposed is when someone voluntarily assumes care of another person. Such a voluntary assumption of care creates a legal duty to act to care and protect the person for whom you are caring. Thus, if you take in a sick friend and do not call for medical help when needed, you have breached a legal duty to act and may be held criminally responsible for what whatever happened to that person. It used to be that to trigger the legal duty to act, the voluntary assumption of care had to be to the exclusion of others, meaning other people could not effectively render aid to the person. But it appears this requirement has been omitted by courts in recent years.

Often, two or more of these methods that impose a legal duty to act might be present simultaneously. Take babysitting, for example. Clearly, when one agrees to act as a babysitter, that person has contractually undertaken a legal duty to act to protect the children in the babysitter's care. The babysitter has also voluntarily assumed care of the child to the exclusion of others (usually, the parents or legal guardians). A babysitter's failure to act can give rise to criminal sanctions under both of these theories.

As with many of the rules of law presented in this book, it is all too easy to say there is no legal duty to act unless one of the four criteria above are met. The application of legal principles to the complexities of real world, however, often leaves room for argument. Consider the following case.

STATE of Connecticut v. Santos MIRANDA
715 A.2d 680 (Conn. 1998).

Katz, Associate Justice.

The issue in this appeal is whether a person who is not the biological or legal parent of a child but who establishes a familial relationship with a woman and her infant child, voluntarily assumes responsibility for the care and welfare of the child, and considers himself the child's stepfather, has a legal duty to protect the child from abuse, such that the breach of that duty exposes the person to criminal liability [not only for child neglect, but also for assault].

The defendant commenced living with his girlfriend and her two children in an apartment in September, 1992. On January 27, 1993, the defendant was twenty-one years old, his girlfriend was sixteen, her son was two, and her daughter, the victim in this case, born on September 21, 1992, was four months old. Although he was not the biological father of either child, the defendant took care of them and considered himself to be their stepfather. He represented himself as such to the people at Meriden Veteran's Memorial Hospital where, on January 27, 1993, the victim was taken for treatment of her injuries following a 911 call by the defendant that the child was choking on milk. Upon examination at the hospital, it was determined that the victim had multiple rib fractures that were approximately two to three weeks old, two skull fractures that were approximately seven to ten days old, a brachial plexus injury to her left arm, a rectal tear that was actively "oozing blood" and bilateral subconjunctival nasal hemorrhages. On the basis of extensive medical evidence, the trial court determined that the injuries had been sustained on three or more occasions and that none of the injuries had been the result of an accident, a fall, events that took place at the time of the child's birth, cardiopulmonary resuscitation, a blocked air passageway or the child choking on milk. Rather, the trial court found that the injuries, many of which created a risk of death, had been caused by great and deliberate force.

The trial court further found in accordance with the medical evidence that, as a result of the nature of these injuries, at the time they were sustained the victim would have screamed inconsolably, and that her injuries would have caused noticeable physical deformities, such as swelling, bruising and poor mobility, and finally, that her intake of food would have been reduced. The court also determined that anyone who saw the child would have had to notice these injuries, the consequent deformities and her reactions. Indeed, the trial court found that the defendant had been aware of the various bruises on her right cheek and the subconjunctival nasal hemorrhages, as well as the swelling of the child's head, that he knew she had suffered a rectal tear, as well as rib fractures posteriorly on the left and right sides, and that he was aware that there existed a substantial and unjustifiable risk that the child was exposed to conduct that created a risk of death. The trial court concluded that despite this knowledge, the defendant "failed to act to help or aid [the child] by promptly notifying authorities of her injuries, taking her for medical care, removing her from her circumstances and guarding her from future abuses. As a result of his failure to help her, the child was exposed to conduct which created a risk of death to her and the child suffered subsequent serious physical injuries . . . ."

The trial court concluded that the defendant had a legal duty to protect the health and well-being of the child based on the undisputed facts that he had established a familial relationship with the child's mother and her two children, that he had voluntarily assumed responsibility for the care and welfare of both children, and that he considered himself the victim's stepfather. On the basis of these circumstances, the trial court found the defendant guilty.

I

The trend of Anglo-American law has been toward enlarging the scope of criminal liability for failure to act in those situations in which the common law or statutes have imposed an affirmative responsibility for the safety and well-being of others. Criminal liability of parents based on a failure to act in accordance with common-law affirmative duties to protect and care for their children is well recognized in many jurisdictions. *See, e.g., People v. Stanciel*, 153 Ill.2d 218, 606 N.E.2d 1201 (1992) (mother guilty of homicide by allowing known abuser to assume role of disciplinarian over child). In light of this duty to protect and care for children, courts in [many] jurisdictions have concluded that, where this duty exists and injury results, the failure to protect the child from harm will be "deemed to be the cause of those injuries" and the person bearing the duty may face criminal sanctions.

Criminal conduct can arise not only through overt acts, but also by an omission to act when there is a legal duty to do so. "Omissions are as capable of producing consequences as overt acts. Thus, the common law rule that there is no general duty to protect limits criminal liability where it would otherwise exist. The special relationship exception to the 'no duty to act' rule represents a choice to retain liability for some omissions, which are considered morally unacceptable." *State v. Williquette*, 129 Wis.2d 239, 385 N.W.2d 145 (1986). Therefore, had the defendant been the victim's parent – someone with an undisputed affirmative legal obligation to protect and provide for his minor child – we would conclude that his failure to protect the child from abuse could constitute a violation of [our assault statute].

II

We next turn to the issue of whether the duty to protect can be imposed on the defendant, an adult member of the household unrelated to the child. The defendant argues that there is no statutory or common-law precept "authorizing the expansion of assault under § 53a-59 (a)(3)." The state argues that there is both. We conclude that, based on the trial court's findings that the defendant had established a family-like relationship with the mother and her two children, that he had voluntarily assumed responsibility for the care and welfare of both children, and that he had considered himself the victim's stepfather, there existed a common-law duty to protect the victim from her mother's abuse, the breach of which can be the basis of a conviction.

"'Duty is a legal conclusion about relationships between individuals, made after the fact . . . . The nature of the duty, and the specific persons to whom it is owed, are determined by the circumstances surrounding the conduct of the individual.'" *Clohessy v. Bachelor*, 237 Conn. 31, 45, 675 A.2d 852 (1996). Although one generally has no legal duty to aid another in peril, even when the aid can be provided without danger or inconvenience to the provider, there are four widely recognized situations in which the failure to act may constitute breach of a legal duty: (1) where one stands in a certain relationship to another; (2) where a statute imposes a duty to help another; (3) where one has assumed a contractual duty; and (4) where one voluntarily has assumed the care of another. The state argues that this case falls within both the first and fourth situations, or some combination thereof.

We begin with the duty based upon the relationship between the parties. One standing in a certain personal relationship to another person has some affirmative duties of care with regard to that person.

It is undisputed that parents have a duty to provide food, shelter and medical aid for their children and to protect them from harm. "The inherent dependency of a child upon his parent to obtain medical aid, i.e., the incapacity of a child to evaluate his condition and summon aid by himself, supports imposition of such a duty upon the parent." *Commonwealth v. Konz*, 498 Pa. 639, 644, 450 A.2d 638 (1982). Additionally, "'[t]he commonly understood general obligations of parenthood entail these minimum attributes: (1) express love and affection for the child; (2) express personal concern over the health, education and general well-being of the child; (3) the duty to supply the necessary food, clothing, and medical care; (4) the duty to provide an adequate domicile; and (5) the duty to furnish social and religious guidance.'" *In re Adoption of Webb*, 14 Wash. App. 651, 653, 544 P.2d 130 (1975). Indeed, the status relationship giving rise to a duty to provide and protect that has been before the courts more often than any other relationship and, at the same time, the one relationship that courts most frequently assume to exist without expressly so stating, is the relationship existing between a parent and a minor child.

In addition to biological and adoptive parents and legal guardians, there may be other adults who establish familial relationships with and assume responsibility for the care of a child, thereby creating a legal duty to protect that child from harm. *See, e.g., Cornell v. State*, 159 Fla. 687, 32 So.2d 610 (1947) (grandmother guilty of manslaughter in death of grandchild where she had assumed care of child but became so intoxicated that she allowed child to smother to death). "Recognizing the primary responsibility of a natural parent does not mean that an unrelated person may not also have some responsibilities incident to the care and custody of a child. Such duties may be regarded as derived from the primary custodian, i.e., the natural parent, or arise from the nature of the circumstances." *People v. Berg*, 171 Ill. App.3d 316, 320, 525 N.E.2d 573 (1988).

Most courts deciding whether, under a particular set of facts, liability for an omission to act may be imposed under a statute that does not itself impose a duty to act, have looked to whether a duty to act exists in another statute, in the common law or in a contract. Of those courts acting outside the context of a statutory or contractual duty that have held a defendant criminally liable for failing to protect a child from injury, most have relied on a combination of both the first and fourth situations as the predicate for the defendant's conviction. More specifically, these courts have examined the nature of the relationship of the defendant to the victim and whether the defendant, as part of that relationship, had assumed a responsibility for the victim. We find the reliance by these courts on this combination of factors persuasive.

In *People v. Salley*, 153 App. Div.2d 704, 544 N.Y.S.2d 680 (1989), the court examined the issue of whether the defendant, a woman who was living with a man named Taylor and Kenneth, a three year old who was the son of Taylor's estranged wife and another man, as well as five other children, was guilty of manslaughter in the second degree for failing to secure medical attention for Kenneth, who was being physically abused by Taylor. Taylor had inflicted approximately seventy bruises on Kenneth and Kenneth died from a combination of a fracture, internal bleeding and various wounds to his body. Because the defendant "had assumed the parental obligations of care for Kenneth," and had been aware of and consciously disregarded the substantial and unjustifiable risk of his death in failing to get Kenneth help during the time he was being abused by Taylor, the court concluded that she properly could be convicted of manslaughter.

47

In *State v. Orosco*, 113 N.M. 789, 833 P.2d 1155 (1991), the court examined whether the defendant, who lived with the victim and his mother and who failed to intervene when one of his friends sexually abused the victim, could be held criminally liable for the abuse. The court held that, by assuming the care and welfare of the child, the defendant stood in the position of a parent.

In *Leet v. State*, 595 So.2d 959 (Fla. App. 1991), the court examined whether the defendant could be held criminally responsible for abuse of a child by his mother although he was not the child's father. The statute at issue required the state to prove "[w]hoever ... by culpable negligence, deprives a child of, or allows a child to be deprived of, necessary food, clothing, shelter, or medical treatment, or who, knowingly or by culpable negligence, inflicts or permits the infliction of physical or mental injury to the child...." *Id.* at 961. Despite the broad language of the statute imposing liability on "whoever," the court discussed at length the nature of the defendant's relationship with the child victim, and his assumption of responsibility for the child's care and held that, because the defendant had "assumed responsibility for [the child's] well-being when he established a family-like relationship with [the child] and his mother," he could be held responsible for permitting the child's abuse by his mother. *Id.* at 962-63. Although the defendant had argued that he was not financially responsible for the child and could not have authorized his medical treatment, the court, nevertheless, concluded that he had the authority, and indeed, the duty to prevent the mother's conduct.

In *People v. Wong*, 182 App. Div.2d 98, 588 N.Y.S.2d 119, *rev'd on other grounds*, 81 N.Y.2d 600, 619 N.E.2d 377, 601 N.Y.S.2d 440 (1993), the court examined whether the defendants, who had been babysitters for the child victim's parents, could be convicted of manslaughter for harming the child and for failing to provide him with necessary medical care. To support a conviction based upon their failure to provide medical attention, the prosecution relied on two theories: (1) that the defendants had contracted with the child's parents to care for the child while the parents worked; and (2) that the defendants voluntarily had assumed care for the child. The court embraced both theories, recognizing that the voluntary assumption of care, as well as a contractual babysitting agreement, were sufficient to trigger a legal duty. The court concluded that by assuming care for the child, the defendants created a legal duty "substantially coextensive with those which would be borne by a parent." *Id.*

As these cases demonstrate, the traditional approach in this country is to restrict the duty to save others from harm to certain very narrow categories of cases. We are not prepared now to adopt a broad general rule covering other circumstances. We conclude only that, in accordance with the trial court findings, when the defendant, who considered himself the victim's parent, established a familial relationship with the victim's mother and her children and assumed the role of a father, he assumed, under the common law, the same legal duty to protect the victim from the abuse as if he were, in fact, the victim's guardian. Under these circumstances, to require the defendant as a matter of law to take affirmative action to prevent harm to the victim or be criminally responsible imposes a reasonable duty. That duty does not depend on an ability to regulate the mother's discipline of the victim or on the defendant having exclusive control of the victim when the injuries occurred. Nor is the duty contingent upon an ability by the state or the mother to look to the defendant for child support. Moreover, whether the defendant had created a total in loco parentis relationship with the victim by January, 1993, is not dispositive of whether the defendant had assumed a responsibility for the victim.

Nor should we reject the concept of a duty in this case because the defendant might not have been able to authorize medical treatment for the victim had he taken her to the hospital. The status required to impose the legal duty to safeguard the victim is not coextensive with the status that permits one to authorize treatment. Quite obviously, had the defendant brought the victim to the hospital at any time throughout the four month period during which she was abused by her mother, a physician would have had the ability to examine and treat her, and the costs would be paid by her parent, guardian or the state, if necessary.

Finally, we recognize the continuing demographic trend reflecting a significant increase in nontraditional alternative family arrangements. Consequently, more and more children will be living with or may depend upon adults who do not qualify as a natural or adoptive parent. The attachment by children to the adults who care for them does not, however, depend exclusively upon whether the caregiver is the natural or adoptive parent or another person who has assumed the caretaker role. Children become attached to people who care for them, and this attachment is "rooted inevitably in the infant's inability to ensure his own survival...." J. Goldstein, A. Freud & A. Solnit, Beyond the Best Interest of the Child 18 (1973). To distinguish among children in deciding which ones are entitled to protection based upon whether their adult caregivers have chosen to have their relationships officially recognized hardly advances the public policy of protecting children from abuse.

QUESTIONS

1.   The majority spent considerable time explaining the imposition of a legal duty to act on Mr. Miranda, even though he was not the biological or adoptive parent of the child in this case. How far should such logic be extended? In *People v. Wong*, as case cited and discussed by the court, babysitters were included in the class of persons having a legal duty to act on behalf of a child in need. But often, babysitter are teenagers – sometime the older siblings or cousins of the children entrusted to the sitter, and sometimes having no familial relationship at all. To what standard of care should a fourteen or fifteen year old be help if he or she fails to act?

2.   The court, even the dissent (whose opinion has been omitted), had no problem finding that Mr. Miranda had committed child neglect by failing to take steps necessary to care for the child. But the majority went beyond this by holding that a person can assault another person by failing to act when there is a legal duty to act to prevent a child victim from harm. Do you think this wise? Why or why not?

3.   As stated by the court, parents have explicit duties they owe to their minor children. Some of these duties, such as providing for food, clothing, shelter, health, education and general well-being of the child, seem non-controversial, if not entirely appropriate. But what should the law do with parents who are financially unable to provide these things for their children? Does a fair reading of the *Miranda* opinion above support a case for criminal liability of parents who live in extreme poverty not only for child neglect, but also, arguably, for criminal assault or battery?

4.   The court included references to parental duties to "express love and affection for the child" and "the duty to furnish social and religious guidance." Do you agree that these are appropriate responsibilities for the law to place on parents? Why or why not? What are the potential consequences of the latter responsibility for parents who are atheists? Suppose a set of parents fail to provide love and affection for a child who then grows up to be a violent criminal and there is a small army of mental health professionals who were willing to testify under oath that "but for" the parents having failed to provide love to their child, then the child would not have been driven to commit his crimes. Should the parents be held criminally liable for the crimes of the child they "caused" to become a violent criminal? Why or why not?

5.   Another duty the court emphasizes is the duty to provide for the health and medical care of a child. What if parents, on the basis of their religion, do not believe in medicine, but rather put the care of their child in the hands of God, often referred to as "prayer healing"? Should these parents be criminally punished for child neglect for allowing a child to suffer rather than be medically treated? What if the child dies from a lack of medical care; should the parents be held criminally responsible for homicide? Nearly all U.S. jurisdictions answer these questions in the affirmative. The law requires parents to subjugate their own religious beliefs and provide medical care to their children. Do you agree with the way the law handles this issue? Why or why not?

C. Essential Elements of a Crime: Mens Rea

As mentioned above, most crimes require not only that some prohibited act occur, but also that the actus reus be accompanied by culpable mental state. The mental state that must exist at the time of the commission of an actus reus is referred to as *mens rea* – Latin for "the guilty mind." It does not, however, refer to all or even some culpable mental states, but rather the term refers to the defendant's state of mind with respect to his or her level of intentionality with respect to having done the actus reus.

1. Specific and General Intent Crimes

The common law and the Model Penal Code differ markedly over their approaches to mens rea. At common law, crimes were either crimes of **general intent** or crimes of **specific intent**. A specific intent crime requires that the actor have formed the intent in his or her mind to engage in specific conduct and to cause a particular result. For example, if you decided you wanted to kill someone, and you took a gun, aimed it at the person you intended to kill, pull the trigger causing a bullet to strike and kill your victim, you have acted with specific intent to kill. If you take and carry away the personal property of another person, say a wallet, and you do so with the intent to permanently deprive the rightful owner of the wallet, then you have acted with the specific intent to steal.

It is quite rare that we have direct evidence of the defendant's state of mind at the time of the commission or attempted commission of a crime. Sometimes, a person declares his or her intent ahead of time or subsequently confesses to the level of intent. When either of these situations arise, we have direct evidence of mens rea. But more often than not, we have no direct evidence of intentionality, meaning that mens rea, including specific intent, must usually be inferred from the facts and circumstances surrounding the defendant's conduct. Doing so, however, is not always easy. Consider the following case.

<hr>

John THACKER v. COMMONWEALTH of Virginia
114 S.E. 504 (Va. 1922).

The accused, in company with two other young men, Doc Campbell and Paul Kelly, was attending a church festival in Allegheny county, at which all three became intoxicated. They left the church between ten and eleven o'clock at night, and walked down the county road about one and one-half miles, when they came to a sharp curve. Located in this curve was a tent in which the said Mrs. J.A. Ratrie, her husband, four children, and a servant were camping for the summer. The husband, though absent, was expected home that night, and Mrs. Ratrie, upon retiring, had placed a lighted lamp on a trunk by the head of her bed. After eleven o'clock, she was awakened by the shots of a pistol and loud talking in the road nearby, and heard a man say, "I am going to shoot that God-damned light out"; and another voice said, "Don't shoot the light out."

The accused and his friends then appeared at the back of the tent, where the flaps of the tent were open, and said they were from Bath county and had lost their way, and asked Mrs. Ratrie if she could take care of them all night. She informed them she was camping for the summer, and had no room for them. One of the three thanked her, and they turned away, but after passing around the tent the accused used some vulgar language and did some cursing and singing. When they got back in the road, the accused said again he was going to shoot the light out, and fired three shots, two of which went through the tent, one Passing through the head of the bed in which Mrs. Ratrie was lying, just missing her head and the head of her baby, who was sleeping with her. The accused did not know Mrs. Ratrie, and had never seen her before. He testified he did not know any of the parties in the tent, and had no ill will against either of them; that he simply shot at the light, without any intent to harm Mrs. Ratrie or any one else; that he would not have shot had he been sober, and regretted his action. The foregoing are the admitted facts in the case.

An attempt to commit a crime is composed of two elements: (1) The intent to commit it; and (2) a direct, ineffectual act done towards its commission. The act must reach far enough towards the accomplishment of the desired result to amount to the commencement of the consummation.

The law can presume the intention so far as realized in the act, but not an intention beyond what was so realized. The law does not presume, because an assault was made with a weapon likely to produce death, that it was an assault with the intent to murder. And where it takes a particular intent to constitute a crime, that particular intent must be proved either by direct or circumstantial evidence, which would warrant the inference of the intent with which the act was done.

When a statute makes an offense to consist of an act combined with a particular intent, that intent is just as necessary to be proved as the act itself, and must be found as a matter of fact before a conviction can be had; and no intent in law or mere legal presumption, differing from the intent in fact, can be allowed to supply the place of the latter.

Mr. Bishop, in his Criminal Law, vol. 1 (8th ed.), at section 729, says:

> When the law makes an act, whether more or less evil in itself, punishable, though done simply from general malevolence, if one takes what, were all accomplished, would be a step towards it, yet if he does not mean to do the whole, no court can justly hold him answerable for more than he does. And when the thing done does not constitute a substantive crime, there is no ground for treating it as an attempt. So that necessarily an act prompted by general malevolence, or by a specific design to do something else, is not an attempt to commit a crime not intended.

> * * *

> When we say that a man attempted to do a given wrong, we mean that he intended to do specifically it, and proceeded a certain way in the doing. The intent in the mind covers the thing in full; the act covers it only in part. Thus, to commit murder, one need not intend to take life, but to be guilty of an attempt to murder, he must so intend. It is not sufficient that his act, had it proved fatal, would have been murder.

> We have seen that the unintended taking of life may be murder, yet there can be no attempt to murder without the specific intent to commit it – a rule the latter branch whereof appears probably in a few of the states to have been interfered with by statutes. For example, if one from a housetop recklessly throws down a billet of wood upon the sidewalk where persons are constantly passing, and it falls upon a person passing by and kills him, this would be the common-law murder, but if, instead of killing, it inflicts only a slight injury, the party could not be convicted of an assault with attempt to commit murder . . . .

The application of the foregoing principles to the facts of the instant case shows clearly, as we think, that the judgment complained of is erroneous. While it might possibly be said that the firing of the shot into the head of Mrs. Ratrie's bed was an act done towards the commission of the offense charged, the evidence falls far short of proving that it was fired with the intent to murder her.

However averse we may be to disturb the verdict of the jury, our obligation to the law compels us to do so. The judgment of guilty of attempting to murder will be reversed, the verdict of the jury set aside, and the case remanded for a new trial therein, if the commonwealth shall be so advised.

QUESTIONS

1.   As this case illustrates, attempt is a crime of specific intent. Assume that Thacker had shot a gun at Mrs. Ratrie with the intention of killing her and, further presume the bullet had, in fact, hit and killed her. Thacker would have acted with specific intent to kill her. But Thacker testified that he had no intent to kill Mrs. Ratrie, only an intent to shoot our the light in her tent, probably to scare her. Without specific intent to kill, he could not be convicted of attempted murder. Do you think, based on the facts, that Thacker's specific intent to kill could be inferred to his actions? Why or why not?

2.   The jury apparently thought that specific intent to kill could be inferred from Thacker's conduct and convicted him accordingly. But based on his testimony, the court reversed Thacker's conviction on appeal. Do you agree with the court that the self-serving testimony of the defendant is sufficient to create reasonable as to the mens rea element of a crime? Why or why not?

In contrast to specific intent, the level of common law mens rea known as general intent only required that a defendant know, in general terms, that type of conduct in which he or she is engaged. This is so even if the actor does not foresee the result that the conduct may produce. The following case illustrates this principle well.

STATE of Hawaii, Appellee, v. Richard Barry ROCKER and Joseph CAVA, Appellants.
475 P.2d 684 (Haw. 1970).

Richardson, Chief Justice.

Defendants-appellants, having waived a jury trial, were tried in the circuit court of the second circuit and found guilty as charged for violation of Hawaii Revised Statutes § 727-1 for creating a common nuisance [for having sunbathed in the nude on a public beach].

It is undisputed that on February 26, 1969, police officers of the Maui Police Department received a phone call from an anonymous person and, thereafter, on the day of the call, proceeded to the Puu Olai beach at Makena to look for nude sunbathers. On reaching their destination, the police surveyed the beach from a ridge using both their naked eyes and binoculars and saw the defendants lying on the beach completely nude, one on his stomach and the other on his back. The officers then approached the defendants and arrested them for indecent exposure. It was admitted by the police officers that defendants were not at any time engaged in any activity other than sunbathing. At the time of the arrest there were several other people on the beach where the defendants were nude. Defendant Rocker was nude at the Puu Olai beach on other days before and after he was arrested on February 26, 1969. Defendant Cava likewise frequently sunbathed in the nude at the same beach prior to his arrest on February 26, 1969.

I. Indecent Exposure: Elements

The first issue we are asked to decide on this appeal is whether defendants created a common nuisance by sunbathing in the nude on a public beach. The statute, § 727-1, reads as follows:

> The offense of common nuisance is the endangering of the public personal safety or health, or doing, causing or promoting, maintaining or continuing what is offensive, or annoying and vexatious, or plainly hurtful to the public; or is a public outrage against common decency or common morality; or tends plainly and directly to the corruption of the morals, honesty, and good habits of the people; the same being without authority or justification by law: As for example: . . . Open lewdness or lascivious behavior, or indecent exposure.

Section 727-1, unlike statutes of most states, incorporates indecent exposure as an example of what the legislature has defined to constitute common nuisances. [Although t]he statute does not specifically delineate the elements of the crime of indecent exposure . . . , to create a common nuisance, there must be an indecent exposure of the person in a public place where it may be seen by others if they pass by, and it need actually be seen by one person only. However, to answer the specific questions presented to us on this appeal and to clarify and examine our construction of the statute in light of recent decisions in this and other jurisdictions, a further discussion of the elements of the crime of indecent exposure is needed.

Sunbathing in the nude is not per se illegal. It must be coupled with the intent to indecently expose oneself. Intent is an element of the crime of common nuisance defined by Section 727-1. The intent necessary is a general intent, not a specific intent; i.e., it is not necessary that the exposure be made with the intent that some particular person see it, but only that the exposure was made where it was likely to be observed by others. Thus, the intent may be inferred from the conduct of the accused and the circumstances and environment of the occurrence. The criminal intent necessary for a conviction of indecent exposure is usually established by some action by which the defendant either (1)

52

draws attention to his exposed condition or (2) by a display in a place so public that it must be presumed it was intended to be seen by others.

The defendants argue that there is no circumstantial evidence in the record from which a trier of fact could conclude that the element of intent had been proved beyond a reasonable doubt. The issue, therefore, is whether defendants' nude sunbathing . . . was at a place so public that a trier of fact could infer it was intended to be seen by others. The prosecution offered testimony of one of the arresting police officers that the beach was a popular location for fishermen and was in fact one of his favorite fishing spots. Defendants testified that the public in general used the beach, that it was used by fishermen and local residents, and that they observed between 20 and 25 people on the beach over a two-month period. Although the Puu Olai beach is isolated by a hill and a ledge, away from the view of the public road and adjoining beaches, it is accessible by a well-worn path and known to be a favorite location of fishermen to cast and throw fish nets. In view of this and other evidence in the record, we cannot agree with defendants' argument that the trier of fact could not find the beach so public as to justify an inference of intent on the part of defendants to be seen by others.

Levinson, Justice (dissenting).

I dissent because I think that the evidence adduced by the government at the close of the prosecution's case was insufficient to sustain a conviction of either defendant. Before proceeding to my analysis of the insufficiency of the evidence offered by the prosecution, I feel compelled to state the facts in the record at the close of the prosecution's case. I do this because I believe that the majority has failed to segregate clearly the prosecution's evidence from that offered by the defense and has omitted a key fact which I believe raises a reasonable doubt as to the defendants' guilt.

The State's case consisted solely of the testimony of the two arresting police officers. They both testified that the Puu Olai beach is isolated by a hill and a ledge, away from the view of the public road and adjoining beach. The beach is accessible by two trails. One is a well-worn path leading over the hill. The other is a trail on the Wailuku side of the beach, which is not well-used and connects the beach to a small road. The officers testified to being able to see, with the naked eye, the nudity of the defendants, from the crest of the hill.

One of the officers, George Matsunaga, testified that this beach was one of his favorite fishing spots and that it was a popular location for other fishermen. He also stated that the fishermen went to the beach in the "day or night." On examination by the court, Officer Matsunaga admitted that he had never seen the beach used for picnics or family recreation, and the only non-fishermen that he recalled having observed on this beach were what he called "hippie type characters." It was on this evidence alone that the State rested its case.

My reading of the majority opinion leads me to conclude that in order to prove a prima facie case against the defendants, it was necessary for the prosecution to demonstrate that the defendants possessed a general intent to expose themselves in a place where it would be likely that they would be observed by others. To prove this, it would be enough for the prosecution to establish the defendants' awareness of sufficient facts and circumstances from which a trier of fact could infer such intent beyond a reasonable doubt. From the evidence in the record at the close of the prosecution's case, I do not think that a trier of fact could be justified in inferring beyond a reasonable doubt that the defendants possessed the necessary general intent to be seen by others.

Although there was testimony that the beach was visited by fishermen, there was no link established between the visits by the fishermen and visits to the beach by the defendants. Officer Matsunaga, one of the fishermen who used the beach, did not testify to ever having observed the defendants on this beach prior to arresting them. Thus, this evidence could not be used to support an inference that the defendants were aware that this beach was used by fishermen and therefore public.

Nor could a trier of fact infer beyond a reasonable doubt that the defendants were aware of the "well-worn" path leading over the hill to the beach and therefore knew that they were sunbathing in an area readily accessible to the public. One of the police officers testified that the beach was accessible by another trail which was not "well-used." There was no other evidence that would eliminate as a reasonable doubt the possibility that the defendants had used this other path and therefore inferred from its unused nature that the public would not be likely to see them. The majority opinion does not mention this possibility in assessing the adequacy of the prosecution's case. In failing to prove that the defendants were aware of the visits of the fishermen or the "well-worn" path I believe the State failed to prove beyond a reasonable doubt defendants' awareness of facts sufficient to establish a general intent to be seen by others.

Since the prosecution failed to prove a prima facie case against the defendants the motion for acquittal was erroneously denied. I would reverse the convictions.

QUESTIONS

1.   In the context of this case, the court described the requisite mens rea by stating it was "not necessary that the exposure be made with the intent that some particular person see it, but only that the exposure was made where it was likely to be observed by others." Do you agree with the majority that when people sunbathe in the nude, even in a fairly remote area of a public beach, that they are generally aware that their nudity is "likely to be observed by others"? Explain you answer.

2.   As the case both states and illustrates, intent must often be inferred from the defendant's conduct and all of the facts and circumstances surrounding it. Taking into account that indecent exposure is a general intent crime, and further considering both the conduct of the two defendants and all of the facts and circumstances brought out by the majority and dissenting opinion, with which decision do you agree, Justice Richardson's or Justice Levinson's?

At common law, there was another category of mens rea in addition to general intent and specific intent. It was known as *malice*. Malice is difficult and somewhat vague concept. It is not taken in the old sense of wickedness or evil. It can refer to states of mind that encompass both specific and general intent. For example, if one acts with specific intent (i.e., purpose to cause a result, such as specific intent to kill), the one can also be said to have acted maliciously. But a lack of specific intent did not mean that a person had *not* acted with malice.

One can act with general intent and still be acting maliciously if one consciously disregards a known risk that a particular harm night occur. As one court phrased it, malice was "a state of mind showing a heart that is without regard for the life and safety of others." *Bowler v. United States*, 480 A.2d 678, 687 (D.C. 1984). Say, for example, you load a revolver with a single bullet and then played Russian Roulette with a friend. If the friend pulls the trigger and dies, it is clear that you did not act with specific intent to kill your friend. But you still acted with malice since you knew, in general terms, that your having put a bullet in the revolver and subsequently playing the game could have caused death to yourself or to your friend.

2. Mens Rea Under the Model Penal Code

The common law levels of mens rea (general intent, specific intent, and malice) are, to say the least, often confusing and difficult to work with. Accordingly, many U.S. jurisdictions abandoned the common law classifications of mens rea adopted those established by the American Law Institute in its Model Penal Code.

(a)   Purpose - Under the Model Penal Code, the highest/most culpable degree of mens rea is called "*purpose*." When someone acts purposefully, the actors acts with the specific intent to engage in conduct and thereby cause a particular result. This is, perhaps, the easiest of the levels of mens rea to understand and is well-illustrated by returning to the same example given for common law specific intent to kill. If you, with the purpose (i.e., specific intent) of killing someone, raise a loaded gun, aim at the intended victim, pull the trigger, and your bullet strikes and kills the person, you have acted purposefully, the highest level of criminal mens rea.

(b)   Knowledge - Also known as "scienter," *knowledge* requires that the actor act knowingly – meaning acting with an "awareness" or "belief" – that he or she is engaging in the conduct, and that the actor knows, believes, or is aware of practical certainty that the result achieved would occur by engaging in the conduct. It includes not only actual knowledge, but also what is known as constructive knowledge. That means that one cannot be "willfully blind" to facts or the high probability of the existence of circumstances by turning the other cheek and consciously ignoring information that would have given the ordinary, reasonable prudent person "knowledge." The following case illustrates the willful blindness doctrine quite succinctly.

Dwyer Frank WETZLER, Appellant, v. STATE of Florida, Appellee.
455 So.2d 511 (Fla. Ct. App. 1984).

Shivers, Judge.

On the morning of March 23, 1983, appellant drove his pickup truck, which was towing a padlocked U-Haul trailer, into the agricultural inspection station off I-10 in Suwannee County. Agricultural Inspector Silas told appellant that he would like to look in the trailer. Appellant told Silas that he did not have the key to the padlock. Silas told appellant that he had a pair of bolt cutters for that purpose and requested appellant to cut the lock with them. Appellant voluntarily cut the padlock, and Silas opened the trailer, observing what he thought to be marijuana plants. Silas told appellant to close the trailer and come into the station. Silas then called the Suwannee County Sheriff. The Sheriff arrived, looked into the trailer, and observed the marijuana plants. After receiving Miranda warnings, appellant told the Sheriff that he had been given $400 to come to Sarasota, rent a U-Haul trailer and leave it hooked to his truck. He told the Sheriff that for a period of time the truck and trailer were out of his possession. The rig was taken, brought back, and he was supposed to have received another $400 when he got back to Atlanta, Georgia. Appellant told the Sheriff that he knew it was a "shady deal" by the way "they wanted to do things by being secret."

Appellant denied any knowledge that there was marijuana in the trailer and asked the Sheriff if the charge was serious. The Sheriff later counted 164 potted, growing marijuana plants in the trailer with a total dry weight of 32 or 36 ounces. Appellant testified in his own defense. He stated that he was living in Atlanta, Georgia, but that his family lived in Bradenton, Florida. He had met a man named Bill in an Atlanta bar who struck up a conversation with appellant about Bradenton and about appellant's new truck. After talking for approximately 45 minutes, appellant agreed to go to Bradenton, rent a trailer, and pick up some furniture for Bill. Bill advanced appellant $400 and told him he would receive another $400 upon delivery. Appellant was to go to Bradenton and park the truck and rented trailer in a certain shopping mall at a certain time. He was to leave the truck key under the floor mat and go inside the mall for two hours. Although appellant was somewhat suspicious about this arrangement and thought it was "just a little bit" shady, he testified that he did not think he was doing anything illegal. He denied any knowledge of the marijuana in the trailer. Appellant did not head directly back to Atlanta because he heard that there was a snowstorm there. Instead, he headed for Tallahassee to see an old girlfriend and thereby ended up at the I-10 agricultural inspection station.

Appellant was in constructive rather than actual possession of the marijuana. Cases of this kind generally turn on whether the constructive possession is determined to be exclusive or joint. This is so because that determination dictates the State's burden of proof on the issue of a defendant's guilty knowledge. As this court said in *Frank v. State*, 199 So.2d 117, 120-21 (Fla. Ct. App. 1967):

[T]he State must establish beyond a reasonable doubt that the accused knew of the presence of the narcotic drugs on premises occupied and controlled by him, either exclusively or jointly with others. If the premises on which the drugs are found are in the exclusive possession and control of the accused, knowledge of their presence on such premises coupled with his ability to maintain control over them may be inferred. Although no further proof of knowledge by the State is required in cases of exclusive possession by the accused, the inference of knowledge is rebuttable and not conclusive. If the premises on which the drugs are found is not in the exclusive but only in the joint possession of the accused, knowledge of the drugs' presence on the premises and the ability to maintain control over them by the accused will not be inferred but must be established by proof. Such proof may consist either of evidence establishing actual knowledge by the accused, or evidence of incriminating statements and circumstances from which a jury might lawfully infer knowledge by the accused of the drugs' presence on the premises.

Appellant contends that the instant case involves joint possession because of claimant's uncontradicted testimony that the trailer was out of his presence and control when it was loaded by others.

* * *

The doctrine of "willful blindness" (also called "deliberate ignorance") is well established in federal criminal law. An extensive discussion of the doctrine and its derivation is contained in *United States v. Jewell*, 532 F.2d 697, 700 (9th Cir.), *cert. denied*, 426 U.S. 951 (1976). "[T]he rule is that if a party has his suspicion aroused but then deliberately omits to make further enquiries, because he wishes to remain in ignorance, he is deemed to have knowledge."

Although our research has uncovered no Florida cases addressing or utilizing the doctrine of willful blindness, we think this doctrine is applicable to constructive possession cases. . . . Appellant's admissions make it clear that his suspicion concerning the transaction was aroused. We think that these admissions together with the other circumstances present in this case indicate that appellant deliberately chose to remain in ignorance. *See United States v. Suttiswad*, 696 F.2d 645 (9th Cir. 1982); *United States v. Murrieta-Bejarano*, 552 F.2d 1323 (9th Cir. 1977). Thus, we find that there was sufficient evidence for the jury to find knowledge on the part of appellant, and that this is true whether the constructive possession involved in the instant case is described as exclusive or joint. Affirmed.

QUESTIONS

1. The court cites *United States v. Jewell*, one of the leading cases on the doctrine of willful blindness. In that case, the defendant testified that while he was in Mexico, he was approached by a man who offered him $100 to drive a car back to the United States. The car had a secret compartment in which marijuana was concealed. The defendant knew of the existence of the secret compartment, but did not actually know there was marijuana in it. He was charged with importing and possessing with intent to distribute a controlled substance. The mens rea for both crimes was purpose or knowledge. His willful blindness to the likelihood of the compartment containing contraband was held to be sufficient "knowledge" to sustain his convictions. Do you agree with the courts in *Jewell* and *Wetzler* that deliberately staying ignorant of the facts should be treated by the criminal law as the functional equivalent of actual knowledge? Explain your reasoning.

2. What are the implications of the willful blindness doctrine for those persons who are not particularly bright . . . in lay terms, "clueless"? Should a modified objective standard be used in determining whether someone was willfully blind such that the inquiry would not be whether the ordinary, reasonable prudent person would have known, but rather whether someone of similar age, intelligence, and experience as the defendant would have known, given all of the facts and circumstances to which the particular defendant had been exposed? What are the benefits of taking such an approach? What are the drawbacks? Do you think using such a modified objective standard undercuts the very purposes for which the willful blindness doctrine exists? Why or why not?

(c)   Recklessness - Under the Model Penal Code, *recklessness* is the mens rea for any material element of an offense unless otherwise it is specifically stated to be another level of mens rea. When one acts recklessly, the actor is aware of a risk that his or her conduct could cause a particular result, but consciously disregards that known risk and acts anyway. Key to criminal recklessness is that the defendant actually (subjectively in his or her own mind) be aware of a substantial and unjustifiable risk, but then act anyway with disregard for the risk he or she perceived. In other words, the reckless actor just doesn't give a damn.

For better or worse, the criminal law has basically recognized two different levels of recklessness: regular or mere recklessness, and gross recklessness. Regular recklessness is defined in the preceding paragraph. Gross recklessness, however, involves something more than a conscious disregard of a substantial and unjustifiable risk. The risk must be so great that the conscious disregard of it rises to the level of manifesting an "extreme indifference to the value of human life." The difference between the two is difficult to define because it is really only a matter of degree. Since reasonable people might differ over what is reckless conduct as opposed to grossly reckless conduct, this is often a question of fact to be resolved by a jury.

(d)   Negligence - *Negligence* is similar to recklessness with the exception that with negligence, the actor is not aware of a risk (and hence could not have consciously disregarded it), but the *actor should have been aware* of the risk. In other words, using an objective standard, the ordinary, reasonable prudent person in the same circumstances as the actor *would have perceived* the risk that the criminally negligent defendant failed to perceive. But the failure to perceive any risk will not suffice for the imposition of liability under the criminal negligence standard. The failure to become aware of the risk must involve some gross deviation from the conduct that a reasonable person would observe in the situation, rather than mere inadvertence, which is the realm of civil negligence under tort law.

As stated above, the lines between grossly reckless conduct, reckless conduct, and criminally negligent conduct are largely a matter of degree. Consider the following case.

STATE of Vermont v. Stephen C. BROOKS.
658 A.2d 22 (Vt. 1995).

Allen, Chief Justice.

In May 1986, defendant purchased a home in Burlington that was equipped with a driveway heater. Hot water, heated by gas in the unit's boiler, flowed through a system of pipes beneath the driveway to melt snow and ice. The unit was located in the attached garage and could be turned on by a switch. Exhaust fumes from the system were supposed to exit through a vent located on the backside of the garage.

On November 27, 1987, defendant turned on the driveway heater before running an errand. While he was gone, another occupant, Jill McDermott, and her infant became ill from noxious fumes that had emanated from the garage. When defendant returned home, McDermott asked him to take her and the baby to the hospital. Defendant took them to the emergency room where they were examined and released; no diagnosis was made. Defendant thought the fumes were caused by a plumbing problem and called C & L Plumbing and Heating (C& L). C & L sent an employee, Ben Linden, to inspect the heater. Linden determined that a dislodged flap in the termination kit was preventing proper exhaust. He explained the malfunction to defendant and told him that repairs should be made and safety features added. Linden then called Vermont Gas Systems (VGS) and met with one of its employees to examine the system. After doing some additional work on the unit, both servicemen decided the gas should remain off until repairs were made. The VGS employee told McDermott the system was not safe to operate and that she was lucky to be alive, "because it was carbon monoxide." McDermott relayed these comments to defendant.

That night, the owner of C& L called defendant and told him that the heater had been improperly installed and VGS would call about necessary repairs. A VGS supervisor also called and explained the dangers of the condition and agreed that it should be repaired. Approximately one month after the accident, Linden returned to defendant's home to service other appliances. When Linden asked defendant about the heater, he admitted that nothing had been done. Linden told defendant he was playing "Russian roulette," to which defendant remarked that "he would have to call the gas company."

In May 1988, defendant hired a real estate agent to sell his home. Defendant did not mention the heater's history to the agent. Instead, defendant instructed the agent to turn the heater on, then off, when demonstrating it to prospective buyers. The heater was a highlighted feature in agent's marketing materials. In August 1988, the agent recommended Karl Sklar, a part-time carpenter, to replace some rotten siding. While Sklar was at defendant's home, defendant told Sklar that the heater had problems and asked Sklar if he would work on the heater. Sklar declined because he lacked experience with such systems.

In July 1988, the agent showed the house to Linda Cifarelli and her parents, the von Albrechts, who were helping their daughter and son-in-law purchase a home. While touring the home, the agent explained and demonstrated the driveway heating system by turning it on for approximately five minutes. During their second showing, defendant, who was present to answer questions, explained and demonstrated the driveway heater again, but did not mention its prior problem or faulty condition.

The von Albrechts made an offer to purchase the house which defendant accepted. The buyers then arranged a professional home inspection. During the inspection, defendant demonstrated the heater, but did not explain how it worked or mention its history. At the September closing, defendant insisted that the Cifarellis return to the house with him for a more detailed showing because "he knew things [the inspector] wouldn't know." Defendant showed Linda Cifarelli and her parents the central vacuum system, the drainage system, and the driveway heater. When showing the heater, he told them it was not necessary to run it for more than two hours.

On the evening of December 9, 1988, Linda Cifarelli and her husband, John, turned on the driveway heater because it was snowing. They put their two young daughters to bed upstairs and followed shortly after. A house guest, Andrew Csermak, stayed awake to watch television. After a while, Csermak became dizzy and nauseous, and eventually vomited. Csermak cracked a window and fell asleep on the downstairs couch. When Csermak awoke at noon, he was concerned because the Cifarellis were not yet awake. He went upstairs and discovered that only the infant daughter was still breathing. Csermak called 911. Upon arrival, the police and firemen discovered the bodies of John and Linda Cifarelli and their four year old daughter. The police also found the garage door dripping with condensation and the driveway heater running. The infant and Csermak were taken to the hospital and diagnosed with carbon monoxide poisoning. Autopsies revealed that Linda and John Cifarelli and their daughter died of carbon monoxide poisoning. Defendant was charged with three counts of involuntary manslaughter by reckless endangerment and convicted by a jury in October 1992.

Defendant raises several issues on appeal. First, he challenges as erroneous the jury instructions pertaining to (1) the mens rea of recklessness, (2) a seller's legal duty to disclose material defects about a house, and (3) the defense of intervening causation. Second, he claims that his motion for acquittal was improperly denied because there was insufficient evidence to prove the essential elements of recklessness and the existence of his legal duty to act. Third, defendant contends that Vermont's manslaughter statute is unconstitutionally vague as applied to the facts of this case. Finally, he argues that the court abused its discretion in denying his unopposed motion to sequester the jury.

I. Jury Instructions

Defendant first contends that the court's definition of reckless intent was erroneous. Defendant was charged with involuntary manslaughter by reckless endangerment. 13 V.S.A. § 2304; *State v. Stanislaw*, 153 Vt. 517, 522, 573 A.2d 286, 289 (1990) (involuntary manslaughter is a killing caused by an unlawful act, but not accompanied by an intent to take life). Because the underlying unlawful act charged was reckless endangerment, 13 V.S.A. § 1025, defendant's conviction could only be sustained upon finding reckless intent. *Stanislaw*, 153 Vt. at 525, 573 A.2d at 291 (mens rea of recklessness or criminal negligence may sustain conviction for involuntary manslaughter). Defendant argues that the instruction defining recklessness was flawed because it incorporated both the criminal negligence and recklessness standards but did not distinguish between the two. Defendant maintains that while recklessness requires an actual awareness of the risk and of the resulting harm, criminal negligence requires a less stringent showing that the actor should have known of the risk and harm. According to defendant, the failure to distinguish between the two levels of intent amounted to plain error, because the jury could have convicted him if it found only that he should have known either that the heater was not repaired, or that the heater posed a risk.

We have endorsed the Model Penal Code's definition of recklessness, which explains:

A person acts recklessly with respect to a material element of an offense when he consciously disregards a substantial and unjustifiable risk that the material element exists or will result from his conduct. The risk must be of such a nature and degree that, considering the nature and purpose of the actor's conduct and the circumstances known to him, its disregard involves a gross deviation from the standard of conduct that a law-abiding person would observe in the actor's situation.

State v. O'Connell, 149 Vt. 114, 115 n. 1, 540 A.2d 1030, 1031 n. 1 (1987) (quoting Model Penal Code § 2.02(2)(c) (defining recklessly)). In contrast, criminal negligence occurs when the actor should be aware that a substantial and unjustifiable risk exists or will result from his conduct. *Stanislaw*, 153 Vt. at 525, 573 A.2d at 291. Disregarding the risk amounts to a gross deviation from the standard of care that a reasonable person would observe in the actor's situation. *Id.*

Contrary to defendant's suggestion, both recklessness and criminal negligence require an objective view of the risk; the difference is one of degree. The more critical distinction between recklessness and criminal negligence is the actor's subjective awareness of the risk. Recklessness requires a conscious disregard of the risk. In contrast, criminal negligence results when an actor is unaware of the risk which the actor should have perceived. *Stanislaw*, 153 Vt. at 525, 573 A.2d at 291.

The court properly instructed the jury to objectively assess the risk and to determine whether defendant consciously disregarded that risk. For further clarification, it referred the jury to the reckless endangerment instruction, which expressly required a finding that defendant "actually knew from the circumstances then existing that the heater had not properly been repaired."

II. Insufficiency of the Evidence

Defendant challenges the court's denial of his motion for acquittal, claiming there was insufficient evidence to convict on the essential element[] of recklessness . . . . Defendant contends, and we agree, that proof of . . . recklessness . . . hinged on finding that he actually knew the driveway heater had not been repaired. Defendant argues, however, that there was insufficient evidence to prove beyond a reasonable doubt that he knew the driveway heating unit had not been repaired. We disagree.

Defendant knew the heater was malfunctioning and emitting fumes when he took McDermott and her infant child to the hospital in November 1987. Representatives from C& L and VGS testified that they explained the exhaust problem to defendant and told him that the system was dangerous and needed repairs. Although there was conflicting testimony about who was responsible for the repairs, resolving this confusion was less important than determining when, and if, defendant thought the repairs were completed.

Defendant's position was that he thought the heater was fixed by VGS shortly after, if not immediately following, the November 1987 accident. Other witnesses, however, testified to conversations with defendant about repairing the heater which refute defendant's position. The C&L

employee, Linden, testified that one month after the accident, defendant told him the heater was still unrepaired. Linden then told defendant he was "playing Russian roulette." Defendant suggests that he construed Linden's conversation with him to mean that Linden had fixed the problem. Linden testified, however, that a reasonable person would not have thought the problem was fixed. In the summer of 1988, at the recommendation of defendant's real estate agent, defendant spoke with Karl Sklar. According to Sklar's testimony, defendant mentioned that there was a problem with the heater and asked Sklar if he would work on it. There was no evidence that either VGS or C& L worked on the heater while the home was on the market or after Sklar's visit. In sum, there was sufficient evidence fairly and reasonably supporting a finding that defendant actually knew the heater had not been repaired when he sold his home to the Cifarellis. With this critical finding and other supporting evidence, the jury could reasonably conclude that defendant had the requisite reckless intent. There was sufficient evidence to support a finding that defendant's failure to disclose the existence of the malfunctioning heater before selling his home amounted to a conscious disregard of a substantial and unjustifiable risk.

Defendant suggests that his continued use of the heater during the winter of 1987 was persuasive evidence, rising to the level of reasonable doubt, that he thought the heater was repaired or that he was unaware of the substantial risk. We disagree. The jury could have reasonably construed such evidence to have the opposite effect. Because defendant understood the exact nature of the problem, the jury could reasonably have inferred that defendant ran the heater only for brief periods to prevent exhaust back-up. His instructions to the real estate agent to run the heater only briefly suggest as much. Additional evidence that defendant checked the exhaust cylinders before and after using the heater reasonably implied that defendant was himself wary of using the machine. Defendant's motion for judgment of acquittal was properly denied. Affirmed.

QUESTIONS

1.   As explained by the court, a conviction for involuntary manslaughter may be based on either on the mens rea level of ordinary recklessness, or on gross negligence. The critical difference between the two is whether the defendant subjectively perceived and then consciously disregarded a substantial and unjustifiable risk. Do you think Brooks was merely "negligent," or was he "reckless"? Explain your answer using the facts of the case to support your reasoning.

2.   Although not an issue in the case, there is an argument to be made that Brooks committed murder in the second degree. Whether someone is liable for murder in the second degree or involuntary manslaughter depends on whether the jury finds a defendant's conduct to be "reckless" using the ordinary recklessness standard, or "grossly reckless" such that the nature of the reckless conduct "manifests an extreme indifference to the value of human life." Do you think there was sufficient evidence to have held Brooks liable for murder in the second degree? How do you differentiate between acts that are "reckless" and "grossly reckless"?

3.   Driving under the influence clearly involves criminal conduct. But if someone dies as a result of a car accident with a driver who was operating a motor vehicle while impaired by drugs or alcohol, what level of mens rea would such a driver be said to have acted with? Is driving under the influence criminally negligent conduct? Is it a conscious disregard of a known, substantial, and unjustifiable risk that would constitute criminal recklessness and, therefore, be deemed an involuntary manslaughter? Or is it grossly reckless conduct that manifests an extreme indifference to the value of human life such that it would warrant a murder in the second degree conviction? Should the level of intoxication be relevant to the determination? For example, might someone "under the influence" at a 0.07% blood alcohol level (and thus not legally drunk in most U.S. jurisdiction) be criminally negligent, while someone over the legal limit be reckless? What is the person is a two or three times the legal limit; would that constitute gross recklessness? See United States v. Flemming, 739 F.2d 945 (4th Cir. 1984) (upholding murder in the second degree conviction against a driver with a .315% blood alcohol concentration who drove at a speed more than 50 miles per hours over the speed limit).

The distinctions between the non-specific intent level of mens rea are further complicated by the fact that criminal negligence is often confused with civil negligence, although the two are distinct. Civil negligence is really nothing more than mere careless. Although such carelessness is sufficient to impose civil liability, it is insufficient to impose criminal liability. Criminal negligence is aimed at morally culpable behavior, not mere inadvertence. Criminal negligence must involve some gross deviation from the conduct that a reasonable person would observe in the situation. Compare and contrast the following two cases to see if you can distinguish between reckless conduct, criminally negligent conduct, and civilly negligent conduct.

STATE of New Mexico, Plaintiff-Appellee v. Robert Leon MAGBY, Defendant-Appellant.
969 P.2d 965 (N.M. 1998).

Franchini, Chief Justice.

Following a horseback-riding accident, Defendant Robert Leon Magby was convicted of child abuse resulting in death. We hold that the trial court improperly refused a jury instruction tendered by defense counsel, resulting in the distinct possibility of juror confusion as to the mens rea necessary for conviction. We therefore reverse Magby's conviction and remand for a new trial.

Four-year-old Heather Naylor was killed when she fell from the back of the horse she was riding with her mother, Cheryl Naylor. According to Cheryl, just prior to the accident Magby had been "joking around" with her and "playfully" removed the bridle and bit from her horse, which was standing still at the time. Suddenly, the horse bolted into a gallop, and without a bridle or bit, Cheryl was unable to control the animal or slow it down. Heather was thrown to the ground, and her mother jumped from the horse to assist her. Heather suffered grievous injuries, and she died soon after being transported to a nearby hospital.

The State filed a criminal information against Magby as follows:

On or about the 10th day of February, 1995, the above-named defendant negligently caused Heather Naylor, a child, to be placed in a situation that might endanger her life or health, resulting in the death of Heather Naylor, contrary to NMSA 1978, § 30-6-1 [1973, as amended through 1989].

Magby was charged with abuse of a child resulting in death, a first-degree felony, contrary to Section 30-6-1(C). Section 30-6-1(C) provides, in pertinent part, that "[a]buse of a child consists of a person knowingly, intentionally or negligently, and without justifiable cause, causing or permitting a child to be . . . placed in a situation that may endanger the child's life or health . . . ."

There were several eyewitnesses who testified at trial, but none had any idea why Cheryl's horse had bolted. Cheryl testified that the horse seemed to be driven by fear. Neither Cheryl nor any other witness, however, observed anything that might have spooked the horse. The horse was uniformly described as a "quiet, gentle horse," "real sweet and gentle," and "real gentle-natured." One witness, however, testified that the only horse that is totally predictable is one that is "stuffed," and Magby's expert witness, a horse trainer, characterized Magby's act of removing the bridle and bit as "unwise" though not "reckless."

The jury was instructed:

To find that Robert Leon Magby negligently caused child abuse to occur, you must find that Robert Leon Magby knew or should have known of the danger involved and acted with a reckless disregard for the safety or health of Heather Naylor; . . .

As we discuss more fully below, the trial court refused defense counsel's tender of an instruction defining the term "reckless disregard."

The jury found Magby guilty of child abuse resulting in death. . . . Magby appealed his conviction, and the New Mexico Court of Appeals certified the case to this Court. We accepted certification and now take this opportunity to clarify the proper jury instructions to be given in proceedings where a defendant is charged with negligent child abuse.

Defense counsel tendered the following instruction:

> For you to find that the Defendant acted recklessly in this case, you must find that he knew or should have known that his conduct created a substantial and foreseeable risk, that he disregarded that risk and that he was wholly indifferent to the consequences of his conduct and to the welfare and safety of others.

Magby argues that the instruction was necessary to prevent the jury from convicting him of mere civil negligence, as opposed to the criminal negligence standard required by *Santillanes v. State*, 115 N.M. 215, 219, 849 P.2d 358, 362 (1993).

In *Santillanes*, this Court construed Section 30-6-1, which remained unchanged at the time of Magby's trial, "as aiming to punish conduct that is morally culpable, not merely inadvertent." 115 N.M. at 222, 849 P.2d at 365. We observed that, "when moral condemnation and social opprobrium attach to the conviction of a crime, the crime should typically reflect a mental state warranting such contempt." Id. Thus, we held: "We interpret the mens rea element of negligence in the child abuse statute, therefore, to require a showing of criminal negligence instead of ordinary civil negligence." *Id.* On this basis, we announced that, to find a defendant guilty of criminal negligence in the context of child abuse, the jury must find that "the defendant knew or should have known of the danger involved and acted with reckless disregard for the safety or health of the child." *Id.*

The facts presented in *Santillanes*, however, did not prompt us to consider the need for an instruction defining "reckless disregard" in cases alleging criminally negligent child abuse. There, we were able to determine, as a matter of law, that "no rational jury could have concluded that *Santillanes* cut his nephew's throat . . . without satisfying the standard of criminal negligence that we have adopted today." 115 N.M. at 223, 849 P.2d at 266.

In this case, Magby calls our attention the possibility of juror confusion over the concept of "reckless disregard." Magby contends [this jury instruction] could confuse jurors on the critical issue of mens rea because it uses the words "negligently" and "with a reckless disregard" in the same sentence, essentially equating the two concepts. The dictionary definitions of these terms are indeed very similar, "negligent" being defined as: "1. Habitually guilty of neglect; lacking in due care or concern. 2. Extremely careless"; and "reckless" as: "a. Heedless or careless. b. Headstrong; rash. 2. Having no regard for consequences; uncontrolled; wild." THE AMERICAN HERITAGE DICTIONARY 879, 1088 (1973).

Magby argues that the ordinary meaning of the terms "negligently" and "reckless disregard" may misdirect jurors as to the standard of negligence required for conviction, thereby rendering [the jury instruction given] fatally ambiguous. We are persuaded by this argument.

In view of the foregoing dictionary definitions of "negligent" and "reckless," there is a distinct possibility that the jury understood the applicable negligence standard to criminalize "careless" conduct or perhaps only "extremely careless" conduct. Neither understanding is correct. See *State v. Yarborough*, 930 P.2d 131 (N.M. 1996) (merely careless driving cannot form basis for involuntary manslaughter conviction, which requires showing of criminal negligence). Under the lone instruction given to the jury, there is no reason to suppose the jury correctly interpreted [the instruction]. It is equally likely that the jurors understood the terms "negligently" and "reckless disregard" to imply some degree of carelessness as it is that they recognized the necessity of finding a culpable mental state in the defendant.

Defense counsel's tendered instruction would have cured this ambiguity by defining the concept "reckless disregard" in detail and in a separate instruction from the confusing reference to "negligently."

In this way, the distinct possibility of juror confusion over the mens rea necessary for conviction could have been avoided. We therefore hold that the trial court improperly refused defense counsel's curative instruction.

We note that virtually every uniform jury instruction that utilizes the terms "reckless" or "recklessly" provides for an express definition of those terms. Of the instructions that do not expressly define "reckless" or "recklessly," only [the one at issue in this case] involve considerations of negligence. An express definition of "reckless disregard" would be particularly appropriate for these instructions because the distinction between criminal negligence and civil negligence turns on an understanding of the concept of recklessness. *See State v. Harris*, 41 N.M. 426, 428, 70 P.2d 757, 757 (1937) (distinguishing, somewhat tautologically, between criminal and civil negligence as follows: criminal negligence involves "conduct . . . so reckless, wanton, and willful, as to show an utter disregard for the safety of [others]," while mere civil negligence is conduct "not amounting a reckless, willful and wanton disregard of consequences . . . .").

The trial court improperly refused defense counsel's tendered instruction defining the term "reckless disregard." We therefore reverse Magby's conviction and remand for a new trial.

The STATE of New Hampshire, Appellee, v. Michael W. PITTERA, Appellant.
651 A.2d 931 (N.H. 1994).

Thayer, Justice.

The defendant, Michael W. Pittera, appeals from his conviction for negligent homicide, RSA 630:3, I(a) (Supp.1993), based on a jury verdict in the Superior Court (Fauver, J.). The defendant argues that . . . the evidence was insufficient as a matter of law to sustain his conviction. We affirm.

The grand jury brought two indictments against the defendant, alleging alternative theories of negligent homicide. The defendant moved to have the indictments dismissed, and the trial court denied these motions. After a jury trial, the defendant was acquitted on the first indictment, which alleged negligence based on operating a boat at excessive speed and excessively close to shore. The defendant was convicted on the second indictment, which alleged that he did negligently cause the death of another, in that the said Michael W. Pittera did operate a boat on Lower Suncook Lake and did fail to pay due attention and fail to see a person in the water, resulting in said boat and its propeller striking Nicholas G. Carpenter, DOB 8/17/80, causing a cervical fracture and a severing of his spinal cord, which caused the death of said Nicholas G. Carpenter.

To have convicted the defendant of negligent homicide, the jury must have found, beyond a reasonable doubt, that the defendant failed to become aware of a substantial and unjustifiable risk that death would result from his conduct. The risk must be such that the "failure to become aware of it constitutes a gross deviation from the conduct that a reasonable person would observe in the situation."

"Whether the defendant failed to become aware of a substantial and unjustifiable risk is determined by an objective test, not by reference to the defendant's subjective perception." *State v. Ebinger*, 135 N.H. 264, 265, 603 A.2d 924, 925 (1992). Using this objective standard, the jury could have found that a reasonable person, in the defendant's place, would have seen Nicholas Carpenter in the water and avoided hitting him. Furthermore, the jury could have combined this finding with the evidence that the defendant was traveling rapidly through a cove area containing numerous docks and adjacent to a known swimming area while watching the shoreline, to conclude that the defendant's "failure to become aware of [the risk] constitute[d] a gross deviation from the conduct that a reasonable person would observe in the situation." RSA 626:2, II(d).

The evidence showed that the victim was swimming with a group of five other people. While there is conflicting testimony as to the water level, at least the victim's mother was visible from the waist up. The victim was located near a known swimming area and members of the group were using assorted visible flotation devices; the group was visible from the shore; and the defendant had turned away from his direction of travel, pointing to property on the shore, prior to the accident.

The acquittal of the defendant on the first count indicates that the evidence of the defendant's excessive speed alone was insufficient to establish his guilt beyond a reasonable doubt. The acquittal, however, did not preclude the jury from considering evidence regarding the defendant's speed in determining whether the defendant was criminally negligent under the second indictment. The evidence supports the jury's finding that the defendant's behavior constituted a gross deviation from the conduct that a reasonable person would have exhibited in the same situation. Therefore, the trial court properly denied the defendant's motions to dismiss. Affirmed.

QUESTIONS

1.   In *Magby*, there was expert testimony that having removed the bridle from the horse was "unwise," but not "reckless." Do you think this "unwise" conduct was merely civilly negligent, or did is rise to the level of being criminally negligent? On what does the distinction turn in your mind?

2.   Do you think that Mr. Magby's conduct could be classified as criminally reckless? Explain your reasoning.

3.   In contrast to *Magby*, the *Pittera* case involved a more clear cut case of, at minimum, criminal negligence. Note, however, that it was not determinative to the court that Mr. Pittera was speeding. Rather, looking at the totality of the circumstance, the court determined there was sufficient evidence to support the jury's finding that he was criminally negligent. What were the facts you think were important to the court's determination?

4.   The *Pittera* court upheld a conviction for criminally negligent homicide. Do yo think Mr. Pittera's conduct criminally negligent, or do you think there were sufficient facts upon which a jury could have found him to having acted recklessly, thereby supporting a conviction for involuntary manslaughter? Explain your reasoning.

3. Strict Liability and Vicarious Liability

As stated earlier in this chapter, nearly all crimes require an union of actus reus and mens rea. But there are a small, yet growing number of criminal offenses that do not follow this rule. This crimes are called *strict liability* offenses. When a crime carries strict liability, a person can be convicted of the crime for having engaged in the proscribed act (the actus reus) even though there was no accompanying criminal intent. Thus, a person can act without any mens rea whatsoever, and still be convicted of a strict liability crime.

Strict liability does not apply to mala in se crimes – those criminal acts that are innately evil, such as rape and murder. *See, e.g., Morisette v. United States*, 342 U.S. 246 (1952). Rather, strict liability has historically attached only to a small number of malum prohibitum crimes (crimes that are not innately "evil" unto themselves). This small range of offenses typically include public health, safety, and welfare offenses, such as traffic violations, serving alcohol to minors, mislabeling food or drugs, etc. Additionally, when the criminal law is used to regulate morality, especially when dealing with sexual offenses, the crimes usually carry strict liability. Thus, for example, in a jurisdiction that retains the common law strict liability rule for statutory rape, it would be no defense to the crime of having engaged in sexual intercourse under the age of consent that the "victim" lied about her age or even produced false identification that she was over the age of consent.

Compare and contrast the following two cases to see if you can identify the legal rationale underlying the imposition of strict liability in the first case, but not in the second one.

Kreisher, P.J.

On February 6, 1948, John Fisher, a driver for above-named defendant, at the direction of defendant, purchased a load of coal at the Gilberton Coal Company Colliery and had the [coal] loaded upon a truck owned by defendant. [Under the state's vehicle code, the truck was] permitted to weigh 15,000 pounds plus five percent, or a gross weight of 15,750 pounds. The load was weighed by a licensed weigh-master at the colliery and the weight was given at 15,200 pounds. Fisher drove the truck to the home of defendant, who was out of town at the time and then placed the weigh slip from the colliery in the compartment of the truck.

The following day, defendant went to the Danville National Bank to do some banking business and observed the Pennsylvania State Police at the northern end of the river bridge checking on trucks. He then returned to his home and drove his truck with the load of coal to the northern end of the river bridge on his way to the borough water department scales for the purpose of having weighed. He states that he was selling the coal in Danville, an pursuant to the requirements of an ordinance in Danville, he had to have a Danville weigh slip. Before reaching the water department scales, a State policeman stopped him and he was directed to the scale where his load was weighed by the officer and the weigh slip was signed by a licensed weigh-master, showing that his gross weight was 16,015 and that he was, therefore, overloaded 265 pounds. The officer lodge an information for his violation of The Vehicle Code. Defendant waived a hearing and the matter is now before us for disposition.

It is contended by counsel for defendant that this prosecution should be dismissed for the reason that defendant had in his possession a weigh bill for this particular load by a duly licensed weighmaster, which was weighed the day before, showing that the gross weight of the truck and the load was within the load allowed by law for this particular truck, and that defendant, relying upon this weigh bill, voluntarily drove to where he knew the police were weighing trucks, and was of the belief that his load was a legal load, and therefore, because of this belief, he is not guilty of the crime charged.

In criminal law we have two distinct types of crimes: The one type of crime being the common-law crimes, which are designated as crimes mala in se, which means that they are crimes because the act is bad in and of itself. The other type of crime which did not exist at common law covers those acts which are made criminal by statute, and are termed crimes mala prohibita, and simply means that they are crimes not because they are bad in and of themselves, but merely because the legislative authority makes the act criminal and penal.

In crimes that are mala in se, two elements are necessary for the commission of the crime, viz., the mental element and the physical element. In this type of crime intent is a necessary element, but in statutory crimes, which are simply mala prohibita, the mental element is not necessary for the commission of the crime, and one who does an act in violation of the statute and is caught and prosecuted, is guilty of the crime irrespective of his intent or belief. The power of the legislature to punish an act as a crime, even though it is not bad in and of itself, is an absolute power of the legislature, the only restriction being the constitutional restrictions, and it is the duty of the court to enforce these enactments irrespective of what the court might personally think about the wisdom of the act.

Except for constitutional limitations, the power of the State legislature is absolute. It may punish any act which in its judgment requires punishment, provided it violates no constitutional restriction, and its enactments must be enforced by the courts. The courts cannot review the discretion of the legislature, or pass upon the expediency, wisdom, or propriety of legislative action in matters within its powers. Neither can the courts pass upon the action of a prosecuting officer who prosecutes a person for the violation of a statute which is violated by that person, even though the court might be of the opinion that the officer should have not instituted the prosecution.

If the testimony shows, as in this case, that defendant violated the law, and is prosecuted for that violation, then the court is bound to enforce the legislative enactments, and cannot in good conscience set itself up as the legislature and excuse one person who has violated the law and find another person guilty for the same violation. It is true that this rule of law may seem harsh and unjustifiable, but the court is powerless to correct it, and, therefore, under our duty as judge, we are obliged to hold that this defendant violated The Vehicle Code by having his truck overloaded, and he is guilty as charged . . . .

The PEOPLE of the State of California, Plaintiff-Respondent, v. Stephen STUART, Defendant-Appellant. 47 Cal. 2d 167, 302 P.2d 5 (1956).

Traynor, Justice.

Defendant was charged by information with manslaughter, Pen. Code, § 192, and the violation of section 380 of the Penal Code. He was convicted of both offenses by the court sitting without a jury. His motions for a new trial and for dismissal were denied, sentence was suspended, and he was placed on probation for two years. He appeals from the judgment of conviction and the order denying his motion for a new trial.

Defendant was licensed as a pharmacist by this state in 1946 and has practiced here since that time. He holds a B.S. degree in chemistry from Long Island University and a B.S. degree in pharmacy from Columbia University. In April, 1954, he was employed as a pharmacist by the Ethical Drug Company in Los Angeles.

On July 16, 1954, he filled a prescription for Irvin Sills. It had been written by Dr. D.M. Goldstein for Sills' eight-day-old child. It called for "Sodium phenobarbital, grains eight. Sodium citrate, drams three. Simple Syrup, ounces two. Aqua peppermint, ounces one. Aqua distillate QS, ounces four." Defendant assembled the necessary drugs to fill the prescription. He believed that the simple syrup called for was unavailable and therefore used syrup of orange. The ingredients were incompatible, and the syrup of orange precipitated out the phenobarbital. Defendant then telephoned Dr. Goldstein to ask if he could use some other flavoring. Dr. Goldstein told him that since it was midnight, if he could not find any simple syrup "it would be just as well to use another substance, elixir mesopine, P.B." Defendant spoke to a clerk and learned that there was simple syrup behind the counter. He mixed the prescription with this syrup, put a label on the bottle according to the prescription, and gave it to Sills. Sills returned home, put a teaspoonful of the prescription in the baby's milk and gave it to the baby. The baby died a few hours later.

Defendant stipulated that there was nitrite in the prescription bottle and that "the cause of death was methemoglobinemia caused by the ingestion of nitrite." When he compounded the prescription, there was a bottle containing sodium nitrite on the shelf near a bottle labeled sodium citrate. He testified that at no time during his employment at the Ethical Drug Company had he filled any prescription calling for sodium nitrite and that he had taken the prescribed three drams of sodium citrate from the bottle so labeled. On August 11, 1954, another pharmacist employed by the Ethical Drug Company filled a prescription identical with the Sills' prescription. He obtained the sodium citrate from the same bottle used by defendant. The prescription was given to an infant. The infant became ill but recovered. In the opinion of Dr. Goldstein, it was suffering from methemoglobinemia. An analysis of this prescription by a University of Southern California chemist disclosed that it contained 5.4 grams of sodium nitrite per 100 cc's and 4.5 grams of sodium citrate per 100 cc's.

An analysis made by the staff of the head toxicologist for the Los Angeles County Coroner of the contents of the bottle given to Sills disclosed that it contained 1.33 drams of sodium citrate and 1.23 of sodium nitrite. An analysis made by Biochemical Procedures, Incorporated, a laboratory, of a sample of the contents of the bottle labeled sodium citrate disclosed that it contained 38.9 milligrams of nitrite per gram of material. Charles Covet, one of the owners of the Ethical Drug Company, testified that on the 17th or 18th of October, 1954, he emptied the contents of the sodium citrate bottle, washed the bottle but not its cap, and put in new sodium citrate. A subsequent analysis of rinsings from the cap gave strong positive tests for nitrite. Covet also testified that when he purchased an interest in the company in April, 1950, the bottle labeled sodium citrate was part of the inventory, that no one had put additional sodium citrate into the bottle from that time until he refilled it after the death of the Sills child and that he had never seen any other supply of sodium citrate in the store.

There is nothing in the record to indicate that the contents of the bottle labeled sodium citrate could have been identified as containing sodium nitrite without laboratory analysis. There was testimony that at first glance sodium citrate and sodium nitrite are identical in appearance, that in form either may consist of small colorless crystals or white crystalline powder, that the granulation of the crystals may vary with the manufacturer, and that there may be a slight difference in color between the two. The substance from the bottle labeled sodium citrate was exhibited to the court, but no attempt was made to compare it with unadulterated sodium citrate or sodium nitrite. A chemist with Biochemical Procedures, Incorporated, testified that the mixture did not appear to be homogeneous but that from visual observation alone he could not identify the crystals as one substance or the other. Defendant testified that he had no occasion before July 16th to examine or fill any prescription from the sodium citrate bottle.

No evidence whatever was introduced that would justify an inference that defendant knew or should have known that the bottle labeled sodium citrate contained sodium nitrite. On the contrary, the undisputed evidence shows conclusively that defendant was morally entirely innocent and that only because of a reasonable mistake or unavoidable accident was the prescription filled with a substance containing sodium nitrite. Section 20 of the Penal Code makes the union of act and intent of criminal negligence an invariable element of every crime unless it is excluded expressly or by necessary implication. Moreover, section 26 of the Penal Code lists among the persons incapable of committing crimes "persons who committed the act or made the omission charged under an ignorance or mistake of fact, which disproves any criminal intent" and "persons who committed the act or made the omission charged through misfortune or by accident, when it appears that there was no evil design, intention, or culpable negligence." The question is thus presented whether a person can be convicted of manslaughter or a violation of section 380 of the Penal Code in the absence of any evidence of criminal intent or criminal negligence.

The answer to this question as it relates to the conviction of manslaughter depends on whether or not defendant committed an "unlawful act" within the meaning of section 192 of the Penal Code when he filled the prescription. The Attorney General contends that even if he had no criminal intent and was not criminally negligent, defendant violated section 26280 of the Health and Safety Code and therefore committed an unlawful act within the meaning of section 192 of the Penal Code.

Section 26280 of the Health and Safety Code provides: "The manufacture, production, preparation, compounding, packing, selling, offering for sale, advertising or keeping for sale within the State of California . . . of any drug or device which is adulterated or misbranded is prohibited." In view of the analyses of the contents of the prescription bottle and the bottle labeled sodium citrate and defendant's stipulation, there can be no doubt that he prepared, compounded, and sold an adulterated and misbranded drug.

Because of the great danger to the public health and safety that the preparation, compounding, or sale of adulterated or misbranded drugs entails, the public interest in demanding that those who prepare, compound, or sell drugs make certain that they are not adulterated or misbranded, and the belief that although an occasional nonculpable offender may be punished, it is necessary to incur that risk by imposing strict liability to prevent the escape of great numbers of culpable offenders, public welfare statutes like section 26280 are not ordinarily governed by section 20 of the Penal Code and therefore call for the sanctions imposed even though the prohibited acts are committed without criminal intent or criminal negligence.

It does not follow, however, that such acts, committed without criminal intent or criminal negligence, are unlawful acts within the meaning of section 192 of the Penal Code . . . . The act in question must be committed with criminal intent or criminal negligence to be an unlawful act within the meaning of section 192. By virtue of its application to both phrases, section 20 precludes the incongruity of imposing on the morally innocent the same penalty, appropriate only for the culpable. Words such as "unlawful act, not amounting to felony" have been included in most definitions of manslaughter since the time of Blackstone and even since the time of Lord Hale, "unlawful act" as it pertains to manslaughter had been interpreted as meaning an act that aside from its unlawfulness was of such a dangerous nature as to justify a conviction of manslaughter if done intentionally or without due caution.

It follows, therefore, that only if defendant had intentionally or through criminal negligence prepared, compounded, or sold an adulterated or misbranded drug, would his violation of section 26280 of the Health and Safety Code be an unlawful act within the meaning of section 192 of the Penal Code. When, as in this case, however, the defendant did not know, and could not reasonably be expected to know, that the sodium citrate bottle contained nitrite, those conditions are not met and there is therefore lacking the culpability necessary to make the act an unlawful act within the meaning of section 192. The judgment and order are reversed.

QUESTIONS

1.   The driver in *Olshefski* was not at fault. Quite the contrary, he went to a licensed weighmaster who made a mistake when weighing the truck. Thus, the driver was not even criminally negligent, because the ordinary, reasonable prudent person in his situation would not have been aware of any risk that he was violating the law. Yet, criminal liability was imposed on upheld on appeal. Do you agree with the outcome of the case? Why or why not?

2.   Mr. Stuart was convicted of "unlawful act" manslaughter. It is a catch-all type of homicide that holds one liable for any death one causes during the commission of an "unlawful act," even though the death was not intended. In this case, the predicate unlawful act was the strict liability offense of selling the adulterated or misbranded drug. Do you think that the sale of such a drug should subject a nonculpable pharmacist to criminal sanctions? Why? Why do you think the California legislature provides for such a penalty, even in the absence of negligence?

3.   The court in *Stuart* determined that the strict liability offense of selling an adulterated or mislabed drug was not an "unlawful act" within the meaning of the unlawful act manslaughter statute. Why? Do you agree with the court's analysis, separate and apart from the result?

4.   Compare the level of culpability of the defendants in *Olshefski* and *Stuart*. Who was more *morally* blameworthy? Why? What reasons can you offer to explain the differences in the outcome of the two cases? Was "justice" done in either case? Explain.

5.   Romeo, a 19 year old male, has sexual intercourse with Juliet in Verona, Calivada, where the age of consent in Verona is 17. Juliet told Romeo that she is 18 years old when she was, in fact, 16 years old. Romeo however, had no reason to believe that his love would lie to him. Is he guilty of statutory rape? Why? Presume that during the time that Romeo and Juliet are having sex, Juliet, totally overcome with passion, dies of a heart attack. If Romeo were charged under the unlawful act manslaughter applicable in *Stuart*, should he be convicted? Explain your answer, using *Olshefski* and *Stuart* as your guiding precedents.

In addition to the regulation of morality and the regulation of the public health, safety, and welfare, there are three other categories of offenses to which strict liability frequently attaches. The first of these three are to elements of crimes that are central to the criminality of the behavior. By "elements of crime that are not central to the criminality of the behavior," we effectively rule out strict liability for the actus reus of a crime (unless one other criteria for imposing strict liability are met, such as it being a crime regulating morality or the public health, safety, and welfare). Thus, this category of things which typically qualify for the imposition of strict liability is really targeted at attendant circumstances, such as those that are used for determining the severity of the punishment.

For example, selling drugs is a crime, but selling drugs near a school is a more serious crime. The actus reus is selling drugs; the mens would be knowing that one is selling a controlled substance. But the defendant need not know that he or she is near a school to be guilty of the more severe crime if he or she engages in the actus reus with the requisite mens rea (i.e., knowingly selling drugs). The attendant circumstance that the crime took place near a school carries strict liability because the location of the sale is not central to the criminality of the act, but rather is an aggravating factor making the sale of drugs more severe than it would have been had it not occurred near a school.

Along the same line of reasoning, elements regarding jurisdiction or venue often carry strict liability. Thus, a defendant need not know that crossing state lines makes something a federal offense which might carry a stiffer penalty than if just committed in one state.

Finally, strict liability attaches when the doctrine of *vicarious liability* is invoked. Vicarious liability holds someone other than the person who actually committed the actus reus of a crime liable for the criminal act. Vicarious liability is normally imposed when there is some legal relationship, and it is deemed socially desirable, for another person to be held criminally responsible for the criminal acts of another. Examples of vicarious liability include holding the president of a corporation criminally liable for toxic dumping by those in his or her employ; holding a parent liable for having negligently entrusted a vehicle to an underage child; holding a bartender liable for serving alcohol to someone underage, even though the server was the one who should have checked for identification.

Jeffrey V. FUREK, Appellant, v. The UNIVERSITY OF DELAWARE, et al., Appellees.
594 A.2d 506 (Del. 1991).

Walsh, Justice:

This is an appeal from a decision of the Superior Court that granted judgment notwithstanding the verdict, thus invalidating a jury award of damages, in an action brought by a student for injuries sustained in a fraternity hazing incident at the University of Delaware. The plaintiff below-appellant, Jeffrey V. Furek ("Furek"), had sought damages against the fraternity, Sigma Phi Epsilon ("Sig Ep"), its national affiliate, Sigma Phi Epsilon Fraternity . . . (the "National Fraternity"), the University of Delaware (the "University") and a fellow student Joseph Donchez ("Donchez"). During trial, the complaint was dismissed as to Sig Ep on jurisdictional grounds. After trial, a jury awarded damages in the amount of $30,000.00, apportioned on the basis of ninety-three percent liability to the University and seven percent to Donchez with no finding of liability as to the National Fraternity.

In a post-trial ruling, the Superior Court granted a motion for judgment n.o.v. in favor of the University leaving Donchez liable for the entire judgment. Furek appeals from that decision as well as from rulings dismissing Sig Ep and denying punitive damages. Furek also challenges the jury's verdict regarding the National Fraternity. The University cross-appeals from the trial court's denial of motions for a directed verdict as to its defenses of contributory negligence and assumption of risk. We affirm the rulings concerning the local and national fraternity but reverse . . . as to the University.

I

. . . . In September, 1979, Furek entered the University as a freshman after receiving a full football scholarship, which included tuition, room and board. During his freshman year, Furek played linebacker for the University football team. In the fall of his sophomore year, Furek decided to join the local chapter of Sig Ep after being encouraged to do so by several of the fraternity's members who were on the football team.

The University chapter of Sig Ep was established in 1908 through a charter issued by the National Fraternity. In 1980, Sig Ep was one of two fraternities located on land owned by the University. The University leased the land to the Sigma Phi Epsilon Alumni Corporation which, in turn, constructed the fraternity house and permitted the members of the fraternity to occupy the house during their stay at the University.

In the fall of 1980, Furek began his pledge period at Sig Ep. The pledge period is an eight week initiation process during which pledges, those seeking to become members of the fraternity, are instructed concerning the history of the fraternity and undergo a process known as "brotherhood development." The pledges are also subjected to various forms of harassment known as "hazing." The culmination of the initiation process is a secret ritual known as "Hell Night" – an extended period of hazing during which the pledges are physically and emotionally abused. After Hell Night, the pledges are considered members of the fraternity. For Furek and the other members of his pledge class, Hell Night took place on December 4, 1980. After assembling across the street from the Sig Ep house, wearing only T-shirts and jeans, the pledges were ordered to crawl on their hands and knees to the fraternity house while being sprayed by a fire extinguisher. Once inside the house, the pledges were ushered to various rooms where they were humiliated and degraded. Among other things, they were paddled, forced to do calisthenics and ordered to eat food out of a toilet.

Donchez, a member of the fraternity, was stationed in the kitchen and assigned the task of pouring food on the pledges. The pledges were escorted into the kitchen blindfolded, and pancake batter, ketchup and other foodstuffs were poured on their heads. During this process, Donchez poured a container containing a lye-based liquid oven cleaner over the back and neck of Furek. Furek was escorted out of the kitchen and allowed to remove his blindfold. While waiting outside the kitchen, he was overcome by a burning sensation on his back and neck. He rushed to the bathroom and upon looking in the mirror observed the discoloration of the skin on his face, neck and back. He was then taken to the hospital and treated for first and second degree chemical burns. As a result of the events of Hell Night, Sig Ep had its charter revoked by the National Fraternity and the University withdrew the registration of the fraternity. Furek, permanently scarred, subsequently withdrew from the University and forfeited his football scholarship.

Although official policy directives from the University and the National Fraternity forbade hazing, Sig Ep and other fraternities on the Newark campus had engaged in various forms of hazing for at least five years previous to the incident in question. Officers of the local fraternity were required to certify annually to the National Fraternity that hazing was not occurring. Apparently, this was done routinely although one former president of the fraternity testified that he returned the certification to the National Fraternity in 1977 with a notation that the "brotherhood development" program was not free of hazing.

In addition to the statements appearing in the Student Guide, the University through its Dean of Students issued a statement concerning sorority and fraternity hazing in 1978. The statement noted that "The Office of the Dean of Students assists fraternities and sororities in developing constructive activities and positive experiences for their members." The statement recited the "concern . . . expressed, both nationally and locally over fraternity and sorority activities which may be deemed 'hazing.'" The directive listed specific instances of hazing which would "not be tolerated either on or off campus." These instances included "paddling or striking . . . mental or emotional intimidation . . . [and] forced participation in humiliating games, performances, stunts or any rough practical jokes."

In April, 1977, the Director of the University Health Service reported to John Worthen, the University Vice President for Student Affairs, that two students had been treated for injuries received during hazing. In one case, a student had been branded on the arm by a hot coat hanger. The following month, Stuart Sharkey, the University's Director of Housing and Residence Life wrote to the presidents of each fraternity sponsored by the University, including Sig Ep, concerning these incidents. Sharkey noted that the "University is appalled and alarmed that in 1977 this activity has occurred on our campus." He requested that each president "conduct a thorough review" of pledging practices and certify to the University that "your chapter will not engage in any form of hazing."

Two years later, in November, 1979, the Assistant Dean of Students again wrote to fraternity presidents to notify them of a "mandatory meeting" to discuss "a number of activities involving 'disruptive conduct' as well as possible instances of hazing pledges or forcing pledges to perform tasks and activities against their better judgment." In May, 1980 after a speech on campus by the mother of a student killed in a hazing incident at another university, the University Dean of Students wrote to the presidents of the Interfraternity Council, with copies to the presidents of local fraternities and sororities endorsing the speaker's stand against hazing and noting the University's willingness to revoke the charter of any fraternity or sorority which "engages in such activity."

Despite the University's public pronouncement and warnings concerning hazing in the three years prior to Furek's injuries, the record reflects that the hazing activities at Sig Ep, and perhaps other fraternities as well, continued unabated on an annual basis. Groups of pledges, carrying paddles, were observed openly marching through the campus and on one occasion lining up on a public street across from the Sig Ep house, and the Sigma Nu house, to start Hell Night. Indeed, on a night prior to Hell Night, Furek and twenty-five other pledges dressed in dark clothes for "sneaking around" were stopped by University Security officers but were permitted to continue when the officers were advised that they were raiding the Sig Ep house as a pledging prank. Apparently, the University Security department was not made aware of the specific directives against hazing nor is there any indication that University Security was asked to investigate incidents of hazing prior to Furek's injury.

After some delay following Furek's hospitalization for his injuries, the hazing incident was reported to the University and eventually to the National Fraternity. The National Fraternity conducted a separate investigation and immediately revoked Sig Ep's charter. As a result, the local fraternity disbanded and ceased to exist as a fraternity at the University. Although the University conducted its own investigation of the incident, it was unable to secure the cooperation of knowledgeable students and thus did not initiate formal disciplinary proceedings against individual students or the local fraternity.

Furek filed his Superior Court action on September 9, 1982, naming as defendants the University, the National Fraternity, Sig Ep and Donchez and seeking both compensatory and punitive damages. In his complaint, Furek alleged that his injuries were proximately caused by the University's negligent and reckless failure to control Sig Ep and its members; the National Fraternity's negligent and reckless failure to monitor Sig Ep; Sig Ep's negligent and reckless failure to take steps to control the dangerous acts of its members; and Donchez's negligent and wanton failure to exercise reasonable care to ascertain what foreign substance he was pouring over Furek's body.

[After a series of pre-trial motions, a trial on the merits, and post-trial motions, the local chapter of Sig Ep was dismissed from the local on procedural grounds; Donchez was held responsible for Furek's injuries; the National Fraternity was absolved of liability for Furek's injuries; and the trial court set aside the jury's verdict imposing liability on the University. Furek appealed on all these issues, while] the University cross-appealed from the trial court's refusal to direct a verdict in its favor as to Furek's contributory negligence and assumption of risk.

II

[The court upheld the dismissal of the case again the local fraternity chapter of Sig Ep on procedural grounds unrelated to the merits of the case].

III

We next consider Furek's challenge to the jury's determination that the National Fraternity was not liable for his injuries. . . . There was disagreement at trial concerning the extent of the National Fraternity's knowledge that hazing was occurring at Sig Ep and the measures it pursued to prevent such activities. The National Fraternity granted charters to local groups who elect their own officers. The National Fraternity provided a measure of oversight through Regional Directors, who visit the local fraternity, and Chapter Counselors, alumni members of the fraternity who provide guidance to the local chapter. As previously noted, officers of Sig Ep were required to certify annually to the National Fraternity that "the brotherhood development program" was free of hazing. Furek points to the fact that in 1977 the then president of Sig Ep, Tony Glenn, reported to the National Fraternity that the local fraternity was not free of hazing. In later years, however, Glenn, acting as Chapter counselor, signed a no-hazing certification. Upon learning of the Furek injuries, in the spring of 1981, the National Fraternity conducted an investigation of the incident and withdrew Sig Ep's charter.

The extent of the National Fraternity's knowledge and control of hazing at the Sig Ep chapter is open to conflicting interpretations. While the National Fraternity was on notice through Glenn's 1977 report and the presence of pledge paddles observed on visits that hazing might be occurring, it did not exercise day to day control over local chapter activities. Moreover, there is evidence to support the National Fraternity's argument that by 1980 it believed its anti-hazing regulations were being observed. Although the extent of the National Fraternity's precise knowledge is disputed, we conclude that substantial evidence was introduced from which a jury could reasonably conclude that the National Fraternity exercised reasonable care to control the activities of the local chapter. Under our standard of review, we find no basis to disturb the jury's verdict respecting the National Fraternity.

IV

The principal dispute in this appeal concerns what, if any, duty the University owed to Furek to protect him from the hazing activities of Sig Ep and its members, including Donchez. The definition of that duty in the Superior Court was subject to a series of rulings which finally resulted in the setting aside of the jury verdict against the University. It remains for this Court to give this novel issue an additional turn.

Negligent behavior is usually defined as the failure to meet the standard of care which the law requires. However, liability for negligence is limited by the scope of the legally defined duty. Thus, an antecedent duty of care with respect to the interest involved must be established before liability is imposed. The scope of the duty of care often turns on the relationship between the party claiming harm and the party charged with negligence. We here confront the broad question of whether the law imposes upon the relationship between university and student a duty, on the part of the university, to make and enforce policies which might protect the student from harm occasioned by the acts of third parties who function under the auspices of the university.

The university-student relationship is certainly unique. While its primary function is to foster intellectual development through an academic curriculum, the institution is involved in all aspects of student life. Through its providing of food, housing, security, and a range of extracurricular activities the modern university provides a setting in which every aspect of student life is, to some degree, university guided. This attempt at control, however, is directed toward a group whose members are adults in the contemplation of law and thus free agents in many aspects of their lives and life styles. Despite the recognition of adulthood, universities continue to make an effort to regulate student life and the courts have utilized diverse theories in attempting to fix the extent of the university's residual duty.

In earlier times of strict university control, the institution was viewed as acting in loco parentis, i.e., the university exercised delegated parental authority with a concomitant duty of broad protection. The concept of university control based on the doctrine of in loco parentis has all but disappeared in the face of the realities of modern college life where students are now regarded as adults in almost every phase of community life. To the extent that the doctrine of in loco parentis is still viable, its application is limited to claims against high school authorities for injuries to students arising out of a failure to supervise.

The University contends that the demise of the doctrine of in loco parentis has dispelled the notion that any special relationship exists between the university and its student body upon which to posit any duty to protect students from activities of their fellow students. It is argued that the student and the university operate at arms-length, with the student responsible for exercising judgment for his or her own protection when dealing with other students or student groups. In granting judgment [for the University], the Superior Court, in effect, agreed with this argument by rejecting Furek's claim that lack of university supervision over the conduct of the fraternity was a proximate cause of his injuries. While we agree that the University's duty is a limited one, we are not persuaded that none exists.

A number of courts have examined whether a university's failure to supervise student activities could be deemed a breach of a duty arising from the student-university relationship. Some courts have been unwilling to impose liability because the university is not an insurer of its students safety, and the students are legally responsible adults who are able to take care of themselves. Thus, these courts have rejected both a duty under the in loco parentis doctrine and a duty of supervision when one assumes responsibility for another's safety or deprives another of a normal opportunity for self-protection.

A leading decision which examined a university's duty of supervision and protection is *Beach v. University of Utah*, 726 P.2d 413 (Ut. 1986). Beach contended that the University, through an accompanying member of the faculty, breached an affirmative duty to supervise and protect her when she became intoxicated and fell from a cliff while participating in a university sponsored field trip. The *Beach* court held that a special relationship did not exist sufficient to impose liability for the failure to protect and supervise the plaintiff once she became intoxicated. Nor did a duty arise because of a university prohibition against alcohol use and her status as a minor under state law. The *Beach* court concluded that "[a] realistic assessment of the relationship between the parties precludes our finding that a special relationship existed between the University and Beach or other adult students." Id. at 419.

The *Beach* court explicitly based its ruling on the social policy analysis set forth in *Bradshaw v. Rawlings*, 612 F.2d at 138-39, holding that the imposition of a duty to supervise extracurricular activities would be unrealistic and impossible to perform since it would place the university in a custodial relationship with its students who are legally adults. For essentially the same reasons, the Colorado Supreme Court sitting en banc in *University of Denver v. Whitlock*, ., 744 P.2d 54 (Colo. 1987), refused to find a breach of a duty of supervision where a student was injured while intoxicated and making use of a trampoline at his fraternity located on university premises. The *Whitlock* court concluded that there was not a relation of dependence sufficient to support a duty to supervise based on the status of the plaintiff as a student.

Cases subsequent to *Bradshaw* which rejected a duty to supervise seem to rely on the policy analysis set out in *Bradshaw* without considering the factual validity of its premises or the accuracy and consistency of its logic. The *Whitlock* court stated that taking away students control over private recreational and personal safety choices would deprive students of their recently recognized authority in these areas. Citing the California Court of Appeals in *Baldwin v. Zoradi*, 123 Cal. App.3d 275, 176 Cal. Rptr. 809, 818 (1981), with approval, the *Whitlock* court agreed with the proposition that "only by giving them responsibility can students grow into responsible adulthood." The *Whitlock* court concluded that taking away this responsibility would "produce a repressive and inhospitable environment, largely inconsistent with the objectives of modern college education." 744 P.2d at 60.

These cases provide no empirical support for the proposition that supervision is inversely related to the maturation of college students. Aside from the opinion in *Bradshaw*, no legal or other authority is cited for the assertion that supervision of potentially dangerous student activities would create an inhospitable environment or would be largely inconsistent with the objectives of college education. It seems equally reasonable to conclude that university supervision of potentially dangerous student activities is not fundamentally at odds with the nature of the parties' relationship, particularly if such supervision advances the health and safety of at least some students.

Beach and *Bradshaw* may also be faulted on the logic of their analysis. In both cases, it was asserted that the major reason for the rejection of a university duty to supervise was that the students were responsible adults. In both cases, the injuries were alcohol-related. However, in the area of activity that was the subject matter of the dispute, alcohol consumption, the students were unquestionably not deemed adults under the law since most, if not all, participants were below the drinking age.

Despite the rejection of the in loco parentis doctrine, some courts continue to recognize the uniqueness of the student-university relationship. In *Mullins v. Pine Manor College*, 389 Mass. 47, 449 N.E.2d 331 (1983), the court upheld a jury verdict against a college for failure to provide adequate security to a student who was assaulted in a dormitory. The Court explicitly recognized a duty arising from the "existing social values and customs" as well as from the student-university relationship. The "consensus" duty resulted from the recognition of the unique situation created by the concentration of young people on a college campus and the ability of the university to protect its students. . . . The *Mullins* court defined the university's duty to include "reasonable care to prevent injury to their students by third persons whether their acts were accidental, negligent, or intentional." *Id.* at 337.

Other courts have recognized, although denied liability under, the duty to supervise arising from the special relationship between university and student. In *Rubtchinsky v. State University of N.Y. at Albany*, 46 Misc.2d 679, 260 N.Y.S.2d 256 (1965), the plaintiff sought damages allegedly arising out of the university's negligent failure to supervise a "push ball game" that was part of student orientation. The *Rubtchinsky* court held that even though the college had control over the activities, there was no duty to supervise "unless such activities are so inherently dangerous that the college authorities are under actual or constructive notice that injuries may result to students." A duty to supervise dormitory activities involving alcohol consumption was also deemed to support a jury verdict of partial university liability in *Zavala v. Regents of the University of Cal.*, 125 Cal. App.3d 646, 178 Cal. Rptr. 185 (1981).

We do not agree . . . that no legal basis exists for imposing on the University a duty to protect Furek under the circumstances of this case. Certain established principles of tort law provide a sufficient basis for the imposition of a duty on the University to use reasonable care to protect resident students against the dangerous acts of third parties. While we acknowledge the apparent weight of decisional authority that there is no duty on the part of a college or university to control its students based merely on the university-student relationship, where there is direct university involvement in, and knowledge of, certain dangerous practices of its students, the university cannot abandon its residual duty of control.

In our view, . . . a more persuasive rationale for University liability [can be based upon] the duty owed by one who assumes direct responsibility for the safety of another through the rendering of services in the area of protection. . . . This [duty] "applies to any undertakings to render service to another which the defendant should recognize as necessary for the protection of the other person" and the harm to be protected against results from negligence in "performance of the undertaking or from failure to exercise reasonable care to complete it or to protect the other when he discontinues it." If one "takes charge and control of [a] situation, he is regarded as entering into a relation which is attenuated with responsibility." W. PROSSER, HANDBOOK OF TORTS, 56 (2nd ed. 1972). This provision of tort law is encapsulated in Restatement § 323 and has been recognized by this Court.

While § 323 provides the basis for a duty of protection once assumed, the University argues that it assumed no responsibility to protect Furek from the dangers of hazing and, given his adult status, Furek could not reasonably have relied upon the University to do so. The evidence in this record, however, strongly suggests that the University not only was knowledgeable of the dangers of hazing but, in repeated communications to students in general and fraternities in particular, emphasized the University policy of discipline for hazing infractions. The University's policy against hazing, like its overall commitment to provide security on its campus, thus constituted an assumed duty which became "an indispensable part of the bundle of services which colleges . . . afford their students." *Mullins v. Pine Manor College*, 449 N.E.2d at 336.

Even though Restatement § 323 provides a basis for the University's assumed obligation toward Furek, and all students subjected to the known dangers of hazing, a claim for recovery in this case may also be posited upon Furek's status as an invitee on University property. A landowner who knows or should know of an unreasonably dangerous condition or use of his property has a duty to invitees to safeguard the invitee against such hazards including the conduct of third parties.

The question of whether a university, [as a] landowner, owes its students a duty extending to invitees is one of first impression in Delaware but has been considered elsewhere. In *Stockwell v. Board of Trustees*, 64 Cal. App.2d 197, 148 P.2d 405 (1944), a student successfully maintained an action against a university for failure to maintain its premises in a safe condition. The student, held to be an invitee, was injured on university property by a BB gun shot by an individual whose presence was known to the university. The finding of liability was predicated on the university's failure to enforce its rules forbidding the use of BB guns and the fact that inadequate security was maintained. In *Peterson v. San Francisco Comm. College Dist.*, 36 Cal.3d 799, 205 Cal. Rptr. 842, 685 P.2d 1193 (1984), a student pursuing a claim for assault by a third party on university property was considered an invitee "to whom the possessor of the premises would ordinarily owe a duty of due care."

While Furek may be deemed an invitee, the University's duty to protect him from dangerous conditions under is not absolute. The duty extends only to the acts of third persons which are both foreseeable and subject to university control. With respect to foreseeability, Comment f to § 344 is instructive:

> Since the possessor is not an insurer of the visitor's safety, he is ordinarily under no duty to exercise any care until he knows or has reason to know that the acts of the third person are occurring, or are about to occur. He may, however, know or have reason to know, from past experience, that there is a likelihood of conduct on the part of third persons in general which is likely to endanger the safety of the visitor, even though he has no reason to expect it on the part of any particular individual. If the place or character of his business, or his past experience, is such that he should reasonably anticipate careless or criminal conduct on the part of the third persons, either generally or at some particular time, he may be under a duty to take precautions against it, and to provide a reasonably sufficient number of servants to afford a reasonable protection.

In view of past hazing incidents involving physical harm to students, the occurrence of the unusual activities preceding fraternity hazing as witnessed by campus security (i.e. students marching with paddles) and the common knowledge on campus that hazing occurred, there was sufficient evidence for jury determination on the issue of whether the hazing which caused injury to Furek was foreseeable.

There remains the question of control, a matter which was hotly disputed at trial and is the principal basis for the trial court's rejection of Furek's claim against the University. On appeal, the University points to the fact that it owned the land on which the fraternity house was built but not the house itself and argues that its status as a landowner conferred no right to control what occurred on the premises. This is too limited a view of the realities of the university-fraternity relationship at the time of Furek's injuries. It is true that the University did not attempt or purport to regulate day-to-day living conditions in the Sig Ep fraternity house. But in the area of general security and of hazing in particular the University's regulation was pervasive. The Sig Ep fraternity house was located within campus boundaries and was thus subject to the University's security department. The University's ban on hazing, as evidenced by its directives to fraternity officers, made no distinction between activities occurring within or outside fraternity buildings. Indeed, in this case the University's unsuccessful attempt to initiate disciplinary proceedings against Sig Ep because of Furek's injuries clearly evidences its belief that it had the authority to enforce anti-hazing regulations for violations occurring within the fraternity house.

Premises control is not determined in absolute terms. A landowner may exercise control in certain areas while relinquishing it in others. . . . If control includes authority to direct, restrict and regulate, the University with its significant involvement in the regulation of fraternity life, particularly in the area of hazing, may be deemed to have exercised supervision over the use of its property to permit "at least the inference of control." For the purpose of testing the sufficiency of the evidence to withstand the granting of a directed verdict, Furek was entitled to the benefit of that inference.

In sum, although the University no longer stands in loco parentis to its students, . . . [and] the university is not an insurer of the safety of its students nor a policeman of student morality, [the relationship is sufficiently close and direct to impose a duty] . . . to regulate and supervise foreseeable dangerous activities occurring on its property. That duty extends to the negligent or intentional activities of third persons. Because of the extensive freedom enjoyed by the modern university student, the duty of the university to regulate and supervise should be limited to those instances where it exercises control. Situations arising out of the ownership of land, and within the contemplation of Restatement § 344, involving student invitees present on the property for the purposes permitted them are within such limitations.

As noted by the *Bradshaw* court, "duty is not sacrosanct in itself, but only the sum total of those considerations of policy which lead the law to say that a particular plaintiff is entitled to protection." 612 F.2d at 138. Even though the policy analysis of *Bradshaw* has been followed by numerous courts, the justification for following that decision has been seriously eroded by changing societal attitudes toward alcohol use and hazing. The likelihood of injury during fraternity activities occurring on university campuses is greater than the utility of university inaction. The magnitude of the burden placed on the university is no greater than to require compliance with self imposed standards. In the light of that standard and our view of the University's duty in this case, we conclude that the Superior Court erred in granting the University's motion for judgment.

IV

The University has cross-appealed from the trial court's refusal to grant a directed verdict on its defenses of contributory negligence and assumption of risk. The burden of proof as to these affirmative defenses was, of course, upon the University. We agree with the Superior Court that while Furek voluntarily participated in the hazing, he was not chargeable with knowledge that he would be exposed to the risk that someone would pour a caustic substance over his head as part of a fraternity ritual. The failure to anticipate another's negligence or dangerous activity does not itself demonstrate such lack of care so as to bar recovery for injury.

V

In summary, we affirm the rulings of the Superior Court which dismissed Furek's claim against Sig Ep, denied recovery of punitive damages and refused to grant a directed verdict on the defenses of contributory negligence and assumption of risk. We also affirm the jury's verdict in favor of the National Fraternity. We reverse and remand for a new trial, limited to the issue of liability, the Superior Court's grant of judgment n.o.v. in favor of the University.

QUESTIONS

1.   *Furek* was a civil, not a criminal case. The application of vicarious liability in the criminal law context is quite limited. In contrast, vicarious liability is a common doctrine in civil tort law. Suppose, however, that the local prosecutor had filed criminal hazing and battery charges against Donchez individually; against the other members of the local chapter of Sig Ep fraternity as accessories; and against the University as a criminal facilitator for knowingly having failed to take action to prevent criminal hazing. How do you think the doctrine of vicarious liability should be applied in such a case?

2.   Although, as the court pointed out, the is a difference of opinion on the duties a college or university owes to its students. Which rationale do you find more persuasive, the one offered in *Beach* and *Bradshaw*, or the one offered by the *Furek* court? Why? What are the public policy implications of adopting either approach?

3.   Suppose that a fraternity or sorority sponsored an off-campus party at the home of one its members at which the members of the organization chipped in to buy kegs of beer. Further suppose that the beer is provided to guests at the party, some of whom are members of the organization and some of whom are not, some of whom are of legal drinking age, and some of whom are not. Finally, presume one of the underage guests leaves the party, gets into an car accident while driving under the influence, and kills the driver of the other car who was not at fault for the accident. It is clear that the driver would face both driving under the influence charges and some non-intentional homicide charge such as involuntary manslaughter. What, if anything, though, should happen to the hosts of the party

who provided the alcohol to the driver? Why? Should the affiliated college or university have any liability, civil or criminal, for this act? *Cf. Wiener v. Gamma Phi Chapter of Alpha Tau Omega Fraternity*, 485 P.2d 18 (Or. 1971).

4.   "Parents may incur liability when they negligently entrust their child with an instrumentality (such as a gun or car) which, because of the child's immaturity or lack of experience, may become a source of danger to others. . . . A parent may also be held responsible for failure to exercise reasonable control over the child when the parent knows, or should know, that injury to another is a probable consequence. . . . Finally, when parents know of the child's wrongdoing and consent to it, direct it or sanction it, they may be held liable." *Huston v. Konieczny*, 556 N.E.2d 505 (Ohio 1990). These statements of law summarize the normal rules of civil tort law. But applying similar reasoning in the application of the doctrine of vicarious liability in the criminal law, what would you do to parents who give their underage child permission to host a party at which alcohol will be served? What if one of the underage guests in attendance at the party leaves and is involved in a fatal accident while driving under the influence; should the parents be held vicariously liable for the death? Why or why not? Be sure to include a discussion of the parents' level of mens rea, if any, in your analysis.

5.   Should it make a difference if both the hosts and the guests at a party at which alcohol is served are all over the legal drinking age? The court in *Kelly v. Gwinnell*, 476 A.2d 1219 (N.J. 1984) held such a social host civilly liable because the host directly served the guest and continued to do so even after the guest was visibly intoxicated. Should criminal charges be filed against such a host if the intoxicated person then drives and kills someone? What if the intoxicated person gets violent at the party and commits a criminal assault and battery on another guest? What if the intoxicated guest rapes another guest? Where should the law draw the line for the imposition of criminal vicarious liability?

6.   In the hypothetical fact patterns presented above in questions 3, 4, and 5, there is an argument to be made that the application of the doctrine of vicarious liability is appropriate in the criminal law because the relevant actors (respectively, the fraternity members, the parents, and the social host) had some degree of culpability. As such, they are being judged based on their own level of mens rea. Recall, however, that strict liability is the imposition of a criminal sanction for a proscribed act without any necessary level of mens rea. The case of *Commonwealth v. Koczwara*, 155 A.2d 825 (Pa. 1959), *cert. denied*, 363 U.S. 848 (1960), better illustrates the application of vicarious criminal liability to a strict liability offense. In *Koczwara*, an individual owner of a store was fined $500 and sentenced to three months in jail for the actions of an employee who sold liquor to a minor. The Pennsylvania Supreme Court upheld his conviction and fine, but found that imprisonment under such facts deprived the defendant of due process. Do you agree with the outcome of the case? Why or why not? Should this logic be extended to the owners of bars and restaurants whose employees serve alcohol to underage patrons? What purpose is served by having such a policy?

4. Transferred Intent

Suppose that you were to shoot at some someone, with the purpose (i.e., specific intent) to kill that person, but due to poor aim, you wind up killing the person sitting next to your intended victim instead. Do you think you could avoid a charge of premeditated murder by arguing that there was not a concurrence of actus reus and mens rea for the killing that occurred since you did not intent to kill the person whom do you did? That would be a rather absurd outcome, would it not? The common law solved this problem by creating the legal fiction of *transferred intent*.

Under the doctrine of transferred intent, the mens rea entertained with respect to doing a particular actus reus with the intent of causing result *A* can be used to satisfy the mens rea requirement of having actually caused result *B*, so long as the same type of intended harm occurred. Thus, to follow up the hypothetical used in the last paragraph, the specific intent to kill you entertained while trying to shoot and kill your intended victim would "transfer" to be the mens rea for the result you actually caused, the death of the person who was sitting next to your intended victim.

There are two limitations on the application of the doctrine of transferred intent that cannot be over-emphasized. First, the doctrine can only be used to transfer the mens rea for one crime to another if the crime to which the mens rea is being transferred carries the same level of mens rea as the original crime, or some lower level of mens rea. Accordingly, mens rea cannot be transferred to impose criminal liability for a crime that carries a higher degree of mental fault than the defendant actually entertained when doing the actus reus. For example, if someone acts purposefully, then we have no problem transferring this mens rea to any other crime since it is the highest level of mental culpability recognized by the criminal law. In contrast, though, if someone acted recklessly in doing some actus reus, the doctrine of transferred intent could not be used to impose criminal liability for any crime that carried purpose or knowledge as the requisite mens rea; such recklessness could only be transferred as the mens rea for other crimes that require the same level of mens rea – recklessness – or a lower level of mens rea, namely negligence. The following case illustrates this point.

Daniel SMITH, Appellant v. STATE of Georgia, Appellee.
419 S.E.2d 74 (Ga. Ct. App. 1992).

Johnson, J.

Clarence Thomas was attempting to restrain his brother, Leonard Thomas, who was charging at appellant Danny Smith in retaliation for a remark made several weeks earlier which tended to impugn his character. Smith, who thought Leonard might be armed with a gun, fired one round from a 20 gauge shotgun at him. Pellets hit both brothers. Smith was indicted on two counts of aggravated assault. Smith's sole defense at trial was justification. A jury found Smith not guilty of aggravated assault on Leonard Thomas, the intended victim, but guilty of aggravated assault on Clarence Thomas. Smith appeals his conviction.

Smith contends that since intent was not shown with respect to the assault upon Clarence Thomas, the evidence was insufficient to support the verdict. Smith argues that since the jury found that the assault on Leonard Thomas was lawful, it necessarily follows that he did not possess the requisite intent to commit an aggravated assault on the bystander.

The theory of transferred intent in criminal law has a long history from *Reg. v. Sauders*, 2 Plowd. 473, 75 Eng. Reprint 706 (1576), (18 A.L.R. 923) in which it was pointed out that if a man maliciously shoots an arrow at another with intent to kill him and a person to whom he bore no malice is killed by it, this would be murder for the person who shot the arrow with intent to kill, and is the same offense as to such person as if he had killed the person he aimed at. More recently, this court has held: "When an unintended victim is struck down as a result of an unlawful act actually directed against someone else, the law prevents the actor from taking advantage of his own wrong and transfers the original intent from the one against whom it was directed to the one who actually suffered from it. 'In legal contemplation, the intent follows the act through to its legitimate results.'" *Fussell v. State*, 369 S.E.2d 511 (Ga. App. 1988).

Can the principle of transferred intent be applied in a case, however, in which the jury finds that the firing of the shot was justified and therefore lawful? "If, in consequence of an assault upon himself which he did not provoke, the accused shot at his assailant, but missed him and the shot killed a bystander, no guilt would attach to him if the assault upon him was such as would have justified him in killing his assailant." *Butler v. State*, 19 S.E. 51 (Ga. 1893).

In our case, the jury did find the defendant's actions to be justified. There was no evidence in the record from which one could divine any intent to injure Clarence. Intent being a requisite element of the aggravated assault charge, and no lesser offense (such as reckless conduct) having been charged, we find that there was insufficient evidence upon which to base a conviction as to that offense. Consequently, defendant's conviction must be reversed.

QUESTIONS

1.   Because Smith was found to have acted justifiably in shooting at Leonard Thomas, he did not entertain criminal mens rea involving an intent to hurt Leonard. Rather, his intent was to protect himself from what he feared was imminent harm. There was, therefore, no specific intent (i.e., purpose) that could be transferred from his intended act of self-defense towards Leonard to his unintended act of assaulting Clarence. But surely the discharge of a shotgun in the general direction of an innocent bystander is reckless conduct. Why could Smith's recklessness not be transferred to satisfy the mens rea component of the crime of assault as applied to Clarence?

2.   Do you agree with the outcome in this case? Why or why not? The court pointed out in its concluding paragraph that no lesser offense had been charged in the indictment. Presume, however, that Smith had been charged with the common law crime of battery, a general intent crime for which acts of recklessness would suffice for criminal liability. Do you think Smith would have been acquitted on the charge of battery of Clarence even though Smith may have been justified with respect to Leonard? Explain your reasoning.

The second limitation on the doctrine of transferred into involves the type of harm actually caused. The doctrine can be applied only situations where the same harm as was intended actually occurred, but on an unintended victim. The following case illustrates this limitation well.

The STATE of South Carolina, Respondent/Petitioner, v. Michael Lee BRYANT, Petitioner/Respondent. 447 S.E.2d 852 (S.C. 1994).

Finney, A.J.

Petitioner-Respondent (Bryant) was convicted of failure to stop for a blue light, resisting arrest, assault and battery of a high and aggravated nature, and malicious injury to personal property. The Court of Appeals reversed the conviction for malicious injury to personal property and affirmed the remaining convictions.

While attempting to arrest Bryant for failure to stop for a blue light, a struggle ensued between the police officer and Bryant. During the course of the struggle, Bryant slammed the officer against the patrol car causing damage in excess of $200.

Bryant moved for a directed verdict on the offense of malicious damage to personal property. The trial court denied his motion. The Court of Appeals reversed the trial court's refusal to direct a verdict of not guilty on that charge.

The State asserts that the Court of Appeals erred in holding that since there was no evidence of intent, the malicious injury to personal property charge should not have been submitted to the jury. We disagree.

The basic rule is that one cannot be convicted of an offense unless his mental state was that required by the particular offense. Whether intent is a necessary element of the statutory crime must be determined from the language of the statute construed in light of its purpose and design. The elements of malicious mischief are willful, unlawful and malicious damage to the property of another. S.C. Code Ann. § 16-11-510 (Supp. 1993). Willful, unlawful, and malicious are not synonyms and each element must be established.

The Court of Appeals found that the State failed to provide any evidence that Bryant intended to cause damage to the patrol car when he threw the officer against it. The only reasonable inference from the evidence is that the damage to the patrol car was an unintended harm. The doctrine of transferred intent applies only in the situation of the same intended harm inflicted on an unintended victim. The intent to assault and batter the police officer cannot be transferred to the property damage since the harm caused was different from the type of harm intended.

We find there was no evidence that Bryant willfully caused harm to the vehicle as required by § 16-11-50. Therefore, it was improper to submit the charge to the jury. Accordingly, we affirm the Court of Appeals' ruling on this issue.

QUESTIONS

1.   Does this limitation make sense to you? After all, Bryant willfully (i.e., purposefully) assaulted and battered an officer of the law. In doing so, Bryant intentionally threw the officer against a police car. Why shouldn't the doctrine of transferred be permitted to transfer Bryant's level of mens rea – purpose, the highest degree of mental fault – to satisfy the mens rea requirement of the damage to property claim?

2.   The elements of malicious mischief under the relevant Georgia statute are willful, unlawful and malicious damage to the property of another. The court construed the statute as requiring proof of all three mens rea elements (i.e., it was willful, purposeful, or deliberate; such damage was unlawful; and the damage was malicious). But suppose the statute permitted conviction without willfulness, allowing malice alone to be sufficient mens rea. Do you think Bryant's conduct would support a conviction for malicious mischief then? Explain your answer.

---

5. Causation

When a crime requires a particular result, such as the death of a human being for any homicide liability to attach, it is not enough for the prosecution to prove the elements of actus reus, mens rea, and result. The prosecution must also prove that the defendant's actus reus, performed with the requisite mens rea, *caused* the required result.

The doctrine of *causation* applicable in criminal law requires two distinct types of causation: cause-in-fact and proximate cause. *Cause-in-fact* is what we normally think of as "causing": if person does some act that directly brings about a particular result, then the person is said to have caused the result. To determine cause-in-fact, ask yourself, "Would the result have occurred 'but for' the defendant's conduct?" If so, the conduct is not cause-in-fact of the result since it would have occurred anyway. In contrast, though, if the answer to the question is no, then conduct is the cause-in-fact of the result since the result would not have occurred "but for" the act.

The law requires more than the line of direct causation embodied in the cause-in-fact analysis above to impose criminal liability. The law also requires what in known as *proximate cause*. Proximate cause is concerned with whether there were other causes that contributed to the result. If there were no other causes contributing to the result other than the defendant's actus reus, then proximate cause is established and liability can be imposed. But if there were factors other than the defendant's actus reus that contributed to the end result, then a careful proximate cause analysis must be undertaken.

When there are factors other than the defendant's actus reus contributing to the result, criminal liability may only be imposed if the contributing factor was "foreseeable" given the original act setting the chain of events into motion. A cause that is sufficiently foreseeable or sufficiently related to the defendant's conduct so as to make it fair to hold the defendant responsible for the result is called a "dependent intervening cause." Accordingly, a dependent, intervening cause will not relieve the defendant of criminal liability.

On the other hand, a cause that is sufficiently independent of the defendant's conduct so as to make it unfair to hold the defendant responsible for the result is deemed to be an "independent, supervening cause" that breaks the chain of causation. Thus, an independent, supervening cause will absolve a defendant of criminal liability. But for a contributing causal factor to be deemed an independent, supervening cause, it has to be rather extraordinary and/or abnormal such that its very occurrence requires that the defendant not be held liable for the end result.

The PEOPLE, Plaintiff and Respondent, v. Claude Alex SCHMIES, Defendant and Appellant.
44 Cal. App. 4th 38, 51 Cal. Rptr. 2d 185 (1996).

Sparks, Acting Presiding Justice.

Factual and Procedural Background

At 4:30 p.m. on October 24, 1992, California Highway Patrol (CHP) Officer Steven Petch was driving southbound on Interstate 5. Another CHP Officer, Christopher Homen, was approximately two-tenths of a mile behind him in another patrol car. Defendant, who was driving a motorcycle, entered the highway and accelerated to a speed of approximately 90 miles per hour. Officer Petch activated his lights for a traffic stop. Defendant slowed down, looked over his shoulder and then sped up. Officer Petch turned on his flashing lights and siren and radioed to Officer Homen, "Here we go." Officer Petch also notified radio dispatch about the pursuit and, after getting behind the motorcycle and obtaining its license number, asked dispatch to check on the vehicle. The report came back clear: the motorcycle had not been reported stolen, nor were there any outstanding warrants.

The pursuit continued along Interstate 5 at speeds in excess of 90 miles per hour. Officer Petch drove alongside defendant to try to keep him on the freeway. He got a clear look at defendant and the motorcycle. Defendant cut in front of Officer Petch and took an exit from the freeway. Both Officer Petch and Officer Homen followed in their cars. Officer Petch had turned on all of his emergency lights as well as his siren. Officer Homen did not have overhead lights, but had activated a light on the side of his car and also turned on his siren.

Defendant drove through stop signs and over double yellow lines to weave around cars. He drove through red lights as well. Defendant went at speeds of up to 95 miles per hour, and came perilously close to falling off his motorcycle on sharp turns. Defendant drove through the intersection of Churncreek and Parsons. Officer Petch followed. A car on Parsons that had been stopped to allow Officer Petch to go through started into the intersection, apparently unaware of the second patrol car driven by Officer Homen. Officer Homen tried to avoid the car but hit it broadside. The driver, Jane Abbett, was killed and Officer Homen was injured.

Defendant drove on, trying to evade Officer Petch. At this point, Officer Petch had pursued defendant for approximately 5.5 miles. Officer Petch was unable to follow when defendant drove down an abandoned road, but saw defendant drive into an apartment complex. Defendant was arrested shortly afterward. He had hidden his motorcycle, helmet and sweatshirt in a wooded area.

Defendant was charged with second degree murder; willful flight from a peace officer causing death; vehicular manslaughter with gross negligence; and reckless driving causing great bodily injury.

At trial, Officers Petch and Homen described their pursuit of defendant and the crash between Homen and Abbett. Defendant did not testify or offer any evidence. He did, however, stipulate to being the driver of the motorcycle involved in the chase, and further stipulated that he knew his driver's license had been revoked at the time of this incident. As discussed in detail below, defendant argued to the jury that Officer Homen's actions in the pursuit were a superceding intervening act, breaking the chain of causation and relieving defendant of liability for the death of Abbett and the injuries to Officer Homen.

The jury acquitted defendant of second degree murder but convicted him of vehicular manslaughter with gross negligence. The jury also convicted defendant of reckless driving causing great bodily injury as charged in count 6. This appeal followed.

Discussion

At trial, defendant attempted to demonstrate that Officer Homen's actions broke the chain of causation, absolving defendant of responsibility for Abbett's death and Officer Homen's injuries. To this end, defendant tried to obtain a complete copy of the CHP's pursuit policy to learn whether Officer Homen's actions violated CHP guidelines. CHP opposed this request, asserting in part that disclosure of the complete policy would jeopardize officer safety. CHP did, however, release a "sanitized" version of the policy to defendant.

Finding this version of the policy unsatisfactory, defendant renewed his request for complete disclosure. The trial court denied the motion, ruling that the policy was irrelevant to determining whether Officer Homen's actions were reasonably foreseeable. Similarly, the court refused to permit defendant's expert witnesses to testify as to the reasonableness of the pursuit. The court distinguished the question of foreseeability from the question of reasonableness, and ruled that while defendant could argue that Officer Homen's conduct was not reasonably foreseeable, he could not introduce evidence relating to the reasonableness of Officer Homen's action, an area the court deemed irrelevant to the issues at hand.

On appeal, defendant challenges the trial court's exclusion of evidence of the CHP pursuit policies as well as evidence relating to the reasonableness of the officers' actions. We find no error.

The reasonableness, or lack thereof, of the officers' conduct is not in itself an issue with respect to defendant's offenses. None of the defenses to crimes that depend upon the behavior of others, such as self-defense, defense of others, defense of property, duress or menace, or entrapment are even arguably presented here. And, "[i]t has been repeatedly held that contributory negligence is not available as a defense or excuse for crime." *People v. Rodgers*, 94 Cal. App.2d 166, 167, 210 P.2d 71 (1949).

The reasonableness of the officers' conduct, as defendant proffered it, would have arguable relevance only with respect to the question of foreseeability of the harm that ensued from defendant's course of conduct. Foreseeability of harm is not itself an element of the offense, but is a recognized factor to be considered in determining whether the defendant acted with gross negligence and, if so, whether his conduct was the proximate or legal cause of the ensuing harm. Defendant focuses on the causation issue as the disputed issue upon which the reasonableness of the officers' conduct is claimed to have had probative value.

The principles of causation apply to crimes as well as torts. Just as in tort law, the defendant's act must be the legally responsible cause ('proximate cause') of the injury, death or other harm which constitutes the crime. Thus, in the language of the standard jury instruction, to constitute a homicide "there must be, in addition to the death of a human being, an unlawful act which was a cause of that death. . . ." [I]n homicide cases, a cause of the [death of the decedent] is an act or omission that sets in motion a chain of events that produces as a direct, natural and probable consequence of the act or omission the death and without which the death would not occur.

In general, proximate cause is clearly established where the act is directly connected with the resulting injury, with no intervening force operating. In this case, there was an intervening force in operation, the pursuit by the CHP officers and the collision between the vehicle of one of the officers and the decedent's car. But that does not end the inquiry because a d defendant may also be criminally liable for a result directly caused by his act, even though there is another contributing cause.

Intervening causes in criminal cases are typically described as either "dependent" or "independent." A dependent intervening cause will not absolve a defendant of criminal liability while an independent intervening cause breaks the chain of causation and does absolve the defendant. An intervening cause may be a normal or involuntary result of the defendant's original act. Such a cause is said to be "dependent," and does not supercede; i.e., the defendant is liable just as in the direct causation case. An "independent" intervening act may be so disconnected and unforeseeable as to be a superceding cause; i.e., in such a case the defendant's act will be a remote, and not the proximate, cause.

[A] defendant is not relieved of liability by a third party's intervening negligence if at the time of his conduct he realized or reasonably should have realized that a third party might so act or the risk of harm was reasonably foreseeable; or a reasonable person knowing the situation existing at the time of the conduct of the third party would not have regarded it as highly extraordinary that the third party had so acted; or the conduct of the third person was not extraordinarily negligent and was a normal consequence of the situation created by defendant. Extraordinary, under this instruction on superceding causes, "means unforeseeable, unpredictable, and statistically extremely improbable."

Defendant claims his defense would have been that "the actions taken by the CHP officers and the decedent, especially Officer Homen, were so inappropriate as to be a superceding cause which would break the chain of proximate cause – i.e., they were the sole proximate cause of the death." But the court's orders, he argues on appeal, "precluded defense counsel from presenting evidence and arguing the 'abnormality' or 'nature' of the conduct of the officers." Thus, "[d]efense counsel was denied the CHP pursuit rules to aid his expert in determining the 'abnormality' of the officer's response to [defendant's] act – including whether the officers intentionally ignored the pursuit policy guidelines."

It is the burden of the proponent of evidence to establish its relevance through an offer of proof or otherwise. Defendant's assertion in the trial court that he should have been permitted to introduce evidence with respect to the "reasonableness" of the officers' conduct is subject to a certain imprecision of terminology. There are two potential concepts that may be referred to within the rubric of the "reasonableness" of the officers' conduct. One of these concepts focuses upon the point of view of the officers, while the other focuses upon the point of view of the defendant. If we were concerned with a tort action, a disciplinary hearing, or even a criminal action against the officers, then we would be focused upon the officers' conduct and the "reasonableness" thereof, from their point of view. In that respect we would consider the harm that was reasonably foreseeable to the officers, and whether their conduct created an unreasonable risk of harm to others. But, we reiterate, the negligence or other fault of the officers is not a defense to the charge against defendant. The fact that the officers may have shared responsibility or fault for the accident does nothing to exonerate defendant for his role. In short, whether the officers' conduct could be described with such labels as negligent, careless, tortious, cause for discipline, or even criminal, in an action against them, is not at issue with respect to the defendant here. In this sense the "reasonableness" of the officers' conduct, focused upon their point of view and their blameworthiness for the death, is not relevant.

The issue with respect to defendant focuses upon his point of view, that is, whether the harm that occurred was a reasonably foreseeable consequence of his conduct at the time he acted. Since the officers' conduct was a direct and specific response to defendant's conduct, the claim that their conduct was a superceding cause of the accident can be supported only through a showing that their conduct was so unusual, abnormal, or extraordinary that it could not have been foreseen.

* * *

[W]ithout more, the fact that the CHP has adopted pursuit policies would not avail defendant. The logical inference to be drawn from the mere existence of pursuit policies would be decidedly adverse to defendant, since those policies were adopted precisely because vehicular pursuit of lawbreakers by officers and the resulting danger to users of the roads are so foreseeable. If it were shown additionally that, at the time he acted, defendant was aware of the CHP pursuit policies, then it could be argued that he could expect the officers would act in accordance with them. However, such a theory was neither expressly tendered nor implicitly suggested by the defense.

Finally, whether the officers violated the CHP pursuit guidelines is immaterial. The question is whether defendant realized or should have realized that the CHP officers would pursue his fleeing motorcycle. In this case the evidence clearly shows that defendant knew, or at the very least, should have known that his flight would cause the officers to pursue him. This is true if for no other reason than the officers were in fact pursuing him and he nevertheless continued to flee. This illegal and dangerous act by defendant caused the officers to pursue him and ultimately caused the fatal accident. It adds not one whit to say that the officers violated the CHP pursuit guidelines. The test, as we have recounted, is not whether the officers acted reasonably but rather whether defendant realized or should have realized that the officers would respond as they did.

Assume, for purposes of illustration, a bank has a written policy that its armed guards should not fire their weapons at an armed robber if the bank is full of customers. Nevertheless, in the course of an armed robbery during business hours the guard, fearing the robber might injure or kill someone, predictably fires at the robber but misses and kills a customer. Can the defendant robber charged with the murder of the customer establish that the shooting by the guard was a superceding cause because it violated the bank's rules? The answer to that hypothetical is the same as the answer to the identical claim in this case: no. Just as the robber has no knowledge of the bank's rules, so too defendant lacks any knowledge of the CHP guidelines. If it is reasonably foreseeable that the guard, in the heat of the frightening moment, will fire at the robber, or that the CHP officers will give chase to a fleeing motorcycle traveling over 90 miles per hour, it is no defense to prove a rule violation. The task of the jury is to determine whether the officers' response was so extraordinary that it was unforeseeable, unpredictable and statistically extremely improbable. A rule violation may give rise to civil liability or disciplinary action, but it has nothing to do with the foreseeability of the officers' conduct.

In summary, in this case defendant, acting with gross negligence, created a situation to which CHP officers responded. As a result of defendant's conduct and the officers' response, a vehicle collision occurred in which a third party was killed and one of the officers was injured. The question whether defendant's conduct is legally responsible for the death and injury depends upon whether the officers' conduct can be regarded as a superceding cause. That issue depends upon whether the danger was reasonably foreseeable to defendant rather than upon the reasonableness of the officers' response. The court made that distinction, explained it carefully in its ruling, and repeatedly advised that evidence and argument with respect to reasonable foreseeability would not be excluded. The defense pointed to no specific relevant evidence that it was dissuaded from presenting by the court's ruling. The jury was expressly instructed that "an intervening act may be so disconnected and unforeseeable as to be a superceding cause," absolving defendant of liability. The jury simply rejected this claim. There is no cause for reversal on this record.

QUESTIONS

1.   Ultimately, the reaction of the police officers to Schmies' unlawful flight was found to be a dependent, intervening cause. Accordingly, the conduct of the police officers did not to break the chain of causation, and Schmies was help responsible for the death of the innocent driver. Do you agree with the outcome in this case? Why or why not?

2.   The court emphasized that because Schmies had no knowledge of the CHP's policies, what was reasonably foreseeable from his point of view was not dependent on whether there was a formal policy in effect banning such high speed chases. But what if Schmies has such knowledge? Would the police officers' violation of such a policy be so disconnected, so aberrant so as to render their reaction unforeseeable such that it would rise to the level of an independent, superceding cause that would break the chain of causation and thereby relive Schmies of liability? Explain you reasoning.

3.   Assume, for the sake of argument, that (a) there was a clear and written no-high-speed pursuit policy in effect at the CHP, and (b) that a criminal prosecution was instituted against the officers for the death of the innocent driver due to their disregard for that policy. With what level of mens rea would the officers have acted with respect to the homicide? Could cause-in-fact be established against

them? What about probable cause? Explain your answers with special attention paid to the role of foreseeability.

4.   One who unlawfully inflicts a dangerous wound upon another is held for the consequences flowing from such injury, whether the sequence be direct or through the operation of intermediate agencies dependent upon and arising out of the original cause.   In other words, the defendant cannot escape the consequences of his wrongful act by relying upon a supervening cause when such cause naturally resulted from his wrongful act. Given these rules, what should be the result in a criminal prosecution of someone who stabs a victim, but the victim dies from medical malpractice suffered at the hands of the emergency room staff treating the victim's stab wounds?

CHAPTER 3
THEORIES OF INCHOATE CRIMINAL LIABILITY

A. Attempt

The crime of attempt is the first of several crimes we will cover that is subsumed under the definition of *inchoate offenses*. Inchoate crimes are not completed criminal offenses in the way that most crimes are; rather, are they are crimes that are only partly in existence. The inchoate offenses criminally punish acts that would, if carried out successfully, would lead to the commission of a crime, but, due to good police work, incompetence of the offender, or the fate of circumstances, the target crime not actually completed.

Attempt is the easiest of the inchoate offenses to conceptualize because all of us know what it means, in everyday parlance and practice, to attempt to do something: to try, but not succeed. The same meaning of attempt applies in the criminal law setting. If a person, acting with the specific intent of committing a crime, actually tries to commit the crime, but fails to do so, then a criminal attempt has occurred. If, on the other hand, one tries to commit a crime and succeeds, then no attempt has taken place. Rather, the target offense has occurred. Thus, one important limitation on the crime of attempt is that is disappears once the target crime has been committed. In other words, a person cannot be convicted for both an attempt and the actual commission of the offense attempted. For example, suppose person *X* decides to kill person *Y* and goes so far as to lie in wait with a gun and fires upon the intended victim. If the bullet misses *Y*, then person *X* attempted to kill *Y* and is, therefore, guilty of the crime of attempted murder. If, on the other hand, the bullet had struck and killed person *Y*, then *X* is not guilty of attempted murder, but rather the crime of murder.

1. Mens Rea for Attempt

No matter what the mens rea level is for the target crime, an attempt to commit that crime necessarily involves specific intent or purpose. And this makes perfect logical sense insofar as it is impossible to try to do something accidently, right? If you are trying to do something, say attempting to kill someone, by definition, your efforts to bring about the desired result are a product of purposeful actions. Thus, the mens rea for the crime of attempt is always purpose.

The rule that one must have purpose to commit the target crime to satisfy the mens rea requirement for the crime of attempt does not tell us, however, to what the purpose requirement attaches. The common law differed in its treatment of this issue from the way in which the Model Penal Code treats the issue.

At common law, a defendant had to have the specific intent to engage in all the elements of the crime in order to be guilty of the crime of attempt, even those elements such as attendant circumstance which carried strict liability. Recall the case of *Thacker v. Commonwealth*, 134 Va. 767 (1922) from Chapter Two. In that case, the defendant was angry at a woman who refused him entry into her tent. He shot a bullet into the tent in, according to him, an attempt to scare her by knocking out a light she had inside the tent. His conviction for attempted murder was reversed on appeal according to the appellate court because the prosecution did prove he had specific intent (i.e., purpose) to kill the woman, only to scare her. The result in the case demonstrates the mens rea requirement that purpose must go to all elements of the crime. Surely Mr. Thacker purposefully shot the gun while aiming at the tent. But that is the conduct element of the offense. To be guilty of attempted murder, he would have also had to have the purpose of causing the woman's death – the result element of the target offense. Without such intent, there is no attempted murder.

But what if the bullet had stuck and killed the woman in the tent? Mr. Thacker could then have been convicted of depraved heart murder (a type of murder in the second degree) or involuntary manslaughter, even though he had no intent to kill. This lack of intent to kill would be immaterial to the homicide charges if she had died since neither murder in the second degree nor involuntary manslaughter requires purpose as its requisite level of mens rea. The crime of attempt, however, does require purpose. Thus, as the *Thacker* case illustrates, the mens rea for the crime of attempt is always purpose even if the target offense carries some lower level of mens rea.

In contrast to the common law, the Model Penal Code requires the mens rea of purpose only with respect to the conduct or the result elements of the target crime, not the attendant circumstances. Rather, the mens rea requirement for attendant circumstances is the same for the crime of attempt as that which is required for the object offense. This means that if the target crime's level of requisite mens rea is recklessness, negligence, or even strict liability respect to any attendant circumstances, the same would apply to the attempt to commit that crime. In short, to be found guilty of the crime of attempt under the Model Penal Code requires either purposeful conduct or purpose to cause a particular result. The following case and the questions following it should serve as a good example of the difference between the common law and Model Penal Code approaches to what elements the mens rea of purpose must attach.

COMMONWEALTH of Massachusetts v. Daniel DUNNE
474 N.E.2d 538 (Mass. 1985).

Lynch, J.

The defendant was convicted by a jury of assault on a child under sixteen with intent to commit a rape on an indictment charging rape of a child under sixteen years of age.

The victim was approximately fifteen years and four months old on April 19, 1982. That evening, she met several friends at Prospect Hill Park in Somerville. Sometime later, the victim and one friend met the defendant at Perry Park. The victim accepted the defendant's invitation to accompany him to a place where drugs could be purchased. While traveling down some railroad tracks in a nonresidential area of the city, the defendant pulled the victim off the railroad tracks and forced her to the ground, where he forcibly removed her clothing below the waist and attempted to have sexual intercourse with her. The defendant admitted to consensual sexual activity, but denied having intercourse with the victim.

After returning to a friend's house, the victim reported to police that she had been raped. The victim was then taken by police to Cambridge Hospital (hospital) where she was examined by a doctor. The doctor found abrasions and dried blood on the victim's labia. The physical examination of the victim revealed no evidence of semen in her vagina. Clothing tests, however, showed evidence of seminal fluid in the crotch of the victim's pants and on the defendant's underwear.

The defendant was arrested on the night the incident took place. On June 16, 1982, a grand jury returned an indictment charging the defendant with statutory rape. . . .. The defendant was [not convicted of statutory rape. However, he was] convicted of assault on a child under sixteen with intent to commit a rape. He argues, however, that for the conviction to stand, the Commonwealth must prove beyond a reasonable doubt that the defendant was aware that the victim was younger than sixteen. We disagree.

[The charge of assault on a child under sixteen with intent to commit a rape is basically the crime of attempted statutory rape. It is defined by our Commonwealth's statutes as the assault of a child under sixteen with intent to commit a rape].

The Commonwealth need only prove two elements to support a conviction under for statutory rape: "(1) sexual intercourse or unnatural sexual intercourse, with (2) a child under sixteen years of age." *Commonwealth v. Miller*, 432 N.E.2d 463 (1982). In that case, we held that in a prosecution for statutory rape "it is immaterial that the defendant reasonably believed that the victim was sixteen years of age or older." *Id.* This is the rule in most jurisdictions [as statutory rape was historically and continues to be in many jurisdictions a crime that carries strict liability with respect to the age of the victim].

Indeed, it would be incongruous for us to posit one rule for the completed act and another for the attempt. For this reason, we have held that the consent of the victim is no more a defense to an assault with intent to commit statutory rape than it is for the completed act. *Commonwealth v. Roosnell*, 8 N.E. 747 (1886). In that case, this court held that "[i]f, as all agree, it is immaterial upon a charge of committing the completed act, which includes an assault, no reason but an extremely technical one can be urged why it should not be so upon a charge of assault with intent to commit the completed act." *Id.* at 41. This is simply a matter of common sense, for the policies underlying the rules in both cases are identical. Judgment affirmed.

QUESTIONS

1.   Massachusetts followed the Model Penal Code formulation for the crime of attempt in this case. That is to say that since the defendant had the purpose to engage in sexual activity with the victim (i.e., he had specific intent with respect to the conduct element of the offense), it is of no consequence for attempt liability whether he had knowledge of the victim's age since the age of the victim is an attendant circumstance to which strict liability attaches for the target crime. The result, however, would have been different under the common law. Why?

2.   Suppose you had the specific intent to kill someone. In order to carry out your intended plan, you fire a loaded gun at your intended victim. The bullet, however, only grazes the skin of your intended victim, leaving the victim alive and in need of only a few stitches. You actually committed the crime of aggravated battery because you caused physical injury to a person using a deadly weapon. Your intent, however, was to kill that person. If charged with both attempted murder and aggravated battery, what should the outcome of your case be and why?

3.   Assume the same facts as in the last paragraph except this time, your intent was to only wound your victim, not to kill. Of what crimes may you be rightfully convicted and why?

4.   Assume the same facts as in the last two paragraphs except this time, with your intent having been only wound your victim, you actually killed the victim even though it was not your intent to do so. As you will learn in Chapter Seven, you will have criminal homicide liability for the victim's death, mostly likely for a murder in the second degree conviction. Assuming you are convicted of murder two, what, if any, criminal liability would there for the crime of attempt? Why?

_____

2. Actus Reus for Attempt

As stated above, attempt is basically purposefully trying to commit a crime, but failing to be successful. The actus reus is the trying. But both the common law and the Model Penal code require more "trying" than acts of mere preparation. For there to be criminal liability for the crime of attempt, a defendant has to take significant steps toward actually committing the target crime.

The common law required the defendant to have come "dangerously close" to actually committing the target crime. This test, often referred to as the proximity test, examined how much further did a defendant have left to go before actually committing the target crime. If there were so few steps left such that the defendant had already come "dangerously close" to committing the intended offense, then the common law proximity test was satisfied and the defendant could, therefore, be convicted of attempt.

The Model Penal Code eased the requirement by imposing liability for taking enough steps such that the defendant could be said to have taken "substantial steps" toward committing the target crime. Unlike the common law proximity test, which looked at how much further the defendant had left to go, the Model Penal Code examines how far the defendant has already gone. Under this approach a defendant no longer had to come dangerously close to committing the intended offense. Rather, so long as the defendant took sufficient steps that, when viewed together, strongly corroborate the mens rea of purpose to commit the substantive offense, then liability for the crime of attempt can be imposed. What constitutes "substantial steps" is a question of fact for a jury to decide.

By comparing and contrasting the following two cases, the differences between the common law proximity test and Model Penal Code's substantial steps test should become more clear.

The PEOPLE of the State of New York v. Charles RIZZO, et al.
158 N.E. 888 (N.Y. 1927).

The police of the city of New York did excellent work in this case by preventing the commission of a serious crime. It is a great satisfaction to realize that we have such wide-awake guardians of our peace. Whether or not the steps which the defendant had taken up to the time of his arrest amounted to the commission of a crime, as defined by our law, is, however, another matter. He has been convicted of an attempt to commit the crime of robbery in the first degree, and sentenced to prison. There is no doubt that he had the intention to commit robbery, if he got the chance. An examination . . . of the facts is necessary to determine whether his acts were in preparation to commit the crime if the opportunity offered, or constituted a crime in itself, known to our law as an attempt to commit robbery in the first degree.

Charles Rizzo, the defendant-appellant, with three others, Anthony J. Dorio, Thomas Milo, and John Thomasello, on January 14th planned to rob one Charles Rao of a pay roll valued at about $1,200 which he was to carry from the bank for the United Lathing Company. These defendants, two of whom had firearms, started out in an automobile, looking for Rao or the man who had the pay roll on that day. Rizzo claimed to be able to identify the man, and was to point him out to the others, who were to do the actual holding up. The four rode about in their car looking for Rao. They went to the bank from which he was supposed to get the money and to various buildings being constructed by the United Lathing Company. At last they came to One Hundred and Eightieth street and Morris Park Avenue. By this time they were watched and followed by two police officers. As Rizzo jumped out of the car and ran into the building, all four were arrested. The defendant was taken out from the building in which he was hiding. Neither Rao nor a man named Previti, who was also supposed to carry a pay roll, were at the place at the time of the arrest. The defendants had not found or seen the man they intended to rob. No person with a pay roll was at any of the places where they had stopped, and no one had been pointed out or identified by Rizzo. The four men intended to rob the pay roll man, whoever he was. They were looking for him, but they had not seen or discovered him up to the time they were arrested.

Does this constitute the crime of an attempt to commit robbery in the first degree? The Penal Law prescribes: "An act, done with intent to commit a crime, and tending but failing to effect its commission, is an attempt to commit that crime." The word "tending" is very indefinite. It is perfectly evident that there will arise differences of opinion as to whether an act in a given case is one tending to commit a crime. "Tending" means to exert activity in a particular direction. Any act in preparation to commit a crime may be said to have a tendency towards its accomplishment. The procuring of the automobile, searching the streets looking for the desired victim, were in reality acts tending toward the commission of the proposed crime. The law, however, had recognized that many acts in the way of preparation are too remote to constitute the crime of attempt. The line has been drawn between those acts which are remote and those which are proximate and near to the consummation. The law must be practical, and therefore considers those acts only as tending to the commission of the crime which are so near to its accomplishment that in all reasonable probability the crime itself would have been committed, but for timely interference. The cases which have been before the courts express this idea in different language, but the idea remains the same. The act or acts must come or advance very near to the accomplishment of the intended crime.

In *People v. Mills*, 178 N.Y. 274, 70 N.E. 786 (1904), it was said: "Felonious intent alone is not enough, but there must be an overt act shown in order to establish even an attempt. An overt act is one done to carry out the intention, and it must be such as would naturally effect that result, unless prevented by some extraneous cause." In *Hyde v. United States,* 225 U.S. 347 (1912), it was stated by the U.S. Supreme Court that the act amounts to an attempt when it is so near to the result that the danger of success is very great. "There must be dangerous proximity to success."

How shall we apply this rule of immediate nearness to this case? The defendants were looking for the pay roll man to rob him of his money. This is the charge in the indictment. Robbery is defined in . . . the Penal Law as "the unlawful taking of personal property from the person or in the presence of another, against his will, by means of force, or violence, or fear of injury, immediate or future, to his person"; and it is made robbery in the first degree . . . when committed by a person aided by accomplices actually present. To constitute the crime of robbery, the money must have been taken from Rao by means of force or violence, or through fear. The crime of attempt to commit robbery was committed, if these defendants did an act tending to the commission of this robbery. Did the acts above described come dangerously near to the taking of Rao's property? Did the acts come so near the commission of robbery that there was reasonable likelihood of its accomplishment but for the interference?

Rao was not found; the defendants were still looking for him; no attempt to rob him could be made, at least until he came in sight; he was not in the building at One Hundred and Eightieth Street and Morris Park Avenue. There was no man there with the pay roll for the United Lathing Company whom these defendants could rob. Apparently no money had been drawn from the bank for the pay roll by anybody at the time of the arrest. In a word, these defendants had planned to commit a crime, and were looking around the city for an opportunity to commit it, but the opportunity fortunately never came. Men would not be guilty of an attempt at burglary if they had planned to break into a building and were arrested while they were hunting about the streets for the building not knowing where it was. Neither would a man be guilty of an attempt to commit murder if he armed himself and started out to find the person whom he had planned to kill but could not find him. So here these defendants were not guilty of an attempt to commit robbery in the first degree when they had not found or reached the presence of the person they intended to rob. *People v. Sullivan*, 173 N.Y. 122, 135, 65 N.E. 989 (1903).

For these reasons, the judgment of conviction of this defendant appellant must be reversed and a new trial granted.

Roger Matthew WALTERS, Petitioner-Appellant, v. Manfred MAASS, Respondent-Appellee.
45 F.3d 1355 (9th Cir. 1995).

Poole, Circuit Judge:

Roger Matthew Walters, an Oregon state prisoner, appeals the district court's denial of his 28 U.S.C. § 2254 habeas corpus petition challenging his conviction and sentence for attempted rape, attempted sodomy, and attempted kidnapping of a thirteen-year old girl.

I

Walters first contends that he was denied a fair trial when the state court admitted evidence that in 1981, he approached another thirteen-year old girl with the ploy of searching for a nonexistent white German shepherd, offered her $ 20, and then kidnapped her, took her to his trailer, and forcibly raped and sodomized her. Walters used the same German shepherd ploy in this case to try to lure the thirteen-year old victim into his truck. The state court admitted the prior bad acts evidence as proof of intent.

The Oregon court did not err by admitting evidence of Walters' 1981 convictions. Walters' use of the German shepherd ploy in 1981 was relevant to show his intent in using the same ploy in 1987. Moreover, the prior act was not too remote in time. Although seven years elapsed between the two crimes, Walters spent almost all of that time in jail serving his sentence for the 1981 crime. The trial court reduced the danger of unfair prejudice by giving a limiting instruction that the evidence could be used only to show "motive, opportunity, intent, preparation, plan, knowledge, or absence of mistake or accident" and could not be used to show Walters' bad character.

II

Walters contends that the evidence was insufficient to support his convictions for attempted first-degree kidnapping, attempted first-degree rape, and attempted first-degree sodomy.

Under Oregon law, conviction for attempt requires proof beyond a reasonable doubt that the defendant "intentionally engaged in conduct which constitutes a substantial step toward commission of the crime." Or. Rev. Stat. § 161.405(1); *State v. Walters*, 804 P.2d 1164, 1167 (Or.), *cert. denied*, 501 U.S. 1209 (1991). To constitute a substantial step toward the commission of a crime, the defendant's conduct must (1) "advance the criminal purpose charged, and (2) provide some verification of the existence of that purpose." *Walters*, 804 P.2d at 1167. Mere preparation is insufficient to constitute a substantial step. *Id.* at 1167-68.

The difference between making preparations and taking a substantial step toward the commission of a crime is one of degree. *Id.* In evaluating whether conduct constitutes a substantial step, we have stated that although behavior need not be incompatible with innocence to be punishable as an attempt, "it must be necessary to the consummation of the crime and be of such a nature that a reasonable observer, viewing it in context[,] could conclude beyond a reasonable doubt that it was undertaken in accordance with a design" to commit the particular crime charged. *United States v. Manley*, 632 F.2d 978, 987-88 (2d Cir. 1980), *cert. denied*, 449 U.S. 1112 (1981). Moreover, a substantial step must entail "an overt act adapted to, approximating, and which in the ordinary and likely course of things will result in, the commission of the particular crime." *Id.*

Walters asserts that the evidence was insufficient to establish his intent to commit the crimes of first-degree kidnapping, rape, and sodomy and to establish that he took a substantial step toward the commission of those crimes.

Certainly Walters' intent is manifested by (1) evidence regarding his use of the German shepherd ruse in 1981 to kidnap, rape, and sodomize another thirteen-year old girl, (2) his persistent attempts to lure the victim into his truck using the same ruse, (3) his actions in following the victim home, (4) his strange speech patterns when he talked to the victim's mother, and (5) his statements to the police officer. In addition, Walters' attempt to entice the victim into his truck clearly advances the criminal purpose of first-degree kidnapping and strongly corroborates the existence of his purpose to commit that crime. Thus, we agree with the Oregon Supreme Court that this conduct constitutes a substantial step toward the commission of the crime of first-degree kidnapping, and we do not disturb Walters' conviction for attempted first-degree kidnapping.

The more troubling question is whether Walters' attempt to entice the victim into his truck constitutes a substantial step toward the commission of the crimes of rape and sodomy when the only evidence of intent to rape and sodomize is Walters' 1981 conviction for kidnapping, raping, and sodomizing another thirteen-year old girl. If in 1981, Walters had committed other crimes (for example, breaking the victim's arm and stealing her wallet), it would be difficult to conclude now that enticement into the truck constituted a substantial step toward the commission of those crimes. At some point, the link between the enticement and the charged crimes becomes too attenuated: we cannot say that the enticement strongly corroborates any intent to commit those crimes such that a reasonable observer, viewing it, in context, could conclude beyond a reasonable doubt that it was undertaken in accordance with a design to commit the crimes.

The only step Walters took toward the commission of the charged crimes was his attempt to entice the victim into his truck. It may be that this act to some extent corroborates Walters' intent to commit some sexual assault, but we cannot agree that it strongly corroborates his intent to commit those crimes. Moreover, attempting to entice the victim into a truck does not, in the ordinary and likely course of events, result in the crimes of rape and sodomy.

In sum, where the only evidence of Walters' intent to commit the crimes of rape and sodomy is the 1981 crimes, we hold that Walters' attempt to entice the victim into his truck is not a substantial step toward the commission of the crimes of rape and sodomy. Accordingly, we direct that the writ be granted with regard to Walters' convictions for attempted rape and attempted sodomy on the ground of constitutional insufficiency of the evidence.

We affirm the district court's determinations concerning the admissibility of the prior bad acts evidence, [and] the sufficiency of the evidence to support Walters' conviction for attempted first-degree kidnapping . . . . We reverse the district court's determination that the evidence was sufficient to support Walters' convictions for attempted first-degree rape and attempted first-degree sodomy.

Tang, Senior Judge, dissenting:

I share Judge Poole's concern with this case; Oregon appears on the verge of criminalizing pure (albeit bad) thought. But in finding sufficient evidence of a "substantial step" toward rape and sodomy in Walters's efforts to have his intended victim get into his truck, the Oregon Supreme Court retains at least a vestige of the actus reus requirement. I therefore respectfully dissent.

The actus reus element of state criminal laws is generally a matter of state law. As the Supreme Court has stated:

> The doctrines of actus reus [and] mens rea . . . have historically provided the tools for a constantly shifting adjustment of the tension between the evolving aims of the criminal law and changing religious, moral, philosophical, and medical views of the nature of man. This process of adjustment has always been thought to be the province of the States.

Powell v. Texas, 392 U.S. 514, 536 (1968). Here, Oregon has declared that "enticement" constitutes one form of the "substantial step" required for an attempt conviction under state law. *State v. Walters*, 311 Ore. 80, 85-86, 804 P.2d 1164, *cert. denied*, 501 U.S. 1209 (1991).

Because there is sufficient evidence to support a finding of enticement under Oregon law, we should defer to state law and uphold Walters's convictions.

QUESTIONS

1.   The *Rizzo* court found insufficient evidence to convict the defendants of attempted bank robbery using the common law proximity test. What effect, if any, on the outcome of the case do you think it would have made if the Model Penal Code's substantial steps test had been in effect at that time? Explain your reasoning.

2.   In the *Maass* case, the court had no problem determining that Mr. Maass' actions were strongly corroborative of his intent to kidnap the girl, and therefore found sufficient evidence to uphold his conviction for attempted kidnapping. Do you agree? Why or why not? Would your opinion differ if you did not know about his previous crimes regarding the same *modus operandi* (i.e., using the German shepherd as a lure)?

3.   Both courts emphasize that "mere preparation" is always insufficient to impose criminal liability for the crime of attempt. But when does "mere preparation" turn into "substantial steps"? The jury convicted Mr. Maass attempted statutory rape and attempted sodomy. Presumably, therefore, the jury was satisfied that his act of enticing the girl to his truck went beyond mere preparation and was strongly corroborative of his intent to commit both target crimes. But the majority of the court of appeals disagreed. Do you think the acts described as "enticing" in the *Maass* case were acts of mere preparation or were they "substantial steps" sufficient to impose criminal liability for attempt? Why?

3. The Defense of Impossibility for the Crime of Attempt

Suppose that, with the specific intent to kill, you walked into a bedroom in which you believed your intended victim to be sleeping and fired at the bed, believing your victim to be in it. As the fates would have it, however, your victim was not in the bed that night. Your bullet merely pierced some pillows and bedding. Are you guilty of attempted murder? Both the common law and the Model Penal Code would answer this question in the affirmative and hold you liable for attempted murder. Circumstances being what they actually were (i.e., the bed was empty), rather than what you believed them to be (i.e., that your intended victim was in the bed) caused it to be factually impossible for you to have killed your intended victim. But *factual impossibility* is not a defense to the crime of attempt under either the common law or the Model Penal Code.

The classic example of the "unlucky pickpocket" is an excellent example of factual impossibility. If the pickpocket picks a pocket that has nothing in it to steal (and, therefore, no theft actually can occur), is the pickpocket liable for attempted theft? Since the pickpocket tried, and failed due to the fact that the pocket from which he attempted to steal was empty, it was factually impossible for him to succeed in his attempt. But since factual impossibility is not a defense, the pickpocket would have criminal responsibility for his attempt.

In both of the above examples, the aim of the actors were both crimes: murder in the first hypothetical; theft in the second. The impossibility of succeeding with their respective turned not on the law, but rather on the facts and circumstances of the case. Hence, the impossibility at issue is factual, not legal impossibility. But what if the law itself made it impossible for an actor to succeed in his or her criminal attempt? Such situations are covered by the defense of legal impossibility.

Can someone be legally convicted of attempting to do something that was, in actuality, not a crime? At first blush, the question seems silly. Why would we punish trying, but failing, to so something that is not illegal? Well, if phrased that way, the obvious answer to the question should be a resounding "no." Neither the common law nor the Model Penal Code impose any criminal liability for attempting to that which is perfectly legal. The law would say there is a *true legal impossibility* to be guilty of the crime of attempt under such circumstances.

But what if someone tries, but fails to commit an act the person believed to be a crime, but wasn't? Should the law punish someone for acting with such criminal intent even though the result turned out not to be illegal? The common law and the Model Penal Code answered this question differently. At common law, if one attempted to do an act that he believed was illegal, but turned out not to be illegal, there was no criminal attempt. In other words, regardless of the actor's guilty state of mind, if one did not try and fail to do an act that was actually illegal, there was no liability for criminal attempt. Thus, at common law, *legal impossibility* was a bona-fide defense to the crime of attempt.

In contrast to the common law's approach, the Model Penal Code sought to eliminate the defense of impossibility in virtually all situations. While it is still a requirement that the result intended or desired by the actor constitute a crime (otherwise there would be true legal impossibility), the Model Penal Code shifted the focus to the defendant's mens rea. Accordingly, attempt liability is now judged not on external circumstances, but rather on whether the defendant's intent warrants criminal sanctioning. The Model Penal Code holds that there is no defense if, under the attendant circumstances, a crime was factually or legally impossible of commission, "if such crime could have been committed had the attendant circumstances been as such person believed them to be." The following case illustrates this approach.

===

The PEOPLE of the State of New York, Appellant, v. Melvin DLUGASH, Respondent.
41 N.Y.2d 725, 363 N.E.2d 1155, 395 N.Y.S.2d 419 (1977).

Jasen, Judge.

Introduction

The criminal law is of ancient origin, but criminal liability for attempt to commit a crime is comparatively recent. At the root of the concept of attempt liability are the very aims and purposes of penal law. The ultimate issue is whether an individual's intentions and actions, though failing to achieve a manifest and malevolent criminal purpose, constitute a danger to organized society of sufficient magnitude to warrant the imposition of criminal sanctions. Difficulties in theoretical analysis and concomitant debate over very pragmatic questions of blameworthiness appear dramatically in reference to situations where the criminal attempt failed to achieve its purpose solely because the factual or legal context in which the individual acted was not as the actor supposed them to be. Phrased somewhat differently, the concern centers on whether an individual should be liable for an attempt to commit a crime when, unknown to him, it was impossible to successfully complete the crime attempted.

For years, serious studies have been made on the subject in an effort to resolve the continuing controversy when, if at all, the impossibility of successfully completing the criminal act should preclude liability for even making the futile attempt. The 1967 revision of the Penal Law approached the impossibility defense to the inchoate crime of attempt in a novel fashion. The statute provides that, if a person engages in conduct which would otherwise constitute an attempt to commit a crime, "it is no defense to a prosecution for such attempt that the crime charged to have been attempted was, under the attendant circumstances, factually or legally impossible of commission, if such crime could have been committed had the attendant circumstances been as such person believed them to be." (Penal Law, § 110.10.) This appeal presents to us, for the first time, a case involving the application of the modern statute. We hold that, under the proof presented by the People at trial, defendant Melvin Dlugash may be held for attempted murder, though the target of the attempt may have already been slain, by the hand of another, when Dlugash made his felonious attempt.

Factual Background

On December 22, 1973, Michael Geller, 25 years old, was found shot to death in the bedroom of his Brooklyn apartment. The body, which had literally been riddled by bullets, was found lying face up on the floor. An autopsy revealed that the victim had been shot in the face and head no less than seven times. Powder burns on the face indicated that the shots had been fired from within one foot of the victim. Four small caliber bullets were recovered from the victim's skull. The victim had also been critically wounded in the chest. One heavy caliber bullet passed through the left lung, penetrated the heart chamber, pierced the left ventricle of the heart upon entrance and again upon exit, and lodged in the victim's torso. A second bullet entered the left lung and passed through to the chest, but without reaching the heart area. Although the second bullet was damaged beyond identification, the bullet tracks indicated that these wounds were also inflicted by a bullet of heavy caliber. A tenth bullet, of unknown caliber, passed through the thumb of the victim's left hand. The autopsy report listed the cause of death as "multiple bullet wounds of head and chest with brain injury and massive bilateral hemothorax with penetration of the heart." Subsequent ballistics examination established that the four bullets recovered from the victim's head were .25 caliber bullets and that the heart-piercing bullet was of .38 caliber.

Detective Joseph Carrasquillo of the New York City Police Department was assigned to investigate the homicide. On December 27, 1973, five days after the discovery of the body, Detective Carrasquillo and a fellow officer went to the defendant's residence in an effort to locate him. The officers arrived at approximately 6:00 p.m. The defendant answered the door and, when informed that the officers were investigating the death of Michael Geller, a friend of his, defendant invited the officers into the house. Detective Carrasquillo informed defendant that the officers desired any information defendant might have regarding the death of Geller and, since defendant was regarded as a suspect, administered the standard preinterrogation warnings. The defendant told the officers that he and another friend, Joe Bush, had just returned from a four or five day trip "upstate someplace" and learned of Geller's death only upon his return. Since Bush was also a suspect in the case and defendant admitted knowing Bush, defendant agreed to accompany the officers to the station house for the purposes of identifying photographs of Bush and of lending assistance to the investigation.

Upon arrival at the police station, Detective Carrasquillo and the defendant went directly into an interview room. Carrasquillo advised the defendant that he had witnesses and information to the effect that as late as 7:00 p.m. on the day before the body was found, defendant had been observed carrying a .25 caliber pistol. Once again, Carrasquillo administered the standard preinterrogation statement of rights. The defendant then proceeded to relate his version of the events which culminated in the death of Geller. Defendant stated that, on the night of December 21, 1973, he, Bush and Geller had been out drinking. Bush had been staying at Geller's apartment and, during the course of the evening, Geller several times demanded that Bush pay $100 towards the rent on the apartment. According to defendant, Bush rejected these demands, telling Geller that "you better shut up or you're going to get a bullet." All three returned to Geller's apartment at approximately midnight, took seats in the bedroom, and continued to drink until sometime between 3:00 and 3:30 in the morning. When Geller again pressed his demand for rent money, Bush drew his .38 caliber pistol, aimed it at Geller and fired three times. Geller fell to the floor. After the passage of a few minutes, perhaps two, perhaps as much as five, defendant walked over to the fallen Geller, drew his .25 caliber pistol, and fired approximately five shots in the victim's head and face. Defendant contended that, by the time he fired the shots, "it looked like Mike Geller was already dead."

After the shots were fired, defendant and Bush walked to the apartment of a female acquaintance. Bush removed his shirt, wrapped the two guns and a knife in it, and left the apartment, telling Dlugash that he intended to dispose of the weapons. Bush returned 10 or 15 minutes later and stated that he had thrown the weapons down a sewer two or three blocks away. After Carrasquillo had taken the bulk of the statement, he asked the defendant why he would do such a thing. According to Carrasquillo, the defendant said, "gee, I really don't know." Carrasquillo repeated the question 10 minutes later, but received the same response. After a while, Carrasquillo asked the question for a third time and defendant replied, "well, gee, I guess it must have been because I was afraid of Joe Bush."

At approximately 9:00 p.m., the defendant repeated the substance of his statement to an Assistant District Attorney. Defendant added that at the time he shot at Geller, Geller was not moving and his eyes were closed. While he did not check for a pulse, defendant stated that Geller had not been doing anything to him at the time he shot because "Mike was dead."

Defendant was indicted by the Grand Jury of Kings County on a single count of murder in that, acting in concert with another person actually present, he intentionally caused the death of Michael Geller. At the trial, there were four principal prosecution witnesses: Detective Carrasquillo, the Assistant District Attorney who took the second admission, and two physicians from the office of the New York City Chief Medical Examiner. For proof of defendant's culpability, the prosecution relied upon defendant's own admissions as related by the detective and the prosecutor. From the physicians, the prosecution sought to establish that Geller was still alive at the time defendant shot at him. Both physicians testified that each of the two chest wounds, for which defendant alleged Bush to be responsible, would have caused death without prompt medical attention. Moreover, the victim would have remained alive until such time as his chest cavity became fully filled with blood. Depending on the circumstances, it might take 5 to 10 minutes for the chest cavity to fill. Neither prosecution witness could state, with medical certainty, that the victim was still alive when, perhaps five minutes after the initial chest wounds were inflicted, the defendant fired at the victim's head.

The defense produced but a single witness, the former Chief Medical Examiner of New York City. This expert stated that, in his view, Geller might have died of the chest wounds "very rapidly" since, in addition to the bleeding, a large bullet going through a lung and the heart would have other adverse medical effects. "Those wounds can be almost immediately or rapidly fatal or they may be delayed in there, in the time it would take for death to occur. But I would say that wounds like that which are described here as having gone through the lungs and the heart would be fatal wounds and in most cases they're rapidly fatal."

The trial court declined to charge the jury, as requested by the prosecution, that defendant could be guilty of murder on the theory that he had aided and abetted the killing of Geller by Bush. Instead, the court submitted only two theories to the jury: that defendant had either intentionally murdered Geller or had attempted to murder Geller.

The jury found the defendant guilty of murder. The defendant then moved to set the verdict aside. He submitted an affidavit in which he contended that he "was absolutely, unequivocally and positively certain that Michael Geller was dead before (he) shot him." Further, the defendant averred that he was in fear for his life when he shot Geller. "This fear stemmed from the fact that Joseph Bush, the admitted killer of Geller, was holding a gun on me and telling me, in no uncertain terms, that if I didn't shoot the dead body I, too, would be killed." This motion was denied.

On appeal, the Appellate Division reversed the judgment of conviction on the law and dismissed the indictment. The court ruled that "the People failed to prove beyond a reasonable doubt that Geller had been alive at the time he was shot by defendant; defendant's conviction of murder thus cannot stand." Further, the court held that the judgment could not be modified to reflect a conviction for attempted murder because "the uncontradicted evidence is that the defendant, at the time that he fired the five shots into the body of the decedent, believed him to be dead, and . . . there is not a scintilla of evidence to contradict his assertion in that regard."

Legal + Factual Impossibility

Discussion

1. Murder Liability

Preliminarily, we state our agreement with the Appellate Division that the evidence did not establish, beyond a reasonable doubt, that Geller was alive at the time defendant fired into his body. To sustain a homicide conviction, it must be established, beyond a reasonable doubt, that the defendant caused the death of another person. (Penal Law, § 125.00; CPL 70.20.) The People were required to establish that the shots fired by defendant Dlugash were a sufficiently direct cause of Geller's death. *People v Stewart*, 40 N.Y.2d 692, 697 (1976). While the defendant admitted firing five shots at the victim approximately two to five minutes after Bush had fired three times, all three medical expert witnesses testified that they could not, with any degree of medical certainty, state whether the victim had been alive at the time the latter shots were fired by the defendant. Thus, the People failed to prove beyond a reasonable doubt that the victim had been alive at the time he was shot by the defendant. Whatever else it may be, it is not murder to shoot a dead body. Man dies but once.

2. Attempt Liability

Legal + Factual Impossibility

. . . . The Revised Penal Law now provides that a person is guilty of an attempt to commit a crime when, with intent to commit a crime, he engages in conduct which tends to effect the commission of such crime. (Penal Law, § 110.10). . . .

The most intriguing attempt cases are those where the attempt to commit a crime was unsuccessful due to mistakes of fact or law on the part of the would-be criminal. A general rule developed in most American jurisdictions that legal impossibility is a good defense but factual impossibility is not. Thus, for example, it was held that defendants who shot at a stuffed deer did not attempt to take a deer out of season, even though they believed the dummy to be a live animal. The court stated that there was no criminal attempt because it was no crime to "take" a stuffed deer, and it is no crime to attempt to do that which is legal. A further example is Francis Wharton's classic hypothetical involving Lady Eldon and her French lace. Lady Eldon, traveling in Europe, purchased a quantity of French lace at a high price, intending to smuggle it into England without payment of the duty. When discovered in a customs search, the lace turned out to be of English origin, of little value and not subject to duty. The traditional view is that Lady Eldon is not liable for an attempt to smuggle.

On the other hand, factual impossibility was no defense. For example, a man was held liable for attempted murder when he shot into the room in which his target usually slept and, fortuitously, the target was sleeping elsewhere in the house that night. Although one bullet struck the target's customary pillow,

96

attainment of the criminal objective was factually impossible. In another case, the defendant agreed to perform an abortion, then a criminal act, upon a female undercover police investigator who was not, in fact, pregnant. The court sustained the conviction, ruling that "when the consequences sought by a defendant are forbidden by the law as criminal, it is no defense that the defendant could not succeed in reaching his goal because of circumstances unknown to him." On the same view, it was held that men who had sexual intercourse with a woman, with the belief that she was alive and did not consent to the intercourse, could be charged for attempted rape when the woman had, in fact, died from an unrelated ailment prior to the acts of intercourse.

As can be seen from even this abbreviated discussion, the distinction between "factual" and "legal" impossibility was a nice one indeed and the courts tended to place a greater value on legal form than on any substantive danger the defendant's actions posed for society. The approach of the draftsmen of the Model Penal Code was to eliminate the defense of impossibility in virtually all situations. Under the code provision, to constitute an attempt, it is still necessary that the result intended or desired by the actor constitute a crime. However, the code suggested a fundamental change to shift the locus of analysis to the actor's mental frame of reference and away from undue dependence upon external considerations. The basic premise of the code provision is that what was in the actor's own mind should be the standard for determining his dangerousness to society and, hence, his liability for attempted criminal conduct. Thus, a person is guilty of an attempt when, with intent to commit a crime, he engages in conduct which tends to effect the commission of such crime. (Penal Law, § 110.00.) It is no defense that, under the attendant circumstances, the crime was factually or legally impossible of commission, "if such crime could have been committed had the attendant circumstances been as such person believed them to be." (Penal Law, § 110.10.) Thus, if defendant believed the victim to be alive at the time of the shooting, it is no defense to the charge of attempted murder that the victim may have been dead.

Turning to the facts of the case before us, we believe that there is sufficient evidence in the record from which the jury could conclude that the defendant believed Geller to be alive at the time defendant fired shots into Geller's head. Defendant admitted firing five shots at a most vital part of the victim's anatomy from virtually point blank range. Although defendant contended that the victim had already been grievously wounded by another, from the defendant's admitted actions, the jury could conclude that the defendant's purpose and intention was to administer the coup de grace. The jury never learned of defendant's subsequent allegation that Bush had a gun on him and directed defendant to fire at Geller on the pain of his own life.

Defendant did not testify and this statement of duress was made only in a postverdict affidavit, which obviously was never placed before the jury. In his admissions that were related to the jury, defendant never made such a claim. Nor did he offer any explanation for his conduct, except for an offhand aside made casually to Detective Carrasquillo. Any remaining doubt as to the question of duress is dispelled by defendant's earlier statement that he and Joe Bush had peacefully spent a few days together on vacation in the country. Moreover, defendant admitted to freely assisting Bush in disposing of the weapons after the murder and, once the weapons were out of the picture, defendant made no effort at all to flee from Bush. Indeed, not only did defendant not come forward with his story immediately, but when the police arrived at his house, he related a false version designed to conceal his and Bush's complicity in the murder. All of these facts indicate a consciousness of guilt which defendant would not have had if he had truly believed that Geller was dead when he shot him.

Defendant argues that the jury was bound to accept, at face value, the indications in his admissions that he believed Geller dead. Certainly, it is true that the defendant was entitled to have the entirety of the admissions, both the inculpatory and the exculpatory portions, placed in evidence before the trier of facts. However, the jury was not required to automatically credit the exculpatory portions of the admissions. The general rule is, of course, that the credibility of witnesses is a question of fact and the jury may choose to believe some, but not all, of a witness' testimony. The general rule applies with equal force to proof of admissions. Thus, it has been stated that "where that part of the declaration which discharges the party making it is in itself highly improbable or is discredited by other evidence the jury may believe one part of the admission and reject the other."

In this case, there is ample other evidence to contradict the defendant's assertion that he believed Geller dead. There were five bullet wounds inflicted with stunning accuracy in a vital part of the victim's anatomy. The medical testimony indicated that Geller may have been alive at the time defendant fired at him. The defendant voluntarily left the jurisdiction immediately after the crime with his coperpetrator. Defendant did not report the crime to the police when left on his own by Bush. Instead, he attempted to conceal his and Bush's involvement with the homicide. In addition, the other portions of defendant's admissions make his contended belief that Geller was dead extremely improbable. Defendant, without a word of instruction from Bush, voluntarily got up from his seat after the passage of just a few minutes and fired five times point blank into the victim's face, snuffing out any remaining chance of life that Geller possessed. Certainly, this alone indicates a callous indifference to the taking of a human life. His admissions are barren of any claim of duress and reflect, instead, an unstinting co-operation in efforts to dispose of vital incriminating evidence. Indeed, defendant maintained a false version of the occurrence until such time as the police informed him that they had evidence that he lately possessed a gun of the same caliber as one of the weapons involved in the shooting. From all of this, the jury was certainly warranted in concluding that the defendant acted in the belief that Geller was yet alive when shot by defendant.

The jury convicted the defendant of murder. Necessarily, they found that defendant intended to kill a live human being. Subsumed within this finding is the conclusion that defendant acted in the belief that Geller was alive. Thus, there is no need for additional fact findings by a jury. Although it was not established beyond a reasonable doubt that Geller was, in fact, alive, such is no defense to attempted murder since a murder would have been committed "had the attendant circumstances been as [the defendant] believed them to be." (Penal Law, § 110.10.) The jury necessarily found that defendant believed Geller to be alive when defendant shot at him.

Legal impossibility than not a defense

QUESTIONS

1.   Because the prosecution could not prove that Geller was alive when Dlugash shot at Geller, he could not be held liable for any homicide charge since it is truly impossible to kill a dead person. But, if the attendant circumstances were as Dlugash believed them to be (i.e., that Geller either was alive or could have been alive – facts the jury found to exist), then what Dlugash did would have been the crime of murder. Hence, he was held liable for attempted murder using the Model Penal Code formulation of the law on the defense of impossibility. But suppose that New York had employed the old common law rule regarding impossibility. Would he have any criminal liability for the crime of attempted murder? Explain your answer.

2.   Suppose a defendant, believing that he was buying drugs, purchased a small, plasticine bag containing a white, powered substance. If the bag actually contained flour or sugar (or some other legal substance), what would be the defendant's liability for the crime of attempt under the common law? Under the Model Penal Code? Explain your reasoning for both answers.

3.   If a male over the statutory age of consent had sexual intercourse with a female under the age of consent, the common law would hold that male liable for the crime of statutory rape. His mens rea would be irrelevant. Even if the underage female lied about her age and produce false identification to show she was age to consent to the intercourse, he will still be guilty of the crime of statutory rape because the female was, in fact, under the age. This was due to the fact that the age of the "victim" was an attendant circumstance that carried strict liability at common law.

In contrast, however, if a male over the age of consent had sexual intercourse with a woman who was also over the age of consent, but he erroneously believed her to be under the age of consent, then no statutory rape occurred. This is due to the fact that the elements of statutory rape are not met under such a fact patter (i.e., no male had sexual intercourse with a female under the age of consent). But this male thought he was committing the crime of statutory rape. He tried to commit the crime, but failed. What would his liability be for the crime of attempted statutory rape under the common law? Under the Model Penal Code? Why?

4. The Defense of Abandonment for the Crime of Attempt

At common law, one could not abandon or withdraw from his or her criminal attempt and assert that as a defense to the crime after the actor had already come "dangerously close" to effectuating the target crime. Accordingly, once the elements of the crime of attempt had occurred, there was no defense to it for not having followed through on one's criminal intentions. Many U.S. jurisdictions continue to follow this common law rule with respect to the crime of attempt.

In contrast to the common law approach, the Model Penal Code recognizes the defense of **abandonment** (sometimes referred to as the defense of renunciation or withdrawal). The rationale for the Model Penal Code approach hinges on the fact that the target offense must have been prevented from the abandonment. If it was, then excusing the defendant from attempt liability is seen as good public policy that benefits society at large because the availability of the defense encourages would-be criminals to stop their attempts, thereby reducing the risk of crime.

In order for the defense to be successfully asserted, the Model Penal Code requires that three criteria be met. The abandonment must be (a) effective; (b) complete; and (c) voluntary. If all three requirements are not met, a defendant cannot successfully assert the defense of abandonment.

By *effective*, the Model Penal Code requires that the actor actually stop his or her criminal attempt at the target crime. And, further, the target crime cannot occur. Abandoning an attempt out of frustration after one has done everything possible to attempt the crime is not an effective abandonment. Similarly, if the actor has put in motion forces that he is powerless to stop, then the attempt has been completed and cannot be effectively abandoned.

Secondly, the defendant's renunciation of his or her criminal intent must be **complete**. That is to say that the defendant must totally abandon all intent to commit the target crime, not just postpone it to a later time or "to transfer the criminal effort to another but similar objective or victim." Model Penal Code § 5.01(4).

And finally, the abandonment must be **voluntary**. It must out of the defendant's own remorse or feeling that he or she should not be doing the crime, not due to the circumstances surrounding the attempt. In the words of the Model Penal Code, an abandonment is not voluntary "if it is motivated, in whole or in part, by circumstances . . . that increase the probability of detection or apprehension or that make more difficult the accomplishment of the criminal purpose." Model Penal Code § 5.01(4).

The PEOPLE of the State of New York, Respondent, v. George TAYLOR, Appellant.
80 N.Y.2d 1, 598 N.E.2d 693, 586 N.Y.S.2d 545 (1992).

[According to the testimony of the victim Elizabeth G], a man forced his way into her apartment on March 2, 1987. Threatening her with a knife, he made aggressive sexual advances. Because of her fear of the knife, she sought to dissuade him – rather than fighting him or screaming – by "trying to make him believe that he could be [her] boyfriend and he did not have to do it this way." Despite these efforts, he carried her into the bedroom where he continued to touch and rub himself against her and tried to pull down her pants. After Ms. G. "told him he could come to [her] house anytime," he relented and they "went back to the living room and started talking." He took off the surgical gloves he had been wearing during the attack, saying that he was "not going to be needing these anymore."

The man apparently accepted Ms. G.'s suggestion that they "go buy a bottle" to celebrate "getting to know each other." When they stepped into the hallway outside the apartment on their way "to buy the bottle," the man had ahold of her upper arm. She slipped back through the door, which was slightly ajar, stating that she had forgotten her pocketbook. The door closed and locked automatically behind her and she stayed inside. As she put it on cross-examination, "I ducked from under his arm and the door closed". The man knocked on the apartment door and tried to get her to open it by telling her to "get him a tissue." She refused to let him back in, called the police, and the man left. At the close of the evidence, the court denied defense counsel's request for a jury charge on renunciation regarding the attempted rape charge. [He was convicted and appealed claiming this failure to instruct the jury on the defense of abandonment was error].

* * *

According to defendant, the evidence shows that he voluntarily and completely abandoned any intention of carrying out the design of raping Elizabeth G. Thus, he argues, the trial court erred in denying his request to charge renunciation as an affirmative defense to the attempted rape count. . . .

* * *

For the defense of renunciation to be effective, it must be shown that the object crime was abandoned "under circumstances manifesting a voluntary and complete renunciation of [the] criminal purpose" (Penal Law § 40.10[3]). To be "voluntary," as that term is used in the statute, the abandonment must reflect a change in the actor's purpose or a change of heart that is not influenced by outside circumstances i.e., the abandonment cannot be motivated in whole or in part by a belief that circumstances exist that increase the probability of detection or apprehension or make more difficult the completion of the crime (Penal Law § 40.10[5]). To be "complete," the abandonment must be permanent, not temporary or contingent, not simply a decision to postpone the criminal conduct until another time or to transfer the criminal effort to another victim. It is essential that the defendant demonstrate that the claimed renunciation resulted in avoidance of the crime (Penal Law § 40.10[3]); in other words, that by abandoning the criminal enterprise he prevented it from being completed. Thus, for example, if the actor fires at the intended victim and misses he has no defense to the charge of criminal attempt. What resulted in the crime's avoidance was the actor's poor aim, not his abandonment of the criminal purpose.

Arguably, there is enough for the jury to have concluded that defendant voluntarily stopped the sexual assault, apparently in response to the victim's intimations concerning future gratification. There is no reasonable view of the proof, however, that the abandonment of the criminal enterprise was complete, or that the culmination of the intended rape was avoided by defendant's abandoning the criminal effort. On these critical issues we have only the testimony of Ms. G. that when she and defendant left the apartment defendant was holding her by the arm, that she managed to duck from under his arm and get back through the apartment door which closed and locked automatically behind her, and that defendant thereafter attempted to regain entry into the apartment by knocking on the door and asking for a tissue. This evidence hardly evinces a complete abandonment by defendant of his criminal purpose. On the contrary, it strongly suggests that the criminal enterprise was continuing and that what prevented its completion was not defendant's intention to abandon it but the victim's escape.

Inasmuch as renunciation is an affirmative defense, we agree with the lower courts that under no reasonable view of the evidence could the jury have found that defendant established by a preponderance of the evidence that the crime was avoided by his abandonment of the criminal effort "under circumstances manifesting a voluntary and complete renunciation of his criminal purpose."

QUESTIONS

1.   The court stated, "Arguably, there is enough for the jury to have concluded that defendant voluntarily stopped the sexual assault, apparently in response to the victim's intimations concerning future gratification." Without considering the criteria of being complete, effective, and voluntary, do you agree that the defendant's conduct – in an of itself – "arguably" forms the basis of a withdrawal from the crime of attempted rape? Why or why not?

2.   The court found that even though the defendant actions may be viewed as an abandonment of his attempt to rape the victim, the abandonment was not "complete." Do you think there was sufficient evidence to label his "abandonment" effective? Voluntary? Why or why not?

3.   An eyewitness testified that she two men knocking on doors and looking in windows in her neighborhood. She then saw them walk around the side of a neighbor's house into the back yard. The neighbor was not at home, so she called the police. When the police arrived at the house, they saw the men "walking towards the back fence of the residence looking over their shoulders." They ordered the men to stop and arrested them. One of the men had a pair of cloth gloves stuffed into the front of his pants; a buck knife in his front pocket, and a plastic bag containing change in his back pocket. The molding from one of the windows near the place then men had walked from had been removed and was lying on the ground beneath the window, and there were fresh scratches in the dust around the window and smudges on the glass. Evaluate the likelihood of success of the defense of abandonment if the men were prosecuted for attempted burglary. *See Thomas v. State*, 708 S.W.2d 861 (Tex. Ct. Crim. App. 1986).

B. Solicitation

Solicitation, as the word connotes, involves an "asking." Basically, asking someone else to do something that is criminal is the actus reus for the crime of solicitation. But "asking" is broadly defined. It need not be an explicit question. It does not even have to involve words, as a solicitation can be accomplished with gestures.

The response of the person being solicited is immaterial to whether the crime of solicitation occurred; the crime is complete once the solicitor entices, advises, incites, induces, urges, or otherwise invites another person to commit a crime so long as the requisite mental state is also present. The mens rea for the crime of solicitation is purpose. In other words, if the actor solicits someone with the specific intent or purpose that the other party engage in the crime, the crime of solicitation has occurred irrespective of the other person's response. However, nearly all U.S. jurisdictions do not allow someone to be convicted of both a criminal solicitation to commit a specific crime and a conspiracy to commit that crime. Thus, although a criminal solicitation occurs when someone asks another person to commit a crime with the requisite mens rea of purpose, a conviction is only proper if the other person refuses the solicitation. If the person agrees to the solicitation, then the crime of solicitation "evaporates" into the more serious crime of conspiracy, covered later in this chapter.

As with the other inchoate offenses, the common law and the Model Penal Code approach the crime of solicitation differently. At common law, it was only a crime to solicit someone to commit a felony or a misdemeanor that tended to breach the peace or to obstruct justice or otherwise to be injurious to the public welfare. The Model Penal Code, in contrast, punishes solicitation to commit any crime.

Some U.S. jurisdictions have adopted the Model Penal Code's formulation of the crime of solicitation and are therefore said to have general solicitation statutes. The majority of U.S. jurisdictions, however, specifically enumerate the target offenses a solicitation to which will qualify for criminal liability under their solicitation statutes.

Another difference between the common law approach to the crime and the Model Penal approach is whether the intended recipient of the solicitation must actually receive the solicitation. The common law would answer the question in the affirmative, while the Model Penal Code would answer it in the negative. But, as the following case illustrates, the common law's approach is the preferred one.

STATE of Oregon, Respondent, v. Delbert Floyd LEE, Appellant.
804 P.2d 1208 (Or. Ct. App. 1991).

Deits , J.

Defendant appeals his conviction for solicitation to commit robbery in the first degree. He argues that a letter that was not delivered can support, at most, a conviction for attempted solicitation.

In July, 1989, defendant, while in jail, wrote letters to an acquaintance who was in the Hillcrest Juvenile Center, outlining plans to rob a store and a residence. The letters were intercepted by Hillcrest personnel and never reached their intended recipient. The first intercepted letter stated:

> I wrote about two weeks ago. I guess you didn't get it. So, I'll tell you again. The job I got set up will get us some guns. On the other page is a picture of the place. And then I want to go to Washington. Okay.

The letter also described plans for robbing a store and burglarizing a residence. The other letter intercepted at Hillcrest also discussed plans for a "job." Defendant admitted that he wrote the letters. [But,] Defendant . . . contends that, because the letters were never received by the addressee, he did not commit the crime of solicitation, but only attempted solicitation. Solicitation is defined in ORS 161.435(1):

> A person commits the crime of solicitation if with the intent of causing another to engage in specific conduct constituting a crime punishable as a felony or as a Class A misdemeanor or an attempt to commit such felony or Class A misdemeanor the person commands or solicits such other person to engage in that conduct.

The statute contains two elements: mens rea and actus reus. Defendant was found by the trial court to have the specified state of mind. He argues, however, that the actus reus proved by the state was insufficient to support a conviction, because the intercepted letters do not constitute a completed solicitation.

The statute provides that a person is guilty of solicitation if that person "commands or solicits" another to engage in criminal conduct constituting a felony or a Class A misdemeanor. However, the terms "command" or "solicit" are not defined in the statute, and it is unclear whether they include circumstances where a communication is not received. Our function is to construe the statute to carry out the legislature's intent. The issue of an unreceived solicitation is not specifically discussed in the commentary to the statute. It is noted in the commentary, however, that the terms "request" and "encourage" were not included in the statute, because the drafters were concerned that such language might be "too open-ended."

It is also noted in the commentary that the word "solicits" was used "because it is an historic legal term that would carry with it the traditional limitations that are intended." At common law, solicitation probably required that the communication be completed:

> What if the solicitor's message never reaches the person intended to be solicit[ed], as where an intermediary fails to pass on the communication or the solicitor's letter is intercepted before it reaches the addressee? The act is nonetheless criminal, although it may be that the solicitor must be prosecuted for an attempt to solicit on such facts.

2 LaFave, SUBSTANTIVE CRIMINAL LAW 12, § 6.1 (1986).

Solicitation in the Oregon Penal Code was based, in part, on the Model Penal Code. Significantly, [however,] the legislature did not adopt the provision of the Model Penal Code that specifically provides that solicitation may be based on an incomplete communication. . . . We [therefore] conclude that a completed communication is required to prove the crime of solicitation. Accordingly, defendant's conviction for solicitation was error. [But, because an] attempt to solicit is necessarily included in the completed crime . . . no new trial is required.

Conviction for solicitation vacated; remanded with instructions to enter a judgment of conviction for attempted solicitation and for resentencing.

QUESTIONS

1.   Do you agree with the majority approach that a solicitation must be received in order for criminal liability to be imposed for the crime of solicitation? Why do you think the drafters of the Model Penal Code decided such receipt was not necessary?

2.   The defendant was adjudged to have committed the crime of attempted solicitation. Since solicitation boils down to asking someone else to commit a crime with the intent that the person solicited do so, what do you believe the logic behind attempted solicitation to be? Does such a crime make sense? Why or why not?

It should be emphasized that soliciting someone is its own offense. As a rule, a mere solicitation, unaccompanied by some acts moving directly toward the commission of the intended crime, does not qualify as a "substantial step" constituting the actus reus element for the crime of attempt. More simply put, merely soliciting someone one to commit a crime does not constitute a criminal attempt to commit the object crime.

Finally, as with the other inchoate offenses, abandonment and impossibility may be the defenses to the charge of solicitation. Just as with the crime of attempt, for abandonment to be a successful defense to the crime of solicitation, it must be complete, effective, and voluntary. Accordingly, the solicitor must prevent the crime solicited from occurring. Some jurisdictions require not only that the solicitor notify the person solicited that the crime should not be carried out, but also require the solicitor to notify law enforcement or make similar efforts to ensure the crime does not occur.

Similarly, as with the crime of attempt, true legal impossibility is a defense to solicitation. Thus, if a defendant encourages behavior that is, in fact, not a crime, a criminal solicitation has not occurred. This is true both at common law and under the Model Penal Code. Also as with the crime of attempt, however, factual impossibility is never a defense to the crime of solicitation. For example, it would not be a defense to an otherwise criminal solicitation that the person solicited is factually incapable of committing the particular offense, such as soliciting the rightful owner of property to "steal" property that rightfully belongs to him or her.

C. Facilitation

Solicitation and facilitation are often confused, perhaps because the two crimes can occur together. But they are separate and distinct criminal offenses. The crime of *facilitation* occurs when someone provides another person with either the means or the opportunity to commit a crime. Providing the means or opportunity for the commission of a crime (such as providing a weapon or drawing a map) is the actus reus for the crime of facilitation.

The mens rea for facilitation is knowledge. That means that in order for liability to be imposed for the crime of facilitation, a defendant must have actual or constructive knowledge that the person to whom they are providing the means and opportunity to commit a crime is actually committing or planning to commit the target offense. Without such knowledge that the other person is committing or plans to commit a crime, giving someone something that subsequently might be used during the commission of crime does not give rise to criminal liability for facilitation.

D. Complicity: Group Criminality, Accomplice Liability, and Post-Offense Charges

Complicity theory is the tool by which one is made legally accountable for the criminal acts of another. The two most frequent ways in which complicity theory operates is by imposing liability on the non-principal actor as an accomplice or co-conspirator. In this section, we will examine the ways in which complicity theory is used to hold someone liable as an accomplice, also known as an "accessory." But it should be noted there are ways, other than accessorial or conspiratorial liability, that one can be held liable for the criminal acts of another, such as via vicarious liability (as discussed in Chapter Two) or by knowing facilitation statutes (discussed above in the previous section). For example, in some U.S. jurisdictions, the crimes of solicitation and facilitation do not exist as separate penal offenses, but rather are included in the definition of an accomplice for the purposes of imposing accessorial liability.

An "*accomplice*" is a person, other than a peace officer acting in his or her official capacity within the scope of his or her authority and in the line of duty, who actually helps or attempts to help someone else with the specific intent (i.e., purpose) to promote or facilitate the commission of an offense. Unlike with conspiracy, which is an offense that punishes forming a crime-related agreement, accessorial liability requires that an accomplice actually give some aid to the principal – the one primarily responsible for the crime.

At the outset, there is a significant limitation on whom can be held liable as an accomplice that should be noted. Those who are "victims" of a crime or who take part in a crime that by its definition "takes two to tango" are not held liable under any theory of complicity. In other words, there is no accomplice liability to those who are incident to an offense; one who is a necessarily party to an offense by definition may not be held an as accessory to the crime. For example, the underage female who is the victim of a statutory rape cannot be charged as an accessory to the male's statutory rape of her, even if she "aided and abetted" him in the crime.

1. Actus Reus for Accessorial Liability

"*Aiding and abetting*" is the traditional way in which the actus reus for accessorial liability is described. The quantity or quality of the aid offered is not measured, nor is its success. Any form of giving aid, however minimal, can satisfy the actus reus requirement. The aid given does not even need to be effective. For example, if person A gives person B a gun to commit a murder, and person B winds up killing the intended victim with person B's own knife, A is still an accomplice to the homicide since actual aid was given by A, even though it was not effective aid.

Similarly, the aid given need not be affirmative aid, such as actually assisting the principal carry out the crime, for the actus reus requirement to be satisfied. Simply giving moral support, advice, or counsel can suffice. It can even be an omission when there is a legal duty to act. For example, a police officer who "turns the other cheek" while witnessing a fellow officer use unlawful force on a suspect becomes an accessory to the principal officer's assault and battery of the suspect. But *some* aid must be given. Mere presence at the scene of a crime, without more (such as a prior agreement with the principal to be at the scene to provide a false eyewitness account of what transpired, or to just provide moral support), is insufficient to qualify as the actus reus for accessorial liability. And this makes perfect logical sense, otherwise simply being at the wrong place at the wrong time could make anyone an accessory. Consider the following case.

John HICKS v. UNITED STATES of America
150 U.S. 442 (1893).

Mr. Justice Shiras delivered the opinion of the court.

In the circuit court of the United States for the western district of Arkansas, John Hicks, an Indian, was jointly indicted with Stand Rowe, also an Indian, for the murder of Andrew J. Colvard, a white man, by shooting him with a gun on the 13th of February, 1892. Rowe was killed by the officers in the attempt to arrest him, and Hicks was tried separately, and found guilty, in March, 1893. We adopt the statement of the facts in the case made in the brief for the government as correct, and as sufficient for our purposes:

It appears that on the night of the 12th of February, 1892, there was a dance at the house of Jim Rowe, in the Cherokee Nation; that Jim Rowe was a brother to Stand

104

Rowe, who was indicted jointly with the defendant; that a large number of men and women were in attendance; that the dance continued until near sunrise the morning of the 13th; that Stand Rowe and the defendant were engaged in what was called "scouting," viz. eluding the United States marshals who were in search of them with warrants for their arrest, and were armed for the purpose of resisting arrest. They appeared at the dance, each armed with a Winchester rifle. They were both Cherokee Indians. The deceased, Andrew J. Colvard, was a white man, who had married a Cherokee woman. He had been engaged in the mercantile business in the Cherokee country until a few months before the homicide. He came to the dance on horseback on the evening of the 12th. A good deal of whisky was drank during the night by the persons present, and Colvard appears to have been drunk at some time during the night. Colvard spoke Cherokee fluently, and appears to have been very friendly with Stand Rowe and the defendant, Hicks.

On the morning of the 13th, as the party were dispersing, Colvard invited Stand Rowe and Hicks to go home with him, and repeated frequently this invitation. Finally he offered as an inducement to Stand Rowe, if he would accompany him home, to give him a suit of clothes, and a hat and boots. The urgency of these invitations appears to have excited the suspicion of the defendant in error, who declared openly that if Colvard persisted in his effort to take Stand Rowe away with him he would shoot him.

Some time after sunrise on the morning of the 13th, about 7 o'clock, S.J. Christian, Benjamin F. Christian, Wm. J. Murphy, and Robert Murphy, all of whom had been at the dance the night before, and had seen there Colvard, Stand Rowe, and the defendant, were standing on the porch of the house of William J. Murphy, about 414 steps west from the house of Jim Rowe, and saw Stand Rowe, coming on horseback in a moderate walk, with his Winchester rifle lying down in front of him, down a "trail," which led into the main traveled road. Before Stand Rowe appeared in sight the men who were on the porch had heard a "whoop" in the direction from which Stand Rowe came, and this "whoop" was responded to by one from the main road in the direction of Jim Rowe's house. Stand Rowe halted within five or six feet of the main road, and the men on the porch saw Mr. Colvard and the defendant, Hicks, riding together down the main road from the direction of Jim Rowe's house.

As Colvard and Hicks approached the point where Stand Rowe was sitting on his horse, Stand Rowe rode out into the road and halted. Colvard then rode up to him in a lope or canter, leaving Hicks, the defendant, some 30 or 40 feet in his rear. The point where the three men were together on their horses was about 100 yards from where the four witnesses stood on the porch. The conversation between the three men on horseback was not fully heard by the four men on the porch, and all that was heard was not understood, because part of it was carried on in the Cherokee tongue; but some part of this conversation was distinctly heard and clearly understood by these witnesses. They saw Stand Rowe twice raise his rifle and aim it at Colvard, and twice he lowered it. They heard Colvard say, "I am a friend to both of you." They saw and heard the defendant, Hicks, laugh aloud when Rowe directed his rifle towards Colvard. They saw Hicks take off his hat, and hit his horse on the neck or shoulder with it. They heard Hicks say to Colvard, "Take off your hat, and die like a man." They saw Stand Rowe raise his rifle for the third time point it at Colvard, and fire it. They saw Colvard's horse wheel and run back in the direction of Jim Rowe's house, 115 or 116 steps. They saw Colvard fall from his horse. They went to where he was lying in the road, and found him dead. They saw Stand Rowe and John Hicks ride off together after the shooting.

Hicks testified in his own behalf, denying that he had encouraged Rowe to shoot Colvard, and alleging that he had endeavored to persuade Rowe not to shoot.

At the trial the government's evidence clearly disclosed that John Hicks, the accused, did not, as charged in the indictment, shoot the deceased, nor take any part in the physical struggle. To secure a conviction it hence became necessary to claim that the evidence showed such participation in the felonious shooting of the deceased as to make the accused an accessory, or that he so acted in aiding and abetting Rowe as to make him guilty as a principal. The prosecution relied on evidence tending to show that Rowe and Hicks cooperated in inducing Colvard to leave the house, where they and a number of others had passed the night in a drunken dance, and to accompany them up the road to the spot where the shooting took place. Evidence was likewise given by two or three men, who, from a house about 100 yards distant, were eyewitnesses of the occurrence, that the three men were seated on their horses a few feet apart; that Rowe twice raised his gun and aimed at Colvard; that Hicks was heard to laugh on both occasions; that Rowe thereupon withdrew his gun; that Hicks pulled off his hat, and, striking his horse with it, said to Colvard, "Pull off your hat, and die like a man"; that there-upon Rowe raised his gun a third time, and fired at Colvard, whose horse then ran some distance before Colvard fell. As the horse ran, Rowe fired a second time. When Colvard's body was subsequently examined, it was found that the first bullet had passed through his chest, inflicting a fatal wound, and that the second had not taken effect.

The language attributed to Hicks, and which he denied having used, cannot be said to have been entirely free from ambiguity. It was addressed, not to Rowe, but to Colvard. Hicks testified that Rowe was in a dangerous mood, and that he did not know whether he would shoot Colvard or Hicks. The remark made – if made – accompanied with the gesture of taking off his own hat, may have been an utterance of desperation, occasioned by his belief that Rowe would shoot one or both of them. That Hicks and Rowe rode off together after seeing Colvard fall was used as a fact against Hicks, pointing to a conspiracy between them. Hicks testified that he did it in fear of his life; that Rowe had demanded that he should show him the road which he wished to travel. Hicks further testified – and in this he was not contradicted – that he separated from Rowe a few minutes afterwards, on the first opportunity, and that he never afterwards had any intercourse with him, nor had he been in the company of Rowe for several weeks before the night of the fatal occurrence.

Two of the assignments of error are especially relied on by the counsel of the accused. One arises out of that portion of the charge wherein the judge sought to instruct the jury as to the evidence relied on as showing that Hicks aided and abetted Rowe in the commission of the crime. . . .

We agree with the counsel for the plaintiff in error in thinking that this instruction was erroneous in two particulars. It omitted to instruct the jury that the acts or words of encouragement and abetting must have been used by the accused with the intention of encouraging and abetting Rowe. So far as the instruction goes, the words may have been used for a different purpose, and yet have had the actual effect of inciting Rowe to commit the murderous act. Hicks, indeed, testified that the expressions used by him were intended to dissuade Rowe from shooting. But the jury were left to find Hicks guilty as a principal because the effect of his words may have had the result of encouraging Rowe to shoot, regardless of Hicks' intention. In another part of the charge the learned judge did make an observation as to the question of intention in the use of the words, saying:

> If the deliberate and intentional use of words was the effect to encourage one man to kill another, he who uttered these words is presumed by the law to have intended that effect, and is responsible therefor.

This statement is itself defective in confounding the intentional use of the words with the intention as respects the effect to be produced. Hicks no doubt intended to use the words he did use, but did he thereby intend that they were to be understood by Rowe as an encouragement to act? However this may be, we do not think this expression of the learned judge availed to cure the defect already noticed in his charge, that the mere use of certain words would suffice to warrant the jury in finding Hicks guilty, regardless of the intention with which they were used.

Another error is contained in that portion of the charge now under review, and that is the statement:

that, if Hicks was actually present at that place at the time of the firing by Stand Rowe, and he was there for the purpose of either aiding, abetting, advising, or encouraging the shooting of Andrew J. Colvard by Stand Rowe, and that, as a matter of fact, he did not do it, but was present for the purpose of aiding or abetting or advising or encouraging his shooting, but he did not do it because it was not necessary, it was done without his assistance, the law says there is a third condition where guilt is fastened to his act in that regard.

We understand this language to mean that where an accomplice is present for the purpose of aiding and abetting in a murder, but refrains from so aiding and abetting because it turned out not to be necessary for the accomplishment of the common purpose, he is equally guilty as if he had actively participated by words or acts of encouragement. Thus understood, the statement might, in some instances, be a correct instruction. Thus, if there had been evidence sufficient to show that there had been a previous conspiracy between Rowe and Hicks to waylay and kill Colvard, Hicks, if present at the time of the killing, would be guilty, even if it was found unnecessary for him to act. But the error of such an instruction, in the present case, is in the fact that there was no evidence on which to base it. The evidence, so far as we are permitted to notice it, as contained in the bills of exception and set forth in the charge, shows no facts from which the jury could have properly found that the rencounter was the result of any previous conspiracy or arrangement. The jury might well, therefore, have thought that they were following the court's instructions in finding the accused guilty because he was present at the time and place of the murder, although he contributed neither by word nor action to the crime, and although there was no substantial evidence of any conspiracy or prior arrangement between him and Rowe.

The judgment of the court below is reversed, and the cause remanded, with directions to set aside the verdict and award a new trial.

QUESTIONS

1. This case involves two complex theories of criminal liability: accessorial liability (complicity theory) and conspiratorial liability (conspiracy theory). What is the difference between the two?

2. As Justice Shiras discusses at some length in the case, it was Hicks having said, "Take off your hat and die like a man" that gave rise to his potential criminal liability. Hicks, however, is not the one who shot Colvard. Could his statement make him accessory, a co-conspirator, or both?

3. The case is remanded by the Supreme Court for a new trial because the jury instructions used in Hicks' trial were flawed. Upon retrial, how should the jury be instructed regarding accessorial liability? Conspiratorial liability?

4. Unless a defendant declares his or her intent to aid in the commission of a criminal offense, how do you think the prosecution can meet its burden in showing that a particular defended subjectively intended to assist another person in committing a crime?

5. If someone is an accomplice to one crime, but an unintended result occurs, should that person be deemed an accomplice to all crimes that wind up occurring? For example, suppose Hicks stumbled across Rowe "beating-up" Colvard at the dance. If Hicks interrupted by giving Rowe a two-by-four he saw off to the side so that Rowe could use it to continue beating-up Colvard, it is clear that Hicks would become an accessory to Rowe's assault and battery. But what if Colvard died from internal bleeding as a result of having been badly beaten? It was Hicks' intent to aid in the commission of an assault and battery; it was not his intent that Colvard die. Should Hicks nonetheless be deemed to be an accessory to a criminal homicide? Why or why not?

6. There is some question as to whether Hicks' "mere presence" at the scene is sufficient aid to justify imposing accessorial liability. Presume that Hicks had not said anything. Would his silent presence at the scene make him an accomplice? The Supreme Court answers that question by saying, "It depends." On what does the answer depend? Do you agree with the Court's criteria? Why?

7.   Does the fact that Hicks did more than merely be present change your view? After all, the defendant Rowe had twice raised his rifle, pointed it at Colvard, and did not shoot him. It was only after Hicks made the statement, "Take off your hat and die like a man" that Rowe fired on Colvard. Do you think, therefore, that Hicks' statement "aided" or "abetted" Rowe in the commission of the homicide? Is that enough to use complicity theory to impose accessorial liability on Hicks?

2. Mens Rea for Accessorial Liability

As stated above, the mens rea required to hold someone liable as an accomplice is purpose. That means the accomplice must have offered some aid, however minimal and regardless of its effectiveness, with the specific intent that the aid offered would facilitate the principal's commission of the target crime. Indifference to the outcome is not sufficient.

Generally speaking, the mens rea applies to the conduct element of the target offense. In other words, one who aids a principal in committing an actus reus for another crime is an accessory to that crime. There need not be any mens rea with respect to either the result elements or the attendant circumstance elements of a crime for accessorial liability to be imposed. For example, suppose X aids and abets his friend Y into having sexual intercourse with a girl under the age of consent, but did so without knowing that she was not of age. Y, of course, is guilty of statutory rape since it is a strict liability crime. But is X guilty as an accessory for aiding and abetting statutory rape? Yes, because he purposely aided and abetted the conduct element of the offense (i.e., encouraged the sexual intercourse). Since strict liability attaches to the attendant circumstance of the victim's age for the principal, it also attaches to the same attendant circumstance for the accomplice.

The same rationale applies with respect to the result element of a crime. Generally, a person who satisfies all the requirements for being an accomplice is an accomplice to all offenses committed by the principal that are the probable consequences of the offense aided. In other words, an accomplice is liable for all of the acts committed by the principal that are reasonably foreseeable in light of the aid given. Thus, so long as the accessory purposefully aided and abetted the conduct element of the principal's crime, the fact that a result occurred other than the one envisioned by the accessory is not relevant so long as it was reasonably foreseeable, as the next case demonstrates.

PEOPLE of the State of New York, Respondent, v. Mark D. ABBOTT, Appellant.
84 A.D.2d 11, 445 N.Y.S.2d 344 (N.Y. App. Div. 1981).

Schnepp, Justice.

The issue for determination is whether a participant in a high-speed automobile race on a public highway is subject to criminal liability when another participant's car is involved in an accident which results in the death of a third-person. The charges in this case arose from a two-car accident involving the vehicle of the defendant Mark D. Abbott. The occupants of the other car were killed.

It appears from the facts established at trial that at approximately 1:00 a.m. on January 19, 1980 defendant Paul T. Moon was traveling alone in his car in an easterly direction on Maple Road in the Town of Amherst when he became involved in a "drag race" with an automobile driven by Abbott. Maple Road, which traverses a residential area, is a four-lane highway with designated speed limits. Traffic is controlled by traffic control signal lights at various intersections. Spaced white lines divide the two eastbound and the two westbound lanes and double yellow lines spaced approximately four feet apart separate the eastbound and westbound lanes. Both Moon and Abbott were observed racing at very high rates of speed by the occupants of at least three other vehicles which were traveling along Maple Road at the time. At one point in particular Moon was observed trying to overtake Abbott's vehicle by crossing over the double yellow line and traveling in the westbound lane. An automobile driven by Patricia A. Hammond, which entered the intersection of Maple Road and Palmdale, was struck broadside by the

Abbott vehicle instantly killing Mrs. Hammond and her two passengers. Moon's vehicle fishtailed through the scene of the accident and avoided collision with the two vehicles. It was described as spinning in a full circle in all four lanes before it stopped facing in a westerly direction. Moon sat in his automobile for a short time until he backed up, made a U-turn and drove away.

Moon and Abbott were jointly indicted for three counts of manslaughter in the second degree in that they, "each being intentionally aided by the other, . . . recklessly caused the death of another person," three counts of criminally negligent homicide in that they, "each being intentionally aided by the other, . . . with criminal negligence, caused the death of another person," and other accident related offenses. Both defendants were acquitted of the manslaughter charges but were convicted of three counts of criminally negligent homicide (Penal Law, § 125.10), reckless driving (Vehicle and Traffic Law, § 1190), and other traffic violations.

The theory of the prosecution against Moon was that he intentionally aided Abbott to engage in the criminally negligent conduct which resulted in the deaths of the three victims. Moon claims that such a theory is "not logical" and that one must be liable by "one's own acts as a principal for criminally negligent homicide or not at all." He contends that his conduct was not of such a nature as to justify a conviction for criminally negligent homicide pursuant to section 20.00 of the Penal Law, which attaches criminal liability for the conduct of another. We disagree with this contention. A person is guilty of criminally negligent homicide under section 125.10 of the Penal Law when "with criminal negligence, he causes the death of another person." Under subdivision 4 of section 15.05 of the Penal Law, a person acts with criminal negligence with respect to a result or circumstance "when he fails to perceive a substantial and unjustifiable risk that such result will occur or that such circumstance exists. The risk must be of such nature and degree that the failure to perceive it constitutes a gross deviation from the standard of care that a reasonable person would observe in the situation." Section 20.00 of the Penal Law provides that when one person engages in conduct which constitutes an offense "another person is criminally liable for such conduct when, acting with the mental culpability required for the commission thereof, he . . . intentionally aids such a person to engage in such conduct."

What amounts to criminal negligence "depends, of course, entirely on the circumstances of the particular conduct. Whether in those circumstances the act or acts causing death involved a substantial and unjustifiable risk, and whether the failure to perceive it was such as to constitute a gross deviation from the standard of care which a reasonable man would have observed under the same circumstances, are questions that generally must be left directly to the trier of the facts. In other words, '[t]he tribunal must evaluate the actor's failure of perception and determine whether, under all the circumstances, it was serious enough to be condemned.'"

Criminal negligence refers to both a subjective state of mind and conduct involving "(1) 'a substantial and unjustifiable risk' that a result or circumstance described by a penal statute will occur or exists, as the case may be, and (2) 'a gross deviation' from the standard of conduct or of care that a reasonable person would observe." It is the combination of the defendant's conduct, that is, the creation of a certain type of risk, together with his mental state, namely his failure to perceive the risk when there is a legal duty of awareness, which constitutes criminal negligence.

A "drag race" involves two or more drivers engaged in a contest of speed with the use of their automobiles. When this activity occurs on a public highway there is an inherent danger of increasing the death-dealing potential of the automobile. The significance of this conduct should be apparent to anyone "who shares the community's general sense of right and wrong." It necessarily evinces a "failure to perceive a substantial and unjustifiable risk, constituting a 'gross deviation from the standard of care that a reasonable person would observe in the situation'" and it is "sufficient to sustain the conviction for criminally negligent homicide."

The statutory scheme permits accessorial liability to attach for criminally negligent homicide provided that the accessory shares the requisite culpable mental state for the crime and intentionally aids in its commission. While Moon did not personally control Abbott's vehicle which struck and killed the three victims, it could reasonably be found that he "intentionally" aided Abbott in the unlawful use of the vehicle by participating in a high-speed race, weaving in and out of traffic, and thus shared Abbott's culpability. Skid marks and other evidence at the scene of the accident permitted expert testimony that the pre-braking speed of Moon's automobile was 80 to 85 miles per hour and that the speed of Abbott's automobile immediately prior to the collision was 93.5 miles per hour. Moon associated himself with the high-speed race on a busy highway and took a part in it for nearly two minutes over a distance in excess of one mile. Actually his conduct made the race possible. He accepted Abbott's challenge and shared in the venture. Without Moon's aid Abbott could not have engaged in the high-speed race which culminated in the tragedy. The accident was "the culmination of a continuum of events" in which both defendant and Abbott participated.

Giving assistance or encouragement to one it is known will thereby engage in conduct dangerous to life should suffice for accomplice liability as to crimes defined in terms of recklessness or negligence. The evidence was, therefore, sufficient for the trier of fact to conclude beyond a reasonable doubt that Moon while acting with the culpable mental state of criminal negligence gave assistance or encouragement to Abbott to engage in conduct dangerous to life. This is sufficient to impose criminal liability.

QUESTIONS

1.   What level of mens rea did the court find Moon and Abbott to have entertained with respect to the conduct of drag racing? With respect to the result of their drag racing? Why are these two levels of mens rea different? Of what significance, if any, is the fact that they are different?

2.   Suppose that *X* gives *Y* his car keys, knowing *Y* is drunk, and *Y* is subsequently in a car accident that kills an innocent third party. *Y* would be liable for driving under the influence and for the homicide, mostly likely for involuntary manslaughter or vehicular homicide. Is *X* an accessory to *Y*'s drunk driving? Why or why not? Should *X* be held criminally liable as an accomplice to *Y*'s homicide? Explain your answer in light of the court's reasoning in *Abbott*.

3.   In both the *Abbott* case and in the hypothetical fact pattern in question # 2, having a rule that imposes liability for unforseen, but foreseeable results of purposeful conduct serves a "fairness" factor in the criminal law by avoiding disparate treatment between the principal and the accomplice. Do you agree the two should be treated in a similar fashion? Why or why not?

3. Guilt and Grading Difference Between Principal and Accomplice

At common law, accessorial liability was **derivative**, meaning that the guilt of the accessory was predicated on the guilt of the principal. But, this rule periodically resulted in a windfall for an accessory when the principal was acquitted on grounds not related to the criminality of the accessory, such as the minority or insanity of the principal, or if the principal died before trial. The Model Penal Code rectified this quirk of the common law by severing the derivative nature of an accomplice's liability and holding the accomplice liable based on his or her own actions and mens rea independent of those of the principal. Most U.S. jurisdictions have adopted the Model Code approach.

Because the guilt of the accessory was derivative at common law, an accessory could not be held liable for any felony more serious than those actually committed by the principal, even if the accessory's level of mens rea was higher than that of the principal (this rule did not apply to misdemeanors). For example, if someone killed another in the heat of passion upon a legally adequate provocation, that person would not be guilty of murder, but of voluntary manslaughter. But if the person was purposefully aided and abetted in the killing, the accessory aided and abetted a murder. The common law would not have allowed the accessory to be convicted of the more severe crime. The Model Penal Code, in contrast, would allow the different convictions, judging accessory and principal on each person's level of culpability independent from the other, as exemplified by the following case.

UNITED STATES of America, Appellant, v. Rayful EDMOND, III, Appellee.
924 F.2d 261 (D.C. 1991).

Randolph, Circuit Judge

On June 20, 1989, Rayful Edmond, III, Columbus Daniels, and twenty-seven others were named as defendants in a forty-three count, superceding indictment. The indictment charged the defendants with participating in a conspiracy to violate federal narcotics laws and with committing various drug-related offenses. Count 21, which is at the center of this appeal, charged Edmond and Daniels with first-degree murder while armed.

* * *

Daniels was tried first on Count 21. On June 21, 1990, the jury returned a special verdict, finding Daniels not guilty of first-degree murder while armed but guilty of the lesser included offense of second-degree murder while armed. This caused Edmond to move for a reduction of the murder charge against him to second-degree murder while armed, to the extent his responsibility rested on aiding and abetting Daniels. The court granted Edmond's motion . . . .

The district court reduced the charge against Edmond to second-degree murder on the ground that District of Columbia law does not permit an aider and abettor to "be tried for an offense greater than that committed by the principal." Daniels' acquittal of first-degree murder therefore relieved Edmond of liability for that offense.

Whether the district court ruled correctly turns on the meaning of D.C. Code § 22-105:

In prosecutions for any criminal offense all persons advising, inciting, or conniving at the offense, or aiding or abetting the principal offender, shall be charged as principals and not as accessories, the intent of this section being that as to all accessories before the fact the law heretofore applicable in cases of misdemeanors only shall apply to all crimes, whatever the punishment may be.

* * *

Standefer v. United States, 447 U.S. 10 (1980), held that a defendant accused of aiding and abetting the commission of a federal offense may be convicted despite the principal's acquittal of that offense. Early common law applied this rule to aiders and abettors of misdemeanors. A more complicated rule governed aiders and abettors of felonies. Principals in the second degree — that is, accessories who were actually or constructively present at the scene of the felony offense — were treated in the same manner as abettors of misdemeanors. Other accessories in felony cases, however, were treated differently. Their liability was considered derivative and their fate depended on the fate of the principals, who were required to be tried first. If the actual perpetrators were never tried, or were acquitted, or were pardoned after conviction, these accessories could not be held criminally liable for the offense. Early in this century, as part of a general reform movement, Congress adopted the common law misdemeanor rule for all federal offenses. The Supreme Court found that the predecessor of 18 U.S.C. § 2(a) had abolished the common law's misdemeanor-felony distinction by directing that whoever aided or abetted the commission of an offense "is a principal." 447 U.S. at 18. Under federal law, acquittal of the direct perpetrator thus became irrelevant in the accessory's prosecution.

Of particular importance to this case, the Court in *Standefer* supported its interpretation of the federal aiding and abetting statute by relying on D.C. Code § 22-105, which Congress passed in 1901. The federal and District of Columbia statutes, although enacted several years apart, were "part and parcel of [the] same reform movement," and both provisions contained language "unmistakably demonstrating" that accessories were to be treated as principals. 447 U.S. at 18.

Only a short time ago, we held that an aiding-and-abetting conviction pursuant to § 22-105 "may stand even where the principal is acquitted in a separate trial." *United States v. Richardson*, 817 F.2d 886, 888 (D.C. Cir. 1987). The proposition was so certain that we summarily rejected an argument against it, citing *Standefer* and *Murchison v. United States*, 486 A.2d 77, 81 (D.C. 1984), which affirmed the conviction of an aider and abettor despite the principal's mistrial.

We would be inclined to dispatch Edmond's argument in the same manner but for the intervening decision in *Morriss v. United States*, 554 A.2d 784 (D.C. 1989), and the significance the district court attributed to it. Morriss was tried for aiding and abetting the murder-for-hire of co-defendant Cole's husband. His role in the murder consisted in procuring the three gunmen Cole hired. In a joint trial, Morriss and Cole were convicted of second-degree murder. The court of appeals reversed Cole's conviction on the ground that a pretrial statement by Morriss, who did not testify, should not have been admitted against her.

Morriss' appeal presented a separate question. Morriss had defended on the basis that he thought Cole only wanted her husband beaten and that he, Morriss, did not know of her intention to have him murdered. Over Morriss' objection, the trial court instructed the jury that an aider and abettor need not intend the particular crime committed by the principal so long as the crime was the natural and probable consequence of his actions. The court of appeals sustained the instruction, rejecting Morriss' argument that an aider and abettor must share, or at least know of, the mens rea of the principal. Nevertheless, the court reversed Morriss' conviction and remanded so that he could be retried with Cole.

The reasoning behind this disposition seems to us rather obscure. Citing *Standefer*, the court of appeals stated that "even the acquittal of a principal does not preclude conviction of an aider and abettor," although the government must show that someone actually committed "the act constituting the offense." 554 A.2d at 790. But the court's reversal of Cole's conviction presented what it described as a "difficulty" with respect to Morriss' conviction. The "difficulty" appears to have been evidentiary in nature. After reciting that the "government's whole theory of Morriss' consequential liability depends upon his solicitation of the killers at [Cole's] behest" and her "participation in arranging for the slaying," the court concluded that Morriss' conviction could not "fairly stand in the wake of trial error in the conviction[] by the same jury of the primary participant[], . . . Cole." *Id.* At this point the court dropped a footnote acknowledging that Morriss' pretrial statement "provided an additional strand of evidence" against him but not Cole and stating that "this" may have been relevant in separate trials "or even in a joint trial where a jury convicted Morriss while acquitting Cole." 554 A.2d at 790 n.13. The footnote concluded, however, that the court could not "tell how the jury interrelated factors in determining the guilt of" Cole and Morriss. Morriss' pretrial statement recounted his connection with Cole and his understanding that Cole only wanted someone to "rough up" her husband. Perhaps the court thought the jury might somehow have misused Morriss' statement in finding him guilty. For example, suppose the jury first erroneously found Cole guilty in light of Morriss' pretrial statement and, using that improper finding, decided that Morriss was also guilty because Cole's actions were the "natural and probable consequence" of Morriss' assistance. The jury could have done this only by violating the instructions, but the court of appeals thought that such a violation might have occurred. If this was the court's thinking in Morriss, it explains why – as the footnote strongly suggests – the court would have sustained Morriss' conviction if he had been tried separately or if, in a
joint trial, Cole had been acquitted.

* * *

The district court's basic mistake was in thinking that, in view of the Daniels verdict, Edmond was being prosecuted for aiding and abetting a first-degree murder that never happened. That view is contrary to District of Columbia law. Whether there has been a first-degree murder remains to be determined – by the jury at Edmond's trial, where the government must prove this offense. This is the point of *Jefferson v. United States*, 558 A.2d 298 (D.C. 1989), *cert. denied*, 493 U.S. 1032 (1990), which the district court cited. *Jefferson* held that one "cannot be convicted of carrying a pistol without a license on an aiding and abetting theory where there is no proof that the person in actual possession of the pistol did not have a license to carry it." 558 A.2d at 303. *Jefferson* simply recognizes that in the abettor's trial, the government must prove the criminal act the defendant is accused of abetting.

The special verdict in Daniels' case is an entirely separate matter. The jury there decided only Daniels' culpability. Its verdict said nothing about Edmond or his alleged role in bringing about Terrell's death. Under § 22-105, Edmond must stand trial as a principal, which means that whether he is guilty and, if so, the degree of his offense, will depend entirely on what the government proves at his trial. That much has been settled in the District of Columbia since 1907.

* * *

The court's judgment reducing the charge against Edmond to second-degree murder while armed . . . are reversed and the case is remanded for further proceedings consistent with this opinion.

QUESTIONS

1.   The court applied local law patterned after the Model Penal Code. What should the result of Edmond's case have been if the common law rules had been applicable in the jurisdiction? Why?

2.   Do you think it is fair to allow someone who aids and abets another to commit a crime to be punished more severely than the principal criminal actor? Why? Under what circumstances, if any, should the law punish an accessory more severely than a principal?

3.   The court stated that "in the abettor's trial, the government must prove the criminal act the defendant is accused of abetting." Although a correct statement of the law, what should be done with an accomplice in circumstances where the principal is acquitted on the basis of some justification, such as acting in self-defense? Suppose, for example, two friends get into a heated argument with a third person. Further suppose the third person unlawfully attacks one of the friends, and the other friend yells, "for God's sake, kill the bastard before he kills you." If the person acting is self-defense is acquitted of all homicide charges on those grounds, should there be any criminal liability for the friend who encouraged the killing? Why or why not?

---

4. The Defense of Abandonment

Both the common law and Model Penal Code recognize the defense of abandonment for aiding and abetting. As with the other inchoate offenses, the abandonment must be effective, complete, and voluntary. But in order to be deemed both effective and complete after one has given aid to another with the intention that a crime be committed, the accessory must take three steps under the common law approach. First, the accessory must inform the principal that the offense should not be committed. Second, the accessory must do everything possible to render all prior aid ineffective. And third, the accessory must accomplish this before it is too late to prevent the offense.

The Model Penal Code requirements for satisfying the effective and complete elements of the defense are even more stringent. The same three criteria the common law required must be satisfied, but in rendering all prior aid ineffective, the Model Penal Code imposes a duty on the accomplice to either (a) give timely warning to law enforcement authorities; or (b) otherwise make a "proper effort" to prevent the commission of the offense, a standard which is not clarified by the Code.

5. Accessories After-the-Fact and Obstruction of Justice

As defined at common law, an *accessory after the fact* was any person who harbored, concealed, or otherwise aided an offender, knowing or having reasonable grounds to believe (i.e., no willful blindness allowed) the offender had committed a *felony*. Further, the aid given with such knowledge had to be given with the specific intent that the offender avoid or escape arrest, trial, or punishment. Under this definition, if one did not actually or constructively know someone had committed a felony, harboring or concealing that person would not have made the person providing the aid an accessory after the fact.

The common law made an exception to the accessory after the fact rule for spouses stemming from the old common law theory of marital unity (i.e., that the two were one). A spouse aiding a husband or a wife did not have choose between breaking the marital unity and being an accessory after the fact for helping the spouse.

Under the Model Penal Code and the modern, majority view, the specific category of being an accessory after the fact has been abolished. *See* Model Penal Code and Commentaries § 2.06, comment 1 (1985). Accordingly, many U.S. jurisdictions treat such behavior as obstruction of justice, applying to all types of crimes, not just felonies. Most jurisdictions following the modern rule, although not all of them, do not exclude spouses from liability the way the common law did. Thus, today, a spouse can be held liable for obstruction of justice in the prosecution of his or her spouse. A handful of U.S. jurisdictions have even expanded the common law spousal exemption to include parent-child relationships.

Regardless of whom can be convicted of the crime in light of their relationship to the principal actor(s), obstruction of justice is a broad crime today. It encompasses not only the common law definition of an accessory after the fact (today often referred to as harboring or concealing), but also other acts. Examine the following statute from the state of New Jersey, modeled after the Model Penal Code, as an example:

N.J.S.A. § 2C:29-3. Hindering apprehension or prosecution

a. A person commits an offense if, with purpose to hinder the apprehension, prosecution, conviction or punishment of another for an offense he:
    (1) Harbors or conceals the other;
    (2) Provides or aids in providing a weapon, money, transportation, disguise or other means of avoiding discovery or apprehension or effecting escape;
    (3) Suppresses, by way of concealment or destruction, any evidence of the crime, or tampers with a witness, informant, document or other source of information, regardless of its admissibility in evidence, which might aid in the discovery or apprehension of such person or in the lodging of a charge against him;
    (4) Warns the other of impending discovery or apprehension, except that this paragraph does not apply to a warning given in connection with an effort to bring another into compliance with law;
    (5) Prevents or obstructs, by means of force, intimidation or deception, anyone from performing an act which might aid in the discovery or apprehension of such person or in the lodging of a charge against him;
    (6) Aids such person to protect or expeditiously profit from an advantage derived from such crime; or
    (7) Volunteers false information to a law enforcement officer.

There are other crimes that obstruct justice that are often punished as separate offense, such as perjury, defined as the giving of a false sworn statement in regard to a material issue, believing it to be false; taking the identity of another person; falsely incriminating another person; filing a false police report; impersonating a public servant; resisting arrest (even if unlawful); and unlawful flight from an officer of the law, also known as "eluding."

Given the rather broad nature of the conduct that may qualify as the actus reus for the crime of obstruction of justice, it should come as no surprise that applying the particularized statutory definitions to facts of particular cases is often challenging, as the following case illustrates.

COMMONWEALTH of Pennsylvania, Appellant, v. John Raymond NECKERAUER, Jr.
617 A.2d 1281 (Pa. Super. Ct. App. Div. 1992).

Ford Elliott, Judge.

The Commonwealth appeals from the October 19, 1990 Order granting John R. Neckerauer, Jr.'s Omnibus Pretrial Motion to Quash Information/Petition For Writ of Habeas Corpus and dismissing the charges. Mr. Neckerauer, appellee, had been charged with obstructing administration of law or other governmental function (18 Pa. C.S.A. § 5101), tampering with or fabricating physical evidence (18 Pa. C.S.A. § 4910), [and] hindering apprehension or prosecution (18 Pa. C.S.A. § 5105(a)(3, 5)). . . .

This case resulted from a Pennsylvania State Police investigation of the disappearance of Ada J. Groomes from Scottdale, Pennsylvania, in October 1988. According to the preliminary hearing testimony of Trooper Hill, the State Police contacted many people and conducted interviews. Donald and Ada Groomes owned a 1976 Dodge motor home which Mr. Groomes reported missing on October 26, 1988. Mrs. Groomes was believed to be missing on October 7, 1988, and the motor home was believed to be missing about one day prior to her disappearance. It was very important to locate the motor home because it might provide evidence as a crime scene or provide information as to the whereabouts of Mrs. Groomes. The police used several methods to locate the missing motor home including the dissemination of fliers with a photo of Mrs. Groomes and of the motor home, and the news media was also contacted.

Police initially talked to appellee by telephone regarding the motor home and Mrs. Groomes' disappearance in early November of 1988. Trooper Hill inquired about a garage rental in Uniontown, and they discussed the two one-hundred dollar bills with the name Bud written on them found in Mr. Groomes' truck; appellee's nickname is Bud. Trooper Hill spoke with appellee again in May 1989 at his residence and in the presence of his girlfriend, Linda Gettemy, regarding Mrs. Groomes and the motor home. Both denied having any knowledge of the location of the woman or the motor home.

Appellee told Trooper Hill that he was familiar with the motor home since Mr. Groomes parked it in his driveway and lived in it on one occasion when Mr. Groomes left his wife. Based upon information from Mr. Groomes, appellee and his girlfriend told the trooper they believed that Mrs. Groomes was driving the motor home out in Arizona because she had joined some kind of a cult.

At the preliminary hearing, Trooper Taylor testified that, in October 1989, a Mr. Lofstead, from Tampa, Florida, indicated that he was in possession of the motor home involved in the Groomes case. Mr. Lofstead informed the trooper that appellee had driven the motor home to his property and told him that the motor home was being stored there for a friend entangled in a divorce dispute and that the friend did not want his wife to have access to the motor home. After Trooper Taylor obtained information that the motor home on Lofstead's property was in fact the Groomes' motor home, he immediately received a call from appellee explaining that he had been in possession of the motor home and had been given the motor home by Mr. Groomes to use two days prior to the disappearance of Mrs. Groomes. Appellee also stated that he was aware of the location of the motor home since that time. Appellee told Trooper Taylor that prior to bringing the motor home to Florida, he had taken the motor home to Virginia where he was working on a construction site. Trooper Taylor asked appellee why he had not apprised Trooper Hill of the location of the motor home when Hill interviewed him earlier, and appellee responded that Hill had never specifically asked him about the motor home, only about Mrs. Groomes' disappearance.

Trooper Craig also testified at the preliminary hearing that he continued the investigation to Williamsburg, Virginia, where he talked to several people. During an interview, Mr. Shaulis, told the trooper that he worked as a mechanic at the job site where appellee was working. Mr. Shaulis became acquainted with appellee in May of 1988 and he saw appellee with the motor home in October of 1988. Appellee's girlfriend, Ms. Gettemy, was also present on two occasions with the motor home. The trooper proceeded to Fair Oaks Campgrounds in Williamsburg where he spoke with a Ms. Rigleman who informed him that, based on her documents, appellee stored a twenty-six foot Diplomat motor home at the campground from November 19, 1988, until March 23, 1989. Upon contacting Mr. Lofstead in Florida by telephone, Trooper Craig was told that appellee transported the motor home to Lofstead's residence on March 27, 1989. None of the Pennsylvania troopers who testified at the preliminary hearing went to look at the motor home after it was found, and, when the motor home was processed by the Hillsborough Sheriff's Department in Florida, they found no evidence of a crime. Mrs. Groomes has not been located.

The magistrate determined that the Commonwealth had presented sufficient evidence to show that appellee and Linda Gettemy willfully concealed evidence knowing that it was the focal point in a police investigation, and that a prima facie case had been established on the charges filed against the defendants. Appellee then filed the omnibus pretrial motion to quash information/habeas corpus petition which was granted by the trial court . . .and the Commonwealth appealed the dismissal of the charges.

Initially, the Commonwealth submits that providing false answers in response to questions by law enforcement officials is conduct constituting the crime of hindering apprehension or prosecution in violation of 18 Pa. C.S.A. § 5105(a)(5), which states:

> (a) Offense defined. person commits an offense if, with intent to hinder the apprehension, prosecution, conviction or punishment of another for crime, ... (5) volunteers false information to a law enforcement officer.

The Commonwealth argues that since false information regarding the location of the motor home was provided by appellee in response to Trooper Hill's questions, that a crime has been made out under the statute.

The Commonwealth disagrees with this court's recent . . . dismissal of the charges against appellee's girlfriend, Linda Gettemy. In that case, we were presented with an issue of first impression and the Commonwealth raises the very same legal question today. Ms. Gettemy argued that section 5105(a)(5) did not apply in her case because she did not volunteer the false information to the police as prohibited by the statute. We agreed with this contention and found it necessary to consider the legislative intent to ascertain exactly what conduct was contemplated and proscribed by section 5105(a)(5). Our analysis began with the definition of the term "to volunteer" and we stated, "[T]o offer (oneself or one's services) for some undertaking or purpose; . . . to give, bestow, or perform without being asked . . . ; to say, tell, or communicate voluntarily. . . . THE RANDOM HOUSE DICTIONARY OF THE ENGLISH LANGUAGE (1981).

We further noted that the courts of New Jersey were faced with this exact issue in *State v. D'Addario*, 482 A.2d 961 (N.J. 1984). The New Jersey Superior Court stated that this definition, particularly the emphasized language, supports the conclusion that the meaning of 'volunteer' as used in N.J.S.A. 2C:29-3a(7), is that the accused must take the initiative in giving false information. We point out that the wording of the New Jersey statute is identical to that of the Pennsylvania statute, as both statutes are derived from the Model Penal Code. The court in *D'Addario*, stated that the statute applied only to those persons who take the initiative in supplying false information to law enforcement officials.

Recognizing that we are not bound by the decisions of a sister state, we, nevertheless find the reasoning of the New Jersey Court to be persuasive. The facts of the instant case make it clear that Appellee did not take the initiative in supplying false information to the law enforcement officers. Her answers, misleading as they were, were given in response to the officers questions.

Additionally, the Official Comment to 18 Pa. C.S. § 5105 states that this section is derived from Section 242.3 of the Model Penal Code. The comment to this section provides: "Paragraph (5) prohibits volunteering false information to the law enforcement authorities. Mere failure to report a crime is not proscribed by this section. Neither is giving misleading or even false answers to inquiries initiated by the police. . . ." This provision is intended to reach those who take the initiative in throwing the police off track. We concluded that providing fallacious statements in response to questions initiated by law enforcement officers does not constitute the type of conduct defined as hindering apprehension or prosecution under 5105.

Appellee also cites the New Jersey supreme court case *State v. Valentin*, 519 A.2d 322 (N.J. 1987), which upheld the rationale promulgated in *D'Addario*, as the leading case on providing false answers in response to police questions. The Commonwealth argues that appellee's reliance on these cases is misplaced. The Commonwealth believes that a grave injustice would be done to police investigations if this court continues to follow these cases, and that law enforcement would be without any means to pursue persons who deliberately provide police with false statements. The Commonwealth further contends that . . . [this policy] does not carry out the public policy of this state to deter individuals from hindering apprehension or prosecution, and [thereby] permits persons who hinder apprehension to avoid being prosecuted due to a technicality. We do not agree.

We are aware that words of a statute must be construed according to their plain meaning. *Commonwealth v. Reeb*, 593 A.2d 853 (Pa. Super. Ct. 1991). However, the word volunteer is ambiguous and capable of more than one meaning. Penal statutes must be strictly construed in favor of the accused.

The Commentary to section 242.3 of the Model Penal Code, expounding upon its reasoning as to why giving false answers to police initiated inquiries did not constitute hindering prosecution or apprehension, stated:

> This solution represents a delicate policy judgment, premised in part on the fear that a wider reach for this subsection would invite abusive charges by police against persons interviewed in the course of investigating crime. It should be borne in mind that the law provides a means of compelling testimony under oath and that a penal policy with respect to unsworn false statements to the police has been carefully developed in Section 241.3 (unsworn falsification to authorities) and Section 241.5 (false reports to law enforcement authorities) of the Model Code. Paragraph (5) of this offense proscribes only the borderline case of volunteered misinformation to the police, which is not covered elsewhere.

Section 5105(a)(5) was enacted to preclude a very specific type of conduct that was not covered by other statutes. We will not enlarge the scope of this statute to reach conduct that our legislators did not intend to prohibit in enacting this particular statute.

Despite the very narrow interpretation of the hindering apprehension or prosecution statute by the Commentators to the Model Penal Code, Pennsylvania adopted the Model Penal Code's version of this statute almost verbatim and duly noted in the Official Comment to section 5105 that it is derived from section 242.3 of the Model Penal Code.

* * *

The statute defining tampering with or fabricating physical evidence states . . . :

> A person commits a misdemeanor of the second degree if, believing that an official proceeding or investigation is pending or about to be instituted, he: (1) alters, destroys, conceals or removes any record, document or thing with intent to impair its verity or availability in such proceeding or investigation; . . . .

18 Pa. C.S.A. § 4910(1).

The Official Comment to this statute indicates that it is derived from section 241.7 of the Model Penal Code which refers to this crime as a form of obstruction of justice. The commentary to the Model Penal Code emphasizes that the prosecution must demonstrate that the actor believed that an official proceeding or investigation was pending or about to be instituted. Elaborating further, the comment states:

Paragraph (1) punishes one who 'alters, destroys, conceals or removes.'.... The range of items protected against tampering includes 'any record, document or thing.'.... The limiting factor in Paragraph (a) is the requirement of specific intent. The statute punishes any kind of tampering with any document or thing, but only if the defendant acts 'with purpose to impair its verity or availability' in an official proceeding or investigation.

Model Penal Code § 241.7.

The Commonwealth asserts that the record in the case contains a number of indications that appellee knew where the motor home was located, and that he was aware of the pending investigation based upon the contact he had with the police. Trooper Hill testified at the preliminary hearing that he initially spoke with appellee on November 2, 1988, by telephone. The trooper informed appellee that he was trying to locate or obtain information concerning Mrs. Groomes and the motor home. During the conversation, Trooper Hill also talked to appellee about a garage rental in Uniontown and the one-hundred dollar bills found in Mr. Groomes' truck with the name "Bud" written on them. Appellee had not provided Trooper Hill with any information regarding Mrs. Groomes or the motor home during this particular conversation even though he was in possession of the motor home or knew where it was located. Trooper Craig testified at the preliminary hearing, and his investigation revealed, that appellee proceeded to Fair Oaks Campground in Williamsburg, Virginia, where he signed documents on November 19, 1988, to store a Diplomat motor home there which was picked up on March 23, 1989.

Contrary to the trial court's findings, the evidence presented was sufficient to establish a prima facie case that appellee tampered with physical evidence. Based upon the testimony at the preliminary hearing, it is apparent, or it can at least be inferred, that when the police initially questioned him by phone that appellee knew a police investigation was pending or about to be instituted. Appellee shortly thereafter removed the motor home from Pennsylvania and had it stored in Virginia and then in Florida, knowing that it was the focus of a police investigation. These facts are sufficient to infer that appellee possessed the requisite specific intent to conceal the motor home and impair its availability in a police investigation.

Appellee was also accused of obstructing administration of law or other governmental function set forth at 18 Pa. C.S.A. § 5101 which provides:

A person commits a misdemeanor of the second degree if he intentionally obstructs, impairs or perverts the administration of law or other governmental function by force, violence, physical interference or obstacle, breach of official duty, or any other unlawful act, except that this section does not apply to flight by a person charged with crime, refusal to submit to arrest, failure to perform a legal duty other than an official duty, or any other means of avoiding compliance with law without affirmative interference with governmental functions.

This section was also substantially based upon the Model Penal Code section 242.1. . . . [T]he provision requires that the actor have a conscious objective to engage in the conduct proscribed by the offense. Section 242.1 further requires that the obstruction actually take place. Preparatory, incomplete, and equivocal conduct is excluded from the offense. The generality of the crime has been confined by limiting its application to (i) violent or physical interference, (ii) breach of official duty, and (iii) any other act that is unlawful independently of a purpose to obstruct the government. Model Penal Code § 242.1.

The Commonwealth argues that appellee's conduct is clearly prohibited by the obstruction statute. As previously stated, appellee, after being informed on November 2, 1988, that the police were investigating the disappearance of Mrs. Groomes and the motor home, appellee promptly removed the motor home and took it to Virginia on November 19, 1988, for storage. Appellee's behavior demonstrates his conscious purpose to obstruct the police investigation. From November 1988 until October 1989, appellee engaged in a course of concealing physical evidence sought in an official investigation thereby obstructing justice. Although appellee did not use force or violence to accomplish this deed, sufficient prima facie evidence was presented at the preliminary hearing to show that appellee unlawfully tampered with physical evidence. Such activity would come within the reach of the obstruction statute which only requires that a person "intentionally obstructs, impairs or perverts the administration of law or other governmental function by force . . . or any other unlawful act . . . ." 18 Pa. C.S.A. § 5101 (emphasis added). Based on this evidence, a prima facie case had been established and appellee was properly bound over for trial.

QUESTIONS

1.   The result in *Neckerauer* turned on the court's interpretation of the word "volunteers" in the phrase "volunteers false information to a law enforcement officer." The court pointed out its duty to strictly construe language in the light most favorable to the accused, an doctrine of statutory interpretation that has its roots in due process concerns with the principle of legality. If the court had decided such a narrow construction of "volunteers" was not required (i.e., it found that giving false information to the police regardless of who approached whom), do you think the principle of legality or any other due process concerns would be violated? Explain your response using the material from Chapter One.

2.   In his classic text *The Limits of the Criminal Sanction* (1968), Herbert Packer explained one of the tensions inherent in our criminal justice system as being between the perception of what the substantive and procedural rules of the criminal law ought to be. On one hand, in what he dubbed the **Crime Control Model**, the criminal law has as its main focus the repression of criminal conduct. Laws prescribe norms. Punishments focuses on incapacitation, deterrence, and retribution. In contrast, the **Due Process Model** emphasizes the protection of individual rights. It asserts that granting too much leeway to law enforcement officials will result in losses of rights and freedoms. Careful consideration of each case, with multiple layers of checks and balances to guard against the infringement of individual rights and liberties, even at the expense of speedy processing of offenders, is emphasized. Punishment focuses on rehabilitation. Which of Packer's two models appears to be a part of the rationale underlying the court's decision in *Neckerauer*? Explain your reasoning.

3.   Just because the conduct at issue in *Neckerauer* was determined not to be obstruction of justice via hindering prosecution clearly did not mean that Mr. Neckerauer would not be criminally prosecuted for misleading the police. The court found that there were sufficient facts to justify trial on both tampering with evidence and obstruction of justice charges. Do you think that Mr. Neckerauer's actions should result in charges of "unsworn falsification to authorities" being brought against him?

===

E. Conspiracy

Conspiracy is a rather odd crime because it punishes what boils down to basically a mental offense. A conspiracy is nothing more than an agreement – a meeting of the minds – with wrongful intent. The object of the agreement must be the commission of an unlawful act, or the commission of a lawful act by illegal means. If two or more people make such an agreement, a conspiracy has occurred.

1. Actus Reus for Conspiracy: Bilateral v. Unilateral Agreements

The actus reus for the crime of conspiracy is making the actual agreement. It need not be an express agreement; it can be implied. And all of the details of a conspiracy need not be known for liability to be imposed. It is sufficient that was a meeting of the minds with the requisite criminal intent.

At common law, for a conspiracy to occur, there had to be a bona-fide agreement between two or more people. This was known as a bilateral conspiracy. While some jurisdictions hold on to this common law view that a conspiracy necessarily "takes two to tango," many jurisdictions have adopted the Model Penal Code's view on **unilateral conspiracies**. This approach allows a conviction for a conspiracy if one party *thinks* there is an agreement, even though the other party did not so agree. The reasons for adopting this approach and the application of it are illustrated by the following case.

Shirley GARCIA, Defendant-Appellant v. STATE of Indiana, Plaintiff-Appellee.
394 N.E.2d 106 (Ind. 1979).

Prentice, Justice.

Defendant was convicted in a trial by jury of conspiracy to commit murder and sentenced to twenty years imprisonment. Her sentence was suspended and she was placed on five years probation. On appeal she raises the following issue[]: Whether the defendant can be convicted of conspiracy when the only person with whom the defendant conspired was a police informant who only feigned his acquiescence in the scheme. . . .

The evidence introduced at trial consisted of the following: On September 30, 1977, State's witness, Allen Young, was first contacted by the defendant with regard to certain marital problems that she was having. She stated that her husband constantly beat her and her children and that she "couldn't take it any longer" that she wanted her husband killed. Young suggested that she go to the police or see an attorney, but she refused, stating that to do so would only make matters worse. Young then mentioned the sum of $5000.00 in an attempt to discourage her. She responded that the amount was out of the question and ended the conversation. Young testified that he had not taken the defendant seriously at that point, because he thought that she was simply upset and needed to "blow off steam."

Young received a second call from the defendant on October 4, 1977. During this conversation, the defendant said that she had $200 in cash and wanted to know whether he had found anyone to kill her husband. Young responded that he did not think he could help her since he did not know anyone who was in that line of "business." She asked him to look around anyway. Young testified that, although he did not directly promise to find someone for her, he probably left her with the impression that he would do so. Shortly after talking with the defendant, Young went to the Whiting Police Department and discussed the matter with two detectives. He offered to call the defendant and let them listen and record the conversation, which they did. During that conversation, Young again asked the defendant if she wanted him to help her find someone to kill her husband, and she responded affirmatively. Young replied that he would try to find someone.

Several more conversations took place between the defendant and Young. On each occasion the defendant reaffirmed her desire to have her husband killed, and she rejected the idea of going to the police instead. At their final meeting, Young, accompanied by a plain-clothed detective, introduced the defendant to the detective, stating that here was a man who might be willing to do the job. The defendant then produced $200, a picture of her husband, and a record of his daily habits and gave them to the detective. She agreed to pay the balance of the contract price when the "job" was completed. Defendant was subsequently arrested. At trial, Young testified that he only feigned his acquiescence in the plan and at no time did he intend to actually carry it out.

The issue is whether the conspiracy section of our new penal code adopts the Model Penal Code's "unilateral" concept or whether it retains the traditional "bilateral" concept. . . . The bilateral concept is the traditional view of conspiracy as derived from common law. It is formulated in terms of two or more persons agreeing to commit a crime, each with intent to do so. In cases where the person or persons with whom the defendant conspired only feigned his acquiescence in the plan, the courts have generally held that neither person could be convicted of conspiracy because there was no "conspiratorial agreement."

Reacting to criticism of this viewpoint, the drafters of the Model Penal Code, though not without internal disagreement, adopted a "unilateral" concept, as follows:

Section 5.03. Criminal Conspiracy.

(1)   Definition of conspiracy. A person is guilty of conspiracy with another person or persons to commit a crime if with the purpose of promoting or facilitating its commission he:

   (a)   agrees with such other person or persons that they or one or more of them will engage in conduct which constitutes such crime or an attempt or solicitation to commit such crime; or

   (b)   agrees to aid such other person or persons in the planning or commission of such crime or of an attempt or solicitation to commit such crime."

Section 5.04. Incapacity, Irresponsibility or Immunity of Party to Solicitation or Conspiracy.

(1)   Except as provided in Subsection (2) of this Section, it is immaterial to the liability of a person who solicits or conspires with another to commit a crime that:

   (a)   he or the person whom he solicits or with whom he conspires does not occupy a particular position or have a particular characteristic which is an element of such crime, if he believes that one of them does; or

   (b)   the person whom he solicits or with whom he conspires is irresponsible or has an immunity to prosecution or conviction for the commission of the crime.

In explanation of their new approach, the Drafters of the Model Penal Code commented:

First: Unilateral Approach of the Draft. The definition of the Draft departs from the traditional view of conspiracy as an entirely bilateral or multilateral relationship, the view inherent in the standard formulation cast in terms of "two or more persons" agreeing or combining to commit a crime. Attention is directed instead to each individual's culpability by framing the definition in terms of the conduct which suffices to establish the liability of any given actor, rather than the conduct of a group of which he is charged to be a part an approach which in this comment we have designated unilateral. "One consequence of this approach is to make it immaterial to the guilt of a conspirator whose culpability has been established that the person or all of the persons with whom he conspired have not been or cannot be convicted. Present law frequently holds otherwise, reasoning from the definition of conspiracy as an agreement between two or more persons that there must be at least two guilty conspirators or none. The problem arises in a number of contexts.

        Second: Where the person with whom the defendant conspired secretly intends not to go through with the plan. In these cases it is generally held that neither party can be convicted because there was no "agreement" between two persons. Under the unilateral approach of the Draft, the culpable party's guilt would not be affected by the fact that the other party's agreement was feigned. He has conspired, within the meaning of the definition, in the belief that the other party was with him; apart from the issue of entrapment often presented in such cases, his culpability is not decreased by the other's secret intention. True enough, the project's chances of success have not been increased by the agreement; indeed, its doom may have been sealed by this turn of events. But the major basis of conspiratorial liability the unequivocal evidence of a firm purpose to commit a crime remains the same. The result would be the same under the Draft if the only co-conspirator established a defense of renunciation under Section 5.03(6). While both the Advisory Committee and the Council support the Draft upon this point, it should be noted that the Council vote was 14-11, the dissenting members deeming mutual agreement on the part of two or more essential to the concept of conspiracy.

Model Penal Code § 5.03, Comments at pp. 104-105.

        The adopted statute [in our state] is similar in all respects relevant herein to the final draft proposed by the Criminal Law Study Commission. The comments accompanying that draft state that the present law is not sought to be changed, and defendant's position is that the Legislature did not adopt the unilateral concept in the act under which she was tried and convicted.

        We are unable to determine with certainty what the commission intended by this comment, i.e., whether the enactment would merely restate the definition, without changing the result, or whether the law relative to the offense, except for the elimination of enumerated defenses, would remain unchanged. If the former was intended by the commenter, it can only be viewed as a mental lapse and proofreading

121

oversight; as it is clear upon the face of the act that defenses available under the multilateral concept were to be eliminated. The inclusion of the "catch-all" sub-proviso (5) can leave no doubt. Clearly "any reason," as recited therein, includes the absence of criminal culpability on the part of a co-conspirator including a sole co-conspirator. The words "agrees" and "agreement" have not been used as words of art denoting a "meeting of the minds" and "contract." Rather, the former is descriptive of the defendant's state of mind at the time he communicated with another in furtherance of the felony; and the latter refers to the defendant's understanding.

Defendant has cited us to numerous cases supporting the bilateral concept requiring "concurrence of sentiment and cooperative conduct in the unlawful and criminal enterprise"; however, those cases were not decided under statutes remotely similar to our own. She has distinguished those cases upholding the unilateral concept upon the basis of better articulated legislative commentary or differences in the wording of the statute under attack which we do not perceive to be material. For example, the Minnesota statute (Minn. St. 609.175, subd, 2) reads: "Whoever conspires with another" whereas our own refers to agreeing with another. Her argument that, by definition, an agreement requires the concurrence of sentiment of at least two individuals could be applied with even greater logic to the Minnesota statute and its use of the word "conspires." It is not persuasive in the light of the express wording of the entire enactment. . . . We find no reversible error. . . . Affirmed.

QUESTIONS

1.   The situation presented in *Garcia* is frequently referred to as the "feigned acquaintances" issue. If someone pretends to agree, but is not actually agreeing with the requisite intent, the common law would hold no conspiracy was formed. But, as the *Garcia* case illustrates, the Model Penal Code's approach to unilateral conspiracies allows a conviction under such circumstances. Some of the rationale for this approach is summarized in the case. What do you think of this approach to the crime of conspiracy? Why? What loopholes of the common law does this approach close?

2.   Suppose person *X* agrees to rob a bank with person *Y*. Both people enter into the agreement with the purpose of carrying out the offense. Unbeknownst to person *X*, however, *Y* is legally insane, believing that by robbing the bank, world hunger will end. If *X* and *Y* are arrested and charged with conspiracy to commit bank robbery and *Y* is acquitted on the grounds of *Y*'s insanity, what should happen to *X* under the common law approach to the crime of conspiracy? Under the Model Penal Code approach? Which approach is more fair, in your opinion? Why?

2. Actus Reus for Conspiracy: Necessary Parties and the Wharton Rule

Because conspiracy punishes the act of agreeing with criminal intent, it is a separate crime from the target offense. Thus, a conspiracy to commit an offense and the subsequent commission of that crime (or attempt to commit that crime) normally do not merge into a single punishable act. This means one may be convicted of conspiracy to commit crime *X* as well as crime *X*, presuming the object crime is committed, or attempted to commit crime *X* if the conspirators try, but fail to commit the object crime. The rationale for punishing conspiracy as its own offense is set for in *Iannelli v. United States*, reproduced below. Before considering *Iannelli*, however, you should know there is an exception that does merge a conspiracy and its target offense into one crime under a doctrine of somewhat limited application known as the ***Wharton Rule***.

Simply put, the Wharton Rule preclude a conviction for conspiracy to commit an offense which, but its nature, requires a concert of action between two people in conspiracy as part of the substantive offense. The crimes of dueling, adultery, fornication, consensual sodomy, and drag-racing are all good examples of offenses to which the Wharton Rule would apply because all of them *necessarily* include a concert of action between two people for the substantive offenses to take place. One cannot duel oneself or commit adultery alone.

The rationale for the Wharton Rule is that a charge of conspiracy involves no additional element unless someone else (i.e., a third party) is involved besides the two persons whose agreement to jointly act is part of the very definition of the substantive crime. Once someone else participates, however, the rationale for the Wharton Rule is inapplicable. Thus, when a conspiracy involves the cooperation of a greater number of persons than is required for commission of the substantive offense, the Wharton Rule will not bar convictions for both conspiracy to commit the crime and the actual crime (or its attempt, when applicable). With these principles in mind, consider the following case.

<hr>

IANNELLI, et al., v. UNITED STATES of America.
420 U.S. 770 (1975).

Mr. Justice Powell delivered the opinion of the Court.

This case requires the Court to consider Wharton's Rule, a doctrine of criminal law enunciating an exception to the general principle that a conspiracy and the substantive offense that is its immediate end are discrete crimes for which separate sanctions may be imposed.

I

Petitioners were tried under a six-count indictment alleging a variety of federal gambling offenses. Each of the eight petitioners . . . was charged with conspiring to violate and [actually] violating 18 U. S. C. § 1955, a federal gambling statute making it a crime for five or more persons to conduct, finance, manage, supervise, direct, or own a gambling business prohibited by state law. Each petitioner was convicted of both offenses, and each was sentenced under both the substantive and conspiracy counts. The Court of Appeals for the Third Circuit affirmed, finding that a recognized exception to Wharton's Rule permitted prosecution and punishment for both offenses, 477 F.2d 999 (3d Cir. 1973). We granted certiorari to resolve the conflicts caused by the federal courts' disparate approaches to the application of Wharton's Rule. For the reasons now to be stated, we affirm.

II

Wharton's Rule owes its name to Francis Wharton, whose treatise on criminal law identified the doctrine and its fundamental rationale:

> When to the idea of an offense plurality of agents is logically necessary, conspiracy, which assumes the voluntary accession of a person to a crime of such a character that it is aggravated by a plurality of agents, cannot be maintained. . . . In other words, when the law says, 'a combination between two persons to effect a particular end shall be called, if the end be effected, by a certain name,' it is not lawful for the prosecution to call it by some other name; and when the law says, such an offense – e.g., adultery – shall have a certain punishment, it is not lawful for the prosecution to evade this limitation by indicting the offense as conspiracy.

2 F. WHARTON, Criminal Law § 1604, p. 1862 (12th ed. 1932).

The Rule has been applied by numerous courts, state and federal alike. It also has been recognized by this Court, although we have had no previous occasion carefully to analyze its justification and proper role in federal law.

The classic formulation of Wharton's Rule requires that the conspiracy indictment be dismissed before trial. Wharton's description of the Rule indicates that, where it is applicable, an indictment for conspiracy "cannot be maintained," a conclusion echoed by . . . statements of this Court as well, *see Gebardi v. United States*, 287 U.S. 112, 122 (1932). Federal courts earlier adhered to this literal interpretation and thus sustained demurrers to conspiracy indictments . . . [but], [m]ore recently, . . . some federal courts have differed over whether Wharton's Rule requires initial dismissal of the conspiracy indictment . . . [holding instead] . . . that the Rule's purposes can be served equally effectively by permitting the prosecution to charge both offenses and instructing the jury that a conviction for the substantive offense necessarily precludes conviction for the conspiracy.

Federal courts likewise have disagreed as to the proper application of the recognized "third-party exception," which renders Wharton's Rule inapplicable when the conspiracy involves the cooperation of a greater number of persons than is required or commission of the substantive offense. *See Gebardi*, 287 U.S. at 122 n.6. In the present case, the Third Circuit concluded that the third-party exception permitted prosecution because the conspiracy involved more than the five persons required to commit the substantive offense, 477 F.2d 999, a view shared by the Second Circuit, *United States v. Becker*, 461 F.2d 230, 234 (1972), *vacated and remanded on other grounds*, 417 U.S. 903 (1974). The Seventh Circuit reached the opposite result, however, reasoning that since § 1955 also covers gambling activities involving more than five persons, the third-party exception is inapplicable. *United States v. Hunter*, 478 F.2d 1019, cert. denied, 414 U.S. 857 (1973). . . . The Courts of Appeals are at odds even over the fundamental question whether Wharton's Rule ever applies to a charge for conspiracy to violate § 1955.

III

Traditionally the law has considered conspiracy and the completed substantive offense to be separate crimes. Conspiracy is an inchoate offense, the essence of which is an agreement to commit an unlawful act. Unlike some crimes that arise in a single transaction, the conspiracy to commit an offense and the subsequent commission of that crime normally do not merge into a single punishable act. Thus, it is well recognized that in most cases separate sentences can be imposed for the conspiracy to do an act and for the subsequent accomplishment of that end.

The consistent rationale of this long line of decisions rests on the very nature of the crime of conspiracy. This Court repeatedly has recognized that a conspiracy poses distinct dangers quite apart from those of the substantive offense.

> This settled principle derives from the reason of things in dealing with socially reprehensible conduct: collective criminal agreement – partnership in crime – presents a greater potential threat to the public than individual delicts. Concerted action both increases the likelihood that the criminal object will be successfully attained and decreases the probability that the individuals involved will depart from their path of criminality. Group association for criminal purposes often, if not normally, makes possible the attainment of ends more complex than those which one criminal could accomplish. Nor is the danger of a conspiratorial group limited to the particular end toward which it has embarked. Combination in crime makes more likely the commission of crimes unrelated to the original purpose for which the group was formed. In sum, the danger which a conspiracy generates is not confined to the substantive offense which is the immediate aim of the enterprise. *Callanan v. United States*, 364 U.S. 587, 593-94 (1961).

The historical difference between the conspiracy and its end has led this Court consistently to attribute to Congress "a tacit purpose – in the absence of any inconsistent expression – to maintain a long-established distinction between offenses essentially different; a distinction whose practical importance in the criminal law is not easily overestimated." *Callanan*, 364 U.S. at 594. Wharton's Rule announces an exception to this general principle.

The Rule traces its origin to the decision of the Pennsylvania Supreme Court in *Shannon v. Commonwealth*, 14 Pa. 226 (1850), a case in which the court ordered dismissal of an indictment alleging conspiracy to commit adultery that was brought after the State had failed to obtain conviction for the substantive offense. Prominent among the concerns voiced in the Shannon opinion is the possibility that the State could force the defendant to undergo subsequent prosecution for a lesser offense after failing to prove the greater. The Shannon court's holding reflects this concern, stating that "where concert is a constituent part of the act to be done, as it is in fornication and adultery, a party acquitted of the major cannot be indicted of the minor." *Id.*, at 227-228.

Wharton's treatise first reported the case as one based on principles of double jeopardy, see F. WHARTON, CRIMINAL LAW 198 (2d ed. 1852), and indicated that it was limited to that context. Subsequently, however, Wharton came to view the principle as one of broader application. The seventh edition of Wharton's treatise reported the more general rule which is repeated in similar form today.

This Court's previous discussions of Wharton's Rule have not elaborated upon its precise role in federal law. In most instances, the Court simply has identified the Rule and described it in terms similar to those used in Wharton's treatise. But in *United States v. Holte*, 236 U.S. 140 (1915), the sole case in which the Court felt compelled specifically to consider the applicability of Wharton's Rule, it declined to adopt an expansive definition of its scope. In that case, Wharton's Rule was advanced as a bar to prosecution of a female for conspiracy to violate the Mann Act. Rejecting that contention, the Court adopted a narrow construction of the Rule that focuses on the statutory requirements of the substantive offense rather than the evidence offered to prove those elements at trial:

> The substantive offence might be committed without the woman's consent, for instance, if she were drugged or taken by force. Therefore the decisions that it is impossible to turn the concurrence necessary to effect certain crimes such as bigamy or dueling into a conspiracy to commit them do not apply.

This Court's prior decisions indicate that the broadly formulated Wharton's Rule does not rest on principles of double jeopardy, *see Pereira v. United States*, 347 U.S. 1, 11 (1954). Instead, it has current vitality only as a judicial presumption, to be applied in the absence of legislative intent to the contrary. The classic Wharton's Rule offenses – adultery, incest, bigamy, dueling – are crimes that are characterized by the general congruence of the agreement and the completed substantive offense. The parties to the agreement are the only persons who participate in commission of the substantive offense, and the immediate consequences of the crime rest on the parties themselves rather than on society at large. *See United States v. Bobo*, 477 F.2d 974, 987 (4th Cir. 1973). Finally, the agreement that attends the substantive offense does not appear likely to pose the distinct kinds of threats to society that the law of conspiracy seeks to avert. It cannot, for example, readily be assumed that an agreement to commit an offense of this nature will produce agreements to engage in a more general pattern of conduct.

The conduct proscribed by § 1955 is significantly different from the offenses to which the Rule traditionally has been applied. Unlike the consequences of the classic Wharton's Rule offenses, the harm attendant upon the commission of the substantive offense is not restricted to the parties to the agreement. Large-scale gambling activities seek to elicit the participation of additional persons – the bettors – who are parties neither to the conspiracy nor to the substantive offense that results from it. Moreover, the parties prosecuted for the conspiracy need not be the same persons who are prosecuted for commission of the substantive offense. An endeavor as complex as a large-scale gambling enterprise might involve persons who have played appreciably different roles, and whose level of culpability varies significantly. It might, therefore, be appropriate to prosecute the owners and organizers of large-scale gambling operations both for the conspiracy and for the substantive offense but to prosecute the lesser participants only for the substantive offense. Nor can it fairly be maintained that agreements to enter into large-scale gambling activities are not likely to generate additional agreements to engage in other criminal endeavors.

Wharton's Rule applies only to offenses that require concerted criminal activity, a plurality of criminal agents. In such cases, a closer relationship exists between the conspiracy and the substantive offense because both require collective criminal activity. The substantive offense therefore presents some of the same threats that the law of conspiracy normally is thought to guard against, and it cannot automatically be assumed that the Legislature intended the conspiracy and the substantive offense to remain as discrete crimes upon consummation of the latter. Thus, absent legislative intent to the contrary, the Rule supports a presumption that the two merge when the substantive offense is proved.

But a legal principle commands less respect when extended beyond the logic that supports it. In this case, the significant differences in characteristics and consequences of the kinds of offenses that gave rise to Wharton's Rule and the activities proscribed by § 1955 counsel against attributing significant weight to the presumption the Rule erects. More important, as the Rule is essentially an aid to the determination of legislative intent, it must defer to a discernible legislative judgment. We turn now to that inquiry.

IV

The basic purpose of the Organized Crime Control Act of 1970 was "to seek the eradication of organized crime in the United States by strengthening the legal tools in the evidence-gathering process, by establishing new penal prohibitions, and by providing enhanced sanctions and new remedies to deal with the unlawful activities of those engaged in organized crime." The content of the Act reflects the dedication with which the Legislature pursued this purpose. In addition to enacting provisions to facilitate the discovery and proof of organized criminal activities, Congress passed a number of relatively severe penalty provisions. . . .

Major gambling activities were a principal focus of congressional concern. Large-scale gambling enterprises were seen to be both a substantive evil and a source of funds for other criminal conduct. Title VIII thus was enacted to give the Federal Government a new substantive weapon, a weapon which will strike at organized crime's principal source of revenue: illegal gambling. In addition to declaring that certain gambling activities violate federal as well as state law, 18 U. S. C. § 1955, Title VIII provides new penalties for conspiracies to obstruct state law enforcement efforts for the purpose of facilitating the conduct of these activities. 18 U. S. C. § 1511.

In drafting the Organized Crime Control Act of 1970, Congress manifested its clear awareness of the distinct nature of a conspiracy and the substantive offenses that might constitute its immediate end. The identification of "special offenders" in Title X speaks both to persons who commit specific felonies during the course of a pattern of criminal activity and to those who enter into conspiracies to engage in patterns of criminal conduct. 18 U. S. C. § 3575 (e). And Congress specifically utilized the law of conspiracy to discourage organized crime's corruption of state and local officials for the purpose of facilitating gambling enterprises. 18 U. S. C. § 1511.

But the § 1955 definition of "gambling activities" pointedly avoids reference to conspiracy or to agreement, the essential element of conspiracy. Moreover, the limited § 1955 definition is repeated in identifying the reach of § 1511, a provision that specifically prohibits conspiracies. Viewed in this context, and in light of the numerous references to conspiracies throughout the extensive consideration of the Organized Crime Control Act, we think that the limited congressional definition of "gambling activities" in § 1955 is significant. The Act is a carefully crafted piece of legislation. Had Congress intended to foreclose the possibility of prosecuting conspiracy offenses under § 371 by merging them into prosecutions under § 1955, we think it would have so indicated explicitly. It chose instead to define the substantive offense punished by § 1955 in a manner that fails specifically to invoke the concerns which underlie the law of conspiracy.

Nor do we find merit to the argument that the congressional requirement of participation of "five or more persons" as an element of the substantive offense under § 1955 represents a legislative attempt to merge the conspiracy and the substantive offense into a single crime. The history of the Act instead reveals that this requirement was designed to restrict federal intervention to cases in which federal interests are substantially implicated. The findings accompanying Title VIII would appear to support the assertion of federal jurisdiction over all illegal gambling activities. Congress did not, however, choose to exercise its power to the fullest. Recognizing that gambling activities normally are matters of state concern, Congress indicated a desire to extend federal criminal jurisdiction to reach only "those who are engaged in an illicit gambling business of major proportions." S. Rep. No. 91-617, p. 73 (1969). It accordingly conditioned the application of § 1955 on a finding that the gambling activities involve five or more persons and that they remain substantially in operation in excess of 30 days or attain gross revenues of $ 2,000 in a single day. 18 U.S.C. § 1955 (b)(1)(iii). Thus the requirement of "concerted activity" in § 1955 reflects no more than a concern to avoid federal prosecution of small-scale gambling activities which pose a limited threat to federal interests and normally can be combated effectively by local law enforcement efforts.

Viewed in the context of this legislation, there simply is no basis for relying on a presumption to reach a result so plainly at odds with congressional intent. We think it evident that Congress intended to retain each offense as an "independent curb" available for use in the strategy against organized crime.

Gore v. United States, 357 U.S. 386, 389 (1958). We conclude, therefore, that the history and structure of the Organized Crime Control Act of 1970 manifest a clear and unmistakable legislative judgment that more than outweighs any presumption of merger between the conspiracy to violate § 1955 and the consummation of that substantive offense. Affirmed.

Mr. Justice Douglas, dissenting.

The eight petitioners in this case were tried, along with other codefendants, on a multiple-count indictment alleging the commission of various offenses in connection with gambling activities. Petitioners were convicted both of participating in an "illegal gambling business," and of conspiring to commit that offense. On both statutory and constitutional grounds, I would hold that the simultaneous convictions under both statutes cannot stand.

I

In my view the Double Jeopardy Clause forbids simultaneous prosecution under §§ 1955 and 371. Wharton's Rule in its original formulation was rooted in the double jeopardy concern of avoiding multiple prosecutions. *Carter v. McClaughry*, 183 U.S. 365, 394-395 (1902), and later cases confine the double jeopardy protection to prohibiting cumulative punishment of offenses that are absolutely identical, but I would not extend those cases so as to permit both convictions in this case to stand.

The evidence against petitioners consisted largely of conversations that involved gambling transactions. The Government's theory of the case was that petitioner Iannelli was the central figure in the enterprise who, through other employees or agents, received bets, arranged payoffs, and parceled out commissions. The evidence established, in the Government's view, "syndicated gambling," the kind of activity proscribed by § 1955. The very same evidence was relied upon to establish the conspiracy – a conspiracy, apparently, enduring as long as the substantive offense continued, and provable by the same acts that established the violation of § 1955. Thus the very same transactions among the defendants gave rise to criminal liability under both statutes.

Under these circumstances, I would require the prosecutor to choose between § 371 and § 1955 as the instrument for criminal punishment. . . . To permit this kind of multiple prosecution is to place in the hands of the Government an arbitrary power to increase punishment. . . .

II

Apart from my views of the Double Jeopardy Clause, I would reverse on the additional ground that Congress did not intend to permit simultaneous convictions under §§ 371 and 1955 for the same acts. The rule that a conspiracy remains separable from the completed crime, thus permitting simultaneous conviction for both, rests on the assumption that the act of conspiring presents special dangers the Legislature did not address in defining the substantive crime and that are not adequately checked by its prosecution. But the rule of separability is one of construction only, an aid to discerning legislative intent. Wharton's Rule teaches that where the substantive crime itself is aimed at the evils traditionally addressed by the law of conspiracy, separability should not be found unless the clearest legislative statement demands it. In my view this case fits the rationale of Wharton's Rule, and there is no legislative statement justifying the inference that Congress intended to permit multiple convictions.

Title 18 U. S. C. § 1955, which creates the substantive offense, is aimed at a particular form of concerted activity. The provision was added by the Organized Crime Control Act of 1970. This statute, as its title indicates, was directed at criminal activity carried out by large organizations, described by Congress as hierarchical in structure and as having their own system of law and independent enforcement institutions. Most of the Act was devoted to altering the powers and procedures of law enforcement institutions to deal with existing offenses. Only a few provisions added new prohibitions of primary conduct. Among these was Title VIII, which appears under the heading "Syndicated Gambling." Section 1955, included in Title VIII, prohibits participation in an "illegal gambling business," which is defined as one involving at least five persons who "conduct, finance, manage, supervise, direct, or own all or part of" the enterprise. Congress thought that federal law enforcement resources would be used to combat large enterprises, "so continuous and so substantial as to be a matter of national concern."

Conviction under § 1955 satisfies, in my view, the social concerns that punishment for conspiracy is supposed to address. The provision was aimed not at the single unlawful wager but at "syndicated gambling." Congress viewed this activity as harmful because on such a scale it was thought to facilitate other forms of illicit activity, one of the reasons traditionally advanced for the separate prosecution of conspiracies. Where § 1955 has been violated, the elements of conspiracy will almost invariably be found. The enterprises to which Congress was referring in § 1955 cannot, as a practical matter, be created and perpetuated without the agreement and coordination that characterize conspiracy. Section 1955 is thus most sensibly viewed as a statute directed at conspiracy in a particular context.

All this the majority seems to concede when it acknowledges a "presumption that the two [crimes] merge when the substantive offense is proved." But the majority concludes that simultaneous conviction is authorized because it is not "explicitly excluded." The majority thus implicitly concedes that the statute is silent on the matter of simultaneous conviction. To infer from silence an intention to permit multiple punishment is, I think, a departure from the "presupposition of our law to resolve doubts in the enforcement of a penal code against the imposition of a harsher punishment," *Bell v. United States*, 349 U.S. 81, 83 (1955). I would adhere to that principle, which is but a specific application of the "ancient rule that a criminal statute is to be strictly construed," *Callanan v. United States*, 364 U.S. 587, 602 (1961) (Stewart, J., dissenting).

* * *

Conspiracy, if charged in a § 1955 prosecution, should be charged as a preparatory offense that merges with the completed crime, and considered by the jury only if it first acquits the defendant of the § 1955 charge. The trial judge did allude to this use of the conspiracy charge, and he did suggest that the jury might defer consideration of the conspiracy count until after deliberation of the § 1955 charge. But that was only a suggestion; the instructions permitted convictions on both charges. The error cannot be corrected merely by vacating the sentences on the conspiracy count; it requires a new trial. We so held in *Milanovich v. United States*, 365 U.S. 551 (1961), where the trial judge had permitted the jury to convict the defendant both of larceny and of receiving stolen goods. We held that simultaneous conviction of both offenses was impermissible and that the proper remedy was a new trial: "[There] is no way of knowing whether a properly instructed jury would have found the wife guilty of larceny or of receiving (or, conceivably, of neither)." *Id.*, at 555.

I would accordingly reverse these convictions.

QUESTIONS

1.   The Wharton Rule would be unnecessary if conspiracy were not treated as a separately punishable offense from the crimes that are the objects of the conspiracy. The rationale for conspiracy being so punished is set forth in *Iannelli*. Do you find this rationale persuasive? Why or why not? Include in your critique a discussion of the relevant material from philosophy and sociology in Chapter One dealing with crime and punishment.

2.   Statutory interpretation is not easy. And, often, reasonable minds can differ of the meanings of words, especially when considering what words were included in a statute, and what words were not. Given your knowledge of the Wharton Rule after reading the history and rationale for it in *Iannelli*, do you think the majority or the dissent got it "right" with respect to the Rule's application to the statute at issue in the case? Why?

3.   The Supreme Court cited *Gebardi v. United States*, 287 U.S. 112 (1932). In that case, the defendants were an unmarried man and woman. They traveled from one state to another and had sex in violation of the Mann Act which made it a crime for a man to transport a woman across state line for "immoral purposes." The Mann Act, however, did not make it a crime for the woman to consent to

this. By its terms, therefore, the Mann act punished the male doing the transporting, not the woman being transported. Both the man and the woman, however, were charged with conspiracy to violate the Mann Act in *Gebardi*. How do you think the court should have ruled on the legality of their conspiracy conviction in light of the Wharton Rule? Explain your reasoning.

4.   Suppose the facts of *Gebardi* were different. Suppose the man and the woman did not have the funds to engage in interstate travel and they asked a friend for help to do so. If this friend purchased train tickets the two with the intent that they would travel to several states in violation of the Mann Act, what charges could be brought against the three actors? Why?

3. Distinguishing The Number and Types of Conspiracies

One of the more difficult issues surrounding the crime of conspiracy is the type of conspiracy that has been formed. In a simple conspiracy, and handful of people agree to do something illegal and then carry out their plan together. For example, if two men conspire to rob a bank, then there is a singular conspiracy to commit bank robbery. If three or four people had been a part of this simple conspiracy, the result would still be that there is one singular conspiracy to commit bank robbery; the only thing that has changed in the number of co-conspirators.

But what if two, three, or four people conspired to commit three separate crimes, say bank robbery, murder, and sexual assault? How many conspiracies are there? Just one, even though the singular conspiracy has three target offenses. The rule is that when two or more people enter into a conspiracy to commit several crimes, there is only one conspiracy, not several conspiracies. *See Braverman v. United States*, 317 U.S. 49 (1942). The rational behind such a rule is that conspiracy punishes agreement, not individual criminal acts which, of course, are punished separately.

Many conspiracies, however, are far more complicated that the conspiracies described in the last two paragraphs. Conspiracies can be quite large and may involve many people who do not even know the identities of the other people who are a part of the conspiracy. The extent of the knowledge, and the degree of interdependence on each other will determine the type of conspiracy that is deemed to exist.

You might be asking yourself why the number and size of conspiracies makes a difference. The answer is quite simple. In any given conspiracy, each co-conspirator is potentially criminally liable for the acts of the co-conspirators. Thus, the more people that can be connected to a large conspiracy, the more charges can be brought against each defendant. This serves several important goals in terms of the administration of the criminal justice system. First, it often gives prosecutors the ability to try many defendants together in a single trial, rather than relitigating the same evidence over and over again in multiple trials. Second, the more charges that can be made to "stick" against each co-conspirator, the longer the potential sentence terms might be, thereby increasing public safety via incapacitation of criminal conspirators. And third, plea bargaining agreements for the minor players in a conspiracy often allow for the dropping of many charges against such defendants in exchange for cooperation in prosecuting the central figures in large criminal conspiracies. While the fairness of such practices is open to debate from both an ethical and legal standpoint, traditional wisdom holds that letting the little fish off lighter to catch the big fish is a worthwhile venture. Moreover, as co-conspirators in a single, large conspiracy, the hearsay rule is not applicable with respect to any one co-conspirator's testimony with respect to what another co-conspirator said. *See* Fed. R. Evid. 801(d)(2)(E).

In a **wheel conspiracy**, there is generally one person (or a small group of people) in the "hub" or center of the wheel. A number of different and unrelated persons (or groups) form separate agreements with those in the hub. When this occurs, there is not one large conspiracy, but several smaller conspiracies between the people in the hub or center of the wheel and the people at the end of each spoke. An organized crime hypothetical provides an excellent example of this type of conspiracy. In the center or hub would be the leader of the organized crime syndicate. Those in the hub might enter into several illegal ventures with separate groups of people: a prostitution ring in Dallas; a drug import and distribution business in Miami; fixed gambling operations in a casino in Las Vegas; a construction contracting company in New York who obtains its contracts illegally; and so on. The people at the end of each spoke of the wheel have conspired with those at the hub, but not necessarily with any of the people who are at the end of a different spoke. Each spoke would represent a separate conspiracy from each other, unless there were a way to "connect" the spokes to form a true wheel.

In order to connect the spokes in a wheel conspiracy, it must be shown that there is not only knowledge of the criminal enterprise at the end of another spoke, but some form of interdependence between those at the end of each spoke to be connected. Thus, when a group of people are related to each other only through their mutual agreements with those in the hub, proof of knowledge of a comprehensive conspiracy is necessary to treat it as one, large. Without such proof, the agreements remain separate, smaller conspiracies. In the organized crime example above, the success of the illegal gambling operation in Las Vegas presumably has nothing to do with the success of the contracting venture in New York. Connecting the two spokes to form a larger conspiracy would be difficult.

In contrast, the other major type of conspiracy is known as the *chain or ladder conspiracy*. Each person in the chain is a link whereby one agrees with another who in turn agrees with another, and so on and so on. It is possible for lots of small conspiracies to exist this way, but it is more likely that persons in the chain are interdependent on each other, making for one big conspiracy. Drug conspiracies frequently operate in this way. At one end of the chain or ladder is the grower. The grower conspires with processors, who in turn conspire with exporters. The exporters conspire with importers who then conspire with distributors. Distributors, in turn, conspire with local dealers who then sell the drugs to the end users. Each person in the chain is dependent upon everyone else in the chain in order for the entire conspiracy to be successful. When this occurs, one large conspiracy is formed, not a number of smaller conspiracies. The following case illustrates the distinction between the two main types of conspiracies.

UNITED STATES of America, Appellee, v. Eugene R. ROSNOW, et al., Appellants.
977 F.2d 399 (8th Cir. 1992).

Per Curiam.

Several defendants challenge their convictions on thirty-four counts arising from conduct relating to filing false tax forms with the Internal Revenue Service (IRS). All of the defendants . . . were convicted of conspiracy to file false IRS forms. 18 U.S.C. § 371 (1988). . . .

BACKGROUND

IRS form 1099 is an informational form used to report to the IRS income or other compensation paid to a non-employee, such as a sub-contractor. The information contained in forms 1099 may be communicated to the IRS through the use of a single summary and transmittal form 1096. The defendants allegedly filed these forms in an effort to cause tax problems for individuals involved in repossessing real estate and other property belonging to defendants following the latter's default on various loans. The victims included creditors, attorneys, judges, sheriffs, law enforcement officials and IRS agents. Frequently, the defendants would mail copies of the forms 1099 to the individuals referenced on the forms as well as the IRS. Except for Juanita Dewey, each of the defendants charged with filing false forms 1096 or 1099 with the IRS submitted forms claiming to have paid out more than $ 4million to the [other defendants].

Most of the defendants are relatively uneducated farmers residing in the same geographic region in northwest Minnesota. It is a point of contention as to how they first became involved in this scheme. The plan was created by unindicted co-conspirators Roger Elvick, Natalie Telemaque and Ron Knutt, who are acquainted with Juanita Dewey. Several defendants indicated that they learned of the scheme through a book published by Elvick entitled "The Redemption Package." Others claim to have learned of the scheme through various newspaper and magazine articles. Elvick, Telemaque and Knutt were convicted in a separate trial in North Dakota. As indicated above, the defendants apparently sought a measure of revenge against those individuals who they believed had committed wrongs against them. As a result of the filings, some of the victims received audit letters from the IRS, and some incurred attorney's fees. Additionally, the IRS found it necessary to instigate new manual procedures and hire new employees to check the veracity of the incoming forms.

IRS officials first became suspicious of the defendants' actions after noticing that an inordinate number of forms stated "request denied" in the space for the referenced individual's social security number. Between February of 1989 and January of 1990, officials at the Kansas City IRS Service Center intercepted forms containing this notation and began forwarding these forms to the criminal investigation unit. After checking the reported payments against the referenced individuals' reported income (usually reported in forms 1040), IRS officials discovered the amounts reported by defendants did not comport with the income reported by the individuals referred to on the forms. A criminal investigation ensued and IRS officials came to believe that the payments or unpaid debts reported by defendants were fictitious.

In March of 1990, law enforcement officers executed search warrants for the residences of six of the defendants who were thought to have sent false forms. At the condominium shared by Juanita Dewey and Melford Haugen, located in Detroit Lakes, Minnesota, a two and one-half hour search yielded a calendar indicating Dewey's acquaintance with several other defendants, correspondence between Dewey and several defendants, IRS forms, court transcripts pertaining to lawsuits of various defendants and blank counterfeit sight drafts allegedly payable out of the United States Treasury. At the Carlson farmhouse located in rural Becker, Minnesota, amongst hundreds of files unrelated to this case, investigators discovered six files each labeled with a defendant's name containing past due statements, tax forms, letters from attorneys and court documents. Apparently as a result of these searches, Carlson, Rosnow and Erickson requested the social security numbers of some of the investigators involved in the search and Dewey and Haugen filed false currency transaction reports (CTR's) and meritless federal tort claims against the investigators. Because of these actions, the named defendants were charged with attempted obstruction of an IRS investigation.

The case proceeded to trial on March 1, 1991. At the close of the government's case, the defendants moved for a judgment of acquittal on the conspiracy charge. The motion was denied. On April 8, 1991, the jury returned a verdict of guilty on all thirty-four counts of the indictment. The sentences imposed range from eleven to twenty-seven months of incarceration.

DISCUSSION

We initially turn to the sole meritorious claim affecting most of the defendants. The defendants argue the government failed to prove the existence of the single overall conspiracy charged in the indictment.

The government argues that all of the defendants shared the common goal of harassing their perceived enemies through the use of fraudulent claims to the IRS and that mutual assistance and dependence existed. The government maintains that Juanita Dewey and Harry Carlson each headed up a core group of defendants and the two groups were linked through various cooperative efforts.

The evidence put forth at trial included the six files discovered at the Carlson residence labeled with the names of defendants Erickson, Hansen, David Rodewald, Kermit Rodewald, Wallace Rodewald and Rosnow. The files contained various tax forms, including forms 1096 and 1040, past due bill statements and notices of bills currently due. At the Dewey-Haugen condominium, investigators found notes written on a calendar which referred to defendants Haugen, Yant, Peters, David Rodewald, Kermit Rodewald and unindicted co-conspirator Knutt. Investigators also discovered letters addressed to Dewey from Morse, Telemaque and Knutt. Also uncovered at the Dewey-Haugen residence, was a piece of paper with Dennis and Roger Sands' address and phone number written on it and a letter addressed to the IRS from Reed Glawe, who the Sands reported having paid over $ 630,000.00, stating that he had not been paid any compensation from the Sands in 1989. Finally, investigators also turned up legal papers relating to adverse decisions against Hansen and Peters, which the government maintains served as the catalyst for those defendants' actions.

The government also presented expert analysis of various typewritten documents prepared by defendants indicating that Carlson, Hansen, Kermit Rodewald, Wallace Rodewald and Rosnow used the same typewriter; while David Rodewald, Haugen, Dewey, Yant, and Peters used another. Additionally, some of the defendants testified to being acquainted with each other and to having discussed the filing of the forms 1099 on occasion, and Rosnow and Erickson had accounts with Common Title Bond and Trust, a fraudulent entity whose promoters, including Harry Carlson, have been enjoined from continuing to do business by the Minnesota Attorney General. Finally, the evidence showed that several defendants functioned as notaries for the others: Kermit Rodewald notarized documents for his brother David, Rosnow, Carlson, Hansen, and Dewey; Carlson's wife, Debra, notarized documents for Rosnow, David Rodewald, Kermit Rodewald, Wallace Rodewald and Hansen; and Erickson notarized documents for Hansen.

While this evidence may show, as the government urges, that Dewey and Carlson each headed up a core group of defendants, the record belies the existence of an overall conspiracy between all of the defendants.

We recognize that in order to prove a single conspiracy it is not necessary to show that all the conspirators were involved in each transaction or that all the conspirators even knew each other. However, for a wheel conspiracy to exist those people who form the wheel's spokes must have been aware of each other and must do something in furtherance of some single, illegal enterprise. Otherwise the conspiracy lacks "the rim of the wheel to enclose the spokes." If there is not some interaction between those conspirators who form the spokes of the wheel as to at least one common illegal object, the "wheel" is incomplete, and two [or more] conspiracies rather than one are charged. Put another way, a "common purpose of a single enterprise must motivate each participant and each act" and "mere knowledge of another similarly motivated conspiracy or an overlap in personnel do [sic] not prove one overall agreement." *United States v. Snider*, 720 F.2d 985, 988 (8th Cir. 1983), *cert. denied*, 465 U.S. 1107 (1984).

The evidence shows that Haugen, Morse, Peters and the Sands brothers were associated only with Dewey; no evidence was presented that they implicitly or explicitly joined any agreement or even knew of, much less interacted with, any other defendant in this case. Nor was sufficient evidence presented to indicate an association between Wallace Rodewald and any other defendant except for Carlson and possibly his brother Kermit.

This case is distinguishable from the typical "chain" conspiracy case, where each member plays a different but pivotal role in the overall success of the group. For example, in the typical drug distribution conspiracy you may find a manufacturer who produces the product; a supplier who buys the contraband from the producer; distributors who buy from the supplier and sell to smaller dealers or users; and security personnel who protect the sale proceeds and see to the members' safety. Whatever the product, the purpose of the conspiracy is to put the commodity into the hands of the ultimate consumer. The success of the group as a whole is dependant upon the ability of each member to fulfill his responsibilities. Thus, unlike the wheel conspiracy, the defendants' knowledge of the existence of remote links in the chain may be inferred solely from the nature of the enterprise.

By comparison, except for Dewey who appears to have been connected with the marketers of this scheme, no member of this group stood to gain a thing by the success of a fellow defendant. Nor was any single defendant's probability of success affected by the success of another defendant. There is no evidence that the defendants were motivated by the "common purpose of a single enterprise." *Snider*, 720 F.2d at 988. They engaged in similar acts for similar reasons. Some were assisted by the same people. Some knew each other. But the evidence fails to indicate that there was mutual assistance or dependence between most of these defendants. It appears that they engaged in these actions in order to benefit themselves individually, to gain revenge on their individual perceived enemies, and not to benefit the group as a whole. They did not care about the success of the other defendants, and for the most part they did not assist the other defendants. Thus, we hold it was mere speculation for the jury to find beyond a reasonable doubt the existence of a single conspiracy between all of the defendants charged.

* * *

[Convictions reversed].

QUESTIONS

1.   *Kotteakos v. United States*, 328 U.S. 750 (1946), is the seminal case in distinguishing wheel from chain conspiracies. Kotteakos involved multiple conspiracies to defraud the Federal Housing Administration. The key figure, Brown, arranged with thirty-two people to submit false loan applications. None of the applicants had any connection with the others, although each had a relationship with Brown. The government, however, charged all the applicants with participation in a single conspiracy Brown at the hub of a wheel, and the various applicants were the spokes. With facts similar to those in *Rosnow*, what do you think the Supreme Court rules with respect to the type of conspiracy that existed? Why?

2.   As stated in the material before *Rosnow*, even when there is a wheel with spokes type of conspiracy, there can still be one, large conspiracy if there is some "rim to enclose the spokes." What type of evidence do you think would have provided such a "rim" in *Rosnow* and *Kotteakos*? Explain your reasoning.

---

4. Mens Rea for Conspiracy and Problems with Inferred Intent

Conviction of the crime of conspiracy requires a showing of specific intent to have agreed to do an illegal act, or a legal act by illegal means. But proving intent to agree, whether express or implied, can be difficult.

Proof by direct evidence, of course, is the best way of proving a conspiracy. But since criminal conspirators rarely write down their plans and sign them in the form of a contract, direct evidence may be hard to come by. The law has dealt with this in several ways. First, the law allows the mens rea of intent to agree to a conspiracy to be proven using hearsay evidence. Second, some conspiracies require an overt act performed in furtherance of the conspiratorial objective as evidence of both the actus reus (the agreement) and of the mens rea of specific intent. And third, under some circumstances, intent to agree may be inferred from conduct. We will address each of these in turn.

Unlike with most crimes, hearsay is generally admissible to prove the existence of a conspiracy. Under Rule 801 of the Federal Rules of Evidence, hearsay is defined as "a statement, other than one made by the declarant while testifying at trial or hearing, offered to prove the truth of the matter asserted." Hearsay is a complicated part of the law of evidence which is beyond the scope of this book. For our purposes, however, you should know that the rules of evidence generally disallow hearsay to be used as substantive proof of a fact in issue at a trial. There are, however, many exceptions to the hearsay rule. One of these exceptions is applies to the crime of conspiracy. Damaging statements made by a co-conspirator may be admissible against other co-conspirators under Rule 801(d)(2)(E). For example, *Bourjaily v. United States*, 483 U.S. 171 (1987), involved an FBI informant who had agreed to sell cocaine to a drug dealer. The dealer talked about a friend who would help him sell the cocaine. The discussion was taped and introduced under the hearsay exception to show that the defendant was the friend discussed on the tape. The Supreme Court upheld the admissibility of the tape.

There is an important limitation on this hearsay exception that should be noted. Its applicability is limited to those statements made before the consummation of the offense that is the target of the conspiracy. *See Krulewitch v. United States*, 336 U.S. 440 (1949). The rationale for this limitation rests,

133

in large part, on the fact that a conspiracy is presumed to include, as part of its nature, an agreement to avoid detection. Once the crime is committed, the participants presumably do not want to get caught. Thus, one might erroneously infer that a new conspiracy is formed to cover up the existence of the original conspiracy and the crimes committed pursuant to it. If this were the case, anything ever said pertaining to the crime between co-conspirators would be admissible hearsay. But since there is no separate or subsidiary conspiracy to prevent detection and punishment, the hearsay exception ends when the target crimes of the conspiracy are completed.

At common law, a conviction for conspiracy generally did not require an **overt act**, but modern laws often do, at least for some crimes. An overt act is an act performed in the furtherance of a conspiratorial objective. The requirement of some conduct that will satisfy the overt act requirement for conspiracy liability is usually satisfied by *any* act, whether legal or illegal, so long as it evidences the conspiratorial agreement. It need not be a substantial act that approaches the substantive crime as is required for conviction of attempt.

The Model Penal Code requires an overt act for a conspiracy conviction if the substantive crime is a minor offense. In contrast, however, the Model Penal Code does not require an overt act if the conspiracy is to commit a felony of the first or second degree.

Even when there is an overt act requirement, however, *inferring intent* to agree from that overt act may be problematic. The Model Penal Code does not allow any inference of intent from conduct because the level of culpability for conspiracy is purpose, not knowledge. The common law, however, allowed inferences of intent for felonies, and for misdemeanors where the accused had a special interest associated with the offense, as the following case illustrates.

The PEOPLE of the State of California, Appellant, v. Louis LAURIA et al., Respondents.
251 Cal. App. 2d 471, 59 Cal. Rptr. 628 (1967).

Fleming, Associate Justice.

In an investigation of call-girl activity prostitutes actively plying their trade on call, each of whom was using Lauria's telephone answering service, presumably for business purposes.

On January 8, 1965, Stella Weeks, a policewoman, signed up for telephone service with Lauria's answering service. Mrs. Weeks, in the course of her conversation with Lauria's office manager, hinted broadly that she was a prostitute concerned with the secrecy of her activities and their concealment from the police. She was assured that the operation of the service was discreet and "about as safe as you can get." It was arranged that Mrs. Weeks need not leave her address with the answering service, but could pick up her calls and pay her bills in person.

On February 11, Mrs. Weeks talked to Lauria on the telephone and told him her business was modeling and she had been referred to the answering service by Terry, one of the three prostitutes under investigation. She complained that because of the operation of the service she had lost two valuable customers, referred to as tricks. Lauria defended his service and said that her friends had probably lied to her about having left calls for her. But he did not respond to Mrs. Weeks' hints that she needed customers in order to make money, other than to invite her to his house for a personal visit in order to get better acquainted. In the course of his talk he said "his business was taking messages."

On February 15, Mrs. Weeks talked on the telephone to Lauria's office manager and again complained of two lost calls, which she described as a $50 and a $100 trick. On investigation the office manager could find nothing wrong, but she said she would alert the switchboard operators about slip-ups on calls. On April 1, Lauria and the three prostitutes were arrested. Lauria complained to the police that this attention was undeserved, stating that Hollywood Call Board had 60 to 70 prostitutes on its board while his own service had only 9 or 10, that he kept separate records for known or suspected prostitutes for the convenience of himself and the police. When asked if his records were available to police who might come to the office to investigate call girls, Lauria replied that they were whenever the police had a specific name. However, his service didn't "arbitrarily tell the police about prostitutes on our board. As long as they pay their bills we tolerate them."

In a subsequent voluntary appearance before the Grand Jury, Lauria testified he had always cooperated with the police. But he admitted he knew some of his customers were prostitutes, and he knew Terry was a prostitute because he had personally used her services, and he knew she was paying for 500 calls a month. Lauria and the three prostitutes were indicted for conspiracy to commit prostitution, and nine overt acts were specified. Subsequently the trial court set aside the indictment as having been brought without reasonable or probable cause. The People have appealed, claiming that a sufficient showing of an unlawful agreement to further prostitution was made.

To establish agreement, the People need show no more than a tacit, mutual understanding between coconspirators to accomplish an unlawful act. Here the People attempted to establish a conspiracy by showing that Lauria, well aware that his codefendants were prostitutes who received business calls from customers through his telephone answering service, continued to furnish them with such service. This approach attempts to equate knowledge of another's criminal activity with conspiracy to further such criminal activity, and poses the question of the criminal responsibility of a furnisher of goods or services who knows his product is being used to assist the operation of an illegal business. Under what circumstances does a supplier become a part of a conspiracy to further an illegal enterprise by furnishing goods or services which he knows are to be used by the buyer for criminal purposes?

The two leading cases on this point face in opposite directions. In *United States v. Falcone*, 311 U.S. 205 (1940), the sellers of large quantities of sugar, yeast, and cans were absolved from participation in a moonshining conspiracy among distillers who bought from them, while in *Direct Sales Co. v. United States*, 319 U.S. 703 (1943), a wholesaler of drugs was convicted of conspiracy to violate the federal narcotic laws by selling drugs in quantity to a codefendant physician who was supplying them to addicts. The distinction between these two cases appears primarily based on the proposition that distributors of such dangerous products as drugs are required to exercise greater discrimination in the conduct of their business than are distributors of innocuous substances like sugar and yeast.

In the earlier case, *Falcone*, the sellers' knowledge of the illegal use of the goods was insufficient by itself to make the sellers participants in a conspiracy with the distillers who bought from them. Such knowledge fell short of proof of a conspiracy, and evidence on the volume of sales was too vague to support a jury finding that respondents knew of the conspiracy from the size of the sales alone.

In the later case of *Direct Sales*, the conviction of a drug wholesaler for conspiracy to violate federal narcotic laws was affirmed on a showing that it had actively promoted the sale of morphine sulphate in quantity and had sold codefendant physician, who practiced in a small town in South Carolina, more than 300 times his normal requirements of the drug, even though it had been repeatedly warned of the dangers of unrestricted sales of the drug. The court contrasted the restricted goods involved in *Direct Sales* with the articles of free commerce involved in *Falcone*: "All articles of commerce may be put to illegal ends," said the court. "But all do not have inherently the same susceptibility to harmful and illegal use. . . . This difference is important for two purposes. One is for making certain that the seller knows the buyer's intended illegal use. The other is to show that by the sale he intends to further, promote and cooperate in it. This intent, when given effect by overt act, is the gist of conspiracy. While it is not identical with mere knowledge that another purposes unlawful action, it is not unrelated to such knowledge. . . . The step from knowledge to intent and agreement may be taken. There is more than suspicion, more than knowledge, acquiescence, carelessness, indifference, lack of concern. There is informed and interested cooperation, stimulation, instigation. And there is also a "stake in the venture" which, even if it may not be essential, is not irrelevant to the question of conspiracy." 319 U.S. at 710-13.

While *Falcone* and *Direct Sales* may not be entirely consistent with each other in their full implications, they do provide us with a framework for the criminal liability of a supplier of lawful goods or services put to unlawful use. Both the element of knowledge of the illegal use of the goods or services and the element of intent to further that use must be present in order to make the supplier a participant in a criminal conspiracy.

Proof of knowledge is ordinarily a question of fact and requires no extended discussion in the present case. The knowledge of the supplier was sufficiently established when Lauria admitted he knew some of his customers were prostitutes and admitted he knew that Terry, an active subscriber to his service, was a prostitute. In the face of these admissions he could scarcely claim to have relied on the normal assumption an operator of a business or service is entitled to make, that his customers are behaving themselves in the eyes of the law. Because Lauria knew in fact that some of his customers were prostitutes, it is a legitimate inference he knew they were subscribing to his answering service for illegal business purposes and were using his service to make assignations for prostitution. On this record we think the prosecution is entitled to claim positive knowledge by Lauria of the use of his service to facilitate the business of prostitution.

The more perplexing issue in the case is the sufficiency of proof of intent to further the criminal enterprise. The element of intent may be proved either by direct evidence, or by evidence of circumstances from which an intent to further a criminal enterprise by supplying lawful goods or services may be inferred. Direct evidence of participation, . . . such as advice from the supplier of legal goods or services to the user of those goods or services on their use for illegal purposes, provides the simplest case. When the intent to further and promote the criminal enterprise comes from the lips of the supplier himself, ambiguities of inference from circumstance need not trouble us. But in cases where direct proof of complicity is lacking, intent to further the conspiracy must be derived from the sale itself and its surrounding circumstances in order to establish the supplier's express or tacit agreement to join the conspiracy.

In the case at bench the prosecution argues that since Lauria knew his customers were using his service for illegal purposes but nevertheless continued to furnish it to them, he must have intended to assist them in carrying out their illegal activities. Thus through a union of knowledge and intent he became a participant in a criminal conspiracy. Essentially, the People argue that knowledge alone of the continuing use of his telephone facilities for criminal purposes provided a sufficient basis from which his intent to participate in those criminal activities could be inferred. In examining precedents in this field we find that sometimes, but not always, the criminal intent of the supplier may be inferred from his knowledge of the unlawful use made of the product he supplies. Some consideration of characteristic patterns may be helpful.

1. Intent may be inferred from knowledge, when the purveyor of legal goods for illegal use has acquired a stake in the venture. For example, in *Regina v. Thomas*, [1957] 2 All Eng. 181, 342, a prosecution for living off the earnings of prostitution, the evidence showed that the accused, knowing the woman to be a convicted prostitute, agreed to let her have the use of his room between the hours of 9 p.m. and 2 a.m. for a charge of £3 a night. The Court of Criminal Appeal refused an appeal from the conviction, holding that when the accused rented a room at a grossly inflated rent to a prostitute for the purpose of carrying on her trade, a jury could find he was living on the earnings of prostitution. In the present case, no proof was offered of inflated charges for the telephone answering services furnished the codefendants.

2. Intent may be inferred from knowledge, when no legitimate use for the goods or services exists. The leading California case is *People v. McLaughlin*, 245 P.2d 1076 (Cal. App. 1952), in which the court upheld a conviction of the suppliers of horse-racing information by wire for conspiracy to promote bookmaking, when it had been established that wireservice information had no other use than to supply information needed by bookmakers to conduct illegal gambling operations.

* * *

In *Shaw v. Director of Public Prosecutions*, [1962] A.C. 220, the defendant was convicted of conspiracy to corrupt public morals and of living on the earnings of prostitution, when he published a directory consisting almost entirely of advertisements of the names, addresses, and specialized talents of prostitutes. Publication of such a directory, said the court, could have no legitimate use and serve no other purpose than to advertise the professional services of the prostitutes whose advertisements appeared in the directory. The publisher could be deemed a participant in the profits from the business activities of his principal advertisers.

Other services of a comparable nature come to mind: the manufacturer of crooked dice and marked cards who sells his product to gambling casinos; the tipster who furnishes information on the movement of law enforcement officers to known lawbreakers. In such cases the supplier must necessarily have an intent to further the illegal enterprise since there is no known honest use for his goods. However, there is nothing in the furnishing of telephone answering service which would necessarily imply assistance in the performance of illegal activities. Nor is any inference to be derived from the use of an answering service by women, either in any particular volume of calls, or outside normal working hours. Night-club entertainers, registered nurses, faith healers, public stenographers, photographic models, and free lance substitute employees, provide examples of women in legitimate occupations whose employment might cause them to receive a volume of telephone calls at irregular hours.

3. Intent may be inferred from knowledge, when the volume of business with the buyer is grossly disproportionate to any legitimate demand, or when sales for illegal use amount to a high proportion of the seller's total business. In such cases an intent to participate in the illegal enterprise may be inferred from the quantity of the business done. For example, in *Direct Sales*, the sale of narcotics to a rural physician in quantities 300 times greater than he would have normal use for provided potent evidence of an intent to further the illegal activity. In the same case, the court also found significant the fact that the wholesaler had attracted as customers a disproportionately large group of physicians who had been convicted of violating the Harrison Act. In *Shaw v. Director of Public Prosecutions*, [1962] A.C. 220, almost the entire business of the directory came from prostitutes.

Inflated charges, the sale of goods with no legitimate use, sales in inflated amounts, each may provide a fact of sufficient moment from which the intent of the seller to participate in the criminal enterprise may be inferred. In such instances participation by the supplier of legal goods to the illegal enterprise may be inferred because in one way or another the supplier has acquired a special interest in the operation of the illegal enterprise. His intent to participate in the crime of which he has knowledge may be inferred from the existence of his special interest.

Yet there are cases in which it cannot reasonably be said that the supplier has a stake in the venture or has acquired a special interest in the enterprise, but in which he has been held liable as a participant on the basis of knowledge alone. Some suggestion of this appears in *Direct Sales*, where both the knowledge of the illegal use of the drugs and the intent of the supplier to aid that use were inferred. In *Regina v. Bainbridge*, (1959) 3 Week. L. 656 [(C.C.A. 6) [3 All Eng. 200, 123 J. P. 499, 43 Crim. App. 194], a supplier of oxygen-cutting equipment to one known to intend to use it to break into a bank was convicted as an accessory to the crime. In *Sykes v. Director of Public Prosecutions*, [1962] A.C. 528, one having knowledge of the theft of 100 pistols, 4 submachine guns, and 1960 rounds of ammunition was convicted of misprision of felony for failure to disclose the theft to the public authorities. It seems apparent from these cases that a supplier who furnishes equipment which he knows will be used to commit a serious crime may be deemed from that knowledge alone to have intended to produce the result. Such proof may justify an inference that the furnisher intended to aid the execution of the crime and that he thereby became a participant. For instance, we think the operator of a telephone answering service with positive knowledge that this service was being used to facilitate the extortion of ransom, the distribution of heroin, or the passing of counterfeit money who continued to furnish the service with knowledge of its use, might be chargeable on knowledge alone with participation in a scheme to extort money, to distribute narcotics, or to pass counterfeit money. The same result would follow the seller of gasoline who knew the buyer was using his product to make Molotov cocktails for terroristic use.

Logically, the same reasoning could be extended to crimes of every description. Yet we do not believe an inference of intent drawn from knowledge of criminal use properly applies to the less serious crimes classified as misdemeanors. The duty to take positive action to dissociate oneself from activities helpful to violations of the criminal law as far stronger and more compelling for felonies than it is for misdemeanors or petty offenses. In this respect, as in others, the distinction between felonies and misdemeanors, between more serious and less serious crime, retains continuing vitality. In historically the most serious felony, treason, an individual with knowledge of the treason can be prosecuted for concealing and failing to disclose it. In other felonies, both at common law and under the criminal laws of the United States, an individual knowing of the commission of a felony is criminally liable for concealing it and failing to make it known to proper authority. But this crime, known as misprision of felony, has always been limited to knowledge and concealment of felony and has never extended to misdemeanor. A similar limitation is found in the criminal liability of an accessory, which is restricted to aid in the escape of a principal who has committed or been charged with a Felony. We believe the distinction between the obligations arising from knowledge of a felony and those arising from knowledge of a misdemeanor continues to reflect basic human feelings about the duties owed by individuals to society.

Heinous crime must be stamped out, and its suppression is the responsibility of all. Venial crime and crime not evil in itself present less of a danger to society, and perhaps the benefits of their suppression through the modern equivalent of the posse, the hue and cry, the informant, and the citizen's arrest, and outweighed by the disruption to everyday life brought about by amateur law enforcement and private officiousness in relatively inconsequential delicts which do not threaten our basic security. The subject has been summarized in an English text on the criminal law: "Failure to reveal a felony to the authorities is now authoritatively determined to be misprision of felony, which is a commonwealth misdemeanour; misprision of treason is punishable with imprisonment for life. . . . No offense is committed in failing to disclose a misdemeanour."

To require everyone, without distinction, as to the nature and degree of the offence, to become an accuser, would be productive of inconvenience in exposing numbers to penal prosecutions, multiplying criminal charges, and engendering private dissension. It may sometimes be more convenient that offenses should be passed over, than that all should indiscriminately be made the subject of prosecution; and a law would be considered to be harsh and impolitic, if not unjust, which compelled every party injured by a criminal act, and, still more so, to compel everyone who happened to know that another had been so injured, to make a public disclosure of the circumstances. Here, therefore, there is reason for limiting the law against mere misprisions to the concealment of such crimes as are of an aggravated complexion.

With respect to misdemeanors, we conclude that positive knowledge of the supplier that his products or services are being used for criminal purposes does not, without more, establish an intent of the supplier to participate in the misdemeanors. With respect to felonies, we do not decide the converse, viz. that in all cases of felony knowledge of criminal use alone may justify an inference of supplier's intent to participate in the crime. The implications of *Falcone* make the matter uncertain with respect to those felonies which care merely prohibited wrongs. But decision on this point is not compelled, and we leave the matter open.

From this analysis of precedent we deduce the following rule: the intent of a supplier who knows of the criminal use to which his supplies are put to participate in the criminal activity connected with the use of his supplies may be established by (1) direct evidence that he intends to participate, or (2) through an inference that he intends to participate based on, (a) his special interest in the activity, or (b) the aggravated nature of the crime itself.

When we review Lauria's activities in the light of this analysis, we find no proof that Lauria took any direct action to further, encourage, or direct the call-girl activities of his codefendants and we find an absence of circumstances from which his special interest in their activities could be inferred. Neither excessive charges for standardized services, nor the furnishing of services without a legitimate use, nor an unusual quantity of business with call girls, are present. The offense which he is charged with furthering is a misdemeanor, a category of crime which has never been made a required subject of positive disclosure to public authority. Under these circumstances, although proof of Lauria's knowledge of the criminal activities of his patrons was sufficient to charge him with that fact, there was insufficient evidence that he intended to further their criminal activities, and hence insufficient proof of his participation in a criminal conspiracy with his codefendants to further prostitution. Since the conspiracy centered around the activities of Lauria's telephone answering service, the charges against his codefendants likewise fail for want of proof.

In absolving Lauria of complicity in a criminal conspiracy, we do not wish to imply that the public authorities are without remedies to combat modern manifestations of the world's oldest profession. Licensing of telephone answering services under the police power, together with the revocation of licenses for the toleration of prostitution, is a possible civil remedy. The furnishing of telephone answering service in aid of prostitution could be made a crime. Other solutions will doubtless occur to vigilant public authorities if the problem of call-girl activity needs further suppression. . . . Affirmed.

QUESTIONS

1.   Mr. Lauria knew that the three prostitutes used his service to arrange meetings with their clients and was charged with conspiracy to promote prostitution accordingly. As you read, the court reversed his conviction. Do you agree with the outcome of this case? Why or why not? What would the potential consequences be if nothing more than mere knowledge that the supplying of lawful goods or services somehow contributed to an illegal venture resulted in conspiratorial liability for the supplier?

2.   In *Direct Sales Co. v. United States*, 319 U.S. 703 (1943), discussed in the *Lauria* case, the conviction of a wholesale drug company for conspiracy to violate the narcotic laws by selling large quantities of drugs to a physician who was supplying addicts was upheld by the Supreme Court. The *Lauria* court distinguished *Direct Sales* case from *United States v. Falcone*, 311 U.S. 205, in which the sellers of large quantities of sugar, yeast, and cans were absolved from participation in a moonshining conspiracy. What do you see as the critical distinctions between these two cases that explains the different outcomes in the two cases? Suppose Mr. Lauria provided answering services to a marijuana dealer with the knowledge that his service was taking messages for such a drug dealer. Given your reading of the *Lauria* case, and its summary of *Direct Sales* and *Falcone*, what would you predict the outcome of such a case to be? Why? Would your response change if the dealer were selling crack cocaine? Why or why not?

3.   The court ruled that intent to participate in the criminal venture could be inferred if a supplier of otherwise lawful goods or services has some "special interest" in the venture, such as charging higher rates than those normally charged, or by the aggravated nature of the offense. Given the outcome of the *Lauria* case, presumably, prostitution is not a sufficiently aggravated offense to trigger liability under the latter rationale. What offenses do you feel would clearly qualify as sufficiently aggravated to trigger such supplier liability? What offenses would clearly fall outside the realm of such liability and be more analogous to the activity at issue in the *Lauria* case? Can you think of any crimes that are in a "gray" area in which the liability of the supplier would depend more on the facts and circumstances of the case, rather than the nature of the target crime?

5. Scope of Conspiracy

Under normal rules of complicity, all co-conspirators are liable for any offenses that are explicitly agreed to as part of the conspiracy. But what of those offenses that occur that were not specifically agreed to as a part of the original conspiracy? The common law and the Model Penal Code take very different approaches to answering this question. The Model Penal Code examines the relative individual culpability of each co-conspirator. That is to say that each person will be judged based on his or her own level of mens rea with respect to crimes that were not a part of the conspiracy.

Only a minority of U.S. jurisdictions, however, have adopted the Model Penal Code approach to the scope of a conspiracy. Most states, and federal criminal law, continue to follow the common law rule known as the *Pinkerton Rule*, which derives its name from the following case.

Walter and Daniel PINKERTON, et al. v. UNITED STATES of America.
328 U.S. 640 (1946).

Mr. Justice Douglas delivered the opinion of the Court.

Walter and Daniel Pinkerton are brothers who live a short distance from each other on Daniel's farm. They were indicted for violations of the Internal Revenue Code. The indictment contained ten substantive counts and one conspiracy count. The jury found Walter guilty on nine of the substantive counts and on the conspiracy count. It found Daniel guilty on six of the substantive counts and on the conspiracy count. Walter was fined $500 and sentenced generally on the substantive counts to imprisonment for thirty months. On the conspiracy count he was given a two year sentence to run concurrently with the other sentence. Daniel was fined $1,000 and sentenced generally on the substantive counts to imprisonment for thirty months. On the conspiracy count he was fined $500 and given a two year sentence to run concurrently with the other sentence. The judgments of conviction were affirmed by the Circuit Court of Appeals. The case is here on a petition for a writ of certiorari which we granted because one of the questions presented involved a conflict between the decision below a case decided by the Circuit Court of Appeals for the Third Circuit.

A single conspiracy was charged and proved. Some of the overt acts charged in the conspiracy count were the same acts charged in the substantive counts. Each of the substantive offenses found was committed pursuant to the conspiracy. Petitioners therefore contend that the substantive counts became merged in the conspiracy count, and that only a single sentence not exceeding the maximum two-year penalty provided by the conspiracy statute could be imposed. Or to state the matter differently, they contend that each of the substantive counts became a separate conspiracy count but since only a single conspiracy was charged and proved, only single sentence for conspiracy could be imposed. They rely on *Braverman v. United States,* 317 U.S. 49 (1942).

In the *Braverman* case, the indictment charged no substantive offense. Each of the several counts charged a conspiracy to violate a different statute. But only one conspiracy was proved. We held that a single conspiracy, charged under the general conspiracy statute, however diverse its objects may be, violates but a single statute and no penalty greater than the maximum provided for one conspiracy may be imposed. That case is not apposite here. For the offenses charged and proved were not only a conspiracy but substantive offenses as well.

Nor can we accept the proposition that the substantive offenses were merged in the conspiracy. There are, of course, instances where a conspiracy charge may not be added to the substantive charge. One is where the agreement of two persons is necessary for the completion of the substantive crime and there is no ingredient in the conspiracy which is not present in the completed crime. *See, United States v. Katz*, 271 U.S. 354, 355-56 (1926). Another is where the definition of the substantive offense excludes from punishment for conspiracy one who voluntarily participates in another's crime. *Gebardi v. United States*, 287 U.S. 112, 121-22 (1932) [(applying the Wharton Rule)]. But those exceptions are of a limited character. The common law rule that the substantive offense, if a felony, was merged in the conspiracy, has little vitality in this country. It has been long and consistently recognized by the Court that the commission of the substantive offense and a conspiracy to commit it are separate and distinct offenses. The power of Congress to separate the two and to affix to each a different penalty is well established. A conviction for the conspiracy may be had though the substantive offense was completed. And the plea of double jeopardy is no defense to a conviction for both offenses. A conspiracy is a partnership in crime. It has ingredients, as well as implications, distinct from the completion of the unlawful project.

* * *

Moreover, it is not material that overt acts charged in the conspiracy counts were also charged and proved as substantive offenses. If the overt act be the offense which was the object of the conspiracy, and is also punished, there is not a double punishment of it. The agreement to do an unlawful act is even then distinct from the doing of the act.

It is contended that there was insufficient evidence to implicate Daniel in the conspiracy. But we think there was enough evidence for submission of the issue to the jury.

There is, however, no evidence to show that Daniel participated directly in the commission of the substantive offenses on which his conviction has been sustained, although there was evidence to show that these substantive offenses were in fact committed by Walter in furtherance of the unlawful agreement or conspiracy existing between the brothers. The question was submitted to the jury on the theory that each petitioner could be found guilty of the substantive offenses, if it was found at the time those offenses were committed petitioners were parties to an unlawful conspiracy and the substantive offenses charged were in fact committed in furtherance of it.

Daniel relies on *United States v. Sall*, 116 F.2d 745 (3d Cir. 1940). That case held that participation in the conspiracy was not itself enough to sustain a conviction for the substantive offense even though it was committed in furtherance of the conspiracy. The court held that, in addition to evidence that the offense was in fact committed in furtherance of the conspiracy, evidence of direct participation in the commission of the substantive offense or other evidence from which participation might fairly be inferred was necessary.

We take a different view. We have here a continuous conspiracy. There is here no evidence of the affirmative action on the part of Daniel which is necessary to establish his withdrawal from it. Having joined in an unlawful scheme, having constituted agents for its performance, scheme and agency to be continuous until full fruition be secured, until he does some act to disavow or defeat the purpose, he is in no situation to claim the delay of the law. As the offense has not been terminated or accomplished, he is still offending. And we think, consciously offending, offending as certainly, as we have said, as at the first moment of his confederation, and consciously through every moment of its existence. And so long as the partnership in crime continues, the partners act for each other in carrying it forward.

It is settled that "an overt act of one partner may be the act of all without any new agreement specifically directed to that act." *United States v. Kissel*, 218 U.S. 601, 608 (1910). Motive or intent may be proved by the acts or declarations of some of the conspirators in furtherance of the common objective. A scheme to use the mails to defraud, which is joined in by more than one person, is a conspiracy. Yet all members are responsible, though only one did the mailing. The governing principle is the same when the substantive offense is committed by one of the conspirators in furtherance of the unlawful project. The criminal intent to do the act is established by the formation of the conspiracy. Each conspirator instigated the commission of the crime. The unlawful agreement contemplated precisely what was done. It was formed for the purpose. The act done was in execution of the enterprise. The rule which holds responsible one who counsels, procures, or commands another to commit a crime is founded on the same principle. That principle is recognized in the law of conspiracy when the overt act of one partner in crime is attributable to all. An overt act is an essential ingredient of the crime of conspiracy under Section 37 of the Criminal Code, 18 U.S.C. § 88. If that can be supplied by the act of one conspirator, we fail to see why the same or other acts in furtherance of the conspiracy are likewise not attributable to the others for the purpose of holding them responsible for the substantive offense.

A different case would arise if the substantive offense committed by one of the conspirators was not in fact done in furtherance of the conspiracy, did not fall within the scope of the unlawful project, or was merely a part of the ramifications of the plan which could not be reasonably foreseen as a necessary or natural consequence of the unlawful agreement. But as we read this record, that is not this case. Affirmed.

Mr. Justice Rutledge, dissenting in part.

The judgment concerning Daniel Pinkerton should be reversed. In my opinion, it is without precedent here and is a dangerous precedent to establish. Daniel and Walter, who were brothers living near each other, were charged in several counts with substantive offenses, and then a conspiracy count was added naming those offenses as overt acts. The proof showed that Walter alone committed the substantive crimes. There was none to establish that Daniel participated in them, aided and abetted Walter in committing them, or knew that he had done so. Daniel in fact was in the penitentiary, under sentence for other crimes, when some of Walter's crimes were done.

There was evidence, however, to show that over several years Daniel and Walter had confederated to commit similar crimes concerned with unlawful possession, transportation, and dealing in whiskey, in fraud of the federal revenues. On this evidence both were convicted of conspiracy. Walter also was convicted on the substantive counts on the proof of his committing the crimes charged. Then, on that evidence without more than the proof of Daniel's criminal agreement with Walter and the latter's overt acts, which were also the substantive offenses charged, the court told the jury they could find Daniel guilty of those substantive offenses. They did so.

I think this ruling violates both the letter and the spirit of what Congress did when it separately defined the three classes of crime, namely, (1) completed substantive offenses; (2) aiding, abetting or counseling another to commit them; and (3) conspiracy to commit them. Not only does this ignore the distinctions Congress has prescribed shall be observed. It either convicts one man for another's crime or punishes the man convicted twice for the same offense.

* * *

The court's theory seems to be that Daniel and Walter became general partners in crime by virtue of their agreement and because of that agreement without more on his part Daniel became criminally responsible as a principal for everything Walter did thereafter in the nature of a criminal offense of the general sort the agreement contemplated, so long as there was not clear evidence that Daniel had withdrawn from or revoked the agreement. Whether or not his commitment to the penitentiary had that effect, the result is a vicarious criminal responsibility as broad as, or broader than, the vicarious civil liability of a partner for acts done by a co-partner in the course of the firm's business.

* * *

Mr. Justice Frankfurter, reserving judgment on the question of double jeopardy, agrees in substance with the views expressed in this dissent.

QUESTIONS

1.   As should be evident from a reading of *Pinkerton*, co-conspirators are criminally liable for all acts of other co-conspirators if, and only if, those acts are both (a) reasonably foreseeable in light of the conspiracy; and (b) in furtherance of the conspiracy. But any test that speaks to reasonable foreseeability invites ambiguity. For example, suppose two co-conspirators plan a burglary of a house with the intent to steal various items from the house. Further suppose that one of the thieves has a history of sexual assault that is known to the other. On the night of the planned burglary, it turns out that someone is home in the house and, although not planned, the person with a history of sexual assault rapes the woman who is home. Is that "reasonably foreseeable"? Why or why not?

2.   Assuming, for the sake of argument, that the sexual assault scenario described in question #1 were deemed to be reasonably foreseeable, would the other co-conspirator have criminal liability for the rape under *Pinkerton*? Why or why not? Separate and apart from conspiratorial liability, would the co-conspirator have any other type of liability for the sexual assault, say, perhaps, as an accomplice? Explain your answer.

142

3.   Suppose a group of three or four people plan to rob a bank and then carry out their plan. Part of their agreement is that, although they would arm themselves, their weapons would not be loaded. In other words, they only carry the guns to scare people in the bank into compliance. They all specifically agree that if anything went wrong, they would surrender, rather than use any actual force, as they sincerely do not want anyone to be hurt, as their true objective is to get money. In spite of this specific agreement, one of the co-conspirators brings with him a loaded weapon and uses it during the robbery to kill an armed security guard. What should the liability of the other co-conspirators be in a *Pinkerton* jurisdiction? In a non-*Pinkerton* jurisdiction? Explain your answers.

6. Defense of Abandonment

Once a conspiracy has occurred, the common law did not recognize abandonment or withdrawal as a defense to the charge of conspiracy. In other words, after the mental offense of conspiracy took place, if the defendants abandoned their efforts to complete the target offence(s), they would still have criminal liability for the crime of conspiracy.

Under the Model Penal Code, however, abandonment can be a limited defense. As with most of the other inchoate offenses under the Model Penal Code, one can successfully withdraw from a conspiracy if the abandonment is complete, effective, and voluntary. In other to be deemed effective, it is not enough that a conspirator renounces his or her criminal purpose. The actor must take affirmative steps to thwart the successful completion of the conspiratorial objectives. This usually requires the person withdrawing from the conspiracy to notify the authorities of the plan. If the conspiracy goes in spite of the withdrawing person's efforts to thwart the success of the conspiracy, then abandonment will not be a valid defense since it was not "effective."

CHAPTER 4
DEFENSES OF EXCUSE I: DEFENSES THAT NEGATE MENS REA

A. Ignorance and Mistake

1. Mistake of Fact

When someone makes a mistake that causes the person to have acted in a manner that might otherwise seem criminal, but it is not due to the nature of the mistake, that person may have a legitimate defense in charged with a crime depending upon the type of mistake made.

When a person makes a mistake regarding a factual matter, he or she can assert the defense known as *mistake of fact* if the mistake negates mens rea. In other words, if the mistake effectively erases or nullifies the criminal intent component of the crime, the criminal law will allow that person to assert their mistake as a defense. But the factual mistake must be both an honest and reasonable mistake. The first requirement, that of an honest mistake, is purely subjective. It requires the defendant to have actually (subjectively) been laboring under some factual mistake. The second requirement is objective. It requires that the person's honest mistaken belief be objectively reasonable. In other words, the mistake must have been one that the ordinary, reasonable, prudent person could have made if in the defendant's situation. If either of these requirements are not met, then the defense should be unsuccessful. Consider the following case:

STATE of New Jersey, Plaintiff-Respondent, v. Joseph PELLETERI, Defendant-Appellant.
683 A.2d 555 (N.J. Super. Ct. App. Div. 1996).

Judge Baime:

On May 30, 1990, our Legislature proscribed the "knowing" possession of "assault firearms." N.J.S.A. 2C:39-5f. Persons legally in possession of such firearms prior to the effective date of the statute could retain these weapons by obtaining the appropriate registration. N.J.S.A. 2C:58-12. Included in the definition of "assault firearm" is "[a] semi-automatic rifle with a fixed magazine capacity exceeding [fifteen] rounds." N.J.S.A. 2C:39-1w(4). Defendant was convicted of "knowingly" having in his possession an assault firearm, a semi-automatic rifle with a magazine capacity of seventeen cartridges. He appeals, contending that the trial judge erred by rejecting his claim[] of . . . mistake of fact, and by instructing the jury it could convict if it found he knowingly possessed the weapon even if he did not know its fixed capacity exceeded fifteen rounds. We affirm.

I

We need not recount the facts at length. Defendant, an expert marksman who at one point was employed as a firearms instructor, won a Marlin semi-automatic rifle in the late 1980's by placing first in a police combat match. An avid gun collector, defendant placed the weapon in his safe. Defendant claimed that he neither inspected nor used the firearm. When the police recovered the gun from defendant's residence in December 1993, it still had the manufacturer's tags and the owner's manual attached to the trigger guard. The owner's manual indicated that the rifle could hold at least seventeen cartridges. Defendant claimed that he never read the manual. While conceding that he knew the rifle was a semi-automatic weapon, defendant contended that he was unaware that the firearm had a magazine capacity exceeding fifteen rounds.

At trial, defendant advanced the defense[] of mistake of . . . fact. He asserted that he made diligent inquiry respecting whether the guns in his collection constituted "assault firearms" when the 1990 legislation was enacted and obtained the requisite registration for some of his weapons. Defendant testified that he did not register the Marlin rifle because he did not know its fixed capacity exceeded fifteen rounds. The trial judge barred the defense[] . . . on the grounds that the statutory prohibition was clearly written and published, and that knowledge of the specific character of the weapon did not

144

constitute an element of the offense. In response to a question propounded by the jury during its deliberations, the judge charged that defendant could be found guilty if he knowingly possessed the firearm but was unaware that its fixed capacity exceeded fifteen rounds. Defendant was convicted and placed on probation.

II
* * *

The common law defense required not only that the defendant subjectively misperceive a fact critical to establishing the offense but also that the error be reasonable. . . . *See State v. Bess*, 247 A.2d 669 (N.J. 1968); *State v. Fair*, 211 A.2d 359 (N.J. 1965). The Criminal Law Revision Commission recommended that the objective test be abrogated and that any "honest" error suffice to exonerate the defendant. Final Report of the New Jersey Criminal Law Revision Commission, comment to 2C:2-4 at 52-53 (1971). Our Legislature rejected that proposal by requiring that the defendant "reasonably arrive[] at the conclusion underlying the mistake." N.J.S.A. 2C:2-4a. Defendant's failure to inspect the weapon or read the owner's manual to determine whether it fell within the statutory definition was unreasonable as a matter of law. We find no error in the trial judge's refusal to submit the issue to the jury.

III

The prosecutor candidly points out that the trial judge instructed the jury that defendant could be found guilty if he knowingly possessed the firearm but was unaware its fixed capacity exceeded fifteen rounds. The question squarely presented is whether the State was required to prove that the defendant knew the gun in his possession was an assault firearm. We hold that knowledge of the character of the weapon is not an element of the offense.

N.J.S.A. 2C:39-5f provides in pertinent part that "any person who knowingly has in his possession an assault firearm is guilty of a crime of the third degree." The word "knowingly" thus modifies the phrase "has in his possession." The Code defines "possession" in terms of whether the "possessor knowingly procured or received the thing possessed or was aware of his control [of it] for a sufficient period to have been able to terminate his possession." N.J.S.A. 2C:2-1c. The Code provides that "a person acts knowingly with respect to the nature of his conduct . . . if he is aware that his conduct is of that nature." N.J.S.A. 2C:2-2b(2).

We are satisfied that the Legislature intended to proscribe knowing possession, as distinguished from knowledge of the illegal character of the article possessed. *Cf. State v. Labato*, 80 A.2d 617 (N.J. 1951). In that context, "knowing possession is not to be confused with criminal intent or guilty knowledge." *Id.* "At common law, scienter [was] an indispensable element." *Id.* But it is within the power of the Legislature to declare an act criminal irrespective of the motive of the actor.

We are concerned here with a statute dealing with gun control. "New Jersey has carefully constructed a 'grid' of regulations" on the subject. *In re Two Seized Firearms*, 127 N.J. 84, 88, 602 A.2d 728, *cert. denied sub nom.*, *Sholtis v. New Jersey*, 506 U.S. 823 (1992). This is an area in which "regulations abound and inquiries are likely," and where the overarching purpose is to insure the public safety and protect against acts and threats of violence. *State v. Hatch*, 313 A.2d 797 (N.J. 1973). . . . "The dangers are so high and the regulations so prevalent that, on balance, the legislative branch may as a matter of sound public policy and without impairing any constitutional guarantees, declare the act itself unlawful without any further requirement of mens rea or its equivalent." *Id.* When dealing with guns, the citizen acts at his peril. In short, we view the statute as a regulatory measure in the interests of the public safety, premised on the thesis that one would hardly be surprised to learn that possession of such a highly dangerous offensive weapon is proscribed absent the requisite license. Affirmed.

QUESTIONS

1.   Mr. Pelleteri argued that he honestly did not know the gun in question held seventeen rounds, rather than the maximum permissible fifteen rounds. Why is this a mistake of fact?

145

2.   Given Mr. Pelleteri's knowledge of both the statute and of guns, the court had no problem holding that even if he honestly (i.e., subjectively) did not know that the weapon in question required registration since it held more than the statutorily allowed number of rounds, such a belief was not objectively reasonable. Do you agree with this conclusion? Why or why not?

3.   If Mr. Pelleteri's mistake of fact had been deemed to be both honest and reasonable, would it have negated the mens rea of the crime as defined by the court? Explain your position. *no, not a*

mistake a fact must have a specific men's rea for the crime
knowing possession men's rea
reasonable factor

4.   The crime of bigamy is typically defined as the marriage of any person who, already having a husband or wife living, marries another person. If a married person remarried under the mistaken belief that his or her spouse were dead (i.e., the spouse thought to be dead is actually alive), under what circumstances might such a person be found guilty of bigamy? Explain. What if that person knew their spouse was alive, but thought they had been divorced in a "quickie-divorce" obtained in Mexico? *See, e.g., State v. DeMao*, 118 A.2d 1 (N.J. 1955).

Because mistake of fact can be a defense when it is both honest and reasonable, it can be asserted as a defense to any crime that has purpose, knowledge, or recklessness as its requisite mens rea. It cannot, however, be used as a defense to crimes that carry negligence or strict liability. The reason for this is simple. Since mistake of fact can only be used as a defense when it negates mens rea, and crimes of strict liability have no concern with the mens rea of the defendant, logic dictates that a mistake should be irrelevant. Consider the common law crime of statutory rape. Even an honest and objectively reasonable mistake as the age of the victim would not bar conviction since statutory rape was (and still is in many jurisdictions) a strict liability crime.

But what of crimes of negligence? By definition, being criminally negligent means that one has failed to act reasonably – that one has failed to perceive some risk that the ordinary, reasonable, prudent person would have perceived in the defendant's shoes. Since mistake of fact can only be a defense if it negates mens rea when it involves an honest and reasonable mistake, and negligent conduct is per se unreasonable, hopefully you can see why it does not work as a defense to crimes that carry negligence is their requisite mens rea.

2. Mistake of Law

There is an old maxim which states: *Ignorantia legis neminem excusat*. Translated from the Latin, it means "ignorance of the law is no excuse." While a good rule of thumb, it somewhat of an overstatement. The general rule is that a mistake as to either the existence of law or its meaning is not a defense to any crime. But there are three limited circumstances under which a *mistake of law* might qualify as a criminal defense.

First, if the definition of the offense requires that the defendant have mens rea as to the existence of the law, its meaning, or its application, then the defendant must actually entertain such mens rea. As you might imagine, such statutes are few and far between.

Secondly, if the law has not been made reasonably available, the principle of legality, inextricably tied to due process (see Chapter 1), might be violated. Accordingly, Section 2.04(3)(a) of the Model Penal Code permits a defense of ignorance of law when the law defining the offense is actually (i.e., subjectively) unknown to the defendant and the law "has not been published or otherwise made available prior to the conduct alleged." Of course, this defense would not apply to any crime published in a jurisdiction's criminal code since such publication is deemed to give constructive knowledge of the existence of all such laws. It may be applicable, in contrast, to local ordinances that are not made reasonably available.

The third exception to the rule that mistake of law is not a criminal defense concerns a mistaken belief with regard to the existence or meaning of a law that is founded upon an official statement of law.

Official statement does not mean one's erroneous interpretation of a statute or even the bad advice of an attorney or police officer. The erroneous interpretation of the law relating to the offense has to be made by a public servant, governmental agency, or official body that is charged with administering, interpreting, or enforcing the law. The following case illustrates the type of mistaken belief that would qualify.

COX v. State of LOUISIANA
379 U.S. 559 (1965)

Mr. Justice Goldberg delivered the opinion of the Supreme Court.

Appellant was convicted of violating a Louisiana statute which provides:

> Whoever, with the intent of interfering with, obstructing, or impeding the administration of justice, or with the intent of influencing any judge, juror, witness, or court officer, in the discharge of his duty pickets or parades in or near a building housing a court of the State of Louisiana . . . shall be fined not more than five thousand dollars or imprisoned not more than one year, or both.

Appellant was convicted on this charge also and was sentenced to the maximum penalty under the statute of one year in jail and a $ 5,000 fine. . . .

* * *

The group of 2,000, led by appellant, paraded and demonstrated before the courthouse. Judges and court officers were in attendance to discharge their respective functions. It is undisputed that a major purpose of the demonstration was to protest what the demonstrators considered an "illegal" arrest of 23 students the previous day. While the students had not been arraigned or their trial set for any day certain, they were charged with violation of the law, and the judges responsible for trying them and passing upon the legality of their arrest were then in the building.

* * *

Appellant was convicted for demonstrating not "in," but "near" the courthouse. It is undisputed that the demonstration took place on the west sidewalk, the far side of the street, exactly 101 feet from the courthouse steps and, judging from the pictures in the record, approximately 125 feet from the courthouse itself. The question is raised as to whether the failure of the statute to define the word "near" renders it unconstitutionally vague. . . . It is clear that there is some lack of specificity in a word such as "near." While this lack of specificity may not render the statute unconstitutionally vague, at least as applied to a demonstration within the sight and hearing of those in the courthouse, it is clear that the statute, with respect to the determination of how near the courthouse a particular demonstration can be, foresees a degree of on-the-spot administrative interpretation by officials charged with responsibility for administering and enforcing it. It is apparent that demonstrators, such as those involved here, would justifiably tend to rely on this administrative interpretation of how "near" the courthouse a particular demonstration might take place. Louisiana's statutory policy of preserving order around the courthouse would counsel encouragement of just such reliance. This administrative discretion to construe the term "near" concerns a limited control of the streets and other areas in the immediate vicinity of the courthouse and is the type of narrow discretion which this Court has recognized as the proper role of responsible officials in making determinations concerning the time, place, duration, and manner of demonstrations. . . . It is not the type of unbridled discretion which would allow an official to pick and choose among expressions of view the ones he will permit to use the streets and other public facilities, which we have invalidated [in the past]. Nor does this limited administrative regulation of traffic which the Court has consistently recognized as necessary and permissible, constitute a waiver of law which is beyond the power of the police. Obviously telling demonstrators how far from the courthouse steps is "near" the courthouse for purposes of a permissible peaceful demonstration is a far cry from allowing one to commit, for example, murder, or robbery.

The record here clearly shows that the officials present gave permission for the demonstration to take place across the street from the courthouse. Cox testified that they gave him permission to conduct the demonstration on the far side of the street. This testimony is not only uncontradicted but is corroborated by the State's witnesses who were present. Police Chief White testified that he told Cox "he must confine" the demonstration "to the west side of the street." James Erwin, news director of radio station WIBR, agreed that Cox was given permission for the assembly as long as it remained within a designated time. When Sheriff Clemmons sought to break up the demonstration, he first announced, "now, you have been allowed to demonstrate." The Sheriff testified that he had "no objection" to the students "being assembled on that side of the street." Finally, in its brief before this Court, the State did not contend that permission was not granted. Rather in its statement of the facts and argument it conceded that the officials gave Cox and his group some time to demonstrate across the street from the courthouse. This agreement by the State that in fact permission had been granted to demonstrate across the street from the courthouse – at least for a limited period of time, which the State contends was set at seven minutes – was confirmed by counsel for the State in oral argument before this Court.

The record shows that at no time did the police recommend, or even suggest, that the demonstration be held further from the courthouse than it actually was. The police admittedly had prior notice that the demonstration was planned to be held in the vicinity of the courthouse. They were prepared for it at that point and so stationed themselves and their equipment as to keep the demonstrators on the far side of the street. As Cox approached the vicinity of the courthouse, he was met by the Chief of Police and other officials. At this point not only was it not suggested that they hold their assembly elsewhere, or disband, but they were affirmatively told that they could hold the demonstration on the sidewalk of the far side of the street, 101 feet from the courthouse steps. This area was effectively blocked off by the police and traffic rerouted. Thus, the highest police officials of the city, in the presence of the Sheriff and Mayor, in effect told the demonstrators that they could meet where they did, 101 feet from the courthouse steps, but could not meet closer to the courthouse. In effect, appellant was advised that a demonstration at the place it was held would not be one "near" the courthouse within the terms of the statute.

In *Raley v. Ohio*, 360 U.S. 423 (1959), this Court held that the Due Process Clause prevented conviction of persons for refusing to answer questions of a state investigating commission when they relied upon assurances of the commission, either express or implied, that they had a privilege under state law to refuse to answer, though in fact this privilege was not available to them. The situation presented here is analogous to that in *Raley*, which we deem to be controlling. As in *Raley*, under all the circumstances of this case, after the public officials acted as they did, to sustain appellant's later conviction for demonstrating where they told him he could "would be to sanction an indefensible sort of entrapment by the State – convicting a citizen for exercising a privilege which the State had clearly told him was available to him." *Id.* at 426. The Due Process Clause does not permit convictions to be obtained under such circumstances. This is not to say that had the appellant, entirely on his own, held the demonstration across the street from the courthouse within the sight and hearing of those inside, or a fortiori, had he defied an order of the police requiring him to hold this demonstration at some point further away out of the sight and hearing of those inside the courthouse, we would reverse the conviction as in this case. In such cases a state interpretation of the statute to apply to the demonstration as being "near" the courthouse would be subject to quite different considerations.

* * *

The application of these principles requires us to reverse the judgment of the Supreme Court of Louisiana.

QUESTIONS

1.	In the *Cox* case, as the Supreme Court stressed, the defendant's reliance on an official statement of law concerned public officials at the highest levels: the police chief, the sheriff, and the mayor. Do you think the result would have been different if Cox had sought the advice of his own attorney? Of a patrolman? At what level should the line be drawn to allow a defendant the ability to assert mistake of law when relying on a public official? Explain your reasoning.

2.   Suppose that someone, diligently researching the legality of his contemplated actions, came across a judicial opinion by a state's intermediate level court of appeals. Relying on that decision, the person goes ahead and acts. Unbeknownst to him, however, the highest court in that state had recently reversed the appellate court's decision, effectively prohibiting the conduct in which the person thought he could lawfully engage. Should he be able to assert mistake of law as a defense? Why or why not?

B. Duress, Coercion, and Necessity

The criminal law recognizes that there are times when someone acts not on his or her free will, but rather due to the coercion of another, or the seemingly necessary circumstances of the moment. When such is the case, the law permits a defendant to argue that his or her conduct should either be excused entirely, or mitigated downward to a less serious charge.

There are four requirements for asserting the *defense of necessity*. First, there must be a bona-fide emergency that threatened the defendant with some imminent harm. The type of harm is usually limited by statute to the use of, or a threat to use, unlawful force against the person or the person of another. Second, there must be a true necessity to commit the crime in order to avoid the harm presented under the emergency situation. In other words, there must be no reasonable opportunity to avoid the harm without committing the crime. Third, the defendant must not be at fault for having brought about the emergency situation that gave rise to the need to act. And finally, the choice to do the crime must be the lesser of two evils; the harm avoided by committing the crime must be more substantial or more serious than that harm caused by the commission of the crime. If all four of these criteria are met, a person may assert the defense of necessity or duress (terms used interchangeably in most jurisdictions). If permitted to do so, the defendant typically bears the burden of persuasion to prove that a person of reasonable firmness in the situation in which the defendant found himself or herself would have been unable to resist doing what was done.

There is an important exception to the usual availability of the duress/necessity defense for most crimes: the defense cannot be used to exonerate a homicide. No one may chose between himself or herself and the life of another. Thus, even if, through no fault of your own, someone has one gun to your head and puts another gun in your hand, instructing you to shoot "that person over there," you may not shoot the other person. The following case is considered to be the seminal case illustrating the rationale behind the homicide exception to the defense of necessity.

REGINA v. DUDLEY and STEPHENS
14 QB.D. 273 (1884).

Lord Coleridce, C.J.

The two prisoners, Thomas Dudley and Edwin Stephens, were indicted for the murder of Richard Parker on the high seas on the 25th of July in the present year. They were tried before my Brother Huddleston at Exeter on the 6th of November, and, under the direction of my learned Brother, the jury returned a special verdict, the legal effect of which has been argued before us, and on which we are now to pronounce judgment.

The special verdict is as follows:

On July 5, 1884, the prisoners, Thomas Dudley and Edward [sic] Stephens, with one Brooks, all able-bodied English seamen, and the deceased also an English boy, between seventeen and eighteen years of age, the crew of an English yacht, a registered English vessel, were cast away in a storm on the high seas 1,600 miles from the Cape of Good Hope, and were compelled to put into an open boat belonging to the said yacht. That in this boat they had no supply of water and no supply of food, except two 1 pound tins of turnips, and for three days they had nothing else to subsist upon. That on the fourth day they caught a small turtle, upon which they subsisted for a few days, and this was the only food they had up to the twentieth day when the act now in question was committed.

That on the twelfth day the remains of the turtle were entirely consumed, and for the next eight days they had nothing to eat. That they had no fresh water, except such rain as they from time to time caught in their oilskin capes. That the boat was drifting on the ocean, and was probably more than 1,000 miles away from land. That on the eighteenth day, when they had been seven days without food and five without water, the prisoners spoke to Brooks as to what should be done if no succour came, and suggested that some one should be sacrificed to save the rest, but Brooks dissented, and the boy, to whom they were understood to refer, was not consulted.

That on the 24th of July, the day before the act now in question, the prisoner Dudley proposed to Stephens and Brooks that lots should be cast who should be put to death to save the rest, but Brooks refused to consent, and it was not put to the boy, and in point of fact there was no drawing of lots. That on the day the prisoners spoke of their families, and suggested it would be better to kill the boy that their lives should be saved, and Dudley proposed that if there was no vessel in sight by the morrow morning, the boy should be killed.

That next day, the 25th of July, to vessel appearing, Dudley told Brooks that he had better go and have a sleep, and made signs to Stephens and Brooks that the boy had better be killed. The prisoner Stephens agreed to the act, but Brooks dissented from it. The boy was then lying at the bottom of the boat quite helpless and extremely weakened by famine and by drinking sea water, and unable to make any resistance, nor did he ever assent to his being killed. The prisoner Dudley offered a prayer asking forgiveness for them all if either of them should be tempted to commit a rash act, and that their souls might be saved. That Dudley, with the assent of Stephens, went to the boy, and telling him that his time was come, put a knife into his throat and killed him then and there; that the three men fed upon the body and blood of the boy for four days.

That on the fourth day after the act had been committed the boat was picked up by a passing vessel, and the prisoners were rescued, still alive, but in the lowest state of prostration. That then, were carried to the port of Falmouth, and committed for trial at Exeter. That if the men had not fed upon the body of the boy they would probably not have survived to be so picked up and rescued, but would within four days have died of famine. That the boy, being in a much weaker condition, was likely to have died before them. That at the time of the act in question there was no sail in sight, nor any reasonable prospect of relief. That under these circumstances there appeared to the prisoners every probability that unless they then fed or very soon fed upon the boy or one of themselves they would die of starvation. That there was no appreciable chance of saving life except by killing some one for the others to eat. That assuming any necessity to kill anybody, there was no greater necessity for killing the boy than any of the other three men. But whether upon the whole matter by the jurors found the killing of Richard Parker by Dudley and Stephens be felony and murder the jurors are ignorant, and pray the advice of the Court thereupon, and if upon the whole matter the Court shall be of opinion that the killing of Richard Parker be felony and murder, then the jurors say that Dudley and Stephens were each guilty of felony and murder as alleged in the indictment.

150

From these facts, stated with the cold precision of a special verdict, it appears sufficiently that the prisoners were subject to terrible temptation, to sufferings which might break down the bodily power of the strongest man, and try the conscience of the best. Other details yet more harrowing, facts still more loathsome and appalling, were presented to the jury, and are to be found recorded in my learned Brother's notes. But nevertheless this is clear, that the prisoners put to death a weak and unoffending boy upon the chance of preserving their own lives by feeding upon his flesh and blood after he was killed, and with the certainty of depriving him of any possible chance of survival.

The verdict finds in terms that "if the men had not fed upon the body of the boy they would *probably* not have survived," and that "the boy being in a much weaker condition was *likely* to have died before them." They might possibly have been picked up next day by a passing ship; they might possibly not have been picked up at all; in either case it is obvious that the killing of the boy would have been an unnecessary and profitless act. It is found by the verdict that the boy was incapable of resistance, and, in fact, made none; and it is not even suggested that his death was due to any violence on his part attempted against, or even so much as feared by, those who killed him. Under these circumstances the jury say that they are ignorant whether those who killed him were guilty of murder, and have referred it to this Court to determine what is the legal consequence which follows from the facts which they have found. . . .

The real question in the case is whether killing under the circumstances set forth in the verdict be or not be murder. The contention that it could be anything else was, to the minds of us all, both new and strange, and we stopped the Attorney General in his negative argument in order that we might hear what could be said in support of a proposition which appeared to us to be at once dangerous, immoral, and opposed to all legal principle and analogy. . . . First it is said that it follows from various definitions of murder in books of authority, which definitions imply, if they do not state, the doctrine, that in order to save your own life you may lawfully take away the life of another, when that other is neither attempting nor threatening yours, nor is guilty of any illegal act whatever towards you or any one else. But if these definitions be looked at they will not be found to sustain this contention.

It is . . . clear . . . that the doctrine contended for receives no support from the great authority of Lord Hale. It is plain that in his view the necessity which justified homicide is that only which has always been and is now considered a justification. Lord Hale regarded the private necessity which justified, and alone justified, the taking the life of another for the safeguard of one's own to be what is commonly called "self-defense." (Hale's Pleas of the Crown, i., 478.)

But if this could be even doubtful upon Lord Hale's words, Lord Hale himself has made it clear. For in the chapter in which he deals with the exemption created by compulsion or necessity he thus expresses himself: "If a man be desperately assaulted and in peril of death, and cannot otherwise escape unless, to satisfy his assailant's fury, he will kill an innocent person then present, the fear and actual force will not acquit him of the crime and punishment of murder, if he commit the act for he ought rather to die himself than kill an innocent; but if he cannot otherwise save his own life the law permits him in his own defense to kill the assailant, for by the violence of the assault, and the offence committed upon him by the assailant himself, the law of nature, and necessity, hath made him his own protector. . . . (Hale's Pleas of the Crown, vol. I., 51.)

But, further still, Lord Hale in the following chapter deals with the position asserted by the casuists, and sanctioned, as he says, by Grotius and Puffendorf, that in a case of extreme necessity, either of hunger or clothing; "theft is no theft, or at least not punishable as theft, as some even of our own lawyers have asserted the same." "But," says Lord Hale, "I take it that here in England, that rule, at least by the laws of England, is false; and therefore, if a person, being under necessity for want of victuals or clothes, shall upon that account clandestinely and animo furandi steal another man's goods, it is felony, and a crime by the laws of England punishable with death." (Hale, Pleas of the Crown, I., 54). If, therefore, Lord Hale is clear – as he is that extreme necessity of hunger does not justify larceny, what would he have said to the doctrine that it justified murder?

151

The one real authority of former time is Lord Bacon, who lays down the law as follows: "Necessity carrieth a privilege in itself. Necessity is of three sorts – necessity of conservation of life, necessity of obedience, and necessity of the act of God or of a stranger. First of conservation of life; if a man steal viands to satisfy his present hunger, this is no felony nor larceny. So if divers be in danger of drowning by the casting away of some boat or barge, and one of them get to some plank, or on the boat's side to keep himself above water, and another to save his life thrust him from it, whereby he is drowned, this is neither se defended nor by misadventure, but justifiable."

Lord Bacon was great even as a lawyer; but it is permissible to much smaller men, relying upon principle and on the authority of others, the equals and even the superiors of Lord Bacon as lawyers, to question the soundness of his dictum. There are many conceivable states of things in which it might possibly be true, but if Lord Bacon meant to lay down the broad proposition that man may save his life by killing, if necessary, an innocent and unoffending neighbor, it certainly is not law at the present day. . . .

Now it is admitted that the deliberate killing of this unoffending and unresisting boy was clearly murder, unless the killing can be justified by some well-recognized excuse admitted by the law. It is further admitted that there was in this case no such excuse, unless the killing was justified by what has been called "necessity." But the temptation to the act which existed here was not what the law has ever called necessity. Nor is this to be regretted. Though law and morality are not the same, and many things may be immoral which are not necessarily illegal, yet the absolute divorce of law from morality would be of fatal consequence; and such divorce would follow if the temptation to murder in this case were to be held by law an absolute defense of it. It is not so. To preserve one's life is generally speaking a duty, but it may be the plainest and the highest duty to sacrifice it. War is full of instances in which it is a man's duty not to live, but to die. The duty, in case of shipwreck, of a captain to his crew, of the crew to the passengers, of soldiers to women and children, as in the noble case of the *Birkenhead*; these duties impose on men the moral necessity, not of the preservation, but of the sacrifice of their lives for others, from which in no country, least of all, it is to be hoped, in England, will men ever shrink, as indeed, they have not shrunk.

It is not correct, therefore, to say that there is any absolute or unqualified necessity to preserve one's life. *"Necesse est ut eam, non ut vivam,"* is a saying of a Roman officer quoted by Lord Bacon himself with high eulogy in the very chapter on necessity to which so much reference has been made. It would be a very easy and cheap display of commonplace learning to quote from Greek and Latin authors, from Horace, from Juvenal, from Cicero, from Euripides, passage after passage, in which the duty of dying for others has been laid down in glowing and emphatic language as resulting from the principles of heathen ethics; it is enough in a Christian country to remind ourselves of the Great Example whom we profess to follow.

It is not needful to point out the awful danger of admitting the principle which has been contended for. Who is to be the judge of this sort of necessity? By what measure is the comparative value of lives to be measured? Is it to be strength, or intellect, or what? It is plain that the principle leaves to him who is to profit by it to determine the necessity which will justify him in deliberately taking another's life to save his own. In this case the weakest, the youngest, the most unresisting, was chosen. Was it more necessary to kill him than one of the grown men? The answer must be "No" –

> So spake the Fiend, and with necessity,
> The tyrant's plea, excused his devilish deeds.

It is not suggested that in this particular case the deeds were "devilish," but it is quite plain that such a principle once admitted might be made the legal cloak for unbridled passion and atrocious crime. There is no safe path for judges to tread but to ascertain the law to the best of their ability and to declare it according to their judgment; and if in any case the law appears to be too severe on individuals, to leave it to the Sovereign to exercise that prerogative of mercy which the Constitution has intrusted to the hands fittest to dispense it.

It must not be supposed that in refusing to admit temptation to be an excuse for crime it is forgotten how terrible the temptation was; how awful the suffering; how hard in such trials to keep the judgment straight and the conduct pure. We are often compelled to set up standards we cannot reach ourselves, and to lay down rules which we could not ourselves satisfy. But a man has no right to declare temptation to be an excuse, though he might himself have yielded to it, nor allow compassion for the criminal to change or weaken in any manner the legal definition of the crime. It is therefore our duty to declare that the prisoners' act in this case was wilful murder, that the facts as stated in the verdict are no legal justification of the homicide; and to say that in our unanimous opinion the prisoners are upon this special verdict guilty of murder.

QUESTIONS

1.   Do you agree with the court's rationale? Why or why not? For an in-depth exploration of the various philosophical arguments concerning the defense of necessity as it relates to homicide, read Lon L. Fuller, *The Case of the Speluncean Explorers*, 62 HARV. L. REV. 616 (1949).

2.   What if you were put in a situation, though no fault of your own, that appeared to necessitate killing some innocent third-party in order to save the life of your own child? The law clearly says you may not choose one life over another. But wouldn't human nature suggest that "reasonable" persons in an emergency situation would act in any way possible to save the life of their own children? How should the law handle such a situation?

3.   The defendants in *Regina v. Dudley and Stephens* were sentenced to death. But the Queen of England thereafter commuted their sentences to six months' imprisonment. Which do you think the more prudent route to be: allowing the defense of necessity to be used so that a jury can decide if criminal liability should be imposed, or not allowing it to be asserted in the hopes that the sentencing court or executive branch will see to it that the sentence is adjusted to "fit" the crime under the circumstances? Why?

4.   Suppose that one were in prison and had been specifically threatened with death, forcible sexual attack, or substantial bodily injury in the immediate future, yet the prison authorities dismissed your pleas for help and there were insufficient time to seek the assistance of the courts. Should such a prisoner be allowed to assert the defense of necessity to the crime of escape if he or she does escape (or attempts to do so) in order to avoid the impending attack? Explain the pros and cons of allowing such a defense. *See United States v. Bailey*, 444 U.S. 394 (1980).

5.   Those who engage in acts of civil disobedience often argue their acts are "necessary" to stop some policy or practice. Should the defense work to excuse disorderly conduct of anti-war protestors? How about animal rights activists? See, e.g., *United States v. Schoon*, 971 F.2d 193 (9th Cir. 1992).

___

C. Intoxication

The criminal law has a relatively short long history of permitting those who are intoxicated to assert that their state of intoxication interfered with their ability to form mens rea. From 1551 until the 1800s, the common law disallowed a defendant from using intoxication as an excuse or justification for an offense. But in the nineteenth century, the common law rule changed and since then, it has allowed evidence of intoxication as a defense to certain crimes. The success of such a defense, however, has always been dependent on two main factors: whether the intoxication was voluntary or involuntary; and the level of mens rea of the crime for which the defense was being asserted.

1. Voluntary Intoxication: Specific v. General Intent Crimes

Intoxication is a generic term in the criminal law. It refers not only to a state induced by alcohol, but also by drugs – both licit and illicit. When one is **voluntarily intoxicated**, he or she has introduced a substance into the body which the person either knew or should have known was likely to have intoxicating effects. Voluntary intoxication was a defense at common law and continues to be a defense in many jurisdictions today so long as the intoxication was "substantial." Thus, how much of the intoxicant was consumed over what period of time is highly relevant. Additional relevant factors include the actor's conduct as perceived by others; results of forensic tests; and the actor's own subjective to recall events.

At common law, voluntary intoxication was a defense to crimes of specific intent. Intoxication could be offered to negate the actus reus (i.e, to show the defendant could not have physically performed the conduct required by the definition of the crime). More frequently, though, it was offered to negate mens rea of specific intent. In other words, the defendant was permitted to assert they he or she was so intoxicated they he or she could not form specific intent to kill, rape, steal, etc. When so offered, however, it was not a complete defense. Rather, voluntary intoxication was used to mitigate a crime of specific intent down to one of general intent.

===

The PEOPLE, Plaintiff-Respondent, v. David Keith HOOD, Defendant-Appellant.
1 Cal.3d 444, 462 P.2d 370, 82 Cal. Rptr. 618 (1969).

Traynor, Chief Justice.

On September 11, 1967, at about 2:00 a.m., defendant, his brother Donald, and a friend, Leo Chilton, all of whom had been drinking for several hours, knocked on the door of the house of Susan Bueno, defendant's former girlfriend, and asked if they could use the bathroom. Susan said no, but defendant forced his way in and started to hit her. He knocked her to the floor and kicked her. Donald Hood then took Susan aside, and defendant, Chilton, and Gene Saunders, a friend of Susan's who was staying at the house, went to the kitchen and sat down.

Gilbert A. Nielsen, Susan's next-door neighbor, was awakened by the sound of Susan's screams and called the police. Officers Elia and Kemper responded to his call. After talking to Nielsen, they went to Susan's house, knocked on the door, which was opened by Stella Gonzales, Susan's cousin, and asked if "Susie" was there. Miss Gonzales said, "Yes, just a minute," and in a few seconds Susan came running to the door crying. Officer Elia asked Susan if she had been beaten and who did it. She pointed to the kitchen and said, "They're in there right now."

The two officers walked through the living room, where Susan, Susan's seven-year-old son Ronnie, and Stella remained, and went into the kitchen. There they observed defendant on the right-hand side of the room leaning against a door. On the left side of the kitchen, the three other men were seated at a table. Officer Elia walked to the middle of the room and questioned the men at the table. Defendant interrupted the questioning and asked Officer Elia if he had a search warrant. Officer Elia replied that he did not need one since the person who rented the house had given him permission to enter. Defendant then directed a stream of obscenities of Officer Elia, who turned and, according to his testimony, started to place defendant under arrest for a violation of Penal Code section 415 (using vulgar, profane, or indecent language within the presence or hearing of women or children). He got no further than to say, "Okay fella, you are . . ." when defendant swung at him with his fist. When Officer Kemper attempted to go to Officer Elia's assistance, Donald Hood jumped on him from behind.

During the ensuing struggle, Officer Elia fell with defendant on top of him in a corner of a pantry adjoining the kitchen at the rear. While struggling on the floor, Officer Elia felt a tug at his gun belt and then heard two shots fired. A third officer, Laurence Crocker, who had arrived at the house shortly after the other two officers, came into the kitchen as the scuffle between Officer Elia and defendant was beginning. After he had control of Donald Hood, he looked across the kitchen and saw defendant with a gun in his right hand. He testified that defendant pointed the gun towards Officer Elia's midsection and pulled the trigger twice.

Both Officers Crocker and Kemper testified that after the shots, defendant's arm came up over his head with the revolver in his hand. The struggle continued into the bathroom. Defendant was finally subdued when Officer Elia regained possession of the gun and held it against the side of defendant's neck. Officer Elia then noticed that defendant had shot him once in each leg. The foregoing evidence is clearly sufficient to support the verdicts. Defendant contends that the court failed properly to instruct the jury with respect to lesser included offenses to the offense charged in Count I, and that it also erred in instructing on the effect of intoxication with respect to the offenses charged in both Counts I and III.

[The California Supreme Court reversed the conviction because the trial court had failed to instruct the jury properly regarding the jury's ability to convict on the lesser-included offense of simple-assault. The Court went on to address the issue of intoxication so there would be no problem on retrial].

The judgment must also be reversed as to Count III, for the court gave hopelessly conflicting instructions on the effect of intoxication. Although the court correctly instructed the jury to consider the evidence that defendant was intoxicated in determining whether he had the specific intent to commit murder, it followed that instruction with the complete text of CALJIC No. 78 (revised), which applies to crimes that require proof only of a general criminal intent. The court in no way made clear to the jury that the latter instruction did not apply to the charge of assault with intent to commit murder. The giving of such conflicting instructions with respect to a crime requiring proof of a specific intent is error. That error was clearly prejudicial in this case.

There was substantial evidence that defendant was drunk. He testified that he was not aware that he ever had the gun in his possession or fired it. Its discharge during the scuffle could be reconciled with an intent to kill, an intent to inflict only bodily injury, or with no intent to fire it at all. Had the jury not been given conflicting instructions on the significance of defendant's intoxication, it is reasonably probable that it would have reached a result more favorable to defendant on Count III.

To guide the trial court on retrial, we consider the question of the effect of intoxication on the crime of assault with a deadly weapon. Many cases have held that neither assault with a deadly weapon nor simple assault is a specific intent crime. A number of these cases held that an assault with a deadly weapon could be predicated on reckless, as well as intentional, conduct.

> Where the act is both unlawful and wrongful, and well calculated to inflict serious personal injury the law will imply malice and an unlawful intention and override any actual intention existing in the mind of the aggressor. Thus, while it is not an assault to fire a gun in the air for the purpose of frightening another, it is an assault, without regard to the aggressor's intention, to fire a gun at another or in the direction in which he is standing. The law will not tolerate such a reckless disregard for human life.

The distinction between specific and general intent crimes evolved as a judicial response to the problem of the intoxicated offender. That problem is to reconcile two competing theories of what is just in the treatment of those who commit crimes while intoxicated. On the one hand, the moral culpability of a drunken criminal is frequently less than that of a sober person effecting a like injury. On the other hand, it is commonly felt that a person who voluntarily gets drunk and while in that state commits a crime should not escape the consequences.

Before the nineteenth century, the common law refused to give any effect to the fact that an accused committed a crime while intoxicated. The judges were apparently troubled by this rigid traditional rule, however, for there were a number of attempts during the early part of the nineteenth century to arrive at a more humane, yet workable, doctrine. The theory that these judges explored was that evidence of intoxication could be considered to negate intent, whenever intent was an element of the crime charged. As Professor Hall notes, however, such an exculpatory doctrine could eventually have undermined the traditional rule entirely, since some form of mens rea is a requisite of all but strict liability offenses. To limit the operation of the doctrine and achieve a compromise between the conflicting feelings of sympathy and reprobation for the intoxicated offender, later courts both in England and this country drew a distinction between so-called specific intent and general intent crimes.

Specific and general intent have been notoriously difficult terms to define and apply, and a number of textwriters recommend that they be abandoned altogether. Too often the characterization of a particular crime as one of specific or general intent is determined solely by the presence or absence of words describing psychological phenomena – "intent" or "malice," for example – in the statutory language of defining the crime. When the definition of a crime consists of only the description of a particular act, without reference to intent to do a further act or achieve a future consequence, we ask whether the defendant intended to do the proscribed act. This intention is deemed to be a general criminal intent. When the definition refers to defendant's intent to do some further act or achieve some additional consequence, the crime is deemed to be one of specific intent. There is no real difference, however, only a linguistic one, between an intent to do an act already performed and an intent to do that same act in the future.

We need not reconsider our position in Carmen that an assault cannot be predicated merely on reckless conduct. Even if assault requires an intent to commit a battery on the victim, it does not follow that the crime is one in which evidence of intoxication ought to be considered in determining whether the defendant had that intent. It is true that in most cases specific intent has come to mean an intention to do a future act or achieve a particular result, and that assault is appropriately characterized as a specific intent crime under this definition. An assault, however, is equally well characterized as a general intent crime under the definition of general intent as an intent merely to do a violent act. Therefore, whatever reality the distinction between specific and general intent may have in other contexts, the difference is chimerical in the case of assault with a deadly weapon or simple assault. Since the definitions of both specific intent and general intent cover the requisite intent to commit a battery, the decision whether or not to give effect to evidence of intoxication must rest on other considerations.

A compelling consideration is the effect of alcohol on human behavior. A significant effect of alcohol is to distort judgment and relax the controls on aggressive and anti-social impulses. Alcohol apparently has less effect on the ability to engage in simple goal-directed behavior, although it may impair the efficiency of that behavior. In other words, a drunk man is capable of forming an intent to do something simple, such as strike another, unless he is so drunk that he was reached the stage of unconsciousness. What he is not as capable as a sober man of doing is exercising judgment about the social consequences of his acts or controlling his impulses toward antisocial acts. He is more likely to act rashly and impulsively and to be susceptible to passion and anger. It would therefore be anomalous to allow evidence of intoxication to relieve a man of responsibility for the crimes of assault with a deadly weapon or simple assault, which are so frequently committed in just such a manner. Whatever ambiguities there may be in distinguishing between specific and general intent to determine whether drunkenness constitutes a defense, an offense of this nature is not one which requires an intent that is susceptible to negation through a showing of voluntary intoxication.

Those crimes that have traditionally been characterized as crimes of specific intent are not affected by our holding here. The difference in mental activity between formulating an intent to commit a battery and formulating an intent to commit a battery for the purpose of raping or killing may be slight, but it is sufficient to justify drawing a line between them and considering evidence of intoxication in the one case and disregarding it in the other. Accordingly, on retrial the court should not instruct the jury to consider evidence of defendant's intoxication in determining whether he committed assault with a deadly weapon on a peace officer or any of the lesser assaults included therein, and any case implying the contrary are disapproved.

The judgment is reversed.

QUESTIONS

1.   The *Hood* case illustrates how a specific intent crime can be lessened to one of general intent when the actor is intoxicated to such a degree that he or she could not form the requisite specific intent. But what if criminal intent is formed before the intoxication? For example, suppose a person formulates the intent to kill but is not sure if he or she can follow through on the plan. So, having formed the intent to kill, the person becomes intoxicated in order to lose his or her inhibitions and thereby get up courage (often referred to as "alcohol guts") to carry out the crime. How should the law handle such a defendant? Why?

2.   As the *Hood* case illustrates, voluntary intoxication cannot be used as a defense to general intent crimes. What are the major public policy reasons underlying the rationale for such a rule?

The Model Penal Code follows a very similar approach to the common law with respect to voluntary intoxication. It allows it to be used as a defense on to disprove the existence of an element of the offense. Thus, as with the common law, it can be used to show that the defendant was too intoxicated to have performed the conduct element of an offense, and thereby disprove actus reus. It can also be used to negate the mens rea elements of any crime of either purpose or knowledge, just as the common law allowed it to be used to disprove specific intent.

The Model Penal Code handling of the defense when dealing with the mens rea level of recklessness, however, is more complex. Recall that recklessness is defined as the conscious disregard of a known risk. If, due to voluntary intoxication, a defendant was not subjectively unaware of the risk required by the definition of recklessness, then voluntary intoxication can be asserted as a defense. But this is allowed to be asserted only under very limited circumstances known as *pathological intoxication*. Intoxication is pathological (even though voluntary) if it is a result of an unforeseeable, grossly excessive reaction to the voluntary ingesting of an intoxicant in light of the amount taken. In other words, even though a person voluntary consumes the intoxicant, the reaction is unforeseeably and grossly disproportionate to the amount consumed. An example would be someone who becomes highly intoxicated after drinking a half a glass of wine. But see that in order to be unforeseeable, and therefore pathological, the defendant could not have known of his or her susceptibility to such a disproportionate reaction.

If the voluntary intoxication is not pathological, then it cannot be used as a defense to any crime of recklessness. This is because the very act of voluntarily consuming the intoxicant to the point of not being able to perceive risks is deemed to be reckless conduct in and of itself. And, given that non-pathological, voluntary intoxication is not a defense to crimes that carry recklessness as their mens rea, it should come as no surprise that the defense will not work for those crimes which have negligence as their requisite level of mens rea. Thus, the intoxicated person will be held to the standard of the ordinary, reasonable, prudent person in a sober state, rendering his or her intoxication irrelevant. And, finally, voluntary intoxication is never a defense to crimes of strict liability, the most obvious of which would be drunk driving.

2. Involuntary Intoxication

The defense of *involuntary intoxication* is relatively rare, but it was recognized as a complete defense to all crimes at common law, and continues to operate in the same fashion today in most U.S. jurisdictions. Involuntary intoxication generally means that the person did not voluntary consume the intoxicant. By this, it is meant that one is involuntarily intoxicated if the state was caused by an intoxicant that the defendant neither knew nor had reason to know that he or she ingested (i.e., drink unbeknownst to defendant that is laced with a drug).

But involuntary intoxication also includes to less obvious definitions. Intoxication is considered involuntary if the actor was forced to consume the intoxicant under duress. Intoxication is also considered involuntary if the intoxication was the *unforeseeable* side-effect of a medically prescribed drug. Note the use of the word unforeseeable as opposed to unforeseen. If the side-effect is one that is warned against on the bottle or in the packaging, then presumable it is not unforeseeable. If the patient failed to education himself or herself on the possible side-effects of the drug being consumed, then it was merely unforeseen by him or her. Similarly, if the consumption of some substance has a stronger effect that the one anticipated does not render the intoxication involuntary.

Regardless of which of the three manners a person become involuntarily intoxicated, the defense has the same effect on criminal responsibility. When involuntary intoxication causes the a substantial incapacity to either appreciate the criminality of the actor's conduct, or to conform the actor's behavior to the requirements of the law, then his or her conduct is excused. Hence, unlike voluntary intoxication which only serves to reduce crimes of specific intent to crimes of general intent, involuntary intoxication is a complete defense.

3. Due Process Considerations

It should be noted that a handful of U.S. jurisdictions have abolished the defense of voluntary intoxication completely. In other words, it cannot be used as a defense to either crimes of specific or general intent. Such abolition of the defense of intoxication has raised federal due process concerns, but in *Montana v. Egelhoff*, 518 U.S. 37 (1996), the Supreme Court held that the Due Process Clause does not require that a criminal defendant be allowed to introduce evidence of intoxication to show that he or she did not entertain the requisite mens rea for a given offense. In doing so, the Court upheld the ability of U.S. jurisdictions to abolish the defense of intoxication.

CHAPTER 5
DEFENSES OF EXCUSE II: MENTAL CAPACITY

A. Infancy

Infancy for legal purposes is quite different from the way the term is used by developmental psychologists, educators, or in common parlance. Under a jurisdiction's civil law, an infant is someone who has not reached the age of majority, usually set at age eighteen. The common law set certain presumptions regarding an infant's capacity to commit a crime.

In the middle ages, the courts of England concluded that of a child under the age of seven did not have the capacity to commit of a crime. This conclusion was rooted in ecclesiastical law and Roman law, both of which presumed a child under the age of seven to lack the capacity to know right from wrong. Today, most states maintain the common law rule in the form of a conclusive presumption. Accordingly, children under the age of seven are generally not charged with crimes.

At the other end of the childhood age spectrum, the common law held that children over the age of fourteen were presumed to be both sane, and capable of formulating the necessary mental intent to commit of a crime. Evidence to the contrary may be presented to rebut the presumption of capacity to show incapacity. Most U.S. jurisdictions continue to follow this approach, although the ages during which the presumption of capacity applies vary from state to state. Regardless of the age at which the presumption of capacity attaches, jurisdiction over such juvenile offenders usually lies with a juvenile court. It should be noted, however, that many states have increasingly been allowing juveniles to be transferred out of their juvenile justice systems to be tried as adults in a court of general criminal jurisdiction.

In most jurisdictions, children between the ages of the conclusive incapacity (usually age seven or younger) and presumed capacity (usually age 14 or older) are presumed incapable of forming criminal intent, but the presumption is a rebuttable one. Thus, generally speaking, children between the ages of seven and fourteen are presumed to be incapable of committing of a crime, but evidence by the state that the child had the mental capacity and the ability to formulate the requisite criminal intent may be introduced to overcome the presumption of incapacity, as it was in the following case.

STATE of Washington, Respondent, v. Carlos LINARES and Isaac Lee PAM, Appellants. 880 P.2d 550 (Wash. Ct. App. 1994).

Carlos Linares and Isaac Pam appeal their juvenile convictions on the grounds that the court erred in concluding that they were capable of committing the crimes with which they were charged.

Section 9A.04.050 [of the Revised Code of Washington] establishes a statutory presumption of incapacity where a child is between 8 and 12 years old. The statutory presumption of incapacity applies in juvenile proceedings. The State has the burden of rebutting the presumption of incapacity by clear and convincing evidence. The standard of review on appeal is whether there was evidence from which a rational trier of fact could find capacity by clear and convincing evidence.

Facts

At Linares' capacity hearing, Officer Sweeney testified that Linares admitted entering the school and taking a radio. He also testified that Linares made the following statement: "I know what I did is wrong. Those things didn't belong to me. I wasn't supposed to be inside the school." Besides Sweeney's testimony, the court heard testimony from Linares, Yolanda Gonzales, Linares' teacher for 2 years, Jaynie Pleasants, a school psychologist, and James Matthews, one of Linares' former teachers. Gonzales testified that after the incident Linares told her that he and a friend – a cousin and his brother had gone into a school. And I asked him why. And he said because they wanted to play inside;

because it was raining outside, and they wanted to go in and play ball. She also testified that Linares told her he knew what he had done was wrong and that he took responsibility for it. She explained that Linares understands rules, but not the consequences of breaking those rules. She also testified that Linares has learning disabilities and was receiving special education at the time.

Pleasants testified that she has observed and tested Linares in conjunction with his special education requirements. He was tested in February 1991; the results of those tests showed that his verbal IQ was in the low-average range and his performance IQ was slightly above the mean for his age. She concluded that Linares "has a lot of difficulty processing and getting into long-term memory things." She also testified that, on a comprehension subtest designed to measure a child's understanding of cultural and social information, Linares scored below a 7-year-old level. Pleasants concluded that Linares may understand that "criminals . . . do wrong things," but he would not understand that they actually broke the law or what the consequences of doing so were. In her opinion, Linares did not have the capacity to understand the crimes with which he was charged.

Linares testified at the capacity hearing. He was asked a series of questions by his attorney about his understanding of his rights and the criminal justice system. To each question asked he simply replied "no." The State asked only a few questions on cross examination. The trial court found that the State had met its burden of rebutting the statutory presumption of incapacity. It further stated that, even if it had not considered Linares' statement to Officer Sweeney, it was still led to conclude that the State had met its burden because the remaining evidence was clear, cogent, and convincing that Linares had the capacity to understand it was wrong both to enter a locked school and to take things.

At Pam's capacity hearing, Officer Phipps testified that he asked Pam if he knew why he was being stopped. Pam replied that "he believed that it was in regards to . . . throwing rocks at a building." Phipps further testified that they first discussed who was throwing the rocks and how many rocks were thrown, and he had indicated that he had also thrown rocks at the same building the day before, on, I believe it was, the 25th, and had broken out some windows, both – both this day and the day before.

> When we finished discussing that, I asked him if he realized his actions were wrong; he stated that he did realize that. We talked about did he think he was going to get in trouble from his parents; he stated yeah, he was going to be in trouble, and he knew when he was doing it that is was something that he could get in trouble for. We also discussed the fact that there are laws in our state, and did he realize that it was against the law to break windows, and he said that he did understand that.

Pam did not testify at the capacity hearing and the State did not present any witnesses besides Phipps.

Discussion

Linares argues that the State did not rebut the statutory presumption of incapacity because it did not establish that he appreciated the quality of his acts at the time he committed them or that he understood the consequences of his acts. He contends that the concept of wrongfulness as used in the context of a juvenile's capacity to commit a crime must include the requirement that the juvenile understand the basic legal prohibition against such action. He also argues that, although the evidence may have shown that he knew his actions were morally wrong, there was no evidence to show that he knew his actions were legally prohibited.

In addressing this issue, we find it instructive to refer to cases interpreting the insanity defense. Although not perfectly analogous, the insanity and infancy defenses have similar origins and functions in the criminal law. Both belong to a class of defenses that focus on the actor's lack of capacity to form the mens rea of a crime. If the actor lacks that capacity, he or she is legally incapable of committing the crime and for that reason is relieved of all criminal responsibility for the act.

Under the infancy statute, the State must show that the child had sufficient capacity both to (1) understand the act or neglect charged and (2) to understand that it was wrong. Here we are concerned only with the portion of the infancy statute that addresses the child's knowledge that the act was wrong.

Capacity determinations, by their nature, are fact-specific inquiries and must be determined on a case by case basis. In addition to the nature of the crime, the following factors are relevant in determining whether a child knew the act he or she was committing was wrong: (1) whether the child evinced a desire for secrecy, (2) the child's age, (3) prior conduct similar to that charged, (4) any consequences that attached to that conduct, and (5) acknowledgment that the behavior is wrong and could lead to detention.

We conclude that there was sufficient evidence presented in Linares' case to enable a rational trier of fact to find capacity by clear and convincing evidence. In addition to Linares' statement to Officer Sweeney, the court considered his statement to Gonzales and the testimony of Linares' teachers and a school psychologist regarding his level of maturity and intellectual development. Although some of these witnesses felt Linares did not understand the legal prohibitions against his acts, none testified that he did not understand that his conduct was wrong. The court was also able to observe Linares' demeanor when he took the stand at the hearing. Linares' conduct during and after the break-in is also highly probative in establishing that he appreciated the wrongfulness of his conduct. The finding of capacity is further supported by the fact that Linares was 11 years old at the time of the incident, the upper end of the age range in which a child is presumed incapable of committing a crime.

The State did not meet its burden in Pam's case. Apart from the fact that Pam was 11 years old at the time of the incident, there was no other evidence presented at the hearing besides his custodial statement on which the court could have based its capacity finding. Pam did not testify at the hearing, and the court did not have an opportunity to observe his demeanor. The court did not hear testimony from any other witness besides Officer Phipps. Although in his statement to Phipps following the incident Pam acknowledged that his actions were wrong, that is insufficient evidence from which a rational trier of fact could have concluded that Pam appreciated the wrongfulness of his act at the time it was committed.

In *State v. K.R.L.*, 67 Wash. App. 721, 725, 840 P.2d 210 (1992), the court held a juvenile's statement to his mother admitting the wrongfulness of his conduct was insufficient to support the finding of capacity. The juvenile in that case was 8 years old, and his statement was made only after he had been beaten by his mother. The court reasoned that K.R.L.'s statement did not establish that he knew what he did was wrong at the time of the act because after he had been beaten he undoubtedly came to the realization that what he had done was wrong. We are certain that this conditioned the child, after the fact, to know that what he did was wrong. That is a far different thing than one['s] appreciating the quality of his or her acts at the time the act is being committed. To the extent that Pam's statements did not establish his appreciation of the wrongfulness of his conduct at the time it was committed, this case is similar to *K.R.L.* Although Pam was not beaten like *K.R.L.*, once the children were separated and given Miranda warnings it must have been obvious to Pam that he had done something wrong. Furthermore, when the police showed up, the children did not try to hide what they had done, lie, or otherwise evidence a desire for secrecy. Nor had they suffered any consequences from the similar behavior the day before, acts which Pam readily admitted. We hold that a child's after-the-fact acknowledgment that he or she understood that the conduct was wrong is insufficient, standing alone, to overcome the presumption of incapacity by clear and convincing evidence.

The disposition in Linares is affirmed and the disposition in Pam is reversed.

QUESTIONS

1.   The court found there was insufficient evidence to uphold a finding of capacity with respect to Isaac Pam. Yet, of the two juveniles, both of whom told the police they knew what they did was "wrong," Linares was the one whose understanding of "right" and "wrong" was questionable in light of his learning disability. Given this, do you think the outcome of this case is fair? Why or why not?

2.   There was specific evidence that Linares had problems processing cultural and social information, especially in terms of understanding the consequences of one's actions. The court

concluded, however, that in spite of such evidence, the state had introduced sufficient evidence to rebut the statutory presumption of incapacity for a juvenile of Linares' age. Upon what evidence did the court rely? Do you agree with the court's conclusion that it rose to the level of clear and convincing evidence? Explain your reasoning.

B. Competency to Stand Trial

The U.S. system of criminal justice requires that one be competent or "fit" to stand trial before one's guilt or innocence is assessed at a criminal trial. Accordingly, when the fitness of a particular criminal defendant to stand trial becomes an issue in a case, his or her competency to stand trial must be determined before a trial can proceed.

The legal bar against trying incompetent defendants dates back to common law England when someone who was "mad" could not be arraigned since he did not understand with what or why he was being charged. Today, since most criminal defendant's enjoy the right to counsel, a right not granted to criminal defendants at English common law, the historical justification seems somewhat unpersuasive a reason for continuing the requirement of competency to stand trial today. Nonetheless, it increases both the reliability and the fairness of the trial when the defendant can meaningfully participate in the process.

Competency to stand trial is often confused with insanity. Although the two doctrines are related insofar as they are both concerned with the mental status of a criminal defendant, they are quite different in terms of their goals, justifications, and processes.

1. Timing

Competency to stand trial concerns itself with a criminal defendant's mental state *at the time of trial*. The central focus of a hearing on competency is to see if the trial court should be deprived of jurisdiction over the defendant due to his/her lack of capacity to stand trial. In contrast, insanity is concerned with the defendant's state of mind *at the time the criminal offense is alleged to have taken place.* The issue of insanity is litigated over the course of a criminal trial in which the defendant's alleged insanity serves as a defense to the crime with which the defendant has been charged. Accordingly, *timing* is a critical distinction between the two doctrines.

Timing is also an important distinction between incompetency to stand trial and insanity in terms of when the respective issues may be raised during the criminal judicial process. Insanity is not a defense that the defendant can spring on the court in the middle of trial. Proper notice must be given by the defense that the insanity defense is going to be used.

> If a defendant intends to rely upon the defense of insanity at the time of the alleged offense, the defendant shall, within the time provided for the filing of pretrial motions or at such later time as the court may direct, notify the attorney for the government in writing of such intention and file a copy of such notice with the clerk. If there is a failure to comply with the requirements of this subdivision, insanity may not be raised as a defense. The court may for cause shown allow late filing of the notice or grant additional time to the parties to prepare for trial or make such other order as may be appropriate.

Fed. R. Crim. Pro. 12.2(a). Thus, if a plea of not guilty by reason of insanity or (its equivalent) is not pled in a timely manner, the defense is deemed to be waived.

Competency to stand trial, however, may be raised at any time in the criminal process, even after conviction. And, while the issue of competency to stand trial is usually raised by the defense, the prosecution can raise the issue, as can the court on its own. This stands in sharp contrast to insanity which, as described above, must be timely pled by the defense. Insanity cannot be forced upon a defendant by the prosecution or by the court, absent extra-ordinary circumstances.

2. Burdens of Proof

Historically, the defendant only bore the burden of production on the insanity defense and the prosecution had to prove the sanity of a criminal defendant beyond a reasonable doubt after the defense raised the issue of insanity. Today, however, largely in response to the not guilty by reason of insanity verdict in the case against John Hinckley for his assassination attempt against President Ronald Reagan, insanity is an affirmative defense. Accordingly, in the federal system and in most U.S. jurisdictions, the defense now bears both the burden of production and the burden of persuasion on the issue of insanity.

In contrast, there is no burden of production when dealing with the issue of incompetency to stand trial. As stated above, the issue of competency can be raised by either the prosecution or the defense, or even by the court on its own. Most requests for a clinical determination of competency go unopposed by opposing counsel and are routinely granted by judges. Once granted the opportunity to have such a determination made, the process of determining competency to stand trial is quite different from the trial process used to determine insanity: clinical evaluations followed by an evidentiary hearing on the issue of competency is the norm.

As a general rule, the prosecution must show at the competency hearing that the defendant is competent to proceed with the criminal trial. This showing must be by a preponderance of the evidence. However, there are some states that have shifted the burden of persuasion to the defense who must show the incompetency of the defendant by a preponderance of the evidence. The Supreme Court specifically approved of this allocation of the burden of persuasion over a due process challenge in *Medina v. California,* 505 U.S. 437, 452 (1992). The Court, however, struck down Oklahoma's subsequent attempt to require the defendant to show his or her competence by clear and convincing evidence, finding it to violate the guarantee of due process. *Cooper v. Oklahoma*, 116 S. Ct. 1373, 1384 (1996). In doing so, it invalidated the laws of the four states – Connecticut, Oklahoma, Pennsylvania, and Rhode Island – that had set the burden unconstitutionally high.

3. Constitutional Implications of Denial of a Hearing

Regardless of whether the prosecution or defense bears the burden of persuasion at the competency hearing, the process unfolds in the manner set forth in the next section of this chapter. Before moving on to the technicalities of the competency hearing, it is necessary to consider what happens when a competency hearing should take place, but does not. As stated above, once requested by either side, judges normally grant a competency determination. But if a judge refuses to order a competency hearing, that refusal can have consequences on the ultimate outcome of a case.

If there are no objective grounds for a judge to order a competency determination, it is highly unlikely that the judge's refusal will have any outcome on a case. On the other hand, if there were grounds upon which the competency of the defendant had been called into question and the judge refused to order a competency hearing, then serious constitutional concerns can be raised that could invalidate a conviction on appeal or via some post-conviction relief mechanism such as a habeas corpus proceeding. The law is clear on this latter point: a failure to conduct an evidentiary hearing where evidence before a trial court raises a "bona fide doubt" about the defendant's competency to stand trial violates due process. While a concise rule, what constitutes a "bona fide doubt" is somewhat ambiguous, as the following case illustrates.

UNITED STATES of America, Appellee, v. Jacobo LOYOLA-DOMINGUEZ, Appellant.
125 F.3d 1315 (9th Cir. 1997).

Reinhardt, Circuit Judge:

On January 9, 1995, INS Special Agent Jerry Lee Kracher contacted Jacobo Loyola-Dominguez at the county jail in Fresno, California, where he was being detained. After Agent Kracher advised him of his rights under *Miranda*, Loyola-Dominguez agreed to submit to questioning. During the interview, Loyola-Dominguez admitted the following facts: (1) he is citizen of Mexico; (2) he was convicted in June 1990 of possessing cocaine for sale, a felony under California law; (3) he was twice deported from the United States, first in 1993, and again in 1994; and (4) he illegally re-entered the United States near Tijuana without inspection on January 3, 1995. On the basis of this information, Loyola-Dominguez was indicted on one count of being a deported alien found in the United States and one count of being a deported alien found in the United States following an aggravated felony conviction.

The trial on these charges was scheduled to begin on the morning of April 16, 1996. On the night of April 15, Loyola-Dominguez tried to commit suicide by hanging himself in his jail cell. In court the next morning, defense counsel advised the district judge that his client had attempted suicide the night before and moved for a hearing to determine competency to stand trial. Defense counsel elaborated on his concerns regarding Loyola-Dominguez's competency:

> And I have additional information, background information, that he's been in the isolation ward. He's been in isolation, in the hole, I think it's called, or administrative segregation since November. And in that particular environment he's not given much exercise, much yard time, much — any educational or social interacting type of opportunities. In fact, it seems like it's just isolation most of the time, except for showers and when he comes to court. And that type of sensory deprivation and isolation, in fact, may have led to what happened last night.
>
> As well, he's advised me that approximately two or three weeks ago there was a fight with himself and another member, a jail staff member. I know that the marshals advised me at one time that, yes, there was a fight at the jail with him and a staff member, a jail guard. He's advised me that his jaw, his nose and his back was hurt in this altercation and that for three weeks he's requested medicine or medical contact and he said he hasn't received it. And then I was advised that last night he attempted suicide.

The court did not immediately grant or deny the motion, but instead briefly questioned Loyola-Dominguez (with the assistance of a translator) in order to determine whether a competency hearing was warranted. The following exchange represents the entire colloquy:

COURT: Mr. Loyola, your attorney asked to continue this matter and send you away for a psychiatric examination. Is it your desire to be examined by a psychiatrist or are you ready to go to trial today?

DEFENDANT: I don't know. Whatever they want to do, because they've already — I've been abused a lot already. What I want to do is get away from here, get out of here.

COURT: Well, then, you want to go ahead with the trial today?

DEFENDANT: Yeah, whatever.

COURT: Well, do you feel — do you know what's going on? Do you know what's going on at the trial?

DEFENDANT: I don't know. I've never been here like this, so I don't know.

COURT: Well, do you feel that you're competent to understand what's going on?

DEFENDANT: How long would it take? Because I just can't stand anymore, the way they have me there. I feel desperate.

Following the exchange, the court appeared inclined to deny the motion; in particular, the court expressed concern about how long it would take to have Loyola-Dominguez examined by a psychiatrist.

COURT: Well, what does it usually take, a 90-day study for psychiatric study?

DEFENSE: I've had one done since I've been here, and it's more than 90 days.

GOV'T:	I'm not sure if he's asking how long the trial was going to take.
COURT:	No, no, how long the psychiatric examination would take. Is it 120 days now?
DEFENSE:	I had one done, your Honor, with Judge Coyle approximately a year ago, and it was about 120 days before he came back. He went to Springfield Medical - Federal Hospital in Missouri.
COURT:	Well, he's always appeared mentally competent when he's been in court as far as I'm concerned and this is the first time that anything like this has happened, and he's been in custody for over a year in the state system without any problem.

Following this brief discussion, the district court determined that there was no cause to question Loyola-Dominguez's competency. It denied the motion for a hearing and summoned the jurors.

At trial, the government relied principally on Agent Kracher to establish its case against Loyola-Dominguez. Agent Kracher testified about his interview with Loyola-Dominguez, and he served as the conduit through which the government introduced documents from the INS's Alien Registry File. (otherwise known as the "A" file). The "A" file contained INS documents relating to Loyola-Dominguez, which the government used to prove that Loyola-Dominguez had previously been deported from the United States. On the stand, Agent Kracher removed each document from the "A" file and explained its significance to the jury.

The trial lasted one day and the jury quickly convicted Loyola-Dominguez on one count of being a deported alien found in the United States following an aggravated felony. Loyola-Dominguez made a motion for judgment of acquittal, which the court denied. This appeal followed.

Discussion

Loyola-Dominguez also argues that the trial court's failure to grant a competency hearing following his suicide attempt on the eve of trial violated his right to due process of law. We agree.

It is well established that a conviction obtained against an incompetent defendant "is a clear violation of the constitutional guarantee of due process." *Hernandez v. Ylst*, 930 F.2d 714, 716 (9th Cir. 1991) (citing *Pate v. Robinson*, 383 U.S. 375, 378 (1966)). Competency requires that the defendant have the "capacity to understand the nature and object of the proceedings against him, to consult with counsel, and to assist in preparing his defense." *Drope v. Missouri*, 420 U.S. 162, 171 (1975). When a trial court is presented with evidence that creates a "bona fide doubt" about the defendant's competency to stand trial, due process requires that the court hold a competency hearing. *Ylst*, 930 F.2d at 716. In *Drope v. Missouri*, the Supreme Court identified several factors that are relevant to determining whether a hearing is necessary, including "evidence of a defendant's irrational behavior, his demeanor at trial, and any prior medical opinion on competence to stand trial." *Drope*, 420 U.S. at 180. The Court further explained that "even one of these factors standing alone may, in some circumstances, be sufficient" to create a reasonable doubt regarding the defendant's competence. *Id.*

An attempted suicide is an extremely serious action. While we do not believe that every suicide attempt inevitably creates a doubt concerning the defendant's competency, we are persuaded that, under the circumstances of this case, such a doubt existed. Of particular significance to our decision are the timing of the attempt and the fact that the trial court did not elicit adequate information, from either defense counsel or Loyola-Dominguez, that would have dispelled the concerns that would ordinarily arise regarding competency. Loyola-Dominguez's responses to the trial court's four questions simply provided further cause to doubt his competency. Especially troubling is Loyola-Dominguez's expressed desire to "get out of here," which, in light of the government's open-and-shut case against him, suggests that he may not have had a full grasp of the nature of the proceedings. Also of concern is his response to the question from the court, "Do you know what's going on?" Loyola-Dominguez answered, "I don't know. I've never been here like this, so I don't know." Indeed, none of Loyola-Dominguez's answers demonstrates that he understood the nature and consequences of the proceedings or that he could assist properly in his own defense.

In explaining why a competency hearing was unnecessary, the trial court noted that Loyola-Dominguez had always seemed fine in the past. However, given his suicide attempt the night before trial, his performance during previous court appearances is at best inconclusive, particularly in view of defense counsel's explanation that Loyola-Dominguez's mental state was probably the result of recent events that had occurred at the jail. Without a meaningful inquiry to determine whether the suicide attempt evidenced a severe decline in Loyola-Dominguez's mental health, the court simply did not have enough information to conclude that a hearing regarding his competency was not warranted.

Conclusion

Loyola-Dominguez's suicide attempt on the eve of trial raised significant doubts regarding his competency to stand trial. In these circumstances, due process required a hearing to ascertain whether or not he was competent. Because he was convicted without such a hearing, and thus without due process of law, his conviction cannot stand. Accordingly, we vacate it.

QUESTIONS

1.   The evidence of incompetency in *Loyola-Dominguez* was the defendant's suicide attempt on the night before trial. Do you agree with the court that "every suicide attempt inevitably creates a doubt concerning the defendant's competency"? Does this invite defendants seeking to avoid trial to feign mental illness in the hopes that they can avoid criminal trial and punishment?

2.   Given the result in *Loyola-Dominguez*, why wouldn't a trial court judge routinely order a competency hearing using a "better safe than sorry" approach? Do you think the time factors discussed in *Loyola-Dominguez* have some impact on that decision? What about the fact that there is much evidence that suggests non-psychological factors, such trial strategy, are often the motivating factors in a request for a determination of competency to stand trial?

4. The Competency Hearing

Once a bona fide issue regarding the defendant's competency to stand trial has been raised, the defendant must be clinically assessed. The assessment of a criminal defendant for competency to stand trial is one of the most important roles mental health professionals play in the criminal process. The assessment of the defendant is normally conducted by clinicians appointed by the court who then submit written reports to the court. The court then decides the issue of competency to stand trial. While statutes usually call for a hearing at which the examining clinician(s) testify and are subjected to cross-examination, courts often decide the issue without such a hearing, often upon stipulation of the parties based on the evaluating clinicians' written reports.

According to the Supreme Court's landmark decision in *Dusky v. United States*, 362 U.S. 402, 402 (1960). to be competent to stand trial, a defendant must have (1) "a rational as well as factual understanding of the proceedings against him" and (2) "sufficient present ability to consult with his lawyer with a reasonable degree of rational understanding." This formulation is followed in nearly all U.S. jurisdictions and has been reaffirmed by the Supreme Court quite recently (in constitutional terms). *See Medina v. California*, 505 U.S. 437, 452 (1992).

The first question – can the defendant understand the proceedings against him or her – is not directed at whether the defendant understands the intricacies of the criminal process. Rather, it is concerned with whether the defendant has a basic understanding of the circumstances in which he or she finds himself or herself. More simply, does the defendant understand that he or she has been charged with a crime and faces government-imposed punishment if convicted?

Although not technically a requirement of the test for competency, mental health professionals often consider whether the defendant is orientated with respect to time, place, and situation as part of their inquiry in this phase of the competency evaluation. In other words, does the defendant know who and where he or she is? Without such orientation, it is unlikely that a defendant understands, even in a basic way, the proceedings against him or her.

The second of the criteria is whether the defendant is capable of assisting in his or her own defense. If the defendant cannot communicate with his or her attorney in a manner that permits the defense lawyer the ability to formulate a defense, there is little likelihood that the defendant will be found competent.

The competency standard as applied in any particular case tends to be flexible. Flexible means there are no set of "fixed" diagnostic criteria that, if satisfied, renders a person either competent of incompetent. In 1961, a federal court in *Wieter v. Settle*, 193 F. Supp. 318, 321-22 (W.D. Mo. 1961), set forth the following factors to explain how it might determine if a defendant were competent to stand trial. The court stated one would be competent to stand trial if the defendant:

(1) has the "mental capacity to appreciate his presence in relation to time, place and things";
(2) has "elementary mental processes are such that he apprehends (i.e., seizes and grasps with what mind he has) that he is in a Court of Justice, charged with a criminal offense";
(3) understands "there is a Judge on the Bench";
(4) understands there is "a prosecutor present who will try to convict him of a criminal charge";
(5) understands "he has a lawyer (self-employed or Court-appointed) who will undertake to defend him against that charge";
(6) understands "he will be expected to tell his lawyer the circumstances, to the best of his mental ability, (whether colored or not by mental aberration) the facts surrounding him at the time and place where the law violation is alleged to have been committed;
(7) understands "there is, or will be, a jury present to pass upon evidence adduced as to his guilt or innocence of such charge"; and
(8) has "memory sufficient to relate those things in his own personal manner."

While helpful guidelines, applying the criteria to the facts of any one case can be difficult, especially in where there is conflicting opinions between different mental health professionals. Consider the case of *United States v. Mason*.

UNITED STATES of America, Appellee, v. Lorenzo Nichols & Howard MASON, Defendant-Appellant.
56 F.3d 403 (2d Cir. 1995).

Walker, Circuit Judge:

Howard Mason appeals from a judgment of conviction and sentence entered in the United States District Court for the Eastern District of New York after a jury trial. Mason argues that the district court erroneously . . . found him competent to stand trial in 1989 and to be sentenced in 1994. We affirm.

Background

According to the evidence adduced at trial, Howard Mason was a leader of the "Bebos" drug gang, which controlled much of the South Jamaica crack trade in Queens during the mid to late 1980's. In 1988, Mason was imprisoned on a state firearms conviction. Following his imprisonment, Mason took revenge by directing Bebos underlings to assassinate a New York City police officer. On February 25, 1988, the Bebos carrying out the order happened upon rookie police officer Edward Byrne, who was on assignment outside the home of a witness in an unrelated drug case. They shot Officer Byrne five times in the head at point-blank range, killing him.

1. Arrest and Detention

On August 11, 1988, Mason, along with other members of the Bebos and another drug gang, was arrested on federal narcotics conspiracy charges. He was detained at the Metropolitan Correctional Center ("MCC"). At the MCC, Mason's disruptive conduct earned him disciplinary segregation. After he attacked two codefendants with a homemade weapon and started a fire in his cell because he was denied access to a phone, Mason was transferred to the Federal Correctional Institute at Otisville, New York on August 7, 1989. His conduct at Otisville placed him once again in disciplinary segregation.

On August 15, 1989, Mason was charged alone in a superseding indictment with, among other crimes, ordering the murder of Officer Byrne. After arraignment on the new charges, Mason was again placed in the MCC. When staff noted a sudden change in his behavior, he was sent to MCC staff psychologist Parry Hess. Dr. Hess noted that Mason displayed "paranoid delusions accompanied by agitation and violent outbursts, selective mutism, social withdrawal, marked weight loss, and poor hygiene" and recommended that he be sent to a forensic psychiatric facility for evaluation.

On September 15, 1989, Mason was transferred to the Medical Center for Federal Prisoners in Springfield, Missouri ("Springfield"). Mason submitted to an initial interview with Dr. Richard D'Andrea, a clinical psychologist at Springfield, but thereafter refused to permit further interviews, psychological tests, or a physical examination. Based on the initial interview and about fifteen brief visits to Mason's cell, Dr. D'Andrea wrote a report that he filed with the district court on October 23, 1989. He concluded that Mason understood the charges against him, that Mason's unwillingness to cooperate with the Springfield staff was "volitional and not due to mental illness," and that he was competent to stand trial.

Mason was returned to the MCC in late October, 1989. On November 3, 1989, Mason was visited in jail by his mother and his court-appointed attorney, Harry Batchelder, Jr. Their purpose was to discuss a government offer to consider making a downward departure motion for Mason's mother, who faced sentencing for a recent narcotics conviction, if Mason would plead guilty. According to an affidavit that Batchelder filed with the district court on November 7, 1989, Mason was uncooperative and abusive during both the November 3 visit and a subsequent meeting three days later. He accused Batchelder of lying about his codefendants' willingness to testify against him at trial and conniving with the district court to have him transferred to the "Bug-House." According to Batchelder, Mason at times had a vacant stare, was unresponsive to questions, and did not comprehend the effect that his insistence on going to trial might have on his mother's sentence. Because he was "professionally uncomfortable" that Mason understood his advice or trusted that he would work in Mason's best interests, Batchelder requested that the district court replace him with another attorney.

On November 7, 1989, Mason appeared before the district court. When Judge Korman remarked, "Your lawyer indicated that you had some problems that you want to raise with me," Mason rejoined, "It's your lawyer, it ain't my lawyer. What can I say[?] All I can do is keep getting torched." Moments later, Judge Korman inquired, "Do you wish Mr. Batchelder to represent you or not?" Mason replied, "I don't wish to go to the hospital and the police be kicking on my doors and hollering and screaming on me. I don't wish a lot of things. I don't have no choice." After noting the strange behavior described in the Batchelder affidavit, the court stated to Mason that "one of our concerns is that you understand what's going on around you so that you could assist your lawyer in preparing a defense." Mason again answered unresponsively: "I cannot prepare for anything. I'm locked in 23 hours a day. How can I prepare for anything? I'm in bug houses. How can I prepare for anything?"

When Judge Korman asked if Mason would submit to another psychiatric examination, Mason did not answer the question. Instead he asked, "What is it I'm charged with? I don't even know what I'm charged with." Judge Korman then read Mason the indictment. After he read Count One, which charged a RICO offense, Mason asked for a definition of racketeering. Mason then expressed confusion as to why, after his initial arrest on state charges, he was facing federal charges other than conspiracy. The district court explained that the government had filed a superseding indictment. As the hearing drew to a close, the court asked Mason if he had any other questions. Mason responded, "Yeah. I just wanted to know my status, why I got to keep going through these tribulations. If you're going to give me life [imprisonment], you're going to give me life anyway." He expressed doubt that he could get a fair trial, and answered questions about whether he wanted to retain Batchelder as his counsel with complaints about having no access to the prison law library and being asked to deal with legal papers which "ain't dealing with the same issue."

Finally, Mason agreed to talk with a psychiatrist who would determine his competency, saying, "Yeah, I got to. I ain't got no choice." Mason's resolve was short-lived. On November 16, when Dr. Naomi Goldstein accompanied Batchelder to the MCC, Mason refused to see her, expressing distrust of her because she worked for the government.

2. Trial

On November 27, 1989, Mason appeared in court for jury selection. Batchelder requested a hearing on the issue of Mason's competency to stand trial. Judge Korman questioned the need for the hearing since Mason had already been found competent. Batchelder responded that he wished to cross-examine Dr. D'Andrea about his report, especially given Mr. Mason's repeated assertions, even after the November 7 hearing, that he did not understand "what he was being tried for." Judge Korman discounted those statements as not indicative of incompetency: "At best that is an ambiguous statement. At best it could reflect that he doesn't think he did anything wrong." Judge Korman then conversed with Mason, who repeated that he did not understand why he was being charged for crimes other than conspiracy and why no codefendants were present.

The court remarked that Mason had been found competent by a psychiatric expert and had appeared competent in his court appearances. It nonetheless called Dr. D'Andrea in for a hearing. The court proceeded to select a jury with Mason present. When proceedings commenced the next day, November 28, 1989, Mason refused to attend. Judge Korman advised Mason that the trial would go on without him and explained at some length that he was only hurting himself by refusing to assist in his defense. Mason replied that he was not prepared for trial and that he could not get a fair trial. He again protested that he was facing new charges: "I come from [state prison] and I don't know what I'm coming to court for and now I have different charges. I know some of these people. I know them." After this interchange, Mason opted to be absent for the trial. The district court adopted Batchelder's suggestion to set up an audio connection to Mason's holding cell so that he could hear the proceedings. The audio connection could not be established that day, during which the jury was sworn and the government called and questioned witnesses outside Mason's presence.

On November 29, 1989, Mason attended the trial in the morning, when several police officers who investigated Officer Byrne's murder testified. During one detective's testimony, Mason stood up, causing the court to call a recess. Batchelder informed the court that Mason wished to return to his cell. The court explained again that Mason's decision was unwise, that he was entitled to participate, that he had missed a significant part of the trial, and that by assisting his attorney he might be able to convince the jury that the government did not carry the burden of proving his guilt beyond a reasonable doubt. Aggrieved that he was being charged with federal charges relating to the murder of Officer Byrne, Mason stated that there was "no sense me going to trial" and that he wanted to return to his cell. Nevertheless, Mason attended the proceedings for the rest of that day.

That afternoon, the court held a competency hearing at which both Dr. D'Andrea and Batchelder testified. Dr. D'Andrea testified that he conducted an initial interview of Mason lasting thirty to forty minutes, saw him at staff meetings, and had brief three to five minute visits with Mason in his cell about twelve to fifteen times. No psychological tests were conducted. Dr. D'Andrea reported his conclusion that Mason was antisocial but not psychotic, that Mason's behavior was volitional, and that he understood the nature of the charges against him. Batchelder testified about Mason's threats against him, an episode in which Mason attempted to attack him physically, and his unresponsiveness and lack of comprehension of the charges against him. After the hearing, the court found that Mason was "entirely competent." Judge Korman expressed concern about Batchelder's relationship with Mason, and asked if Mason's conduct since coming back from Otisville had any detrimental impact on his ability to prepare the case. Batchelder said that it did not.

Mason did not attend the trial after November 29, 1989. On November 30 and December 1, only legal arguments were made because the government's next witness was unavailable. By December 4, the next day of trial, a closed-circuit camera had been added to allow Mason to see the trial from the holding cell. Mason did in fact watch some of the trial in this manner, although technical problems caused him to miss the summations and one day in which evidence was taken. The jury found Mason guilty on all counts in the indictment.

3. Post-Trial Proceedings and Evaluations

Shortly after his conviction, Mason's behavior became more erratic. He refused to shower, change his clothes, clean his cell, or interact with MCC staff or inmates. When denied cosmetic items, Mason broke a window and threatened to kill a corrections officer. As a result of Mason's behavior, the government asked for a report from the MCC on his mental status. The court ordered Dr. Daniel Schwartz, a forensic psychiatrist, to evaluate Mason's competency to be sentenced.

Dr. Schwartz examined Mason on May 23, 1990, and found him "apparently so overwhelmed by his rage and paranoid beliefs that he could not address himself to the reality of his legal situation." Dr. Schwartz noted that Mason had "apparently regressed to the point of massive denial of stressful reality," particularly the fact of his conviction, and "ranted and raved about revenge."

On May 30, 1990, prior to filing his report, Dr. Schwartz testified about his evaluation at a hearing before the district court. At one point, Dr. Schwartz mentioned that he was not questioning the finding that Mason was fit to stand trial. Judge Korman interrupted him, saying, "Please stop. I didn't make a final judgment on his fitness to stand trial. I sort of wanted to have the record completed on that. I want to ask you what your judgment about that is, to the extent that you can give one."

Judge Korman then went on to remark that, as a layman, he was satisfied that Mason understood the charges against him, but "the part that I never quite put to rest in my own mind was his ability to assist in his own defense." Dr. Schwartz stated that he was inclined to defer to the court and Dr. D'Andrea, who had not only interviewed Mason prior to trial but had observed him at Springfield. Nevertheless, at the court's prompting, Dr. Schwartz addressed the issue of Mason's competency to stand trial in his report of July 27, 1990. Dr. Schwartz concluded that, although Mason was unfit to be sentenced at that time, he was competent at the time of trial in November and December of 1989.

In the meantime, Mason was returned to Springfield for further evaluation. In Springfield, forensic psychologist Dr. Michael Morrison evaluated him between June 12 and July 9, 1990. Mason again refused to submit to physical examinations or psychological testing. While noting the difficulties of evaluating a recalcitrant subject, Dr. Morrison concluded that Mason's lack of cooperation was volitional and that Mason was antisocial but not psychotic or suffering from any major mental illness.

On November 16, 1990, Mason appeared before the district court for a status conference. Discerning a "distinct difference" from prior appearances during which he had been able to converse rationally with Mason, Judge Korman now described Mason as "ranting and raving." Judge Korman ordered another psychiatric examination of Mason.

At Mason's request, the court appointed Dr. Abraham Halpern, a psychiatrist, to conduct an examination, which occurred on January 17, 1991 in the courthouse holding cell. Dr. Halpern diagnosed Mason as having "bipolar disease, manic," and pronounced him incompetent to be sentenced. Furthermore, after reviewing prior reports, affidavits, and trial transcripts, Dr. Halpern declared Mason incompetent at the time of trial. He discounted Mason's seeming rationality in court appearances as manifestations of "fluctuating competency" and not indicative of general competency to stand trial. At a competency hearing on February 24, 1992, the court questioned Dr. Halpern at length about how one distinguishes volitional disruptive behavior from psychotic conduct. Judge Korman voiced his view that some of Mason's irregular conduct was susceptible of rational explanation.

In a court hearing held in March, 1992, another psychiatrist weighed in with an evaluation of Mason. Dr. John Phelan, in consultation with other Springfield staff, evaluated Mason during the latter's stay in Springfield from May 3, 1991 to January, 1992. Dr. Phelan concluded that Mason was antisocial but rejected Dr. Halpern's diagnosis of bipolar disorder, since such a disorder is unlikely to develop suddenly in an adult of Mason's age who has no prior history of the disease. Dr. Phelan explained Mason's past ranting and raving, which did not recur during his observation of Mason at Springfield, as perhaps a "brief reactive psychosis," but not conclusive evidence of a major mental disorder. Contrary to Dr. Halpern's conclusion, he also said that Mason's on-and-off irrational behavior observed by the court tended to show that he was malingering and not suffering from mental illness.

In April of 1992, the court reappointed Dr. Naomi Goldstein to evaluate Mason. Mason was polite and cooperative in an interview Dr. Goldstein conducted on September 11, 1992. He understood that he had been convicted of ordering the murder of Officer Byrne but denied guilt. He was able to explain the functions of the judge, jury, and counsel, and discussed his relationship with his attorneys. Dr. Goldstein diagnosed Mason as suffering from an antisocial personality disorder and probable atypical psychosis, but not active psychosis. She believed that he was not clearly psychotic in 1989, although she could not rule out the possibility of psychosis, especially after his conviction. She reported that Mason's paranoia may have reached delusional intensity some time that year and that he also may have regressed in isolation, becoming neglectful of his personal hygiene. Nonetheless, Dr. Goldstein decided that, in the aftermath of his trial, "Mason understood only too well what has happened and has had some difficulty adjusting to the prospect of a lifetime incarceration and to the betrayal of his friends." She noted that Mason had been stable since winter and spring of 1992. In sum, Mason was probably neither a malingerer nor psychotic, but more likely he was "so preoccupied with being respected, with power, strength and violence, [that he] had suddenly lost external control and decided that the only way to deal with it was to resist and not participate actively in a lost cause, a conscious decision over which he had control." Dr. Goldstein concluded that he was competent at the time of trial, though probably depressed, and was currently competent to be sentenced.

On January 7, 1994, weighing all the evidence, the district court ruled that Mason had been competent to stand trial and was competent to be sentenced. The district court sentenced Mason to life imprisonment. This appeal followed.

Discussion

In making a determination of competency, the district court may rely on a number of factors, including medical opinion and the court's observation of the defendant's comportment. *United States v. Hemsi*, 901 F.2d 293, 295 (2d Cir. 1990). We will uphold a district court's finding unless clearly erroneous. *United States v. Gold*, 790 F.2d 235, 239-40 (2d Cir. 1986). "Where there are two permissible views of the evidence as to competency, the court's choice between them cannot be deemed clearly erroneous." *United States v. Villegas*, 899 F.2d 1324, 1341 (2d Cir.), *cert. denied*, 498 U.S. 991 (1990).

1. Competency to Stand Trial

Mason attacks the district court's finding that he was competent to stand trial on a number of grounds. He argues that the district court's conclusion that he was malingering was unsupported by any of the psychiatric testimony and inconsistent with Mason's behavior during his detention. It is also, in his view, inconsistent with psychiatric evaluations beginning in 1977 in which experts found evidence of mental illness and delusional behavior. Finally, he faults Dr. Goldstein's conclusion that Mason was competent both to be tried and to be sentenced, upon which the district court placed great weight, as unreliable since Dr. Goldstein admitted that she could not determine precisely what ailed Mason. Mason argues that the district court should instead have credited the testimony of Dr. Halpern, who in 1991 found that Mason was incompetent at the time of trial, and Dr. Schwartz, who in 1990 found him incompetent to be sentenced.

The district court's conclusion that Mason's non-cooperation at trial was a "deliberate and calculated act" was not clearly erroneous. First, Judge Korman was entitled to rely on his own observations and questioning of Mason, as he expressly did in making his final finding of competency on January 7, 1994. *See Hemsi*, 901 F.2d at 295. Second, Mason's claim that all of the psychiatric reports contradict a finding of deliberate, calculated action is factually inaccurate. Dr. D'Andrea had concluded that Mason had an antisocial personality disorder and that his acts of non-cooperation were volitional, findings that the district court specifically adopted as consistent with his own observations of Mason's conduct. Dr. Phelan testified that "on-and-off" acts of non-cooperation tended to show malingering and not mental illness. Finally, the district court specifically relied on Dr. Goldstein's conclusion that, while outright malingering could explain his behavior, the better view was that Mason, "so preoccupied with being respected, with power, strength, and violence, had suddenly lost external control and decided that the only way to deal with it was to resist or not participate actively in a lost cause, a conscious decision over which he had control." Substantial medical opinion thus supported the district court's finding of competency.

The fact that five of the six reports cited by Mason that were conducted between 1977 and 1994 indicated evidence of paranoia or paranoid delusions, and that two indicated the possible onset of psychosis at certain periods, does not undermine the district court's finding of competency. "It is well-established that some degree of mental illness cannot be equated with incompetence to stand trial." *United States v. Vamos*, 797 F.2d 1146, 1150 (2d Cir. 1986), *cert. denied*, 479 U.S. 1036 (1987). The mental illness must deprive the defendant of the ability to consult with his lawyer "with a reasonable degree of rational understanding" and to understand the proceedings against him rationally as well as factually. *Dusky v. United States*, 362 U.S. 402, 402 (1960). Moreover, while the district court may consider psychiatric history in its deliberations, *see Newfield v. United States*, 565 F.2d 203, 206 (2d Cir. 1977), "the question of competency to stand trial is limited to the defendant's abilities at the time of trial," *Vamos*, 797 F.2d at 1150.

The 1977 evaluation preceded the trial by twelve years. More importantly, its impact is weakened by a longer psychiatric report in 1982 which found that Mason did not suffer from mental illness. Two of the reports Mason cites – Dr. Schwartz's diagnosis of Mason as suffering paranoid delusions and an adjustment disorder "apparently of psychotic proportions" six months after trial, and Dr. Goldstein's opinion that he may have had psychotic episodes between 1989 and 1994 during periods of exceptional stress – also do not directly bear upon Mason's competency at the time of trial. Significantly, both Dr. Schwartz and Dr. Goldstein opined that Mason's mental problems did not render him incompetent to stand trial.

The other three reports also do not show the district court's finding to be clearly erroneous. Dr. Hess offered no opinion as to whether Mason's display of paranoid delusions in August, 1989 adversely affected his legal competency; moreover, his reports on Mason were considered by Dr. Schwartz and Dr. Goldstein, who both found him competent. Judge Korman was also entitled to discount the November, 1989 observation of paranoid delusions and hallucinations made by an MCC psychiatrist, Dr. Quinones, in light of Judge Korman's own impressions and the more comprehensive evaluations by other medical experts.

The sixth report, issued by Dr. Halpern, followed a thorough psychiatric evaluation in which Dr. Halpern deemed Mason incompetent to have stood trial in 1989. Judge Korman gave detailed reasons for discrediting Dr. Halpern's testimony and report. First, making a credibility determination that we cannot question on appeal, he noted that Dr. Halpern "impressed [him] as a paid defense witness who was doing his best to come up with answers that would help the party who retained him." Second, he criticized Dr. Halpern for failing to take account of key court proceedings and testimony. Third, Judge Korman faulted Dr. Halpern for placing undue weight on the testimony of Mason's attorney, Batchelder, which Judge Korman dismissed as "flatly inaccurate in some respects and exaggerated in others." This

172

lone diagnosis of incompetency at the time of trial by "one member of an uncertain profession," which conflicts with opinions of other qualified experts, "is too pale a shadow to darken" the district court's judgment of competency. *Reese v. Wainwright*, 600 F.2d 1085, 1094 (5th Cir.), *cert. denied*, 444 U.S. 983 (1979).

Finally, Mason argues that the transcripts of the early court appearances, together with the Batchelder affidavit, demonstrate his mental incoherence and his failure to comprehend the charges against him. While that is one plausible reading, it is at least equally plausible to read Mason's statements as evincing resignation and frustration but not irrationality. We must in these circumstances defer to the judgment of the district court, which had the benefit of examining Mason and hearing from the fact and expert witnesses in person. In summary, the district court was entitled to rely upon its own impressions of Mason and the supporting opinions of Drs. D'Andrea, Morrison, Phelan, Schwartz, and Goldstein in concluding that Mason had a rational understanding of the charges against him and the ability to assist his lawyer in mounting his defense. No clear error was committed in the determination that Mason was competent at the time of trial.

2. Competency to Be Sentenced

There is also no basis for overturning the district court's finding that Mason was competent to be sentenced in January of 1994. In Dr. Goldstein's July, 1993 report, which was the only medical evaluation of Mason performed near the time of Mason's sentencing, she found that "there is no evidence of active psychosis or manic depressive illness at this time and he appears to be in better control than he has been previously." She concluded that Mason was competent to understand and participate in his sentencing. In addition, during the January, 1994 hearing, Judge Korman reviewed numerous statements that evinced Mason's understanding of criminal responsibility, sentencing, and the consequences that sentencing would have in terms of his future incarceration.

Mason did interrupt the court in the midst of its oral decision with rambling statements of his innocence and the pervasiveness of drugs in the neighborhood where he grew up. Mason's attorney at sentencing, Ivan Fisher, then noted for the record that "during this proceeding as well as [another], the defendant has on numerous occasions gotten on all fours, put his head close to the floor, and then stood up again." Judge Korman stated that he was willing to accept a more moderate view of Mason's condition but that his own view was that Mason's behavior was "all calculated fakery." Consequently, he adhered to his determination that Mason was competent to be sentenced.

On the cold record on appeal, and in light of Judge Korman's extended effort to secure a range of medical opinion about Mason's competency, we are not prepared to find clear error in this determination. . . . Accordingly, we affirm.

QUESTIONS

1.   As the appeals court pointed out, they are limited on review of factual findings of a trial court to reverse only those that are "clearly erroneous." Given the precedent, the appeals court probably reached the correct decision. But, unconstrained by the clearly erroneous standard of review, do you agree with the district court's decision that Mason was competent to stand trial? Explain your answer, citing the specific factors upon which you rely for conclusions.

2.   This case is one of many in which there is conflicting expert testimony regarding a criminal defendant's state of mind. As the district judge pointed out, he was a layman assessing Mason, not a mental health professional. Which of the two, in your opinion, is better equipped to make a determination about competency to stand trial? Why? Note the court's dismissal of Dr. Halpern's testimony as a "hired gun." What, if anything, do you think can be done about the hired gun issue in nearly all cases that involve the interplay of law and psychology/psychiatry?

5. After a Competency Determination

If, after evaluation and a hearing, the defendant is found competent, the case proceeds to trial. Such a determination of competency does not prevent the defendant from asserting the insanity defense for many of the reasons discussed above, the most important of which is the issue of timing since competency deals with the defendant's state of mind at the time of trial and insanity deals with the defendant's state of mind at the time of the alleged offense.

The more difficult scenario is when a defendant is found to be incompetent. The normal course of events in such a case is that the criminal case is held in abeyance while the defendant is remanded into inpatient custody for treatment that is designed to restore competency. If, after a period of evaluation often set by statute, the psychiatric staff feels the defendant can be respired to competency, the defendant will remain for treatment and the government must report to the court on the defendant's progress at regular intervals, often every six months. Assuming the original belief of the psychiatric staff was correct and the defendant recovers (i.e., is restored to competency), he or she will then face trial.

If, however, the defendant's condition is fixed, and the psychiatric staff does not believe the defendant's condition will improve, the defendant may not be held indefinitely. This was not always the case, though. Until the Supreme Court's decision in *Jackson v. Indiana*, 406 U.S. 715 (1972), defendants found incompetent to stand trial were routinely kept hospitalized indefinitely, often for a period of time that was in excess of the maximum sentence that could have been imposed had they been convicted (a fact especially so for defendants charged with misdemeanors). And in some cases, such defendants were kept hospitalized for the remainder of their lives. *Jackson* changed that by holding a defendant committed after a finding of incompetency to stand trial could not "be held more than a reasonable period of time necessary to determine whether there is a substantial probability that he will attain that capacity in the foreseeable future."

Since *Jackson*, then, a defendant found incompetent to stand trial can only be kept confined if the treatment he or she is receiving while committed is likely to restore capacity "in the foreseeable future" – not at some distant point-in-time. If the treatment being provided to the defendant either does not advance the defendant toward competency, or does so, but without a fair probability that competency will be restored in the foreseeable future, then the state has two options. First, it can drop the criminal charges against the defendant and release him or her. Or second, it can seek to have the defendant involuntarily committed to a mental institution using civil commitment procedures. While beyond the scope of this text, civil commitment requires the state to prove, by clear and convincing evidence, that a person poses a danger to himself or herself, or to others.

C. Insanity

1. Overview

Insanity is a *legal term* – not a psychological or medical one. Unlike competency to stand trial, which examines the state of mind of the defendant at the time of the criminal prosecution of a case, insanity refers to the defendant's state of mind *at the time of the offense*. Thus, the very nature of the defense is retrospective. The law requires the trier-of-fact (usually a jury) to go back in time to evaluate the defendant's state of mind in the past. Accordingly, mental health experts are used to assist the trier-of-fact in reconstructing the defendant's past mental state. This task is complicated, at best, because as time passes, whatever psychological tests are given to the defendant are less likely to indicate his or her mental state at the time of the offense.

2. Justifications for the Insanity Defense

Why do we have an insanity defense? While answers to this question can take volumes of writing, an oversimplified answer can be given in three parts. First, it is unfair to punish people for acts that result from mental illness. Why? The rational decision-making model of a person of free-will is

174

inapplicable when dealing with someone who is severely mentally ill. With the very premise of human action taken by the criminal law undercut or totally gone, the criminal law's reasons for imposing a sanction are no longer applicable.

Second, in terms of the major theoretical justifications for punishment, all seem inapplicable to the mentally ill criminal offender. From the standpoint of retribution theory, what evil is there to punish if someone acted not out of criminal intent, but rather out of a delusionary or otherwise psychotic thought process? Punishment of the mentally ill also cannot be justified under deterrence theory because it is nearly impossible to deter acts resulting from mental illness. Deterrence as a theory is predicated on the utilitarian notion of rational choice, a presupposition that is not applicable to the insane defendant. Since the treatment of the mentally ill in the correctional setting leaves much to be desired, charitably speaking, rehabilitation is better accomplished through the mental health system, not in jails or prisons. Substantially the same argument applies to incapacitation theory.

Third, those who commit criminal acts as a result of their mental illness do not fit nicely into the criminal law's doctrinal definitions of mens rea. Those who are mentally ill may or may not form mens rea, and even if they do, it may be formed defectively.

3. Common Misperceptions Regarding the Insanity Defense

One of the most common misperceptions about the insanity defense is that it is an overused defense that allows many defendants to escape criminal liability. But, the insanity defense is invoked quite rarely. It is raised in approximately one percent (1%) of all felony cases and, when invoked, it is successful less than 25% of the time. Thus, contrary to popular misperceptions, the insanity defense is infrequently raised and, even when it is raised, it is unsuccessful three-quarters of the time.

There is also much public concern about defendants who fake their mental illnesses in order to "get away with" their crimes and simply hire clinicians to engage in a the proverbial "battle of the experts" at trial. While such cases make for good media play, they are the rare exception and not the rule. There is overwhelming agreement on a clinical diagnosis between clinicians on both sides of the criminal dispute, with clinician agreement rates around ninety percent (90%). Moreover, the fears of a defendant feigning mental illness to avoid criminal punishment, called malingering, is ill-founded. Malingering among insanity defendants is rare, and even when defendants do fake mental illness, it is extraordinarily difficult for them to get away with it, as modern diagnostic instruments and procedures allow clinicians to correctly classify those truly mentally as, as opposed to those who are faking, between ninety-two percent (92%) to ninety-five percent (95%) of the time.

4. The Wild Beast Defense

The insanity defense has a long history, having roots in Moslem, Hebrew, and Roman law. It dates back to 13th century England. Justice Tracy, a judge in King Edward's court, formulated what became known as the "wild beast" test in a case referred to today as Arnold's case, *Rex v. Arnold*, Y.B. 10 Geo. 1 (1724). In it, the defendant attempted to kill a British Lord. Judge Tracy instructed the jury that the defendant should be acquitted if he were "a man that [was] totally deprived of his understanding and memory, and doth not know what he is doing, no more than an infant, than *a brute, or a wild beast,* such a one is never the object of punishment."

The defense evolved significantly in May of 1800 when James Hadfield shot King George III. He believed he had acted on orders from God. At his trial for treason, defense counsel argued that Hadfield's delusions, brought about as a result of head trauma he received in battle, were the cause of his actions. Several physicians testified corroboratively regarding the head trauma. The jury acquitted Hadfield, departing from the Wild Beast Defense in two important ways. First, Hadfield was not totally deprived of his mental faculties in the way a wild beast or brute would be. Second, it was the first time that a verdict of not guilty by reasons of insanity became its own verdict of acquittal. Within a few years of the *Hadfield* decision, however, Justice Tracy's Wild Beast Test, which did require a near complete

175

deprivation of mental faculties for an acquittal, was restored, yet the special verdict of not guilty by reason of insanity remained.

5. The M'Naghten Rule

In 1843, the landmark case of Daniel M'Naghten was decided, M'Naghten's Case, 8 Eng. Rep. 718 (1843).[1] The legal standard for insanity set forth in the case is still used in many jurisdictions today. M'Naghten was indicted for the first-degree murder of Edward Drummond. Drummond was the secretary to Sir Robert Peel, the Prime Minister of England at the time. M'Naghten had intended to kill Peel, but mistook Drummond for him. He explained to the police that he wanted to kill the prime minister as a result of persecutory delusions he suffered which caused him to believe the prime minister and his party were trying to kill him. At his trial, he was represented by several distinguished barristers who called many medical experts on his behalf. None of the expert testimony was rebutted by prosecution expert witnesses. The jury found M'Naghten not guilty by reason of insanity. M'Naghten was committed to Bedlam, the notorious asylum, where he eventually died more than twenty years later.

There was much public outrage over M'Naghten's acquittal, including condemnation of the case from Queen Victoria who herself had be the target of assassination attempts. The House of Lords subsequently set down what became known as the M'Naghten Rule test for insanity. The M'Naghten "right-wrong" test for insanity can be stated in terms of elements:

a)   A person is not responsible for criminal conduct if, *at the time of the offense*
b)   the defendant suffered from *a mental disease or defect*
c)   that *caused* the defendant either:
    (1)   not to know the nature and quality of the act he or she committed; or
    (2)   knowing the quality or nature of the act, nonetheless not to know that the act was wrong.

As discussed above, the first element sets forth the fact that the insanity defense is not concerned with the time of trial, but rather with the defendant's state of mind at the time the criminal act is alleged to have taken place. The second element required that the defendant suffer from a "mental disease or defect." What constitutes a mental disease or defect for the purposes of the insanity defense is somewhat complicated matter that will be addressed later in this chapter.

The third part of the test concerns the legal doctrine of causation (see Chapter 2). In terms of insanity, the mental disease or defect that existed at the time of the offense (elements # 1 and # 2 of the M'Naghten Rule), must have *caused* one of two results. It either had to cause the defendant not to know the nature and quality of the act he or she committed, or if the defendant knew the quality or nature of his or her acts, the mental disease or defect had to *cause* the defendant not to know right from wrong.

The first part of the M'Naghten causation test relieves the defendant of liability when the defendant is incapable of forming mens rea. If one does not know the quality of one's acts, how can one be criminally reckless, negligent, or purposeful? For example, if a man strangled another person believing that he is squeezing the juice out of an orange, he did not understand the nature and quality of his act. As you might surmise, such a situation is rare and would require a significant psychosis for someone to be so removed from reality as to not know what he or she was even doing. Take Daniel M'Naghten's case, for example, he knew the nature and quality of his act. He wanted to kill the prime minister and attempted to do so.

Given the relative rarity of someone not knowing the nature and quality of his or her acts, the second part of the M'Naghten causation test – the right-wrong component – is usually at the crux of an insanity defense, as it was in M'Naghten's case. This part of the insanity test relieves a defendant from

---

[1]   There are at least twelve different spellings of Daniel M'Naghten's last name, something that he himself likely contributed to since he spelled his own name differently on several occasions. RICHARD MORAN, KNOWING RIGHT FROM WRONG: THE INSANITY DEFENSE OF DANIEL MCNAUGHTAN (1981).

criminal liability even if the person forms the requisite mens rea (as Daniel M'Naghten formed intent to kill), but forms mens rea without the understanding that act, committed with intent, is wrong.

The M'Naghten test for insanity was criticized for years in that it only looked at the *cognitive* aspect of the defendant's actions (i.e., did the defendant "know" right from wrong). The test had no affective element, looking at the *volition* of the defendant. It was therefore criticized as incomplete because a defendant might be aware of the wrongfulness of behavior, but still be unable to restrain himself or herself from engaging in it. The M'Naghten Rule was also criticized for being too rigid, as by its very terms, it would only exclude those the most profoundly impaired of defendants. And, finally, the M'Naghten Rule was criticized for its focus on "right" as opposed to "wrong," a standard that often required clinicians to make moral judgments about defendants. These problems with M'Naghten led to the development of other formulations of the insanity defense that included an affective component.

6. The Short-Lived Durham Rule

Dissatisfied with the M'Naghten Rule, the U.S. Court of Appeals for the District of Columbia Circuit formulated a new insanity test in *Durham v. United States*, 214 F.2d 862, 874-75 (D.C. Cir. 1954), *overruled, United States v. Brawner*, 471 F.2d 969, 981 (D.C. Cir. 1972). In it, the court announced what came to be known as the "product test" (a/k/a the Durham Rule). It held that "an accused is not criminally responsible if his unlawful act was the product of a mental disease or defect."

While the Durham Rule did away with both the cognitive focus of the M'Naghten Rule and the moral judgments involved in determinations of right and wrong embedded in the M'Naghten Rule, it proved to be an unworkable standard. It led to an "influx of psychiatrists and clinical psychologists into the courtroom as expert witnesses . . . [whose] testimony . . . usurp[ed] the jury's fact-finding function."[2]

The product test of *Durham* was not widely accepted and was overruled by the D.C. Court of Appeals in 1972 in *United States v. Brawner*, 471 F.2d 969, 981 (D.C. Cir. 1972), which adopted a formulation of the insanity defense based on the one suggested by the American Law Institute in its Model Penal Code.

7. The ALI/MPC Affective Test

The Model Penal Code formulation of the insanity defense is usually referred to as the ALI or MPC Affective Test. It provides that "a person is not responsible for criminal conduct if, at the time of such conduct as of a result of a mental disease or defect, [the defendant] lacks the substantial capacity to appreciate the criminality [wrongfulness] of his conduct or to conform his conduct to the requirements of law."

Additionally, although the ALI/MPC formulation of the insanity defense did not define what a mental disease or defect was (just as the M'Naghten Rule failed to do), it did include a provision purposefully excluding those who were then-termed psychopaths or sociopaths (today referred to as suffering from antisocial personality disorder) from being considered to have a mental disease or defect. Specifically, it stated "the terms mental disease or defect do not include any abnormality manifested only by repeated criminal or otherwise antisocial conduct."

Because it is often easier for the student of the insanity defense to view crimes and defenses in terms of numbered elements, for pedagogical purposes (and for the sake of being able to make element by element comparisons among the various formulations of the insanity defense as set forth in this book), the ALI/MPC Affective Test can be expressed in this way:

---

[2]   LAWRENCE S. WRIGHTSMAN, ET AL., PSYCHOLOGY AND THE LEGAL SYSTEM 297 (4th ed. 1998).

a)   A person is not responsible for criminal conduct if, *at the time of the offense*;

b)   the defendant suffered from *a mental disease or defect* (other than antisocial personality disorder and/or any other abnormality manifested only by repeated criminal or otherwise antisocial conduct);

c)   that *caused* the defendant either:

     (1)   to lack the *substantial capacity* to *appreciate* the criminality [wrongfulness] of his or her conduct; or

     (2)   [having substantial capacity to appreciate the criminality of his or her conduct], to lack the *substantial capacity* to *conform his conduct to the requirements of law*.

As should be evident, the first two elements of the ALI/MPC formulation of the insanity defense are the same as those required under the M'Naghten formulation. Both look at the defendant's conduct at the time of the offense, and both require a mental disease or defect. The only difference in the mental disease or defect requirement between the M'Naghten and ALI formulations of the insanity defense is that the latter specifically excludes antisocial personality disorder (known as psychopathic or sociopathic personalities at the time the ALI formulation was set forth). The main difference between the two formulation is in the third element.

As discussed earlier in this chapter, M'Naghten focused on the cognitive aspects of behavior: did the defendant *know* what he or she was doing, and if so, did the defendant *know* it was wrong. It was an all-or-nothing-at-all test that required total (or near total) impairment. The ALI/MPC formulation avoided a purely cognitive focus by adding elements of affect. Further, it avoided the all-or-nothing-at-all problem by requiring "substantial" rather than total impairment.

By replacing M'Naghten's requirement of knowledge with one that requires that the defendant lack the "substantial capacity to appreciate," mental health experts and, ultimately, juries, were permitted to consider factors other than the defendant's strict knowledge of right and wrong. In other words, it recognized there were differing levels of mental impairment and allowed for acquittal in circumstances short of total impairment.

Additionally, the ALI/ MPC test is less strict than the M'Naghten test since it allows even those who both know and appreciate that their acts were wrong to assert the insanity defense by claiming they were unable to abide by the law. This aspect is known as the **irresistible impulse test**. Its inclusion in the MPC was an explicit recognition of the evolving state of psychological/psychiatric knowledge that one's *volition* (i.e., free will) is often impacted by mental illness.

The ALI/MPC formulation of the insanity defense was repeatedly criticized for the inclusion of the irresistible impulse test. These critics argue that an irresistible impulse is really just an impulse that was not, in fact, resisted. Even the American Bar Association and the American Psychiatric Association joined in this criticism of the volitional aspect of the ALI/MPC test. In spite of the criticisms, the ALI/MPC formulation of the insanity defense was eventually adopted in all but one federal circuit and in a majority of the states.

8. The Modern Federal Formulation of the Insanity Defense

In the late 1970s John Hinckley became obsessed with the characters in the movie *Taxi Driver*, and, in particular, Jodie Foster, one of the starts of the film. He made several attempts to woo Jodie Foster while she was a first-year student at Yale University in New Haven, Connecticut, that included sending her love letters, poems, and having two phone conversations with her. When Foster rebuffed his overtures, Hinckley decided he needed to do something that would make an impression on her – some "historic deed [that would] finally gain her respect and love for him."[3] On March 30, 1981, he

---

[3]   Peter Low, et al., The Trial of John W. Hinckley, Jr.: A Case Study in the Insanity Defense 23-24 (1986).

carried out his plan by attempting to assassinate then President Ronald Reagan as he was leaving the Washington Hilton Hotel in Washington, D.C.

At his trial for attempted murder, Hinckley asserted the insanity defense. The ALI/MPC formulation of the insanity defense governed his trial. Moreover, under *Brawner*, once the issue of insanity was raised by the defense, the government had to prove that Hinckley was sane, beyond a reasonable doubt, at the time he made his assassination attempt on Reagan. Hinckley was found not guilty by reason of insanity. Public outrage over his acquittal followed.

In the wake of the Hinckley verdict, the insanity defense underwent sweeping reforms in both the federal system and in many states. After twenty-six different pieces of legislation were introduced in Congress to either abolish or restrict the insanity defense at the federal level, Congress enacted the Insanity Defense Reform Act of 1984 ("IDRA"). In doing so, Congress codified the federal insanity defense for the first time and legislatively overruled the application of the ALI/MPC formulation of the insanity defense in all federal cases.

The modern federal formulation of the insanity defense as enacted in IDRA provides: "At the time of the commission of the acts constituting the offense, the defendant, as of a result of a severe mental disease or defect, was unable to appreciate the nature and quality or the wrongfulness of his acts. Mental disease or defect does not otherwise constitute of a defense." 18 U.S.C. § 17.

Again, for pedagogical and comparative purposes, it is helpful to consider the requirements of this formulation of the insanity defense in terms of elements.

a) A person is not responsible for criminal conduct if, *at the time of acts constituting the offense*;
b) the defendant suffered from *a <u>severe</u> mental disease or defect*
c) that *caused* the defendant to be *unable to appreciate* either:
    (1) the nature and quality of his or her acts; or
    (2) the wrongfulness of his or her acts [which presumes being able to appreciate the nature and quality of his or her acts].

In effect, the IDRA returned the law of insanity to being very close to where it was at the time the M'Naghten Rule was adopted. As with all of the other insanity defense formulations, the first element looks at the mental state of the defendant at the time of the commission of the offense.

The second element, just like M'Naghten and the ALI/MPC formulation of the insanity defense, requires a mental disease or defect. But the IDRA added the requirement that the mental disease or defect be *severe*. This requirement of severity effectively limited the applicability of the defense to people suffering from psychoses and mental retardation, thereby eliminating neurosis, disabilities, and personality disorders from qualifying as predicate mental diseases or defects.

The third element is similar to all prior formulations of the insanity defense insofar as there must be, as always, a causal nexus between the mental illness and the crime committed. But the third element changed the insanity defense as it existed in the federal courts quite significantly in two important ways.

First, the third element effectively abolished the volitional aspect of the ALI/MPC insanity defense as expressed in the irresistible impulse test. Thus, under the IDRA, no longer will an inability to conform one's conduct to the requirements of law allow one to use the insanity defense in federal courts.

Second, it basically reinstated the M'Naghten Rule with a slight modification. Instead of requiring a lack of "knowledge" that one's conduct is wrong to qualify as legally insane, the IDRA requires an inability to "appreciate" the wrongfulness of one's conduct, thus leaving the slightest door open for some affective component to the defense, rather than exclusively focusing on the cognitive the way M'Naghten originally did.

In addition to changing the elements of the insanity defense and standardizing the defense for the federal system, the IDRA also made a critical change in procedure regarding the way the insanity defense is litigated. Up until the time of the IDRA, once the defense announced its intention to use the insanity defense (i.e., once the defense met its burden of production), the prosecution bore the burden of persuasion to prove a defendant was legally sane at the time of a criminal offense beyond a reasonable doubt. But the IDRA shifted both the burden of production and the burden of persuasion to the defense by making insanity an affirmative defense. Accordingly, the *defense* must now prove that the defendant was *insane* at the time of the criminal offense by *clear and convincing evidence.*

Finally, the IDRA made a change to the law of evidence. "No expert witness testifying with respect to the mental state or condition of a defendant in a criminal case may state an opinion or inference as to whether the defendant did or did not have the mental state or condition constituting an element of the crime charged or of a defense thereto. Such ultimate issues are matters for the trier of fact alone." FED. R. EVID. 704(b). But at least two studies using simulated trials have demonstrated that this change in the law of evidence regarding the "ultimate issue" has had no significant effects on jury verdicts.[4]

By 1985, 33 states had followed the lead of Congress and evaluated the insanity defense as it applied in their respective jurisdictions. Many states followed the IDRA and made insanity an affirmative defense, thereby shifting the burden of persuasion from the prosecution to the defense to prove the defendant's insanity, usually by a preponderance of the evidence. Other states left the burden of persuasion with the government to show the defendant's sanity, but tightened the substantive test for insanity by requiring a "severe" mental disease or defect or some equivalent. Twelve states replaced the insanity defense with a "guilty, but mentally ill" verdict. And three states – Utah, Montana and Idaho – abolished the insanity defense altogether.

9. Guilty But Mentally Ill & Guilty Except Insane

In August of 1975, Michigan was the first U.S. state to add a third possible verdict in criminal cases in which the defendant was mentally ill. Up until that time, using the traditional insanity defense, a jury had to find a defendant either guilty or not guilty by reason of insanity. Michigan did not abolish the latter verdict, but instead supplemented it by adding another alternative it termed "guilty but mentally ill."

Under the Michigan law, a verdict of guilty but mentally ill was supposed to be returned by the trier of fact if the following three criteria were found beyond a reasonable doubt: "(a) That the defendant is guilty of an offense[;] (b) That the defendant was mentally ill at the time of the commission of the offense[; and] (c) That the defendant was *not* legally insane at the time of the commission of the offense." This verdict allowed a jury to completely acquit those defendants who were clearly legally insane under a tradition not guilty by reason of insanity verdict, but gave jurors a middle ground or compromise verdict to convict those who were not clearly legally insane, but did suffer from a mental illness at the time of the commission of a criminal offense.

Under the Michigan schema, someone adjudicated guilty but mentally ill is to be sentenced just as if he or she had been found guilty of the crime with one exception: the court is to make a determination if the defendant needs treatment. If the court so finds, then the defendant is supposed to be remanded either into the custody of the department of corrections or the state's department of mental health services for treatment. Interestingly, though, after treatment, the defendant must serve whatever time remains on his or her sentence in a correctional facility. The law, however, provides that a judge can order the remainder of the term to be served on probation if the defendant continues with mandatory mental health treatment.

---

[4]   *See* Richard Rogers, et al., *Effects of Ultimate Opinions on Juror Perceptions Of Insanity*, 13 INT'L J. L. & PSYCHIATRY 225 (1990); Solomon M. Fulero & Norman J. Finkel, *Barring Ultimate Issue Testimony: An "Insane" Rule?* 15 LAW & HUM. BEHAV. 495 (1991).

Michigan adopted the GBMI verdict before the Hinckley case. Eleven other states followed its lead, although some of these jurisdictions required the state only to prove the first element – the guilt of the defendant – beyond a reasonable doubt, and then shifted the burden to the defendant to prove that he or she was mentally ill at the time of the offense by a preponderance of the evidence.

The GBMI verdict received much criticism from scholars. Notably, empirical research demonstrated that the verdict had little if any effect on the insanity acquittal rate. Moreover, one of the primary objectives of the guilty but mentally ill verdict was to get treatment for those defendants who, although mentally ill, did not have their cognitive abilities so impaired as to be rendered legally insane. Yet, in reality, treatment of such defendants does not appear to be materially different from those of other inmates.

Not all states structured their variations on the guilty but mentally ill verdict the way that Michigan originally did. Consider Arizona's approach. Under it, a person may be found "Guilty Except Insane" if :

(a)   at the time of the commission of the criminal act
(b)   the person was afflicted with a mental disease or defect of such severity
(c)   that the person did not know the criminal act was wrong.
(d)   A mental disease or defect constituting legal insanity is an affirmative defense. The defendant shall prove the defendant's legal insanity by clear and convincing evidence.
(e)   Mental disease or defect does not include disorders that result from acute voluntary intoxication or withdrawal from alcohol or drugs, character defects, psychosexual disorders or impulse control disorders. Conditions that do not constitute legal insanity include but are not limited to momentary, temporary conditions arising from the pressure of the circumstances, moral decadence, depravity or passion growing out of anger, jealousy, revenge, hatred or other motives in a person who does not suffer from a mental disease or defect or an abnormality that is manifested only by criminal conduct.

ARIZ. REV. STAT. ANN. § 13-502 (West Supp. 1997) (broken out into elements above not specified in the statute for pedagogical purposes).

This guilty except insane verdict abolished the not guilty by reason of insanity verdict in its entirety. It paradoxically holds the person responsible (i.e., "guilty"), but simultaneously exempts the legally insane (under the narrow definition set forth in the statute) from criminal punishment. This ostensible oxymoron aside, the statute is one of the most restrictive insanity-related ones in the United States in some aspects, while being arguably the most progressive in other ways.

Arizona's statute returns to the M'Naghten concept of defining insanity as not knowing right from wrong. As a result, it suffers from the same criticisms levied at the M'Naghten Rule for its exclusive focus on cognitive aspects of thought and behavior to the exclusion of affective elements. But Arizona's guilty except insane statute is more restrictive than both M'Naghten and the modern federal variation of the old M'Naghten Rule.

For one thing, it eliminates the first prong of M'Naghten (i.e., not knowing the nature and quality of one's acts) from the definition of legal insanity. But since that first prong was clearly the more difficult to satisfy, the impact of its elimination may be of little consequence – essentially a change in form over substance. Second, like the modern federal formulation of the insanity defense under the IDRA, a "severe" mental disease or defect is required. Also like the modern federal formulation of the insanity defense, Arizona's guilty except insane statute make the defense an affirmative one, placing the burden of persuasion on the defendant to prove his or her insanity by clear and convincing evidence. And, finally, it contains the most restrictive exclusions of mental disorders that will not qualify as a "mental disease or defect" for insanity purposes, ranging from antisocial personality disorder, psychosexual disorders, and or impulse control disorders, to "disorders that result from acute voluntary intoxication or withdrawal from alcohol or drugs, character defects, . . . momentary, temporary conditions arising from the pressure of the circumstances, moral decadence, depravity or passion growing out of anger, jealousy, revenge, hatred or other motives."

While the Arizona approach seems harsh compared to the approaches taken in other states that adopted a GBMI verdict, the treatment of the offender after a guilty except insane verdict is actually more humane that in other jurisdictions. A defendant found guilty except insane of a crime involving a death or physical injury does not go to correctional institution under Arizona law, but rather is remanded into the custody of a state-run mental health facility. A person remains confined until it is shown by clear and convincing evidence that he or she no longer suffers from the mental disease or defect, although a conditional release is available if the person is still mentally ill, but the illness is under control and the person poses no danger to himself or herself or to others. If the person's crime did not involve a death or physical injury, then the person is released if he or she poses no risk of danger to himself/herself or to others. If, on the other hand, there is a risk of dangerousness, civil commitment proceedings, with its strict due process supervision requirements, are instituted.

These post-verdict procedures are among the most progressive in the United States. Arizona's statute is clearly designed to ensure those who need mental health care actually get it – quite a different result than appears to occur in other guilty but mentally ill jurisdictions. Equally importantly, the length of any period of detention in the mental health facility is not tied to any potential criminal sentence, but rather to the person's recovery. And finally, some adjudicated guilty except insane does not serve any time in a correctional institution, even if a fast recovery is made. Thus, although the law labels someone "guilty," its aim is clearly not to punish someone who is insane under is definition of insanity, a fact further concretized by the provision of the law which states, "A guilty except insane verdict is not a criminal conviction for sentencing enhancement purposes [for future crimes, if any]. . . ."

10. What Is a Mental Disease or Defect?

What constitutes a mental disease or defect for the purposes of the insanity defense? Unfortunately, the question is difficult to answer. Rarely is there an answer to this question that turns on a pure matter of law. Courts have consistently refused to precisely define the term "mental disease or defect." Instead, they have held that the issue of whether a person is suffering from a mental disease is a question of fact to be decided at trial.

Although the courts are reluctant to rely exclusively on psychiatric diagnoses in insanity determinations, there is much legal reliance on the American Psychiatric Association's Diagnostic and Statistical Manual ("DSM"). While an oversimplification, it seems fair to state that while the law does not recognize all psychiatric conditions in the DSM as a qualifying mental disease or defect, it does usually require the condition being offered as a qualifying mental disease or defect to be recognized by the psychiatric community in DSM.

Bruce Winick, one of the foremost scholars on the intersection of law and mental health, has suggested that courts view mental diseases and defects with "a traditional medical model of illness" in mind . . . one that may be limited to conditions that until recently were labeled *psychoses*. These major mental disorders – schizophrenia, major depressive disorders, and bipolar disorder – seem to be the paradigmatic cases of mental illness."[5] In support of the proposition that the modern conceptualization of mental illness involves psychoses, Winick cites The American Psychiatric Association's *American Psychiatric Glossary* which defines a psychosis as follows:

A major *mental disorder* of *organic* or *emotional* origin in which a person's ability to think, respond emotionally, remember, communicate, interpret reality, and behave appropriately is sufficiently impaired so as to interfere grossly with the capacity to meet the ordinary demands of life. Often characterized by *regressive* behavior, inappropriate *mood*, diminished impulse control, and such

---

[5]   Bruce Winick, *Ambiguities in the Legal Meaning and Significance of Mental Illness*, 1 PSYCH. PUB. POL. & L. 534, 558-59 (1995).

abnormal mental content as *delusions* and *hallucinations*. The term is applicable to conditions having a wide range of severity and duration. See also *schizophrenia, bipolar disorder, depression, organic mental disorder*, and *reality testing*.[6]

While there can be no doubt that courts accept psychoses as "mental diseases or defects," it is important to keep in mind that the existence of a psychosis is not, in and of itself, sufficient to establish legal incompetency or insanity. The other criteria, notably the psychosis *causing* the defendant's inability to distinguish right from wrong, for example, must also be satisfied.

Psychoses, however, are easily handled by the legal system given its orientation toward the medical model of deviance. The more problematic situations for the law is deciding if other psychiatric disorders qualify as a "mental disease or defect" for insanity purposes. Perhaps the most challenging of these other diagnoses concern personality disorders.

Some federal circuit courts of appeals have specifically held that personality disorders are not "mental diseases or defects" within the meaning of the insanity defense. Other federal circuit courts have determined that although personality disorders are mental diseases or defects, they are not severe enough under the modern federal formulation of the insanity defense to serve as the basis for an insanity defense. And it appears that at least one federal circuit (the Ninth) refuses to have a rule covering personality disorders as a class of psychiatric diagnoses, considering instead the specific diagnosis on a case-by-case basis. *See United States v. Murdoch*, 98 F.3d 472, 478 (9th Cir. 1996), *cert. denied*, 117 S. Ct. 2518 (1997). Regardless of the different approaches taken by the various federal circuits, it is clear that under federal law, antisocial personality disorder is not a qualifying mental disease or defect for insanity defense purposes. *See Foucha v. Louisiana*, 504 U.S. 71 (1992) (dicta).

DSM-IV classifies alcoholism and numerous drug addictions as Axis I "substance related disorders." The defense of intoxication is discussed in Chapter 4. It should be noted here, however, that separate and apart from the criminal defense of intoxication, two issues regarding intoxication and insanity continue to divide U.S. courts. The first is whether an addiction to drugs or alcohol can qualify as a mental disease or defect for the purposes of an insanity defense. The second is whether a drug or alcohol-induced psychosis (when unaccompanied by some other mental illness) is a qualifying mental disease or defect for an insanity defense. The overwhelming number of U.S. jurisdictions answer both questions in the negative. The follow case of sheds light on why that is.

Donald W. BIEBER, v. The PEOPLE of the State of Colorado
856 P.2d 811 (Colo. 1993).

Justice Mullarkey delivered the opinion of the Colorado Supreme Court.

Defendant Donald W. Bieber appeals his convictions for first-degree murder, aggravated robbery and second-degree aggravated motor vehicle theft on the grounds that the trial court erred in denying his request for a jury instruction on the defense of settled insanity. The three-member panel of the court of appeals issued three separate opinions in the case – one dispositive, one concurring and one dissenting – revolving around the question of whether settled insanity is a tenable defense under our statutory scheme and case law. *People v. Bieber*, 835 P.2d 542 (Colo. App. 1992). We granted certiorari in order to resolve the evident conflict.

I

The following facts are undisputed. On September 25, 1986 around 4:30 a.m., Bieber walked up to a truck in which William Ellis was sitting and shot Ellis in the back of his head. After opening the

---

[6]   *Id.* (*citing* AM. PSYCHIATRIC ASS'N, AMERICAN PSYCHIATRIC GLOSSARY 139 (6th ed. 1988)).

truck's door and allowing Ellis' body to fall onto the ground, Bieber proceeded to get into the truck and drive away. Bieber did not know Ellis.

For several hours prior and subsequent to the murder, Bieber had come into contact with various individuals at different locations. In addition to singing "God Bless America" and the "Marine Hymn," he told these people that he was a prisoner of war and that he was being followed by communists. He also fired shots at some of the people, without injuring anyone, and aimed his gun toward others. After the murder, he told people that he had killed a communist on "War Memorial Highway." Ellis' body was found around 6:00 a.m. and Bieber was arrested at approximately 8:00 a.m. Tests conducted later that day revealed no trace of amphetamines in his body, but did indicate heavy long-term marihuana use.[7]

Bieber has a long history of drug abuse. He began using drugs as a teenager, including amphetamines. As an adult, his heavy drug-use continued, and his primary means of income was through the sale of illegal drugs. Several years before the homicide, Bieber voluntarily sought treatment for mental impairment arising out of his substance abuse. He entered the hospital stating that he was afraid that he might hurt someone. His drug psychosis apparently cleared rapidly, and he was released into a long-term drug treatment program.

As a result of the events of the morning of September 25, Bieber was charged with first-degree murder after deliberation, felony murder, two counts of aggravated robbery and aggravated motor vehicle theft. He pled not guilty by reason of insanity. At his sanity trial, Bieber argued that due to a variety of causes, particularly his long-term drug use, he was not intoxicated at the time of the murder, but rather legally insane.

Bieber contended that he was suffering from "amphetamine delusional disorder," ("ADD") which was described by his expert witness in the following manner:

A delusional disorder is a mental disorder which is characterized by delusional beliefs. A delusional belief is a belief held by an individual that is out of character for their sociocultural economic background and is held in a very rigid way and the person doesn't change their belief in the face of reasoning.

And it's a false belief. That is what a delusion is. There's a number of causes of delusional thinking. One cause of delusional thinking is what used to be called amphetamine psychosis. It's now called amphetamine delusional disorder. And what that is from, some people when they use amphetamines on a chronic basis, begin to get very paranoid and delusional. And if that happens, it's associated with the use of amphetamines. It's called an amphetamine delusional disorder.

According to the Diagnostic and Statistical Manual of Mental Disorders of the American Psychiatric Association (3rd Rev. Ed. 1987) ("DSM-III"), one of the criteria for diagnosing ADD is the recent use of amphetamines during a period of long-term use of moderate to high doses of amphetamines or like drugs. The disorder abates over time, usually within a few days or weeks. Because Bieber allegedly was suffering from ADD at the time of the homicide, he argued that he was unable to distinguish right from wrong at the time of the homicide.

The prosecution's psychiatric expert conceded that it was possible that Bieber could have been suffering from ADD at the time. His opinion, however, was that Bieber actually suffered from an antisocial personality disorder, which did not prevent him from knowing right from wrong at the time that he shot Ellis.

---

[7]   The prosecution notes that amphetamines pass through the body within two to five days. It contends that Bieber could have been under the influence of amphetamines at the time of the homicide, but the drug then passed out of his system before the urinalysis was done.

Based on his plea of insanity and its alleged cause of prolonged drug use, Bieber proffered the following jury instruction:

> Insanity produced by long-continued use of amphetamines affects responsibility in the same way as insanity produced by any other cause if the mental disease or defect causing the insanity is "settled."

> "Settled "does not mean permanent or incurable, but means that the mental disease or defect resulting in insanity exists independently of the contemporaneous use of the drug. One who is actually insane does not lose the defense of insanity simply because, at the time he committed the act in question, he may also have been intoxicated. It is immaterial that the use of amphetamines may have caused the insanity, as long as the insanity was of a settled nature and qualifies as insanity as defined [elsewhere in these instructions].

This instruction was rejected by the trial court. Instead, the trial court instructed the jury in accordance with the legal test for insanity set forth in section 16-8-101, 8A C.R.S. (1986), which states in relevant part:

> A person who is so diseased or defective in mind at the time of the commission of the act as to be incapable of distinguishing right from wrong with respect to that act is not accountable. But care should be taken not to confuse such mental disease or defect with moral obliquity, mental depravity, or passion growing out of anger, revenge, hatred, or other motives, and kindred evil conditions, for when the act is induced by any of these causes the person is accountable to the law.

The trial court also instructed the jury that, "Intoxication does not, in itself, constitute a mental disease or defect within the meaning of a plea of not guilty by reason of insanity." The jury found Bieber to be sane.

In the guilt phase of the proceedings against Bieber, the jury found him guilty of felony murder, aggravated robbery and aggravated motor vehicle theft. Bieber was sentenced to life imprisonment on the felony murder and aggravated robbery convictions, and sentenced to six months, to be served concurrently, for the aggravated motor vehicle theft conviction. Bieber appealed to the court of appeals, contending that the trial court wrongly refused to give an instruction on "settled insanity." The court of appeals affirmed his convictions in a three-way opinion, and we agree with the dispositive judgment of that court, finding that our statutory scheme does not recognize "settled insanity" as a defense.

* * *

III

The doctrine of "settled insanity" draws a distinction between voluntary intoxication, universally recognized as not constituting a defense, and "insanity" arising from the long-term use of intoxicants but separate from immediate intoxication. The reasoning behind this distinction has been set forth in many jurisdictions. For example, in *People v. Lim Dum Dong*, 26 Cal. App. 2d 135, 78 P.2d 1026, 1028 (Cal. App. 1938), the court stated as follows: There is, in truth, no injustice in holding a person responsible for his acts committed in a state of voluntary intoxication. It is a duty which every one owes to his fellow men, and to society, to say nothing of more solemn obligations, to preserve so far as lies in his power, the inestimable gift of reason. If it is perverted or destroyed by fixed disease, though brought on by his own vices, the law holds him not accountable, but if, by a voluntary act, he temporarily casts off the restraints of reason and conscience, no wrong is done him if he is considered answerable for any injury which, in that state, he may do to others or to society. It must be "settled insanity," and not merely a temporary mental condition . . . which would relieve one of the responsibility of his criminal act.

We recognize that the substantial weight of precedent from other jurisdictions that have considered the "settled insanity" defense lies in acceptance of that doctrine. We find, however, that the "settled insanity" defense is not reconcilable with our statutory scheme and its underlying policy concerns.

185

Colorado does recognize the defense of insanity, as embodied in our criminal code. The doctrine of "settled insanity," while ostensibly falling under the insanity statute, also invokes the question of intoxication, since its cause is the prolonged use of intoxicants. The General Assembly has definitively addressed the issue of intoxication as a defense.

Section 18- 1-804, 8B C.R.S. (1986) provides as follows:

(1) Intoxication of the accused is not a defense to a criminal charge, except as provided in subsection (3) of this section, but in any prosecution for an offense, evidence of intoxication of the defendant may be offered by the defendant when it is relevant to negative the existence of a specific intent if such intent is an element of the crime charged.
(2) Intoxication does not, in itself, constitute mental disease or defect within the meaning of section 18-1-802 [the insanity defense].
(3) A person is not criminally responsible for his conduct if, by reason of intoxication that is not self-induced at the time he acts, he lacks capacity to conform his conduct to the requirements of the law.
(4) "Intoxication," as used in this section means a disturbance of mental or physical capacities resulting from the introduction of any substance into the body.
(5) "Self-induced intoxication" means intoxication caused by substances which the defendant knows or ought to know have the tendency to cause intoxication and which he knowingly introduced or allowed to be introduced into his body, unless they were introduced pursuant to medical advice or under circumstances that would afford a defense to a charge of crime.

A straight-forward reading of the statute indicates that "settled insanity" cannot be maintained as a defense. In subsection (4), "intoxication" is defined as "a disturbance of mental or physical capacities resulting from the introduction of any substance into the body." Bieber's condition falls directly into this definition – his alleged "settled insanity" resulted from his use of amphetamines and, as such, may be regarded as an "intoxication." Such intoxication was "self-induced" under subsection (5), since Bieber knew of the effect that the drugs, which he took voluntarily, would have and were having on his body and mind. This point is evidenced in particular by Bieber's earlier drug treatment, which he sought because he was afraid that he would hurt someone.

We do not see any qualitative difference between a person who drinks or takes drugs knowing that he or she will be momentarily "mentally defective" as an immediate result, and one who drinks or takes drugs knowing that he or she may be "mentally defective" as an eventual, long-term result. In both cases, the person is aware of the possible consequences of his or her actions. We do not believe that in the latter case, such knowledge should be excused simply because the resulting affliction is more severe.

Our research has disclosed a number of states with intoxication statutes similar enough to ours to be of relevance. Of these states, Connecticut, Hawaii and Maine have not yet addressed the "settled insanity" issue. The remaining states have found "settled insanity" to be a viable defense. It is important to note, however, that these states recognized the defense of "settled insanity" well before they enacted their present criminal codes. *See Beasley v. State*, 50 Ala. 149 (1876); *Byrd v. State*, 76 Ark. 286, 88 S.W. 974 (Ark. 1905); *State v. White*, 27 N.J. 158, 142 A.2d 65 (N.J. 1958). For these latter states, by virtue of their settled caselaw, their interpretation of their statute was already moulded. We are not in such a position, but must approach our statute from its plain meaning.

As a matter of public policy, we cannot excuse a defendant's actions, which endanger others in his or her community, based upon a mental disturbance or illness that he or she actively and voluntarily contracted. There is no principled basis to distinguish between the short-term and long-term effects of voluntary intoxication by punishing the first and excusing the second. If anything, the moral blameworthiness would seem to be even greater with respect to the long-term effects of many, repeated instances of voluntary intoxication occurring over an extended period of time.

Another point we find to be important in our analysis is the fact that, as argued by defense counsel, this particular form of "settled insanity" – ADD – is similar to the condition of temporary insanity. According to one of the expert witnesses as well as the DSM-III, ADD lasts between a few days and several weeks. It is not a permanent disorder, and thus, even if it were considered to be "insanity," is not a permanent or even long-term insanity. We have previously addressed, in a succinct fashion, the defense of temporary insanity in this state. In *People v. Low*, 732 P.2d 622 (Colo. 1987), we stated that, "temporary insanity is not part of the statutory framework for resolving a defendant's nonresponsibility for a criminal act, and was not a proper ground for the trial court's entry of judgment of acquittal."

The General Assembly has so far chosen not to redress this gap in our criminal code, and we must assume that its inaction is purposeful. Because temporary insanity is not recognized as a valid defense in this state, it would be inconsistent and erroneous to permit "settled insanity," which embraces principles similar to those of temporary insanity, as a valid defense. . . . The judgment of the court of appeals is affirmed.

Justice Lohr dissenting:

The majority upholds the judgment of conviction in this case based on its conclusion that "settled insanity" does not constitute a valid defense to a criminal charge because a recognition of that defense would conflict with statutory provisions that limit the use of intoxication as a defense, and would contravene its view of our public policy. Not only do I disagree that by that statute the General Assembly has precluded settled insanity from constituting a defense, but I believe that under the dictates of due process the trial court was constitutionally obligated to instruct the jury on that defense, as the defendant requested. Accordingly, I dissent from the majority opinion and conclude in contrast that the defendant's convictions for first-degree murder, aggravated robbery, and second-degree aggravated motor vehicle theft should be reversed and that this case should be remanded for a new trial on the sanity issue.

A fundamental tenet of our system of justice is that a person may not be held criminally responsible for actions performed while insane. This is because at some point a person's mind may be so impaired by disease or defect that he is incapable of entertaining criminal intent. *See Ryan v. People*, 60 Colo. 425, 427, 153 P. 756, 755 (1915). The General Assembly has determined, however, and we have accordingly held, that although a person may become temporarily incapacitated by the use of alcohol or drugs, voluntary intoxication does not constitute an affirmative defense to a crime and may be used only to negate specific intent when that intent is an element of the crime charged. See § 18-1-804(1); *Hendershott v. People*, 653 P.2d 385, 396 (Colo. 1982), *cert. denied*, 459 U.S. 1225 (1983); *People v. DelGuidice*, 199 Colo. 41, 45, 606 P.2d 840, 843 (1979). In the present case, the defendant did not contend that his conduct should be excused or the basis that he was intoxicated at the time he committed the offenses. Rather, he asserted that he should not be held accountable for his actions because he was legally insane at the time. Because he claimed that his insanity was the result of a long-continued use of amphetamines, the defendant requested an instruction to inform the jury that the cause of the condition was immaterial as long as the insanity was settled.

The defendant's proffered instruction rests on a distinction between an intoxicated condition caused by the voluntary ingestion of alcohol or drugs at or near the time of an offense and a mental condition that exists independent of current use and results from a previous long-term consumption of such substances. The California Supreme Court described this distinction and the rationale for affording it different legal consequences in *People v. Kelly*, 10 Cal. 3d 565, 111 Cal. Rptr. 171, 516 P.2d 875, 882 (Cal. 1973), stating that in the former situation the "mental impairment does not extend beyond the period of intoxication," but in the latter, when long-term intoxication results in insanity, the mental disorder remains even after the effects of the drug or alcohol have worn off. The actor is "legally insane," and the traditional justifications for criminal punishment are inapplicable because of his inability to conform . . . to accepted social behavior. The Maryland Court of Appeals has characterized the distinction as "one between the direct results of drinking, which are voluntarily sought after, and its remote and undesired consequences." *Porreca v. State*, 49 Md. App. 522, 433 A.2d 1204, 1207 (Md. App. 1981).

Thus, even though the direct and short-term consequence of the use of a drug or alcohol – the state of intoxication – will not provide an excuse for resultant conduct because the voluntary nature of the use of that substance to obtain its immediate effects supports holding that person responsible for his actions, when that use develops into a condition that meets the definition of insanity, our society has determined that there is no longer any justification for holding the person legally accountable. As stated by LaFave and Scott, "the defense of intoxication is quite different from the defense of insanity, yet excessive drinking may bring on actual insanity . . .; in such a case, if a defendant does not know right from wrong (in a M'Naghten test jurisdiction), he is not guilty of a crime because of his otherwise criminal conduct. Wayne R. LaFave & Austin W. Scott, Jr., Criminal Law § 410(g), at 395 (2d ed. 1986) (footnotes omitted).

Although I see no need to define specifically the type of conditions that may constitute settled insanity and believe that the only relevant question is whether a person meets the test set forth in § 16-8-101, I am satisfied that the distinctions between legal insanity and intoxication provide ample support for treating persons suffering from these conditions differently.

Although the majority recognizes this distinction in the case now before us, it declines to give it effect. In contrast to the majority's position, I believe that when a person suffers from an actual disease or defect of the mind, regardless of whether it is attributable to prior alcohol or drug use, so that he meets the legal definition of insanity, and when that condition exists independent of any intoxicated state, any limitations on the ability to assert intoxication as a defense are inapplicable.

* * *

The majority goes on to support its position by analogizing the particular form of settled insanity asserted in this case, amphetamine delusional disorder, to temporary insanity, which we have stated at least in passing is not a viable defense under our statutes. *People v. Low*, 732 P.2d 622, 632 (Colo. 1987). Because evidence was presented that settled insanity is not a permanent condition, the majority concludes that it would be "erroneous" to find that it constitutes a valid defense. I disagree with this argument. . . . Not only is there no requirement in our statutory law that a person's insanity be permanent before it may be asserted as an affirmative defense, see §§ 16-8-101 to -107, 8A C.R.S. (1986 & 1992 Supp.), but such a requirement would undermine the assumption implicit in our statutory scheme that a person adjudged insane can be treated and at some point safely returned to society. As Judge Dubofsky well stated, the proper focus is not on "the extent of the period of manifest insanity," but rather is on "when the drugs or alcohol were ingested in time relationship to the criminal offense." Bieber, 835 P.2d at 550. Consequently, I am not persuaded that any similarity between temporary insanity and the condition that the defendant in this case alleged requires preclusion of his assertion of settled insanity as a defense.

Justice Erickson and Justice Kirshbaum join in this dissent.

QUESTIONS

1.   The majority of jurisdictions do not recognize drug or alcohol-induced psychosis (when unaccompanied by some other mental illness) to be a sufficient predicate for an insanity defense. But as the court in *Bieber* pointed out, a number of jurisdictions recognize the concept of settled insanity. Do you agree with the majority or the dissent that Colorado's statutory framework precluded the court from recognizing settled insanity as a criminal defense? Why?

2.   The *Bieber* majority wrote, "there is no principled basis to distinguish between the short-term and long-term effects of voluntary intoxication by punishing the first and excusing the second. If anything, the moral blameworthiness would seem to be even greater with respect to the long-term effects of many, repeated instances of voluntary intoxication occurring over an extended period of time." Critically evaluate this statement.

3.   The legal issue of temporary insanity in this case is, of course, limited to Colorado law. Do you feel that a temporary psychosis induced by drug or alcohol abuse such as amphetamine delusional disorder *should* qualify as a mental disease or defect for insanity purposes? Why or why not? Analyze your reasons using the four main theoretical perspectives on crime and punishment (i.e., retribution, deterrence, rehabilitation, and incapacitation).

4.   The majority did not "see any qualitative difference between a person who drinks or takes drugs knowing that he or she will be momentarily 'mentally defective' as an immediate result, and one who drinks or takes drugs knowing that he or she may be 'mentally defective' as an eventual, long-term result." Do you agree that in both cases, the person is aware of the possible consequences of his or her actions? If a defendant is not actually aware of the difference between short and long-term effects of an intoxicant regulatory consumed, should that make a difference in terms of criminal responsibility in terms of an intoxicant-produced psychosis? Why?

11. What is "Wrong"?

What is right, just, good, moral, and so on is a question that has perplexed philosophers for eons. The counter-question, what is bad, wrong, or immoral is not easier to answer. The law, however, often avoids complex philosophical issues leaving it to scholars to debate. It certainly does so in defining what is meant by "wrong" for the purposes of the insanity defense requirement that a mental disease or defect render a defendant unable to "know right from wrong" or to "appreciate the wrongfulness" of his or her acts. The law simply looks at whether the defendant knew the act was wrong by societal standards. Consider the following case.

STATE of Washington, Respondent, v. Rodney K. CRENSHAW, Petitioner.
659 P.2d 488 (Wash. 1983).

Brachtenbach, Justice.

Rodney Crenshaw pleaded not guilty and not guilty by reason of insanity to the charge of first degree murder of his wife, Karen Crenshaw. A jury found him guilty. Petitioner appealed his conviction, assigning error to a number of the trial court's rulings. After the Court of Appeals affirmed the trial court in all respects, petitioner raised the same issues before this court.

While defendant and his wife were on their honeymoon in Canada, petitioner was deported as a result of his participation in a brawl. He secured a motel room in Blaine, Washington and waited for his wife to join him. When she arrived 2 days later, he immediately thought she had been unfaithful – he sensed "it wasn't the same Karen . . . she'd been with someone else." Petitioner did not mention his suspicions to his wife, instead he took her to the motel room and beat her unconscious. He then went to a nearby store, stole a knife, and returned to stab his wife 24 times, inflicting a fatal wound. He left again, drove to a nearby farm where he had been employed and borrowed an ax. Upon returning to the motel room, he decapitated his wife with such force that the ax marks cut into the concrete floor under the carpet and splattered blood throughout the room.

Petitioner then proceeded to conceal his actions. He placed the body in a blanket, the head in a pillowcase, and put both in his wife's car. Next, he went to a service station, borrowed a bucket and sponge, and cleaned the room of blood and fingerprints. Before leaving, petitioner also spoke with the motel manager about a phone bill, then chatted with him for awhile over a beer.

When Crenshaw left the motel, he drove to a remote area 25 miles away where he hid the two parts of the body in thick brush. He then fled, driving to the Hoquiam area, about 200 miles from the scene of the crime. There he picked up two hitchhikers, told them of his crime, and enlisted their aid in disposing of his wife's car in a river. The hitchhikers contacted the police and Crenshaw was apprehended shortly thereafter. He voluntarily confessed to the crime. The defense of not guilty by reason of insanity was a major issue at trial. Crenshaw testified that he followed the Muscovite religious faith, and that it would be improper for a Muscovite not to kill his wife if she committed adultery. Crenshaw also has a history of mental problems, for which he has been hospitalized in the past. The jury, however, rejected petitioner's insanity defense, and found him guilty of murder in the first degree.

A. Insanity Defense Instruction

Insanity is an affirmative defense the defendant must establish by a preponderance of the evidence [in Washington State at the time relevant to this case]. Sanity is presumed, even with a history of prior institutional commitments from which the individual was released upon sufficient recovery. The insanity defense is not available to all who are mentally deficient or deranged; legal insanity has a different meaning and a different purpose than the concept of medical insanity. A verdict of not guilty by reason of insanity completely absolves a defendant of any criminal responsibility. Therefore, the defense is available only to those persons who have lost contact with reality so completely that they are beyond any of the influences of the criminal law.

Petitioner assigned error to insanity defense instruction 10 which reads: In addition to the plea of not guilty, the defendant has entered a plea of insanity existing at the time of the act charged. Insanity existing at the time of the commission of the act charged is a defense. For a defendant to be found not guilty by reason of insanity you must find that, as a result of mental disease or defect, the defendant's mind was affected to such an extent that the defendant was unable to perceive the nature and quality of the acts with which the defendant is charged or was unable to tell right from wrong with reference to the particular acts with which defendant is charged.

What is meant by the terms "right and wrong" refers to knowledge of a person at the time of committing an act that he was acting contrary to the law. [The M'Naghten test codified]. Petitioner contends, however, that the trial court erred in defining "right and wrong" as legal right and wrong rather than in the moral sense.

We find this instruction was not reversible error on three, alternative grounds: (1) The M'Naghten opinion amply supports the "legal" wrong definition as used in this case, (2) under these facts, "moral" wrong and "legal" wrong are synonymous, therefore the "legal" wrong definition did not alter the meaning of the test, and (3) because Crenshaw failed to prove other elements of the insanity defense, any error in the definition of wrong was harmless.

I

The definition of the term "wrong" in the M'Naghten test has been considered and disputed by many legal scholars. Courts from other jurisdictions are divided on the issue. In Washington, we have not addressed this issue previously. The confusion arises from apparent inconsistencies in the original M'Naghten case. In response to the House of Lords' first question, the justices replied that if an accused knew he was acting contrary to law but acted under a partial insane delusion that he was redressing or revenging some supposed grievance or injury, or producing some supposed public benefit, "he is nevertheless punishable . . . if he knew at the time of committing such crime that he was acting contrary to . . . the law of the land." In this answer, the justices appear to approve the legal standard of wrong when there is evidence that the accused knew he was acting contrary to the law.

This has been characterized as inconsistent with the justices' response to the second and third questions, regarding how a jury should be instructed on the insanity defense: If the question were to be put [to a jury] as to the knowledge of the accused solely and exclusively with reference to the law of the land, it might tend to confound the jury, by inducing them to believe that an actual knowledge of the law of the land was essential in order to lead to a conviction; whereas the law is administered upon the principle that everyone must be taken conclusively to know it, without proof that he does know it. If the accused was conscious that the act was one which he ought not to do, and if that act was at the same time contrary to the law of the land, he is punishable; and the usual course therefore has been to leave the question to the jury, whether the party accused had a sufficient degree of reason to know that he was doing an act that was wrong: and this course we think is correct, accompanied with such observations and explanations as the circumstances of each particular case may require. This response appears to require both that the accused be "conscious that the act was one which he ought not to do" and that the act be "contrary to the law."

A close examination of these answers, however, shows they are reconcilable in the context of this case. First, the similarities between the hypothetical in the first question and Crenshaw's situation should afford that answer great weight. If, arguendo, Crenshaw was delusional, his delusion was only partial, for it related only to his perceptions of his wife's infidelity. His behavior towards others, i.e., the motel manager and the woman who loaned him the ax, at the time of the killing was normal. Crenshaw also "knew he was acting contrary to law," as evidenced by his sophisticated attempts to hide his crime and by the expert, psychiatric testimony. Furthermore, he acted with a view of redressing or revenging the supposed grievance of his wife's infidelity. Thus, the Crenshaw situation fits perfectly into the first hypothetical, and the trial court understandably relied on this passage in approving the challenged instruction.

Second, the answers to the second and third questions certainly do not forbid the additional comment found in instruction 10. The justices expressly provided that the instruction could be "accompanied with such observations and explanations as the circumstances of each particular case may require." In addition, the justices' hesitance to state the question exclusively with reference to the law stemmed from a fear that "it might tend to confound the jury, by inducing them to believe that an actual knowledge of the law of the land was essential in order to lead to a conviction." Therefore, in cases such as this where actual knowledge of the law is not an issue, an instruction in terms of legal wrong would not be improper.

In short, M'Naghten supports the propriety of the trial court's instruction in several ways: (1) the justices' answer to the first question was more analogous to Crenshaw's fact situation, and that answer referred only to legal wrong, (2) the M'Naghten justices provided that in some cases an additional statement by the court would be acceptable, and (3) in this case there was no danger that the jury would be induced to believe that actual knowledge of the law was essential, since Crenshaw demonstrated that he knew the illegality of his acts. Thus, the facts here permit resolution of the inconsistencies in M'Naghten in favor of the "legal" wrong standard. Such an interpretation is consistent with Washington's strict application of M'Naghten. This court's view has been that when M'Naghten is used, all who might possibly be deterred from the commission of criminal acts are included within the sanctions of the criminal law. Only those persons who have lost contact with reality so completely that they are beyond any of the influences of the criminal law, may have the benefit of the insanity defense in a criminal case. Given this perspective, the trial court could assume that one who knew the illegality of his act was not necessarily "beyond any of the influences of the criminal law," thus finding support for the statement in instruction 10.

II

Alternatively, the statement in instruction 10 may be approved because, in this case, legal wrong is synonymous with moral wrong. This conclusion is premised on two grounds.

First, in discussing the term "moral" wrong, it is important to note that it is society's morals, and not the individual's morals, that are the standard for judging moral wrong under M'Naghten. If wrong meant moral wrong judged by the individual's own conscience, this would seriously undermine the criminal law, for it would allow one who violated the law to be excused from criminal responsibility solely because, in his own conscience, his act was not morally wrong. This principle was emphasized by Justice Cardozo: The anarchist is not at liberty to break the law because he reasons that all government is wrong. The devotee of a religious cult that enjoins polygamy or human sacrifice as a duty is not thereby relieved from responsibility before the law . . . . More recently the Arizona Supreme Court stated: We find no authority upholding the defendant's position that one suffering from a mental disease could be declared legally insane if he knew that the act was morally and legally wrong but he personally

191

believed that act right. We believe that this would not be a sound rule, because it approaches the position of exonerating a defendant for his personal beliefs and does not take account of society's determination of defendant's capacity to conform his conduct to the law.

There is evidence on the record that Crenshaw knew his actions were wrong according to society's standards, as well as legally wrong. Dr. Belden testified: "I think Mr. Crenshaw is quite aware on one level that he is in conflict with the law and with people. However, this is not something that he personally invests his emotions in." We conclude that Crenshaw knew his acts were morally wrong from society's viewpoint and also knew his acts were illegal. His personal belief that it was his duty to kill his wife for her alleged infidelity cannot serve to exculpate him from legal responsibility for his acts.

A narrow exception to the societal standard of moral wrong has been drawn for instances wherein a party performs a criminal act, knowing it is morally and legally wrong, but believing, because of a mental defect, that the act is ordained by God: such would be the situation with a mother who kills her infant child to whom she is devotedly attached, believing that God has spoken to her and decreed the act. Although the woman knows that the law and society condemn the act, it would be unrealistic to hold her responsible for the crime, since her free will has been subsumed by her belief in the deific decree.

This exception is not available to Crenshaw, however. Crenshaw argued only that he followed the Muscovite faith and that Muscovites believe it is their duty to kill an unfaithful wife. This is not the same as acting under a deific command. Instead, it is akin to the devotee of a religious cult that enjoins . . . human sacrifice as a duty [and] is not thereby relieved from responsibility before the law. Crenshaw's personal "Muscovite" beliefs are not equivalent to a deific decree and do not relieve him from responsibility for his acts. Once moral wrong is equated with society's morals, the next step, equating moral and legal wrong, follows logically. The law is, for the most part, an expression of collective morality.

Most cases involving the insanity defense involve serious crimes for which society's moral judgment is identical with the legal standard. Therefore, a number of scholars have concluded that, as a practical matter, the way in which a court interprets the word wrong will have little effect on the eventual outcome of a case. As one scholar explained: "Since by far the vast majority of cases in which insanity is pleaded as a defense to criminal prosecutions involves acts which are universally regarded as morally wicked as well as illegal, the hair-splitting distinction between legal and moral wrong need not be given much attention."

Society's morals and legal wrong are interchangeable concepts in the context of this case. Petitioner's crime, killing his wife by stabbing her 24 times then hacking off her head, is clearly contrary to society's morals as well as the law. Therefore by defining wrong in terms of legal wrong, the trial court did not alter the meaning of the M'Naghten test.

III

We also find that, under any definition of wrong, Crenshaw did not qualify for the insanity defense under M'Naghten; therefore, any alleged error in that definition must be viewed as harmless. The alleged error here involved the interpretation of the statutory definition of the insanity defense. Crenshaw's right to an insanity defense instruction is not at issue. Therefore, the stringent, constitutional harmless error analysis is inapplicable. A nonconstitutional error does not require reversal of a criminal conviction unless, within reasonable probabilities, the outcome of the trial would have been materially affected had the error not occurred.

Here, any error is harmless for two alternate reasons. First, Crenshaw failed to prove an essential element of the defense because he did not prove his alleged delusions stemmed from a mental defect; second, he did not prove by a preponderance of the evidence that he was legally insane at the time of the crime.

In addition to an incapacity to know right from wrong, M'Naghten requires that such incapacity stem from a mental disease or defect. Assuming, arguendo, that Crenshaw did not know right from wrong, he failed to prove that a mental defect was the cause of this inability. Petitioner's insanity argument is premised on the following facts: (1) he is a Muscovite and Muscovites believe it is their duty to assassinate an unfaithful spouse; (2) he "knew", without asking, that his wife had been unfaithful when he met her in Blaine and this was equivalent to an insane delusion; and (3) at other times in his life, he had been diagnosed as a paranoid personality and had been committed to mental institutions. A conscientious application of the M'Naghten rule demonstrates, however, that these factors do not afford petitioner the sanctuary of the insanity defense.

To begin, petitioner's Muscovite beliefs are irrelevant to the insanity defense, because they are not insane delusions. Some notion of morality, unrelated to a mental illness, which disagrees with the law and mores of our society is not an insane delusion. Nor was petitioner's belief that his wife was unfaithful an insane delusion. Dr. Trowbridge, a psychiatrist, explained: "A man suspects his wife of being unfaithful. Certainly such suspicions are not necessarily delusional, even if they're ill based. Just because he suspected his wife of being unfaithful doesn't mean that he was crazy. Certainly when a man kills his wife he doesn't do it in a rational way. No one ever does that rationally. But that is not to suggest that every time a man kills his wife he was insane."

Finally, evidence of prior commitments to mental institutions is not proof that one was legally insane at the time the criminal act was committed. . . . Those who are commonly regarded as "odd" or "unsound" or even "deranged" would not normally qualify for the insanity defense. Many, if not most, mentally ill persons presently being treated in the mental institutions of this state who are there under the test of "likelihood of serious harm to the person detained or to others," . . . would not meet the M'Naghten test, if charged with a crime. Thus, petitioner does not establish the necessary connection between his criminal acts and his psychological problems to qualify for the insanity defense.

In addition, the preponderance of the evidence weighs against finding Crenshaw legally insane. All of the psychological experts, save one, testified that defendant was not insane at the time of the murder. The only doctor who concluded defendant (petitioner) was legally insane, Dr. Hunter, was a psychologist who had not examined petitioner for a year and a half. Given the various qualifications of the experts, the time they spent with the petitioner, and the proximity in time of their examinations to the murder, the testimony does not establish by a preponderance of the evidence that petitioner was legally insane at the time of the murder.

Furthermore, in addition to the expert testimony, there was lay testimony that petitioner appeared rational at the time of the killing. After cleaning the motel room, Crenshaw resolved a phone bill dispute with the manager, then shared a beer with him without arousing any suspicion in the manager's mind. Also, the woman who gave him the ax testified as to his behavior the day before the murder: "Well, he seemed very normal or I certainly wouldn't have handed him an ax or a hoe. He was polite, he done his work. He didn't, I wasn't afraid of him or anything. I mean we were just out there working and I certainly wouldn't have handed him an ax or anything like that if I would have thought that there was anything even remotely peculiar about him. Thus, at the same time that he was embroiled in the act of murdering his wife, he was rational, coherent, and sane in his dealings with others.

Finally, evidence of petitioner's calculated execution of the crime and his sophisticated attempts to avert discovery support a finding of sanity. Crenshaw performed the murder methodically, leaving the motel room twice to acquire the knife and ax necessary to perform the deed. Then, after the killing he scrubbed the motel room to clean up the blood and remove his fingerprints. Next, he drove 25 miles to hide the body in thick brush in a remote area. Finally, he drove several hundred miles and ditched the car in a river. Such attempts to hide evidence of a crime manifest an awareness that the act was legally wrong. Moreover, petitioner testified that he did these things because he "didn't want to get caught."

* * *

Finding no reversible error was committed by the trial court, we affirm the judgment.

QUESTIONS

1. *Crenshaw* stands for the proposition that "wrong" by societal standards, not "wrong" by one's personal standards, is what is meant by the terms in the insanity context. Mr. Crenshaw thought his wife was having an affair – behavior that is "wrong" by societal standards. His response, however, was to kill her – something he justified by the subjective standards of his own belief system. Clearly allowing one's own views on what is right or wrong, even if they stem from verifiable religious beliefs, is unacceptable. If it weren't, consider the impact of professing one's faith as a Satanic worshiper. One could conceivably justify all types of killing. But what if the killing of one's spouse for adultery were not "wrong" by societal standards? After all, there was a time, up to quite recently in some U.S. jurisdictions in the Deep South, when a husband was considered justified in killing his wife upon the discovery of adultery (the converse, of course, was not true). What impact, if any, do you think it would have had on this case if that out-dated and sexist view had been in effect in Washington at the time Crenshaw killed his wife?

2. The majority explained that Crenshaw's behavior towards others (i.e., the motel manager and the woman who loaned him the ax, at the time of the killing) was "normal." Clinically assess such behavior. Does such "normal" conduct mean that Crenshaw was not suffering from a qualifying mental disease or defect?

3. The majority felt that Crenshaw "'knew he was acting contrary to law,' as evidenced by his sophisticated attempts to hide his crime." Under a M'Naghten-type approach, such cognitive knowledge deprives Crenshaw of an bona-fide claim to insanity. Given both Crenshaw's religious beliefs and possible delusionary belief system, do you think Crenshaw was legally insane under the ALI/MPC formulation of the insanity defense? Why?

4. Assume for the sake of argument that Crenshaw did, in fact, suffer from a psychotic delusional disorder. Further assume that he was compelled to kill his wife to escape constant tauntings of his psyche stemming from his mental illness. With these two assumptions in mind, do you think Crenshaw would have been found not guilty by reason of insanity using the standard in effect in Washington at the time he committed the homicide? Explain your answer. How would your answer differ, if at all, if the ALI/MPC formulation of the insanity defense were applied?

---

12. Abolition of the Insanity Defense: The Mens Rea Approach

Montana, Idaho, and Utah have abolished the defense and allow evidence of mental illness only to be used to show that the level of mens rea the state is required to prove as an element of a crime was not entertained by the defendant due to his or her mental condition. The mechanics of how this mens rea approach works, and the constitutionality of it, were addressed by the Montana Supreme Court in 1984 in the following case.

STATE of Montana, Plaintiff-Respondent, v. Jerry T. KORELL, Defendant-Appellant.
690 P.2d 992 (Mont. 1984).

Judge Haswell delivered the opinion of the Montana Supreme Court.

Jerry Korell appeals the judgment of the Ravalli County District Court finding him guilty of attempted deliberate homicide and aggravated assault. Korell was sentenced to concurrent sentences of thirty-five and fifteen years at the Montana State Prison. Korell's defense at trial was that he lacked the requisite criminal mental state by reason of his insanity. On appeal his primary contention is that the Montana statutory scheme deprived him of a constitutional right to raise insanity as an independent defense.

Jerry Korell is a Viet Nam veteran who had several disturbing experiences during his tour of duty. The exact nature of the trauma was never fully documented. Friends and family agree that he was a different person when he returned from the service. Between Korell's honorable discharge in 1970 and the present events, he was twice admitted to VA hospitals for psychological problems and treated with anti-psychotic drugs. In 1976 he was jailed briefly in Boise, Idaho, for harassing and threatening the late Senator Frank Church.

The basic nature of Korell's problems was that he would periodically slip into paranoid phases during which he had trouble relating to male authority figures. His mental health varied dramatically. In the poorer times his family entertained thoughts about having him civilly committed. His VA hospitalizations were voluntary and neither of the stays were of such length that he was fully evaluated or treated.

In 1980 Korell entered a community college program for echocardiology in Spokane, Washington. Echocardiology is the skill associated with recording and interpreting sonograms of the heart for diagnostic purposes. In March 1982 he was sent to Missoula to serve a clinical externship at St. Patrick's Hospital. Korell's supervisor at the hospital was Greg Lockwood, the eventual victim of this crime.

Korell's relationship with Lockwood deteriorated for a variety of work-related reasons. Foremost was Korell's belief that he was worked excessively by Lockwood. At this time Korell was subjected to what expert testimony labeled psychological stressors: a divorce by his wife, financial problems and the pressures of graduation requirements.

In April 1982 Korell wrote a letter to the hospital administrator complaining about his supervisor, Lockwood. Korell was transferred to an externship in Spokane, and Lockwood was placed on probation. Both men retained very bitter feelings about the incident. Lockwood stated to friends he would see to it that Korell was never hired anywhere in echocardiology. Korell may have learned of Lockwood's statements.

Korell's actions in the next two months indicate a great deal of confusion. He set fire to a laundromat because he lost nine quarters in a machine and was tired of being ripped off. He set fire to a former home of his wife because she had bad feelings about it.

Released on bail from these incidents, he returned to Missoula in June 1982. Psychiatric testimony introduced at trial indicates that Korell felt he had to kill Lockwood before Lockwood killed him. He removed a handgun from a friend's home, had another acquaintance purchase ammunition, and on the evening of June 25, 1982, drove to the Lockwood home in the Eagle Watch area of the Bitterroot Valley. Shirley Lockwood, Greg's wife, saw the unfamiliar vehicle approach the house. Greg Lockwood was lying on the living room floor at the time watching television. Korell entered the house through a side door and began firing. Although wounded, Greg Lockwood managed to engage the defendant in a struggle. A shot was fired in the direction of Lockwood's wife. Korell grabbed a kitchen knife and both men were further injured before Lockwood was able to subdue Korell.

Korell was charged with attempted deliberate homicide and aggravated assault. The defendant gave notice of his intent to rely on a mental disease or defect to prove that he did not have the particular state of mind which is an essential element of the offense charged. Prior to trial he sought a writ of supervisory control declaring that he had a right to rely on the defense that he was suffering from a mental disease or defect at the time he committed the acts charged. The writ was denied by this court on December 20, 1982, and the case proceeded to trial.

Several psychologists and psychiatrists testified on Korell's mental condition. The defense sought to establish by its expert witnesses and numerous character witnesses that Korell was a disturbed man who was psychotic at the time the crimes were committed. It was argued that his actions when he entered the Lockwood home were not voluntary acts. The State produced its own expert witnesses who testified on Korell's mental condition. Four doctors testified in all, two for the prosecution and two for the defense. Three of the four stated Korell had the capacity to act knowingly or purposely, the requisite mental state for the offenses, when he entered the Lockwood home.

Without giving prior notice, the State produced Cedric Hames as a rebuttal witness who testified that he purchased ammunition for the defendant several days before the shooting. A motion for mistrial was made by the defense. The court denied the motion but offered the defense a continuance. The offer was refused by defendant's counsel.

In keeping with Montana's current law on mental disease or defect, the jury was instructed that they could consider mental disease or defect only insofar as it negated the defendant's requisite state of mind. The jury returned guilty verdicts for the attempted deliberate homicide and aggravated assault.

CONSTITUTIONAL CHALLENGE

Background

In 1979 the Forty-Sixth Session of the Legislature enacted House Bill 877. This Bill abolished use of the traditional insanity defense in Montana and substituted alternative procedures for considering a criminal defendant's mental condition. Evidence of mental disease or defect is now considered at three phases of a criminal proceeding.

Before trial, evidence may be presented to show that the defendant is not fit to proceed to trial. Anyone who is unable to understand the proceedings against him or assist in his defense may not be prosecuted.

During trial, evidence of mental disease or defect is admissible when relevant to prove that, at the time of the offense charged, the defendant did not have the state of mind that is an element of the crime charged, e.g., that the defendant did not act purposely or knowingly. The State retains the burden of proving each element of the offense beyond a reasonable doubt. Defendant may, of course, present evidence to contradict the State's proof that he committed the offense and that he had the requisite state of mind at that time.

Whenever the jury finds that the State has failed to prove beyond a reasonable doubt that the defendant had the requisite state of mind at the time he committed the offense, it is instructed to return a special verdict of not guilty "for the reason that due to a mental disease or defect he could not have a particular state of mind that is an essential element of the offense charged . . . ."

Finally at the dispositional stage following the trial and conviction, the sentencing judge must consider any relevant evidence presented at the trial, plus any additional evidence presented at the sentencing hearing, to determine whether the defendant was able to appreciate the criminality of his acts or to conform his conduct to the law at the time he committed the offense for which he was convicted.

The sentencing judge's consideration of the evidence is not the same as that of the jury. The jury determines whether the defendant committed the offense with the requisite state of mind, e.g., whether he acted purposely or knowingly. The sentencing judge determines whether, at the time the defendant committed the offense, he was able to appreciate its criminality or conform his conduct to the law.

If the court concludes the defendant was not suffering from a mental disease or defect that rendered him unable to appreciate the criminality of his conduct or to conform his conduct to the requirements of law, normal, criminal sentencing procedures are invoked.

Whenever the sentencing court finds the defendant was suffering from mental disease or defect which rendered him unable to appreciate the criminality of his conduct or to conform his conduct to the requirements of law, mandatory minimum sentences are waived. The defendant is committed to the custody of the director of institutions and placed in an appropriate institution for custody, care and treatment not to exceed the maximum possible sentence.

As a practical matter, this means the defendant may be placed in the Warm Springs State Hospital under the alternative sentencing procedures. The institutionalized defendant may later petition the District Court for release from the hospital upon a showing that the individual has been cured of the mental disease or defect. If the petition is granted, the court must transfer the defendant to the state prison or place the defendant under alternative confinement or supervision. The length of this confinement or supervision must equal the original sentence.

In summary, while Montana has abolished the traditional use of insanity as a defense, alternative procedures have been enacted to deal with insane individuals who commit criminal acts.

Review of our case law reveals that the constitutionality of the legislature's abolition of the affirmative defense of insanity has not previously been decided. Korell's present challenge is based on the Fourteenth Amendment guarantee of due process of law and the Eighth Amendment prohibition against cruel and unusual punishment.

Due Process Considerations

1. Fundamental Rights

The due process clause of the Fourteenth Amendment was intended in part to protect certain fundamental rights long recognized under the common law. *Powell v. Alabama*, 287 U.S. 45 (1932). Appellant contends that the insanity defense is so embedded in our legal history that it should be afforded status as a fundamental right. He argues that the defense was firmly established as a part of the common law long before our federal constitution was adopted and is essential to our present system of ordered liberty.

The United States Supreme Court has never held that there is a constitutional right to plea an insanity defense. Moreover, the Court has noted that the significance of the defense is properly left to the states: "We cannot cast aside the centuries-long evolution of the collection of interlocking and overlapping concepts which the common law has utilized to assess the moral accountability of an individual for his antisocial deeds. The doctrines of actus reus, mens rea, insanity, mistake, justification, and duress have historically provided the tools for a constantly shifting adjustment of the tension between the evolving aims of the criminal law and changing religions, moral, philosophical, and medical views of the nature of man. This process of adjustment has always been thought to be the province of the States." *Powell v. Texas* 392 U.S. 514, 535-536 (1968).

The United States Supreme Court refused in 1952 to accept the argument that the Due Process Clause required the use of a particular insanity test or allocation of burden of proof. *Leland v. Oregon*, 343 U.S. 790 (1952). The Oregon statute upheld in *Leland* required the defendant to prove insanity beyond a reasonable doubt. This allocation of proof was found constitutionally sound because the State retained the burden to prove the requisite state of mind and other essential criminal elements. The State's due process burden of proof was further emphasized in *In Re Winship*, 397 U.S. 358 (1970). *Winship* established that the prosecution must prove beyond a reasonable doubt every element constituting the crime charged.

The Montana statutory scheme is consistent with the dictates of *Leland* and *Winship*. The 1979 amendments to the criminal code do not unconstitutionally shift the State's burden of proof of the necessary elements of the offense. The State retains its traditional burden of proving all elements beyond a reasonable doubt.

2. The Delusional Defendant

In addition to asserting that the insanity defense is a fundamental constitutional right, the appellant contends that insanity is a broader concept than mens rea. Korell argues that individuals may be clearly insane yet also be capable of forming the requisite intent to commit a crime. For example, an accused may form intent to harm under a completely delusional perception of reality or act without volitional control. It is defendant's position that the due process of these defendants is compromised by state law which permits conviction of delusional defendants and those who act without volitional control.

Addressing the delusional defendant first, we note that planning, deliberation, and a studied intent are often found in cases where the defendant lacks the capacity to understand the wrongfulness of his acts. Fink & Larene, *In Defense of the Insanity Defense*, 62 MICH. B.J. 199 (1983). Illustrations include the assassin acting under instructions of God, the mother drowning her demonically-possessed child, and the man charging up Montana Avenue on a shooting spree believing he is Teddy Roosevelt on San Juan Hill. Defendant contends that these people could properly be found guilty by a jury under current Montana law.

As some commentators have noted, the 1979 amendments to the law on mental disease or defect may actually have lowered the hurdle mentally disturbed defendants must clear to be exculpated. In order to be acquitted, the defendant need only cast a reasonable doubt in the minds of the jurors that he had the requisite mental state. As a practical matter, the prosecutor who seeks a conviction of a delusional and psychotic defendant will be faced with a heavy burden of proof.

Assuming the delusional defendant is found guilty by a jury, factors of mitigation must be considered by the sentencing judge. The fact that the proven criminal state of mind was formed by a deranged mind would certainly be considered. In addition, a defendant can be sentenced to imprisonment only after the sentencing judge specifically finds that the defendant was not suffering, at the time he committed the offense, from a mental disease that rendered him unable to appreciate the criminality of his conduct or to conform his conduct to the requirements of law.

3. The Volitionally-Impaired Defendant

The test of mental disease or defect that was afforded defendants prior to 1979 read as follows: "A person is not responsible for criminal conduct if at the time of such conduct as a result of mental disease or defect he is unable either to appreciate the criminality of his conduct or to conform his conduct to the requirements of the law." It is the second prong of this standard, the volitional aspect of mental disease or defect, that appellant claims has been eliminated. He argues that there are those who lack the ability to conform their conduct to the law and that elimination of the involuntariness defense is unconstitutional.

The volitional aspect of mental disease or defect has not been eliminated from our criminal law. Consideration of a defendant's ability to conform his conduct to the law has been moved from the jury to the sentencing judge. The United States Supreme Court found in *Leland*, 343 U.S. at 801, that the "irresistible impulse" test of insanity was not implicit in the concept of ordered liberty. . . . To the extent that the 1979 criminal code revisions allegedly eliminated the defense of insanity-induced volitional impairment, we find no abrogation of a constitutional right.

Eighth Amendment Considerations

Appellant next contends that abolition of the affirmative defense of insanity violates the Eighth Amendment's prohibition of cruel and unusual punishment. In *Robinson v. California*, 370 U.S. 660 (1962), the Supreme Court held that punishment for the status crime of drug addiction violated the Eighth Amendment prohibition. The Court declared that any law which created a criminal offense of being mentally ill would also constitute cruel and unusual punishment. The Court noted that had the California statute under which Robinson was convicted required proof of the actual use of narcotics, it would have been valid. In *Powell v. Texas*, 392 U.S. at 532, a statute imposing a fine for public intoxication was found to not violate the Eighth Amendment. There the Court reasoned that although alcoholism might be a disease, the statute was valid because it punished an act, not the status of being an alcoholic.

The Montana Criminal Code does not permit punishment of a mentally ill person who has not committed a criminal act. As such, the statutes avoid the constitutional infirmities discussed in *Robinson v. California* and *Powell v. Texas*.

Prior to sentencing, the court is required to consider the convicted defendant's mental condition at the time the offense was committed. This review is mandatory whenever a claim of mental disease or defect is raised. The plain language of the statute reads: ". . . the sentencing court *shall* consider any relevant evidence . . ." (emphasis added). Whenever the sentencing court finds the defendant suffered from a mental disease or defect, the defendant must be placed in an ". . . appropriate institution for custody, care and treatment . . . ."

These requirements place a heavy burden on the courts and the department of institutions. They serve to prevent imposition of cruel and unusual punishment upon the insane. Since the jury is properly preoccupied with proof of state of mind, it is imperative that the sentencing court discharge its responsibility to independently review the defendant's mental condition.

It is further argued that subjecting the insane to the stigma of a criminal conviction violates fundamental principles of justice. We cannot agree. The legislature has made a conscious decision to hold individuals who act with a proven criminal state of mind accountable for their acts, regardless of motivation or mental condition. Arguably, this policy does not further criminal justice goals of deterrence and prevention in cases where an accused suffers from a mental disease that renders him incapable of appreciating the criminality of his conduct. However, the policy does further goals of protection of society and education. One State Supreme Court Justice who wrestled with this dilemma observed: "In a very real sense, the confinement of the insane is the punishment of the innocent; the release of the insane is the punishment of society." *State v. Stacy*, 601 S.W.2d 696, 704 (Tenn. 1980) (Henry J., dissenting).

Our legislature has acted to assure that the attendant stigma of a criminal conviction is mitigated by the sentencing judge's personal consideration of the defendant's mental condition and provision for commitment to an appropriate institution for treatment, as an alternative to a sentence of imprisonment.

For the foregoing reasons we hold that Montana's abolition of the insanity defense neither deprives a defendant of his Fourteenth Amendment right to due process nor violates the Eighth Amendment proscription against cruel and unusual punishment. There is no independent constitutional right to plead insanity.

SENTENCING

Four doctors testified before the jury concerning Korell's mental condition. These expert witnesses were allowed to express their opinions concerning Korell's medical diagnosis, whether he suffered from mental disease or defect at the time of the shooting, his capacity to form the requisite intent and his ability to control his behavior. Additionally, Dr. Stratford was called to testify at the sentencing hearing on his recommendations for treatment of Korell. All the doctors filed written evaluations with the court. Immediately after announcing sentence, the trial judge stated:

> I'm going to address myself in regard to your mental condition. Let me say that the jury heard the evidence by all of the various doctors in regard to your mental condition. The jury reached their conclusion after some twenty-four to twenty-six hours, and in that conclusion they found that you were responsible and that you did have the mental state required by the statute. For me to indulge otherwise would amount to nothing but nullification of the jury's effort, and I will not do so.

This pronouncement flies in the face of the court's basic duty to independently evaluate the defendant's mental condition. The trial judge's refusal to act compels this Court to vacate the defendant's sentence and remand for resentencing.

The jury has a narrow duty under the statutes: to consider mental disease or defect insofar as it relates to criminal state of mind. The fact that a jury has found the existence of a requisite mental state does not conclusively establish the defendant's sanity or fitness for penal punishment. That determination must be independently made by the sentencing judge and the record must reflect the deliberative process. If problems of cruel and unusual punishment of the insane are to be avoided, the sentencing judge must faithfully discharge the review duties of Sections 46-14-311 and 46-14-312, MCA. The sentence is vacated.

Mr. Justice Sheehy, dissenting:

It is a matter of coincidence that I dictate this dissent on Sunday, November 11, 1984. This used to be called Armistice Day, and the television news is full of reports of a reunion of Viet Nam war veterans in Washington D.C. Coincident with their reunion is the dedication of a memorial statuary to Viet Nam war veterans, the seven-foot tall representation of three Viet Nam war servicemen who seem to be peering intently at an earlier Viet Nam war memorial on which is inscribed the names of more than 58,000 servicemen who lost their lives in that war.

It was a war in which nothing was won and much was lost. A part of that loss, not recognized or admitted by the authorities at first, was the damaging effect to the cognitive abilities of some that served in the war. Only recently has there been positive acceptance that there does exist in some ex-servicemen a post-Viet Nam war traumatic syndrome.

Jerry Korell, the evidence is clear, is a victim of that syndrome. Before his term of service, he was a mentally functional citizen. After his return from service, he is mentally dysfunctional. We can measure our maturity about how we meet such problems by the fact that Jerry Korell now will inevitably spend a great part of his life in jail for his actions arising out of that dysfunction.

Jerry Korell's dysfunction can be traced almost directly to the Viet Nam war. There are thousands of others whose mental aberrations have no such distinct origins. From genes, from force of environment, from physical trauma, or from countless other causes, their actions do not meet the norm. You know them well – the strange, the different, the weird ones.

Sometimes (not really often it should be said) these mentally aberrant persons commit a criminal act. If the criminal act is the product of mental aberration, and not of a straight-thinking cognitive direction, it would seem plausible that society should offer treatment, but if not treatment, at least not punishment. The State of Montana is not such a society.

I would hold that Montana's treatment of the insanity defense is unconstitutional . . . [and] would reverse the conviction of Jerry Korell, and return this cause for a trial on his insanity defense.

QUESTIONS

1.   Montana's abolition of the insanity defense was held constitutional because the mens rea approach left in its place provided procedures to deal with insane individuals who commit criminal acts. Normally, the type of cases to which the insanity defense and Montana's approach would apply would overlap. However, in at least one instance, they do not, as touched on by the majority opinion. Consider if you were to kill another person because you delusionally thought you were under order from God to kill that person. What would be the result under a traditional insanity defense (whether M'Naghten, the ALI/MPC, or the modern federal formulation of the defense)? What would the result be under Montana law? Compare and contrast your responses, evaluating the fairness of the outcomes from both a due process and clinical perspective.

2.   Even though the court went to great lengths to explain why Montana's approach (mirrored in Utah and Idaho) was not fundamentally unfair to insane defendants. But even though the sentencing judge is supposed to make insanity-like evaluations, as the *Korell* case illustrates, they don't always do so. Do you think having a jury better safeguards the rights of a defendant than a judge, or do you think jurors often fail to understand the complexities of insanity law and a judge is more apt to see that "justice" is done? Why?

3.   Even if a defendant is found to be insane by the sentencing judge, and is sentenced "therapeutically," that defendant still has a criminal conviction on his or her record. How can this be justified in light of both the common law history of the insanity defense, and the four major philosophical views that seek to justify punishment (i.e., retribution, deterrence, rehabilitation, and incapacitation)?

Numerous articles have critiqued the abolition of the insanity defense, both pro and con. There can be, however, no "right" or "wrong" answer (to use the lingo of the insanity defense) since how one feels toward the defense is largely a matter of philosophy toward crime, punishment, and mental illness. Empirical research has shown, however, that in Montana since the insanity defense has been abolished, there has been an increase in the number of defendants declared incompetent to stand trial. So, perhaps, insanity is with us to stay in one way, shape, or form.

13. After an Insanity Verdict

The disposition of defendants under Arizona's "guilty except insane" statue and under those states that have adopted GBMI verdicts was discussed above. But what happens to those persons in the majority of U.S. states upon a verdict of not guilty by reason of insanity?

One of the major criticisms of the insanity defense is based on the misperception that people found not guilty by reason of insanity go free. Such is not the case. Take John Hinckley, for example. He was acquitted on insanity grounds in 1981. In 1999, he is still institutionalized in St. Elizabeth's Hospital in their wing for the criminally insane. Hinckley is not unique as his example is the rule, not the exception. Most states automatically commit someone found not guilty by reason of insanity for at least a 60 day period of time and then place the burden on the person committed to show when they are no longer mentally ill and dangerous.

> Unlike guilty defendants whose confinement is limited to a specified term of years, insanity acquittees face an uncertain fate. They are confined for an indeterminate period – potentially for life – until they are no longer dangerous. Typically, insanity acquittees are confined for lengthy periods of time, often spending more time confined than persons found guilty of the same crimes. For example, in New York, the median length of confinement for guilty defendants is 819 days; for insanity acquittees, 1729 days. In California, the median length of confinement for guilty defendants is 610 days; for insanity acquittees, 1359 days. A multistate, longitudinal study revealed that the seriousness of the insanity acquittal offense significantly influenced the insanity acquittee's length of confinement. In each of the seven states studied, longer confinements resulted from insanity acquittals of more serious offenses. In fact, seriousness of the offense was a more significant release factor than seriousness of the patient's mental disorder. Thus, the study suggested that insanity acquittees are being labeled as dangerous and punished for the serious offenses for which they were found insane and supposedly not punishable.[8]

---

[8]   Grant H. Morris, *Placed in Purgatory: Conditional Release of Insanity Acquittees*, 39 Ariz. L. Rev. 1061 (1997) (*citing* Eric Silver, *Punishment or Treatment? Comparing the Lengths of Confinement of Successful and Unsuccessful Insanity Defendants*, 19 Law & Hum. Behav. 375, 382-85 (1995); Grant T. Harris et al., *Length of Detention in Matched Groups of Insanity Acquittees and Convicted Offenders*, 14 Int'l J.L. & Psychiatry 223, 225, 234 (1991).

A minority of states do not automatically commit someone to a mental facility upon a not guilty by reason of insanity verdict. New Jersey's statute is representative of this minority approach:

2C:4-8. Commitment of a Person by Reason of Insanity

a.   After acquittal by reason of insanity, the court shall order that the defendant undergo a psychiatric examination by a psychiatrist of the prosecutor's choice. . . . The defendant, pursuant to this section, may also be examined by a psychiatrist of his own choice.

b.   The court shall dispose of the defendant in the following manner:

    (1)   If the court finds that the defendant may be released without danger to the community or himself without supervision, the court shall so release the defendant; or

    (2)   If the court finds that the defendant may be released without danger to the community or to himself under supervision or under conditions, the court shall so order; or

    (3)   If the court finds that the defendant cannot be released with or without supervision or conditions without posing a danger to the community or to himself, it shall commit the defendant to a mental health facility approved for this purpose by the Commissioner of Human Services to be treated as a person civilly committed. In all proceedings conducted pursuant to this section and pursuant to section N.J.S.2C:4-6 concerning a defendant who lacks the fitness to proceed, including any periodic review proceeding, the prosecuting attorney shall have the right to appear and be heard. The defendant's continued commitment, under the law governing civil commitment, shall be established by a preponderance of the evidence, during the maximum period of imprisonment that could have been imposed, as an ordinary term of imprisonment, for any charge on which the defendant has been acquitted by reason of insanity. Expiration of that maximum period of imprisonment shall be calculated by crediting the defendant with any time spent in confinement for the charge or charges on which the defendant has been acquitted by reason of insanity.

c.   No person committed under this section shall be confined within any penal or correctional institution or any part thereof.

Eleven states specifically state that one cannot be committed to a mental health facility following a verdict of not guilty by reason of insanity for longer than the maximum potential sentence would have been if the defendant had be convicted of the offense. But the remainder of the states usually impose a period of treatment of "one day to life." Under this standard, the defendant who is committed as a mentally ill and posing a risk of danger to himself or to others remains committed in that mental institution until he or she is no longer mentally ill or no longer dangerous. Normally, state law presumes a person so committed remains both mentally ill and dangerous and places the burden of proving otherwise on the person committed.

D. Diminished Capacity[9]

1. Overview

By design, the restrictions of the insanity defense exclude offenders whose conditions do not rise to the level of legal insanity. Some such defendants, however, suffer from mental illness that some would argue render them less culpable than a non-mentally ill defendant. The diminished capacity defense was formulated to deal with these special offenders.

The term diminished capacity is actually used to encompass a number of related claims including diminished responsibility and partial responsibility. The defense is most often used in those

---

[9]   The author acknowledges and thanks Brian McIntyre, J.D., for his research and writing contributions to this section of the Chapter on diminished capacity.

cases where some mental disease or defect that does not rise to the level of legal insanity nonetheless impaired a defendant's ability to form mens rea. For example, a learning-disability generally does not constitute a "mental disease or defect" for insanity purposes. But if a learned-disabled person strikes another, but is unable to know that the blow could kill as a result of his or her disability, he or she might be able to assert diminished capacity to negate the mens rea of intent to kill if charged with assault with intent to kill (if the victim lived) or of murder in the first degree (if the victim died). *See State v. Breakiron*, 108 N.J. 591, 600-01; 532 A.2d 199 (1987).

There are a wide variety of approaches to the defense in the United States. Some states, like Ohio and California, prohibit all evidence of mental impairment short insanity. Accordingly, diminished capacity is not a defense at all in such jurisdictions. Some states restrict the use of the defense to situations where it is used to negate the mental state for crimes of specific intent. And still other jurisdictions follow the Model Penal Code formulation of the diminished capacity defense which allows its use in any case where the defendant's mental state is at issue.

STATE of New Jersey, Plaintiff-Respondent, v. Steven Anthony GALLOWAY, Defendant-Appellant
628 A.2d 735 (N.J. 1993).

Justice Handler wrote for the Court:

On December 19, 1987, defendant, Steven Galloway, was at the home of his girlfriend, Diane Brazilian. At 11:40 p.m., Ms. Brazilian went out to pick up her younger sister. She left the victim, her three-month-old child, Steven, asleep in the room adjacent to where defendant was watching television. Ms. Brazilian's parents had gone upstairs to bed. At some point, the child began to cry, and defendant went over and picked up the child. Defendant stated that he fell while carrying the child, causing the child to cry harder. He admitted shaking the child hard to stop the crying. That shaking caused the child's head to bob back and forth rapidly, causing hemorrhaging of the blood vessels of the child's brain, commonly known as the "shaken baby syndrome."

. . . . Defendant [subsequently] gave a written statement concerning the baby's injury. In that statement, defendant admitted to wanting to hurt the child and to squeezing and shaking the child very hard. Defendant reviewed the statement and signed it. The police then took defendant to the Monmouth County Correctional Facility where, the next day, defendant recounted to Thomas Fatigante, a corrections officer, that he had committed the offense because his girlfriend had been raped and the baby was a product of the rape, and that he had always intended to do it.

Defendant was charged with murder and third-degree endangering the welfare of a child. At trial, he sought through expert witnesses to establish that his mental condition at the time warranted the defense of diminished capacity. Defendant was convicted of both charges and received a thirty-year sentence without possibility of parole for the murder conviction and a concurrent five-year sentence on the remaining charge.

A major issue implicating the validity of defendant's conviction involves the defense of diminished capacity. The diminished capacity statute in effect at the time of defendant's trial, N.J.S.A. 2C:4-2, stated:

> Evidence that the defendant suffered from a mental disease or defect is admissible whenever it is relevant to prove that the defendant did not have the state of mind which is an element of the offense. In the absence of such evidence, it may be assumed that the defendant had no mental disease or defect which would negate a state of mind which is an element of the offense. Mental disease or defect is an affirmative defense which must be proved by a preponderance of the evidence.

[We have previously held] that although the diminished-capacity statute required the State to prove beyond a reasonable doubt that the defendant had acted with the necessary mental state despite the presence of a mental disease or defect, it also required the defendant to establish the existence of that mental disease or defect. Subsequently, however, the court held that the imposition of a burden of proof on the defendant violated a defendant's due-process rights. Our courts now adhere to that ruling, and the conforming statutory amendment of the defense of diminished capacity. Thus, the Appellate Division correctly found that the trial court's jury instruction on the burden of proof had been in error. Nevertheless, it determined that the error had been harmless because defendant had not submitted sufficient evidence to warrant a jury charge on diminished capacity.

The Appellate Division placed great emphasis on the fact that defendant's mental condition had been characterized by the expert testimony as a "personality disorder" and could not, therefore, be considered a "mental disease or defect." The Appellate Division further found that the evidence presented related only to a loss of impulse control and was not the type of mental disease that has been recognized by our law as diminishing mental capacity by affecting the cognitive faculties.

We disagree with both aspects of that decision. The legislative history of the Code and our subsequent decisions demonstrate that the term "mental disease or defect" does not preclude evidence of a mental condition consisting of a borderline personality disorder as such. The Court [has previously] commented on the breadth of the phrase "mental disease or defect," observing that the statutory defense of diminished capacity contemplates a broad range of mental conditions that can be a basis for the defense. . . .

* * *

The Model Penal Code refrained from defining the content of the phrase "mental disease or defect." Rather, those terms are left open to accommodate developing medical understanding. The MPC Commentary also notes that most jurisdictions relying on its formulation have not provided a definition of mental disease or defect. Further, the MPC's proposed jury charge instructs that "the law does not attempt to say what failures or conditions of the mind are properly to be regarded as disease."

In addition to the Model Penal Code, the New Jersey Code drew heavily on existing New Jersey law in adopting the diminished-capacity defense. That law also demonstrates an expansive understanding of the kinds of mental deficiencies that might sustain a defense. In *State v. DiPaolo*, 34 N.J. 279, 295, 168 A.2d 401 (1961), the Court strongly approved the admission of psychiatric evidence pertaining to the defendant's mental state:

> The judiciary cannot bar evidence which rationally bears upon the factual inquiry the legislature has ordered. The capacity of an individual to premeditate, to deliberate, or to will to execute a homicidal design or any deficiency in that capacity, may bear upon the question whether he in fact did so act. Hence evidence of any defect, deficiency, trait, condition, or illness which rationally bears upon the question whether those mental operations did in fact occur must be accepted. Such evidence could be excluded only upon the thesis that it is too unreliable for the courtroom . . . .

Acknowledging those sources, the Court [has] recognized that the Code declined to define "mental disease or defect" and, in eschewing technical definitions of mental disease or defect, intended to leave that determination to the finders of fact.

Against that background, we conclude that the Legislature by its use of the term "mental disease or defect" did not intend to preclude evidence of a mental condition consisting of a "disorder" as such. Forms of psychopathology other than clinically-defined mental diseases or defects may affect the mental process and diminish cognitive capacity, and therefore may be regarded as a mental disease or defect in the statutory or legal sense.

In addition, the determination that a condition constitutes a mental disease or defect is one to be made in each case by the jury after the court has determined that the evidence of the condition in

204

question is relevant and sufficiently accepted within the psychiatric community to be found reliable for courtroom use.

In keeping with the intended application of the diminished-capacity defense, we also reject the State's assertion that because the revised Diagnostic and Statistical Manual of Mental Disorders (DSM) gives borderline personality disorder a V-Code diagnosis, i.e., a condition described as "a behavioral and psychological problem . . . not attributable to a mental disorder," the evidence failed to show a mental defect or disease. We are not persuaded that the label suggested by the DSM should determine whether defendant's mental state constitutes a mental defect or disease under the diminished-capacity defense. The DSM itself cautions that [i]t is to be understood that inclusion here, for clinical and research purposes, of a diagnostic category . . . does not imply that the condition meets legal or other nonmedical criteria for what constitutes mental disease, mental disorder, or mental disability.

Consistent with the legislative understanding that informed the Code, our cases recognize the broad range of mental conditions that can satisfy the Code standard of "mental disease or defect." "Personality disorders" have been among those conditions that have formed the basis for a diminished-capacity defense. For example, in *State v. Moore*, 122 N.J. 420, 585 A.2d 864 (1991), defendant had killed his wife and son with a hammer. The defense expert testified that the defendant had been diagnosed as suffering from a borderline personality disorder that had caused a stress-induced psychosis. The Court found that the evidence, including that diagnosis, was sufficient to warrant a jury instruction on the diminished-capacity defense. . . . It noted that "as thin as the evidence was, it contained a diagnosis of a 'brief reactive psychosis' that defendant suffered at the time of the murder," and that that could be found to have impaired his cognitive function. Accordingly, the Court concluded that the defendant had offered evidence from which a jury could have determined that the State had failed to prove the requisite state of mind beyond a reasonable doubt.

The Appellate Division here determined that the expert testimony did not justify the diminished capacity defense because it did not show an actual impairment of defendant's cognitive faculties. Rather, the testimony on defendant's mental condition demonstrated that defendant had suffered a "loss of impulse control." The Appellate Division stated, "While it can be said in a general sense that loss of impulse control interferes with a person's ability to think clearly, this is not the type of mental disease or defect which has been recognized by the law as affecting cognitive faculties." In expressing that view, the court relied on and quoted from another Appellate Division case, *State v. Carroll*, 577 A.2d 862 (N.J. Super. App. Div. 1990), which stated:

> We . . . distinguish between a case in which there is evidence of mental disease or defect which impairs the cognition required to act knowingly, purposely or with whatever other mental state is required to commit a particular offense, thus requiring the defense of diminished capacity to be submitted to the jury, and a case in which there is evidence of a mental disease or defect which produces an emotive reaction such as rage or impassioned impulse, where a diminished capacity defense is not required to be submitted to the jury.

The Appellate Division in this case may have read the *Carroll* opinion too broadly. In *Carroll*, the defendant's impairment, aside from its characterization as a mental disease, did not prevent him from being cognizant of the fact that he was hitting his stepdaughter over the head with a scale and stabbing her in the throat with a knife or from being practically certain his actions would cause death or serious bodily injury.

The Appellate Division here may also have misread [other precedent] in concluding that those decisions had ruled that a personality disorder as such could not constitute a mental disease or defect that can diminish mental capacity. Our cases . . . are consistent with the theory that a jury instruction is warranted when defendant has presented evidence of a mental disease or defect that interferes with cognitive ability sufficient to prevent or interfere with the formation of the requisite intent or mens rea. We now hold that all mental deficiencies, including conditions that cause a loss of emotional control, may satisfy the diminished-capacity defense if the record shows that experts in the psychological field believe that that kind of mental deficiency can affect a person's cognitive faculties, and the record contains evidence that the claimed deficiency did affect the defendant's cognitive capacity to form the mental state necessary for the commission of the crime.

We conclude that defendant did provide expert testimony sufficient to warrant a jury instruction on diminished capacity. Defendant's first expert witness, Dr. Slonim, a clinical psychologist, clearly stated on cross-examination that defendant suffered not from a loss of cognitive abilities but rather from an inability to control his conduct. Dr. Chamberlain, however, a forensic psychiatrist and Director of the Forensic Hospital for the State of New Jersey, offered evidence to support the jury charge on diminished capacity.

Dr. Chamberlain agreed with Dr. Slonim that defendant's primary diagnosis was borderline personality disorder with a secondary diagnosis of isolated explosive disorder. He stated that a person with a borderline personality disorder is very vulnerable to stress and that condition could affect cognitive functions. He explained:

> Well, the whole area of intending to do something, which an intent, at least in my understanding of it, means the rational cognitive ability to formulate a plan or to do something. When a borderline begins to regress and become overwhelmed, it's not just one aspect of the person that is overwhelmed. It's the whole personality that is overwhelmed. They regress. So all of the functions are impaired, including their ability to think, to reason, to plan or to control themselves. They're all integrated with each other. And we don't just impair one without impairing the other.
>
> * * *
>
> [W]hen you have someone who is vulnerable in those ways because he's not really matured or developed as he should have, than when they're stressed they regress even further back and they become flooded in all areas of their personality, including ability to recognize things, to formulate intent, to rationally weigh consequences, to even sometimes perceive what is going on in a realistic way.

That pattern, according to Dr. Chamberlain, applied to defendant's conduct in this case. Defendant was under a great deal of stress at the time of the occurrence. "As he became flooded, he lost the ability to intend to do things" and "[w]as unable to formulate the intention to even harm the baby under those circumstances." As defendant began to regress and was overwhelmed, he thereby lost "the rational cognitive ability to formulate a plan or to do something." Dr. Chamberlain also said of defendant, "He simply couldn't keep track what was going on and in a rational way understand what he was doing. I don't think he understood he would particularly harm the baby."

In *Moore*, the Court concluded that comparable evidence had been sufficient to allow the jury to determine that the defendant had neither formed an intent to commit his homicidal acts, nor had sufficient knowledge of those acts. The Court observed that the defendant's expert witness, a psychiatrist, testified that the fact that the defendant had killed his son in the course of killing his wife indicated "that he was not aware of what he was doing or not in control of what he was doing, because he certainly felt the opposite toward Kory [his son] [than he felt toward Melva [his wife]]." The Court noted the expert's testimony: "'But [he] knew what he was doing?' Answer: 'I think not. But there is always a continuum. He could have been aware, minimally aware.'"

Viewing the evidence in the light most favorable to defendant, we find that it offers at least the suggestion that defendant's faculties were sufficiently affected to preclude him from engaging in purposeful or knowing conduct when he harmed the infant. That suggestion is present in Dr. Chamberlain's testimony: "he lost the ability to intend to do things"; he was "unable to formulate the intention to even harm the baby under those circumstances"; he did not "understand" he would particularly harm the baby. That evidence is sufficient to allow a jury to consider and determine whether defendant suffered from a mental disease or defect that impaired his cognitive capacity and prevented him from forming the intent or knowing that his acts would cause the death of the child.

Accordingly, we find that the improper instruction withdrawing the defense of diminished capacity from the jury constituted harmful error and requires the reversal of defendant's conviction for murder.

* * *

We reverse the judgment of the Appellate Division, which sustained the convictions for murder and third-degree child endangerment, and remand the matter for a new trial.

QUESTIONS

1.   The court took issue with the lower court's conclusion that a "personality disorder" could not be considered a "mental disease or defect" for diminished capacity purposes. It held that "evidence of any defect, deficiency, trait, condition, or illness which rationally bears upon the question whether those mental operations did in fact occur must be accepted," so long as scientifically reliable. The court specifically included "conditions that cause a loss of emotional control" in this holding covering the diminished capacity defense. What do you think of this holding? Why? Critique it from both a public policy and clinical viewpoint.

2.   Look up the diagnostic criteria of Borderline Personality Disorder in the DSM-IV. How do you think such a diagnosis might interfere with a defendant's ability to form mens rea?

3.   A question not addressed in the *Galloway* case is whether Anti-Social Personality Disorder can serve as the basis of a diminished capacity defense. Look up the diagnostic criteria of this disorder in the DSM-IV. Do you think it should qualify as a sufficient mental disease or defect to invoke the defense of diminished capacity? Why or why not?

2. Beyond Diminished Capacity

The rationale of the diminished capacity defense has been applied, in some cases rather tenuously, to specific situations that have since becomes labeled as their own defenses. In essence, however, these defenses are really just extensions of the diminished capacity defense. They seek a finding on non-criminal culpability due to some extenuating circumstance that allegedly rendered the defendant unable to form the requisite mens rea of a crime, or led to it being formed defectively – as a result of some mental condition rather than out of "normal" criminal intent.

The Post-Traumatic Stress Disorder Defense ("PTSDD") is a good example. It was originally applied to veterans of wars, who experienced intense "flashbacks" from combat. During these flashbacks, individuals were known to have violent outbreaks. For example, in *State v. Phipps*, 883 S.W. 2d 138 (Tenn. Crim. App. 1994), the defendant, a gulf war veteran, was convicted of first degree murder for beating his wife's lover to death. On the day of the murder, Phipps went to his wife's home. At the house, he got into an argument with his wife's lover, Presson. Presson threatened Phipps with a stick; Phipps took the stick from him and hit him repeatedly with it. At trial, the defense presented expert testimony that Phipps suffered from depression and post-traumatic stress disorder. Even the prosecution's expert testified that "[Phipps's] depression was 'of sufficient level to significantly affect his thinking, reasoning, judgment, and emotional well-being,' and that the 'components of his post-traumatic stress disorder may have lessened his threshold or made him more sensitive to defending himself and protecting himself and increased the likelihood of him over-reacting to a real or perceived threat." The judge in the trial court refused to allow a jury instruction to allow consideration of the evidence in relation to whether Phipps possessed the required mens rea for first-degree murder. The Tennessee Court of Appeals reversed the decision, holding that evidence of the defendant's mental state at the time of the offense is admissible to refute elements of specific intent in first degree murder cases. In spite of the such acceptance of PTSD as a mental condition, it is highly subjective and often not subject to scientific confirmation, leaving many people critical of using it as the basis of a legal defense.

In contrast to PTSDD, which has a recognized DSM diagnosis at its core, the diminished capacity defense has been extended to several circumstances that have led to wide-spread criticism of the defense. Consider, for example, The Twinkie Defense. In 1979, Dan White, a member of the San Francisco Board of Supervisors, killed San Francisco Mayor George Moscone and fellow City Supervisor

Harvey Milk. His trial for two counts of first degree murder resulted only in convictions for voluntary manslaughter after the jury ostensibly found White, a hypoglycemic, to have suffered from diminished capacity in a sugar and caffeine induced reactive psychosis brought about by a combination of depression and having gorged himself on Twinkies and Coca-Cola.

The PMS Defense is another extension of diminished capacity. In France, premenstrual syndrome is recognized as a form of legal insanity. There are many symptoms characteristic of PMS, the ailments of which are distinguishable from "normal" premenstrual discomfort experienced by most menstruating women. In the summer of 1994, the APA published DSM-IV which added premenstrual dysphoric disorder (PMDD), a severe form of premenstrual syndrome, to the list of depressive disorders. It is characterized by markedly depressed mood, feelings of hopelessness, or self-depreciating thoughts; marked anxiety, tension, feelings of being "keyed up," or "on edge"; marked affective lability (e.g., feeling suddenly sad or tearful or increased sensitivity to rejection); persistent and marked anger or irritability or increased interpersonal conflicts; decreased interest in usual activities (e.g., work, school, friends, hobbies); subjective sense of difficulty in concentrating; lethargy, easy fatigability, or marked lack of energy; marked change in appetite, overeating, or specific food cravings; hypersomnia or insomnia; a subjective sense of being overwhelmed or out-of-control; and other physical symptoms, such as breast tenderness or swelling, headaches, joint or muscle pain, a sensation of "bloating," or weight gain.

In England, PMS has successfully been used as a type of diminished capacity defense. But in the United States, the defense has not been successfully asserted with the exception of one case. In a 1991 unreported decision, a court in Virginia acquitted Dr. Geraldine Richter of driving while intoxicated concluding that either intoxication or PMS could have caused her erratic driving and assaultive behavior toward a police officer, thereby raising a "reasonable doubt" concerning her guilt. It is important to note that Virginia did not accept diminished capacity as a defense at the time of Dr. Richter's case. Evidence of PMS was not permitted to be used to show that mens rea was not formed, but rather it was used in an effort to explain why the defendant's behavior occurred. The case, although the subject of some scholarly debate, has not been cited in any other subsequent case as precedent. The viability of the defense in the U.S. remains highly questionable. And the social impact of viewing PMS or PMDD as a mental illness has caused some scholars concern. For example, it could be used as a justification to deny women who suffer from it certain jobs or custody of their children. It might be used as a basis to invoke a "heat of passion" defense by men who kill female victims who are suffering from the disorder, thereby mitigating murder down to voluntary manslaughter. And it could even become viewed as an aggravating factor, rather than a mitigating one, if women act while suffering from PMS or PMDD, because they failed to take reasonable measures to control their disorder once they had knowledge of the impact of it on their behavior.

Another variant on the diminished capacity defense is the XYY defense. Under this theory of genetic abnormality, an extra Y chromosome creates a "super male" who is so charged with testosterone that he is biologically driven toward acts of aggression that he cannot control. To date, the defense has not been accepted in U.S. courts, largely due to the fact that research on XYY males has largely been performed on prison populations without control groups for comparisons. But the ongoing Human Genome Project and similar research into biological causes of human behavior might one day offer a scientific basis for a genetically-related diminished capacity defense.

The Black Rage Defense is another example of a variation on the diminished capacity defense. It postulates that after years of systematic and pervasive racism resulting in oppression and abuse, African-Americans might lash out violently against their oppressors. Although the defense received much press due to the case of Colin Ferguson, it has not really been tested in court. Ferguson killed six people and wounded seventeen in a shooting spree on a Long Island commuter train. Ferguson was initially represented by the William Kunstler. Kunstler made headlines by asserting that at trial he would present evidence that Ferguson's actions were the result of years of oppression and racism causing Ferguson to lash out in Black Rage. But Ferguson dropped both the Black Rage defense and Kunstler as his attorney, he proceeded to represent himself at his criminal trial. He was convicted and sentenced to over 200 years in prison.

Although untested in the courtroom, Black Rage has been subjected to much criticism. Like PTSDD, it is a subjective claim without a scientific method for confirming the condition. Furthermore, the defense has sparked the ire of some in the African-American community who fear that accepting Black Rage as a defense will further acceptance of the violent black male stereotype and thereby exacerbate racism by pointing to those who allegedly suffer from Black Rage to the exclusion of millions of law-abiding African-Americans. Finally, similar to problems with the XYY genetic defense, proponents of Black Rage have not been able to scientifically support their theories to the satisfaction of the courts or the public.

CHAPTER 6
DEFENSES OF JUSTIFICATION

A. Self-Defense

1. The General Rule on Use of Physical Force in Self-Defense

The law of self-defense can be summed up in one sentence: A person is privileged to use a *reasonable amount of physical force* when *necessary* to prevent an *imminent attack* upon himself or herself from *unlawful force.* This one sentence, however, contains a number of terms that have very specific meanings in the criminal law.

First and foremost, whenever someone acts in self defense, he or she is privileged to use only a reasonable amount of physical force (deadly force is covered in the next section of this chapter). Thus, if a person acts unreasonably, his or her actions will not be justified under the law. But what is reasonable? Reasonability requires a two-part analysis that is comprised both of a subjective and objective standard. The defendant must have honestly believed that he or she was in imminent danger from unlawful force and that it was necessary to respond to this imminent threat by using force. This is purely a subjective standard that simply examines what the defendant thought in his or her own mind.

The other part of the reasonability test, however, is an objective one. Would the ordinary, reasonable, prudent person in the same circumstances as the defendant have also believed that the use of such force was necessary to protect against the imminent application of unlawful force? If the answer to this question is yes, then the defendant acted reasonably; if the answer is no, then the defendant acted unreasonably. Given this standard, it should be evident to you that the defendant is not deprived of the defense just because he or she was mistaken. Recall that an honest and reasonable mistake of fact is a defense to a crime when it negates mens rea. Presuming the mistake was an honest and reasonable one, then the criteria for invoking the defense of self defense are satisfied since the defense similarly requires that the defendant have acted honestly (subjectively speaking) and reasonably (objectively speaking).

What if the defendant makes a subjectively honest, but objectively unreasonable mistake? The common law and the Model Penal Code answer this question differently. At common law, the defendant would be deprived of the defense in its entirety unless charged with a homicide. An unreasonable mistake regarding the defendant's acting in self defense that resulted in the death of another was called *imperfect self defense* at common law. It reduced a charge of murder to manslaughter or reckless homicide.

The Model Penal Code, in contrast, would hold that someone who did not make an honest and reasonable mistake acted with at least criminal negligence. It would hold such a defendant liable for the those crimes that has criminal negligence as their requisite mens rea. In other words, the Model Penal Code would hold a defendant who makes an unreasonable mistake liable for whatever crimes that have the actual mens rea of the defendant as the requisite mens rea of the crimes.

The level of objectivity to be applied when assessing the reasonableness of the defendant's actions has been the subject of debate for many years. In fact, even today, not all states agree whether it should be a purely objective standard (i.e., the ordinary, reasonable, prudent person standard), or some modified objective standard that takes into account the unique character of the defendant, such as his or her age, intelligence, level of education, past experiences, etc. No U.S. jurisdiction, however, uses a purely subjective standard. The difference between the two objective standards (purely objective verses the modified objective) is explored later in this chapter in case of *People v. Goetz.*

Second, the use of the word "necessary" requires that actual physical force be needed to defend oneself. One has per se acted unreasonably if one uses force when no force was necessary at all. For example, using force to "defend against" name-calling would be deemed both unnecessary and unreasonable. Third, the privilege to use reasonable force in self defense applies only to immediate attack, not threats of future harm. Again, the immediacy of the attack must be viewed from the perspective of the defendant. An honest and reasonable mistake as to the imminency of the attack is permissible and will not deprive the defendant of the defense. Finally, the force to be defended against has to be unlawful force. Thus, if lawful force is being applied (e.g., police effectuating a legal arrest), then one has no privilege to act in self defense.

2. Exceptions to the Rule: When Self-Defense Is Not Available as a Criminal Defense

There are several limitations on the privilege to act in self defense. One may not use force against force applied by a police officer (i.e., resisting arrest). This is true regardless of whether the arrest is lawful or unlawful, unless the physical force used by the police officer exceeds that allowed by law (i.e., if excessive force is being used by a police officer, then it is not "lawful force," thereby allowing one to invoke the defense of self defense.

One may also not use physical force if one is a trespasser being forcibly evicted from the property upon which he trespassed. This is so because the owner of the property is privileged to use a reasonable amount of physical force to effectuate the removal of the trespasser from the owner's property. Accordingly, the owner's use of force is not "unlawful force." But as with police who use excessive force, the trespasser may use force to resist the eviction if threatened with death or serious bodily harm, since that level of force would be "unlawful."

Mere words are rarely, if ever, sufficient provocation to justify the use of physical force. As the school yard rhyme goes, "stick and stone may break my bones, but words can never hurt me." The critique of this maxim by critical theorists aside, the criminal law holds true to it. Thus, verbal provocation alone (without more, such as an assault), will not justify the use of physical force.

A major exception to the availability of the defense of self defense concerns those who are at fault in bringing about the emergency situation against which he or she feels it necessary to defend using physical force. Such a person is called the initial aggressor. The initial aggressor may not use force if he or she wrongfully caused the confrontation unless one of two situations arise. The initial aggressor may use force to defend himself or herself if he or she withdrew from the encounter, thereby effectively ending the confrontation. If the other person still pursues the initial aggressor after such a withdrawal, then the other person is viewed as the "new" aggressor, and the initial aggressor is free to defend himself or herself against the attacks of the other. It should be noted that actual withdrawal by the initial aggressor is not necessary, since it cannot always be accomplished. If the initial aggressor clearly communicates to the other his or her intent to withdraw from the encounter, that will be sufficient.

The other major situation in which the initial aggressor exception will not apply is when other person responds in a grossly disproportionate manner to the force used by the initial aggressor. For example, if the initial aggressor slaps the other person across the face, and then the other person takes out a baseball bat and assaults the initial aggressor, the response is grossly disproportionate to the provocation of the initial aggressor. The other person has, therefore, exceeded the scope of his or her privilege to act in self defense since the response was unreasonable, making this grossly disproportionate response "unlawful." Under such circumstances, the initial aggressor is free to defend himself or herself.

3. Special Rules for Use of Deadly Force

The general rules governing self defense discussed above all apply to the use of deadly force. But when deadly force is an issue, there are additional rules that govern its use. The common law held that deadly force may only be used when the actor reasonably perceives it necessary to defend against deadly force. The Model Penal Code expanded the ability to use deadly force to defend against not only death, but also serious bodily harm, kidnapping, and/or rape. Some jurisdictions have added additional crimes to the list that justifies the use of deadly force, such as arson of an occupied dwelling, kidnapping, and armed robbery.

Even if the actor meets all of the criteria above, some jurisdictions still limit his or her ability to use deadly force in self defense. Some jurisdictions, for example, require the actor to give a *warning* to the assailant before using deadly force (i.e., "Stop or I'll shoot"). Most jurisdictions that require such a warning, however, recognize that there are times when giving the warning might mean the difference between having the opportunity to act in self defense by using the deadly force and being deprived of that opportunity by having been victimized. So, in warning jurisdictions, the warning is not required to be given if doing so would be useless or in vain.

A minority of U.S. jurisdictions require a person to *retreat* if they can do so in complete safety before using deadly force in self-defense. The rationale behind this rule is that it is better to retreat and be perceived as a coward than to take a life when doing so was not absolutely necessary. But if retreat to safety is not a possibility, then the actor may use deadly force in self defense, presuming the other criteria for doing so are met.

Even in retreat jurisdictions, however, there is an exception on the duty to retreat known as the *castle doctrine*. One's home is one's castle. No one has a legal duty to retreat from his or her own home before using deadly force in self defense, provided he or she was not the initial aggressor.

As with the use of physical force, deadly force may only be used when reasonable. But as discussed above, reasonability is a relative term. The Model Penal Code and most U.S. jurisdictions do not use a purely objective standard (i.e., that of the ordinary, reasonable, prudent person). Rather, a modified objective standard is used in most states. This standard asks the trier-of-fact, usually a jury, to judge the reasonableness of the defendant's actions from the defendant's perspective. The jurors are asked to put themselves in the defendant's shoes and look at the totality of the circumstances surrounding the defendant's use of force. This involves not only an examination of all of the facts and circumstances surround the incident itself, but also consideration of how a reasonable person would have reacted in the same situation if they were the same size, gender, intelligence, and educational level of the defendant and had undergone the same prior experiences as the defendant. The following case illustrates the application of the modified objective standard quite well.

The PEOPLE of the State of New York, Appellant, v. Bernhard GOETZ, Respondent.
68 N.Y.2d 96, 506 N.Y.S.2d, 497 N.E.2d 41 (1986).

Chief Judge Wachtler

A Grand Jury has indicted defendant on attempted murder, assault, and other charges for having shot and wounded four youths on a New York City subway train after one or two of the youths approached him and asked for $5. The lower courts, concluding that the prosecutor's charge to the Grand Jury on the defense of justification was erroneous, have dismissed the attempted murder, assault and weapons possession charges. We now reverse and reinstate all counts of the indictment.

I

The precise circumstances of the incident giving rise to the charges against defendant are disputed, and ultimately it will be for a trial jury to determine what occurred. We feel it necessary, however, to provide some factual background to properly frame the legal issues before us. Accordingly, we have summarized the facts as they appear from the evidence before the Grand Jury. We stress, however, that we do not purport to reach any conclusions or holding as to exactly what transpired or whether defendant is blameworthy. The credibility of witnesses and the reasonableness of defendant's conduct are to be resolved by the trial jury.

On Saturday afternoon, December 22, 1984, Troy Canty, Darryl Cabey, James Ramseur, and Barry Allen boarded an IRT express subway train in The Bronx and headed south toward lower Manhattan. The four youths rode together in the rear portion of the seventh car of the train. Two of the four, Ramseur and Cabey, had screwdrivers inside their coats, which they said were to be used to break into the coin boxes of video machines.

Defendant Bernhard Goetz boarded this subway train at 14th Street in Manhattan and sat down on a bench towards the rear section of the same car occupied by the four youths. Goetz was carrying an unlicenced .38 caliber pistol loaded with five rounds of ammunition in a waistband holster. The train left the 14th Street station and headed towards Chambers Street.

It appears from the evidence before the Grand Jury that Canty approached Goetz, possibly with Allen beside him, and stated "give me five dollars." Neither Canty nor any of the other youths displayed a weapon. Goetz responded by standing up, pulling out his handgun and firing four shots in rapid succession. The first shot hit Canty in the chest; the second struck Allen in the back; the third went through Ramseur's arm and into his left side; the fourth was fired at Cabey, who apparently was then standing in the corner of the car, but missed, deflecting instead off of a wall of the conductor's cab. After Goetz briefly surveyed the scene around him, he fired another shot at Cabey, who then was sitting on the end bench of the car. The bullet entered the rear of Cabey's side and severed his spinal cord.

All but two of the other passengers fled the car when, or immediately after, the shots were fired. The conductor, who had been in the next car, heard the shots and instructed the motorman to radio for emergency assistance. The conductor then went into the car where the shooting occurred and saw Goetz sitting on a bench, the injured youths lying on the floor or slumped against a seat, and two women who had apparently taken cover, also lying on the floor. Goetz told the conductor that the four youths had tried to rob him. While the conductor was aiding the youths, Goetz headed towards the front of the car. The train had stopped just before the Chambers Street station and Goetz went between two of the cars, jumped onto the tracks and fled. Police and ambulance crews arrived at the scene shortly thereafter. Ramseur and Canty, initially listed in critical condition, have fully recovered. Cabey remains paralyzed, and has suffered some degree of brain damage.

On December 31, 1984, Goetz surrendered to police in Concord, New Hampshire, identifying himself as the gunman being sought for the subway shootings in New York nine days earlier. Later that day, after receiving Miranda warnings, he made two lengthy statements, both of which were tape recorded with his permission. In the statements, which are substantially similar, Goetz admitted that he had been illegally carrying a handgun in New York City for three years. He stated that he had first purchased a gun in 1981 after he had been injured in a mugging. Goetz also revealed that twice between 1981 and 1984 he had successfully warded off assailants simply by displaying the pistol. According to Goetz's statement, the first contact he had with the four youths came when Canty, sitting or lying on the bench across from him, asked "how are you," to which he replied "fine." Shortly thereafter, Canty, followed by one of the other youths, walked over to the defendant and stood to his left, while the other two youths remained to his right, in the corner of the subway car. Canty then said "give me five dollars." Goetz stated that he knew from the smile on Canty's face that they wanted to "play with me." Although he was certain that none of the youths had a gun, he had a fear, based on prior experiences, of being "maimed."

Goetz then established "a pattern of fire," deciding specifically to fire from left to right. His stated intention at that point was to "murder [the four youths], to hurt them, to make them suffer as much as possible." When Canty again requested money, Goetz stood up, drew his weapon, and began firing, aiming for the center of the body of each of the four. Goetz recalled that the first two he shot "tried to run through the crowd [but] they had nowhere to run." Goetz then turned to his right to "go after the other two." One of these two "tried to run through the wall of the train, but . . . he had nowhere to go." The other youth (Cabey) "tried pretending that he wasn't with [the others]" by standing still, holding on to one of the subway hand straps, and not looking at Goetz. Goetz nonetheless fired his fourth shot at him. He then ran back to the first two youths to make sure they had been "taken care of." Seeing that they had both been shot, he spun back to check on the latter two. Goetz noticed that the youth who had been standing still was now sitting on a bench and seemed unhurt. As Goetz told the police, "I said '[y]ou seem to be all right, here's another,'" and he then fired the shot which severed Cabey's spinal cord. Goetz added that "if I was a little more under self-control . . . I would have put the barrel against his forehead and fired." He also admitted that "if I had had more [bullets], I would have shot them again, and again, and again."

II

After waiving extradition, Goetz was brought back to New York and arraigned on a felony complaint charging him with attempted murder and criminal possession of a weapon. The matter was presented to a Grand Jury in January 1985, with the prosecutor seeking an indictment for attempted murder, assault, reckless endangerment, and criminal possession of a weapon. Neither the defendant nor any of the wounded youths testified before this Grand Jury. On January 25, 1985, the Grand Jury indicted defendant on one count of criminal possession of a weapon in the third degree for possessing the gun used in the subway shootings, and two counts of criminal possession of a weapon in the fourth degree for possessing two other guns in his apartment building. It dismissed, however, the attempted murder and other charges stemming from the shootings themselves.

Several weeks after the Grand Jury's action, the People, asserting that they had newly available evidence, moved for an order authorizing them to resubmit the dismissed charges to a second Grand Jury. Supreme Court, Criminal Term, after conducting an in camera inquiry, granted the motion. Presentation of the case to the second Grand Jury began on March 14, 1985. Two of the four youths, Canty and Ramseur, testified. Among the other witnesses were four passengers from the seventh car of the subway who had seen some portions of the incident. Goetz again chose not to testify, though the tapes of his two statements were played for the grand jurors, as had been done with the first Grand Jury.

On March 27, 1985, the second Grand Jury filed a 10-count indictment, containing four charges of attempted murder, four charges of assault in the first degree, one charge of reckless endangerment in the first degree, and one charge of criminal possession of a weapon in the second degree. Goetz was arraigned on this indictment on March 28, 1985, and it was consolidated with the earlier three-count indictment.

On October 14, 1985, Goetz moved to dismiss the charges contained in the second indictment alleging, among other things, that the evidence before the second Grand Jury was not legally sufficient to establish the offenses charged, and that the prosecutor's instructions to that Grand Jury on the defense of justification were erroneous and prejudicial to the defendant so as to render its proceedings defective.

On November 25, 1985, while the motion to dismiss was pending before Criminal Term, a column appeared in the *New York Daily News* containing an interview which the columnist had conducted with Darryl Cabey the previous day in Cabey's hospital room. The columnist claimed that Cabey had told him in this interview that the other three youths had all approached Goetz with the intention of robbing him. The day after the column was published, a New York City police officer informed the prosecutor that he had been one of the first police officers to enter the subway car after the shootings, and that Canty had said to him "we were going to rob [Goetz]." The prosecutor immediately disclosed this information to the court and to defense counsel, adding that this was the first time his office had been told of this alleged statement and that none of the police reports filed on the incident contained any such information. Goetz then orally expanded his motion to dismiss, asserting that resubmission of the charges voted by the second Grand Jury was required . . . because it appeared from this new information that Ramseur and Canty had committed perjury.

In an order dated January 21, 1986, Criminal Term granted Goetz's motion to the extent that it dismissed all counts of the second indictment, other than the reckless endangerment charge, with leave to resubmit these charges to a third Grand Jury. The court, after inspection of the Grand Jury minutes, first rejected Goetz's contention that there was not legally sufficient evidence to support the charges. It held, however, that the prosecutor, in a supplemental charge elaborating upon the justification defense, had erroneously introduced an objective element into this defense by instructing the grand jurors to consider whether Goetz's conduct was that of a "reasonable man in [Goetz's] situation." The court, citing prior decisions from both the First and Second Departments . . . , concluded that the statutory test for whether the use of deadly force is justified to protect a person should be wholly subjective, focusing entirely on the defendant's state of mind when he used such force. It concluded that dismissal was required for this error because the justification issue was at the heart of the case.

* * *

On appeal by the People, a divided Appellate Division affirmed Criminal Term's dismissal of the charges. . . . Justice Asch, in a dissenting opinion in which Justice Wallach concurred, disagreed with both bases for dismissal relied upon by Criminal Term. On the justification question, he opined that the statute requires consideration of both the defendant's subjective beliefs and whether a reasonable person in defendant's situation would have had such beliefs. Accordingly, he found no error in the prosecutor's introduction of an objective element into the justification defense. . . . Justice Asch granted the People leave to appeal to this court. We agree with the dissenters that neither the prosecutor's charge to the Grand Jury on justification nor the information which came to light while the motion to dismiss was pending required dismissal of any of the charges in the second indictment.

III

Penal Law article 35 recognizes the defense of justification, which "permits the use of force under certain circumstances." One such set of circumstances pertains to the use of force in defense of a person, encompassing both self-defense and defense of a third person. Penal Law Section 35.15(1) sets forth the general principles governing all such uses of force: "a person may . . . use physical force upon another person when and to the extent he *reasonably believes* such to be necessary to defend himself or a third person from what he reasonably believes to be the use or imminent use of unlawful physical force by such other person."

Section 35.15(2) sets forth further limitations on these general principles with respect to the use of "deadly physical force": "A person may not use deadly physical force upon another person under circumstances specified in subdivision one unless (a) He reasonably believes that such other person is using or about to use deadly physical force . . . or (b) He *reasonably believes* that such other person is committing or attempting to commit a kidnapping, forcible rape, forcible sodomy or robbery."

Thus, consistent with most justification provisions, Penal Law Section 35.15 permits the use of deadly physical force only where requirements as to triggering conditions and the necessity of a particular response are met. . . . As to the triggering conditions, the statute requires that the actor "reasonably believes" that another person either is using or about to use deadly physical force or is committing or attempting to commit one of certain enumerated felonies, including robbery. As to the need for the use of deadly physical force as a response, the statute requires that the actor "reasonably believes" that such force is necessary to avert the perceived threat.

Because the evidence before the second Grand Jury included statements by Goetz that he acted to protect himself from being maimed or to avert a robbery, the prosecutor correctly chose to charge the justification defense in section 35.15 to the Grand Jury. . . . The prosecutor properly instructed the grand jurors to consider whether the use of deadly physical force was justified to prevent either serious physical injury or a robbery, and, in doing so, to separately analyze the defense with respect to each of the charges. He elaborated upon the prerequisites for the use of deadly physical force essentially by reading or paraphrasing the language in Section 35.15. The defense does not contend that he committed any error in this portion of the charge.

When the prosecutor had completed his charge, one of the grand jurors asked for clarification of the term "reasonably believes." The prosecutor responded by instructing the grand jurors that they were to consider the circumstances of the incident and determine "whether the defendant's conduct was that of a reasonable man in the defendant's situation." It is this response by the prosecutor – and specifically his use of "a reasonable man" – which is the basis for the dismissal of the charges by the lower courts. As

215

expressed repeatedly in the Appellate Division's plurality opinion, because section 35.15 uses the term "*he* reasonably believes," the appropriate test, according to that court, is whether a defendant's beliefs and reactions were "reasonable to *him*." Under that reading of the statute, a jury which believed a defendant's testimony that he felt that his own actions were warranted and were reasonable would have to acquit him, regardless of what anyone else in defendant's situation might have concluded. Such an interpretation defies the ordinary meaning and significance of the term "reasonably" in a statute, and misconstrues the clear intent of the Legislature, in enacting section 35.15, to retain an objective element as part of any provision authorizing the use of deadly physical force.

Penal statutes in New York have long codified the right recognized at common law to use deadly physical force, under appropriate circumstances, in self-defense. . . . These provisions have never required that an actor's belief as to the intention of another person to inflict serious injury be correct in order for the use of deadly force to be justified, but they have uniformly required that the belief comport with an objective notion of reasonableness. The 1829 statute, using language which was followed almost in its entirety until the 1965 recodification of the Penal Law, provided that the use of deadly force was justified in self-defense or in the defense of specified third persons "when there shall be a reasonable ground to apprehend a design to commit a felony, or to do some great personal injury, and there shall be imminent danger of such design being accomplished."

[W]e [have previously] emphasized that deadly force could be justified under the statute even if the actor's beliefs as to the intentions of another turned out to be wrong, but noted there had to be a reasonable basis, viewed objectively, for the beliefs. We explicitly rejected the position that the defendant's own belief that the use of deadly force was necessary sufficed to justify such force regardless of the reasonableness of the beliefs.

In 1881, New York reexamined the many criminal provisions set forth in the revised statutes and enacted, for the first time, a separate Penal Code. The provision in the 1881 Penal Code for the use of deadly force in self-defense or to defend a third person was virtually a reenactment of the language in the 1829 statutes, and the "reasonable ground" requirement was maintained.

The 1909 Penal Law replaced the 1881 Penal Code. The language of section 205 of the 1881 code pertaining to the use of deadly force in self-defense or in defense of a third person was reenacted, verbatim, as part of section 1055 of the new Penal Law. Several cases from this court interpreting the 1909 provision demonstrate unmistakably that an objective element of reasonableness was a vital part of any claim of self-defense. . . .

* * *

In 1961 the Legislature established a Commission to undertake a complete revision of the Penal Law and the Criminal Code. The impetus for the decision to update the Penal Law came in part from the drafting of the Model Penal Code by the American Law Institute, as well as from the fact that the existing law was poorly organized and in many aspects antiquated. . . . Following the submission by the Commission of several reports and proposals, the Legislature approved the present Penal Law in 1965 and it became effective on September 1, 1967. The drafting of the general provisions of the new Penal Law, including the article on justification, was particularly influenced by the Model Penal Code. . . . While using the Model Penal Code provisions on justification as general guidelines, however, the drafters of the new Penal Law did not simply adopt them verbatim.

The provisions of the Model Penal Code with respect to the use of deadly force in self-defense reflect the position of its drafters that any culpability which arises from a mistaken belief in the need to use such force should be no greater than the culpability such a mistake would give rise to if it were made with respect to an element of a crime. . . . Accordingly, under Model Penal Code § 3.04(2)(b), a defendant charged with murder (or attempted murder) need only show that he "*believe[d]* that [the use of deadly force] was necessary to protect himself against death, serious bodily injury, kidnapping or [forcible] sexual intercourse" to prevail on a self-defense claim. If the defendant's belief was wrong, and was recklessly, or negligently formed, however, he may be convicted of the type of homicide charge requiring only a reckless or negligent, as the case may be, criminal intent.

The drafters of the Model Penal Code recognized that the wholly subjective test set forth in section 3.04 differed from the existing law in most States by its omission of any requirement of reasonableness. The drafters were also keenly aware that requiring that the actor have a "reasonable belief" rather than just a "belief" would alter the wholly subjective test. This basic distinction was recognized years earlier by the New York Law Revision Commission and continues to be noted by the commentators.

New York did not follow the Model Penal Code's equation of a mistake as to the need to use deadly force with a mistake negating an element of a crime, choosing instead to use a single statutory section which would provide either a complete defense or no defense at all to a defendant charged with any crime involving the use of deadly force. The drafters of the new Penal Law adopted in large part the structure and content of Model Penal Code § 3.04, but, crucially, inserted the word "reasonably" before "believes."

The plurality below agreed with defendant's argument that the change in the statutory language from "reasonable ground," used prior to 1965, to "he reasonably believes" in Penal Law § 35.15 evinced a legislative intent to conform to the subjective standard contained in Model Penal Code § 3.04. This argument, however, ignores the plain significance of the insertion of "reasonably." Had the drafters of section 35.15 wanted to adopt a subjective standard, they could have simply used the language of section 3.04. "Believes" by itself requires an honest or genuine belief by a defendant as to the need to use deadly force. Interpreting the statute to require only that the defendant's belief was "reasonable to him," as done by the plurality below, would hardly be different from requiring only a genuine belief; in either case, the defendant's own perceptions could completely exonerate him from any criminal liability.

We cannot lightly impute to the Legislature an intent to fundamentally alter the principles of justification to allow the perpetrator of a serious crime to go free simply because that person believed his actions were reasonable and necessary to prevent some perceived harm. To completely exonerate such an individual, no matter how aberrational or bizarre his thought patterns, would allow citizens to set their own standards for the permissible use of force. It would also allow a legally competent defendant suffering from delusions to kill or perform acts of violence with impunity, contrary to fundamental principles of justice and criminal law.

We can only conclude that the Legislature retained a reasonableness requirement to avoid giving a license for such actions. The plurality's interpretation, as the dissenters below recognized, excises the impact of the word "reasonably. . . ."

* * *

Goetz also argues that the introduction of an objective element will preclude a jury from considering factors such as the prior experiences of a given actor and thus, require it to make a determination of "reasonableness" without regard to the actual circumstances of a particular incident. This argument, however, falsely presupposes that an objective standard means that the background and other relevant characteristics of a particular actor must be ignored. To the contrary, we have frequently noted that a determination of reasonableness must be based on the "circumstances" facing a defendant or his "situation. . . ." Such terms encompass more than the physical movements of the potential assailant. As just discussed, these terms include any relevant knowledge the defendant had about that person. They also necessarily bring in the physical attributes of all persons involved, including the defendant. Furthermore, the defendant's circumstances encompass any prior experiences he had which could provide a reasonable basis for a belief that another person's intentions were to injure or rob him or that the use of deadly force was necessary under the circumstances.

Accordingly, a jury should be instructed to consider this type of evidence in weighing the defendant's actions. The jury must first determine whether the defendant had the requisite beliefs under section 35.15, that is, whether he believed deadly force was necessary to avert the imminent use of deadly force or the commission of one of the felonies enumerated therein. If the People do not prove beyond a reasonable doubt that he did not have such beliefs, then the jury must also consider whether these beliefs were reasonable. The jury would have to determine, in light of all the "circumstances," as explicated above, if a reasonable person could have had these beliefs.

The prosecutor's instruction to the second Grand Jury that it had to determine whether, under the circumstances, Goetz's conduct was that of a reasonable man in his situation was thus essentially an accurate charge. It is true that the prosecutor did not elaborate on the meaning of "circumstances" or "situation" and inform the grand jurors that they could consider, for example, the prior experiences Goetz related in his statement to the police. We have held, however, that a Grand Jury need not be instructed on the law with the same degree of precision as the petit jury. . . . This lesser standard is premised upon the different functions of the Grand Jury and the petit jury: the former determines whether sufficient evidence exists to accuse a person of a crime and thereby subject him to criminal prosecution; the latter ultimately determines the guilt or innocence of the accused, and may convict only where the People have proven his guilt beyond a reasonable doubt. . . .

* * *

Accordingly, the order of the Appellate Division should be reversed, and the dismissed counts of the indictment reinstated.

QUESTIONS

1.   The essence of the reasoning applied in *Goetz* is that prior victimization may provide someone with special "expertise" in assessing a situation that the ordinary, reasonable, prudent person would not have. Do you agree? Why? What are the benefits of allowing such prior experiences to be considered by a jury? What are the drawbacks?

2.   Some have argued that by allowing the defendant's past to come into evidence, the focus of a trial shifts away from his or her culpability for the crime(s) in question, to the culpability of others who may not be around to defend themselves. Take, for example, the trials of Lyle and Eric Menendez. After they killed their parents, they argued that years of physical and sexual abuse drove them to act as they did. Do you think such prior abuse should be considered in assessing the reasonability of a defendant's actions when self defense is claimed? Explain your reasoning. Would it make a difference to you if the defendant was the repeated victim of spousal abuse? Why or why not?

3.   The *Goetz* court, following the Model Penal Code approach, adopted the modified objective standard for assessing the reasonableness of a defendant's actions. Do you think jurors are capable of putting themselves in the shoes of a defendant who has had experiences that the typical juror has not had? Why?

4.   Basic biology calls into question the position that the prosecution took in the *Goetz* case. The limbic system controls the "flight/fight" response when one perceives oneself to be in danger. The response is autonomic (i.e., not under one's voluntary control). Given that the flight/fight response can be a directing force for a substantial period of time, is it "reasonable" to expect that someone can rationally assess when then are out of danger and withdraw from acting in self defense accordingly? Explain your response, including the public policy implications of having expert witnesses testify as to this function of neuro-anatomy.

B. Defense of Others

One may act to defend another person in much the same way one may act in self defense. Thus, one may use force to defend another person when one reasonably perceives it necessary to protect the other person from imminent bodily harm. But recall the privilege to act in self defense applies only when the imminent harm to be defended against stems from unlawful force. The same holds true for defense of others. But this can lead to a bizarre situation when the person coming to the aid of another reasonably believes it necessary to defend the other person, but that person had no right to act in self defense to begin with, perhaps because he or she was the initial aggressor, was a trespasser, or was resisting arrest. Even if the person coming to the aid of such a person makes an honest and reasonable mistake, the law will generally not allow him or her to assert defense of others. This is called the *mistaken intervener rule*.

Under the mistaken intervener rule, also referred to as the "Alter-Ego Rule," the intervener acts at his or her own risk when stepping into the shoes of the person being defended. The mistaken intervener, as the alter-ego of the person being defended, only has whatever privilege to act in defense of the other person as that person would have had to act in self defense. The actor will be subject to prosecution for the use of force if his or assumptions turn out to be mistaken, even if the mistake was both an honest and reasonable one, as the following case illustrates.

===

The PEOPLE of the State of New York, Appellant, v. Gerald A. YOUNG, Respondent.
11 N.Y.2d 274, 299 N.Y.S.2d 1, 183 N.E.2d 319 (1962).

Per Curiam.

Whether one, who in good faith aggressively intervenes in a struggle between another person and a police officer in civilian dress attempting to effect the lawful arrest of the third person, may be properly convicted of assault in the third degree is a question of law of first impression here.

The opinions in the court below in the absence of precedents in this State carefully expound the opposing views found in other jurisdictions. The majority in the Appellate Division have adopted the minority rule in the other States that one who intervenes in a struggle between strangers under the mistaken but reasonable belief that he is protecting another who he assumes is being unlawfully beaten is thereby exonerated from criminal liability. The weight of authority holds with the dissenters below that one who goes to the aid of a third person does so at his own peril.

While the doctrine espoused by the majority of the court below may have support in some States, we feel that such a policy would not be conducive to an orderly society. We agree with the settled policy of law in most jurisdictions that the right of a person to defend another ordinarily should not be greater than such person's right to defend himself.

In this case there can be no doubt that the defendant intended to assault the police officer in civilian dress. The resulting assault was forceful. Hence motive or mistake of fact is of no significance as the defendant was not charged with a crime requiring such intent or knowledge. To be guilty of third degree assault "it is sufficient that the defendant voluntarily intended to commit the unlawful act of touching." Since in these circumstances the aggression was inexcusable the defendant was properly convicted.

Accordingly, the order of the Appellate Division should be reversed and the information reinstated.

Froessel, Judge (dissenting).

The law is clear that one may kill in defense of another when there is reasonable, though mistaken, ground for believing that the person slain is about to commit a felony or to do some great personal injury to the apparent victim (Penal Law, § 1055); yet the majority now hold, for the first time, that in the event of a simple assault under similar circumstances, the mistaken belief, no matter how reasonable, is no defense.

Briefly, the relevant facts are these: On a Friday afternoon at about 3:40, Detectives Driscoll and Murphy, not in uniform, observed an argument taking place between a motorist and one McGriff in the street in front of premises 64 West 54th Street, in midtown Manhattan. Driscoll attempted to chase McGriff out of the roadway in order to allow traffic to pass, but McGriff refused to move back; his actions caused a crowd to collect. After identifying himself to McGriff, Driscoll placed him under arrest. As McGriff resisted, defendant, "came out of the crowd" from Driscoll's rear and struck Murphy about the head with his fist. In the ensuing struggle Driscoll's right kneecap was injured when defendant fell on top of him. At the station house, defendant said he had not known or thought Driscoll and Murphy were police officers.

Defendant testified that while he was proceeding on 54th Street he observed two white men, who appeared to be 45 or 50 years old, pulling on a "colored boy" (McGriff), who appeared to be a lad about 18, whom he did not know. The men had nearly pulled McGriff's pants off, and he was crying. Defendant admitted he knew nothing of what had transpired between the officers and McGriff, and made no inquiry of anyone; he just came there and pulled the officer away from McGriff.

Defendant was convicted of assault third degree. In reversing upon the law and dismissing the information, the Appellate Division held that one is not "criminally liable for assault in the third degree if he goes to the aid of another who he mistakenly, but reasonably, believes is being unlawfully beaten, and thereby injures one of the apparent assaulters." While in my opinion the majority below correctly stated the law, I would reverse here and remit so that the Appellate Division may pass on the question of whether or not defendant's conduct was reasonable in light of the circumstances presented at the trial.

As the majority below pointed out, assault is a crime derived from the common law. Basic to the imposition of criminal liability both at common law and under our statutory law is the existence in the one whom committed the prohibited act of what has been variously termed a guilty mind, a mens rea or a criminal intent. Criminal intent requires an awareness of wrongdoing. When conduct is based upon mistake of fact reasonably entertained, there can be no such awareness and, therefore, no criminal culpability. An honest and reasonable belief in the existence of circumstances which, if true, would make the act for which the defendant is prosecuted innocent, would be a good defense.

It is undisputed that defendant did not known that Driscoll and Murphy were detectives in plain clothes engaged in lawfully apprehending an alleged disorderly person. If, therefore, defendant reasonably believed he was lawfully assisting another, he would not have been guilty of a crime. Subdivision 3 of section 246 of the Penal Law provides that it is not unlawful to use force 'When committed either by the party about to be injured or by another person in his aid or defense, in preventing or attempting to prevent an offense against his person, . . . if the force or violence used is not more than sufficient to prevent such offense." The law is thus clear that if defendant entertained an "honest and reasonable belief" that the facts were as he perceived them to be, he would be exonerated from criminal liability.

By ignoring one of the most basic principles of criminal law that crimes mala in se require proof of at least general criminal intent, the majority now hold that the defense of mistake of fact is "of no significance." We are not here dealing with one of a narrow class of exceptions where the Legislature has created crimes which do not depend on criminal intent but which are complete on the mere intentional doing of an act malum prohibitum.

There is no need, in my opinion, to consider the law of other States, for New York policy clearly supports the view that one may act on appearances reasonably ascertained, as does New Jersey. Our Penal Law (§ 1055), to which I have already alluded, is a statement of that policy.

Although the majority of our courts are now purporting to fashion a policy "conducive to an orderly society," by their decision they have defeated their avowed purpose. What public interest is promoted by a principle which would deter one from coming to the aid of a fellow citizen who he has reasonable ground to apprehend is in imminent danger of personal injury at the hands of assailants? Is it reasonable to denominate, as justifiable homicide, a slaying committed under a mistaken but reasonably held belief, and deny this same defense of justification to one using less force? Logic, as well as historical background and related precedent, dictates that the rule and policy expressed by our Legislature in the case of homicide, which is an assault resulting in death, should likewise be applicable to a much less serious assault not resulting in death.

I would reverse the order appealed from and remit the case to the Appellate Division pursuant to section 543-b of the Code of Criminal Procedure for determination upon the questions of fact raised in that court.

QUESTIONS

1.   The *Young* case demonstrates the risk one assumes when coming to the aid of another person. What do you think the rationale is that underlies the mistaken intervener rule? What public policy concerns are addressed by having such a rule that can serve to criminally punish someone who mistakenly thought he or she was acting as a good Samaritan?

2.   Given the fact that the mistaken intervener rule fails to parallel the rule regarding honest and reasonable mistakes for those acting in self defense, do you think the rule is unfair? Explain.

3.   The New York State Assembly legislatively overruled the *Young* case by adopting the Model Penal Code approach to the mistaken intervener situation. Under this approach, the actor is excused for mistakenly intervening if he or she reasonably believed it necessary to prevent unlawful harm to the third party. This approach, however, remains the minority approach in the United States. Why do you think that is?

C. Defense of Property

As with the rule on self defense, the law on defense of property can similarly be summarized in a single sentence. One may use of a *reasonable amount* of *non-deadly force* to prevent *unlawful interference* with one's *property*. This means that deadly force can never be used to defend property. As the following case illustrates, the rationale underlying such a prohibition is that life should be valued more than property or possessions.

The PEOPLE, Plaintiff and Respondent, v. Don Louis CEBALLOS, Defendant and Appellant.
12 Cal.3d 470, 526 P.2d 241, 116 Cal. Rptr. 233 (1974).

Burke, Justice.

Don Ceballos was found guilty by a jury of assault with a deadly weapon. Imposition of sentence was suspended and he was placed on probation. He appeals from the judgment, contending primarily that his conduct was not unlawful because the alleged victim was attempting to commit burglary when hit by a trap gun mounted in the garage of defendant's dwelling and that the court erred in instructing the jury. We have concluded that the former argument lacks merit, that the court did not commit prejudicial error in instructing the jury, and that the judgment should be affirmed.

Defendant lived alone in a home in San Anselmo. The regular living quarters were above the garage, but defendant sometimes slept in the garage and had about $2,000 worth of property there.

In March 1970 some tools were stolen from defendant's home. On May 12, 1970, he noticed the lock on his garage doors was bent and pry marks were on one of the doors. The next day he mounted a loaded .22 caliber pistol in the garage. The pistol was aimed at the center of the garage doors and was connected by a wire to one of the doors so that the pistol would discharge if the door was opened several inches.

The damage to defendant's lock had been done by a 16-year-old boy named Stephen and a 15-year-old boy named Robert. On the afternoon of May 15, 1970, the boys returned to defendant's house while he was away. Neither boy was armed with a gun or knife. After looking in the windows and seeing no one, Stephen succeeded in removing the lock on the garage doors with a crowbar, and, as he pulled the door outward, he was hit in the face with a bullet from the pistol. Stephen testified: He intended to go into the garage "for musical equipment" because he had a debt to pay to a friend. His "way of paying that debt would be to take [defendant's] property and sell it" and use the proceeds to pay the debt. He "wasn't going to do it (i.e., steal) for sure, necessarily." He was there "to look around," and "getting in, I don't know if I would have actually stolen."

Defendant, testifying in his own behalf, admitted having set up the trap gun. He stated that after noticing the pry marks on his garage door on May 12, he felt he should "set up some kind of a trap, something to keep the burglar out of my home." When asked why he was trying to keep the burglar out, he replied, ". . . because somebody was trying to steal my property . . . and I don't want to come home some night and have the thief in there . . . usually a thief is pretty desperate . . . and . . . they just pick up a weapon . . . if they don't have one . . . and do the best they can."

When asked by the police shortly after the shooting why he assembled the trap gun, defendant stated that "he didn't have much and he wanted to protect what he did have."

As heretofore appears, the jury found defendant guilty of assault with a deadly weapon. An assault is "an unlawful attempt, coupled with a present ability, to commit a violent injury on the person of another."

Defendant contends that had he been present he would have been justified in shooting Stephen since Stephen was attempting to commit burglary, and that defendant had a right to do indirectly what he could have done directly, and that therefore any attempt by him to commit a violent injury upon Stephen was not "unlawful" and hence not an assault. The People argue that as a matter of law, a trap gun constitutes excessive force, and that in any event the circumstances were not in fact such as to warrant the use of deadly force.

The issue of criminal liability under statutes such as Penal Code section 245 where the instrument employed is a trap gun or other deadly mechanical device appears to be one of first impression in this state, but in other jurisdictions courts have considered the question of criminal and civil liability for death or injuries inflicted by such a device.

At common law in England it was held that a trespasser, having knowledge that there are spring guns in a wood, cannot maintain an action for an injury received in consequence of his accidentally stepping on the wire of such gun. That case aroused such a protest in England that it was abrogated seven years later by a statute, which made it a misdemeanor to set spring guns with intent to inflict grievous bodily injury but excluded from its operation a spring gun set between sunset and sunrise in a dwelling house for the protection thereof.

In the United States, courts have concluded that a person may be held criminally liable under statutes proscribing homicides and shooting with intent to injure, or civilly liable, if he sets upon his premises a deadly mechanical device and that device kills or injures another. However, an exception to the rule that there may be criminal and civil liability for death or injuries caused by such a device has been recognized where the intrusion is, in fact, such that the person, were he present, would be justified in taking the life or inflicting the bodily harm with his own hands. The phrase "were he present" does not hypothesize the actual presence of the person, but is used in setting forth in an indirect manner the principle that a person may do indirectly that which he is privileged to do directly.

Allowing persons, at their own risk, to employ deadly mechanical devices imperils the lives of children, firemen and policemen acting within the scope of their employment, and others. Where the actor is present, there is always the possibility he will realize that deadly force is not necessary, but deadly mechanical devices are without mercy or discretion. Such devices "are silent instrumentalities of death. They deal death and destruction to the innocent as well as the criminal intruder without the slightest warning. The taking of human life (or infliction of great bodily injury) by such means is brutally savage and inhuman."

It seems clear that the use of such devices should not be encouraged. Moreover, whatever may be thought in torts, the foregoing rule setting forth an exception to liability for death or injuries inflicted by such devices "is inappropriate in penal law for it is obvious that it does not prescribe a workable standard of conduct; liability depends upon fortuitous results." We therefore decline to adopt that rule in criminal cases.

Furthermore, even if that rule were applied here, as we shall see, defendant was not justified in shooting Stephen. Penal Code section 197 provides:

> Homicide is . . . justifiable . . . 1. When resisting any attempt to murder any person, or to commit a felony, or to do some great bodily injury upon any person; or, 2. When committed in defense of habitation, property, or person, against one who manifestly intends or endeavors, by violence or surprise, to commit a felony . . . .

Since a homicide is justifiable under the circumstances specified in section 197, a fortiori, an attempt to commit a violent injury upon another under those circumstances is justifiable.

By its terms subdivision 1 of Penal Code section 197 appears to permit killing to prevent any felony, but in view of the large number of felonies today and the inclusion of many that do not involve a danger of serious bodily harm, a literal reading of the section is undesirable. We must look further into the character of the crime, and the manner of its perpetration. When these do not reasonably create a fear of great bodily harm, as they could not if defendant apprehended only a misdemeanor assault, there is no cause for the exaction of a human life.

Examples of forcible and atrocious crimes are murder, mayhem, rape and robbery. In such crimes "from their atrocity and violence human life (or personal safety from great harm) either is, or is presumed to be, in peril." Burglary has been included in the list of such crimes. However, in view of the wide scope of burglary under Penal Code section 459, as compared with the common law definition of that offense, in our opinion it cannot be said that under all circumstances burglary under section 459 constitutes a forcible and atrocious crime. Where the character and manner of the burglary do not reasonably create a fear of great bodily harm, there is no cause for exaction of human life or for the use of deadly force. The character and manner of the burglary could not reasonably create such a fear unless the burglary threatened, or was reasonably believed to threaten, death or serious bodily harm.

In the instant case the asserted burglary did not threaten death or serious bodily harm, since no one but Stephen and Robert was then on the premises. A defendant is not protected from liability merely by the fact that the intruder's conduct is such as would justify the defendant, were he present, in believing that the intrusion threatened death or serious bodily injury. There is ordinarily the possibility that the defendant, were he present, would realize the true state of affairs and recognize the intruder as one whom he would not be justified in killing or wounding.

We thus conclude that defendant was not justified under Penal Code section 197, subdivisions 1 or 2, in shooting Stephen to prevent him from committing burglary. Our conclusion is in accord with dictum indicating that there may be no privilege to use a deadly mechanical device to prevent a burglary of a dwelling house in which no one is present.

Defendant also does not, and could not properly, contend that the intrusion was in fact such that, were he present, he would be justified under Civil Code section 50 in using deadly force. That section

223

provides, "any necessary force may be used to protect from wrongful injury the person or property of oneself . . . ." This section also should be read in the light of the common law, and at common law in general deadly force could not be used solely for the protection of property. "The preservation of human life and limb from grievous harm is of more importance to society than the protection of property."

At common law an exception to the foregoing principle that deadly force could not be used solely for the protection of property was recognized where the property was a dwelling house in some circumstances. According to the older interpretation of the common law, even extreme force may be used to prevent dispossession of the dwelling house. Also at common law, if another attempted to burn a dwelling the owner was privileged to use deadly force if this seemed necessary to defend his "castle" against the threatened harm. Further, deadly force was privileged it if was, or reasonably seemed, necessary to protect the dwelling against a burglar.

Here we are not concerned with dispossession or burning of a dwelling, and, as heretofore concluded, the asserted burglary in this case was not of such a character as to warrant the use of deadly force. We therefore conclude that as a matter of law the exception to the rule of liability for injuries inflicted by a deadly mechanical device does not apply under the circumstances here appearing. The judgment is affirmed.

QUESTIONS

1.   As the court explained, mechanical devices used to defend property are per se unreasonable because of the risk they pose to innocent persons, such as children who unwittingly trespass on property; public servants such as firefighters, police, and first-aid workers; and public utility workers. How far may a property owner go, then, to defend his or her property while away without running afoul the law? Give specific examples of devices you feel would be appropriate to have at one's home in light of *Ceballos*.

2.   Burglary presents a difficult scenario for the criminal law. Technically, burglary is a crime against property and habitation in which someone breaks into the home of another person with the intent to commit some crime once inside, usually a theft. But what if someone is home at the time the burglary takes place? What level of force could the homeowner use under such circumstances? Why, especially in light of the castle doctrine?

D. Law Enforcement and the Use of Force

In general, police are permitted to use as much physical force as is reasonably necessary to subdue a suspect from resisting arrest. The reasonableness of the actions of the police will always require an examination of the totality of the circumstances. But there are limits on the use of deadly force by police. Law enforcement officers may use deadly force in self defense to the same extent that an ordinary citizen can. Law enforcement officers may also use deadly force to defend another person without having to worry about the mistaken intervener rule since it is their job to protect others. Accordingly, if the police make an honest and reasonable mistake by defending someone who had no privilege to act in self defense, they will not be subjected to criminal liability.

Unlike ordinary citizens, however, police, by the nature of the duties, are empowered to use deadly force to stop a fleeing suspect under limited circumstances. As the following case illustrates, the use of deadly by police is justified when there is probable cause (thereby making it is reasonable) to believe that a fleeing felon poses some sort of danger. Either the felon must be dangerous or the felony must be dangerous. Accordingly, police may not use deadly force to apprehend a fleeing suspect of a misdemeanor, or to stop a suspected felon who poses no immediate threat of death or serious bodily harm. Moreover, an honest and reasonable mistake will not subject the officer to criminal liability. Thus, even if a police officer uses deadly force on someone who did not commit a crime, the officer will be excused if he or she acted reasonably when making the assessment. This stands in sharp contrast to private persons who would be held accountable for their mistakes, even if they were reasonable mistakes, since private citizens act at their own peril.

State of TENNESSEE, Appellant, v. Cleamtee GARNER, et al.
471 U.S. 1 (1985).

Justice White delivered the opinion of the Supreme Court.

This case requires us to determine the constitutionality of the use of deadly force to prevent the escape of an apparently unarmed suspected felon. We conclude that such force may not be used unless it is necessary to prevent the escape and the officer has probable cause to believe that the suspect poses a significant threat of death or serious physical injury to the officer or others.

I

At about 10:45 p.m. on October 3, 1974, Memphis Police Officers Elton Hymon and Leslie Wright were dispatched to answer a "prowler inside call." Upon arriving at the scene, they saw a woman standing on her porch and gesturing toward the adjacent house. She told them she had heard glass breaking and that "they" or "someone" was breaking in next door. While Wright radioed the dispatcher to say that they were on the scene, Hymon went behind the house. He heard a door slam and saw someone run across the backyard. The fleeing suspect, who was appellee-respondent's decedent, Edward Garner, stopped at a 6-feet-high chain link fence at the edge of the yard. With the aid of a flashlight, Hymon was able to see Garner's face and hands. He saw no sign of a weapon, and, though not certain, was "reasonably sure" and "figured" that Garner was unarmed. He thought Garner was 17 or 18 years old and about 5'5" or 5'7" tall.

While Garner was crouched at the base of the fence, Hymon called out "police, halt" and took a few steps toward him. Garner then began to climb over the fence. Convinced that if Garner made it over the fence he would elude capture, Hymon shot him. The bullet hit Garner in the back of the head. Garner was taken by ambulance to a hospital, where he died on the operating table. Ten dollars and a purse taken from the house were found on his body.

In using deadly force to prevent the escape, Hymon was acting under the authority of a Tennessee statute and pursuant to Police Department policy. The statute provides that "[i]f, after notice of the intention to arrest the defendant, he either flee or forcibly resist, the officer may use all the necessary means to effect the arrest." Tenn. Code Ann. § 40-7-108 (1982). The Department policy was slightly more restrictive than the statute, but still allowed the use of deadly force in cases of burglary. The incident was reviewed by the Memphis Police Firearm's Review Board and presented to a grand jury. Neither took any action.

Garner's father then brought this action in the Federal District Court for the Western District of Tennessee, seeking damages under 42 U.S.C. § 1983 for asserted violations of Garner's constitutional rights. The complaint alleged that the shooting violated the Fourth, Fifth, Sixth, Eighth, and Fourteenth Amendments of the United States Constitution. It named as defendants Officer Hymon, the Police Department, its Director, and the Mayor and city of Memphis. After a 3-day bench trial, the District Court entered judgment for all defendants. It dismissed the claims against the Mayor and the Director for lack of evidence. It then concluded that Hymon's actions were authorized by the Tennessee statute, which in turn was constitutional. Hymon had employed the only reasonable and practicable means of preventing Garner's escape. Garner had "recklessly and heedlessly attempted to vault over the fence to escape, thereby assuming the risk of being fired upon."

The Court of Appeals for the Sixth Circuit affirmed with regard to Hymon, finding that he had acted in good-faith reliance on the Tennessee statute and was therefore within the scope of his qualified immunity. It remanded for reconsideration of the possible liability of the city, however, in light of *Monell v. New York City Dept. of Social Services*, 436 U.S. 658 (1978), which had come down after the District

Court's decision. The District Court was directed to consider whether a city enjoyed a qualified immunity, whether the use of deadly force and hollow point bullets in these circumstances was constitutional, and whether any unconstitutional municipal conduct flowed from a "policy or custom" as required for liability under *Monell*.

The District Court concluded that *Monell* did not affect its decision. While acknowledging some doubt as to the possible immunity of the city, it found that the statute, and Hymon's actions, were constitutional. Given this conclusion, it declined to consider the "policy or custom" question.

The Court of Appeals reversed and remanded. It reasoned that the killing of a fleeing suspect is a "seizure" under the Fourth Amendment, and is therefore constitutional only if "reasonable." The Tennessee statute failed as applied to this case because it did not adequately limit the use of deadly force by distinguishing between felonies of different magnitudes – "the facts, as found, did not justify the use of deadly force under the Fourth Amendment." Officers cannot resort to deadly force unless they "have probable cause . . . to believe that the suspect [has committed a felony and] poses a threat to the safety of the officers or a danger to the community if left at large."

The State of Tennessee, which had intervened to defend the statute, appealed to this Court. The city filed a petition for certiorari. We noted probable jurisdiction in the appeal and granted the petition.

II

Whenever an officer restrains the freedom of a person to walk away, he has seized that person. While it is not always clear just when minimal police interference becomes a seizure, there can be no question that apprehension by the use of deadly force is a seizure subject to the reasonableness requirement of the Fourth Amendment.

A. A police officer may arrest a person if he has probable cause to believe that person committed a crime. Petitioners and appellant argue that if this requirement is satisfied the Fourth Amendment has nothing to say about how that seizure is made. This submission ignores the many cases in which this Court, by balancing the extent of the intrusion against the need for it, has examined the reasonableness of the manner in which a search or seizure is conducted. To determine the constitutionality of a seizure "[w]e must balance the nature and quality of the intrusion on the individual's Fourth Amendment interests against the importance of the governmental interests alleged to justify the intrusion." We have described "the balancing of competing interests" as "the key principle of the Fourth Amendment. Because one of the factors is the extent of the intrusion, it is plain that reasonableness depends on not only when a seizure is made, but also how it is carried out.

Applying these principles to particular facts, the Court has held that governmental interests did not support a lengthy detention of luggage, an airport seizure not "carefully tailored to its underlying justification," surgery under general anesthesia to obtain evidence, or detention for fingerprinting without probable cause. On the other hand, under the same approach it has upheld the taking of fingernail scrapings from a suspect, an unannounced entry into a home to prevent the destruction of evidence, administrative housing inspections without probable cause to believe that a code violation will be found, and a blood test of a drunken-driving suspect. In each of these cases, the question was whether the totality of the circumstances justified a particular sort of search or seizure.

B. The same balancing process applied in the cases cited above demonstrates that, notwithstanding probable cause to seize a suspect, an officer may not always do so by killing him. The intrusiveness of a seizure by means of deadly force is unmatched. The suspect's fundamental interest in his own life need not be elaborated upon. The use of deadly force also frustrates the interest of the individual, and of society, in judicial determination of guilt and punishment. Against these interests are ranged governmental interests in effective law enforcement.

It is argued that overall violence will be reduced by encouraging the peaceful submission of suspects who know that they may be shot if they flee. Effectiveness in making arrests requires the resort to deadly force, or at least the meaningful threat thereof. "Being able to arrest such individuals is a condition precedent to the state's entire system of law enforcement." Without in any way disparaging the importance of these goals, we are not convinced that the use of deadly force is a sufficiently productive means of accomplishing them to justify the killing of nonviolent suspects. The use of deadly force is a self-defeating way of apprehending a suspect and so setting the criminal justice mechanism in motion. If successful, it guarantees that mechanism will not be set in motion. And while the meaningful threat of deadly force might be thought to lead to the arrest of more live suspects by discouraging escape attempts, the presently available evidence does not support this thesis. The fact is that a majority of police departments in this country have forbidden the use of deadly force against nonviolent suspects. If those charged with the enforcement of the criminal law have abjured the use of deadly force in arresting nondangerous felons, there is a substantial basis for doubting that the use of such force is an essential attribute of the arrest power in all felony cases. Petitioners and appellant have not persuaded us that shooting nondangerous fleeing suspects is so vital as to outweigh the suspect's interest in his own life.

This lenient approach does avoid the anomaly of automatically transforming every fleeing misdemeanant into a fleeing felon – subject, under the common-law rule, to apprehension by deadly force – solely by virtue of his flight. However, it is in real tension with the harsh consequences of flight in cases where deadly force is employed. For example, Tennessee does not outlaw fleeing from arrest. The Memphis City Code does, subjecting the offender to a maximum fine of $50. Thus, Garner's attempted escape subjected him to (a) a $50 fine, and (b) being shot.

The use of deadly force to prevent the escape of all felony suspects, whatever the circumstances, is constitutionally unreasonable. It is not better that all felony suspects die than that they escape. Where the suspect poses no immediate threat to the officer and no threat to others, the harm resulting from failing to apprehend him does not justify the use of deadly force to do so. It is no doubt unfortunate when a suspect who is in sight escapes, but the fact that the police arrive a little late or are a little slower afoot does not always justify killing the suspect. A police officer may not seize an unarmed, nondangerous suspect by shooting him dead. The Tennessee statute is unconstitutional insofar as it authorizes the use of deadly force against such fleeing suspects.

It is not, however, unconstitutional on its face. Where the officer has probable cause to believe that the suspect poses a threat of serious physical harm, either to the officer or to others, it is not constitutionally unreasonable to prevent escape by using deadly force. Thus, if the suspect threatens the officer with a weapon or there is probable cause to believe that he has committed a crime involving the infliction or threatened infliction of serious physical harm, deadly force may be used if necessary to prevent escape, and if, where feasible, some warning has been given. As applied in such circumstances, the Tennessee statute would pass constitutional muster.

III

A.   It is insisted that the Fourth Amendment must be construed in light of the common-law rule, which allowed the use of whatever force was necessary to effect the arrest of a fleeing felon, though not a misdemeanant. As stated in Hale's posthumously published Pleas of the Crown:

> [I]f persons that are pursued by these officers for felony or the just suspicion thereof . . . shall not yield themselves to these officers, but shall either resist or fly before they are apprehended or being apprehended shall rescue themselves and resist or fly, so that they cannot be otherwise apprehended, and are upon necessity slain therein, because they cannot be otherwise taken, it is no felony.

Most American jurisdictions also imposed a flat prohibition against the use of deadly force to stop a fleeing misdemeanant, coupled with a general privilege to use such force to stop a fleeing felon.

The State and city argue that because this was the prevailing rule at the time of the adoption of the Fourth Amendment and for some time thereafter, and is still in force in some States, use of deadly force against a fleeing felon must be "reasonable." It is true that this Court has often looked to the common law in evaluating the reasonableness, for Fourth Amendment purposes, of police activity. On the other hand, it "has not simply frozen into constitutional law those law enforcement practices that existed at the time of the Fourth Amendment's passage." Because of sweeping change in the legal and technological context, reliance on the common-law rule in this case would be a mistaken literalism that ignores the purposes of a historical inquiry.

B.   It has been pointed out many times that the common-law rule is best understood in light of the fact that it arose at a time when virtually all felonies were punishable by death. "Though effected without the protections and formalities of an orderly trial and conviction, the killing of a resisting or fleeing felon resulted in no greater consequences than those authorized for punishment of the felony of which the individual was charged or suspected." Courts have also justified the common-law rule by emphasizing the relative dangerousness of felons.

Neither of these justifications makes sense today. Almost all crimes formerly punishable by death no longer are or can be. And while in earlier times "the gulf between the felonies and the minor offenses was broad and deep," today the distinction is minor and often arbitrary. Many crimes classified as misdemeanors, or nonexistent, at common law are now felonies. These changes have undermined the concept, which was questionable to begin with, that use of deadly force against a fleeing felon is merely a speedier execution of someone who has already forfeited his life. They have also made the assumption that a "felon" is more dangerous than a misdemeanant untenable. Indeed, numerous misdemeanors involve conduct more dangerous than many felonies.

There is an additional reason why the common-law rule cannot be directly translated to the present day. The common-law rule developed at a time when weapons were rudimentary. Deadly force could be inflicted almost solely in a hand-to-hand struggle during which, necessarily, the safety of the arresting officer was at risk. Handguns were not carried by police officers until the latter half of the last century. Only then did it become possible to use deadly force from a distance as a means of apprehension. As a practical matter, the use of deadly force under the standard articulation of the common-law rule has an altogether different meaning – and harsher consequences – now than in past centuries.

One other aspect of the common-law rule bears emphasis. It forbids the use of deadly force to apprehend a misdemeanant, condemning such action as disproportionately severe. In short, though the common-law pedigree of Tennessee's rule is pure on its face, changes in the legal and technological context mean the rule is distorted almost beyond recognition when literally applied.

C.   It cannot be said that there is a constant or overwhelming trend away from the common-law rule. In recent years, some States have reviewed their laws and expressly rejected abandonment of the common-law rule. Nonetheless, the long-term movement has been away from the rule that deadly force may be used against any fleeing felon, and that remains the rule in less than half the States.

This trend is more evident and impressive when viewed in light of the policies adopted by the police departments themselves. Overwhelmingly, these are more restrictive than the common-law rule. The Federal Bureau of Investigation and the New York City Police Department, for example, both forbid the use of firearms except when necessary to prevent death or grievous bodily harm. For accreditation by the Commission on Accreditation for Law Enforcement Agencies, a department must restrict the use of deadly force to situations where "the officer reasonably believes that the action is in defense of human life . . . or in defense of any person in immediate danger of serious physical injury." A 1974 study reported that the police department regulations in a majority of the large cities of the United States allowed the firing of a weapon only when a felon presented a threat of death or serious bodily harm. Overall, only 7.5% of departmental and municipal policies explicitly permit the use of deadly force against any felon; 86.8% explicitly do not. In light of the rules adopted by those who must actually administer them, the older and fading common-law view is a dubious indicium of the constitutionality of the Tennessee statute now before us.

D.   Actual departmental policies are important for an additional reason. We would hesitate to declare a police practice of long standing "unreasonable" if doing so would severely hamper effective law enforcement. But the indications are to the contrary. There has been no suggestion that crime has worsened in any way in jurisdictions that have adopted, by legislation or departmental policy, rules similar to that announced today. Amici noted that "[a]fter extensive research and consideration, [they] have concluded that laws permitting police officers to use deadly force to apprehend unarmed, non-violent fleeing felony suspects actually do not protect citizens or law enforcement officers, do not deter crime or alleviate problems caused by crime, and do not improve the crime-fighting ability of law enforcement agencies." The submission is that the obvious state interests in apprehension are not sufficiently served to warrant the use of lethal weapons against all fleeing felons.

Nor do we agree with petitioners and appellant that the rule we have adopted requires the police to make impossible, split-second evaluations of unknowable facts. We do not deny the practical difficulties of attempting to assess the suspect's dangerousness. However, similarly difficult judgments must be made by the police in equally uncertain circumstances. Nor is there any indication that in States that allow the use of deadly force only against dangerous suspects, the standard has been difficult to apply or has led to a rash of litigation involving inappropriate second-guessing of police officers' split-second decisions. Moreover, the highly technical felony/misdemeanor distinction is equally, if not more, difficult to apply in the field. An officer is in no position to know, for example, the precise value of property stolen, or whether the crime was a first or second offense. Finally, as noted above, this claim must be viewed with suspicion in light of the similar self-imposed limitations of so many police departments.

IV

The District Court concluded that Hymon was justified in shooting Garner because state law allows, and the Federal Constitution does not forbid, the use of deadly force to prevent the escape of a fleeing felony suspect if no alternative means of apprehension is available. This conclusion made a determination of Garner's apparent dangerousness unnecessary. The court did find, however, that Garner appeared to be unarmed, though Hymon could not be certain that was the case. Restated in Fourth Amendment terms, this means Hymon had no articulable basis to think Garner was armed.

In reversing, the Court of Appeals accepted the District Court's factual conclusions and held that "the facts, as found, did not justify the use of deadly force." We agree. Officer Hymon could not reasonably have believed that Garner – young, slight, and unarmed – posed any threat. Indeed, Hymon never attempted to justify his actions on any basis other than the need to prevent an escape. The District Court stated in passing that "[t]he facts of this case did not indicate to Officer Hymon that Garner was 'non-dangerous.'" This conclusion is not explained, and seems to be based solely on the fact that Garner had broken into a house at night. However, the fact that Garner was a suspected burglar could not, without regard to the other circumstances, automatically justify the use of deadly force. Hymon did not have probable cause to believe that Garner, whom he correctly believed to be unarmed, posed any physical danger to himself or others.

The dissent argues that the shooting was justified by the fact that Officer Hymon had probable cause to believe that Garner had committed a nighttime burglary. While we agree that burglary is a serious crime, we cannot agree that it is so dangerous as automatically to justify the use of deadly force. The FBI classifies burglary as a "property" rather than a "violent" crime. Although the armed burglar would present a different situation, the fact that an unarmed suspect has broken into a dwelling at night does not automatically mean he is physically dangerous. This case demonstrates as much. In fact, the available statistics demonstrate that burglaries only rarely involve physical violence. During the 10-year period from 1973-1982, only 3.8% of all burglaries involved violent crime.

V

We wish to make clear what our holding means in the context of this case. The complaint has been dismissed as to all the individual defendants. The State is a party only by virtue of 28 U.S.C. § 2403(b) and is not subject to liability. The possible liability of the remaining defendants – the Police

Department and the city of Memphis – hinges on *Monell v. New York City Dept. of Social Services*, and is left for remand. We hold that the statute is invalid insofar as it purported to give Hymon the authority to act as he did. As for the policy of the Police Department, the absence of any discussion of this issue by the courts below, and the uncertain state of the record, preclude any consideration of its validity.

The judgment of the Court of Appeals is affirmed, and the case is remanded for further proceedings consistent with this opinion. So ordered.

Justice O'Connor, with whom The Chief Justice and Justice Rehnquist join, dissenting.

The Court today holds that the Fourth Amendment prohibits a police officer from using deadly force as a last resort to apprehend a criminal suspect who refuses to halt when fleeing the scene of a nighttime burglary. This conclusion rests on the majority's balancing of the interests of the suspect and the public interest in effective law enforcement. Notwithstanding the venerable common-law rule authorizing the use of deadly force if necessary to apprehend a fleeing felon, and continued acceptance of this rule by nearly half the States, the majority concludes that Tennessee's statute is unconstitutional inasmuch as it allows the use of such force to apprehend a burglary suspect who is not obviously armed or otherwise dangerous. Although the circumstances of this case are unquestionably tragic and unfortunate, our constitutional holdings must be sensitive both to the history of the Fourth Amendment and to the general implications of the Court's reasoning. By disregarding the serious and dangerous nature of residential burglaries and the longstanding practice of many States, the Court effectively creates a Fourth Amendment right allowing a burglary suspect to flee unimpeded from a police officer who has probable cause to arrest, who has ordered the suspect to halt, and who has no means short of firing his weapon to prevent escape. I do not believe that the Fourth Amendment supports such a right, and I accordingly dissent.

The clarity of hindsight cannot provide the standard for judging the reasonableness of police decisions made in uncertain and often dangerous circumstances. Moreover, I am far more reluctant than is the Court to conclude that the Fourth Amendment proscribes a police practice that was accepted at the time of the adoption of the Bill of Rights and has continued to receive the support of many state legislatures. Although the Court has recognized that the requirements of the Fourth Amendment must respond to the reality of social and technological change, fidelity to the notion of constitutional – as opposed to purely judicial – limits on governmental action requires us to impose a heavy burden on those who claim that practices accepted when the Fourth Amendment was adopted are now constitutionally impermissible.

The public interest involved in the use of deadly force as a last resort to apprehend a fleeing burglary suspect relates primarily to the serious nature of the crime. Household burglaries not only represent the illegal entry into a person's home, but also "pose real risk of serious harm to others." According to recent Department of Justice statistics, "[t]hree-fifths of all rapes in the home, three-fifths of all home robberies, and about a third of home aggravated and simple assaults are committed by burglars." During the period 1973-1982, 2.8 million such violent crimes were committed in the course of burglaries. Victims of a forcible intrusion into their home by a nighttime prowler will find little consolation in the majority's confident assertion that "burglaries only rarely involve physical violence." Moreover, even if a particular burglary, when viewed in retrospect, does not involve physical harm to others, the "harsh potentialities for violence" inherent in the forced entry into a home preclude characterization of the crime as "innocuous, inconsequential, minor, or 'nonviolent.'"

Because burglary is a serious and dangerous felony, the public interest in the prevention and detection of the crime is of compelling importance. Where a police officer has probable cause to arrest a suspected burglar, the use of deadly force as a last resort might well be the only means of apprehending the suspect. With respect to a particular burglary, subsequent investigation simply cannot represent a substitute for immediate apprehension of the criminal suspect at the scene. Indeed, the Captain of the Memphis Police Department testified that in his city, if apprehension is not immediate, it is likely that the suspect will not be caught. Although some law enforcement agencies may choose to assume the risk that a criminal will remain at large, the Tennessee statute reflects a legislative determination that the use of deadly force in prescribed circumstances will serve generally to protect the public. Such statutes assist the police in apprehending suspected perpetrators of serious crimes and provide notice that a lawful police order to stop and submit to arrest may not be ignored with impunity.

The Court unconvincingly dismisses the general deterrence effects by stating that "the presently available evidence does not support [the] thesis" that the threat of force discourages escape and that "there is a substantial basis for doubting that the use of such force is an essential attribute to the arrest power in all felony cases." There is no question that the effectiveness of police use of deadly force is arguable and that many States or individual police departments have decided not to authorize it in circumstances similar to those presented here. But it should go without saying that the effectiveness or popularity of a particular police practice does not determine its constitutionality. Moreover, the fact that police conduct pursuant to a state statute is challenged on constitutional grounds does not impose a burden on the State to produce social science statistics or to dispel any possible doubts about the necessity of the conduct. This observation, I believe, has particular force where the challenged practice both predates enactment of the Bill of Rights and continues to be accepted by a substantial number of the States.

Against the strong public interests justifying the conduct at issue here must be weighed the individual interests implicated in the use of deadly force by police officers. The majority declares that "[t]he suspect's fundamental interest in his own life need not be elaborated upon." This blithe assertion hardly provides an adequate substitute for the majority's failure to acknowledge the distinctive manner in which the suspect's interest in his life is even exposed to risk. For purposes of this case, we must recall that the police officer, in the course of investigating a nighttime burglary, had reasonable cause to arrest the suspect and ordered him to halt. The officer's use of force resulted because the suspected burglar refused to heed this command and the officer reasonably believed that there was no means short of firing his weapon to apprehend the suspect. Without questioning the importance of a person's interest in his life, I do not think this interest encompasses a right to flee unimpeded from the scene of a burglary. The legitimate interests of the suspect in these circumstances are adequately accommodated by the Tennessee statute: to avoid the use of deadly force and the consequent risk to his life, the suspect need merely obey the valid order to halt.

A proper balancing of the interests involved suggests that use of deadly force as a last resort to apprehend a criminal suspect fleeing from the scene of a nighttime burglary is not unreasonable within the meaning of the Fourth Amendment. Admittedly, the events giving rise to this case are in retrospect deeply regrettable. No one can view the death of an unarmed and apparently nonviolent 15-year-old without sorrow, much less disapproval. Nonetheless, the reasonableness of Officer Hymon's conduct for purposes of the Fourth Amendment cannot be evaluated by what later appears to have been a preferable course of police action. The officer pursued a suspect in the darkened backyard of a house that from all indications had just been burglarized. The police officer was not certain whether the suspect was alone or unarmed; nor did he know what had transpired inside the house. He ordered the suspect to halt, and when the suspect refused to obey and attempted to flee into the night, the officer fired his weapon to prevent escape. The reasonableness of this action for purposes of the Fourth Amendment is not determined by the unfortunate nature of this particular case; instead, the question is whether it is constitutionally impermissible for police officers, as a last resort, to shoot a burglary suspect fleeing the scene of the crime.

Even if I agreed that the Fourth Amendment was violated under the circumstances of this case, I would be unable to join the Court's opinion. The Court holds that deadly force may be used only if the suspect "threatens the officer with a weapon or there is probable cause to believe that he has committed a crime involving the infliction or threatened infliction of serious physical harm." The Court ignores the more general implications of its reasoning. Relying on the Fourth Amendment, the majority asserts that it is constitutionally unreasonable to use deadly force against fleeing criminal suspects who do not appear to pose a threat of serious physical harm to others. By declining to limit its holding to the use of firearms, the Court unnecessarily implies that the Fourth Amendment constrains the use of any police practice that is potentially lethal, no matter how remote the risk.

Although it is unclear from the language of the opinion, I assume that the majority intends the word "use" to include only those circumstances in which the suspect is actually apprehended. Absent apprehension of the suspect, there is no "seizure" for Fourth Amendment purposes. I doubt that the Court intends to allow criminal suspects who successfully escape to return later with Section 1983 claims against officers who used, albeit unsuccessfully, deadly force in their futile attempt to capture the fleeing suspect. The Court's opinion, despite its broad language, actually decides only that the shooting of a fleeing burglary suspect who was in fact neither armed nor dangerous can support a s 1983 action.

The Court's silence on critical factors in the decision to use deadly force simply invites second-guessing of difficult police decisions that must be made quickly in the most trying of circumstances. Police are given no guidance for determining which objects, among an array of potentially lethal weapons ranging from guns to knives to baseball bats to rope, will justify the use of deadly force. The Court also declines to outline the additional factors necessary to provide "probable cause" for believing that a suspect "poses a significant threat of death or serious physical injury," when the officer has probable cause to arrest and the suspect refuses to obey an order to halt. But even if it were appropriate in this case to limit the use of deadly force to that ambiguous class of suspects, I believe the class should include nighttime residential burglars who resist arrest by attempting to flee the scene of the crime. We can expect an escalating volume of litigation as the lower courts struggle to determine if a police officer's split-second decision to shoot was justified by the danger posed by a particular object and other facts related to the crime. Thus, the majority opinion portends a burgeoning area of Fourth Amendment doctrine concerning the circumstances in which police officers can reasonably employ deadly force.

The Court's opinion sweeps broadly to adopt an entirely new standard for the constitutionality of the use of deadly force to apprehend fleeing felons. Thus, the Court lightly brushes aside, a long-standing police practice that predates the Fourth Amendment and continues to receive the approval of nearly half of the state legislatures. I cannot accept the majority's creation of a constitutional right to flight for burglary suspects seeking to avoid capture at the scene of the crime. Whatever the constitutional limits on police use of deadly force in order to apprehend a fleeing felon, I do not believe they are exceeded in a case in which a police officer has probable cause to arrest a suspect at the scene of a residential burglary, orders the suspect to halt, and then fires his weapon as a last resort to prevent the suspect's escape into the night. I respectfully dissent.

QUESTIONS

1.   While the rule posited by the majority may seem like a good one, the dissent points out that expecting a police officer to make split-second determinations of reasonableness and dangerousness is unrealistic. The decision made by a police officer in the haste of the moment when tensions are running high may or may not seem objectively reasonable when viewed in hindsight by a judge or jury. Given this, do you agree with the dissent that the *Tennessee v. Garner* standard is an unworkable one for police? Why or why not?

2.   The *Garner* case involved a burglary, clearly one of the more difficult crimes to assess the dangerousness of the perpetrator. When the felony itself is an inherently dangerous one, this case would allow the police to use deadly force to apprehend a fleeing suspect. Which felonies do you think should qualify? Which ones should not?

3.   The Supreme Court also held that police may use deadly force to apprehend a dangerous felon who is fleeing. Thus, even if the crime itself is not inherently dangerous, but the fleeing felon is, deadly force may be used. But, before the use of such deadly force would be reasonable according to the majority opinion, the police would need probable cause to believe that such a fleeing felon posed a risk of danger. How might a police officer assess the dangerousness of the felon separate and apart from the instant crime? What if the police officer was wrong?

E. Battered Women's Syndrome

1. The Cycle of Violence

Why do people stay in abusive relationships? That question is at the forefront of jurors' minds when they are faced with a defendant who killed an abusive partner. To people unfamiliar with domestic violence, it is quite difficult for them to figure out why the abused person just didn't leave. To help jurors understand why victims of domestic violence feel an inability to escape (or in legal terms, "retreat"), it is necessary for them to be educated about various sociological and psychological issues that help to explain the seemingly irrational behavior of the abused person. The following case is considered to be the seminal case in U.S. jurisprudence explaining not only many of these psycho-social factors, but also the legal mechanism by which they may be brought to a jury for consideration. When reading it, pay particular attention to the three phases of the *cycle of violence* and the condition known as *learned helplessness* as explained by the New Jersey Supreme Court in section III of its decision.

STATE of New Jersey v. Gladys KELLY
478 A.2d 364 (N.J. 1984).

Wilentz, C.J.

The central issue before us is whether expert testimony about the battered-woman's syndrome is admissible to help establish a claim of self-defense in a homicide case. The question is one of first impression in this state. We hold, based on the limited record before us (the State not having had a full opportunity to prove the contrary), that the battered-woman's syndrome is an appropriate subject for expert testimony; that the experts' conclusions, despite the relative newness of the field, are sufficiently reliable under New Jersey's standards for scientific testimony; and that defendant's expert was sufficiently qualified. Accordingly, we reverse and remand for a new trial. If on retrial after a full examination of these issues the evidence continues to support these conclusions, the expert's testimony on the battered-woman's syndrome shall be admitted as relevant to the honesty and reasonableness of defendant's belief that deadly force was necessary to protect her against death or serious bodily harm.

I

On May 24, 1980, defendant, Gladys Kelly, stabbed her husband, Ernest, with a pair of scissors. He died shortly thereafter at a nearby hospital. The couple had been married for seven years, during which time Ernest had periodically attacked Gladys. According to Ms. Kelly, he assaulted her that afternoon, and she stabbed him in self-defense, fearing that he would kill her if she did not act.

Ms. Kelly was indicted for murder. At trial, she did not deny stabbing her husband, but asserted that her action was in self-defense. To establish the requisite state of mind for her self-defense claim, Ms. Kelly called Dr. Lois Veronen as an expert witness to testify about the battered-woman's syndrome. After hearing a lengthy voir dire examination of Dr. Veronen, the trial court ruled that expert testimony concerning the syndrome was inadmissible on the self-defense issue. Apparently the court believed that the sole purpose of this testimony was to explain and justify defendant's perception of the danger rather than to show the objective reasonableness of that perception.

Ms. Kelly was convicted of reckless manslaughter. In an unreported decision, the Appellate Division affirmed the conviction. We granted certification and now reverse.

II

The Kellys had a stormy marriage. Some of the details of their relationship, especially the stabbing, are disputed. The following is Ms. Kelly's version of what happened – a version that the jury could have accepted and, if they had, a version that would make the proffered expert testimony not only relevant, but critical.

The day after the marriage, Mr. Kelly got drunk and knocked Ms. Kelly down. Although a period of calm followed the initial attack, the next seven years were accompanied by periodic and frequent beatings, sometimes as often as once a week. During the attacks, which generally occurred when Mr. Kelly was drunk, he threatened to kill Ms. Kelly and to cut off parts of her body if she tried to leave him. Mr. Kelly often moved out of the house after an attack, later returning with a promise that he would change his ways. Until the day of the homicide, only one of the attacks had taken place in public.

The day before the stabbing, Gladys and Ernest went shopping. They did not have enough money to buy food for the entire week, so Ernest said he would give his wife more money the next day.

The following morning he left for work. Ms. Kelly next saw her husband late that afternoon at a friend's house. She had gone there with her daughter, Annette, to ask Ernest for money to buy food. He told her to wait until they got home, and shortly thereafter the Kellys left. After walking past several houses, Mr. Kelly, who was drunk, angrily asked "What the hell did you come around here for?" He then grabbed the collar of her dress, and the two fell to the ground. He choked her by pushing his fingers against her throat, punched or hit her face, and bit her leg.

A crowd gathered on the street. Two men from the crowd separated them, just as Gladys felt that she was "passing out" from being choked. Fearing that Annette had been pushed around in the crowd, Gladys then left to look for her. Upon finding Annette, defendant noticed that Annette had defendant's pocketbook. Gladys had dropped it during the fight. Annette had retrieved it and gave her mother the pocketbook.

After finding her daughter, Ms. Kelly then observed Mr. Kelly running toward her with his hands raised. Within seconds he was right next to her. Unsure of whether he had armed himself while she was looking for their daughter, and thinking that he had come back to kill her, she grabbed a pair of scissors from her pocketbook. She tried to scare him away, but instead stabbed him.

This version of the homicide – with a drunk Mr. Kelly as the aggressor both in pushing Ms. Kelly to the ground and again in rushing at her with his hands in a threatening position after the two had been separated – is sharply disputed by the State. The prosecution presented testimony intended to show that the initial scuffle was started by Gladys; that upon disentanglement, while she was restrained by bystanders, she stated that she intended to kill Ernest; that she then chased after him, and upon catching up with him stabbed him with a pair of scissors taken from her pocketbook.

III

The central question in this case is whether the trial court erred in its exclusion of expert testimony on the battered-woman's syndrome. That testimony was intended to explain defendant's state of mind and bolster her claim of self-defense. We shall first examine the nature of the battered-woman's syndrome and then consider the expert testimony proffered in this case and its relevancy.

In the past decade social scientists and the legal community began to examine the forces that generate and perpetuate wife beating and violence in the family. What has been revealed is that the problem affects many more people than had been thought and that the victims of the violence are not only the battered family members (almost always either the wife or the children). There are also many other strangers to the family who feel the devastating impact, often in the form of violence, of the psychological damage suffered by the victims.

[In enacting the Prevention of Domestic Violence Act, the New Jersey Legislature recognized the pervasiveness and seriousness of domestic violence:

> The Legislature finds and declares that domestic violence is a serious crime against society; that there are thousands of persons in this State who are regularly beaten, tortured and in some cases even killed by their spouses or cohabitants; that a significant number of women who are assaulted are pregnant; that victims of domestic violence come from all societal and economic backgrounds and ethnic groups; that there is a positive correlation between spouse

234

abuse and child abuse; and that children, even when they are not themselves physically assaulted, suffer deep and lasting emotional effects from exposure to domestic violence. It is therefore, the intent of the Legislature to assure the victims of domestic violence the maximum protection from abuse the law can provide. N.J.S.A. § 2C:25-2].

Due to the high incidence of unreported abuse (the FBI and other law enforcement experts believe that wife abuse is the most unreported crime in the United States), estimates vary of the number of American women who are beaten regularly by their husband, boyfriend, or the dominant male figure in their lives. One recent estimate puts the number of women beaten yearly at over one million. The state police statistics show more than 18,000 reported cases of domestic violence in New Jersey during the first nine months of 1983, in 83% of which the victim was female. It is clear that the American home, once assumed to be the cornerstone of our society, is often a violent place.

While common law notions that assigned an inferior status to women, and to wives in particular, no longer represent the state of the law as reflected in statutes and cases, many commentators assert that a bias against battered women still exists, institutionalized in the attitudes of law enforcement agencies unwilling to pursue or uninterested in pursuing wife beating cases.

Another problem is the currency enjoyed by stereotypes and myths concerning the characteristics of battered women and their reasons for staying in battering relationships. Some popular misconceptions about battered women include the beliefs that they are masochistic and actually enjoy their beatings, that they purposely provoke their husbands into violent behavior, and, most critically, as we shall soon see, that women who remain in battering relationships are free to leave their abusers at any time.

As these cases so tragically suggest, not only do many women suffer physical abuse at the hands of their mates, but a significant number of women kill (or are killed by) their husbands. In 1978, murders between husband and wife or girlfriend and boyfriend constituted 13% of all murders committed in the United States. Undoubtedly some of these arose from battering incidents. Men were the victims in 48% of these killings.

As the problem of battered women has begun to receive more attention, sociologists and psychologists have begun to focus on the effects a sustained pattern of physical and psychological abuse can have on a woman. The effects of such abuse are what some scientific observers have termed "the battered-woman's syndrome," a series of common characteristics that appear in women who are abused physically and psychologically over an extended period of time by the dominant male figure in their lives. Dr. Lenore Walker, a prominent writer on the battered-woman's syndrome, defines the battered woman as one

who is repeatedly subjected to any forceful physical or psychological behavior by a man in order to coerce her to do something he wants her to do without concern for her rights. Battered women include wives or women in any form of intimate relationships with men. Furthermore, in order to be classified as a battered woman, the couple must go through the battering cycle at least twice. Any woman may find herself in an abusive relationship with a man once. If it occurs a second time, and she remains in the situation, she is defined as a battered woman.

According to Dr. Walker, relationships characterized by physical abuse tend to develop battering cycles. Violent behavior directed at the woman occurs in three distinct and repetitive stages that vary both in duration and intensity depending on the individuals involved.

Phase one of the battering cycle is referred to as the "tension-building stage," during which the battering male engages in minor battering incidents and verbal abuse while the woman, beset by fear and tension, attempts to be as placating and passive as possible in order to stave off more serious violence.

Phase two of the battering cycle is the "acute battering incident." At some point during phase one, the tension between the battered woman and the batterer becomes intolerable and more serious violence inevitable. The triggering event that initiates phase two is most often an internal or external event in the life of the battering male, but provocation for more severe violence is sometimes provided by the woman who can no longer tolerate or control her phase-one anger and anxiety.

Phase three of the battering cycle is characterized by extreme contrition and loving behavior on the part of the battering male. During this period the man will often mix his pleas for forgiveness and protestations of devotion with promises to seek professional help, to stop drinking, and to refrain from further violence. For some couples, this period of relative calm may last as long as several months, but in a battering relationship the affection and contrition of the man will eventually fade and phase one of the cycle will start anew.

The cyclical nature of battering behavior helps explain why more women simply do not leave their abusers. The loving behavior demonstrated by the batterer during phase three reinforces whatever hopes these women might have for their mate's reform and keeps them bound to the relationship.

Some women may even perceive the battering cycle as normal, especially if they grew up in a violent household. Or they may simply not wish to acknowledge the reality of their situation. Other women, however, become so demoralized and degraded by the fact that they cannot predict or control the violence that they sink into a state of psychological paralysis and become unable to take any action at all to improve or alter the situation. There is a tendency in battered women to believe in the omnipotence or strength of their battering husbands and thus to feel that any attempt to resist them is hopeless.

In addition to these psychological impacts, external social and economic factors often make it difficult for some women to extricate themselves from battering relationships. A woman without independent financial resources who wishes to leave her husband often finds it difficult to do so because of a lack of material and social resources. Even with the progress of the last decade, women typically make less money and hold less prestigious jobs than men, and are more responsible for child care. Thus, in a violent confrontation where the first reaction might be to flee, women realize soon that there may be no place to go. Moreover, the stigma that attaches to a woman who leaves the family unit without her children undoubtedly acts as a further deterrent to moving out.

In addition, battered women, when they want to leave the relationship, are typically unwilling to reach out and confide in their friends, family, or the police, either out of shame and humiliation, fear of reprisal by their husband, or the feeling they will not be believed.

Dr. Walker and other commentators have identified several common personality traits of the battered woman: low self-esteem, traditional beliefs about the home, the family, and the female sex role, tremendous feelings of guilt that their marriages are failing, and the tendency to accept responsibility for the batterer's actions.

Finally, battered women are often hesitant to leave a battering relationship because, in addition to their hope of reform on the part of their spouse, they harbor a deep concern about the possible response leaving might provoke in their mates. They literally become trapped by their own fear. Case histories are replete with instances in which a battered wife left her husband only to have him pursue her and subject her to an even more brutal attack.

The combination of all these symptoms – resulting from sustained psychological and physical trauma compounded by aggravating social and economic factors – constitutes the battered-woman's syndrome. Only by understanding these unique pressures that force battered women to remain with their mates, despite their long-standing and reasonable fear of severe bodily harm and the isolation that being a battered woman creates, can a battered woman's state of mind be accurately and fairly understood.

The voir dire testimony of Dr. Veronen, sought to be introduced by defendant Gladys Kelly, conformed essentially to this outline of the battered-woman's syndrome. Dr. Vernonen, after establishing her credentials, described in general terms the component parts of the battered-woman's syndrome and its effects on a woman's physical and mental health. The witness then documented, based on her own considerable experience in counseling, treating, and studying battered women, and her familiarity with the work of others in the field, the feelings of anxiety, self-blame, isolation, and, above all, fear that plagues these women and leaves them prey to a psychological paralysis that hinders their ability to break free or seek help.

Dr. Veronen stated that the problems of battered women are aggravated by a lack of understanding among the general public concerning both the prevalence of violence against women and the nature of battering relationships. She cited several myths concerning battered women that enjoy popular acceptance – primarily that such women are masochistic and enjoy the abuse they receive and that they are free to leave their husbands but choose not to. Dr. Veronen described the various psychological tests and examinations she had performed in connection with her independent research. These tests and their methodology, including their interpretation, are, according to Dr. Veronen, widely accepted by clinical psychologists. Applying this methodology to defendant (who was subjected to all of the tests, including a five-hour interview), Dr. Veronen concluded that defendant was a battered woman and subject to the battered-woman's syndrome.

In addition, Dr. Veronen was prepared to testify as to how, as a battered woman, Gladys Kelly perceived her situation at the time of the stabbing, and why, in her opinion, defendant did not leave her husband despite the constant beatings she endured.

IV

Whether expert testimony on the battered-woman's syndrome should be admitted in this case depends on whether it is relevant to defendant's claim of self-defense, and, in any event, on whether the proffer meets the standards for admission of expert testimony in this state. We examine first the law of self-defense and consider whether the expert testimony is relevant.

The present rules governing the use of force in self-defense are set out in the justification section of the Code of Criminal Justice. The use of force against another in self-defense is justifiable "when the actor reasonably believes that such force is immediately necessary for the purpose of protecting himself against the use of unlawful force by such other person on the present occasion." N.J.S.A. § 2C:3-4(a). Further limitations exist when deadly force is used in self-defense. The use of such deadly force is not justifiable "unless the actor reasonably believes that such force is necessary to protect himself against death or serious bodily harm . . . ." N.J.S.A. § 2C:3-4(b)(2).

These principles codify decades of prior case law development of the elements of self-defense. We focus here on the critical requirement that the actor reasonably believe deadly force to be necessary to prevent death or serious bodily harm, for the proffer of expert testimony was argued to be relevant on this point.

Self-defense exonerates a person who kills in the reasonable belief that such action was necessary to prevent his or her death or serious injury, even though this belief was later proven mistaken. "Detached reflection cannot be demanded in the presence of an uplifted knife," Justice Holmes aptly said, *Brown v. United States*, 256 U.S. 335, 343 (1921); and the law accordingly requires only a reasonable, not necessarily a correct, judgment. *See State v. Hipplewith*, 33 N.J. 300, 316-17 (1960).

While it is not imperative that actual necessity exist, a valid plea of self-defense will not lie absent an actual (that is, honest) belief on the part of the defendant in the necessity of using force. While no case in New Jersey has addressed the point directly, the privilege of self-defense does not exist where the defendant's action is not prompted by a belief in its necessity: "He has no defense when he intentionally kills his enemy in complete ignorance of the fact that his enemy, when killed, was about to launch a deadly attack upon him." W. LAFAVE & A. SCOTT, CRIMINAL LAW § 53, at 394 (1972).The intent of the drafters of the present Code was that a necessity to act should not give rise to a meritorious plea of self-defense where the defendant was unaware of that necessity. Ultimately, of course, it is for the jury to determine if the defendant actually did believe in the necessity of acting with deadly force to prevent an imminent, grave attack. *See, e.g., State v. Fair*, 45 N.J. 77, 93 (1965).

Honesty alone, however, does not suffice. A defendant claiming the privilege of self-defense must also establish that her belief in the necessity to use force was reasonable. As originally proposed, the new Code of Criminal Justice would have eliminated the reasonableness requirement, allowing self-defense whenever the defendant honestly believed in the imminent need to act. This proposed change in the law was not accepted by the Legislature. N.J.S.A. Section 2C:3-4 as finally enacted retains the requirement that the defendant's belief be reasonable.

Thus, even when the defendant's belief in the need to kill in self-defense is conceded to be sincere, if it is found to have been unreasonable under the circumstances, such a belief cannot be held to constitute complete justification for a homicide. As with the determination of the existence of the defendant's belief, the question of the reasonableness of this belief "is to be determined by the jury, not the defendant, in light of the circumstances existing at the time of the homicide."

It is perhaps worth emphasizing here that for defendant to prevail, the jury need not find beyond a reasonable doubt that the defendant's belief was honest and reasonable. Rather, if any evidence raising the issue of self-defense is adduced, either in the State's or the defendant's case, then the jury must be instructed that the State is required to prove beyond a reasonable doubt that the self-defense claim does not accord with the facts; acquittal is required if there remains a reasonable doubt whether the defendant acted in self-defense.

With the foregoing standards in mind, we turn to an examination of the relevance of the proffered expert testimony to Gladys Kelly's claim of self-defense.

V

Gladys Kelly claims that she stabbed her husband in self-defense, believing he was about to kill her. The gist of the State's case was that Gladys Kelly was the aggressor, that she consciously intended to kill her husband, and that she certainly was not acting in self-defense.

The credibility of Gladys Kelly is a critical issue in this case. If the jury does not believe Gladys Kelly's account, it cannot find she acted in self-defense. The expert testimony offered was directly relevant to one of the critical elements of that account, namely, what Gladys Kelly believed at the time of the stabbing, and was thus material to establish the honesty of her stated belief that she was in imminent danger of death.

The State argues that there is no need to bolster defendant's credibility with expert testimony concerning the battering because the State did not attempt to undermine defendant's testimony concerning her prior mistreatment at the hands of her husband. The State's claim is simply untrue.

In her summation, the prosecutor suggested that had Ernest Kelly lived, he might have told a different story from the one Gladys told. (In its brief, the State argues that evidence in the case suggests that Gladys Kelly's claims of abuse could have been contradicted by her husband.) This is obviously a direct attempt to undermine defendant's testimony about her prior mistreatment. Moreover, defendant's credibility was also attacked in other ways. Gladys Kelly's prior conviction for conspiracy to commit robbery was admitted into evidence for the express purpose of impeachment, even though this conviction had occurred nine years before the stabbing. Other questions, about Gladys Kelly's use of alcohol and drugs and about her premarital sexual conduct, were clearly efforts to impeach credibility.

As can be seen from our discussion of the expert testimony, Dr. Veronen would have bolstered Gladys Kelly's credibility. Specifically, by showing that her experience, although concededly difficult to comprehend, was common to that of other women who had been in similarly abusive relationships, Dr. Veronen would have helped the jury understand that Gladys Kelly could have honestly feared that she would suffer serious bodily harm from her husband's attacks, yet still remain with him. This, in turn, would support Ms. Kelly's testimony about her state of mind (that is, that she honestly feared serious bodily harm) at the time of the stabbing.

On the facts in this case, we find that the expert testimony was relevant to Gladys Kelly's state of mind, namely, it was admissible to show she honestly believed she was in imminent danger of death. Moreover, we find that because this testimony was central to the defendant's claim of self-defense, its exclusion, if otherwise admissible, cannot be held to be harmless error.

We also find the expert testimony relevant to the reasonableness of defendant's belief that she was in imminent danger of death or serious injury. We do not mean that the expert's testimony could be used to show that it was understandable that a battered woman might believe that her life was in danger when indeed it was not and when a reasonable person would not have so believed, for admission for that purpose would clearly violate the rule set forth in *State v. Bess*, 53 N.J. 10, 247 A.2d 669 (1968). Expert testimony in that direction would be relevant solely to the honesty of defendant's belief, not its objective reasonableness. Rather, our conclusion is that the expert's testimony, if accepted by the jury, would have aided it in determining whether, under the circumstances, a reasonable person would have believed there was imminent danger to her life.

At the heart of the claim of self-defense was defendant's story that she had been repeatedly subjected to "beatings" over the course of her marriage. While defendant's testimony was somewhat lacking in detail, a juror could infer from the use of the word "beatings," as well as the detail given concerning some of these events (the choking, the biting, the use of fists), that these physical assaults posed a risk of serious injury or death. When that regular pattern of serious physical abuse is combined with defendant's claim that the decedent sometimes threatened to kill her, defendant's statement that on this occasion she thought she might be killed when she saw Mr. Kelly running toward her could be found to reflect a reasonable fear; that is, it could so be found if the jury believed Gladys Kelly's story of the prior beatings, if it believed her story of the prior threats, and, of course, if it believed her story of the events of that particular day.

The crucial issue of fact on which this expert's testimony would bear is why, given such allegedly severe and constant beatings, combined with threats to kill, defendant had not long ago left decedent. Whether raised by the prosecutor as a factual issue or not, our own common knowledge tells us that most of us, including the ordinary juror, would ask himself or herself just such a question. And our knowledge is bolstered by the experts' knowledge, for the experts point out that one of the common myths, apparently believed by most people, is that battered wives are free to leave. To some, this misconception is followed by the observation that the battered wife is masochistic, proven by her refusal to leave despite the severe beatings; to others, however, the fact that the battered wife stays on unquestionably suggests that the "beatings" could not have been too bad for if they had been, she certainly would have left. The expert could clear up these myths, by explaining that one of the common characteristics of a battered wife is her inability to leave despite such constant beatings; her "learned helplessness"; her lack of anywhere to go; her feeling that if she tried to leave, she would be subjected to even more merciless treatment; her belief in the omnipotence of her battering husband; and sometimes her hope that her husband will change his ways.

Unfortunately, in this case the State reinforced the myths about battered women. On cross-examination, when discussing an occasion when Mr. Kelly temporarily moved out of the house, the State repeatedly asked Ms. Kelly: "You wanted him back, didn't you?" The implication was clear: domestic life could not have been too bad if she wanted him back. In its closing argument, the State trivialized the severity of the beatings, saying:

> I'm not going to say they happened or they didn't happen, but life isn't pretty. Life is not a bowl of cherries. We each and every person who takes a breath has problems. Defense

counsel says bruised and battered. Is there any one of us who hasn't been battered by life in some manner or means?

Even had the State not taken this approach, however, expert testimony would be essential to rebut the general misconceptions regarding battered women. The difficulty with the expert's testimony is that it sounds as if an expert is giving knowledge to a jury about something the jury knows as well as anyone else, namely, the reasonableness of a person's fear of imminent serious danger. That is not at all, however, what this testimony is directly aimed at. It is aimed at an area where the purported common knowledge of the jury may be very much mistaken, an area where jurors' logic, drawn from their own experience, may lead to a wholly incorrect conclusion, an area where expert knowledge would enable the jurors to disregard their prior conclusions as being common myths rather than common knowledge. After hearing the expert, instead of saying Gladys Kelly could not have been beaten up so badly for if she had, she certainly would have left, the jury could conclude that her failure to leave was very much part and parcel of her life as a battered wife. The jury could conclude that instead of casting doubt on the accuracy of her testimony about the severity and frequency of prior beatings, her failure to leave actually reinforced her credibility.

Since a retrial is necessary, we think it advisable to indicate the limit of the expert's testimony on this issue of reasonableness. It would not be proper for the expert to express the opinion that defendant's belief on that day was reasonable, not because this is the ultimate issue, but because the area of *expert* knowledge relates, in this regard, to the reasons for defendant's failure to leave her husband. Either the jury accepts or rejects that explanation and, based on that, credits defendant's stories about the beatings she suffered. No expert is needed, however, once the jury has made up its mind on those issues, to tell the jury the logical conclusion, namely, that a person who has in fact been severely and continuously beaten might very well reasonably fear that the imminent beating she was about to suffer could be either life-threatening or pose a risk of serious injury. What the expert could state was that defendant had the battered-woman's syndrome, and could explain that syndrome in detail, relating its characteristics to defendant, but only to enable the jury better to determine the honesty and reasonableness of defendant's belief. Depending on its content, the expert's testimony might also enable the jury to find that the battered wife, because of the prior beatings, numerous beatings, as often as once a week, for seven years, from the day they were married to the day he died, is particularly able to predict accurately the likely extent of violence in any attack on her. That conclusion could significantly affect the jury's evaluation of the reasonableness of defendant's fear for her life.

VI

Having determined that testimony about the battered-woman's syndrome is relevant, we now consider whether Dr. Veronen's testimony satisfies the limitations placed on expert testimony by Evidence Rule 56(2) and by applicable case law. *See State v. Cavallo*, 443 A.2d 1020 (N.J. 1982).

Evidence Rule 56(2) provides that an expert may testify "as to matters requiring scientific, technical or other specialized knowledge if such testimony will assist the trier of fact to understand the evidence or determine a fact in issue." In effect, this Rule imposes three basic requirements for the admission of expert testimony: (1) the intended testimony must concern a subject matter that is beyond the ken of the average juror; (2) the field testified to must be at a state of the art such that an expert's testimony could be sufficiently reliable; and (3) the witness must have sufficient expertise to offer the intended testimony.

The primary justification for permitting expert testimony is that the average juror is relatively helpless in dealing with a subject that is not a matter of common knowledge. Thus, the proponent of expert testimony must demonstrate that testimony would "enhance the knowledge and understanding of lay jurors with respect to other testimony of a special nature normally outside of the usual lay sphere." *State v. Griffin*, 120 N.J. Super. 13, 20, 293 A.2d 217 (App. Div. 1972).

As previously discussed, a battering relationship embodies psychological and societal features that are not well understood by lay observers. Indeed, these features are subject to a large group of myths and stereotypes. It is clear that this subject is beyond the ken of the average juror and thus is suitable for explanation through expert testimony.

The second requirement that must be met before expert testimony is permitted is a showing that the proposed expert's testimony would be reliable. The rationale for this requirement is that expert testimony seeks to assist the trier of fact. An expert opinion that is not reliable is of no assistance to anyone.

To meet the requirement that the expert's testimony be sufficiently reliable, defense counsel must show that the testimony satisfies New Jersey's standard of acceptability for scientific evidence. The technique or mode of analysis used by the expert must have a sufficient scientific basis to produce uniform and reasonably reliable results so as to contribute materially to the ascertainment of the truth.

In a relatively new field of research, such as that of the battered-woman's syndrome, there are three ways a proponent of scientific evidence can prove its general acceptance and thereby its reliability: (1) by expert testimony as to the general acceptance, among those in the profession, of the premises on which the proffered expert witness based his or her analysis; (2) by authoritative scientific and legal writings indicating that the scientific community accepts the premises underlying the proffered testimony; and (3) by judicial opinions that indicate the expert's premises have gained general acceptance.

Applying those methods to the case at bar, we note that judicial opinions thus far have been split concerning the scientific acceptability of the syndrome and the methodology used by the researchers in this area. On the other hand, Dr. Veronen, the proffered expert, testified that the battered-woman's syndrome is acknowledged and accepted by practitioners and professors in the fields of psychology and psychiatry. Dr. Veronen also brought to the court's attention the findings of several researchers who have published reports confirming the presence of the battered-woman's syndrome. She further noted that the battered-woman's syndrome has been discussed at several symposia since 1977, sponsored by such organizations as the Association for the Advancement of Behavior Therapy and the American Sociological Association. Briefs submitted to this Court indicate that there are at least five books and almost seventy scientific articles and papers about the battered-woman's syndrome.

Thus, the record before us reveals that the battered woman's syndrome has a sufficient scientific basis to produce uniform and reasonably reliable results. The numerous books, articles and papers referred to earlier indicate the presence of a growing field of study and research about the battered woman's syndrome and recognition of the syndrome in the scientific field. However, while the record before us could require such a ruling, we refrain from conclusively ruling that Dr. Veronen's proffered testimony about the battered-woman's syndrome would satisfy New Jersey's standard of acceptability for scientific evidence. This is because the State was not given a full opportunity in the trial court to question Dr. Veronen's methodology in studying battered women or her implicit assertion that the battered-woman's syndrome has been accepted by the relevant scientific community.

Finally, before expert testimony may be presented, there must be a showing that the proffered expert witness has sufficient expertise to offer the intended testimony. In this case, it appears that Dr. Veronen is qualified to testify as an expert. She has a Ph.D. in clinical psychology, as well as an M.A. from North Texas State. She is a member of four professional associations. As of 1980, when she was offered as a witness at Ms. Kelly's trial, Dr. Veronen had been an assistant professor at the medical school at the University of South Carolina for three years. Twenty percent of her time at the University was spent teaching, some of it on topics related to the battered-woman's syndrome, and 80% of her time was spent conducting research, most of it on the psychological reaction of women who are victims of violent assaults. She had spent two years studying the battered-woman's syndrome, with the goal of changing the patterns of fear and anxiety of battered women. Dr. Veronen is a clinical psychologist, licensed to practice in two states, and in that capacity had, by 1980, treated approximately thirty battered women and seen seventy others. Because these thirty women have several important characteristics in common with Ms. Kelly (the thirty women had all been in battering relationships for more than two years, were beaten more than six times, and were within the same age group as Ms. Kelly), Dr. Veronen is familiar with battered women who share Ms. Kelly's background.

* * *

[Accordingly, Ms. Kelly's conviction is reversed, and the case is remanded for retrial.]

QUESTIONS

1.   Even if expert testimony helped the trier-of-fact understand the cycle of violence, some people have a difficult time understanding why a victim of domestic violence even allows himself or herself to fall into the cycle in the first place. The common statement to the effect that "If he ever hit me, I'd be out of there right away," expresses a sentiment with which many people can relate. After reading *State v. Kelly*, explain why (a) a woman might not leave after the first battering incident; and (b) why, after it happens again, she may stay anyway.

2.   What is the *legal* role of expert testimony in Battered Woman Syndrome cases? In other words, at what elements of self-defense is such expert testimony aimed?

3.   When the victim of domestic abuse is the wife who suffers such abuse at the hands of her husband, the various psycho-social factors contributing to the formation of learned helplessness appear to be more easily accepted by juries than when the victim of the abuse is a man being abused by a woman, or when a homosexual couple are involved. Why do you think that is? Should these facts be legally relevant? Explain your answer.

2. The Problem with the "Imminent Danger" Requirement

At common law and under the statutory penal codes of nearly all U.S. jurisdictions, before a person can take the life of another, it must reasonably appear that he or she was in imminent danger of some great bodily injury or loss of life from the hands of the person killed. Thus, the general rule regarding the law of self-defense is that no one can attack and kill another because a person fears injury at some future time. But this imminency requirement in the context of the battered woman's syndrome presents special problems, as the following case illustrates.

STATE of Kansas, Appellant, v. Peggy STEWART, Appellee.
763 P.2d 572 (Kan. 1988).

Lockett, Justice.

A direct appeal by the prosecution upon a question reserved asks whether the statutory justification for the use of deadly force in self-defense provided by K.S.A. § 21-3211 excuses a homicide committed by a battered wife where there is no evidence of a deadly threat or imminent danger contemporaneous with the killing.

Peggy Stewart fatally shot her husband, Mike Stewart, while he was sleeping. She was charged with murder in the first degree, K.S.A. § 21-3401. Defendant pled not guilty, contending that she shot her husband in self-defense. Expert evidence showed that Peggy Stewart suffered from the battered woman syndrome. Based upon the battered woman syndrome, the trial judge instructed the jury on self-defense. The jury found Peggy Stewart not guilty.

The State stipulates that Stewart "suffered considerable abuse at the hands of her husband," but contends that the trial court erred in giving a self-defense instruction since Peggy Stewart was in no imminent danger when she shot her sleeping husband. We agree that under the facts of this case the giving of the self-defense instruction was erroneous. We further hold that the trial judge's self-defense instruction improperly allowed the jury to determine the reasonableness of defendant's belief that she was in imminent danger from her individual subjective viewpoint rather than the viewpoint of a reasonable person in her circumstances.

Following an annulment from her first husband and two subsequent divorces in which she was the petitioner, Peggy Stewart married Mike Stewart in 1974. Evidence at trial disclosed a long history of abuse by Mike against Peggy and her two daughters from one of her prior marriages. Laura, one of Peggy's daughters, testified that early in the marriage Mike hit and kicked Peggy, and that after the first year of the marriage Peggy exhibited signs of severe psychological problems.

Subsequently, Peggy was hospitalized and diagnosed as having symptoms of paranoid schizophrenia; she responded to treatment and was soon released. It appeared to Laura, however, that Mike was encouraging Peggy to take more than her prescribed dosage of medication. In 1977, two social workers informed Peggy that they had received reports that Mike was taking indecent liberties with her daughters. Because the social workers did not want Mike to be left alone with the girls, Peggy quit her job. In 1978, Mike began to taunt Peggy by stating that Carla, her 12-year-old daughter, was "more of a wife" to him than Peggy.

Later, Carla was placed in a detention center, and Mike forbade Peggy and Laura to visit her. When Mike finally allowed Carla to return home in the middle of summer, he forced her to sleep in an un-air conditioned room with the windows nailed shut, to wear a heavy flannel nightgown, and to cover herself with heavy blankets. Mike would then wake Carla at 5:30 a.m. and force her to do all the housework. Peggy and Laura were not allowed to help Carla or speak to her.

When Peggy confronted Mike and demanded that the situation cease, Mike responded by holding a shotgun to Peggy's head and threatening to kill her. Mike once kicked Peggy so violently in the chest and ribs that she required hospitalization. Finally, when Mike ordered Peggy to kill and bury Carla, she filed for divorce.

Peggy's attorney in the divorce action testified in the murder trial that Peggy was afraid for both her and her children's lives. One night, in a fit of anger, Mike threw Carla out of the house. Carla, who was not yet in her teens, was forced out of the home with no money, no coat, and no place to go. When the family heard that Carla was in Colorado, Mike refused to allow Peggy to contact or even talk about Carla.

Mike's intimidation of Peggy continued to escalate. One morning, Laura found her mother hiding on the school bus, terrified and begging the driver to take her to a neighbor's home. That Christmas, Mike threw the turkey dinner to the floor, chased Peggy outside, grabbed her by the hair, rubbed her face in the dirt, and then kicked and beat her.

After Laura moved away, Peggy's life became even more isolated. Once, when Peggy was working at a café, Mike came in and ran all the customers off with a gun because he wanted Peggy to go home and have sex with him right that minute. He abused both drugs and alcohol, and amused himself by terrifying Peggy, once waking her from a sound sleep by beating her with a baseball bat. He shot one of Peggy's pet cats, and then held the gun against her head and threatened to pull the trigger. Peggy told friends that Mike would hold a shotgun to her head and threaten to blow it off, and indicated that one day he would probably do it.

In May 1986, Peggy left Mike and ran away to Laura's home in Oklahoma. It was the first time Peggy had left Mike without telling him. Because Peggy was suicidal, Laura had her admitted to a hospital. There, she was diagnosed as having toxic psychosis as a result of an overdose of her medication. On May 30, 1986, Mike called to say he was coming to get her. Peggy agreed to return to Kansas. Peggy told a nurse she felt like she wanted to shoot her husband. At trial, she testified that she decided to return with Mike because she was not able to get the medical help she needed in Oklahoma.

When Mike arrived at the hospital, he told the staff that he "needed his housekeeper." The hospital released Peggy to Mike's care, and he immediately drove her back to Kansas. Mike told Peggy that all her problems were in her head and he would be the one to tell her what was good for her, not the doctors. Peggy testified that Mike threatened to kill her if she ever ran away again. As soon as they arrived at the house, Mike forced Peggy into the house and forced her to have oral sex several times.

The next morning, Peggy discovered a loaded .357 magnum. She testified she was afraid of the gun. She hid the gun under the mattress of the bed in a spare room. Later that morning, as she cleaned house, Mike kept making remarks that she should not bother because she would not be there long, or that she should not bother with her things because she could not take them with her. She testified she was afraid Mike was going to kill her.

Mike's parents visited Mike and Peggy that afternoon. Mike's father testified that Peggy and Mike were affectionate with each other during the visit. Later, after Mike's parents had left, Mike forced Peggy to perform oral sex. After watching television, Mike and Peggy went to bed at 8:00 p.m. As Mike slept, Peggy thought about suicide and heard voices in her head repeating over and over, "kill or be killed." At this time, there were two vehicles in the driveway and Peggy had access to the car keys. About 10:00 p.m., Peggy went to the spare bedroom and removed the gun from under the mattress, walked back to the bedroom, and killed her husband while he slept. She then ran to the home of a neighbor, who called the police.

When the police questioned Peggy regarding the events leading up to the shooting, Peggy stated that things had not gone quite right that day, and that when she got the chance she hid the gun under the mattress. She stated that she shot Mike to "get this over with, this misery and this torment." When asked why she got the gun out, Peggy stated to the police: "I'm not sure exactly what . . . led up to it . . . and my head started playing games with me and I got to thinking about things and I said I didn't want to be by myself again . . . . I got the gun out because there had been remarks made about me being out there alone. It was as if Mike was going to do something again like had been done before. He had gotten me down here from McPherson one time and he went and told them that I had done something and he had me put out of the house and was taking everything I had. And it was like he was going to pull the same thing over again."

Two expert witnesses testified during the trial. The expert for the defense, psychologist Marilyn Hutchinson, diagnosed Peggy as suffering from "battered woman syndrome," or post-traumatic stress syndrome. Dr. Hutchinson testified that Mike was preparing to escalate the violence in retaliation for Peggy's running away. She testified that loaded guns, veiled threats, and increased sexual demands are indicators of the escalation of the cycle. Dr. Hutchinson believed Peggy had a repressed knowledge that she was in a "really grave lethal situation."

The State's expert, psychiatrist Herbert Modlin, neither subscribed to a belief in the battered woman syndrome nor to a theory of learned helplessness as an explanation for why women do not leave an abusive relationship. Dr. Modlin testified that abuse such as repeated forced oral sex would not be trauma sufficient to trigger a post-traumatic stress disorder. He also believed Peggy was erroneously diagnosed as suffering from toxic psychosis. He stated that Peggy was unable to escape the abuse because she suffered from schizophrenia, rather than the battered woman syndrome.

* * *

At defense counsel's request, the trial judge gave an instruction on self-defense to the jury. The jury found Peggy not guilty.

Although the State may not appeal an acquittal, it may reserve questions for appeal. We will not entertain an appeal by the prosecution merely to determine whether the trial court committed error. The appeal by the prosecution must raise a question of statewide interest, the answer to which is essential to the just administration of criminal law.

The question reserved is whether the trial judge erred in instructing on self-defense when there was no imminent threat to the defendant and no evidence of any argument or altercation between the defendant and the victim contemporaneous with the killing. We find this question and the related question of the extent to which evidence of the battered woman syndrome will be allowed to expand the statutory justification for the use of deadly force in self-defense are questions of statewide importance [and exercise jurisdiction accordingly].

The State claims that under the facts the instruction should not have been given because there was no lethal threat to defendant contemporaneous with the killing. The State points out that Peggy's annulment and divorces from former husbands, and her filing for divorce after leaving Mike, proved that Peggy knew there were non-lethal methods by which she could extricate herself from the abusive relationship.

Under the common law, the excuse for killing in self-defense is founded upon necessity, be it real or apparent. Early Kansas cases held that killing in self-defense was justifiable when the defendant had reasonable grounds to believe that an aggressor (1) had a design to take the defendant's life, (2) attempted to execute the design or was in an apparent situation to do so, and (3) induced in the defendant a reasonable belief that he intended to do so immediately.

> [B]efore a person can take the life of another, it must reasonably appear that his own life must have been in imminent danger, or that he was in imminent danger of some great bodily injury from the hands of the person killed. No one can attack and kill another because he may fear injury at some future time.

The perceived imminent danger had to occur in the present time, specifically during the time in which the defendant and the deceased were engaged in their final conflict. These common-law principles were codified in K.S.A. § 21-3211, which provides:

> A person is justified in the use of force against an aggressor when and to the extent it appears to him and he reasonably believes that such conduct is necessary to defend himself or another against such aggressor's imminent use of unlawful force.

The traditional concept of self-defense has posited one-time conflicts between persons of somewhat equal size and strength. When the defendant claiming self-defense is a victim of long-term domestic violence, such as a battered spouse, such traditional concepts may not apply. Because of the prior history of abuse, and the difference in strength and size between the abused and the abuser, the accused in such cases may choose to defend during a momentary lull in the abuse, rather than during a conflict. However, in order to warrant the giving of a self-defense instruction, the facts of the case must still show that the spouse was in imminent danger close to the time of the killing.

A person is justified in using force against an aggressor when it appears to that person and he or she reasonably believes such force to be necessary. A reasonable belief implies both an honest belief and the existence of facts which would persuade a reasonable person to that belief. A self-defense instruction must be given if there is any evidence to support a claim of self-defense, even if that evidence consists solely of the defendant's testimony.

Where self-defense is asserted, evidence of the deceased's long-term cruelty and violence towards the defendant is admissible. In cases involving battered spouses, expert evidence of the battered woman syndrome is relevant to a determination of the reasonableness of the defendant's perception of danger. However, no jurisdictions have held that the existence of the battered woman syndrome in and of itself operates as a defense to murder.

In order to instruct a jury on self-defense, there must be some showing of an imminent threat or a confrontational circumstance involving an overt act by an aggressor. There is no exception to this requirement where the defendant has suffered long-term domestic abuse and the victim is the abuser. In such cases, the issue is not whether the defendant believes homicide is the solution to past or future problems with the batterer, but rather whether circumstances surrounding the killing were sufficient to create a reasonable belief in the defendant that the use of deadly force was necessary.

In three recent Kansas cases where battered women shot their husbands, the women were clearly threatened in the moments prior to the shootings. . . .

* * *

Here, however, there is an absence of imminent danger to defendant: Peggy told a nurse at the Oklahoma hospital of her desire to kill Mike. She later voluntarily agreed to return home with Mike when he telephoned her. She stated that after leaving the hospital Mike threatened to kill her if she left him again. Peggy showed no inclination to leave. In fact, immediately after the shooting, Peggy told the police that she was upset because she thought Mike would leave her. Prior to the shooting, Peggy hid the loaded gun. The cars were in the driveway and Peggy had access to the car keys. After being abused, Peggy went to bed with Mike at 8 p.m. Peggy lay there for two hours, then retrieved the gun from where she had hidden it and shot Mike while he slept.

Under these facts, the giving of the self-defense instruction was erroneous. Under such circumstances, a battered woman cannot reasonably fear imminent life-threatening danger from her sleeping spouse. We note that other courts have held that the sole fact that the victim was asleep does not preclude a self-defense instruction. In *State v. Norman*, 366 S.E.2d 586 (N.C. Ct. App. 1988), cited by defendant, the defendant's evidence disclosed a long history of abuse. Each time defendant attempted to escape, her husband found and beat her. On the day of the shooting, the husband beat defendant continually throughout the day, and threatened either to cut her throat, kill her, or cut off her breast. In the afternoon, defendant shot her husband while he napped. The North Carolina Court of Appeals held it was reversible error to fail to instruct on self-defense. The court found that, although the decedent was napping at the time defendant shot him, defendant's unlawful act was closely related in time to an assault and threat of death by decedent against defendant and that the decedent's nap was "but a momentary hiatus in a continuous reign of terror."

There is no doubt that the North Carolina court determined that the sleeping husband was an evil man who deserved the justice he received from his battered wife. Here, similar comparable and compelling facts exist. But, as one court has stated: "To permit capital punishment to be imposed upon the subjective conclusion of the [abused] individual that prior acts and conduct of the deceased justified the killing would amount to a leap into the abyss of anarchy." *Jahnke v. State*, 682 P.2d 991, 997 (Wyo. 1984). Finally, our legislature has not provided for capital punishment for even the most heinous crimes. We must, therefore, hold that when a battered woman kills her sleeping spouse when there is no imminent danger, the killing is not reasonably necessary and a self-defense instruction may not be given. To hold otherwise in this case would in effect allow the execution of the abuser for past or future acts and conduct.

One additional issue must be addressed. In its amicus curiae brief, the Kansas County and District Attorney Association contends the instruction given by the trial court improperly modified the law of self-defense to be more generous to one suffering from the battered woman syndrome than to any other defendant relying on self-defense. We agree. . . .

The trial judge gave the [following] instruction:

The defendant has claimed her conduct was justified as self-defense. A person is justified in the use of force against an aggressor when and to the extent it appears to him and he reasonably believes that such conduct is necessary to defend himself or another against such aggressor's imminent use of unlawful force. Such justification requires both a belief on the part of the defendant and the existence of facts that would persuade a reasonable person to that belief.

The trial judge then added the following:

You must determine, from the viewpoint of the defendant's mental state, whether the defendant's belief in the need to defend herself was reasonable in light of her subjective impressions and the facts and circumstances known to her.

This addition was apparently encouraged by the following language in *State v. Hodges*, 239 Kan. 63, [16 P.2d 563], Syl. para. 4:

Where the battered woman syndrome is an issue in the case, the standard for reasonableness concerning an accused's belief in asserting self-defense is not an objective, but a subjective standard. The jury must determine, from the viewpoint of defendant's mental state, whether defendant's belief in the need to defend herself was reasonable.

The statement that the reasonableness of defendant's belief in asserting self-defense should be measured from the defendant's own individual subjective viewpoint conflicts with prior law. Our test for self-defense is a two-pronged one. We first use a subjective standard to determine whether the defendant sincerely and honestly believed it necessary to kill in order to defend. We then use an objective standard to determine whether defendant's belief was reasonable – specifically, whether a reasonable person in defendant's circumstances would have perceived self-defense as necessary. . . . We [have] stated that, in cases involving battered spouses, "[t]he objective test is how a reasonably prudent battered wife would perceive the aggressor's demeanor."

. . . [I]t was error for the trial court to instruct the jury to employ solely a subjective test in determining the reasonableness of defendant's actions. Insofar as the above-quoted language can be read to sanction a subjective test, this language is disapproved.

Herd, Justice, dissenting:

The sole issue before us on the question reserved is whether the trial court erred in giving a jury instruction on self-defense. We have a well-established rule that a defendant is entitled to a self-defense instruction if there is any evidence to support it, even though the evidence consists solely of the defendant's testimony. It is for the jury to determine the sincerity of the defendant's belief she needed to act in self-defense, and the reasonableness of that belief in light of all the circumstances.

It is not within the scope of appellate review to weigh the evidence. An appellate court's function is to merely examine the record and determine if there is any evidence to support the theory of self-defense. If the record discloses any competent evidence upon which self-defense could be based, then the instruction must be given. In judging the evidence for this purpose, all inferences should be resolved in favor of the defendant.

It is evident from prior case law appellee met her burden of showing some competent evidence that she acted in self-defense, thus making her defense a jury question. She testified she acted in fear for her life, and Dr. Hutchinson corroborated this testimony. The evidence of Mike's past abuse, the escalation of violence, his threat of killing her should she attempt to leave him, and Dr. Hutchinson's testimony that appellee was indeed in a "lethal situation" more than met the minimal standard of "any evidence" to allow an instruction to be given to the jury.

Appellee introduced much uncontroverted evidence of the violent nature of the deceased and how he had brutalized her throughout their married life. It is well settled in Kansas that when self-defense is asserted, evidence of the cruel and violent nature of the deceased toward the defendant is admissible. The evidence showed Mike had a "Dr. Jekyll and Mr. Hyde" personality. He was usually very friendly and ingratiating when non-family persons were around, but was belligerent and domineering to family members. He had a violent temper and would blow up without reason. Mike was cruel to his two stepdaughters, Carla and Laura, as well as to the appellee. He took pride in hurting them or anything they held dear, such as their pets.

Mike's violence toward appellee and her daughters caused appellee to have emotional problems with symptoms of paranoid schizophrenia. He would overdose appellee on her medication and then cut her off it altogether. Mike's cruelty would culminate in an outburst of violence, and then he would suddenly become very loving and considerate. This was very confusing to appellee. She lived in constant dread of the next outburst. Appellee became progressively more passive and helpless during the marriage but finally became desperate enough to confront Mike and tell him the cruelty to her daughters had to stop. Mike responded by holding a shotgun to her head and threatening to kill her in front of the girls. The violence escalated. At one point, Mike kicked appellee so violently in the chest and ribs that she required hospitalization.

Mike threw twelve-year-old Carla out of the house without resources, and Laura left home as soon as she could. Mike would not let appellee see her daughters and ran Laura off with a shotgun when she tried to visit. Appellee's life became even more isolated. Towards the end, both the phone and utilities were disconnected from the house.

Appellee finally took the car and ran away to Laura's home in Oklahoma. It was the first time she had ever left Mike without telling him. She was suicidal and again hearing voices, and Laura had her admitted to a hospital. She was diagnosed as having toxic psychosis from a bad reaction to her medication. She soon felt better, but was not fully recovered, when Mike found out where she was and called her to say he was coming to get her. She told a nurse she felt like she wanted to shoot him, but the nurse noted her major emotion was one of hopelessness.

The hospital nevertheless released appellee to Mike's care, and he immediately drove her back to Kansas, telling her on the way she was going to have to "settle down now" and listen to him because he was the boss. He said if she ever ran away again, he would kill her.

When they reached the house, Mike would not let appellee bring in her suitcases and forced her to have oral sex four or five times in the next 36 hours, with such violence that the inside of her mouth was bruised. The next morning, appellee found a box of bullets in the car that had not been there before. She then discovered a loaded .357 magnum. This frightened her, because Mike had promised to keep his guns unloaded. She did not know how to unload the gun, so she hid it under the mattress of the bed in a spare room. As she cleaned house, Mike remarked she should not bother, because she would not be there long. He told her she should not bother with her things, because she could not take them with her. She took these statements to mean she would soon be dead and she grew progressively more terrified. Throughout the day Mike continued to force her to have oral sex, while telling her how he preferred sex with other women.

The sexual abuse stopped when Mike's parents came to visit. Mike's father testified everything seemed normal during their stay. After the visit, Mike again forced appellee to perform oral sex and then demanded at 8:00 p.m. she come to bed with him. The cumulative effect of Mike's past history, coupled with his current abusive conduct, justified appellee's belief that a violent explosion was imminent. As he slept, appellee was terrified and thought about suicide and heard voices in her head repeating over and over, "kill or be killed." The voices warned her there was going to be killing and to get away.

She went to the spare bedroom and removed the gun from under the mattress, walked back to the bedroom, and fatally shot Mike. After the first shot, she thought he was coming after her so she shot again and fled wildly outside, barefoot, wearing only her underwear. Ignoring the truck and car outside, although she had the keys in her purse inside, she ran over a mile to the neighbors' house and pled with them to keep Mike from killing her. She thought she had heard him chasing her. The neighbor woman took the gun from appellee's hand and gave her a robe while her husband called the sheriff. The neighbor testified appellee appeared frightened for her life and was certain Mike was alive and looking for her.

Psychologist Marilyn Hutchinson qualified as an expert on the battered woman syndrome and analyzed the uncontroverted facts for the jury. She concluded appellee was a victim of the syndrome and reasonably believed she was in imminent danger. In *State v. Hodges*, we held it appropriate to permit expert testimony on the battered woman syndrome to prove the reasonableness of the defendant's belief she was in imminent danger. Most courts which have addressed the issue are in accord.

The majority implies its decision is necessary to keep the battered woman syndrome from operating as a defense in and of itself. It has always been clear the syndrome is not a defense itself. Evidence of the syndrome is admissible only because of its relevance to the issue of self-defense. The majority of jurisdictions have held it beyond the ordinary jury's understanding why a battered woman may feel she cannot escape, and have held evidence of the battered woman syndrome proper to explain it. The expert testimony explains how people react to circumstances in which the average juror has not been involved. It assists the jury in evaluating the sincerity of the defendant's belief she was in imminent danger requiring self-defense and whether she was in fact in imminent danger.

Dr. Hutchinson explained to the jury at appellee's trial the "cycle of violence" which induces a state of "learned helplessness" and keeps a battered woman in the relationship. She testified appellee was caught in such a cycle. The cycle begins with an initial building of tension and violence, culminates in an explosion, and ends with a "honeymoon." The woman becomes conditioned to trying to make it through one more violent explosion with its battering in order to be rewarded by the "honeymoon phase," with its expressions of remorse and eternal love and the standard promise of "never again." After all promises are broken time after time and she is beaten again and again, the battered woman falls into a state of learned helplessness where she gives up trying to extract herself from the cycle of violence. She learns fighting back only delays the honeymoon and escalates the violence. If she tries to leave the relationship, she is located and returned and the violence increases. She is a captive. She begins to believe her husband is omnipotent, and resistance will be futile at best.

It is a jury question to determine if the battered woman who kills her husband as he sleeps fears he will find and kill her if she leaves, as is usually claimed. Under such circumstances the battered woman is not under actual physical attack when she kills but such attack is imminent, and as a result she believes her life is in imminent danger. She may kill during the tension-building stage when the abuse is apparently not as severe as it sometimes has been, but nevertheless has escalated so that she is afraid the acute stage to come will be fatal to her. She only acts on such fear if she has some survival instinct remaining after the husband-induced "learned helplessness."

Dr. Hutchinson testified the typical batterer has a dichotomous personality, in which he only shows his violent side to his wife or his family. A batterer's major characteristic is the need to blame all frustration on someone else. In a typical battering relationship, she said, the husband and wife are in traditional sex roles, the wife has low self-esteem, and the husband abuses drugs or alcohol. The husband believes the wife is his property and what he does to her is no one's business. There is usually a sense of isolation, with the woman not allowed to speak with friends or children. Overlying the violence is the intimation of death, often created by threats with weapons. It was Dr. Hutchinson's opinion Mike was planning to escalate his violence in retaliation against appellee for running away. She testified that Mike's threats against appellee's life, his brutal sexual acts, and appellee's discovery of the loaded gun were all indicators to appellee the violence had escalated and she was in danger. Dr. Hutchinson believed appellee had a repressed knowledge she was in what was really a gravely lethal situation. She testified appellee was convinced she must "kill or be killed."

The majority claims permitting a jury to consider self-defense under these facts would permit anarchy. This underestimates the jury's ability to recognize an invalid claim of self-defense. Although this is a case of first impression where an appeal by the State has been allowed, there have been several similar cases in which the defendant appealed on other grounds. In each of these cases where a battered woman killed the sleeping batterer, a self-defense instruction has been given when requested by the defendant. The most recent case on this issue is *State v. Norman* which held the trial court erred in refusing to instruct on self-defense where a battered wife shot her husband as he slept. The court stated:

[W]ith the battered spouse there can be, under certain circumstances, an unlawful killing of a passive victim that does not preclude the defense of perfect self-defense. Given the characteristics of battered spouse syndrome, we do not believe that a battered person must wait until a deadly attack occurs or that the victim must in all cases be actually attacking or threatening to attack at the very moment defendant commits the unlawful act for the battered person to act in self-defense. Such a standard, in our view, would ignore the realities of the condition. This position is in accord with other jurisdictions that have addressed the issue.

The majority bases its opinion on its conclusion appellee was not in imminent danger, usurping the right of the jury to make that determination of fact. The majority believes a person could not be in imminent danger from an aggressor merely because the aggressor dropped off to sleep. This is a fallacious conclusion. For instance, picture a hostage situation where the armed guard inadvertently drops off to sleep and the hostage grabs his gun and shoots him. The majority opinion would preclude the use of self-defense in such a case.

The majority attempts to buttress its conclusion appellee was not in imminent danger by citing 19th Century law. The old requirement of "immediate" danger is not in accord with our statute on self-defense and has been emphatically overruled by case law. Yet this standard permeates the majority's reasoning. A review of the law in this state on the requirement of imminent rather than immediate danger to justify self-defense is therefore required. I will limit my discussion to those cases involving battered wives.

The first case, *State v. Hundley*, 693 P.2d 475 (Kan. 1985), involved a battered wife who shot her husband when he threatened her and reached for a beer bottle. Hundley pled self-defense. We held it was error for the trial court to instruct that self-defense was justified if a defendant reasonably believed his conduct was necessary to defend himself against an aggressor's immediate use of force. We held this instruction improperly excluded from the jury's consideration the effect that Hundley's many years as a battered wife had upon her perception of the dangerousness of her husband's actions. We held the statutory word "imminent" should be used, rather than "immediate."

The next case in which a battered wife claimed self-defense was *State v. Osbey*, 710 P.2d 676 (Kan. 1985). The husband had a gun and had threatened to kill Osbey. After an argument while the husband was moving out, Osbey threw a chair towards his van. She shot him when he walked towards her and reached behind some record albums he was carrying. We again held the trial court erred in using the word "immediate" rather than "imminent" in the self-defense instruction to the jury.

In the most recent case, *State v. Hodges*, 716 P.2d 563 (1986), the battered wife was kicked and beaten before making her way into another room. When her husband ordered her to return to him, she shot him. When her first trial resulted in a hung jury, she was retried and convicted of voluntary manslaughter. On appeal, we again held the trial court's use of "immediate" in instructing the jury on self-defense was reversible error. Such usage "places undue emphasis on the decedent's immediate conduct and obliterates the build-up of terror and fear the decedent systematically injected into the relationship over a long period of time."

In *State v. Hundley*, we joined other enlightened jurisdictions in recognizing that the jury in homicide cases where a battered woman ultimately kills her batterer is entitled to all the facts about the battering relationship in rendering its verdict. The jury also needs to know about the nature of the cumulative terror under which a battered woman exists and that a batterer's threats and brutality can make life-threatening danger imminent to the victim of that brutality even though, at the moment, the batterer is passive. Where a person believes she must kill or be killed, and there is the slightest basis in fact for this belief, it is a question for the jury as to whether the danger was imminent. I confess I am an advocate for the constitutional principle that in a criminal prosecution determination of the facts is a function of the jury, not the appellate court.

QUESTIONS

1.   The battered woman's syndrome defense is widely accepted today in the courts of most U.S. jurisdictions. Thus, the approach taken in *State v. Stewart* is clearly a minority approach to self-defense and the battered woman. When a woman defends herself – even if she uses deadly force – during an acute battering incident, it is likely that she will be able to meet the standard requirements of the defense of self defense. But when a battered woman kills under circumstances that appear to the layperson not to meet the "imminent danger" requirement, as Peggy Stewart did, self defense is not likely to be an effective defense. Expert testimony helps the trier-of-fact see why a woman might kill in the "lull" period, going to the "reasonableness" of her actions. Do you agree that it is "reasonable" for an abused person to use deadly force against a batterer while the abuser is not engaged in an acute battering incident, say, for example, when the batterer is sleeping? Why or why not?

2.   The problems faced by a battered woman in asserting self defense under circumstances that do not appear to present imminent danger are complicated further in those jurisdictions that require retreat before the use of deadly force can be deemed justified. Based on your readings of the *Kelly* and *Stewart* cases, explain how you think defense counsel would address the issue of retreat.

3.   The problem with the imminent requirement is not limited to battered women as illustrated by *State v. Schroeder*, 199 Neb. 822, 261 N.W.2d 759 (1978). In *Schroeder*, a 19-year-old inmate stabbed his older cell-mate at 1:00 a.m. while the cell-mate was sleeping. The cell-mate had a reputation for violence, including rape, and had threatened Schroeder that day by saying he would make a "punk" out of him due to an unpaid gambling debt. Schroeder's self defense argument was rejected, and he was convicted of assault with intent to inflict great bodily harm. His conviction was upheld on appeal. Critique this result.

4.   The case of *Jahnke v. State*, 682 P.2d 991 (Wyo. 1984), was discussed by the *Stewart* court. Jahnke was sixteen years old. He waited with a loaded shotgun in his home for his parents to return from dinner. When his father walked in, Jahnke shot him. The evidence showed that the father has physically and psychologically abused Jahnke for most of his life. Jahnke unsuccessfully attempted to assert a "battered person syndrome" defense. On appeal, the Wyoming Supreme Court upheld his conviction, with one judge stating it was a "textbook case of first-degree murder." Do you think the battered woman's syndrome defense should be extended to situations like Jahnke's? Why or why not? Consider the case of the Menendez brothers in your response.

5.   Just as the battered person's syndrome defense has been met with hostility when used by children who kill their parents or by inmates who kill other inmates, it has been met with similar hostility when used by the abused partner in a homosexual relationship. *See* Denise Bricker, *Fatal Defense: An Analysis of Battered Woman's Syndrome Expert Testimony for Gay Men and Lesbians Who Kill Abusive Partners*, 58 BROOK. L. REV. 1379 (Winter 1993). What do you think the unique challenges of using a battering defense would be in a case involving a gay or lesbian couple? Explain your answers interdisciplinarily, incorporating law, sociology, economics, and psychology into your response.

CHAPTER 7
HOMICIDE

A. The Killing of a Person

1. A Life in Being

The term "*homicide*" refers to the killing of a human being – referred to as a "person" in some homicide statutes. While a simple enough definitional statement, the preceding sentence contains two terms that have a specific definition in the criminal law arena. First, "killing" means to cause a premature end to another human's life. If life is at all shortened – even by a few seconds – then a killing has taken place. This element – the killing of a human being – is a common element to all forms of criminal homicide. But how do we know when someone is dead? At common law, death was defined as the cessation of heart and respiratory functions. But today, we know that the heart is not the body's most vital organ, especially since (1) it can be transplanted, and (2) it can be kept functioning by artificial means, such as a respirator. The brain is now considered to be the body's most important organ. Thus, under modern law, death is now taken to mean an absence of brain activity, otherwise known as "brain death."

Second, a human being must be the victim of the killing for homicide liability to attach. Accordingly, as much as one might love one's pet, if someone killed the family dog, no homicide would be deemed to have taken place. But without delving into the realm of the existentialism, what counts as a "person" for criminal law purposes requires further exploration. Consider the following case.

The PEOPLE of The State of Illinois, Appellee, v. Alan GREER, Appellant.
402 N.E.2d 203 (Ill. 1980).

Justice Underwood, writing for the majority of the court:

The defendant, Alan Greer, was charged in separate informations with the murders of Sharon Moss and her 8½-month-old fetus. He was found guilty of both murders by a jury in the circuit court of Massac County and was sentenced to death.

The issue [in this appeal] is whether the commission of acts which result in the death of a fetus before its birth may constitute murder. The answer to that question depends upon the proper construction of the homicide statute. [It] provides that "[a] person who kills an individual without lawful justification commits murder . . . ." The use of the word "individual" rather than "person" to designate the victim is not significant; the two words are [synonymous], and the drafters merely used one to designate the perpetrator and the other to designate the victim in order to avoid confusion. Since this court has not considered previously the question now before us, we must turn to the common law to determine whether an unborn fetus is an "individual" within the meaning of our homicide statute.

At common law the killing of a fetus was not murder unless the child was born alive and then expired as a result of the injuries previously sustained. This rule may produce apparently incongruous results depending on the precise time when the fetus expires. If the fetus survives long enough to be born and take a single breath, the defendant committed homicide. If, however, the fetus expires during birth, or just before, homicide has not occurred. Some States have avoided this anomaly by expressly including a fetus within the definition of victims of homicide or by passing a separate feticide statute. In the absence of such a legislative enactment, however, no court of last resort in this country has held that the killing of a fetus is murder unless the fetus is born alive and then expires.

The State contends, however, that the born-alive rule developed in the common law simply reflected the inadequacies of contemporary medical knowledge. Given the high infant mortality rates prevalent in the 18th century and the lack of medical knowledge, the judges who formulated the common law were unwilling to consider the killing of a fetus murder and rationalized that result by creating a presumption that the fetus would die in childbirth.

Although the killing of a fetus was not homicide at common law, the abortion of a quickened child was punished as a "great misprision." The common law also protected the rights of the unborn child in a variety of other ways. The unborn child could take property by devise and intestate succession, and the child was considered a life in being for purposes of the Rule Against Perpetuities. Moreover, Blackstone maintained that as a general proposition "life . . . begins in contemplation of law as soon as an infant is able to stir in the mother's womb." The State argues that the medical basis for the common law's reluctance to punish as murder the killing of a fetus no longer exists today. A fetus which has reached the stage of viability, generally thought to be about six months of age, has a high probability of survival upon premature birth. Modern medicine regards the fetus as a distinct individual since it has a separate circulatory system which does not intermix with the mother's. The State concludes therefore that a fetus which has reached the age of viability should be protected by the homicide statute.

[The court went on to summarize the other arguments of the State which focused on the fact that civil law, specifically tort law, had come to consider a fetus a "person" and the fact that Illinois law governing abortion until the time of *Roe v. Wade* had declared an unborn child a "human being" from the moment of conception.]

Although the arguments advanced by the State have considerable merit, we cannot concur in its conclusion. The extent to which the unborn child is to be accorded the legal status of one already born is one of the most debated questions of our time, and one to which we do not find any completely consistent response. As the State points out, the protections and remedies of tort law have expanded to include the unborn, sometimes subject to a viability standard and other times not. Doubtlessly the unborn also enjoy substantial rights under the law of property. On the other hand the United States Supreme Court has held that the unborn, whether or not viable, are not persons protected by the Fourteenth Amendment to the United States Constitution. *Roe v. Wade* (1973), 410 U.S. 113. Furthermore, a woman's constitutional right to privacy prevents the State from interfering with her decision to abort a previable fetus, even though that decision ordinarily results in its death. [*Id.*]

Equally significant, these opposing tendencies to protect the fetus in some instances and not in others have long coexisted. The common law that protected certain property rights of the fetus also declined to apply the penalties for homicide to one who destroyed the fetus. As earlier noted, American courts which have extended the benefits of tort law to fetuses have also, in the absence of specifically inclusive statutory language, uniformly refused to change the born-alive rule in criminal cases, four of them within the last 10 years. We do not imply that this divergence between tort law and criminal law is necessarily inconsistent. Differing objectives and considerations in tort and criminal law foster the development of different principles governing the same factual situation.

If the General Assembly was aware when it enacted our homicide statute that the unborn enjoy extensive rights in the law of tort and property, it was also aware that under the common law and the decisional law of this country the crime of homicide does not encompass causing the death of a fetus unless the fetus is born alive and subsequently expires. Nevertheless, the General Assembly declined to specifically include the unborn within the potential victims of homicide or to create a separate offense of feticide. We cannot alter that decision or create a new offense.

After considering the status of the unborn in the common law, the uniform decisions of the courts of last resort in our sister States, and the attitude toward the unborn reflected in our abortion statute, we conclude that taking the life of a fetus is not murder under our current statute unless the fetus is born alive and subsequently expires as a result of the injuries inflicted.

* * *

We therefore . . .reverse that judgment insofar as it found defendant guilty of the murder of baby girl Moss, vacate the death sentence, and remand the cause to the trial court for resentencing.

Mr. Justice Clark, concurring in part and dissenting in part:

I must dissent from the reversal of the conviction for the murder of the fetus. The essential question here is when a fetus becomes a human being so that it is entitled to protection under the law. This question is certainly no stranger to controversy. At various times in history it has been promoted as doctrinal truth that humanity attaches at conception (immediate animation), at quickening (mediate animation) and at birth (animation at birth). No single view has achieved total acceptance in the law at any one time, and any harmony of thought seems remote in our time. However, it is not necessary to plumb the depths of one's reason to reach the conclusion that it is wrong for there to be such a sizeable gap in our criminal law that a person may destroy a viable, 8½-month-old fetus with impunity. Even *Roe v. Wade*, the decision which legalized abortion to a limited extent, contained the restriction that, once viability occurs, the State may proscribe all abortions except those necessary to preserve the life or health of the mother. The reasoning of the court was that, once the fetus is viable, that is, able to live or survive apart from its mother the State's interest in potential life is compelling. I believe the viability argument takes on even greater force in the instant context, where a violent attack was made which destroyed the fetus. Such an attack should be punishable as murder.

What I find to be particularly puzzling is that the majority discusses at length the persuasive arguments of the State as to why this fetus should be considered to be a human being, concedes that there is "considerable merit" to these arguments, but then rejects the conclusion to be drawn from them. . . . We are not dealing with the intentional termination of a pregnancy by the use of any instrument, medicine, drug or any other substance or device that is, as a medical procedure, performed by a physician and with the consent of the woman. Rather, we are here concerned with a violent attack upon the person of a woman who had carried a fetus for 8 ½ months, to the point where the fetus was fully viable.

I think the destruction of the fully viable fetus in this case constituted murder. To hold otherwise is to resolve a doubt against the preservation of fetal life rather than in favor of it. To hold otherwise also absolves the defendant herein of any wrongdoing, although he cruelly denied a viable fetus, with the unbounded potential for life, of the opportunity to enjoy what rightfully belonged to it. I do not think the law of Illinois should countenance such a result.

Mr. Justice Moran, concurring in part and dissenting in part:

For all applications within the Criminal Code of 1961, the legislature defined "person" as "an individual." Within the Criminal Code, the legislative intent is clear. Therein, the General Assembly, in 1975, reaffirmed the long-standing public policy which recognizes the fetus, from conception, as a human being and a legal person for purpose of a right to life. The sole exception to this policy was expressly – and reluctantly – carved out for the abortion provision mandated by the United States Supreme Court ruling in *Roe v. Wade*. It is my opinion that, but for the single exception, the public policy of this State has recognized and continues to recognize a fetus as a human being, a person, an individual.

QUESTIONS

1.   As mentioned before the case, the common law used to consider cessation of heart functioning to be the definition of "death," while today brain death is the standard. The law of homicide, therefore, evolved as the passage of time brought medical progress. This was one of the arguments raised by the State of Illinois in seeking to have Greer's conviction affirmed. If scientific progress is permitted to affect the evolution of the criminal law in one area of homicide law, why do you think that the majority refused to apply similar reasoning to include a fetus in the definition of a "person" in being?

2.   This case presents what is known as an issue of statutory construction because a statute (a written law enacted by the state legislature, the state's murder law in this case), had to be "construed" to figure out what was meant by the words actually used. The court noted that at common law, a life had

to be "in being" for a homicide to be deemed to have occurred. A fetus was not a life in being at common law. The majority reasoned that, with such knowledge of the common law, the legislature of the state of Illinois did not include the killing of a fetus in its homicide statute to overcome the common law tradition the way other states had done. Do you agree that the legislature's failure to include a fetus in its definition of murder means it did not want people like the defendant to be held criminally liable for the death of an unborn fetus? Why or why not?

3.　　　Civil law played an important role in both the reasoning of the majority and the two dissenters. Specifically, the civil law at issue in the case involved tort law, property law, and constitutional law as a function of the Supreme Court's decision in *Roe v. Wade*. Do you feel it is appropriate to use civil law to determine what criminal law should be? Why? If not, how do you reconcile the inconsistencies in the treatment of the same issue, such as whether a fetus is a human life in being, by the criminal law and the civil law?

4.　　　At common law, if the victim of an attack died within one year and one day of the attack, the person responsible for the attack on the victim could be held liable for the death. But if the person lived for more than one year and a day, then no homicide was deemed to have taken place. Today, most states have either abolished this rule, or have adopted some variation of the rule, such as creating a three-year or five-year limit on how long the victim may live before the perpetrator cannot be tried on homicide charges. Why do you think the common law had the "year and a day" rule? What purposes were served by having such a rule? Is the logic underlying such a rule compromised by the modern trend in either extending the period during which death must occur, or abolishing it in its entirety? Why or why not?

2. Corpus Delicti

Corpus Delicti is Latin for "the body (or substance) of the crime." In homicide cases, the corpus delicti is the dead body of a human being. There is no presumption of corpus delicti in homicide cases; it must be proven beyond of a reasonable doubt in all cases. Doing so is easy when there is a dead body. The introduction into evidence of a death certificate, or the testimony of the medical examiner or coroner establishes corpus delicti. But what if there is no body? Corpus delicti can be proven by circumstantial evidence, but doing so is difficult.

The PEOPLE of the State of New York, Appellant, v. Leonard LIPSKY, Respondent
57 N.Y.2d 560, 443 N.E.2d 925, 457 N.Y.S.2d 451 (1982).

Judge Meyer delivered the opinion of the Court:

I

The question at issue being the sufficiency of the evidence to sustain the jury's verdict finding defendant guilty of murder in the second degree, the evidence is to be viewed in the light most favorable to the People. What follows is a recital of the evidence as so viewed.

Mary Robinson, a lifelong resident of Rochester, was last heard from at 1:30 a.m. on June 10, 1976. Married to Larry Robinson in October, 1971, she had worked as a telephone solicitor for about a year and then as a waitress until, following her father's death in 1974, she inherited an interest in seven houses. Thereafter she collected the rents and took care of the maintenance of the houses. For about a year and a half before her father's death, Mary's sister, Frances, lived with Mary and her husband. In 1973, Larry Robinson began living as husband and wife with Frances and told Mary he did not wish to continue such a relationship with her. Mary, nevertheless, remained in the same living quarters with Larry and Frances. In early June, 1976, Larry and Frances began working at a massage parlor and in order to be closer to where they worked moved from the apartment in which the three of them were then living to a hotel. Frances was working as a prostitute. Mary, who had again been working as a waitress, was told by Frances and Larry what they were doing and she also started in early June, 1976, working as a prostitute, mainly at several downtown Rochester hotels. Although she had remained in the apartment in order to close it up, she was going to move in with Frances and Larry when that was done. Larry testified that he was in daily contact with her and that her emotional and physical condition was good.

Between 6 and 7 p.m. on June 9, 1976, Larry received a call from Mary and at 8:30 p.m., he and Frances met and spoke with Mary in the park near the two hotels she frequented. She was wearing her glasses, a dress, a light jacket and white sandals and was carrying a white purse. Larry and Frances then returned to their hotel room. At 1:30 a.m. on June 10, Larry had a 5 to 10 minute telephone conversation with Mary. When he had not heard further from her by about 3 a.m., he and Frances went looking for Mary, checking with the security guards at the two hotels. When she had neither called nor come to their hotel by 7:30 a.m., Larry and Frances went to the apartment. They found no one there but found nothing missing from it other than the glasses and clothing she wore, the purse she carried when they met in the park the night before and the reddish plaid wallet she carried in her purse. Mary's mother had died giving birth to her and the wedding picture of her mother and father which she always kept at her bedside was in its regular place on the nightstand in her bedroom. Larry and Frances remained at the apartment until 11 a.m. the next day, June 11, and then reported Mary to the police as a missing person. Neither Larry nor Frances, nor Mary's sister-in-law and mother-in-law, all of whom saw her frequently before June 9, have had any contact with her since, nor was any money paid into her Social Security account after the quarter ending in June, 1976, nor any claim for benefits made against the account.

Defendant Lipsky was an accounting student at Monroe Community College in Rochester in 1976, and was living in an apartment at 77 Brooks Avenue. In April, 1976, he became engaged to Marsha Hanrahan and when the gas and electricity was turned off at 77 Brooks Avenue, he moved into her apartment. On June 1, 1976, Ms. Hanrahan left Rochester for Cape Cod where she stayed until June 14 or 15. Her relationship with defendant was not going well when she left. When she returned to Rochester, defendant was at her apartment but seemed upset and emotionally overwrought, and at times cried. He told her he wanted to go to Arizona and work at his parents' motel and asked her to come. Shortly thereafter he left. Ms. Hanrahan did not go with him, but she did go to the 77 Brooks Avenue apartment to help him clean it up, pack the things he wanted to take and discard the things he did not want. While doing so she found in a cupboard in the room across the hall from defendant's room a purse, some white sandals and some girls' socks. Inside the purse was a pair of wire frame glasses and a red plaid wallet in which was a police identification card bearing a photograph and the name of Mary C. Robinson and some family pictures. She asked defendant whose the articles were and he replied that they belonged to a former tenant and had been abandoned. He told her she could keep them, which she did, asking a number of friends whether they had ever seen the girl identified by the police card. Defendant left Rochester for Arizona a few days later.

In August, 1978, defendant, who had married in the interim, was working in Provo, Utah, for a distribution company. On October 16, 1978, as the result of an incident that occurred on the campus of Brigham Young University, defendant was arrested for aggravated assault. He pleaded guilty and was ordered held pending presentence evaluation. During a conference with the psychiatric social worker in January, 1979, defendant told him that he had committed a previous crime which he wished to clear up. Warned that his statements could not be kept confidential and after discussing the matter with his wife, defendant met with the social worker and his probation officer on February 7, 1979, and informed them that he had murdered a woman, that she was a prostitute whom he had paid to have intercourse with him, but that he became angry when she wanted to leave and attacked her and then strangled her for fear that someone in her family might retaliate against him. Questioned as to the name, date and place, he wrote on a legal pad: "Mary Robinson, June 14, 1976, Rochester, N.Y.," and gave the place in Rochester as his apartment at 77 Brooks Avenue. Asked what he had done with the body, defendant said he had placed it in the trunk of his car and driven three hours to a point south of Rochester, where he dumped the body down a gully.

After the Rochester police were notified by Utah authorities, the Rochester Democrat and Chronicle carried an article on the matter including a photograph of Mary C. Robinson. As a result Ms.

Hanrahan turned over to the Rochester police the articles defendant had given her when his apartment was cleaned out, all of which were introduced at trial and identified by Larry Robinson as belonging to Mary Robinson. The People also presented testimony of two of defendant's co-workers at the Provo distribution company that on separate occasions defendant had stated that he could not join the Mormon church because he had killed someone. The first, who testified to a conversation at the warehouse, asked defendant what was the reason, to which defendant responded that he was afraid he would be caught and so, though he considered backing out, had gone through with it. The second, who testified to a conversation at his own apartment, asked why he was being told about such things, to which defendant responded: "well, go ahead and try to pin it on me, you can't because there isn't a body so there wouldn't be any evidence."

Also introduced was a poem written by defendant, found during a consensual search of defendant's apartment by the Utah police after the October 16, 1978 arrest, which read (punctuation added):

> To crush out a life with a hand or a heel;
> To be carelessly senseless and not even feel;
> To treat one as nothing and not even real;
> To be as a jackal, a thief who did steal.
> I was such a man, and it's a part of me now.
> I was such a fool and can't even tell how I did such a thing.
> Now, it weighs on my brow and I think of the peace such an act won't allow.
> But still I live on and remember it well.
> Yet still I must live to remember the hell.
> I can never let go of the body that fell, and it tears me to pieces where my thoughts on this dwell.
> I can never be free of this feeling inside.
> I will never be able to successfully hide.
> And there is no way to share the tears that I've cried.
> So I now live for two; by my hand one has died.

In addition to the confession and admissions, the People's case included testimony of defendant's former roommates at 77 Brooks Avenue, that they had never met Mary Robinson or seen the articles found by Ms. Hanrahan; of defendant's landlord at that address, who testified Mary Robinson had never been a tenant there, that he cleaned out the apartment before defendant moved in and did not see those articles and that though defendant was obligated to give him a month's notice prior to moving he gave only a week to 10 days' notice; of several witnesses that Mary Robinson wore the wire frame glasses all the time and could not see well without them; and of unsuccessful efforts of the New York and Pennsylvania police to locate Mary Robinson's body.

Prior to trial, defendant's attorney moved to suppress his February 7 confession to the Provo, Utah, authorities. The motion was denied, the Trial Judge finding the confession completely voluntary and made in a knowing and reflective manner. No issue as to that ruling is involved on this appeal. When defendant thereafter moved for a trial order of dismissal at the close of the evidence, the Trial Judge reserved decision and the jury returned a verdict of guilty. Defendant then moved for judgment notwithstanding the verdict on the ground that there was no evidence other than defendant's confession and admissions to establish either Mary Robinson's death or any criminal act of defendant in relation to her. The Trial Judge reluctantly agreed after reviewing the trial transcript that there was neither direct proof of death nor proof that death was caused by a criminal act. He therefore dismissed the indictment.

The Appellate Division affirmed by a divided court. Two Judges writing for affirmance agreed with the Trial Judge that the requirement of CPL 60.50 had not been met, that section requiring either "direct proof of one or the other of the element of the corpus delicti or, in the absence of such proof, that the circumstantial evidence of the corpus delicti be 'strong and unequivocal.'" The two dissenters . . . held . . . the circumstantial evidence sufficient, when considered in connection with the confession, to meet the requirements of the CPL. We agree with that conclusion and, therefore, reverse.

II

This case involves two related but distinct rules which are often confused. The first is the common-law rule . . . that a defendant cannot be convicted of murder "without direct proof of the death, or of the violence or other act of the defendant which is alleged to have produced death." Although the rule has often been said to preclude conviction for murder unless the body has been found, that is an oversimplification. Exceptions were recognized as where the murder has been on the high seas, at a great distance from the shore, and the body had been thrown overboard, or where the body had been entirely consumed by fire, or so far that it was impossible to identify it, in which case direct evidence of death and accounting for the absence of the body would suffice. Moreover, the rule required no more than direct proof which would, of course, include eyewitness testimony.

* * *

The second is the confession-corroboration rule. . . carried forward into the present Criminal Procedure Law as section 60.50. That section proscribes conviction "of any offense solely upon evidence of a confession or admission made by him [the defendant] without additional proof that the offense charged has been committed." The purpose sought to be served by its provision is "to avert 'the danger that a crime may be confessed when [in fact] no such crime . . . has been committed by any one.'" *People v. Reade*, 13 N.Y.2d 42, 43 (1963). It is said to have stemmed from a general distrust of extrajudicial confessions, which might be erroneously reported or construed, involuntary, mistaken or the workings of a disturbed or insane mind, as well as from rare but widely reported cases in which after conviction of the defendant his "victim" returned alive.

* * *

Under CPL 60.50 no additional proof need connect the defendant with the crime. . . . Evidence in addition to the confession is, moreover, sufficient "even though it fails to exclude every reasonable hypothesis save that of guilt." *People v Cuozzo*, 292 N.Y. 85, 92 (1944). Indeed, the statute is satisfied "by the production of some proof, of whatever weight, that a crime was committed by someone." *People v Daniels*, 37 NY2d 624, 629 (1975). . . . In final analysis, of course, the additional evidence of the crime together with the confession must be sufficient to establish defendant's guilt beyond a reasonable doubt . . . , but "when, in addition to the confession, there is proof of circumstances which, although they may have an innocent construction, are nevertheless calculated to suggest the commission of crime, and for the explanation of which the confession furnishes the key, the case cannot be taken from the jury for a non-compliance with the requirement of the statute.'" *People v. Reade*, 13 N.Y.2d at 45.

III

Measured against that template, the evidence was sufficient to present a question for the jury, notwithstanding that Mary Robinson's body has not been found and that, apart from defendant's confession and admissions, there was no direct proof of death or of criminal agency.

The circumstances of Mary Robinson's disappearance not only meet Reade's "calculated to suggest" standard, they are strongly suggestive of the commission of crime, for the evidence is wholly inconsistent with the possibility that she left Rochester of her own free will. Since the early morning hours of June 10, 1976, she has never been heard from. She was a lifelong resident of Rochester, the owner of property in that city, and had strong social ties in the community. That nothing but the articles she wore or carried on June 9 were missing from her apartment, that her glasses, which she regularly wore, purse, wallet and shoes were not with her but in defendant's possession, and that the family picture she treasured was still on her night table provide sufficient evidence that she did not intentionally leave Rochester. Indeed, the fact that she had communicated three times during the evening of June 9 and early morning of June 10 with her husband, who expected to hear further from her, is inconsistent with an intent on her part to leave. Of some significance also in view of the fact that she had worked in several legitimate positions is the total absence of any activity in her Social Security account after her disappearance, although the fact that she had become a prostitute just before she disappeared reduces the weight that can be given to that factor.

Equally sufficient is the evidence that her disappearance was the result of criminal agency. Despite evidence ruling out any connection, other than through defendant, of Mary Robinson with 77 Brooks Avenue, her purse, sandals, wallet, glasses, identification card and other personal effects were found in his apartment there within a week after her disappearance and the explanation he offered Ms. Hanrahan for their presence was proven false. Although he had given no indication of an intention to leave Rochester and, indeed, had preregistered for the fall 1976 semester at Monroe Community College, he left for Arizona precipitously within a week to 10 days after Mary Robinson's disappearance and gave evidence of being emotionally overwrought before doing so. Defendant argues that the breakup of his relationship with Ms. Hanrahan could account for that, but the jury could have found from her testimony that their relationship was not going well before she left on June 1 for Cape Cod, the more particularly so in view of the presence of Robinson's clothing and effects in defendant's apartment.

To be sure, the evidence other than the confession does not establish Mary Robinson's death or that defendant was the cause of it. But the question with respect to circumstantial evidence is "whether common human experience would lead a reasonable man, putting his mind to it, to reject or accept the inferences asserted for the established facts." *People v. Wachowicz*, 22 N.Y.2d 369, 372 (1968). The evidence reviewed above, when read with defendant's confession, the poem he composed and his admissions to his two Provo co-workers, sufficiently establishes both Mary Robinson's death and defendant's strangulation of her as the cause of it to take the issues to the jury.

For the foregoing reasons, the order of the Appellate Division should be reversed and the verdict reinstated.

QUESTIONS "High seas, fire"

1.   The circumstantial evidence of Mr. Lipsky's guilt was particularly strong in this case. But what if the only evidence against him had been his confession? Why do you think confessions alone, without some corroboration, are generally insufficient to establish corpus delicti?

2.   How much circumstantial evidence (and what types of it) do you think is necessary before corpus delicti can be deemed proven beyond a reasonable doubt? Give specific examples.

B. Murder

1. Premeditation and Murder in the First Degree

Murder is defined as the commission of a homicide with ***malice aforethought***. Malice aforethought is typically construed to mean the premeditated killing of another human being; but it is actually a broader term. "Malice" is the presence of the required malevolent state of mind coupled with the absence of legally adequate justification, excuse, or circumstances of mitigation. Most states presume that all intentional killings are not, in fact, murders in the first degree, but rather murders in the second degree until some aggravating factor that qualifies as malice aforethought is proven. Premeditation is the most common of these aggravating factors, but it is not the only one. For example, New York law allows for a murder in the first degree conviction not upon a showing of premeditation, but rather based on the status of the victim – the killing a police officer killed in the line of duty. Other jurisdictions hold there to be malice aforethought even if the killing was an unintentional one if it occurred during the commission of certain inherently dangerous felonies. These jurisdictional variations aside, however, most states' definition of murder in the first degree turns on whether the killing was premeditated.

There is considerable disagreement on what constitutes premeditation and/or how long premeditation must be entertained before a conviction for murder in the first degree is permissible. The majority approach to this issue holds that premeditation need not exist for any substantial period of time, while the minority approach requires some time for measured, unhurried thinking. Under the former approach, if intent to kill is formed, reflected upon even momentarily, and then acted upon, the defendant would be said to have acted premeditatedly. Under the latter approach, however, premeditation requires some showing of the defendant's prior actions in planning the killing, a motive or reason from which of a jury could infer that the defendant intended to kill, or some manner of killing from which the jury could infer the wounds were deliberately calculated to result in death (e.g., ambush, time-bomb). *See People v. Anderson*, 70 Cal. 2d 15, 447 P.2d 942 (1968).

Thomas GREEN, Plaintiff in Error, v. STATE of Tennessee, Defendant in Error
450 S.W.2d 27 (Tenn. Ct. Crim. App. 1969).

Judge Walker, Presiding Judge:

The defendant below, Thomas Green, was found guilty of murder in the first degree and sentenced to 25 years in the penitentiary, from which judgment he appeals to this court. He contends that the evidence did not warrant a conviction for murder in the first degree, particularly that no premeditation was shown.

The deceased, Morris Snow, age 21 and three other young men (Sylvester Hill, Tommy Lee Billups, and Larry Code) were at Velma's Tea Room in Chattanooga in the early morning hours of January 19, 1968. There was some disagreement between Snow and the defendant. Billups says that the defendant and two other people came to Snow's table and the defendant argued with him, telling Snow: "My brother killed a man the other night, and you're going to mess around here and get killed, too." After this the defendant and Snow shook hands and the defendant said to forget it. He then returned to his table in another part of the room and the deceased, Snow, sat at his table with his three friends and was drinking a bottle of beer.

A short time later, estimated by the witnesses from four to twenty minutes, the defendant returned to the table where Snow was seated and told him to go home, to which Snow replied that he was grown and didn't have to go home. The defendant asked the deceased to repeat himself and he again said he was grown. All of the witnesses agree that the defendant pulled a pistol and shot the deceased while he was seated at the table with his hands on it. The defendant fired several shots, one striking the deceased back of the left ear and another back of the left shoulder. The second shot was fired after Snow had fallen to the floor. The defendant and one of his friends ran out of the building.

Of course, to support a verdict finding a defendant guilty of murder in the first degree, there must be an evidentiary basis for a conclusion that the killing was willful, deliberate, malicious and premeditated, unless effected by poison or lying in wait or in the perpetration of one of the felonies named in the defining statute, in which cases the specified circumstances make it otherwise unnecessary to prove deliberation and premeditation.

Here the defendant had had an argument, during which he threatened to kill the deceased. After some minutes and time to become cool, he returned and shot the deceased. The jury was well warranted in concluding the killing came from deliberation and premeditation. It is not necessary that the design or intention to kill should have been conceived or have pre-existed in the mind any definite time anterior to its execution. It is sufficient if it preceded the assault, however short the interval, and the length of time is not the essence of this constituent of the offense. The design may be conceived and deliberately formed in an instant. Hence it is not material that the interval of premeditation was brief.

Judge Oliver, concurring:

With respect to the element of premeditation, I am in complete agreement that under the evidence in this record the jury was fully warranted in finding that the defendant deliberately and premeditatedly murdered the deceased. As pointed out in the opinion, the Supreme Court of this State has held many times that the elements of premeditation and deliberation may be inferred from the circumstances of the killing.

Concerning the weight and sufficiency of evidence to establish premeditation, and particularly with reference to the nature of the act causing death, many courts have held that deliberation and premeditation may be inferred from the manner in which the killing was committed; and that repeated shots, blows, and other acts of violence are sufficient evidence of premeditation. Such matters as the atrocity, cruelty, and malignity, appearing in the circumstances under which the killing took place have been passed on frequently by the courts in considering the sufficiency of the evidence to sustain a conviction for first degree murder. In this case the defendant deliberately shot the deceased in the head, mortally wounding him, callously shot him again in the back after he fell from his chair to the floor, and then fled the premises.

Judge Galbreath, dissenting:

I must dissent. The facts of this homicide case and the law are correctly stated in the majority opinion but it is strongly felt that an erroneous conclusion has been reached. Here we have a somewhat usual murder case, if murder can ever be said to be usual. In a tavern disagreement one angry man drew a deadly weapon and killed another. This is a serious crime, and is deserving of serious punishment in order to deter others from such conduct, but it is not that most serious crime involving the taking of a human life, murder in the first degree.

From the facts of the case it would appear the jury, lower court and the majority here presumed premeditation or inferred it from proof that does not seem to this writer to suggest its existence at the time of the killing. Premeditation may not be presumed, it must be proved. True, the defendant killed the deceased with a deadly weapon following a quarrel. But, from these facts only murder in the second degree may be presumed.

Where the state proves the commission of a homicide, there arises a presumption of second degree murder. To reduce homicide from second degree murder there must be evidence of justification or mitigation. The burden is on the state to raise the offense to murder in the first degree. Admission of deliberate killing is sufficient so as to raise the offense, as is evidence of killing in an attempt at robbery, or to otherwise gain deceased's property. The offense is not raised by proof of killing with a deadly weapon. The burden of reducing the offense to manslaughter is on the defendant, but defendant sustains the burden by raising a reasonable doubt in the jury's mind whether defendant is guilty of second degree murder.

What is the proof in the record that proves premeditation? There is none. On the contrary, there is undisputed proof from which it may plainly be inferred that an instant before the shooting there was no plan in the mind of the defendant to kill the victim. Green walked up to the table at which the victim was seated and said simply, "Go home." It is submitted for logical consideration that these actions and words mitigate against a previously designed plan to kill. If the defendant had acceded to the imperious request to go home, nothing appears in the record to suggest that he would not be alive today. Of course, he had every right not to go home, and for the defendant to become angry enough to kill him for not obeying his dictatorial order he should be subjected to such punishment as the law provides for taking the life of another under such circumstances. He should not, in my judgment, be subjected to the same punishment reserved for the felon who carefully plans to insure his child's life and then kills it to collect money. Or the depraved killer who lies in wait to slay his victim from ambush. Or the bandit who kills his robbery victim to conceal his guilt of that crime. These are more serious matters than the rash, impulsive, stupid, impetuous act described in the record before us.

True, it is not necessary to prove premeditation existed for any definite period of time. But it is necessary to prove that it did exist. This is a relatively difficult matter to prove. It involves proving the mental state of the killer just prior to the act of killing. The fact that a killing is unexplainable from a reasonable consideration of the facts and circumstances, that it was pointless and useless, that the killer had nothing to gain from his act, that the killing was executed in a particularly bloody manner as in this case by shooting again and again do not constitute facts that tend to prove first degree murder; on the contrary, the more irrational and pointless a killing is, the more likely is it to lack the planning and deliberation necessary to constitute premeditation. Juries, and I fear courts, are inclined to let natural prejudices against violence effect their judgment to such an extent that they view a murder in which the victim is left mutilated and butchered after a drunken brawl as a more serious crime than one involving the administration of a not too unpleasant tasting poison to a vexatious spouse in such a manner as to leave a good looking corpse, and a large insurance benefit.

Premeditation should not, as the majority herein seems to do, when their opinion holds that the design or intention to kill need not have pre-existed for any definite time, be treated as synonymous with intent. Intent, unlike premeditation, is also one of the elements of second degree murder and intent must be accompanied by a deliberate preconceived plan to kill in order to raise the degree to the highest level of murder. [P]remeditated design denotes pre-existing reflection and deliberation encompassing more than the mere intent to kill.

Murder in the second degree is all murder other than the precisely defined murder in the first degree. There are only some nine ways in which murder in the first degree may be committed, one of them requiring premeditation. All other murders are of the lesser degree. The Supreme Court of Alabama in discussing the difficulty of proving the narrow elements necessary to establish murder in the first degree, other than those committed in connection with a defined felony, said:

> [T]he taking of life must been willful, deliberate, malicious, and premeditated. These must concur and co-exist or, whatever other offense may be committed, this offense of statutory creation is not committed. There is no possible state of facts from which the law presumes their concurrence and co-existence.

Premeditation may, of course, be inferred from the acts and words of the killer. Nowhere in the record from the point the defendant shook hands with the deceased and told him to forget an argument they had concluded does anything at all appear to indicate the defendant's state of mind. If he had stood up and announced, "I am going over and kill Snow"; or if he had taken his pistol out and walked over to Snow's table in a threatening way, these facts would justify the jury in concluding a previously formulated design to kill had taken shape. Instead of such actions or words the circumstances prove without dispute that the defendant walked over and did something that completely dispels the notion that he planned to kill; he told the deceased to leave!

QUESTIONS

1.   As should be evident from the case, Tennessee follows the majority approach to premeditation, holding that it need not exist for any appreciable period of time. The dissent makes a strong argument, however, there was no premeditation in the case. With whom do you side – the majority or the dissent? Why?

2.   As mentioned before the case and alluded to in the concurring opinion, premeditation can be deemed to exist from the manner of the killing if it was accomplished in such a manner that it appears the fatal wounds were deliberately calculated to result in death. What qualifies? The concurring opinion states that Green "deliberately shot the deceased in the head, mortally wounding him, callously shot him again in the back after he fell from his chair to the floor, and then fled the premises." Do you agree that the manner of this killing demonstrates premeditation, or can it alternatively be explained as a killing in the heat of the moment? How about if someone stabbed a victim dozens of times? Do you think such repeated stab wounds were deliberately calculated to result in death? Why or why not? *See People v. Anderson*, 70 Cal. 2d 15, 447 P.2d 942 (1968) (holding 60 stabs wounds in the victim to be evidence of heat-of-passion and not the non-premeditated nature of the killing). In light of *Anderson*, from what manners of killing would you be comfortable in inferring premeditation?

3.   Usually, juries want to know the *motive* for a killing. Motive, however, is not an element of any criminal homicide, but rather is only circumstantial evidence of guilt. Why do you think it is so important to show a motive? What is its relationship, if any, to premeditation?

2. Murder in the Second Degree

Murder in the second degree is a broad type of homicide. It is defined in several different ways depending on the jurisdiction. The three most common definitions of murder in the second degree mirror the common law definitions of it. First, murder in the second degree can be founded upon a specific intent to kill that was formed and acted upon without deliberation. Thus, it is *not* the absence or presence of intent to kill that differentiates murder in the first from murder in the second, but rather the existence of some aggravating factor, such as premeditation.

The second way in which a conviction for murder in the second degree can be obtained is upon of showing of intent to do serious bodily harm. If a defendant has no actual intent to kill, but intends to seriously hurt someone (say, beat the victim severely), but the victim then dies from the beating, the perpetrator is guilty of murder. The malice the defendant entertained when specifically intended to inflict serious bodily harm is deemed to be sufficient to impose murder liability on him or her, even though there was no specific intent to kill.

The third and finally main way in which a conviction for murder in the second degree can be obtained is known as "*depraved heart murder*." Under this formulation, the defendant neither entertained specific intent to kill nor specific intent to inflict serious bodily harm. Instead, the defendant acted with such *gross recklessness as to manifest an extreme indifference to the value of human life*. See that this does not require either purpose or knowledge as the requisite mens rea. A person acting with general intent – gross recklessness – can be convicted of murder in the second degree, as the following case illustrates.

Kinte Leeon BROWN, Appellant, v. COMMONWEALTH of Kentucky, Appellee.
975 S.W.2d 922 (Ky. 1998).

Graves, Justice.

Appellant, Kinte Brown, was convicted in the Jefferson Circuit Court of wanton murder and sentenced to twenty years imprisonment. He appeals to this Court as a matter of right. The facts surrounding the murder are not in dispute. On November 20, 1996, Appellant and several others were at a friend's house watching television. Dwayne Cardine took Appellant's pager from him and, after making a "playfully insulting remark," returned it upon request. Thereafter, Appellant reached under a couch and pulled out a .38 caliber handgun. Appellant placed the barrel of the gun at or near Cardine's head. According to Appellant and several witnesses, Appellant used his thumb to pull back the hammer of the gun. He was in the process of lowering the hammer when the gun discharged, striking Cardine in the head and causing his death. Appellant was subsequently charged with the intentional or wanton murder of Cardine.

At trial, Appellant testified that he had held the gun near Cardine's head but that the shooting was an accident. Appellant stated that he did not know whether the gun was loaded, but did concede that he was aware of some problem with the gun. The jury was instructed on wanton murder, second-degree manslaughter and reckless homicide. Appellant objected to the wanton murder instruction on the grounds that the Commonwealth had not proven the element of extreme indifference to human life. The jury subsequently convicted him of wanton murder and recommended a sentence of twenty years imprisonment. The trial court entered judgment accordingly.

* * *

263

Wanton murder is distinguished from second-degree (involuntary) manslaughter, KRS 507.040, which also punishes "wantonly caus[ing] the death of another person," by the additional element described in the phrase "under circumstances manifesting extreme indifference to human life." To punish wanton conduct as murder, it must be conduct as culpable as intentional murder. "[T]he culpable mental state defined in KRS 507.020 as 'wantonness,' . . . without more, will suffice for a conviction of manslaughter in the second degree but not for murder because, to qualify as 'murder,' 'a capital offense,' it must be accompanied by further 'circumstances manifesting extreme indifference to human life.'" *McGinnis v. Commonwealth*, 875 S.W.2d 518, 520 (Ky. 1994).

Appellant is correct in his observation that extreme indifference to human life is not a phrase capable of precise definition, and the drafter of the Model Penal Code and the Kentucky Penal code admitted as much.

> There is a kind of [wanton] homicide that cannot fairly be distinguished . . . from homicides committed [intentionally]. [Wantonness] . . . presupposes an awareness of the creation of substantial homicidal risk, a risk too great to be deemed justifiable by any valid purpose that the actor's conduct serves. Since risk, however, is a matter of degree and the motives for risk creation may be infinite in variation, some formula is needed to identify the case where [wantonness] should be assimilated to [intention]. The conception that the draft employs is that of extreme indifference to the value of human life. The significance of [intention] is that, cases of provocation apart, it demonstrates precisely such indifference. Whether recklessness is so extreme that it demonstrates similar indifference is not a question that, in our view, can be further clarified; it must be left directly to the trier of the facts. If recklessness exists but is not so extreme, the homicide is manslaughter . . . .

Commentary; Model Penal Code, § 201.2, Comment 2.

. . . [T]he Commentary to the Model Penal Code of the American Law Institute notes that to qualify as "circumstances manifesting extreme indifference to human life," wanton killing must exhibit "purposeful or knowing" indifference, "conduct evidencing a 'depraved heart' with no regard for human life." A.L.I., Model Penal Code & Commentaries, Part II, § 210.2 (1980 ed.). Moreover, attempting to emphasize that only the highest levels of unjustifiable homicidal risk should render an actor eligible for a murder conviction, the drafters of KRS 507.020(1)(b) provided illustrations of conduct sufficient to support findings of extreme indifference:

> Typical of conduct contemplated for inclusion in "wanton" murder is shooting into a crowd, an occupied building or an occupied automobile; placing a time bomb in a public place; or derailing a speeding locomotive.

Setting this conduct apart from behavior that would not warrant an unintentional murder conviction are the following characteristics: (i) homicidal risk that is exceptionally high; (ii) circumstances known to the actor that clearly show awareness of the magnitude of the risk; and (iii) minimal or non-existent social utility in the conduct. Such conduct plainly reflects more than mere awareness and conscious disregard of a substantial and unjustifiable risk of death. It manifests a high disregard for life and evinces what the common law chose to call a depravity of mind or heart. As stated in a recent case, "a conviction of wanton murder is reserved exclusively for offenders who manifest virtually no concern for the value of human life." *Johnson v. Commonwealth*, 885 S.W.2d 951, 952 (Ky. 1994).

* * *

Appellant's conduct in this case clearly justified his conviction for wanton murder. The conviction and sentence of the Jefferson Circuit Court is affirmed.

QUESTIONS

1.   Brown stated that he did not know whether the gun was loaded, but did know that there was some problem with the gun. Given the unanimous affirmance of Brown's conviction, the court

apparently had not problem concluding his conduct was so grossly reckless as to manifest an extreme indifference to the value of human life. But where should the line between grossly reckless conduct, sufficient for a murder in the second degree conviction, be drawn as compared to "regular" reckless conduct that does not rise to the level of manifesting an extreme indifference to the value of human life, and therefore only be sufficient to impose liability for involuntary manslaughter? Would playing "Russian Roulette" qualify? Why or why not? *See Commonwealth v. Malone*, 354 Pa. 180, 47 A.2d 445 (1946).

2.   As several courts have stated, the difference between recklessness sufficient for a manslaughter conviction, and gross recklessness that manifests an extreme indifference to the value of human life sufficient for a murder in the second degree conviction is one of degree. Consider the act of driving under the influence of a controlled substance. At a .06% blood alcohol concentration ("B.A.C."), one is not "legally intoxicated" on most U.S. jurisdictions, but can still be held liable for driving under the influence. At a .10% B.A.C., one would be legally drunk in all U.S. jurisdictions. If a car accident occurred in which someone were killed as a result of the driver's operating the motor vehicle under the influence of alcohol, what level of homicide liability should be imposed? Why? Would your response change if the person were driving at two or three times the legal limit? *See United States v. Flemming*, 739 F.2d 945 (4th Cir. 1984) (upholding depraved heart murder conviction for driver with a .315% B.A.C.).

3. Felony Murder

When someone is killed during the commission or attempt to commit a felony that, by its nature, poses an inherent risk to human life, then the killing, even if unintentional, is deemed to be a type of murder called felony murder. The mens rea the defendant had to commit the underlying felony transfers to satisfy the mens rea for felony murder. It is important to note that some jurisdictions have a statutory offense called "*felony murder*," while other states have merged the definition of felony murder into one of the other types of murder definitions. For example, some states consider any qualifying felony murder one of the "aggravating circumstances" sufficient to elevate an unintentional homicide to murder in the first degree.

Given the harshness of the felony murder doctrine at English common law, most U.S. jurisdictions developed a number of limitations on it. First, as already stated, the underlying felony generally has to be one that is "inherently dangerous," such as burglary, arson, robbery, sexual assault, and kidnaping. Some jurisdictions have very broad felony murder statutes, adding crimes like escape, drug trafficking, aggravated child abuse, and unlawful flight/eluding police. But statutes do not enumerate qualifying felonies and instead apply the "inherently dangerous" test, determining what constitutes an inherently dangerous felony is not always a clear-cut task as the following case illustrates.

STATE of Wisconsin, Plaintiff-Respondent, v. Monte L. NOREN, Defendant-Appellant.
371 N.W.2d 381 (Wisc. Ct. App. 1985).

Cane, Presiding Judge.

Monte Noren appeals a judgment convicting him of [felony] murder. The jury found that Noren killed Joseph Lebakken as a natural and probable consequence of the commission of a felony. The underlying felony was robbery. Noren argues that the evidence was insufficient to prove beyond a reasonable doubt that Lebakken's death was the natural and probable consequence of the robbery.

. . . The record shows that Noren struck Lebakken on the head three times during a robbery. He struck the blows with his closed fist, causing his knuckles to bleed. A witness to the crime was concerned that Noren's blows would kill Lebakken. Lebakken was extremely drunk at the time of the robbery. His blood alcohol content was .38% and his urine alcohol content was .48% at the time of death. Noren knew that Lebakken was very drunk. Noren's blows caused Lebakken to lose consciousness and to become comatose. His extreme intoxication contributed to the loss of consciousness. Lebakken suffered from a preexisting respiratory disease that impeded the removal of mucus from his lungs. This condition, in association with the coma, caused death by asphyxiation. Noren did not know about Lebakken's respiratory disease.

Natural & Probable Consequence

. . . . Noren contends that death is not a natural and probable consequence of striking a person's head with a fist. The phrase "natural and probable" has not been defined under the felony-murder statute. The parties concede that to be a natural consequence of a felony, death must be proximately caused by the defendant's conduct. The test of cause is whether the defendant's conduct was a substantial factor in causing the death. *See State v. Serebin*, 350 N.W.2d 65, 70 (Wis. 1984). It is undisputed on appeal that Noren's conduct caused Lebakken's death. The critical issue therefore is whether death was a probable consequence of striking Lebakken's head.

Although the parties agree that "probable" relates to the foreseeability of death, they disagree about how foreseeable death must be. We agree that foreseeability requires different degrees of certainty in different contexts. To constitute negligence, harm must be probable rather than merely possible. . . . Negligent homicide requires that conduct create a high probability of death or great bodily harm. *Hart v. State*, 249 N.W.2d 810, 815 (Wis. 1977). "High probability" is defined as a probability that the ordinary person, having in mind all the circumstances, including the seriousness of the consequences, would consider unreasonable. It does not mean that the mathematical probability of the consequences must be greater than fifty percent. *Id.* at 815 n.4. Death caused by conduct evincing a depraved mind, requires that the defendant's conduct be imminently dangerous to human life. "Imminently dangerous" means that the conduct is dangerous in and of itself; it must have been inherently, apparently, and consciously dangerous to life and not such as might casually produce death by misadventure. *Balistreri v. State*, 265 N.W.2d 290, 296 (Wis. 1978). No Wisconsin appellate decision has addressed the certainty required for death to be foreseeable under the present felony-murder statute.

The statutory requirement that death be a probable consequence of a felony is intended to limit felony-murder liability to situations where the defendant's conduct creates some measure of foreseeable risk of death. See Model Penal Code § 201.2 Comment 4C at 37 (Tent. Draft No. 9 1959). Under the predecessor felony-murder statute, a defendant committed murder when death resulted from the commission of any felony. *Pliemling v. State*, 1 N.W. 278, 279 (Wis. 1879). This rule was modified because it imposed severe criminal sanctions without considering the moral culpability of the defendant.

Because felony-murder is a Class B felony, we conclude that the level of foreseeability should be the same as for depraved mind murder, which is also a Class B felony. Under this test, the acts causing death must be inherently dangerous to life. We apply this test to felony-murder because it requires a high degree of foreseeability, thereby implicitly requiring greater culpability than lesser grades of homicide. Our supreme court applied this standard under the predecessor felony-murder statute when it stated that the act constituting the felony must be in itself dangerous to life. *Pliemling*, 1 N.W. at 281.

Our conclusion is supported by the fact that most other jurisdictions apply the inherently dangerous test in felony murder cases. . . . Most courts that have recognized the inherently dangerous test have relied on language from an English case, *Regina v. Serne*, 16 Cox Crim. Cases 311 (Central Crim. Ct.1887), as stating the basis of the modern felony-murder rule. In [that case], the court stated:

> [I]nstead of saying that any act done with intent to commit a felony and which causes death amounts to murder, it would be reasonable to say that any act known to be dangerous to life, and likely in itself to cause death, done for the purpose of committing a felony which causes death, should be murder.

Regina, 16 Cox Crim. Cases at 313. We are persuaded that Wisconsin's felony-murder statute originates from this case and that the inherently dangerous test applies.

Sufficiency of the Evidence

The trial court correctly instructed the jury in this case that the acts constituting the robbery must have been "in and of themselves dangerous to the life of Joseph Lebakken." Whether Noren's conduct was inherently dangerous must be determined from the conduct itself and the surrounding circumstances. *Wagner v. State*, 250 N.W.2d 331, 339 (Wis. 1977). Whether the conduct was inherently dangerous is not determined by considering only the abstract qualities of the underlying felony. . . . We review the evidence to determine whether a reasonable jury could be convinced beyond a reasonable doubt that Noren's conduct was inherently dangerous.

Noren argues that striking a person's head three times with a fist is not inherently dangerous. He relies on *Beauregard v. State*, 131 N.W. 347, 351 (1911), where our supreme court stated that striking a person's head with a gun barrel generally would not cause death. The state argues that striking a very intoxicated person who has a respiratory disease is inherently dangerous. According to this argument, the specific traits of the victim must be considered when deciding whether conduct is dangerous. The state also argues that one who commits a violent crime takes his victim as he finds him. *See State v. Berry*, 309 N.W.2d 777, 784 n.4 (Minn. 1981).

We agree that generally death is not the natural and probable result of a blow with a hand. *See* 40 Am. Jur. 2d HOMICIDE § 268 (1968). Our inquiry is not complete, however, because the particular traits of the victim also must be considered. Conduct that is unlikely to cause the death of a healthy adult may be dangerous to others. *Virgil v. State*, 267 N.W.2d 852, 857 (Wis. 1978). Only special attributes that the defendant was aware of may be considered. *Id.* Conduct does not become inherently dangerous on the basis of latent danger. *Wangerin v. State*, 243 N.W.2d 448, 452 (Wis. 1976). The truism that a defendant takes his victim as he finds him, therefore, does not apply to this case. The proposition applies in tort law when assessing damages. It also applies in criminal law when deciding the issue of causation. *See Berry*, 309 N.W.2d at 784. The unknown qualities of a victim, however, are irrelevant to the issue of foreseeability of death.

Applying the inherently dangerous test to this case, we conclude that sufficient evidence supports Noren's conviction. Although Lebakken's respiratory disease was irrelevant to the issue of inherent danger, his extreme intoxication was a factor that distinguished him from a healthy adult. Striking an intoxicated person exposes him to familiar risks that a sober person would not face. He may fall and fatally strike his head. He also may asphyxiate from vomit while unconscious. Although Lebakken did not die from either of these causes, the jury could consider such possibilities when determining whether Noren's conduct was inherently dangerous. We conclude that a reasonable jury could have been convinced beyond a reasonable doubt that his conduct was inherently dangerous.

* * *

Judgment affirmed.

QUESTIONS

1.   Key to the court's reasoning was the defendant's knowledge that the victim was intoxicated. Do you agree that knowledge of such data should be the key to determining whether the assault and battery that took place rose to the level of being an "inherently dangerous" felony? Why or why not?

2.   Research the laws of your jurisdiction to identify felony offenses that are, in your opinion, not "inherently dangerous" by their nature, but could be if facts – such as the ones in this case – were known to the defendant that the victim was particularly susceptible to serious injury in a manner that is not typically foreseeable.

3.   What of the suspect who commits the felony of unlawful flight, known as eluding in some jurisdictions? This crime occurs when one "takes off," rather than stopping for police when directed to do so. If a high speed chase ensues in which someone is killed, what should the liability be of the person evading the police? Why? Suppose the police struck and killed someone while in a high-speed pursuit of someone unlawfully fleeing them. Should the law enforcement officers operating that vehicle have any homicide liability? Explain your answer, including a discussion of public policy concerns that such chases raise.

Even when an inherently dangerous felony is found to have occurred, there are other limitations on the felony murder rule that might limit a defendant's liability for the crime. As with all homicide offense, causation must be proven. In other words, the acts or omissions (presuming a legal duty to act) of the defendant must have caused the death of the victim. As was illustrated in the *Noren* case above, normal principles of criminal law causation apply (see Chapter 2).

Another limitation is that of timing. Whatever act the defendant did to cause the death of another had to have occurred during the commission or attempt to commit an inherently dangerous felony, or during immediate flight therefrom. As with the determination of what constitutes an inherently dangerous felony, what constitutes "during" either the attempt or actual commission of a crime, or "immediate flight therefrom" leaves some room for argumentation, as the following case illustrates.

STATE of Tennessee, Appellee, v. Donald C. LEE, Appellant.
969 S.W.2d 414 (Tenn. Ct. Crim. App. 1997).

Summers, Judge.

The appellant, Donald C. Lee, was convicted by a jury of felony murder, robbery, reckless endangerment, aggravated assault, and vehicular homicide. He was sentenced to life for the felony murder conviction. This sentence was ordered to run consecutively to the 37 years he received on the other convictions. He appeals . . . . and we affirm.

The appellant entered the Super-X drug store in Knoxville. He forced the pharmacist to open the safe and give him all Schedule II, III, and IV narcotics. A witness saw him leaving the pharmacy in a white truck. The driver of the white truck let the appellant out in an adjacent parking lot. The police immediately apprehended the driver. He informed the police that the appellant left in a brown Ford containing one passenger. Approximately 25 minutes later the appellant was spotted by the police and a high-speed chase ensued. In an effort to get away, the appellant struck the side of the police car. He erratically cut in front of other motorists. He slammed on his brakes causing the police car to slam into the rear of his car. The appellant eventually swerved into the oncoming lane of traffic and struck a Jeep. The appellant's passenger and the driver of the Jeep were killed in the head-on collision.

In his first issue the appellant contends that the evidence was insufficient to support a conviction for felony murder. He argues that the killing of the victim did not occur during the perpetration of the robbery. He claims that he had successfully completed the robbery and made a successful getaway when the police chase ensued. We disagree.

The purpose of Tennessee's felony murder statute is to prevent the death of innocent persons likely to occur during the commission of certain inherently dangerous felonies. The applicable statute reads in pertinent part:

First degree murder. (a) First degree murder is defined as:

(2)   A reckless killing of another committed in the perpetration of, or attempt to perpetrate any first degree murder, arson, rape, robbery, burglary, theft, kidnaping or aircraft piracy.

Tenn. Code Ann. § 39-13-202(a)(2) (1991). The appellant's contention is simply that the robbery had been completed when he collided with the Jeep causing the death of its driver. We note that the protraction of events over time and distance accentuate the problem of determining whether the underlying felony had reached completion before the death occurred. However, other jurisdictions have held that a person is engaged in the commission or perpetration of a robbery while the criminal is trying to escape with the property taken in such robbery. *Campbell v. State*, 227 So.2d 873 (Fla. 1969).

Factors to be considered in determining whether there has been a break in the chain of circumstances include the relationship between the underlying felony and the homicide in point of time, place, and causation. One commentator suggests that in the case of flight, the most important consideration is whether the fleeing felon has reached a "place of temporary safety." LaFave, Substantive Criminal Law, § 7.5 (1986). We also note that the determination of whether the act of escape or flight is a continuous part of the accomplished crime or whether the defendant has reached a place of temporary safety is a question for the trier of fact. See *Commonwealth v. Dellelo*, 209 N.E.2d 303 (1965).

In this case the appellant was spotted by a police officer approximately 25 minutes after the robbery occurred. The appellant, in his brief, states that he and his accomplice planned to rendezvous and split up the fruits of the robbery. We find that a rational trier of fact could find, and indeed did find, that the homicide occurred in furtherance of the robbery. Nothing in the record indicates that the appellant had reached a place of temporary safety. The homicide was clearly a result of the high-speed chase necessitated by the appellant's attempt to flee the area of the crime. It is a legitimate and logical assumption that one who plans a robbery and carries it out has also planned to escape from the scene of the crime. His flight is an integral part of the crime. Since asportation is an element of robbery, the felony is still in progress while the defendant is fleeing from the scene with the stolen property. We find the evidence sufficient to support the appellant's felony murder conviction.

* * *

Accordingly, we affirm the judgment of the trial court.

Temporary place of safety test ＊

QUESTIONS

1.   Why do you think nearly all U.S. jurisdictions limit felony murder liability to those deaths that occur during the commission of a qualifying felony, or immediate flight therefrom? What do you think about this limitation? Why?

2.   How do we know when immediate flight from the scene of a felony is over? The court in this case determined there was sufficient evidence that the defendant had not reached a "temporary place of safety," and thus, he was still in immediate flight from the robbery. What do you think of this rule that examines a place of temporary safety? Explain your answer.

Three final limitations on the felony murder rule require attention. First, some jurisdictions limit the application of the rule to when innocent, third parties are killed. Thus, if an accomplice or co-conspirator dies during the actual or attempted commission of an inherently dangerous felony, then no felony murder will be deemed to have taken place. Second, if one is being charged with felony murder due to the actions of an accomplice and/or co-conspirator, some states require that the killing be "in furtherance of" the felony before liability for felony murder can be imputed via complicity theory. This effectively eliminates complicity liability for felony murder for any homicide that occurs outside the common plan of the felony.

And, lastly, there is limitation on felony murder liability known as the *merger rule*. Plainly stated, manslaughter cannot be "merged" to serve as the underlying/qualifying felony in felony murder. The reason for this is simple. If manslaughter qualified as one of the inherently dangerous felonies that triggered the application of the felony murder rule, then no one would ever escape liability for murder since even manslaughter killings – those without malice – would then trigger the application of the felony murder rule. Accordingly, the merger rule prohibits manslaughter from ever so qualifying as the underlying felony.

C. Manslaughter

Manslaughter is defined as the killing of a human being without malice. There are three types of manslaughter: voluntary manslaughter, involuntary manslaughter, and unlawful act manslaughter. We will address each of these in turn.

1. Voluntary Manslaughter

Voluntary manslaughter is a type of homicide in which the defendant entertains specific intent to kill, but the intent is formed under special circumstances which the law recognizes as mitigating factors. There are three types of situations in which recognizes someone might form intent to kill and act on it, yet does not deserve to punished for murder.

The first of the three situations which mitigates what would otherwise be murder down to manslaughter is called "imperfect self defense." Recall that if one acts in self defense, but is mistaken either about either the nature or existence of imminent harm, or the reasonableness of the force used, he or she is not deprived of the defense just because the actor was mistaken. The mistake of fact, if both honest and reasonable, can be a defense. But when a defendant makes a subjectively honest, but objectively unreasonable mistake, the common law would label the homicide as being one of voluntary manslaughter due to the doctrine of *imperfect self defense*. Under this doctrine, an unreasonable mistake regarding the defendant's acting in self defense that resulted in the death of another reduced a charge of murder to manslaughter.

The second circumstance is when the defendant was provoked into killing the victim and the provocation is deemed "legally adequate." Legally adequate provocation is quite limited, such as when the defendant is the victim of some unlawful act. In some jurisdictions, the criminal statutes enumerate the crimes which qualify as legally adequate provocation, often limiting them to battery, mutual combat, and sudden discovery of adultery.

The final circumstance under which murder may be mitigated to voluntary manslaughter is when the intent to kill is formed during the "heat of passion" due to the actions of the person killed. Heat of passion is defined as anything that would cause the ordinary, reasonable, prudent person to have formed the desire to kill under similar circumstances. The following case demonstrates the fine lines that the law will draw when one argues a killing in the heat of passion, even upon what might otherwise qualify as legally adequate provocation.

The PEOPLE of the State of Illinois, Plaintiff-Appellee, v. William SIMPSON, Defendant-Appellant. 473 N.E.2d 350 (Ill. Ct. App. 1984).

Judge Romiti:

Defendant was convicted for the murder of William Drake. The evidence produced at the suppression hearing and at trial established that the defendant had suspected Drake of having an adulterous relationship with the defendant's wife, Tecumseh Berry. Defendant and Berry were married on August 7, 1979, while defendant was incarcerated in the penitentiary. Berry testified that she had known Drake for about 16 to 17 years and had been having an affair with him, but that it terminated in August 1980. The defendant was released from prison in August 1980 and moved in with Berry, who was living with her mother and son (defendant was not the father of Berry's son). The record is unclear whether the defendant suspected the involvement between Berry and the decedent prior to his release from the penitentiary or only after he was released and began living with Berry. The record also does not disclose explicitly whether the defendant was aware of their prior involvement when he married Berry, although there was evidence that the defendant did not personally know Drake or his specific identity before his release. In any event, the record establishes that the defendant, once released, suspected that the relationship had not terminated.

The record indicates that during the first few months that the defendant lived with Berry, the defendant on more than one occasion confronted Berry with his suspicions of her relationship with Drake; when Berry denied any involvement, defendant would become angry. There is some evidence in the record that on at least one occasion the defendant became violent and threatened Berry with a knife during the course of the confrontation. There is also evidence in the record that on at least a few occasions the defendant threatened to "get" Drake because of his relationship with Berry, or made some equivalent threat against him.

The last confrontation between the parties occurred on October 16 or 17, 1980, roughly two weeks before Drake was killed. At that time, Berry, her mother, and Drake were talking in Berry's living room. The defendant entered the room; apparently he had returned to gather his belongings because he was moving out of the residence, since the defendant and Berry were considering divorce. When defendant entered the room and discovered Drake in the presence of Berry and her mother, defendant crudely informed Drake that he wanted Drake to terminate his involvement with his wife. Drake responded that the defendant should not use vulgar language about Berry in front of her mother, and told the defendant that they could discuss the matter outside the presence of the others. The defendant answered that he would "see you [Drake] later" and went to another room to gather his possessions. He then departed from the apartment.

On October 29, 1980, Drake was found lying on the street at the corner of 71st Street and Stewart Avenue. He had one gunshot wound in the lower back. It was stipulated at trial that the gunshot wound was the cause of death. There were no eyewitnesses to the incident, nor anyone who had seen Drake or any other individual at or near the scene near the time of death. No fingerprints were recovered from the scene, nor any weapon. No firearm linked to the event was ever recovered.

Detectives of the Chicago police department initially assigned to investigate the homicide spoke with Berry, her mother, and her son a few days after the incident and learned from them of the confrontations between the defendant, Berry, and Drake regarding her relationship with Drake. Although the officers attempted to locate the defendant to speak with him regarding the incident, they were unable to find him. As a result, they left word at the home of his mother that they wished to speak with him. They also issued a stop order – an internal police notification to fellow officers that the individual is wanted for questioning.

On December 28, 1980, at roughly 3:30 p.m., defendant and a companion were arrested for shoplifting from a grocery store and taken to the Sixth District station. The defendant gave the name of "Oscar Williamson" and gave an incorrect date as his date of birth. He was charged with theft and fingerprinted. At roughly 10 p.m., officers of the Sixth District determined that his true identity was William Simpson and that he was wanted by Area 3 officers for questioning regarding the Drake homicide. The defendant was transported by Detectives Brankin and Moser of Area 3 to that station house at roughly 11:30 p.m. that evening. When the defendant inquired about the reasons for such transportation, the detectives told him he was wanted for questioning and advised him of his rights under *Miranda*.

Defendant was questioned regarding the homicide at approximately 9:30 a.m. the following morning. At that time, he was questioned by Detectives McWeeny and Higgins, who first advised him of his *Miranda* rights. According to the officers, the defendant voluntarily explained to them that he had shot Drake on October 29. The defendant specifically told them, in substance, the following sequence of events which culminated in Drake's death. Defendant stated that following his confrontation with Drake in the presence of Berry and her mother on October 16 or 17, he contacted Drake and arranged to meet with him at the corner of 71st Street and Stewart Avenue at 11 p.m. on October 29, 1980. At this encounter, the defendant again informed Drake that he wanted him to end his relationship with Berry. Drake responded that he had known Berry longer than the defendant had. The defendant stated that this was not important since Berry was his wife. Drake then asked whether the defendant was threatening him; the defendant responded that Drake could "take it any way he wanted to." Drake then turned away from the defendant and opened the door and reached into his van, next to which the two had been standing during the conversation. As Drake reached into the van, the defendant shot him in the back. The defendant then fled the scene. The defendant gave substantially the same explanation of his commission of the crime to Assistant State's Attorney Dane Cleven, to whom the defendant spoke later on the morning of December 30. The defendant refused to sign a written confession.

At the trial, defendant testified on his own behalf. He denied knowing whether Berry was having an affair, denied knowing Drake, denied making any threats of harm to Drake, and denied confronting Drake about his relationship with Berry in the living room of Berry's apartment on October 16 or 17. He also maintained that he had not shot Drake but presented the alibi that he had been at his mother's house playing cards on the night in question. Following a jury trial, defendant was found guilty of murder and sentenced to 32 years' imprisonment. His notice of appeal was timely filed.

Defendant argues that the trial court committed reversible error in its refusal to give defendant's tendered jury instructions on voluntary manslaughter based upon unreasonable belief in self-defense and sudden and intense passion resulting from serious provocation. Defendant claims that the testimony of two State's witnesses, Officer James Higgins and Assistant State's Attorney Dane Cleven, provided the evidence which would have supported such instructions. Both Higgins and Cleven testified to the inculpatory statements of the defendant during custodial interrogation. Higgins stated that the defendant said that he met Drake at approximately 11 p.m. on October 29 to discuss Drake's involvement with the defendant's wife. According to Higgins, the defendant stated that he said to Drake:

> You f--- around with my wife and I don't want you doing that. [Drake then said:] Listen I've known her longer than you have and [the defendant] said that doesn't matter you're f--- around with her and I want you to stop. [Drake] says are you threatening me and [the defendant] says you can take it any way you want and with this [Drake] turned around toward the van opened up the door and started to reach in and [the defendant] says I pulled my gun and shot him, shot him in the back. I didn't want to give him a chance.

Cleven's testimony of the defendant's statement was substantially similar, but he also stated that the defendant told him that Drake had not threatened him and that he did not see that Drake had a weapon. (No weapon was recovered from the scene or from the defendant.)

The defendant first argues that this testimony was sufficient to support a jury instruction for voluntary manslaughter based on unreasonable belief in self-defense. We disagree.

Voluntary manslaughter occurs where a person intentionally or knowingly kills an individual [because] at the time of the killing he believes the circumstances to be such that, if they existed, would justify or exonerate the killing, but his belief is unreasonable. An individual is justified in the use of force which is intended or likely to cause death or great bodily harm only if he reasonably believes that such force is necessary to prevent imminent death or great bodily harm to himself or another or the commission of a forcible felony.

Here, the trial court concluded that there was no evidence justifying a voluntary manslaughter instruction, and we cannot say that this conclusion was manifestly erroneous. The defendant's argument, in our view, is based upon the mere factual reference of Officer Higgins to Drake's movement away from the defendant in order to reach into his van. According to Cleven, however, the defendant stated that Drake did not threaten him and that he did not see that Drake had a weapon. Consequently, there was nothing in the testimony from which the jury reasonably could have concluded that the defendant subjectively believed at the time that Drake was about to commit an aggressive act or that the defendant subjectively believed the use of force was necessary for his own self-defense. As a result, there was insufficient evidence in the record to justify a voluntary manslaughter instruction based on a mistaken belief in self-defense.

Defendant also claims that the trial court should have given the jury a voluntary manslaughter instruction based on sudden and intense passion resulting from serious provocation. He argues that such passion resulted from his discovery that Drake was having an adulterous relationship with his wife, Berry. We disagree.

An instruction based on discovery-of-adultery provocation has generally been limited to instances where the parties are discovered in the act of adultery or immediately before or after such act, and the killing immediately follows such discovery. This general rule has been the subject of exception in limited circumstances where the revelation of adultery was but one of a series of statements or circumstances found by the courts to be so provoking as to constitute an exception to the general rule in Illinois that words alone cannot constitute sufficient provocation to reduce a murder to voluntary manslaughter. Here, the facts do not establish that the defendant shot Drake immediately following discovery of the parties in an adulterous act. Nor do the facts indicate a series of exceptionally provoking statements or circumstances within the limited exception justifying a voluntary manslaughter instruction. As a result, we find no error in the trial court's refusal to give a voluntary manslaughter instruction based upon discovery-of-adultery provocation.

QUESTIONS

1. Simpson argued two grounds for a voluntary manslaughter instruction: imperfect self defense and sudden discovery of adultery. Why were both rejected by the court? Do you agree with the court's analysis of both issues? Why or why not?

2. Simpson's own statements were the main evidence against him. Prior to his having made inculpatory statements to the police during questioning, the only real evidence against him was circumstantial – the threats he allegedly made to his wife and the victim, Drake. The court pointed out "[t]here were no eyewitnesses to the incident, nor anyone who had seen Drake or any other individual at or near the scene near the time of death. No fingerprints were recovered from the scene, nor any weapon. No firearm linked to the event was ever recovered." Assume that Drake had not made any statements to the police. Do you think there would have been enough evidence to convict Simpson? Why or why not?

2. Involuntary Manslaughter and Criminally Negligent Homicide

Involuntary manslaughter is the unintended killing of another human being. Accordingly, intent to kill *never* exists for this crime. The victim's death was not intended, but the actions causing the victim's death were grossly negligent or reckless such that it is fair to hold the defendant liable for the killing.

There are at least three types of homicides in which the victim's death was unintentional. The difference between the three levels of homicide is, therefore, not the result, but rather the defendant's mens rea. As covered above, if the defendant acted so grossly recklessly such that the conduct manifests and extreme indifference to the value of human life, then the person can be held liable for murder in the second degree under the depraved heart murder rule. But if the person was simply reckless (as opposed to grossly reckless), then the crime is involuntary manslaughter. In other words, if the defendant consciously disregarded a known risk of death or serious bodily injury that did not rise to the level of manifesting an extreme disregard for the value of human life, then the mens rea requirement for involuntary manslaughter is satisfied.

In addition to acts of regular criminal recklessness, acts of gross negligence – an objective standard – can also qualify for involuntary manslaughter liability. As with recklessness and gross recklessness, the difference between negligence and gross negligence is one of degree, not one of kind. Gross negligence is present when some inherently dangerous instrumentality (e.g., a deadly weapon) is used. When someone's grossly negligent acts unintentionally causes the death of another human being, an involuntary manslaughter will be deemed to have taken place.

In contrast to acts of gross negligence, if someone is merely criminally negligent, then the requisite mens rea involuntary manslaughter is not met. Such acts are the realm of another homicide crime called *criminally negligent homicide*. A person commits criminally negligent homicide when he or she, acting with criminal negligence, causes the death of another person. This "catch all" type of homicide offense does not exist in all jurisdictions.

Before illustrating the application of an involuntary manslaughter law with a case, it should be pointed out that involuntary manslaughter is often the crime with which people are charged when someone dies in a car accident. By definition, a car accident is just that – an accident; no intent to kill is present. But whether there will be homicide liability for a car accident depends upon the level of mens rea entertained by driver-at-fault. If the driver was grossly reckless (e.g., drag racing), a conviction for murder in the second degree would be proper. If the driver was reckless (e.g., speeding and tail-gaiting), then an involuntary manslaughter conviction would be proper. If the driver was criminally negligent (e.g., running a red light that the driver didn't see because he or she wasn't paying attention), then the law might deem that a criminal negligent homicide, although since a motor vehicle is an inherently dangerous instrumentality, such conduct might be deemed grossly negligent. Where would you put driving under the influence of alcohol or a controlled substance? Some states have passed special laws to cover deaths that occur while driving called *vehicular manslaughter* laws. Criminal homicide constitutes vehicular homicide when it is caused by driving a vehicle or vessel recklessly. Not all states have such a law, as such conduct is easily subsumed into their existing involuntary manslaughter statutes.

COMMONWEALTH of Massachusetts v. David R. TWITCHELL and Ginger TWITCHELL
617 N.E.2d 609 (Mass. 1993).

Wilkins, J.

David and Ginger Twitchell appeal from their convictions of involuntary manslaughter in connection with the April 8, 1986, death of their two and one-half year old son Robyn. Robyn died of the consequences of peritonitis caused by the perforation of his bowel which had been obstructed as a result of an anomaly known as Meckel's diverticulum. There was evidence that the condition could be corrected by surgery with a high success rate.

The defendants are practicing Christian Scientists who grew up in Christian Science families. They believe in healing by spiritual treatment. During Robyn's five-day illness from Friday, April 4, through Tuesday, April 8, they retained a Christian Science practitioner, a Christian Science nurse, and at one time consulted with Nathan Talbot, who held a position in the church known as the "Committee on Publication." As a result of that consultation, David Twitchell read a church publication concerning the legal rights and obligations of Christian Scientists in Massachusetts. That publication quoted a portion of [our state's criminal law][1] which, at least in the context of the crimes described, accepted remedial treatment by spiritual means alone as satisfying any parental obligation not to neglect a child or to provide a child with physical care. We shall subsequently discuss this statute in connection with the

---

[1] The spiritual treatment provision then read, as it does now, as follows: "A child shall not be deemed to be neglected or lack proper physical care for the sole reason that he is being provided remedial treatment by spiritual means alone in accordance with the tenets and practice of a recognized church or religious denomination by a duly accredited practitioner thereof." G. L. c. 273, § 1 (1992 ed.).

defendants' claim, rejected by the trial judge, that the spiritual treatment provision in [that law] protects them from criminal liability for manslaughter.

We need not recite in detail the circumstances of Robyn's illness. The jury would have been warranted in concluding that Robyn was in considerable distress and that, in the absence of their belief in and reliance on spiritual treatment, the parents of a child in his condition would normally have sought medical treatment in sufficient time to save that child's life. There was also evidence that the intensity of Robyn's distress ebbed and flowed, perhaps causing his parents to believe that prayer would lead to the healing of the illness. On the other hand, the jury would have been warranted in finding that the Twitchells were wanton or reckless in failing to provide medical care for Robyn, if parents have a legal duty to provide a child with medical care in such circumstances . . . .

We shall conclude that parents have a duty to seek medical attention for a child in Robyn's circumstances, the violation of which, if their conduct was wanton or reckless, could support a conviction of involuntary manslaughter and that the spiritual healing provision in G. L. c. 273, § 1, did not bar a prosecution for manslaughter in these circumstances. We further conclude, however, that special circumstances in this case would justify a jury's finding that the Twitchells reasonably believed that they could rely on spiritual treatment without fear of criminal prosecution. This affirmative defense should have been asserted and presented to the jury. Because it was not, there is a substantial risk of a miscarriage of justice in this case, and, therefore, the judgments must be reversed.

We shall first consider whether the law generally imposes a parental duty to provide medical services to a child, the breach of which can be the basis of a conviction for involuntary manslaughter. We thus put aside temporarily the question of what, if any, application the spiritual treatment provision in G. L. c. 273, § 1, has to this case.

The Commonwealth presented its case on the theory that each defendant was guilty of involuntary manslaughter because the intentional failure of each to seek medical attention for their son involved such "a high degree of likelihood that substantial harm will result to" him as to be wanton or reckless conduct. *Commonwealth v. Welansky*, 316 Mass. 383, 399, 55 N.E.2d 902 (1944). Our definition of involuntary manslaughter derives from the common law. A charge of involuntary manslaughter based on an omission to act can be proved only if the defendant had a duty to act and did not do so. That duty, however, is not limited to those duties whose violation would create civil liability.

The Commonwealth claims that the defendants owed an affirmative duty of care to their son which they wantonly or recklessly failed to perform. The duty to provide sufficient support for a child is legally enforceable in a civil proceeding against a parent. A breach of that duty is a misdemeanor. Where necessary to protect a child's well-being, the Commonwealth may intervene, over the parents' objections, to assure that needed services are provided. More important, for our current purposes, a parental duty of care has been recognized in the common law of homicide in this Commonwealth.

The defendants argue, however, that any common law duty of care does not include a duty to provide medical treatment and that there is no statute imposing such a duty except G. L. c. 273, § 1, which, in turn, in their view, provides them with complete protection against any criminal charge based on their failure to seek medical treatment for their son. In their argument that the common law of the Commonwealth does not include a duty to provide medical treatment, the defendants overlook *Commonwealth v. Gallison*, 383 Mass. 659, 421 N.E.2d 757 (1981). In that case, we upheld a conviction of manslaughter, saying that a parent who "made no effort to obtain medical help, knowing that her child was gravely ill," could be found guilty of wanton or reckless involuntary manslaughter for her child's death caused by her omission to meet her "duty to provide for the care and welfare of her child." The *Gallison* opinion did not rely on § 1 as the basis of the parent's duty to provide medical care. It relied rather on the more general duty of care underlying civil and criminal liability. There is, consequently, quite apart from § 1, a common law duty to provide medical services for a child, the breach of which can be the basis, in the appropriate circumstances, for the conviction of a parent for involuntary manslaughter.

We, therefore, consider the impact, if any, of G. L. c. 273, § 1, on this case. The defendants argue that the spiritual treatment provision in § 1 bars any involuntary manslaughter charge against a parent who relies, as they did, on spiritual treatment and who does not seek medical attention for his or her child, even if the parent's failure to seek such care would otherwise be wanton or reckless conduct. We disagree.

The Commonwealth asks us to eliminate any application of the spiritual treatment provision to this case by holding that the spiritual treatment provision is unconstitutional. The argument is based solely on the establishment of religion clause of the First Amendment to the Constitution of the United States and the equal protection clause of the Fourteenth Amendment to the Constitution of the United States. Apparently, the latter theory was not raised below, and the former was raised but was not decided. These claims of unconstitutionality place the Commonwealth in the position of challenging the constitutionality of its own duly enacted statute. Issues of timeliness and standing are obvious. The retroactive invalidation of a statute on which a criminal defendant relied in justification of his conduct would present a serious fairness issue. Because we shall conclude that the spiritual treatment provision does not apply to foreclose a charge of involuntary manslaughter, we need resolve neither these preliminary questions nor the underlying constitutional one.

Section 1 of G. L. c. 273 provides no complete protection to a parent against a charge of involuntary manslaughter that is based on the parent's wanton or reckless failure to provide medical services to a child. Section 1 concerns child support and care in a chapter of the General Laws that deals not so much with the punishment of criminal conduct as with motivating parents to fulfil their natural obligations of support. On the other hand, the principle underlying involuntary manslaughter is the Commonwealth's interest that persons within its territory should not be killed by the wanton and reckless conduct of others. It is unlikely that the Legislature placed the spiritual treatment provision in § 1 to provide a defense to, or to alter any definition of, common law homicide. There is no history to § 1 that suggests that the spiritual treatment provision carries any message beyond § 1 itself. The act that added the spiritual treatment provision was entitled "An Act defining the term 'proper physical care' under the law relative to care of children by a parent." The amendment's concern seems focused on the subject matter of § 1 and certainly not directed toward changing the common law of homicide. Indeed, that was the view expressed at the time by a representative of the Christian Science Church.

The spiritual treatment provision refers to neglect and lack of proper physical care, which are concepts set forth earlier in § 1, as then amended, as bases for punishment: (1) neglect to provide support and (2) wilful failure to provide necessary and proper physical care. These concepts do not underlie involuntary manslaughter. Wanton or reckless conduct is not a form of negligence. Wanton or reckless conduct does not involve a wilful intention to cause the resulting harm. *See Commonwealth v. Welansky*, 316 Mass. 383, 397-398, 55 N.E.2d 902 (1944). An involuntary manslaughter verdict does not require proof of wilfulness. Thus, by its terms, the spiritual treatment provision in § 1 does not apply to involuntary manslaughter.

The defendants argue that the failure to extend the protection of the spiritual treatment provision to them in this case would be a denial of due process of law because they lacked "fair warning" that their use of spiritual treatment could form the basis for a prosecution for manslaughter. Fair warning is part of the due process doctrine of vagueness, which requires that a penal statute define the criminal offense with sufficient definiteness that ordinary people can understand what conduct is prohibited and in a manner that does not encourage arbitrary and discriminatory enforcement. Many fair warning challenges involve statutes that are unconstitutionally vague on their face, such as vagrancy statutes. Even if a statute is clear on its face, there may not be fair warning in the circumstances of particular defendants. The defendants here argue that they have been denied fair warning in three different ways. They contend that fair warning (1) would be denied by an unforeseeable retroactive judicial interpretation that the spiritual treatment provision does not protect them(2) is denied by the existence of contradictory commands in the law of the Commonwealth, (3) is denied because they were officially misled by an opinion of the Attorney General of the Commonwealth. We find some merit only in the last of these contentions.

The defendants claim that a statute (G. L. c. 273, § 1) that clearly provided protection against criminal prosecution for a statutory crime did not give fair warning that it did not provide similar protection against prosecution for a more serious common law crime. For the reasons we have given, a charge of common law involuntary manslaughter is not barred by the spiritual treatment provision of § 1. That conclusion is not a surprise judicial interpretation of the kind that due process of law directs may not be applied retroactively.

There is no mixed signal from the coexistence of the spiritual treatment provision and the common law definition of involuntary manslaughter. The spiritual treatment provision protects against criminal charges of neglect and of wilful failure to provide proper medical care and says nothing about protection against criminal charges based on wanton or reckless conduct. The fact that at some point in a given case a parent's conduct may lose the protection of the spiritual treatment provision and may become subject to the application of the common law of homicide is not a circumstance that presents a due process of law "fair warning" violation.

The defendants argue that they were misled by an opinion of the Attorney General that caused them to conclude that they were protected by the spiritual treatment provision. The claim is that their manslaughter convictions violated their due process right to fair warning because they were entrapped for exercising a privilege which the State clearly had told them was available. There is, however, no evidence to support the contention that they relied directly on that opinion or that they knew of the Attorney General's opinion. Indeed it does not appear that the defendants made any argument to the trial judge that they relied on an official interpretation of the law.

Although the Twitchells were not aware of the Attorney General's opinion, they knew of a Christian Science publication called "Legal Rights and Obligations of Christian Scientists in Massachusetts." The defense offered the publication in evidence. The judge held a voir dire on the question whether to admit that portion of the publication which concerned the furnishing of proper physical care to a child and which David Twitchell had read on the Sunday or Monday before Robyn's death. The judge excluded the evidence, and, although the defendants objected at trial, they have not argued to us that the exclusion was error.

The relevant portion of the publication, after quoting G. L. c. 273, § 1, added, repeating, precisely but without citation, a portion of the Attorney General's opinion, that this criminal statute "expressly precludes imposition of criminal liability as a negligent parent for failure to provide medical care because of religious beliefs. But this does not prohibit the court from ordering medical treatment for children." There is no mention of potential criminal liability for involuntary manslaughter.

Although we have held that the law of the Commonwealth was not so unclear as to bar the prosecution of the defendants on due process of law principles, the Attorney General's opinion presents an additional element to the fairness assessment. It is obvious that the Christian Science Church's publication on the legal rights and obligations of Christian Scientists in Massachusetts relied on the Attorney General's 1975 opinion. That opinion was arguably misleading because of what it did not say concerning criminal liability for manslaughter. If the Attorney General had issued a caveat concerning manslaughter liability, the publication (which, based on such portions of it as appear in the record, is balanced and fair) would have referred to it in all reasonable likelihood. Nathan Talbot, who served as the Committee on Publication for the church and with whom the Twitchells spoke on the Sunday or Monday before Robyn's death, might well have given the Twitchells different advice.

Although it has long been held that "ignorance of the law is no defense," there is substantial justification for treating as a defense the belief that conduct is not a violation of law when a defendant has reasonably relied on an official statement of the law, later determined to be wrong, contained in an official interpretation of the public official who is charged by law with the responsibility for the interpretation or enforcement of the law defining the offense. See Model Penal Code § 2.04 (3) (b).

The Twitchells were entitled to present such an affirmative defense to the jury. The Attorney General was acting in an area of his official responsibilities. He is the chief law officer of the Commonwealth, with the power to set a unified and consistent legal policy for the Commonwealth. He is statutorily empowered to "give his opinion upon questions of law submitted to him" by the executive branch or the Legislature. G. L. c. 12, § 9 (1992 ed.). Whether a person would reasonably conclude that the Attorney General had ruled that § 1 provided protection against a manslaughter charge is a question of fact. Whether the defendants in turn reasonably relied on the church's publication and on the advice of the Committee on Publication, assuming that the construction of the Attorney General's opinion was reasonable, also presents questions of fact. In the resolution of these factual questions, the relevant portion of the Attorney General's opinion and the relevant portion of the church's publication will be admissible. The jury should also be advised of the terms of the spiritual treatment provision of § 1.

The Twitchells were entitled to present such an affirmative defense to the jury. We can hardly fault the judge for not doing so because the defense did not make such an argument or request a jury instruction on that defense. The issue was one that, if presented to them, could well have changed the jury's verdicts. Evidence showed that the defendants were deeply motivated toward helping their child, while at the same time seeking to practice their religion within the limits of what they were advised that the law permitted. The issue of their reliance on advice that had origins in the Attorney General's opinion should have been before the jury. Therefore, the failure to present the affirmative defense to the jury, along with the relevant portion of the church's publication which the judge excluded, created a substantial risk of a miscarriage of justice requiring that we reverse the convictions, even in the absence of a request for jury instruction on the subject. For these reasons, the judgments must be reversed, the verdicts must be set aside, and the cases remanded for a new trial, if the district attorney concludes that such a prosecution is necessary in the interests of justice.

QUESTIONS

1.   The death of the Twitchell's child could have been prevented by medical intervention. The Twitchells, however, did not believe in seeking medical attention for religious reasons. Because there were due process concerns based on the principle of legality (see Chapter 1), their convictions were overturned and a new trial was ordered. But the court made it clear that their religious beliefs do not excuse them from their legal duty to provide care – including medical treatment – to their child. A parent opting of spiritual healing once informed of a risk of death or serious bodily injury, therefore, can be the basis of involuntary manslaughter liability. Critique this rule. In your analysis, be sure to include a discussion of the First Amendment's protections regarding the free exercise of one's religion. Also include a discussion of the rights of the child.

2.   Recall that mistake of law is rarely a defense to a crime. There are, however, some limited circumstances when a mistake as to the existence or meaning of a criminal law can be a defense to a crime, two of which arguably applicable in this case: a mistake of law founded upon an official misstatement of the law, and a law that is so vague as to render it violative of the principle of legality embedded in the constitutional guarantee of due process. How did the court deal with each of these issues? Critique the outcome on both.

3.   What if a parent is unaware that his or her child is so sick that there is a risk of death? If the ordinary, reasonable prudent parent would have been aware of the risk, then the parent was criminally negligent. But "regular" criminal negligence is insufficient for involuntary manslaughter liability; it would only be enough for a conviction for criminally negligent homicide. But how do we know what was going through a parent's mind? Can a parent be so grossly negligent, under an objective standard, to justify involuntary manslaughter liability? Explain your answer, giving a specific example to illustrate your position.

4.   The *Twitchell* court cited the case of *Commonwealth v. Welansky*, 55 N.E.2d 902 (Mass. 1944). In *Welansky*, the defendant operated a nightclub. He ordered his employees to block or lock all of the fire doors to the club so customers could not leave without paying. One night, a match ignited

flammable decorations in the club, starting a fire. Many patrons were killed since they could not escape through the fire doors. The defendant's conviction for involuntary manslaughter was upheld on appeal because his conduct was deemed to be reckless in light of the substantial likelihood of resulting harm. Do you think that *Welansky* and *Twitchell* stand for the proposition that an objective standard of recklessness (rather than the normal subjective standard of recklessness that requires conscious disregard of a known risk) can be used to impose liability for involuntary manslaughter? If so, why? If not, how else might the results in these cases be explained in terms of the applicable mens rea standards?

3. Unlawful Act Manslaughter

Although this crime is disappearing today, approximately half of the states have an unlawful act manslaughter law. These laws are similar to felony murder laws insofar as they impose homicide liability on an actor who unintentionally causes the death of another human being during the commission of an unlawful act. Recall that felony murder liability is predicated on the underlying act being an inherently dangerous felony. Those unlawful acts that do not so qualify – felonies that are not inherently dangerous and misdemeanors – can be the basis of unlawful act manslaughter liability.

Recall, though, that since manslaughter, even unlawful act manslaughter, is considered to be a *mala in se* crime, the underlying unlawful act must not be one of strict liability for the doctrine of transferred intent to work. There must be some criminal mens rea for the underlying unlawful act, even if only negligence. *See People v. Stuart,* 302 P.2d 5 (Cal. 1956), in Chapter 2.

D. Suicide, Assisting Suicide, and Euthanasia

Criminal law was developed at a time when medicine was not able to keep people alive via artificial means. As science has progressed, the criminal law has also had to adapt. Courts are hesitant to step into this arena, though, often finding it the realm of legislatures. With the exception a very small minority of jurisdictions, nearly all states have clung to the common law tradition that suicide, assisted suicide, and active euthanasia are all criminal offenses.

At common law, **suicide** was a crime. Of course, if successful, the defendant was dead, so one might think it was a crime only in theory. But actually, the trial for the crime could go forward against the defendant *in absentia*. If convicted, the decedent's estate could be forfeited to the crown. The logic underlying such a law was that one of the King's taxpayers, who should be alive and paying taxes, no longer was. Suicide laws allowed the crown to collect monies from those who ended their own lives prematurely as a penalty for have "cheated" the crown out of the taxed that would have been paid until the decedent had died a natural death. Today, many states continue to criminally prohibit suicide. Prosecutions, however, are exceedingly rare. Of course, a suicide attempt is therefore also a crime. But if someone attempts to commit suicide, again, it is very rare that a criminal prosecution takes place, as police and prosecutorial discretion are exercised in a manner that attempts to get treatment for such a person, not inflict punishment.

Because suicide is illegal, assisting someone in the commission of suicide is also illegal. Normal rules of complicity – aiding and abetting – apply to such acts, making the person who assists another in a suicide an accomplice. But what if the assistance one gives another is done out of a sense of compassion, say to ease the suffering of a terminally ill person? Such conduct is referred to as **euthanasia**.

Passive euthanasia is legal in the United States. It is defined as the withdrawal of medical aid and/or treatment such that nature can take its course. Living wills and durable health care powers of attorney are documents designed to insure that someone's constitutional right to refuse medical treatment is honored. *See Cruzan v. Director of Missouri Dept. of Health*, 497 U.S. 261 (1990). In contrast, active euthanasia, or mercy killing, is illegal in the United States. The rule is clear: one who intentionally kills another, even if their purpose is to end suffering, is guilty of murder.

Some Scandinavian countries and Australia have recently legalized active euthanasia. And Oregon voters passed a referendum permitting active euthanasia under limited circumstances, although the validity of the Oregon law is being challenged in the courts at the time of the writing of this book. Dr. Jack Kevorkian has nearly single-handedly brought the issue of active euthanasia into the national spotlight in the last decade or so. He has been acquitted of murder a few times on the basis that his intent, in assisting terminally ill people to commit suicide, was not to kill, but to ease suffering. While, as stated just a few sentences ago, that distinction is technically legally irrelevant, jury nullification clearly played a large role in his acquittals.

While there is a distinction made between actively killing, and passively allowing someone to die, as illustrated by the following case, some critics have argued the difference is one that asserts form over substance. At least two United States Circuit Courts of Appeals thought so when they declared there to be a constitutional right to commit suicide, one under a right to privacy analysis, the other under an equal protection analysis. The Michigan Supreme Court in *People v. Kevorkian*, 527 N. W. 2d 714 (1994), *cert. denied*, 514 U.S. 1083 (1995), disagreed. The Supreme Court resolved these conflicting ruling in the following companion cases.

WASHINGTON, et al., Petitioners, v. Harold GLUCKSBERG et al.
117 S. Ct. 2258 (1997),
and the companion case of
Dennis C. VACCO, Attorney General of New York, et al., Petitioners, v. Timothy E. QUILL, et al.
117 S. Ct. 2293 (1997).

[The Due Process Clause Part of the Decision: *Washington v. Glucksberg*]

The question presented in this case is whether Washington's prohibition against "causing" or "aiding" a suicide offends the Fourteenth Amendment to the United States Constitution. We hold that it does not.

It has always been a crime to assist a suicide in the State of Washington. In 1854, Washington's first Territorial Legislature outlawed "assisting another in the commission of self-murder." Today, Washington law provides: "A person is guilty of promoting a suicide attempt when he knowingly causes or aids another person to attempt suicide." Promoting a suicide attempt is a felony, punishable by up to five years' imprisonment and up to a $10,000 fine. At the same time, Washington's Natural Death Act, enacted in 1979, states that the "withholding or withdrawal of life-sustaining treatment" at a patient's direction "shall not, for any purpose, constitute a suicide."

Under Washington's Natural Death Act, "adult persons have the fundamental right to control the decisions relating to the rendering of their own health care, including the decision to have life-sustaining treatment withheld or withdrawn in instances of a terminal condition or permanent unconscious condition." In Washington, "any adult person may execute a directive directing the withholding or withdrawal of life-sustaining treatment in a terminal condition or permanent unconscious condition," and a physician who, in accordance with such a directive, participates in the withholding or withdrawal of life-sustaining treatment is immune from civil, criminal, or professional liability.

John Doe, Jane Roe, and James Poe, plaintiffs in the District Court, were then in the terminal phases of serious and painful illnesses. They declared that they were mentally competent and desired assistance in ending their lives. The plaintiffs asserted "the existence of a liberty interest protected by the Fourteenth Amendment which extends to a personal choice by a mentally competent, terminally ill adult to commit physician-assisted suicide." Relying primarily on *Planned Parenthood v. Casey*, 505 U.S. 833 (1992), and *Cruzan v. Director, Missouri Dept. of Health*, 497 U.S. 261 (1990), the District Court agreed and concluded that Washington's assisted-suicide ban is unconstitutional because it "places an undue burden on the exercise of [that] constitutionally protected liberty interest." The District Court also decided that the Washington statute violated the Equal Protection Clause's requirement that "'all persons similarly situated . . . be treated alike.'"

A panel of the Court of Appeals for the Ninth Circuit reversed, emphasizing that "in the two hundred and five years of our existence no constitutional right to aid in killing oneself has ever been asserted and upheld by a court of final jurisdiction." The Ninth Circuit reheard the case en banc, reversed the panel's decision, and affirmed the District Court. Like the District Court, the en banc Court of Appeals emphasized our *Casey* and *Cruzan* decisions. The court also discussed what it described as "historical" and "current societal attitudes" toward suicide and assisted suicide, concluded that "the Constitution encompasses a due process liberty interest in controlling the time and manner of one's death — that there is, in short, a constitutionally-recognized 'right to die.'" After "weighing and then balancing" this interest against Washington's various interests, the court held that the State's assisted-suicide ban was unconstitutional "as applied to terminally ill competent adults who wish to hasten their deaths with medication prescribed by their physicians." The court did not reach the District Court's equal-protection holding. We granted certiorari, and now reverse.

I

We begin, as we do in all due-process cases, by examining our Nation's history, legal traditions, and practices. In almost every State — indeed, in almost every western democracy — it is a crime to assist a suicide. The States' assisted-suicide bans are not innovations. Rather, they are longstanding expressions of the States' commitment to the protection and preservation of all human life. Indeed, opposition to and condemnation of suicide — and, therefore, of assisting suicide — are consistent and enduring themes of our philosophical, legal, and cultural heritages.

More specifically, for over 700 years, the Anglo-American common-law tradition has punished or otherwise disapproved of both suicide and assisting suicide. In the 13th century, Henry de Bracton, one of the first legal-treatise writers, observed that "just as a man may commit felony by slaying another so may he do so by slaying himself." The real and personal property of one who killed himself to avoid conviction and punishment for a crime were forfeit to the king; however, thought Bracton, "if a man slays himself in weariness of life or because he is unwilling to endure further bodily pain . . . [only] his movable goods [were] confiscated." Thus, "the principle that suicide of a sane person, for whatever reason, was a punishable felony was . . . introduced into English common law." Centuries later, Sir William Blackstone, whose Commentaries on the Laws of England not only provided a definitive summary of the common law but was also a primary legal authority for 18th and 19th century American lawyers, referred to suicide as "self-murder" and "the pretended heroism, but real cowardice, of the Stoic philosophers, who destroyed themselves to avoid those ills which they had not the fortitude to endure . . . ." Blackstone emphasized that "the law has . . . ranked [suicide] among the highest crimes," although, anticipating later developments, he conceded that the harsh and shameful punishments imposed for suicide "border a little upon severity."

For the most part, the early American colonies adopted the common-law approach. For example, the legislators of the Providence Plantations, which would later become Rhode Island, declared, in 1647, that "self-murder is by all agreed to be the most unnatural, and it is by this present Assembly declared, to be that, wherein he that doth it, kills himself out of a premeditated hatred against his own life or other humor: . . . his goods and chattels are the king's custom, but not his debts nor lands; but in case he be an infant, a lunatic, mad or distracted man, he forfeits nothing." Virginia also required ignominious burial for suicides, and their estates were forfeit to the crown.

Over time, however, the American colonies abolished these harsh common-law penalties. William Penn abandoned the criminal-forfeiture sanction in Pennsylvania in 1701, and the other colonies (and later, the other States) eventually followed this example. Zephaniah Swift, who would later become Chief Justice of Connecticut, wrote in 1796 that there can be no act more contemptible, than to attempt to punish an offender for a crime, by exercising a mean act of revenge upon lifeless clay, that is insensible of the punishment. There can be no greater cruelty, than the inflicting [of] a punishment, as the forfeiture of goods, which must fall solely on the innocent offspring of the offender. . . . [Suicide] is so abhorrent to the feelings of mankind, and that strong love of life which is implanted in the human heart, that it cannot be so frequently committed, as to become dangerous to society. There can of course be no necessity of any punishment.

This statement makes it clear, however, that the movement away from the common law's harsh sanctions did not represent an acceptance of suicide; rather, as Chief Justice Swift observed, this change reflected the growing consensus that it was unfair to punish the suicide's family for his wrongdoing. Nonetheless, although States moved away from Blackstone's treatment of suicide, courts continued to condemn it as a grave public wrong.

That suicide remained a grievous, though nonfelonious, wrong is confirmed by the fact that colonial and early state legislatures and courts did not retreat from prohibiting assisting suicide. Swift, in his early 19th century treatise on the laws of Connecticut, stated that "if one counsels another to commit suicide, and the other by reason of the advice kills himself, the advisor is guilty of murder as principal." This was the well established common-law view, as was the similar principle that the consent of a homicide victim is "wholly immaterial to the guilt of the person who caused [his death]. And the prohibitions against assisting suicide never contained exceptions for those who were near death. Rather, "the life of those to whom life had become a burden – of those who [were] hopelessly diseased or fatally wounded – nay, even the lives of criminals condemned to death, [were] under the protection of law, equally as the lives of those who [were] in the full tide of life's enjoyment, and anxious to continue to live."

The earliest American statute explicitly to outlaw assisting suicide was enacted in New York in 1828, and many of the new States and Territories followed New York's example. Between 1857 and 1865, a New York commission led by Dudley Field drafted a criminal code that prohibited "aiding" a suicide and, specifically, "furnishing another person with any deadly weapon or poisonous drug, knowing that such person intends to use such weapon or drug in taking his own life." By the time the Fourteenth Amendment was ratified, it was a crime in most States to assist a suicide. . . . In this century, the Model Penal Code also prohibited "aiding" suicide, prompting many States to enact or revise their assisted-suicide bans. The Code's drafters observed that "the interests in the sanctity of life that are represented by the criminal homicide laws are threatened by one who expresses a willingness to participate in taking the life of another, even though the act may be accomplished with the consent, or at the request, of the suicide victim."

Though deeply rooted, the States' assisted-suicide bans have in recent years been reexamined and, generally, reaffirmed. Because of advances in medicine and technology, Americans today are increasingly likely to die in institutions, from chronic illnesses. Public concern and democratic action are therefore sharply focused on how best to protect dignity and independence at the end of life, with the result that there have been many significant changes in state laws and in the attitudes these laws reflect. Many States, for example, now permit "living wills," surrogate health-care decision-making, and the withdrawal or refusal of life-sustaining medical treatment. At the same time, however, voters and legislators continue for the most part to reaffirm their States' prohibitions on assisting suicide.

The Washington statute at issue in this case was enacted in 1975 as part of a revision of that State's criminal code. Four years later, Washington passed its Natural Death Act, which specifically stated that the "withholding or withdrawal of life-sustaining treatment . . . shall not, for any purpose, constitute a suicide" and that "nothing in this chapter shall be construed to condone, authorize, or approve mercy killing . . . ." In 1991, Washington voters rejected a ballot initiative which, had it passed, would have permitted a form of physician-assisted suicide. Washington then added a provision to the Natural Death Act expressly excluding physician-assisted suicide.

California voters rejected an assisted-suicide initiative similar to Washington's in 1993. On the other hand, in 1994, voters in Oregon enacted, also through ballot initiative, that State's "Death With Dignity Act," which legalized physician-assisted suicide for competent, terminally ill adults. Since the Oregon vote, many proposals to legalize assisted-suicide have been and continue to be introduced in the States' legislatures, but none has been enacted. And just last year, Iowa and Rhode Island joined the overwhelming majority of States explicitly prohibiting assisted suicide. President Clinton signed the Federal Assisted Suicide Funding Restriction Act of 1997, which prohibits the use of federal funds in support of physician-assisted suicide.

II

The Due Process Clause guarantees more than fair process, and the "liberty" it protects includes more than the absence of physical restraint. The Clause also provides heightened protection against government interference with certain fundamental rights and liberty interests. In a long line of cases, we have held that, in addition to the specific freedoms protected by the Bill of Rights, the "liberty" specially protected by the Due Process Clause includes the rights to marry; to have children; to direct the education and upbringing of one's children; to marital privacy; to use contraception, to bodily integrity; and to abortion. We have also assumed, and strongly suggested, that the Due Process Clause protects the traditional right to refuse unwanted lifesaving medical treatment.

But we "have always been reluctant to expand the concept of substantive due process because guideposts for responsible decision-making in this unchartered area are scarce and open-ended." By extending constitutional protection to an asserted right or liberty interest, we, to a great extent, place the matter outside the arena of public debate and legislative action. We must therefore "exercise the utmost care whenever we are asked to break new ground in this field," lest the liberty protected by the Due Process Clause be subtly transformed into the policy preferences of the members of this Court.

Our established method of substantive-due-process analysis has two primary features: First, we have regularly observed that the Due Process Clause specially protects those fundamental rights and liberties which are, objectively, "deeply rooted in this Nation's history and tradition." Second, we have required in substantive-due-process cases a "careful description" of the asserted fundamental liberty interest. Our Nation's history, legal traditions, and practices thus provide the crucial "guideposts for responsible decision-making" that direct and restrain our exposition of the Due Process Clause.

Turning to the claim at issue here, the Court of Appeals stated that "properly analyzed, the first issue to be resolved is whether there is a liberty interest in determining the time and manner of one's death," or, in other words, "is there a right to die?" Similarly, respondents assert a "liberty to choose how to die" and a right to "control of one's final days," and describe the asserted liberty as "the right to choose a humane, dignified death," and "the liberty to shape death." As noted above, we have a tradition of carefully formulating the interest at stake in substantive-due-process cases. For example, although *Cruzan* is often described as a "right to die" case, we were, in fact, more precise: we assumed that the Constitution granted competent persons a "constitutionally protected right to refuse lifesaving hydration and nutrition." The Washington statute at issue in this case prohibits "aiding another person to attempt suicide," and, thus, the question before us is whether the "liberty" specially protected by the Due Process Clause includes a right to commit suicide which itself includes a right to assistance in doing so.

We now inquire whether this asserted right has any place in our Nation's traditions. Here, as discussed above, we are confronted with a consistent and almost universal tradition that has long rejected the asserted right, and continues explicitly to reject it today, even for terminally ill, mentally competent adults. To hold for respondents, we would have to reverse centuries of legal doctrine and practice, and strike down the considered policy choice of almost every State.

Respondents contend, however, that the liberty interest they assert is consistent with this Court's substantive-due-process line of cases, if not with this Nation's history and practice. Pointing to *Casey* and *Cruzan*, respondents read our jurisprudence in this area as reflecting a general tradition of "self-sovereignty," and as teaching that the "liberty" protected by the Due Process Clause includes "basic and intimate exercises of personal autonomy." According to respondents, our liberty jurisprudence, and the broad, individualistic principles it reflects, protects the "liberty of competent, terminally ill adults to make end-of-life decisions free of undue government interference." The question presented in this case, however, is whether the protections of the Due Process Clause include a right to commit suicide with another's assistance. With this "careful description" of respondents' claim in mind, we turn to *Casey* and *Cruzan*.

In *Cruzan*, we considered whether Nancy Beth Cruzan, who had been severely injured in an automobile accident and was in a persistive vegetative state, "had a right under the United States Constitution which would require the hospital to withdraw life-sustaining treatment" at her parents' request. We began with the observation that "at common law, even the touching of one person by another without consent and without legal justification was a battery." We then discussed the related rule that "informed consent is generally required for medical treatment." After reviewing a long line of relevant state cases, we concluded that "the common-law doctrine of informed consent is viewed as generally encompassing the right of a competent individual to refuse medical treatment." Next, we reviewed our own cases on the subject, and stated that "the principle that a competent person has a constitutionally protected liberty interest in refusing unwanted medical treatment may be inferred from our prior decisions." Therefore, "for purposes of [that] case, we assumed that the United States Constitution would grant a competent person a constitutionally protected right to refuse lifesaving hydration and nutrition." We concluded that, notwithstanding this right, the Constitution permitted Missouri to require clear and convincing evidence of an incompetent patient's wishes concerning the withdrawal of life-sustaining treatment.

Respondents contend that in *Cruzan* we "acknowledged that competent, dying persons have the right to direct the removal of life-sustaining medical treatment and thus hasten death," and that "the constitutional principle behind recognizing the patient's liberty to direct the withdrawal of artificial life support applies at least as strongly to the choice to hasten impending death by consuming lethal medication." Similarly, the Court of Appeals concluded that "*Cruzan*, by recognizing a liberty interest that includes the refusal of artificial provision of life-sustaining food and water, necessarily recognized a liberty interest in hastening one's own death."

The right assumed in *Cruzan*, however, was not simply deduced from abstract concepts of personal autonomy. Given the common-law rule that forced medication was a battery, and the long legal tradition protecting the decision to refuse unwanted medical treatment, our assumption was entirely consistent with this Nation's history and constitutional traditions. The decision to commit suicide with the assistance of another may be just as personal and profound as the decision to refuse unwanted medical treatment, but it has never enjoyed similar legal protection. Indeed, the two acts are widely and reasonably regarded as quite distinct. *See Quill v. Vacco*. In *Cruzan* itself, we recognized that most States outlawed assisted suicide – and even more do today – and we certainly gave no intimation that the right to refuse unwanted medical treatment could be somehow transmuted into a right to assistance in committing suicide.

Respondents also rely on *Casey*. There, the Court's opinion concluded that "the essential holding of *Roe v. Wade* should be retained and once again reaffirmed." We held, first, that a woman has a right, before her fetus is viable, to an abortion "without undue interference from the State"; second, that States may restrict post-viability abortions, so long as exceptions are made to protect a woman's life and health; and third, that the State has legitimate interests throughout a pregnancy in protecting the health of the woman and the life of the unborn child. In reaching this conclusion, the opinion discussed in some detail this Court's substantive-due-process tradition of interpreting the Due Process Clause to protect certain fundamental rights and "personal decisions relating to marriage, procreation, contraception, family relationships, child rearing, and education," and noted that many of those rights and liberties "involve the most intimate and personal choices a person may make in a lifetime."

The Court of Appeals, like the District Court, found Casey "'highly instructive'" and "'almost prescriptive'" for determining "'what liberty interest may inhere in a terminally ill person's choice to commit suicide'": "Like the decision of whether or not to have an abortion, the decision how and when to die is one of 'the most intimate and personal choices a person may make in a lifetime,' a choice 'central to personal dignity and autonomy.'" Similarly, respondents emphasize the statement in *Casey* that: "At the heart of liberty is the right to define one's own concept of existence, of meaning, of the universe, and of the mystery of human life. Beliefs about these matters could not define the attributes of personhood were they formed under compulsion of the State."

By choosing this language, the Court's opinion in *Casey* described, in a general way and in light of our prior cases, those personal activities and decisions that this Court has identified as so deeply rooted in our history and traditions, or so fundamental to our concept of constitutionally ordered liberty, that they are protected by the Fourteenth Amendment. The opinion moved from the recognition that liberty necessarily includes freedom of conscience and belief about ultimate considerations to the observation that "though the abortion decision may originate within the zone of conscience and belief, it is more than a philosophic exercise." That many of the rights and liberties protected by the Due Process Clause sound in personal autonomy does not warrant the sweeping conclusion that any and all important, intimate, and personal decisions are so protected, and Casey did not suggest otherwise.

The history of the law's treatment of assisted suicide in this country has been and continues to be one of the rejection of nearly all efforts to permit it. That being the case, our decisions lead us to conclude that the asserted "right" to assistance in committing suicide is not a fundamental liberty interest protected by the Due Process Clause. The Constitution also requires, however, that Washington's assisted-suicide ban be rationally related to legitimate government interests. This requirement is unquestionably met here. As the court below recognized, Washington's assisted-suicide ban implicates a number of state interests.

First, Washington has an "unqualified interest in the preservation of human life." The State's prohibition on assisted suicide, like all homicide laws, both reflects and advances its commitment to this interest. This interest is symbolic and aspirational as well as practical: "While suicide is no longer prohibited or penalized, the ban against assisted suicide and euthanasia shores up the notion of limits in human relationships. It reflects the gravity with which we view the decision to take one's own life or the life of another, and our reluctance to encourage or promote these decisions."

Respondents admit that "the State has a real interest in preserving the lives of those who can still contribute to society and enjoy life." The Court of Appeals also recognized Washington's interest in protecting life, but held that the "weight" of this interest depends on the "medical condition and the wishes of the person whose life is at stake." Washington, however, has rejected this sliding-scale approach and, through its assisted-suicide ban, insists that all persons' lives, from beginning to end, regardless of physical or mental condition, are under the full protection of the law. As we have previously affirmed, the States "may properly decline to make judgments about the 'quality' of life that a particular individual may enjoy." This remains true, as *Cruzan* makes clear, even for those who are near death.

Relatedly, all admit that suicide is a serious public-health problem, especially among persons in otherwise vulnerable groups. The State has an interest in preventing suicide, and in studying, identifying, and treating its causes. Those who attempt suicide – terminally ill or not – often suffer from depression or other mental disorders. The New York Task Force, however, expressed its concern that, because depression is difficult to diagnose, physicians and medical professionals often fail to respond adequately to seriously ill patients' needs. Thus, legal physician-assisted suicide could make it more difficult for the State to protect depressed or mentally ill persons, or those who are suffering from untreated pain, from suicidal impulses.

The State also has an interest in protecting the integrity and ethics of the medical profession. In contrast to the Court of Appeals' conclusion that "the integrity of the medical profession would [not] be threatened in any way by [physician-assisted suicide]," the American Medical Association, like many

285

other medical and physicians' groups, has concluded that "physician-assisted suicide is fundamentally incompatible with the physician's role as healer."

Next, the State has an interest in protecting vulnerable groups – including the poor, the elderly, and disabled persons – from abuse, neglect, and mistakes. The Court of Appeals dismissed the State's concern that disadvantaged persons might be pressured into physician-assisted suicide as "ludicrous on its face." We have recognized, however, the real risk of subtle coercion and undue influence in end-of-life situations. Similarly, the New York Task Force warned that "legalizing physician-assisted suicide would pose profound risks to many individuals who are ill and vulnerable. . . . The risk of harm is greatest for the many individuals in our society whose autonomy and well-being are already compromised by poverty, lack of access to good medical care, advanced age, or membership in a stigmatized social group." If physician-assisted suicide were permitted, many might resort to it to spare their families the substantial financial burden of end-of-life health-care costs. The State's interest here goes beyond protecting the vulnerable from coercion; it extends to protecting disabled and terminally ill people from prejudice, negative and inaccurate stereotypes, and "societal indifference." The State's assisted-suicide ban reflects and reinforces its policy that the lives of terminally ill, disabled, and elderly people must be no less valued than the lives of the young and healthy, and that a seriously disabled person's suicidal impulses should be interpreted and treated the same way as anyone else's.

Finally, the State may fear that permitting assisted suicide will start it down the path to voluntary and perhaps even involuntary euthanasia. The Court of Appeals struck down Washington's assisted-suicide ban only "as applied to competent, terminally ill adults who wish to hasten their deaths by obtaining medication prescribed by their doctors." Washington insists, however, that the impact of the court's decision will not and cannot be so limited. If suicide is protected as a matter of constitutional right, it is argued, "every man and woman in the United States must enjoy it." The Court of Appeals' decision, and its expansive reasoning, provide ample support for the State's concerns. The court noted, for example, that the "decision of a duly appointed surrogate decision maker is for all legal purposes the decision of the patient himself," that "in some instances, the patient may be unable to self-administer the drugs and . . . administration by the physician . . . may be the only way the patient may be able to receive them"; and that not only physicians, but also family members and loved ones, will inevitably participate in assisting suicide. Thus, it turns out that what is couched as a limited right to "physician-assisted suicide" is likely, in effect, a much broader license, which could prove extremely difficult to police and contain. Washington's ban on assisting suicide prevents such erosion.

We need not weigh exactly the relative strengths of these various interests. They are unquestionably important and legitimate, and Washington's ban on assisted suicide is at least reasonably related to their promotion and protection. We therefore hold that Wash. Rev. Code § 9A.36.060(1) (1994) does not violate the Fourteenth Amendment, either on its face or "as applied to competent, terminally ill adults who wish to hasten their deaths by obtaining medication prescribed by their doctors."

Throughout the Nation, Americans are engaged in an earnest and profound debate about the morality, legality, and practicality of physician-assisted suicide. Our holding permits this debate to continue, as it should in a democratic society. The decision of the en banc Court of Appeals is reversed, and the case is remanded for further proceedings consistent with this opinion.

[The Equal Protection Clause Part of the Decision: *Vacco v. Quill*]

In New York, as in most States, it is a crime to aid another to commit or attempt suicide,[2] but patients may refuse even lifesaving medical treatment. The question presented by this case is whether

---

[2]   N. Y. Penal Law § 125.15 (McKinney 1987) ("Manslaughter in the second degree") provides: "A person is guilty of manslaughter in the second degree when . . . (3) He intentionally causes or aids another person to commit suicide. Manslaughter in the second degree is a class C felony." Section 120.30 ("Promoting a suicide attempt") states: "A person is guilty of promoting a suicide attempt when he intentionally causes or aids another person to attempt suicide. Promoting a suicide attempt is a Class E felony."

New York's prohibition on assisting suicide therefore violates the Equal Protection Clause of the Fourteenth Amendment. We hold that it does not.

Petitioners are various New York public officials. Respondents Timothy E. Quill, Samuel C. Klagsbrun, and Howard A. Grossman are physicians who practice in New York. They assert that although it would be "consistent with the standards of [their] medical practices" to prescribe lethal medication for "mentally competent, terminally ill patients" who are suffering great pain and desire a doctor's help in taking their own lives, they are deterred from doing so by New York's ban on assisting suicide. Respondents, and three gravely ill patients who have since died, sued the State's Attorney General in the United States District Court. They urged that because New York permits a competent person to refuse life-sustaining medical treatment, and because the refusal of such treatment is "essentially the same thing" as physician-assisted suicide, New York's assisted-suicide ban violates the Equal Protection Clause.

The District Court disagreed: "It is hardly unreasonable or irrational for the State to recognize a difference between allowing nature to take its course, even in the most severe situations, and intentionally using an artificial death-producing device." The court noted New York's "obvious legitimate interests in preserving life, and in protecting vulnerable persons," and concluded that "under the United States Constitution and the federal system it establishes, the resolution of this issue is left to the normal democratic processes within the State."

The Court of Appeals for the Second Circuit reversed. 80 F.3d 716 (1996). The court determined that, despite the assisted-suicide ban's apparent general applicability, "New York law does not treat equally all competent persons who are in the final stages of fatal illness and wish to hasten their deaths," because "those in the final stages of terminal illness who are on life-support systems are allowed to hasten their deaths by directing the removal of such systems; but those who are similarly situated, except for the previous attachment of life-sustaining equipment, are not allowed to hasten death by self-administering prescribed drugs." In the court's view, "the ending of life by [the withdrawal of life-support systems] is nothing more nor less than assisted suicide." The Court of Appeals then examined whether this supposed unequal treatment was rationally related to any legitimate state interests, and concluded that "to the extent that [New York's statutes] prohibit a physician from prescribing medications to be self-administered by a mentally competent, terminally-ill person in the final stages of his terminal illness, they are not rationally related to any legitimate state interest." We granted certiorari, and now reverse.

The Equal Protection Clause commands that no State shall "deny to any person within its jurisdiction the equal protection of the laws." This provision creates no substantive rights. Instead, it embodies a general rule that States must treat like cases alike but may treat unlike cases accordingly.

New York's statutes outlawing assisting suicide affect and address matters of profound significance to all New Yorkers alike. They neither infringe fundamental rights nor involve suspect classifications. These laws are therefore entitled to a "strong presumption of validity."

On their faces, neither New York's ban on assisting suicide nor its statutes permitting patients to refuse medical treatment treat anyone differently than anyone else or draw any distinctions between persons. Everyone, regardless of physical condition, is entitled, if competent, to refuse unwanted lifesaving medical treatment; no one is permitted to assist a suicide. Generally speaking, laws that apply evenhandedly to all "unquestionably comply" with the Equal Protection Clause.

The Court of Appeals, however, concluded that some terminally ill people – those who are on life-support systems – are treated differently than those who are not, in that the former may "hasten death" by ending treatment, but the latter may not "hasten death" through physician-assisted suicide. This conclusion depends on the submission that ending or refusing lifesaving medical treatment "is nothing more nor less than assisted suicide." Unlike the Court of Appeals, we think the distinction between assisting suicide and withdrawing life-sustaining treatment, a distinction widely recognized and endorsed in the medical profession and in our legal traditions, is both important and logical; it is certainly rational.

The distinction comports with fundamental legal principles of causation and intent. First, when a patient refuses life-sustaining medical treatment, he dies from an underlying fatal disease or pathology; but if a patient ingests lethal medication prescribed by a physician, he is killed by that medication. Furthermore, a physician who withdraws, or honors a patient's refusal to begin, life-sustaining medical treatment purposefully intends, or may so intend, only to respect his patient's wishes and "to cease doing useless and futile or degrading things to the patient when [the patient] no longer stands to benefit from them." The same is true when a doctor provides aggressive palliative care; in some cases, painkilling drugs may hasten a patient's death, but the physician's purpose and intent is, or may be, only to ease his patient's pain. A doctor who assists a suicide, however, "must, necessarily and indubitably, intend primarily that the patient be made dead." Similarly, a patient who commits suicide with a doctor's aid necessarily has the specific intent to end his or her own life, while a patient who refuses or discontinues treatment might not.

The law has long used actors' intent or purpose to distinguish between two acts that may have the same result. Put differently, the law distinguishes actions taken "because of" a given end from actions taken "in spite of" their unintended but foreseen consequences. Given these general principles, it is not surprising that many courts, including New York courts, have carefully distinguished refusing life-sustaining treatment from suicide. And recently, the Michigan Supreme Court also rejected the argument that the distinction "between acts that artificially sustain life and acts that artificially curtail life" is merely a "distinction without constitutional significance – a meaningless exercise in semantic gymnastics," insisting that "the Cruzan majority disagreed and so do we." *People v. Kevorkian*, 447 Mich. 436, 471, 527 N. W. 2d 714, 728 (1994), *cert. denied*, 514 U.S. 1083 (1995).

Similarly, the overwhelming majority of state legislatures have drawn a clear line between assisting suicide and withdrawing or permitting the refusal of unwanted lifesaving medical treatment by prohibiting the former and permitting the latter. And "nearly all states expressly disapprove of suicide and assisted suicide either in statutes dealing with durable powers of attorney in health-care situations, or in 'living will' statutes." Thus, even as the States move to protect and promote patients' dignity at the end of life, they remain opposed to physician-assisted suicide.

New York is a case in point. The State enacted its current assisted-suicide statutes in 1965. Since then, New York has acted several times to protect patients' common-law right to refuse treatment [by allowing "Do Not Resuscitate Orders" and "Health Care Agents and Proxies"]. In so doing, however, the State has neither endorsed a general right to "hasten death" nor approved physician-assisted suicide. Quite the opposite: The State has reaffirmed the line between "killing" and "letting die."

This Court has also recognized, at least implicitly, the distinction between letting a patient die and making that patient die. In *Cruzan v. Director of Missouri Dept. of Health*, 497 U.S. 261, 278 (1990), we concluded that "the principle that a competent person has a constitutionally protected liberty interest in refusing unwanted medical treatment may be inferred from our prior decisions," and we assumed the existence of such a right for purposes of that case. But our assumption of a right to refuse treatment was grounded not, as the Court of Appeals supposed, on the proposition that patients have a general and abstract "right to hasten death," but on well established, traditional rights to bodily integrity and freedom from unwanted touching. In fact, we observed that "the majority of States in this country have laws imposing criminal penalties on one who assists another to commit suicide." *Cruzan* therefore provides no support for the notion that refusing life-sustaining medical treatment is "nothing more nor less than suicide."

For all these reasons, we disagree with respondents' claim that the distinction between refusing lifesaving medical treatment and assisted suicide is "arbitrary" and "irrational." Granted, in some cases, the line between the two may not be clear, but certainty is not required, even were it possible. Logic and contemporary practice support New York's judgment that the two acts are different, and New York may therefore, consistent with the Constitution, treat them differently. By permitting everyone to refuse unwanted medical treatment while prohibiting anyone from assisting a suicide, New York law follows a longstanding and rational distinction.

The judgment of the Court of Appeals is reversed. It is so ordered. Justices O'Connor, Stevens, Souter, Ginsburg, and Breyer concur in the judgment.

Justice O'Connor, concurring:[3]

Death will be different for each of us. For many, the last days will be spent in physical pain and perhaps the despair that accompanies physical deterioration and a loss of control of basic bodily and mental functions. Some will seek medication to alleviate that pain and other symptoms.

The Court frames the issue in this case as whether the Due Process Clause of the Constitution protects a "right to commit suicide which itself includes a right to assistance in doing so," and concludes that our Nation's history, legal traditions, and practices do not support the existence of such a right. I join the Court's opinions because I agree that there is no generalized right to "commit suicide." But respondents urge us to address the narrower question whether a mentally competent person who is experiencing great suffering has a constitutionally cognizable interest in controlling the circumstances of his or her imminent death. I see no need to reach that question in the context of the facial challenges to the New York and Washington laws at issue here. The parties and amici agree that in these States a patient who is suffering from a terminal illness and who is experiencing great pain has no legal barriers to obtaining medication, from qualified physicians, to alleviate that suffering, even to the point of causing unconsciousness and hastening death. In this light, even assuming that we would recognize such an interest, I agree that the State's interests in protecting those who are not truly competent or facing imminent death, or those whose decisions to hasten death would not truly be voluntary, are sufficiently weighty to justify a prohibition against physician-assisted suicide.

Every one of us at some point may be affected by our own or a family member's terminal illness. There is no reason to think the democratic process will not strike the proper balance between the interests of terminally ill, mentally competent individuals who would seek to end their suffering and the State's interests in protecting those who might seek to end life mistakenly or under pressure. As the Court recognizes, States are presently undertaking extensive and serious evaluation of physician-assisted suicide and other related issues. In such circumstances, "the . . . challenging task of crafting appropriate procedures for safeguarding . . . liberty interests is entrusted to the 'laboratory' of the States . . . in the first instance."

In sum, there is no need to address the question whether suffering patients have a constitutionally cognizable interest in obtaining relief from the suffering that they may experience in the last days of their lives. There is no dispute that dying patients in Washington and New York can obtain palliative care, even when doing so would hasten their deaths. The difficulty in defining terminal illness and the risk that a dying patient's request for assistance in ending his or her life might not be truly voluntary justifies the prohibitions on assisted suicide we uphold here.

Justice Stevens, concurring in the judgments.

The Court ends its opinion with the important observation that our holding today is fully consistent with a continuation of the vigorous debate about the "morality, legality, and practicality of physician-assisted suicide" in a democratic society. I write separately to make it clear that there is also room for further debate about the limits that the Constitution places on the power of the States to punish the practice.

---

[3]   Justice Ginsburg concurs in the Court's judgments substantially for the reasons stated in this Opinion. Justice Breyer joins this opinion except insofar as it joins the opinions of the Court.

I

The morality, legality, and practicality of capital punishment have been the subject of debate for many years. In 1976, this Court upheld the constitutionality of the practice in cases coming to us from Georgia, Florida, and Texas. In those cases we concluded that a State does have the power to place a lesser value on some lives than on others; there is no absolute requirement that a State treat all human life as having an equal right to preservation. Because the state legislatures had sufficiently narrowed the category of lives that the State could terminate, and had enacted special procedures to ensure that the defendant belonged in that limited category, we concluded that the statutes were not unconstitutional on their face. In later cases coming to us from each of those States, however, we found that some applications of the statutes were unconstitutional.

Today, the Court decides that Washington's statute prohibiting assisted suicide is not invalid "on its face," that is to say, in all or most cases in which it might be applied. That holding, however, does not foreclose the possibility that some applications of the statute might well be invalid.

As originally filed, this case presented a challenge to the Washington statute on its face and as it applied to three terminally ill, mentally competent patients and to four physicians who treat terminally ill patients. After the District Court issued its opinion holding that the statute placed an undue burden on the right to commit physician-assisted suicide, the three patients died. Although the Court of Appeals considered the constitutionality of the statute "as applied to the prescription of life-ending medication for use by terminally ill, competent adult patients who wish to hasten their deaths," the court did not have before it any individual plaintiff seeking to hasten her death or any doctor who was threatened with prosecution for assisting in the suicide of a particular patient; its analysis and eventual holding that the statute was unconstitutional was not limited to a particular set of plaintiffs before it.

History and tradition provide ample support for refusing to recognize an open-ended constitutional right to commit suicide. Much more than the State's paternalistic interest in protecting the individual from the irrevocable consequences of an ill-advised decision motivated by temporary concerns is at stake. There is truth in John Donne's observation that "No man is an island." The State has an interest in preserving and fostering the benefits that every human being may provide to the community – a community that thrives on the exchange of ideas, expressions of affection, shared memories and humorous incidents as well as on the material contributions that its members create and support. The value to others of a person's life is far too precious to allow the individual to claim a constitutional entitlement to complete autonomy in making a decision to end that life. Thus, I fully agree with the Court that the "liberty" protected by the Due Process Clause does not include a categorical "right to commit suicide which itself includes a right to assistance in doing so."

But just as our conclusion that capital punishment is not always unconstitutional did not preclude later decisions holding that it is sometimes impermissibly cruel, so is it equally clear that a decision upholding a general statutory prohibition of assisted suicide does not mean that every possible application of the statute would be valid. A State, like Washington, that has authorized the death penalty and thereby has concluded that the sanctity of human life does not require that it always be preserved, must acknowledge that there are situations in which an interest in hastening death is legitimate. Indeed, not only is that interest sometimes legitimate, I am also convinced that there are times when it is entitled to constitutional protection.

II

In *Cruzan*, the Court assumed that the interest in liberty protected by the Fourteenth Amendment encompassed the right of a terminally ill patient to direct the withdrawal of life-sustaining treatment. As the Court correctly observes today, that assumption "was not simply deduced from abstract concepts of personal autonomy." Instead, it was supported by the common-law tradition protecting the individual's general right to refuse unwanted medical treatment. We have recognized, however, that this common-law right to refuse treatment is neither absolute nor always sufficiently weighty to overcome valid countervailing state interests. As Justice Brennan pointed out in his *Cruzan* dissent, we have upheld legislation imposing punishment on persons refusing to be vaccinated, and as Justice Scalia pointed out in his concurrence, the State ordinarily has the right to interfere with an attempt to commit suicide by, for example, forcibly placing a bandage on a self-inflicted wound to stop the flow of blood. In most cases, the individual's constitutionally protected interest in his or her own physical autonomy, including the right to refuse unwanted medical treatment, will give way to the State's interest in preserving human life.

Cruzan, however, was not the normal case. Given the irreversible nature of her illness and the progressive character of her suffering, Nancy Cruzan's interest in refusing medical care was incidental to her more basic interest in controlling the manner and timing of her death. In finding that her best interests would be served by cutting off the nourishment that kept her alive, the trial court did more than simply vindicate Cruzan's interest in refusing medical treatment; the court, in essence, authorized affirmative conduct that would hasten her death. When this Court reviewed the case and upheld Missouri's requirement that there be clear and convincing evidence establishing Nancy Cruzan's intent to have life-sustaining nourishment withdrawn, it made two important assumptions: (1) that there was a "liberty interest" in refusing unwanted treatment protected by the Due Process Clause; and (2) that this liberty interest did not "end the inquiry" because it might be outweighed by relevant state interests. I agree with both of those assumptions, but I insist that the source of Nancy Cruzan's right to refuse treatment was not just a common-law rule. Rather, this right is an aspect of a far broader and more basic concept of freedom that is even older than the common law. This freedom embraces, not merely a person's right to refuse a particular kind of unwanted treatment, but also her interest in dignity, and in determining the character of the memories that will survive long after her death. In recognizing that the State's interests did not outweigh Nancy Cruzan's liberty interest in refusing medical treatment, *Cruzan* rested not simply on the common-law right to refuse medical treatment, but – at least implicitly – on the even more fundamental right to make this "deeply personal decision."

Thus, the common-law right to protection from battery, which included the right to refuse medical treatment in most circumstances, did not mark "the outer limits of the substantive sphere of liberty" that supported the Cruzan family's decision to hasten Nancy's death. Those limits have never been precisely defined. They are generally identified by the importance and character of the decision confronted by the individual. Whatever the outer limits of the concept may be, it definitely includes protection for matters "central to personal dignity and autonomy."

The Cruzan case demonstrated that some state intrusions on the right to decide how death will be encountered are also intolerable. The now-deceased plaintiffs in this action may in fact have had a liberty interest even stronger than Nancy Cruzan's because, not only were they terminally ill, they were suffering constant and severe pain. Avoiding intolerable pain and the indignity of living one's final days incapacitated and in agony is certainly "at the heart of [the] liberty . . . to define one's own concept of existence, of meaning, of the universe, and of the mystery of human life."

While I agree with the Court that *Cruzan* does not decide the issue presented by these cases, *Cruzan* did give recognition, not just to vague, unbridled notions of autonomy, but to the more specific interest in making decisions about how to confront an imminent death. Although there is no absolute right to physician-assisted suicide, *Cruzan* makes it clear that some individuals who no longer have the option of deciding whether to live or to die because they are already on the threshold of death have a constitutionally protected interest that may outweigh the State's interest in preserving life at all costs. The liberty interest at stake in a case like this differs from, and is stronger than, both the common-law right to refuse medical treatment and the unbridled interest in deciding whether to live or die. It is an interest in deciding how, rather than whether, a critical threshold shall be crossed.

III

The state interests supporting a general rule banning the practice of physician-assisted suicide do not have the same force in all cases. First and foremost of these interests is the "'unqualified interest in the preservation of human life,'" which is equated with "'the sanctity of life.'" That interest not only justifies – it commands – maximum protection of every individual's interest in remaining alive, which in turn commands the same protection for decisions about whether to commence or to terminate

291

life-support systems or to administer pain medication that may hasten death. Properly viewed, however, this interest is not a collective interest that should always outweigh the interests of a person who because of pain, incapacity, or sedation finds her life intolerable, but rather, an aspect of individual freedom.

Many terminally ill people find their lives meaningful even if filled with pain or dependence on others. Some find value in living through suffering; some have an abiding desire to witness particular events in their families' lives; many believe it a sin to hasten death. Individuals of different religious faiths make different judgments and choices about whether to live on under such circumstances. There are those who will want to continue aggressive treatment; those who would prefer terminal sedation; and those who will seek withdrawal from life-support systems and death by gradual starvation and dehydration. Although as a general matter the State's interest in the contributions each person may make to society outweighs the person's interest in ending her life, this interest does not have the same force for a terminally ill patient faced not with the choice of whether to live, only of how to die. Allowing the individual, rather than the State, to make judgments " 'about the "quality" of life that a particular individual may enjoy,'" does not mean that the lives of terminally-ill, disabled people have less value than the lives of those who are healthy. Rather, it gives proper recognition to the individual's interest in choosing a final chapter that accords with her life story, rather than one that demeans her values and poisons memories of her.

Similarly, the State's legitimate interests in preventing suicide, protecting the vulnerable from coercion and abuse, and preventing euthanasia are less significant in this context. I agree that the State has a compelling interest in preventing persons from committing suicide because of depression, or coercion by third parties. But the State's legitimate interest in preventing abuse does not apply to an individual who is not victimized by abuse, who is not suffering from depression, and who makes a rational and voluntary decision to seek assistance in dying. Although, as the New York Task Force report discusses, diagnosing depression and other mental illness is not always easy, mental health workers and other professionals expert in working with dying patients can help patients cope with depression and pain, and help patients assess their options.

Relatedly, the State and amici express the concern that patients whose physical pain is inadequately treated will be more likely to request assisted suicide. Encouraging the development and ensuring the availability of adequate pain treatment is of utmost importance; palliative care, however, cannot alleviate all pain and suffering. An individual adequately informed of the care alternatives thus might make a rational choice for assisted suicide. For such an individual, the State's interest in preventing potential abuse and mistake is only minimally implicated.

The final major interest asserted by the State is its interest in preserving the traditional integrity of the medical profession. The fear is that a rule permitting physicians to assist in suicide is inconsistent with the perception that they serve their patients solely as healers. But for some patients, it would be a physician's refusal to dispense medication to ease their suffering and make their death tolerable and dignified that would be inconsistent with the healing role For doctors who have long-standing relationships with their patients, who have given their patients advice on alternative treatments, who are attentive to their patient's individualized needs, and who are knowledgeable about pain symptom management and palliative care options, heeding a patient's desire to assist in her suicide would not serve to harm the physician-patient relationship.

Furthermore, because physicians are already involved in making decisions that hasten the death of terminally ill patients – through termination of life support, withholding of medical treatment, and terminal sedation – there is in fact significant tension between the traditional view of the physician's role and the actual practice in a growing number of cases.

IV

In New York, a doctor must respect a competent person's decision to refuse or to discontinue medical treatment even though death will thereby ensue, but the same doctor would be guilty of a felony if she provided her patient assistance in committing suicide. Today we hold that the Equal Protection

Clause is not violated by the resulting disparate treatment of two classes of terminally ill people who may have the same interest in hastening death. I agree that the distinction between permitting death to ensue from an underlying fatal disease and causing it to occur by the administration of medication or other means provides a constitutionally sufficient basis for the State's classification. Unlike the Court, however, I am not persuaded that in all cases there will in fact be a significant difference between the intent of the physicians, the patients or the families in the two situations.

There may be little distinction between the intent of a terminally-ill patient who decides to remove her life-support and one who seeks the assistance of a doctor in ending her life; in both situations, the patient is seeking to hasten a certain, impending death. The doctor's intent might also be the same in prescribing lethal medication as it is in terminating life support. A doctor who fails to administer medical treatment to one who is dying from a disease could be doing so with an intent to harm or kill that patient. Conversely, a doctor who prescribes lethal medication does not necessarily intend the patient's death – rather that doctor may seek simply to ease the patient's suffering and to comply with her wishes. The illusory character of any differences in intent or causation is confirmed by the fact that the American Medical Association unequivocally endorses the practice of terminal sedation – the administration of sufficient dosages of pain-killing medication to terminally ill patients to protect them from excruciating pain even when it is clear that the time of death will be advanced. The purpose of terminal sedation is to ease the suffering of the patient and comply with her wishes, and the actual cause of death is the administration of heavy doses of lethal sedatives. This same intent and causation may exist when a doctor complies with a patient's request for lethal medication to hasten her death.

Thus, although the differences the majority notes in causation and intent between terminating life-support and assisting in suicide support the Court's rejection of the respondents' facial challenge, these distinctions may be inapplicable to particular terminally ill patients and their doctors. Our holding today that the Equal Protection Clause is not violated by New York's classification, just like our holding in *Washington v. Glucksberg* that the Washington statute is not invalid on its face, does not foreclose the possibility that some applications of the New York statute may impose an intolerable intrusion on the patient's freedom.

. There remains room for vigorous debate about the outcome of particular cases that are not necessarily resolved by the opinions announced today. How such cases may be decided will depend on their specific facts. In my judgment, however, it is clear that the so-called "unqualified interest in the preservation of human life" is not itself sufficient to outweigh the interest in liberty that may justify the only possible means of preserving a dying patient's dignity and alleviating her intolerable suffering.

Justice Souter, concurring in the judgment:

Even though I do not conclude that assisted suicide is a fundamental right entitled to recognition at this time, I accord the claims raised by the patients and physicians in this case a high degree of importance, requiring a commensurate justification. The reasons that lead me to conclude that the prohibition on assisted suicide is not arbitrary under the due process standard also support the distinction between assistance to suicide, which is banned, and practices such as termination of artificial life support and death-hastening pain medication, which are permitted. I accordingly concur in the judgment.

QUESTIONS

1.   Separate and apart from the law, do you support or oppose active euthanasia? Why? Do you think it should be the province of the criminal law to regulate such activity? Why? Include in your response a discussion of the legislation of morality that encompasses the arguments of H.L.A. Hart, and Lord Patrick Devlin, and the other philosophers of law discussed in Chapter 1.

2.   Using *Glucksberg* and *Vacco*, write an essay in support of or in opposition to active euthanasia. Include a discussion of both due process privacy interests, and of equal protection interests, paying particular attention of *Roe v. Wade, Bowers v. Hardwick,* and *Cruzan v. Missouri* as precedent.

CHAPTER 8
RAPE AND SEX-RELATED CRIMES

A. Rape and Sexual Assault

1. The Elements of Rape

The common law crime of *rape* has undergone significant evolution as the criminal law has developed over time. The common law crime of rape can be broken down into the following elements:

a)   Actus Reus: The unlawful carnal knowledge of a woman;
b)   Attendant Circumstance: by man who is not her husband;
c)   Mens Rea: without her effective consent.   *penetration*

Two terms used in this definition of rape require explication. The "unlawful carnal knowledge of a woman," the actus reus, was defined as "the penetration, however slight, of the vagina by a penis." And "without her effective consent" required a woman to resist the man "to the utmost."   *resistance of the utmost*

Several things should be evident from this definition that illustrates why the law of rape needed to be updated from its common law roots. Only a man could perpetrate a rape; only a woman could be the victim of a rape; rape required penile-vaginal penetration; a husband could not rape his wife; and "effective consent" was defined so narrowly that the victim was often put on trial for not having resisted to the "utmost."

Modern rape laws have abolished such antiquated notions of sexual assault. Most states today reject the common law notion that a husband cannot rape his wife. Only a minority of states still exclude a spouse from their general rape statutes. And of these, a few have passed spousal rape laws that deal especially with the particular instance when one is raped by one's spouse. Most states have also gone to gender neutral rape laws, recognizing that either sex may commit a rape or be the victim of a rape.

Modern rape statutes no longer define the actus reus of rape as the unlawful carnal knowledge of a woman. Instead, the actus reus for rape is typically defined as "unlawful sexual intercourse." This definition still requires a penetration, however slight, but it does not narrowly limit the penetration to one of penile-vaginal penetration. Forcible cunnilingus, fellatio, anal intercourse, digital penetration, or the insertion of a foreign object into the genital or anal opening of another thus qualifies as rape in many jurisdictions today.

Arguably the most important evolution of the law of rape that has occurred concerns the antiquated notion that required resistance to the utmost in order for the element "without consent" to be proven. Today, resistance to the utmost is no longer required. Lack of effective consent can be proven when: (a) intercourse is accomplished by actual force; (b) intercourse is accomplished by threats of great and immediate bodily harm; (c) the victim was incapable of consenting due to unconsciousness (including sleep), intoxication (drugs or alcohol), or mental condition; (d) the victim is fraudulently caused to believe that the act is not intercourse; or (e) the victim is intentionally deceived to erroneously believe that the person is the victim's spouse. Consider the following case in examining the meaning of "without consent."

STATE of Connecticut v. Richard T. SMITH.
554 A.2d 713 (Conn. 1989).

Shea, Associate Justice.

After a jury trial, the defendant was convicted of sexual assault in the first degree in violation of General Statutes § 53a-70. In this appeal he claims error in (1) the denial of his motion for a judgment of acquittal for insufficiency of the evidence on the element of lack of consent; (2) the application of a statute, § 53a-70, claimed to be unconstitutionally vague, to the facts of this case; (3) the instructions to the jury, as well as the argument of the prosecutor, concerning certain evidence of consciousness of guilt; and (4) the charge upon reasonable doubt. We find no error.

Upon the evidence presented the jury could reasonably have found the following facts. On March 18, 1987, the victim, T, a twenty-six year old woman, and her girlfriend, A, a visitor from Idaho, went to a bar in West Haven. T was introduced by a friend to the defendant, who bought her a drink. The defendant invited her and A, together with a male acquaintance A had met at the bar, to dinner at a restaurant across the street. After dinner, the defendant having paid for T's share, the four left the restaurant. The defendant proposed that they all go to his apartment in West Haven. Because A's acquaintance had a motorcycle, the defendant gave them directions to the apartment so that they could ride there, while he and T walked.

After a twenty minute walk, the defendant and T arrived at the apartment at about 10 p.m. A and her acquaintance were not there and never arrived at the apartment. When T and the defendant had entered the apartment they sat on the couch in the living room to watch television. After a while the defendant put his arm around T and told her he wanted a kiss. She gave him a kiss. She testified that "He wouldn't back off. He wouldn't let go of me. So I said, look, I am not kidding. I really don't want to do anything. I don't know you and whatnot." The defendant still held onto T. She testified that he was "still right in my face wanting to kiss me. You know, saying so, saying that you don't think I paid for dinner for nothing, do you."

T testified that she was scared: "At first I didn't know what to do. I did spit in his face and he didn't even take it seriously. Then I tried kicking him off, which was to no avail. He was way too big for me." T described the defendant as "at least six foot two" and "at least two hundred pounds." She testified: "He told me he could make it hard on me or I could make it easy on myself, which I finally decided was probably my best bet." T understood that the defendant was determined to "have sex" with her and that either he would hurt her or she "was going to go along with it." At the point where T ceased resistance, she was "down on the couch" and the defendant was "on top of" her. T testified that she had informed the defendant that she had to pick up her daughter, had insulted him, and had told him that he was "a big man to have to force a woman." She testified, however, that after she decided to "give in," she tried to convince the defendant that she was not going to fight and "was going to go along with him and enjoy it."

The defendant removed T's clothing as she remained on the couch and led her into the bedroom. When she declined his request for oral sex, he did not insist upon it, but proceeded to engage in vaginal intercourse with her. After completion of the act, the defendant said that he knew the victim felt that she had been raped, but that she could not prove it and had really enjoyed herself. After they both had dressed, the defendant requested T's telephone number, but she gave him a number she concocted as a pretense. He also offered her some sherbet, which she accepted and ate while she waited for a cab that the defendant had called. T, however, placed her pink cigarette lighter underneath the couch, so that she would be able to prove she had been in the apartment. When the cab arrived, she left the apartment.

She told the cab driver to take her to the police station because she had been raped. At the station she gave her account of the event to the police. The defendant was arrested. The police found T's lighter under the couch in his living room, where T had informed them it was located.

I

Although the defendant claims insufficiency of the evidence as the basis for his claim that he was entitled to an acquittal, he actually seeks to have this court impose a requirement of mens rea, or guilty intent, as an essential element of the crime of sexual assault in the first degree. In fact, he concedes in his reply brief that, if conviction for sexual assault in the first degree requires only a general intent, he cannot prevail on his claim that the evidence was insufficient to support his conviction. This court has held that our statute, § 53a-70, requires proof of only a general intent to perform the physical acts that constitute that crime. *State v. Carter*, 458 A.2d 369 (Conn. 1983). "No specific intent is made an element of the crime of first degree sexual assault . . . ." "It is well settled that first degree sexual assault is a general intent crime." *State v. Rothenberg*, 487 A.2d 545 (Conn. 1985). . . .

The defendant, nevertheless, urges that we adopt a construction of § 53a-70 making the mental state of the defendant the touchstone for the resolution of the issue of consent when presented in a prosecution for first degree sexual assault. He refers to this mental state as a mens rea, a guilty mind, and describes it as an awareness on the part of a man that he is forcing sex upon a woman against her will and that he intends to do so. In the context of the evidence in this case, the defendant claims, though he did not testify at trial, that he honestly believed that at the time the sexual act occurred that T had consented to it. He bases this claim upon her testimony that, after their preliminary encounter on the couch, and his remark that he could "make it hard" for her or she could "make it easy" on herself, she ceased resisting his advances and decided to "go along with it." T also testified that, once she decided to "give in," she acted as if she were "going to go along with him and enjoy it."

The position advocated by the defendant that the requisite mens rea should be an element of the crime of sexual assault in the first degree is supported by a widely publicized decision of the British House of Lords in 1975, *Director of Public Prosecutions v. Morgan*, 1976 App. Cas. 182, 205, 2 W.L.R. 913, 2 All E.R. 347 (H.L.1975). A majority of the court held that a defendant cannot properly be convicted of rape if he in fact believed that the woman had consented, even though the basis for his belief may not have been reasonable. Lord Hailsham expressed the view that, for the crime of rape at common law, "the prohibited act is and always has been intercourse without the consent of the victim and the mental element is and always has been the intention to commit that act, or the equivalent intention to have intercourse willy-nilly, not caring whether the victim consents or no." *Id.*, 215. A similar position has been adopted in Alaska, where it is held that the state has the burden of proving at least "that the defendant acted 'recklessly' regarding his putative victim's lack of consent." *Reynolds v. State*, 664 P.2d 621, 625 (Ala. App.1983). The Supreme Court of California has concluded that a wrongful intent is an element of a rape offense, but, contrary to *Morgan*, has held that this element would be negated if a defendant entertained a "reasonable and bona fide belief" that the complainant had consented. *People v. Mayberry*, 15 Cal.3d 143, 145, 125 Cal. Rptr. 745, 542 P.2d 1337 (1975). A recent commentary on the subject of rape also has suggested that the focus of the inquiry regarding consent in such cases should be upon the mens rea of the defendant rather than upon the attitude of the victim. Susan Estrich, "Rape," 95 YALE L.J. 1087, 1094-1132 (1986).

Most courts have rejected the proposition that a specific intention to have intercourse without the consent of the victim is an element of the crime of rape or sexual assault [citations omitted]. This court has implicitly discountenanced such a claim. One of the complications that might arise, if such a mental element were required, involves the problem of intoxication, which is generally held to be relevant to negate a crime of specific intent but not a crime of general intent. The difficulty of convicting a thoroughly intoxicated person of rape, if awareness of lack of consent were an element of the crime, would diminish the protection that our statutes presently afford to potential victims from lustful drunkards. Another related problem would be the admissibility of evidence of other similar behavior of a defendant charged with rape to prove his intent to disregard any lack of consent. Such evidence is now usually excluded as more prejudicial than probative, because only a general intent is necessary to constitute the offense.

Although the Supreme Judicial Court of Massachusetts has rejected the contention that a specific intent to have nonconsensual intercourse is an essential element of the crime of rape that the state must prove, it has expressly left open the question "[w]hether a reasonable good faith mistake of fact as to the fact of consent is a defense to the crime . . . ." *Commonwealth v. Grant*, 464 N.E.2d 33 (1984). The California Supreme Court, in holding that a wrongful intent is an element of the crime of rape in *People v. Mayberry, supra*, construed the California penal code to embody the principle that a mistake of fact based upon a reasonable and good faith belief as to consent negates the existence of the requisite wrongful intent. A corresponding provision of our own penal code, General Statutes § 53a-6(a),[1] allows the defense that a person has engaged in conduct otherwise criminal under a mistaken belief of fact where "[s]uch factual mistake negates the mental state required for the commission of an offense." This statute, however, applies only to specific intent crimes. Unless we should conclude, contrary to our precedent, that the mental state required of the actor for sexual assault in the first degree includes an awareness of lack of consent, even a reasonably founded, but nonetheless mistaken, belief as to that fact would not be available as a defense under § 53a-6(a).

Our first degree sexual assault statute, § 53a-70, applies to a person who "compels another person to engage in sexual intercourse by the use of force . . . or by the threat of use of force which . . . reasonably causes such person to fear physical injury . . . ." Although the consent of the complainant is not expressly made a defense to such a crime, it is abundantly clear that the draftsmen of our penal code endorsed the principle that "non- commercial sexual activity in private, whether heterosexual or homosexual, between consenting, competent adults, not involving corruption of the young by older persons, is no business of the criminal law." COMMISSION TO REVISE THE CRIMINAL STATUTES, PENAL CODE COMMENTS, CONNECTICUT GENERAL STATUTES (1969), [at] 38. A finding that a complainant had consented would implicitly negate a claim that the actor had compelled the complainant by force or threat to engage in sexual intercourse. Consent is not made an affirmative defense under our sex offense statutes, so, as in the case of the defense of alibi, the burden is upon the state to prove lack of consent beyond a reasonable doubt whenever the issue is raised.

While the word "consent" is commonly regarded as referring to the state of mind of the complainant in a sexual assault case, it cannot be viewed as a wholly subjective concept. Although the actual state of mind of the actor in a criminal case may in many instances be the issue upon which culpability depends, a defendant is not chargeable with knowledge of the internal workings of the minds of others except to the extent that he should reasonably have gained such knowledge from his observations of their conduct. . . . [W]hether a complainant has consented to intercourse depends upon her manifestations of such consent as reasonably construed. If the conduct of the complainant under all the circumstances should reasonably be viewed as indicating consent to the act of intercourse, a defendant should not be found guilty because of some undisclosed mental reservation on the part of the complainant. Reasonable conduct ought not to be deemed criminal.

It is likely that juries in considering the defense of consent in sexual assault cases, though visualizing the issue in terms of actual consent by the complainant, have reached their verdicts on the basis of inferences that a reasonable person would draw from the conduct of the complainant and the defendant under the surrounding circumstances. It is doubtful that jurors would ever convict a defendant who had in their view acted in reasonable reliance upon words or conduct of the complainant indicating consent, even though there had been some concealed reluctance on her part. If a defendant were concerned about such a possibility, however, he would be entitled, once the issue is raised, to request a jury instruction that the state must prove beyond a reasonable doubt that the conduct of the complainant would not have justified a reasonable belief that she had consented. Thus we adhere to the view expressed in our earlier decisions that no specific intent, but only a general intent to perform the physical acts constituting the crime, is necessary for the crime of first degree sexual assault. We reject the position of the British courts, as well as that adopted in Alaska, that the state must prove either an actual awareness on the part of the defendant that the complainant had not consented or a reckless disregard of her nonconsenting status. We agree, however, with the California courts that a defendant is entitled to a jury instruction that a defendant may not be convicted of this crime if the words or conduct of the complainant under all the circumstances would justify a reasonable belief that she had consented.

---

[1] General Statutes § 53a-6(a) provides: "A person shall not be relieved of criminal liability for conduct because he engages in such conduct under a mistaken belief of fact, unless: (1) Such factual mistake negates the mental state required for the commission of an offense; or (2) the statute defining the offense or a statute related thereto expressly provides that such factual mistake constitutes a defense or exemption; or (3) such factual mistake is of a kind that supports a defense of justification."

We arrive at that result, however, not on the basis of our penal code provision relating to a mistake of fact, § 53a-6(a), which is applicable only to specific intent crimes, but on the ground that whether a complainant should be found to have consented depends upon how her behavior would have been viewed by a reasonable person under the surrounding circumstances.

The defendant in this case made no request to charge upon the issue of the mental state required for the crime of sexual assault in the first degree or upon the issue of consent, nor did he except in these respects to the charge as given. On appeal his claim that a realization by a defendant of the absence of consent, or its recklessness equivalent, should be an element of the crime, as courts in Great Britain and Alaska have held, is necessarily limited to the sufficiency of the evidence to establish either an actual awareness[2] that T had not consented or a reckless disregard of her manifestations of nonconsent. Since we have rejected the subjective standard for determining the issue of consent, however, the question for us is whether the evidence is sufficient to prove that a reasonable person would not have believed that T's conduct under all the circumstances indicated her consent.

From our review of the evidence detailed previously, it is clear that the jury could properly have found beyond a reasonable doubt that T's words and actions could not reasonably be viewed to indicate her consent to intercourse with the defendant. According to her uncontradicted testimony, she expressly declined his advances, explaining that she did not know him and wanted to pick up her child. She spat in his face and "tried kicking him off." She "gave in" only after the defendant declared that "he could make it hard" for her if she continued to resist. This statement she could reasonably have regarded as a threat of physical injury. Only by entertaining the fantasy that "no" meant "yes," and that a display of distaste meant affection, could the defendant have believed that T's behavior toward him indicated consent. Such a distorted view of her conduct would not have been reasonable. The evidence was more than sufficient to support the verdict.

II

The defendant's second claim, that § 53a-70, our first degree sexual assault statute, is unconstitutionally vague, is closely related to the first. He contends that, unless the statute is construed to require proof of a guilty mind, "every act of sexual intercourse can be punishable as a class B felony regardless of the mind set of the accused, because all that would be required to establish guilt is the act of sexual intercourse coupled with the statement of the victim that she felt threatened." He suggests that the reasonableness of the complainant's fear of physical injury generated by the threat "could readily be established simply by the differences in size between the man and the woman or the strangeness to the victim of the place she had gone to." The horrendous scenario postulated by the defendant that a sexual assault conviction may be based wholly upon a statement by the complainant of feeling threatened because of the greater size of the person accused, combined with the strangeness of the surroundings, is contrary to the conclusion we have reached in Part I. There we held that the crux of the inquiry on the issue of consent was not the subjective state of mind of the complainant but rather her manifestations of lack of consent by words or conduct as reasonably construed.

Further, since § 53a-70 requires that one compel another person to engage in sexual intercourse "by the use of force . . . or by the threat of use of force . . . which reasonably causes such person to fear physical injury," it is clear that a defendant must either use force or threaten its use by words or conduct that would reasonably generate fear of physical injury.

* * *

We conclude that the defendant's claim that § 53a-70 is void for vagueness is without merit in the context of the circumstances of this case.

---

[2]   The testimony of T that the defendant had told her, after completion of the sexual act, that "he knew that [T] felt [she] was raped but [she] couldn't prove it" is significant evidence that the defendant subjectively may have realized that T had not consented to intercourse. We hold, however, that actual awareness of lack of consent is not essential.

QUESTIONS

1.   At common law, Smith clearly would not have been found guilty of raping the victim in this case because there came a point when she "gave in," fearing that if she resisted any further, she would be hurt even more seriously than the rape itself. This "giving in" would have defeated the resistence to the utmost requirement which was required to prove non-consent. But how much resistence should be necessary for a finding of non-consent? The court in this case found her verbal actions along with her spitting at the defendant and her kicking him to be sufficient. Do you agree? Why or why not?

2.   A small minority of states allow non-consent to be proven simply by the victim's testimony that he or she did not consent. But most states, as the *Smith* case illustrates, require a showing of some resistence to prove non-consent. Which approach do you think is best? Why? In a jurisdiction that requires some resistence, how much is enough? Would you have upheld Smith's conviction if the victim hadn't spat on him or kicked him? Explain the reasoning underlying your response.

3.   In *State v. Rusk*, 424 A.2d 720 (Md. 1981), the victim drove the defendant to his home in an area with which she was unfamiliar. He took her car keys from her and asked her to come up to his place. The victim testified that he had a "look" on his face when he made the request that scared her into complying. Once up in the apartment, he left the room for a few minutes, yet she did not run out of the apartment or call the police. When he returned, he pulled her by the arm to the bed and began to undress her. She removed his pants because "he asker her to do it." She then engaged in sexual activity after the defendant began "to lightly choke her." She testified that she began to cry and asked if he would let her go without killing her if she did what he wanted. He allegedly did not respond to the question. The defendant was convicted. The Maryland Supreme Court upheld the conviction reasoning that a rape victim need not offer any resistence when in fear that doing so may result in death or serious bodily harm. Do you agree with the outcome of this case? Why or why not? Of what relevance to you are the facts that the victim drove him home; went up to the apartment rather than honking the horn or calling for help; and remained in his apartment instead of running out?

4.   The *Smith* court cited the case of *Regina v. Morgan*, 1976 App. Cas. 182, 205, 2 W.L.R. 913, 2 All E.R. 347 (H.L.1975). In that case, there were four defendants, all of whom were members of the Royal Air Force. One of them defendant invited the other three back to his home to have sexual intercourse with his wife. He explained to them that she would protest, but that it was all part of a fantasy he had agreed to provide for her. Thus, the men honestly believed that the wife wanted to have sex with them. All four men had forcible sex with her over her objections. They were charged with rape and conspiracy to commit rape. The three men who were not the woman's husband defended themselves by citing the husband's representations to them. Thus, they argued, they had formed a mistaken belief as to the wife's consent. They were acquitted on appeal upon a rationale that they had made honest, but unreasonable mistakes regarding the wife's consent. The case was widely criticized and led Parliament to change the law to require criminal recklessness as the mens rea for rape, requiring an honest and reasonable mistake to negate such mens rea. How is the *Smith* court's handling of mens rea different from that taken by England and, as described in the *Smith* case, some U.S. jurisdictions like Alaska? How about the differences in the handling of the mistake of fact regarding whether there was consent? Which approach do you think is best? Why?

---

2. Issues of Proof and Rape Shield Laws

Proving rape is very difficult. In fact, it has one of the highest acquittal rate of all crimes. Often, forensic evidence is not particularly helpful because the defendant admits that some sex act took place, but defends on the grounds that the act was consensual. Even when there is some evidence of a struggle, a "rough sex" defense can create reasonable doubt.

Another tactic that was often used by the defense in rape cases was to put the victim on trial. Factual issues such as the victim's past sexual conduct and/or the victim's manner and style of dress were made the focal points of the trial by the defense in an attempt to create reasonable doubt with regard to the matter of consent. Most jurisdictions today have enacted *rape shield laws* designed to prevent the victim and his or her past sexual conduct from being put on trial, thereby focusing attention at trial on the facts of the incident in question.

Generally speaking, rape shield laws prohibit the introduction of any evidence of the alleged victim's past sexual conduct. Most jurisdictions, however, recognize exceptions to this general bar and admit evidence of the alleged victim's past sexual conduct with the accused, reasoning the past sexual history between the accused and the accuser is highly relevant. Some states also admit evidence of the alleged victim's prior sexual conduct: (a) to rebut the State's argument of chastity if such an argument is made; (b) when the defendant argues the victim consented to an act of prostitution; (c) to show that the alleged victim had made an unsubstantiated charge of rape in the past; and (d) to refute physical or scientific evidence (such as the victim's virginity, the origin of semen found, the presence of disease or pregnancy, etc.).

Although such laws have routinely been upheld, defendants continually challenge their constitutionality as applied to their particular cases if they operate in such a manner as to interfere with a defendant's constitutional rights. The following case illustrates such a challenge.

Adrian WILLIAMS, Appellant-Defendant, v. STATE of Indiana, Appellee-Plaintiff.
681 N.E.2d 195 (Ind. 1997).

Boehm, Justice.

A jury convicted defendant Adrian Williams of attempted criminal deviate conduct, a Class A felony, and criminal confinement, a Class B felony. A majority of the Court of Appeals reversed the convictions on the grounds that the trial court erred in excluding certain evidence. Because we conclude that the evidence was properly excluded and no other reversible error occurred, we now grant transfer, vacate the opinion of the Court of Appeals, and reinstate the convictions.

Factual and Procedural History

During the early morning hours on January 9, 1993, the victim was working as a topless dancer at a nightclub in downtown Indianapolis. The following is her version of the events of that night. When she finished work at approximately 2:45 a.m., she walked out into the parking lot and asked two strangers, Williams and co-defendant Antoine Edmondson, for a ride home. The two men agreed and she got into the car. Williams did not drive the car directly to the victim's home. Instead, he told her that "they had to make a stop." He drove into an alley behind a different club where Edmondson exited the car. The victim then attempted to run away but Edmondson grabbed her arms and pulled her into the back seat of the car. As the victim struggled with Edmondson in the car, Williams drove to a public park and stopped the car in a dark area of its parking lot. The two then ordered the victim to engage in sexual acts with them simultaneously. Edmondson pulled a gun out of his pocket and placed it on the arm rest of the front seat. He then removed the victim's shoe and sock and pulled her right pants leg off. The victim managed to grab the gun, open the car door, and run away. As she ran, she fired the gun behind her and, although she apparently had never fired a weapon before, shot Edmondson in the jaw. Williams and Edmondson were subsequently arrested and each was charged with two counts of attempted criminal deviate conduct, criminal confinement, and carrying a handgun without a license. The two men were tried together.

Three days before trial, the State filed two motions in limine. In the first motion, the State sought to exclude evidence of the victim's sexual history pursuant to Indiana's Rape Shield Rule, Indiana Evidence Rule 412. Williams did not object to this motion. In the second motion, the State sought to exclude evidence of the victim's history of drug use. Williams did object to this motion, arguing that the victim's cocaine habit "would obviously make a difference as to her ability to recall facts, that it's something that the jury should consider in determining whether she is able to relate facts in an appropriate, truthful, factual manner." The trial court granted both motions and excluded the evidence of both the victim's sexual history and her prior drug use. However, Williams was allowed to question the victim about drug use at the time of the incident.

During the trial of the two defendants, the victim testified on cross- examination that she did not use cocaine on the day of the incident or on the day of the trial. At defense counsel's request, the court conducted a hearing outside the presence of the jury regarding the exclusion of evidence of the victim's prior drug use. Williams joined in Edmondson's argument that the victim's prior drug use was pertinent to her credibility. Williams specifically argued that she had "a poor recall of the facts because of her cocaine habit." The trial court stood by its original decision to exclude the evidence. Thereafter, defense counsel made an offer of proof and the victim testified, outside the hearing of the jury, that she was previously addicted to cocaine and had received treatment. Later during the trial, both Williams and Edmondson testified that the victim wanted the men to locate some cocaine for her and when they could not find any, the men agreed to give her money in exchange for sex. Williams requested that the trial court lift its proscription on testimony as to prior drug use because the victim's prior drug use and alleged acts of prostitution were now at issue. The trial court denied the request. Defense counsel then made another offer of proof that a friend of the victim would testify that the victim had previously committed acts of prostitution in exchange for money or cocaine. This evidence was also excluded by the trial court. The jury found Williams guilty of one count of attempted deviate conduct and criminal confinement.

Evidence of the Victim's Prior Drug Use

Williams argues that he is entitled to a new trial because the trial court erred by refusing to allow the defense to inquire into the victim's prior drug use. The trial court allowed defense counsel to elicit testimony regarding the victim's use of drugs on the day of the incident because it was relevant to her ability to perceive and recall the events in dispute. However, prior drug use was held irrelevant. Relevant evidence means "evidence having any tendency to make the existence of any fact that is of consequence to the determination of the action more probable or less probable than it would be without the evidence." Ind. Evidence Rule 401. Before the adoption of the Indiana Rules of Evidence, Indiana courts consistently upheld decisions of trial courts excluding evidence of a witness' past drug use as irrelevant. *Kimble v. State*, 569 N.E.2d 653, 654 (Ind. 1991) (victim's wife could be questioned regarding her drug use on the night in question but any questions about her past drug use were irrelevant) . . . .

In this case, the victim testified that she did not use drugs on the day of the incident. The defense's effort to question the victim about her prior drug use was justified solely on the basis of challenging her credibility. The jury had ample opportunity to assess the credibility of her testimony as defense counsel repeatedly challenged the accuracy of her memory. Moreover, there was no showing that the victim's consumption of drugs on prior occasions was of such a degree that it substantially affected her current ability to perceive, remember, or testify. Indeed, the trial court noted that there was no evidence presented of the victim's inability to recall the incident. Therefore, the trial court did not abuse its discretion in excluding the evidence.

Additionally, the trial court properly excluded testimony of the victim's friend who would have testified about the victim's prior drug use. The trial court again found such testimony irrelevant unless the friend could testify that the victim used drugs on the date in question. As discussed above, the fact that the victim had used drugs, in and of itself, is not relevant. Accordingly, the trial court properly excluded the friend's testimony.

Evidence of the Victim's Past Sexual Conduct

The trial court also properly excluded the friend's testimony that on prior occasions the victim had committed acts of prostitution in exchange for money or cocaine. Williams claims this testimony supports his defense that the victim consented and accompanied the men because they had promised to obtain drugs for her. The trial court excluded the friend's testimony regarding the victim's prior alleged acts of prostitution because evidence of a victim's past sexual conduct is not admissible except as provided in Indiana's Rape Shield Rule, Indiana Evidence Rule 412. Rule 412 provides that in prosecutions for a sex crime, evidence of a victim's or witness' past sexual conduct is inadmissible, except in the following circumstances: 1) evidence of the victim's or witness' past sexual conduct with the defendant; 2) evidence that shows that some person other than the defendant committed the act upon which the prosecution is founded; 3) evidence that the victim's pregnancy at the time of trial was not caused by the defendant; or 4) evidence of a conviction for a crime offered for impeachment under Rule 609. Otherwise stated, past incidents of consent, except in these limited circumstances, are not permitted to imply consent on the date in question.

None of the exceptions to Rule 412's general prohibition of inquiry into the victim's sexual history apply here. The evidence offered here was of the classic sort precluded by the Rape Shield Rule: purported incidents with other men at other times offered simply to show that the victim had consented in the past in the hope the inference will be drawn that she consented here. Rule 412 was enacted to prevent just this kind of generalized inquiry into the reputation or past sexual conduct of the victim in order to avoid embarrassing the victim and subjecting the victim to possible public denigration. *Stephens v. Miller*, 13 F.3d 998, 1002 (7th Cir.), *cert. denied*, 513 U.S. 808 (1994). The Rule reflects a policy first embodied in Indiana's Rape Shield Act, Indiana Code § 35-37- 4-4, that inquiry into a victim's prior sexual activity is sufficiently problematic that it should not be permitted to become a focus of the defense. Rule 412 is intended to prevent the victim from being put on trial, to protect the victim against surprise, harassment, and unnecessary invasion of privacy, and, importantly, to remove obstacles to reporting sex crimes.

Balanced against these considerations is the defendant's right to present relevant evidence. For this reason, Rule 412 permits evidence of the defendant's past experience with the victim, but does not permit a defendant to base his defense of consent on the victim's past sexual experiences with third persons. The allegation of prostitution does not affect this calculus. We agree with the Fourth Circuit's view that it is "intolerable to suggest that because the victim is a prostitute, she automatically is assumed to have consented with anyone at any time." *United States v. Saunders*, 943 F.2d 388, 392 (4th Cir. 1991), *cert. denied*, 502 U.S. 1105 (1992). Moreover, even when evidence does fall within one of Rule 412's exceptions and is admissible, it is still subject to Evidence Rules 401 and 403. In this case, the evidence would shift the jury's attention away from the defendants' actions to the past acts of the victim. Any probative value is "substantially outweighed by the danger of unfair prejudice." Evid. R. 403. Thus, the trial court properly excluded the evidence.

Williams contends that the trial court's application of Indiana's Rape Shield Rule violates his Sixth Amendment right to present witnesses. Indiana's Rape Shield Rule has repeatedly been held facially constitutional. *Moore v. Duckworth*, 687 F.2d 1063, 1067 (7th Cir. 1982). However, "the constitutionality of such a law as applied to preclude particular exculpatory evidence remains subject to examination on a case by case basis." *Tague v. Richards*, 3 F.3d 1133, 1137 (7th Cir. 1993). . . . Many jurisdictions acknowledge that a rape shield statute or rule serves to emphasize the general irrelevance of a victim's sexual history. . . . Although there are instances where the application of the Rape Shield Rule may violate a defendant's Sixth Amendment right, this is not one of them. For example, admission of such evidence may be constitutionally required where the evidence is offered not to show the victim's consent but to establish some other point such as that an injury could have been inflicted by someone other than the defendant. . . . It may also be required when the trial court restricts a defendant from giving his own account of the events at issue. . . . And the Sixth Amendment may be implicated when a defendant establishes that the victim engaged in a similar pattern of sexual acts. *Cf. Jeffries v. Nix*, 912 F.2d 982, 987-88 (8th Cir. 1990) (essentially finding a victim's sexual history irrelevant in the absence of compelling evidence of modus operandi); *People v. Sandoval*, 552 N.E.2d 726, 738 (Ill. 1990) (prior pattern exception applies to the admission of certain evidence which reveals activity marked by characteristics tending to show an individual's unique "signature").

In this case, there was no restriction on the ability of the defense to present evidence of the incident. The trial court allowed both defendants to testify that the victim agreed to perform sex acts in exchange for money. The jury was informed through testimony of the defendants and the victim that the victim voluntarily entered a car with two strange men at 2 a.m. in the parking lot of a topless club. Whatever her initial motive, at some point, according to her, she clearly communicated her lack of consent to proceeding as the men directed. Whatever her sexual past, if the jury accepted that story, conviction was proper. As noted above, the excluded evidence did not serve to explain any physical evidence. Under these facts, exclusion of the victim's past sexual experiences with third persons is not unconstitutional. . . . We do not agree that an alleged prostitute's prior sexual history becomes fair game simply by reason of her prior actions, or that there is any constitutional right to present evidence of past consensual sex with other persons for that reason alone. Accordingly, Williams' constitutional right to present witnesses was not violated.

The Court of Appeals reversed Williams' convictions because the majority concluded that evidence of the victim's cocaine addiction was admissible as a pertinent character trait of the victim offered by the accused under Indiana Evidence Rule 404(a)(2). . . . The court held that "evidence of the victim's severe (and obviously expensive) addiction to smoking cocaine is relevant to and extremely probative of Williams' consent defense that the victim agreed to have sex with the men in exchange for cocaine or money." However Williams' consent defense does not ultimately turn on the victim's drug use. The evidence of the victim's prior drug use is relevant only to the extent it is offered to show the reason for her past sexual conduct. Money for drugs is one motivation to consent to sex. There are plenty of others. The reasoning of the Court of Appeals would permit evidence of the victim's past sexual conduct to support the theory that the victim consented to the sex acts on the night in question for the same reason as she had allegedly consented in the past. Similar reasoning would subject any complaining victim with an allegedly promiscuous past to unfettered examination of sexual history. That is precisely what Evidence Rule 412 prevents. Where a specific rule – Evidence Rule 412 – makes the past sexual conduct of a victim or witness inadmissible, except under specified circumstances, a party cannot circumvent the requirements of Rule 412(b) by relying on the general doctrines of Rule 404(b). We conclude that the trial court properly excluded evidence of the victim's prior drug history and past sexual conduct pursuant to Indiana's Evidence Rules.

Transfer is granted. The Court of Appeals opinion is vacated and Williams' convictions for attempted criminal deviate conduct and criminal confinement are affirmed.

QUESTIONS

1.   This court disagreed with the court of appeals. What are the merits of the Supreme Court of Indiana's opinion? How about those of the court of appeals? Which approach do you think is the more "fair"?

2.   Indiana's rape shield law did not bar the evidence of the alleged victim's drug use; another rule of evidence was used to exclude it based upon the court's determination that it was not relevant to the issue of rape. Do you agree with that conclusion? Why or why not?

3.   The court cites approvingly precedent that holds the status of the victim as being a prostitute is not relevant to determining the issue of consent. Do you feel the fact that an alleged victim is a prostitute has any relevance on the issue of consent in a rape prosecution? When such an allegation is made, should the jury be informed that the accuser is a prostitute, or would such information unfairly bias the jury? Explain your answers.

3. Modern Sexual Assault/Sexual Battery Laws

Nearly half of all U.S. states have sexual assault or sexual battery laws instead of traditional rape statutes. Under most of these laws, the modern definition of rape – sexual intercourse via penetration, however slight, without the consent of the victim – is termed "sexual assault" or "sexual battery" in the first degree. Sexual assault in the second degree is often defined as the "offensive touching" of an "intimate part" or "private part" of the body for the purpose of arousing or gratifying sexual desire in either party. But such a definition is troublesome. Sexual assault is typically a crime of power, and thus is not really one committed for sexual gratification. The statutory intent is therefore problematic.

Other jurisdictions differentiate between a sexual assault and an "aggravated sexual assault" not based on the type of offensive touching that occurred, but rather based on the amount of force used or on the age of the victim. For example, a sexual assault might be deemed to have occurred if the perpetrator used physical force or coercion, but the victim did not sustain severe personal injury. On the other hand, if the amount of force used to perpetrate the rape resulted in severe physical injury to the victim, then an aggravated sexual assault would be deemed to have occurred. Other circumstances that might raise such a crime to level of being an aggravated sexual assault would include those acts performed on a child under a certain age (e.g., 13 or 14); those involving the actual or threatened use of a deadly weapon, or those that are committed during the commission or attempted commission of another felony; or those in which there are multiple attackers.

B. Sodomy

As discussed in Chapter 1 where the cases of *Commonwealth v. Bonadio*, 415 A.2d 47 (Pa. 1980), and *Bowers v. Hardwick*, 478 U.S. 186 (1986), were presented, sodomy has a long history of being criminalized. Some states call sodomy the "crimes against nature." Sodomy is a broad term that actually encompasses anal intercourse, oral intercourse, or intercourse with an animal. It was a crime at English common law and was a crime in all U.S. jurisdictions until the 1960s.

When rape was narrowly defined as requiring a penile-vaginal penetration, sodomy laws were used to prosecute offenders whose forcible acts involved other types of penetrations, or those whose forcible sex acts were performed on a member of the same sex. But as the definition of rape evolved to encompass a broad range of non-consensual sexual acts and were broadened so that not just a woman could be the victim of rape at the hands of a man, the usefulness of sodomy laws in prosecuting forcible sex acts (i.e., those in which the parties did not consensually participate) waned. Some jurisdictions, however, continue to define the crime of rape as the penetration, however slight, of the vagina by a penis. Some of these jurisdictions have enacted special statutes to cover the forcible rape of a male by another male, or of a female by another female, called *homosexual sodomy* or *aggravated sodomy* laws.

But sodomy laws also cover consensual acts. Thus, those who desire to engage in oral sex or anal sex in the privacy of one's own home – whether married or unmarried; whether heterosexual or homosexual; whether the active performer or the passive recipient – all commit the crime of sodomy. Because many feel that the criminal law should not reach private sexual conduct between consenting adults, more than half the states have decriminalized sodomy since the 1960s – twenty-five states via legislative repeal of the statutes, and seven via the action of courts declaring such laws unconstitutional on state constitutional law grounds. But as illustrated by *Bowers v. Hardwick*, the right to privacy under the federal constitution has been interpreted as not providing any protection for consenting adults who wish to engage in such conduct.

As of the writing of this text, 18 states and Puerto Rico still criminalize consensual sodomy. Of these states, five (Arkansas, Kansas, Missouri, Oklahoma, and Texas) have laws that explicitly target homosexual sodomy. Court challenges to several of these laws are ongoing at the time of this writing. The other fourteen U.S. jurisdictions that continue to criminalize consensual sodomy do so regardless of the sexual orientation of the participants (Alabama, Arizona, Florida, Idaho, Louisiana, Michigan, Massachusetts, Minnesota, Mississippi, North Carolina, Puerto Rico, South Carolina, Utah, and Virginia). The penalties for violating these sodomy laws range from $200 fines to 20 years imprisonment.

C. Fornication and Adultery

Like laws banning consensual sodomy, the crimes of fornication and adultery have been disappearing. *Fornication* is committed by both parties to a sexual intercourse between unmarried persons. In other words, it criminalizes pre-marital sex. If, however, one or both of the parties to the sexual coupling are married to someone who is not a participant, then the crime is *adultery*. Accordingly, adultery is committed by parties to a sexual intercourse if either party is validly married to someone else. In many jurisdictions, the adultery has to be "open and notorious" to be a crime.

D. Statutory Rape

At common law, statutory rape was the carnal knowledge of a female under the age of consent. *Statutory rape* differs from rape or sexual assault because no force is used. But the coupling cannot be labeled "consensual" because the law deems people under a certain age incapable of being able to validly consent to sex. The age of consent varies throughout the United States. Some states have an age of consent as low as fourteen, while others have it as high as eighteen.

Statutory rape was a strict liability crime at common law and continues to be to be a strict liability offense in many U.S. jurisdictions today. Some states have gone to gender-neutral laws, but many states continue to use the common law definition of the crime insofar as holding that only a male may statutorily rape a female. Penalizing only the male for statutory rape would appear to raise equal protection concerns under the Fourteenth Amendment to the U.S. Constitution. But the Supreme Court, in the following case, upheld such laws over an Equal Protection Clause challenge.

MICHAEL M. v. SUPERIOR COURT of Sonoma County, California
450 U.S. 464 (1981).

Justice Rehnquist announced the judgment of the Supreme Court and delivered an opinion in which the Chief Justice, Justice Stewart, and Justice Powell joined.

The question presented in this case is whether California's "statutory rape" law, § 261.5 of the California Penal Code, violates the Equal Protection Clause of the Fourteenth Amendment. Section 261.5 defines unlawful sexual intercourse as "an act of sexual intercourse accomplished with a female not the wife of the perpetrator, where the female is under the age of 18 years." The statute thus makes men alone criminally liable for the act of sexual intercourse.

In July 1978, a complaint was filed in the Municipal Court of Sonoma County, Cal., alleging that petitioner, then a 17½ year old male, had had unlawful sexual intercourse with a female under the age of 18, in violation of § 261.5. . . . Prior to trial, petitioner sought to set aside the information on both state and federal constitutional grounds, asserting that § 261.5 unlawfully discriminated on the basis of gender. The trial court and the California Court of Appeal denied petitioner's request for relief and petitioner sought review in the Supreme Court of California . . . [which upheld the statute].

As is evident from our opinions, the Court has had some difficulty in agreeing upon the proper approach and analysis in cases involving challenges to gender-based classifications. . . . [W]e have not held that gender-based classifications are "inherently suspect" and thus we do not apply so-called "strict scrutiny" to those classifications. Our cases have held, however, that the traditional minimum rationality test takes on a somewhat "sharper focus" when gender-based classifications are challenged. *See Craig v. Boren*, 429 U.S. 190, 210 (1976). In *Reed v. Reed,* 404 U.S. 71 (1971), for example, the Court stated that a gender-based classification will be upheld if it bears a "fair and substantial relationship" to legitimate state ends, while in *Craig v. Boren,* [429 U.S.] at 197, the Court restated the test to require the classification to bear a "substantial relationship" to "important governmental objectives."

Underlying these decisions is the principle that a legislature may not "make overbroad generalizations based on sex which are entirely unrelated to any differences between men and women or which demean the ability or social status of the affected class." *Parham v. Hughes*, 441 U.S. 347, 354 (1979). But because the Equal Protection Clause does not "demand that a statute necessarily apply equally to all persons" or require "things which are different in fact to be treated in law as though they were the same." *Rinaldi v. Yeager*, 384 U.S. 305, 309 (1966). This Court has consistently upheld statutes where the gender classification is not invidious, but rather realistically reflects the fact that the sexes are not similarly situated in certain circumstances. *Parham v. Hughes*, 441 U.S. 347 (1979); *Califano v. Webster*, 430 U.S. 313 (1977). . . . As the Court has stated, a legislature may "provide for the special problems of women." *Weinberger v. Wiesenfeld*, 420 U.S. 636, 653 (1975).

Applying those principles to this case, the fact that the California Legislature criminalized the act of illicit sexual intercourse with a minor female is a sure indication of its intent or purpose to discourage that conduct. Precisely why the legislature desired that result is of course somewhat less clear. This Court has long recognized that "inquiries into congressional motives or purposes are a hazardous matter," *United States v. O'Brien*, 91 U.S. 367, 383-384 (1968); *Palmer v. Thompson*, 403 U.S. 217, 224 (1971), and the search for the "actual" or "primary" purpose of a statute is likely to be elusive. . . . Here, for example, the individual legislators may have voted for the statute for a variety of reasons. Some legislators may have been concerned about preventing teenage pregnancies, others about protecting young females from physical injury or from the loss of "chastity," and still others about promoting various religious and moral attitudes towards premarital sex.

The justification for the statute offered by the State, and accepted by the Supreme Court of California, is that the legislature sought to prevent illegitimate teenage pregnancies. That finding, of course, is entitled to great deference. . . . And although our cases establish that the State's asserted reason for the enactment of a statute may be rejected, "if it could not have been a goal of the legislation," *Weinberger v. Wiesenfeld*, [420 U.S.] at 648, this is not such a case.

We are satisfied not only that the prevention of illegitimate pregnancy is at least one of the "purposes" of the statute, but that the State has a strong interest in preventing such pregnancy. At the risk of stating the obvious, teenage pregnancies, which have increased dramatically over the last two decades, have significant social, medical and economic consequences for both the mother and her child, and the State. Of particular concern to the State is that approximately half of all teenage pregnancies end in abortion. And of those children who are born, their illegitimacy makes them likely candidates to become wards of the State.

We need not be medical doctors to discern that young men and young women are not similarly situated with respect to the problems and the risks of sexual intercourse. Only women may become pregnant and they suffer disproportionately the profound physical, emotional and psychological consequences of sexual activity. The statute at issue here protects women from sexual intercourse at an age when those consequences are particularly severe.[3]

The question thus boils down to whether a State may attack the problem of sexual intercourse and teenage pregnancy directly by prohibiting a male from having sexual intercourse with a minor

---

[3] Although petitioner concedes that the State has a "compelling" interest in preventing teenage pregnancy, he contends that the "true" purpose of § 261.5 is to protect the virtue and chastity of young women. As such, the statute is unjustifiable because it rests on archaic stereotypes. What we have said above is enough to dispose of that contention. The question for us – and the only question under the Federal Constitution – is whether the legislation violates the Equal Protection Clause of the Fourteenth Amendment, not whether its supporters may have endorsed it for reasons no longer generally accepted. Even if the preservation of female chastity were one of the motives of the statute, and even if that motive be impermissible, petitioner's argument must fail because "it is a familiar practice of constitutional law that this Court will not strike down an otherwise constitutional statute on the basis of an alleged illicit legislative motive." *United States v. O'Brien*, 391 U.S. 367, 383 (1968). . . .

female.[4] We hold that such a statute is sufficiently related to the State's objectives to pass constitutional muster.

Because virtually all of the significant harmful and inescapably identifiable consequences of teenage pregnancy fall on the young female, a legislature acts well within its authority when it elects to punish only the participant who, by nature, suffers few of the consequences of his conduct. It is hardly unreasonable for a legislature acting to protect minor females to exclude them from punishment. Moreover, the risk of pregnancy itself constitutes a substantial deterrence to young females. No similar natural sanctions deter males. A criminal sanction imposed solely on males thus serves to roughly "equalize" the deterrents on the sexes.

We are unable to accept petitioner's contention that the statute is impermissibly under-inclusive and must, in order to pass judicial scrutiny, be *broadened* so as to hold the female as criminally liable as the male. It is argued that this statute is not *necessary* to deter teenage pregnancy because a gender-neutral statute, where both male and female would be subject to prosecution, would serve that goal equally well. The relevant inquiry, however, is not whether the statute is drawn as precisely as it might have been, but whether the line chosen by the California Legislature is within constitutional limitations. *Kahn v. Shevin,* 416 U.S. at 356, n. 10.

In any event, we cannot say that a gender-neutral statute would be as effective as the statute California has chosen to enact. The State persuasively contends that a gender-neutral statute would frustrate its interest in effective enforcement. Its view is that a female is surely less likely to report violations of the statute if she herself would be subject to criminal prosecution. In an area already fraught with prosecutorial difficulties, we decline to hold that the Equal Protection Clause requires a legislature to enact a statute so broad that it may well be incapable of enforcement.

* * *

In upholding the California statute we also recognize that this is not a case where a statute is being challenged on the grounds that it "invidiously discriminates" against females. To the contrary, the statute places a burden on males which is not shared by females. But we find nothing to suggest that men, because of past discrimination or peculiar disadvantages, are in need of the special solicitude of the courts. Nor is this a case where the gender classification is made "solely for administrative convenience," or rests on "the baggage of sexual stereotypes," *Orr v. Orr,* 440 U.S. at 283. As we have held, the statute instead reasonably reflects the fact that the consequences of sexual intercourse and pregnancy fall more heavily on the female than on the male. Accordingly the judgment of the California Supreme Court is affirmed.

Justice Stewart, concurring.

* * *

The Constitution is violated when government, state or federal, invidiously classifies similarly situated people on the basis of the immutable characteristics with which they were born. Thus, detrimental racial classifications by government always violate the Constitution, for the simple reason that, so far as the Constitution is concerned, people of different races are always similarly situated. See *Fullilove v. Klutznick,* 448 U.S. 448, 522 (1980) (dissenting opinion). By contrast, while detrimental gender classifications by government often violate the Constitution, they do not always do so, for the reason that there are differences between males and females that the Constitution necessarily recognizes. In this case we deal with the most basic of these differences: females can become pregnant as the result of sexual intercourse; males cannot.

---

[4]   We do not understand petitioner to question a state's authority to make sexual intercourse among teenagers a criminal act, at least on a gender-neutral basis. . . . The Court has long recognized that a State has even broader authority to protect the physical, mental, and moral well-being of its youth, than of its adults. . . .

. . . . [W]e have recognized that in certain narrow circumstances men and women are *not* similarly situated, and in these circumstances a gender classification based on clear differences between the sexes is not invidious, and a legislative classification realistically based upon those differences is not unconstitutional.

Applying these principles to the classification enacted by the California Legislature, it is readily apparent that § 261.5 does not violate the Equal Protection Clause. Young women and men are not similarly situated with respect to the problems and risk associated with intercourse and pregnancy, and the statute is realistically related to the legitimate state purpose of reducing those problems and risks. . . .

Justice Brennan, with whom Justices White and Marshall join, dissenting.

It is disturbing to find the Court so splintered on a case that presents such a straightforward issue: whether the admittedly gender-based classification in Cal. Penal Code § 261.5 bears a sufficient relationship to the State's asserted goal of preventing teenage pregnancies to survive the "mid-level" constitutional scrutiny mandated by *Craig v. Boren,* 429 U.S. 190 (1976). Applying the analytical framework provided by our precedents, I am convinced that there is only one proper resolution of this issue: the classification must be declared unconstitutional. I fear that the plurality and Justices Stewart and Blackmun reach the opposite result by placing too much emphasis on the desirability of achieving the State's asserted statutory goal – prevention of teenage pregnancy – and not enough emphasis on the fundamental question of whether the sex-based discrimination in the California statute is *substantially* related to the achievement of that goal.

. . . . [E]ven assuming that prevention of teenage pregnancy is an important governmental objective and that it is in fact an objective of § 261.5, California still has the burden of proving that there are fewer teenage pregnancies under its gender-based statutory rape law than there would be if the law were gender-neutral. To meet this burden, the State must show that because its statutory rape law punishes only males, and not females, it more effectively deters minor females from having sexual intercourse. . . .

However, a State's bare assertion that its gender-based statutory classification substantially furthers an important governmental interest is not enough to meet its burden of proof under *Craig v. Boren.* Rather, the State must produce evidence that will persuade the Court that its assertion is true. The State has not produced such evidence in this case. Moreover, there are at least two serious flaws in the State's assertion that law enforcement problems created by a gender-neutral statutory rape law would make such a statute less effective than a gender-based statute in deterring sexual activity.

First, the experience of other jurisdictions, and California itself, belies the plurality's conclusion that a gender-neutral statutory rape law "may well be incapable of enforcement." There are now at least 37 States that have enacted gender-neutral statutory rape laws. California has introduced no evidence that those states have been handicapped by the enforcement problems the plurality finds so persuasive. Surely, if those States could provide such evidence, we might expect that California would have introduced it. In addition, the California Legislature in recent years has revised other sections of the Penal Code to make them gender-neutral. For example, Cal. Penal Code §§ 286(b)(1) and 288a(b)(1), prohibiting sodomy and oral copulation with a "person who is under 18 years of age," could cause two minor homosexuals to be subjected to criminal sanctions for engaging in mutually consensual conduct. Again, the State has introduced no evidence to explain why a gender-neutral statutory rape law would be any more difficult to enforce than those statutes.

The second flaw in the State's assertion is that even assuming that a gender-neutral statute would be more difficult to enforce, the State has still not shown that those enforcement problems would make such a statute less effective than a gender-based statute in deterring minor females from engaging in sexual intercourse. Common sense, however, suggests that a gender-neutral statutory rape law is potentially a *greater* deterrent of sexual activity than a gender-based law, for the simple reason that a gender-neutral law subjects both men and women to criminal sanctions and thus arguably has a deterrent effect on twice as many potential violators. Even if fewer persons were prosecuted under the gender-neutral law, as the State suggests, it would still be true that twice as many persons would be *subject* to arrest. The State's failure to prove that a gender-neutral law would be a less effective deterrent than a gender-based law, like the State's failure to prove that a gender-neutral law would be difficult to enforce, should have led this Court to invalidate § 261.5.

* * *

Justice Stevens, dissenting.

* * *

In my judgment, the fact that a class of persons is especially vulnerable to a risk that a statute is designed to avoid is a reason for making the statute applicable to that class. The argument that a special need for protection provides a rational explanation for an exemption is one I simply do not comprehend. In this case, the fact that a female confronts a greater risk of harm than a male is a reason for applying the prohibition to her – not a reason for granting her a license to use her own judgment on whether or not to assume the risk. Surely, if we examine the problem from the point of view of society's interest in preventing the risk-creating conduct from occurring at all, it is irrational to exempt 50% of the potential violators. And, if we view the government's interest as that of a *parens patriae* seeking to protect its subjects from harming themselves, the discrimination is actually perverse. Would a rational parent making rules for the conduct of twin children of opposite sex simultaneously forbid the son and authorize the daughter to engage in conduct that is especially harmful to the daughter? That is the effect of this statutory classification.

In my opinion, the only acceptable justification for a general rule requiring disparate treatment of the two participants in a joint act must be a legislative judgment that one is more guilty than the other. The risk-creating conduct that this statute is designed to prevent requires the participation of two persons – one male and one female. In many situations it is probably true that one is the aggressor and the other is either an unwilling, or at least a less willing, participant in the joint act. If a statute authorized punishment of only one participant and required the prosecutor to prove that that participant had been the aggressor, I assume that the discrimination would be valid. Although the question is less clear, I also assume, for the purpose of deciding this case, that it would be permissible to punish only the male participant, if one element of the offense were proof that he had been the aggressor, or at least in some respects the more responsible participant in the joint act. The statute at issue in this case, however, requires no such proof. The question raised by this statute is whether the State, consistently with the Federal Constitution, may always punish the male and never the female when they are equally responsible or when the female is the more responsible of the two.

It would seem to me that an impartial lawmaker could give only one answer to that question. The fact that the California Legislature has decided to apply its prohibition only to the male may reflect a legislative judgment that in the typical case the male is actually the more guilty party. Any such judgment must, in turn, assume that the decision to engage in the risk-creating conduct is always – or at least typically – a male decision. If that assumption is valid, the statutory classification should also be valid. But what is the support for the assumption? It is not contained in the record of this case or in any legislative history or scholarly study that has been called to our attention. I think it is supported to some extent by traditional attitudes toward male-female relationships. But the possibility that such an habitual attitude may reflect nothing more than an irrational prejudice makes it an insufficient justification for discriminatory treatment that is otherwise blatantly unfair. For, as I read this statute, it requires that one, and only one, of two equally guilty wrongdoers be stigmatized by a criminal conviction.

* * *

Nor do I find at all persuasive the suggestion that this discrimination is adequately justified by the desire to encourage females to inform against their male partners. Even if the concept of a wholesale informant's exemption were an acceptable enforcement device, what is the justification for defining the exempt class entirely by reference to sex rather than by reference to a more neutral criterion such as relative innocence? Indeed, if the exempt class is to be composed entirely of members of one sex, what is there to support the view that the statutory purpose will be better served by granting the informing license to females rather than to males? If a discarded male partner informs on a promiscuous female, a timely threat of prosecution might will prevent the precise harm the statue is intended to minimize.

Finally, even if my logic is faulty and there actually is some speculative basis for treating equally guilty males and females differently, I still believe that any such speculative justification would be outweighed by the paramount interest in evenhanded enforcement of the law. A rule that authorizes punishment of only one of two equally guilty wrongdoers violates the essence of the constitutional requirement that the sovereign must govern impartially.

I respectfully dissent.

QUESTIONS

1.   The primary rationale offered by the majority for punishing males but not females for non-forcible sexual relations with someone under the legal age of consent was the prevention of teen pregnancy. Do you agree with the majority or the dissent that the sexes are not "similarly situated" when it comes to this issue and, thus, discrimination on the basis of gender as applied to statutory rape laws is not constitutionally impermissible? Explain your reasons.

2.   The majority opinion stated that it was not basing its opinion on the stereotype that the male is frequently the aggressor in teenage sexual relations. Do you agree, or do you think that stereotype played some role in the decision. Why or why not? Do you think such a stereotype a valid one? Explain.

3.   As stated in the text above this case, traditional statutory rape laws, like the one at issue in *Michael M.*, have been modified in many jurisdictions to be gender-neutral, even though not constitutionally required to be so under the holding of this case. Which approach do you think is the wiser? Why?

E. Miscellaneous Sex Offenses

1. Child Molestation

Child molestation is technically covered by sexual assault/rape laws. Some states, though, have statutorily created a special offense for child molestation. It is typically punished more severely than a sexual assault on an adult.

2. Incest

Incest is defined as either the marriage or the engaging in sexual acts between closely related persons. The degree of kinship required by statutes varies by jurisdiction. As a general rule, most states do not permit any coupling of persons who are first cousins or any closer degree of kinship.

3. Lewd and Lascivious Conduct

A person who commits any lewd and offensive act which he or she knows or reasonably expects is likely to be observed by other non-consenting persons who would be affronted or alarmed by such conduct is guilty of lewd and lascivious conduct. In some states, this crime includes indecent exposure. On other states, indecent exposure is its own offense, leaving a lewd and lascivious conduct statute limited to acts such as masturbation in a public place. Some states also have "public sexual indecency" laws which punish many forms of sexual expression as crimes if they are done in public. Public sexual indecency can be committed by someone who is reckless about whether a third-party would see the act and would, as a reasonable person, be offended or alarmed by the act.

4. Prostitution

"Prostitution" is sexual activity with another person in exchange for something of economic value. Technically, therefore, both the person offering the sexual activity in exchange for the thing of value, and the person offering the thing of value in exchange for the sexual activity, are guilty of the crime of prostitution. And, of course, inchoate liability may be affixed on anyone who solicits, knowingly facilitates, or purposefully aids or abets the crime of prostitution.

F. Sexually Dangerous Person Laws

"Megan's Law" was enacted by the New Jersey state legislature in the wake of the death of Megan Kanka, a girl who was killed by a sex offender after his release from prison. The law enacted a system of registration to permit law enforcement officials to identify and alert the public of the release of those offenders who commit other predatory acts against children when necessary for the public safety.

The federal government mandated that similar laws be adopted by all states to qualify for certain types of funding. Accordingly, nearly all states have adopted some requirement that people convicted of certain sex crimes register as a sex offender or as a "sexually dangerous person." The constitutionality of such registration schemes has been fought in many courts, but they have been upheld in large part.

Another strategy designed to protect the public from sexually dangerous persons was adopted by Kansas. Their law provided for the civil commitment of "sexually violent predators" upon the completion of their period of criminal incarceration. The statute was upheld by the Supreme Court in following case.

The State of KANSAS, Petitioner, v. Leroy HENDRICKS, Respondent.
117 S. Ct. 2072 (1997).

Justice Thomas delivered the opinion of the Supreme Court.

In 1994, Kansas enacted the Sexually Violent Predator Act, which establishes procedures for the civil commitment of persons who, due to a "mental abnormality" or a "personality disorder," are likely to engage in "predatory acts of sexual violence." Kan. Stat. Ann. § 59-29a01 et seq. (1994). The State invoked the Act for the first time to commit Leroy Hendricks, an inmate who had a long history of sexually molesting children, and who was scheduled for release from prison shortly after the Act became law. Hendricks challenged his commitment on, inter alia, "substantive" due process, double jeopardy, and ex post facto grounds. The Kansas Supreme Court invalidated the Act, holding that its pre-commitment condition of a "mental abnormality" did not satisfy what the court perceived to be the "substantive" due process requirement that involuntary civil commitment must be predicated on a finding of "mental illness." *In re Hendricks*, 912 P.2d 129, 138 (1996). The State of Kansas petitioned for certiorari. Hendricks subsequently filed a cross-petition in which he reasserted his federal double jeopardy and ex post facto claims. We granted certiorari on both the petition and the cross-petition, and now reverse the judgment below.

I

The Kansas Legislature enacted the Sexually Violent Predator Act (Act) in 1994 to grapple with the problem of managing repeat sexual offenders. Although Kansas already had a statute addressing the involuntary commitment of those defined as "mentally ill," the legislature determined that existing civil commitment procedures were inadequate to confront the risks presented by "sexually violent predators." In the Act's preamble, the legislature explained:

> [A] small but extremely dangerous group of sexually violent predators exist who do not have a
> mental disease or defect that renders them appropriate for involuntary treatment pursuant to the
> [general involuntary civil commitment statute] . . . . In contrast to persons appropriate for civil
> commitment under the [general involuntary civil commitment statute], sexually violent predators

311

generally have anti-social personality features which are unamenable to existing mental illness treatment modalities and those features render them likely to engage in sexually violent behavior. The legislature further finds that sexually violent predators' likelihood of engaging in repeat acts of predatory sexual violence is high. The existing involuntary commitment procedure . . . is inadequate to address the risk these sexually violent predators pose to society. The legislature further finds that the prognosis for rehabilitating sexually violent predators in a prison setting is poor, the treatment needs of this population are very long term and the treatment modalities for this population are very different than the traditional treatment modalities for people appropriate for commitment under the [general involuntary civil commitment statute].

Kan. Stat. Ann. § 59-29a01 (1994).

As a result, the Legislature found it necessary to establish "a civil commitment procedure for the long-term care and treatment of the sexually violent predator." The Act defined a "sexually violent predator" as: "any person who has been convicted of or charged with a sexually violent offense and who suffers from a mental abnormality or personality disorder which makes the person likely to engage in the predatory acts of sexual violence." A "mental abnormality" was defined, in turn, as a "congenital or acquired condition affecting the emotional or volitional capacity which predisposes the person to commit sexually violent offenses in a degree constituting such person a menace to the health and safety of others."

As originally structured, the Act's civil commitment procedures pertained to: (1) a presently confined person who, like Hendricks, "has been convicted of a sexually violent offense" and is scheduled for release; (2) a person who has been "charged with a sexually violent offense" but has been found incompetent to stand trial; (3) a person who has been found "not guilty by reason of insanity of a sexually violent offense"; and (4) a person found "not guilty" of a sexually violent offense because of a mental disease or defect.

The initial version of the Act, as applied to a currently confined person such as Hendricks, was designed to initiate a specific series of procedures. The custodial agency was required to notify the local prosecutor 60 days before the anticipated release of a person who might have met the Act's criteria. The prosecutor was then obligated, within 45 days, to decide whether to file a petition in state court seeking the person's involuntary commitment. If such a petition were filed, the court was to determine whether "probable cause" existed to support a finding that the person was a "sexually violent predator" and thus eligible for civil commitment. Upon such a determination, transfer of the individual to a secure facility for professional evaluation would occur. After that evaluation, a trial would be held to determine beyond a reasonable doubt whether the individual was a sexually violent predator. If that determination were made, the person would then be transferred to the custody of the Secretary of Social and Rehabilitation Services (Secretary) for "control, care and treatment until such time as the person's mental abnormality or personality disorder has so changed that the person is safe to be at large." § 59-29a07(a).

In addition to placing the burden of proof upon the State, the Act afforded the individual a number of other procedural safeguards. In the case of an indigent person, the State was required to provide, at public expense, the assistance of counsel and an examination by mental health care professionals. The individual also received the right to present and cross-examine witnesses, and the opportunity to review documentary evidence presented by the State. Once an individual was confined, the Act required that "the involuntary detention or commitment . . . shall conform to constitutional requirements for care and treatment." Confined persons were afforded three different avenues of review: First, the committing court was obligated to conduct an annual review to determine whether continued detention was warranted. Second, the Secretary was permitted, at any time, to decide that the confined individual's condition had so changed that release was appropriate, and could then authorize the person to petition for release. Finally, even without the Secretary's permission, the confined person could at any time file a release petition. If the court found that the State could no longer satisfy its burden under the initial commitment standard, the individual would be freed from confinement.

In 1984, Hendricks was convicted of taking "indecent liberties" with two 13-year-old boys. After serving nearly 10 years of his sentence, he was slated for release to a halfway house. Shortly before his scheduled release, however, the State filed a petition in state court seeking Hendricks' civil confinement as a sexually violent predator. On August 19, 1994, Hendricks appeared before the court with counsel and moved to dismiss the petition on the grounds that the Act violated various federal constitutional provisions. Although the court reserved ruling on the Act's constitutionality, it concluded that there was probable cause to support a finding that Hendricks was a sexually violent predator, and therefore ordered that he be evaluated at the Larned State Security Hospital.

Hendricks subsequently requested a jury trial to determine whether he qualified as a sexually violent predator. During that trial, Hendricks' own testimony revealed a chilling history of repeated child sexual molestation and abuse, beginning in 1955 when he exposed his genitals to two young girls. At that time, he pleaded guilty to indecent exposure. Then, in 1957, he was convicted of lewdness involving a young girl and received a brief jail sentence. In 1960, he molested two young boys while he worked for a carnival. After serving two years in prison for that offense, he was paroled, only to be rearrested for molesting a 7-year-old girl. Attempts were made to treat him for his sexual deviance, and in 1965 he was considered "safe to be at large," and was discharged from a state psychiatric hospital. Shortly thereafter, however, Hendricks sexually assaulted another young boy and girl – he performed oral sex on the 8-year-old girl and fondled the 11-year-old boy. He was again imprisoned in 1967, but refused to participate in a sex offender treatment program, and thus remained incarcerated until his parole in 1972. Diagnosed as a pedophile, Hendricks entered into, but then abandoned, a treatment program. He testified that despite having received professional help for his pedophilia, he continued to harbor sexual desires for children. Indeed, soon after his 1972 parole, Hendricks began to abuse his own stepdaughter and stepson. He forced the children to engage in sexual activity with him over a period of approximately four years. Then, as noted above, Hendricks was convicted of "taking indecent liberties" with two adolescent boys after he attempted to fondle them. As a result of that conviction, he was once again imprisoned, and was serving that sentence when he reached his conditional release date in September 1994.

Hendricks admitted that he had repeatedly abused children whenever he was not confined. He explained that when he "gets stressed out," he "can't control the urge" to molest children. Although Hendricks recognized that his behavior harms children, and he hoped he would not sexually molest children again, he stated that the only sure way he could keep from sexually abusing children in the future was "to die." Hendricks readily agreed with the state physician's diagnosis that he suffers from pedophilia and that he is not cured of the condition; indeed, he told the physician that "treatment is bull-." The jury unanimously found beyond a reasonable doubt that Hendricks was a sexually violent predator. The trial court subsequently determined, as a matter of state law, that pedophilia qualifies as a "mental abnormality" as defined by the Act, and thus ordered Hendricks committed to the Secretary's custody.

Hendricks appealed, claiming, among other things, that application of the Act to him violated the Federal Constitution's Due Process, Double Jeopardy, and Ex Post Facto Clauses. The Kansas Supreme Court accepted Hendricks' due process claim. The court declared that in order to commit a person involuntarily in a civil proceeding, a State is required by "substantive" due process to prove by clear and convincing evidence that the person is both (1) mentally ill, and (2) a danger to himself or to others. The court then determined that the Act's definition of "mental abnormality" did not satisfy what it perceived to be this Court's "mental illness" requirement in the civil commitment context. As a result, the court held that "the Act violates Hendricks' substantive due process rights."

II

Kansas argues that the Act's definition of "mental abnormality" satisfies "substantive" due process requirements. We agree. Although freedom from physical restraint "has always been at the core of the liberty protected by the Due Process Clause from arbitrary governmental action," *Foucha v. Louisiana*, 504 U.S. 71, 80, (1992), that liberty interest is not absolute. . . .

Accordingly, States have in certain narrow circumstances provided for the forcible civil detainment of people who are unable to control their behavior and who thereby pose a danger to the public health and safety. . . . We have consistently upheld such involuntary commitment statutes provided the confinement takes place pursuant to proper procedures and evidentiary standards. *See Foucha, supra,* at 80; *Addington v. Texas,* 441 U.S. 418, 426-427 (1979). It thus cannot be said that the involuntary civil confinement of a limited subclass of dangerous persons is contrary to our understanding of ordered liberty.

The challenged Act unambiguously requires a finding of dangerousness either to one's self or to others as a prerequisite to involuntary confinement. Commitment proceedings can be initiated only when a person "has been convicted of or charged with a sexually violent offense," and "suffers from a mental abnormality or personality disorder which makes the person likely to engage in the predatory acts of sexual violence." The statute thus requires proof of more than a mere predisposition to violence; rather, it requires evidence of past sexually violent behavior and a present mental condition that creates a likelihood of such conduct in the future if the person is not incapacitated. As we have recognized, "previous instances of violent behavior are an important indicator of future violent tendencies." *Heller v. Doe,* 509 U.S. 312, 323 (1993). A finding of dangerousness, standing alone, is ordinarily not a sufficient ground upon which to justify indefinite involuntary commitment. We have sustained civil commitment statutes when they have coupled proof of dangerousness with the proof of some additional factor, such as a "mental illness" or "mental abnormality." *See, e.g., Heller, supra,* 314-315. . . . These added statutory requirements serve to limit involuntary civil confinement to those who suffer from a volitional impairment rendering them dangerous beyond their control. The Kansas Act is plainly of a kind with these other civil commitment statutes: It requires a finding of future dangerousness, and then links that finding to the existence of a "mental abnormality" or "personality disorder" that makes it difficult, if not impossible, for the person to control his dangerous behavior. The precommitment requirement of a "mental abnormality" or "personality disorder" is consistent with the requirements of these other statutes that we have upheld in that it narrows the class of persons eligible for confinement to those who are unable to control their dangerousness.

Hendricks nonetheless argues that our earlier cases dictate a finding of "mental illness" as a prerequisite for civil commitment, citing *Foucha,* and *Addington.* He then asserts that a "mental abnormality" is not equivalent to a "mental illness" because it is a term coined by the Kansas Legislature, rather than by the psychiatric community. Contrary to Hendricks' assertion, the term "mental illness" is devoid of any talismanic significance. Not only do "psychiatrists disagree widely and frequently on what constitutes mental illness," *Ake v. Oklahoma,* 470 U.S. 68, 81 (1985), but the Court itself has used a variety of expressions to describe the mental condition of those properly subject to civil confinement. . . .

To the extent that the civil commitment statutes we have considered set forth criteria relating to an individual's inability to control his dangerousness, the Kansas Act sets forth comparable criteria and Hendricks' condition doubtless satisfies those criteria. The mental health professionals who evaluated Hendricks diagnosed him as suffering from pedophilia, a condition the psychiatric profession itself classifies as a serious mental disorder. Hendricks even conceded that, when he becomes "stressed out," he cannot "control the urge" to molest children. This admitted lack of volitional control, coupled with a prediction of future dangerousness, adequately distinguishes Hendricks from other dangerous persons who are perhaps more properly dealt with exclusively through criminal proceedings. Hendricks' diagnosis as a pedophile, which qualifies as a "mental abnormality" under the Act, thus plainly suffices for due process purposes.

We granted Hendricks' cross-petition to determine whether the Act violates the Constitution's double jeopardy prohibition or its ban on ex post facto lawmaking. The thrust of Hendricks' argument is that the Act establishes criminal proceedings; hence confinement under it necessarily constitutes punishment. He contends that where, as here, newly enacted "punishment" is predicated upon past conduct for which he has already been convicted and forced to serve a prison sentence, the Constitution's Double Jeopardy and Ex Post Facto Clauses are violated. We are unpersuaded by Hendricks' argument that Kansas has established criminal proceedings.

* * *

.... Those persons committed under the Act are, by definition, suffering from a "mental abnormality" or a "personality disorder" that prevents them from exercising adequate control over their behavior. Such persons are therefore unlikely to be deterred by the threat of confinement. And the conditions surrounding that confinement do not suggest a punitive purpose on the State's part. The State has represented that an individual confined under the Act is not subject to the more restrictive conditions placed on state prisoners, but instead experiences essentially the same conditions as any involuntarily committed patient in the state mental institution. Because none of the parties argues that people institutionalized under the Kansas general civil commitment statute are subject to punitive conditions, even though they may be involuntarily confined, it is difficult to conclude that persons confined under this Act are being "punished."

Although the civil commitment scheme at issue here does involve an affirmative restraint, "the mere fact that a person is detained does not inexorably lead to the conclusion that the government has imposed punishment." *United States v. Salerno*, 481 U.S. 739, 746 (1987). The State may take measures to restrict the freedom of the dangerously mentally ill. This is a legitimate non-punitive governmental objective and has been historically so regarded. The Court has, in fact, cited the confinement of "mentally unstable individuals who present a danger to the public" as one classic example of nonpunitive detention. *Id.* at 748-749. If detention for the purpose of protecting the community from harm necessarily constituted punishment, then all involuntary civil commitments would have to be considered punishment. But we have never so held.

Hendricks focuses on his confinement's potentially indefinite duration as evidence of the State's punitive intent. That focus, however, is misplaced. Far from any punitive objective, the confinement's duration is instead linked to the stated purposes of the commitment, namely, to hold the person until his mental abnormality no longer causes him to be a threat to others. If, at any time, the confined person is adjudged "safe to be at large," he is statutorily entitled to immediate release.

Furthermore, commitment under the Act is only potentially indefinite. The maximum amount of time an individual can be incapacitated pursuant to a single judicial proceeding is one year. If Kansas seeks to continue the detention beyond that year, a court must once again determine beyond a reasonable doubt that the detainee satisfies the same standards as required for the initial confinement. This requirement again demonstrates that Kansas does not intend an individual committed pursuant to the Act to remain confined any longer than he suffers from a mental abnormality rendering him unable to control his dangerousness.

* * *

Finally, Hendricks argues that the Act is necessarily punitive because it fails to offer any legitimate "treatment." Without such treatment, Hendricks asserts, confinement under the Act amounts to little more than disguised punishment. Hendricks' argument assumes that treatment for his condition is available, but that the State has failed (or refused) to provide it. The Kansas Supreme Court, however, apparently rejected this assumption, explaining: "It is clear that the overriding concern of the legislature is to continue the segregation of sexually violent offenders from the public. Treatment with the goal of reintegrating them into society is incidental, at best. The record reflects that treatment for sexually violent predators is all but nonexistent. The legislature concedes that sexually violent predators are not amenable to treatment under [the existing Kansas involuntary commitment statute]. If there is nothing to treat under [that statute], then there is no mental illness. In that light, the provisions of the Act for treatment appear somewhat disingenuous." It is possible to read this passage as a determination that Hendricks' condition was untreatable under the existing Kansas civil commitment statute, and thus the Act's sole purpose was incapacitation. Absent a treatable mental illness, the Kansas court concluded Hendricks could not be detained against his will.

Accepting the Kansas court's apparent determination that treatment is not possible for this category of individuals does not obligate us to adopt its legal conclusions. We have already observed that, under the appropriate circumstances and when accompanied by proper procedures, incapacitation

315

may be a legitimate end of the civil law. Accordingly, the Kansas court's determination that the Act's "overriding concern" was the continued "segregation of sexually violent offenders" is consistent with our conclusion that the Act establishes civil proceedings, especially when that concern is coupled with the State's ancillary goal of providing treatment to those offenders, if such is possible. While we have upheld state civil commitment statutes that aim both to incapacitate and to treat, we have never held that the Constitution prevents a State from civilly detaining those for whom no treatment is available, but who nevertheless pose a danger to others. A State could hardly be seen as furthering a "punitive" purpose by involuntarily confining persons afflicted with an untreatable, highly contagious disease. . . .

Although the treatment program initially offered Hendricks may have seemed somewhat meager, it must be remembered that he was the first person committed under the Act. That the State did not have all of its treatment procedures in place is thus not surprising. What is significant, however, is that Hendricks was placed under the supervision of the Kansas Department of Health and Social and Rehabilitative Services, housed in a unit segregated from the general prison population and operated not by employees of the Department of Corrections, but by other trained individuals. And, before this Court, Kansas declared "absolutely" that persons committed under the Act are now receiving in the neighborhood of "31.5 hours of treatment per week."

Where the State has "disavowed any punitive intent"; limited confinement to a small segment of particularly dangerous individuals; provided strict procedural safeguards; directed that confined persons be segregated from the general prison population and afforded the same status as others who have been civilly committed; recommended treatment if such is possible; and permitted immediate release upon a showing that the individual is no longer dangerous or mentally impaired, we cannot say that it acted with punitive intent. We therefore hold that the Act does not establish criminal proceedings and that involuntary confinement pursuant to the Act is not punitive. Our conclusion that the Act is nonpunitive thus removes an essential prerequisite for both Hendricks' double jeopardy and ex post facto claims.

* * *

We hold that the Kansas Sexually Violent Predator Act comports with due process requirements and neither runs afoul of double jeopardy principles nor constitutes an exercise in impermissible ex post facto lawmaking. Accordingly, the judgment of the Kansas Supreme Court is reversed.

Justice Breyer, with whom Justices Stevens, Souter and Ginsburg join dissenting.

I agree with the majority that the Kansas Act's "definition of 'mental abnormality'" satisfies the "substantive" requirements of the Due Process Clause. 8. Kansas, however, concedes that Hendricks' condition is treatable; yet the Act did not provide Hendricks (or others like him) with any treatment until after his release date from prison and only inadequate treatment thereafter. These, and certain other, special features of the Act convince me that it was not simply an effort to commit Hendricks civilly, but rather an effort to inflict further punishment upon him. The Ex Post Facto Clause therefore prohibits the Act's application to Hendricks, who committed his crimes prior to its enactment.

* * *

Kansas' 1994 Act violates the Federal Constitution's prohibition of "any . . . ex post facto Law" if it "inflicts" upon Hendricks "a greater punishment" than did the law "annexed to" his "crimes" when he "committed" those crimes in 1984. *Calder v. Bull*, 3 U.S. 386 (1798); U.S. Const., Art. I, § 10. The majority agrees that the Clause "'forbids the application of any new punitive measure to a crime already consummated.'" *California Dept. of Corrections v. Morales*, 514 U.S. 499 (1995). But it finds the Act is not "punitive." With respect to that basic question, I disagree with the majority.

Certain resemblances between the Act's "civil commitment" and traditional criminal punishments are obvious. Like criminal imprisonment, the Act's civil commitment amounts to "secure" confinement, and "incarceration against one's will." *In re Gault*, 387 U.S. 1, 50 (1967). . . . In addition, a basic objective of the Act is incapacitation, which, as Blackstone said in describing an objective of criminal law, is to "deprive the party injuring of the power to do future mischief." 4 W. BLACKSTONE, COMMENTARIES

*11- *12. . . . Moreover, the Act, like criminal punishment, imposes its confinement (or sanction) only upon an individual who has previously committed a criminal offense. . . . And the Act imposes that confinement through the use of persons (county prosecutors), procedural guarantees (trial by jury, assistance of counsel, psychiatric evaluations), and standards ("beyond a reasonable doubt") traditionally associated with the criminal law.

These obvious resemblances by themselves, however, are not legally sufficient to transform what the Act calls "civil commitment" into a criminal punishment. Civil commitment of dangerous, mentally ill individuals by its very nature involves confinement and incapacitation. Yet "civil commitment," from a constitutional perspective, nonetheless remains civil. *Allen v. Illinois*, 478 U.S. 364 (1986). Nor does the fact that criminal behavior triggers the Act make the critical difference. The Act's insistence upon a prior crime, by screening out those whose past behavior does not concretely demonstrate the existence of a mental problem or potential future danger, may serve an important noncriminal evidentiary purpose. Neither is the presence of criminal law-type procedures determinative. Those procedures can serve an important purpose that in this context one might consider noncriminal, namely helping to prevent judgmental mistakes that would wrongly deprive a person of important liberty.

* * *

To find that the confinement the Act imposes upon Hendricks is "punishment" is to find a violation of the Ex Post Facto Clause. Kansas does not deny that the 1994 Act changed the legal consequences that attached to Hendricks earlier crimes, and in a way that significantly "disadvantaged the offender," *Weaver v. Graham*, 450 U.S. 24, 29 (1981). To find a violation of that Clause here, however, is not to hold that the Clause prevents Kansas, or other States, from enacting dangerous sexual offender statutes. A statute that operates prospectively, for example, does not offend the Ex Post Facto Clause. Neither does it offend the Ex Post Facto Clause for a State to sentence offenders to the fully authorized sentence, to seek consecutive, rather than concurrent, sentences, or to invoke recidivism statutes to lengthen imprisonment. Moreover, a statute that operates retroactively, like Kansas' statute, nonetheless does not offend the Clause if the confinement that it imposes is not punishment – if, that is to say, the legislature does not simply add a later criminal punishment to an earlier one. I therefore would affirm the judgment below.

QUESTIONS

1.   Recall from Chapter 5 that diagnoses of anti-social personality disorder and pedophilia do not qualify as qualifying "mental diseases or defects" for the purposes of the insanity defense. Why should they for involuntary commitment after a prison term has been served?

2.   The majority of the *Hendricks* court upheld the Kansas statute over ex post facto and double jeopardy challenges on the grounds that involuntary civil commitment of sexually dangerous predators was not "punishment." Do you agree? Why or why not?

3.   Given that involuntary commitment was deemed not to be "punishment" by the *Hendricks* court, do you think any challenges to sex offender registration and notification laws, like Megan's Law, can be successfully challenged using a constitutional argument? Explain your reasoning.

G. Obscenity, Pornography, and Indecency

In evaluating the free speech rights of adults, the Supreme Court has held that sexually explicit expression which is "indecent" but not "obscene" is protected by the First Amendment. Where the line is drawn between indecency and obscenity, though, is not subject to easy explication.

Under the Model Penal Code, "Material is obscene if, considered as a whole, its predominant appeal is to prurient interest, that is, a shameful or morbid interest, in nudity, sex, or excretion, and if, in addition, it foes substantially beyond customary limits of candor in describing or representing such matters." Such material "cannot [knowingly or recklessly be] sold, exhibited, advertised, or otherwise publically disseminated." Exemptions are made for "institutions or person having scientific, educational, governmental, or other similar justification for possession obscene materials" and "non-commercial dissemination to personal associates of the actor." Laws seeking to regulate material or conduct that does not fit into this definition of obscenity may run afoul the freedom of speech and expression protections of the First Amendment to the United States Constitution, no matter how well-intentioned the law might be, as illustrated by the following case.

Janet RENO, Attorney General of the United States v. AMERICAN CIVIL LIBERTIES UNION, et al. 521 U.S. 844 (1997).

Justice Stevens delivered the opinion of the Supreme Court.

At issue is the constitutionality of two statutory provisions enacted to protect minors from "indecent" and "patently offensive" communications on the Internet. Notwithstanding the legitimacy and importance of the congressional goal of protecting children from harmful materials, we agree with the three-judge District Court that the statute abridges "the freedom of speech" protected by the First Amendment.

I

The District Court made extensive findings of fact, most of which were based on a detailed stipulation prepared by the parties. The findings describe the character and the dimensions of the Internet, the availability of sexually explicit material in that medium, and the problems confronting age verification for recipients of Internet communications. Because those findings provide the underpinnings for the legal issues, we begin with a summary of the undisputed facts.

* * *

Sexually explicit material on the Internet includes text, pictures, and chat and "extends from the modestly titillating to the hardest-core." These files are created, named, and posted in the same manner as material that is not sexually explicit, and may be accessed either deliberately or unintentionally during the course of an imprecise search. "Once a provider posts its content on the Internet, it cannot prevent that content from entering any community." Thus, for example, "when the UCR/California Museum of Photography posts to its Web site nudes by Edward Weston and Robert Mapplethorpe to announce that its new exhibit will travel to Baltimore and New York City, those images are available not only in Los Angeles, Baltimore, and New York City, but also in Cincinnati, Mobile, or Beijing – wherever Internet users live. Similarly, the safer sex instructions that Critical Path posts to its Web site, written in street language so that the teenage receiver can understand them, are available not just in Philadelphia, but also in Provo and Prague."

Though such material is widely available, users seldom encounter such content accidentally. "A document's title or a description of the document will usually appear before the document itself . . . and in many cases the user will receive detailed information about a site's content before he or she need take the step to access the document. Almost all sexually explicit images are preceded by warnings as to the content." For that reason, the "odds are slim" that a user would enter a sexually explicit site by accident. Unlike communications received by radio or television, "the receipt of information on the Internet requires a series of affirmative steps more deliberate and directed than merely turning a dial. A child requires some sophistication and some ability to read to retrieve material and thereby to use the Internet unattended."

Systems have been developed to help parents control the material that may be available on a home computer with Internet access. A system may either limit a computer's access to an approved list of sources that have been identified as containing no adult material, it may block designated inappropriate sites, or it may attempt to block messages containing identifiable objectionable features. "Although parental control software currently can screen for certain suggestive words or for known sexually explicit sites, it cannot now screen for sexually explicit images." Nevertheless, the evidence indicates that "a reasonably effective method by which parents can prevent their children from accessing sexually explicit and other material which parents may believe is inappropriate for their children will soon be available."

* * *

II

The Telecommunications Act of 1996, Pub. L. 104-104, 110 Stat. 56, was an unusually important legislative enactment. As stated on the first of its 103 pages, its primary purpose was to reduce regulation and encourage "the rapid deployment of new telecommunications technologies." The major components of the statute have nothing to do with the Internet; they were designed to promote competition in the local telephone service market, the multichannel video market, and the market for over-the-air broadcasting. The Act includes seven Titles, six of which are the product of extensive committee hearings and the subject of discussion in Reports prepared by Committees of the Senate and the House of Representatives. By contrast, Title V – known as the "Communications Decency Act of 1996" (CDA) – contains provisions that were either added in executive committee after the hearings were concluded or as amendments offered during floor debate on the legislation. An amendment offered in the Senate was the source of the two statutory provisions challenged in this case. They are informally described as the "indecent transmission" provision and the "patently offensive display" provision.

The first, 47 U.S.C. A. § 223(a) (Supp. 1997), prohibits the knowing transmission of obscene or indecent messages to any recipient under 18 years of age. It provides in pertinent part:

> Whoever . . . makes, creates, or solicits, . . . [or] . . . initiates the transmission of, any comment, request, suggestion, proposal, image, or other communication which is obscene or indecent, knowing that the recipient of the communication is under 18 years of age, regardless of whether the maker of such communication placed the call or initiated the communication;. . .. [or] knowingly permits any telecommunications facility under his control to be used for any activity prohibited by paragraph (1) with the intent that it be used for such activity, shall be fined under Title 18, or imprisoned not more than two years, or both.

The second provision, § 223(d), prohibits the knowing sending or displaying of patently offensive messages in a manner that is available to a person under 18 years of age. It provides:

> Whoever . . . knowingly . . . uses an interactive computer service to send to a specific person or persons under 18 years of age, or uses any interactive computer service to display in a   manner available to a person under 18 years of age, any comment, request, suggestion, proposal, image, or other communication that, in context, depicts or describes, in terms patently offensive as measured by contemporary community standards, sexual or excretory activities or organs, regardless of whether the user of such service placed the call or initiated the communication; or knowingly permits any telecommunications facility under such person's control to be used for an activity prohibited by paragraph 29 with the intent that it be used for such activity, shall be fined under Title 18, or imprisoned not more than two years, or both.

The breadth of these prohibitions is qualified by two affirmative defenses. One covers those who take "good faith, reasonable, effective, and appropriate actions" to restrict access by minors to the prohibited communications. § 223(e)(5)(A). The other covers those who restrict access to covered material by requiring certain designated forms of age proof, such as a verified credit card or an adult identification number or code. § 223(e)(5)(B).

III

On February 8, 1996, immediately after the President signed the statute, 20 plaintiffs filed suit against the Attorney General of the United States and the Department of Justice challenging the constitutionality of §§ 223(a)(1) and 223(d). A week later, based on his conclusion that the term "indecent" was too vague to provide the basis for a criminal prosecution, District Judge Buckwalter entered a temporary restraining order against enforcement of § 223(a)(1)(B)(ii) insofar as it applies to indecent communications. A second suit was then filed by 27 additional plaintiffs, the two cases were consolidated, and a three-judge District Court was convened pursuant to § 561 of the Act. After an evidentiary hearing, that Court entered a preliminary injunction against enforcement of both of the challenged provisions. Each of the three judges wrote a separate opinion, but their judgment was unanimous.

Chief Judge Sloviter doubted the strength of the Government's interest in regulating "the vast range of online material covered or potentially covered by the CDA," but acknowledged that the interest was "compelling" with respect to some of that material. She concluded, nonetheless, that the statute "sweeps more broadly than necessary and thereby chills the expression of adults" and that the terms "patently offensive" and "indecent" were "inherently vague." She also determined that the affirmative defenses were not "technologically or economically feasible for most providers," specifically considering and rejecting an argument that providers could avoid liability by "tagging" their material in a manner that would allow potential readers to screen out unwanted transmissions. Chief Judge Sloviter also rejected the Government's suggestion that the scope of the statute could be narrowed by construing it to apply only to commercial pornographers.

Judge Buckwalter concluded that the word "indecent" in § 223(a)(1)(B) and the terms "patently offensive" and "in context" in § 223(d)(1) were so vague that criminal enforcement of either section would violate the "fundamental constitutional principle" of "simple fairness," and the specific protections of the First and Fifth Amendments. He found no statutory basis for the Government's argument that the challenged provisions would be applied only to "pornographic" materials, noting that, unlike obscenity, "indecency has not been defined to exclude works of serious literary, artistic, political or scientific value." Moreover, the Government's claim that the work must be considered patently offensive "in context" was itself vague because the relevant context might "refer to, among other things, the nature of the communication as a whole, the time of day it was conveyed, the medium used, the identity of the speaker, or whether or not it is accompanied by appropriate warnings." He believed that the unique nature of the Internet aggravated the vagueness of the statute.

Judge Dalzell's review of "the special attributes of Internet communication" disclosed by the evidence convinced him that the First Amendment denies Congress the power to regulate the content of protected speech on the Internet. His opinion explained at length why he believed the Act would abridge significant protected speech, particularly by noncommercial speakers, while "perversely, commercial pornographers would remain relatively unaffected." He construed our cases as requiring a "medium-specific" approach to the analysis of the regulation of mass communication, and concluded that the Internet – "the most participatory form of mass speech yet developed," is entitled to "the highest protection from governmental intrusion."

The judgment of the District Court enjoins the Government from enforcing the prohibitions in § 223(a)(1)(B) insofar as they relate to "indecent" communications, but expressly preserves the Government's right to investigate and prosecute the obscenity or child pornography activities prohibited therein. The injunction against enforcement of §§ 223(d)(1) and (2) is unqualified because those provisions contain no separate reference to obscenity or child pornography.

The Government appealed under the Act's special review provisions, and we noted probable jurisdiction. In its appeal, the Government argues that the District Court erred in holding that the CDA violated both the First Amendment because it is overbroad and the Fifth Amendment because it is vague. While we discuss the vagueness of the CDA because of its relevance to the First Amendment overbreadth inquiry, we conclude that the judgment should be affirmed without reaching the Fifth Amendment issue. We begin our analysis by reviewing the principal authorities on which the Government relies. Then, after describing the overbreadth of the CDA, we consider the Government's specific contentions, including its submission that we save portions of the statute either by severance or by fashioning judicial limitations on the scope of its coverage.

IV

In arguing for reversal, the Government contends that the CDA is plainly constitutional under three of our prior decisions: (1) *Ginsberg v. New York*, 390 U.S. 629 (1968); (2) *FCC v. Pacifica Foundation*, 438 U.S. 726 (1978); and (3) *Renton v. Playtime Theatres, Inc.*, 475 U.S. 41 (1986). A close look at these cases, however, raises – rather than relieves – doubts concerning the constitutionality of the CDA.

In *Ginsberg*, we upheld the constitutionality of a New York statute that prohibited selling to minors under 17 years of age material that was considered obscene as to them even if not obscene as to adults. We rejected the defendant's broad submission that "the scope of the constitutional freedom of expression secured to a citizen to read or see material concerned with sex cannot be made to depend on whether the citizen is an adult or a minor." 390 U.S. at 636. In rejecting that contention, we relied not only on the State's independent interest in the well-being of its youth, but also on our consistent recognition of the principle that "the parents' claim to authority in their own household to direct the rearing of their children is basic in the structure of our society."

In four important respects, the statute upheld in *Ginsberg* was narrower than the CDA. First, we noted in Ginsberg that "the prohibition against sales to minors does not bar parents who so desire from purchasing the magazines for their children." Id., at 639. Under the CDA, by contrast, neither the parents' consent -- nor even their participation – in the communication would avoid the application of the statute. Second, the New York statute applied only to commercial transactions, whereas the CDA contains no such limitation. Third, the New York statute cabined its definition of material that is harmful to minors with the requirement that it be "utterly without redeeming social importance for minors." The CDA fails to provide us with any definition of the term "indecent" as used in § 223(a)(1) and, importantly, omits any requirement that the "patently offensive" material covered by § 223(d) lack serious literary, artistic, political, or scientific value. Fourth, the New York statute defined a minor as a person under the age of 17, whereas the in applying to all those under 18 years, includes an additional year of those nearest majority.

In *Pacifica*, we upheld a declaratory order of the Federal Communications Commission, holding that the broadcast of a recording of a 12-minute monologue entitled "Filthy Words" that had previously been delivered to a live audience "could have been the subject of administrative sanctions." 438 U.S. at 730 (internal quotations omitted). The Commission had found that the repetitive use of certain words referring to excretory or sexual activities or organs "in an afternoon broadcast when children are in the audience was patently offensive" and concluded that the monologue was indecent "as broadcast." The respondent did not quarrel with the finding that the afternoon broadcast was patently offensive, but contended that it was not "indecent" within the meaning of the relevant statutes because it contained no prurient appeal. After rejecting respondent's statutory arguments, we confronted its two constitutional arguments: (1) that the Commission's construction of its authority to ban indecent speech was so broad that its order had to be set aside even if the broadcast at issue was unprotected; and (2) that since the recording was not obscene, the First Amendment forbade any abridgement of the right to broadcast it on the radio.

In the portion of the lead opinion not joined by Justices Powell and Blackmun, the plurality stated that the First Amendment does not prohibit all governmental regulation that depends on the content of speech. Accordingly, the availability of constitutional protection for a vulgar and offensive monologue that was not obscene depended on the context of the broadcast. Relying on the premise that "of all forms of communication" broadcasting had received the most limited First Amendment protection, the Court concluded that the ease with which children may obtain access to broadcasts, "coupled with the concerns recognized in *Ginsberg*," justified special treatment of indecent broadcasting.

As with the New York statute at issue in *Ginsberg*, there are significant differences between the order upheld in *Pacifica* and the CDA. First, the order in *Pacifica*, issued by an agency that had been regulating radio stations for decades, targeted a specific broadcast that represented a rather dramatic departure from traditional program content in order to designate when – rather than whether – it would be

321

permissible to air such a program in that particular medium. The CDA's broad categorical prohibitions are not limited to particular times and are not dependent on any evaluation by an agency familiar with the unique characteristics of the Internet. Second, unlike the CDA, the Commission's declaratory order was not punitive; we expressly refused to decide whether the indecent broadcast "would justify a criminal prosecution." Finally, the Commission's order applied to a medium which as a matter of history had "received the most limited First Amendment protection," in large part because warnings could not adequately protect the listener from unexpected program content. The Internet, however, has no comparable history. Moreover, the District Court found that the risk of encountering indecent material by accident is remote because a series of affirmative steps is required to access specific material.

In *Renton*, we upheld a zoning ordinance that kept adult movie theatres out of residential neighborhoods. The ordinance was aimed, not at the content of the films shown in the theaters, but rather at the "secondary effects" – such as crime and deteriorating property values – that these theaters fostered: "It is the secondary effect which these zoning ordinances attempt to avoid, not the dissemination of 'offensive' speech.'" 475 U.S. at 49. According to the Government, the CDA is constitutional because it constitutes a sort of "cyberzoning" on the Internet. But the CDA applies broadly to the entire universe of cyberspace. And the purpose of the CDA is to protect children from the primary effects of "indecent" and "patently offensive" speech, rather than any "secondary" effect of such speech. Thus, the CDA is a content-based blanket restriction on speech, and, as such, cannot be "properly analyzed as a form of time, place, and manner regulation." 475 U.S. at 46. *See also Boos v. Barry*, 485 U.S. 312, 321 (1988) ("Regulations that focus on the direct impact of speech on its audience" are not properly analyzed under *Renton*).

These precedents, then, surely do not require us to uphold the CDA and are fully consistent with the application of the most stringent review of its provisions.

V

In *Southeastern Promotions, Ltd. v. Conrad*, 420 U.S. 546, 557 (1975), we observed that "each medium of expression . . . may present its own problems." Thus, some of our cases have recognized special justifications for regulation of the broadcast media that are not applicable to other speakers. . . . In [prior] cases, the Court relied on the history of extensive government regulation of the broadcast medium, . . . and its "invasive" nature.

Those factors are not present in cyberspace. Neither before nor after the enactment of the CDA have the vast democratic fora of the Internet been subject to the type of government supervision and regulation that has attended the broadcast industry. Moreover, the Internet is not as "invasive" as radio or television. The District Court specifically found that "communications over the Internet do not 'invade' an individual's home or appear on one's computer screen unbidden. Users seldom encounter content 'by accident.'" It also found that "almost all sexually explicit images are preceded by warnings as to the content," and cited testimony that "'odds are slim' that a user would come across a sexually explicit sight by accident."

We distinguished *Pacifica* in *Sable*, 492 U.S. at 128, on just this basis. In *Sable*, a company engaged in the business of offering sexually oriented prerecorded telephone messages (popularly known as "dial-a-porn") challenged the constitutionality of an amendment to the Communications Act that imposed a blanket prohibition on indecent as well as obscene interstate commercial telephone messages. We held that the statute was constitutional insofar as it applied to obscene messages but invalid as applied to indecent messages. In attempting to justify the complete ban and criminalization of indecent commercial telephone messages, the Government relied on *Pacifica*, arguing that the ban was necessary to prevent children from gaining access to such messages. We agreed that "there is a compelling interest in protecting the physical and psychological well-being of minors" which extended to shielding them from indecent messages that are not obscene by adult standards, 492 U.S. at 126, but distinguished our "emphatically narrow holding" in *Pacifica* because it did not involve a complete ban and because it involved a different medium of communication. We explained that "the dial-it medium requires the listener to take affirmative steps to receive the communication." "Placing a telephone call," we continued, "is not the same as turning on a radio and being taken by surprise by an indecent message."

Finally, unlike the conditions that prevailed when Congress first authorized regulation of the broadcast spectrum, the Internet can hardly be considered a "scarce" expressive commodity. It provides relatively unlimited, low-cost capacity for communication of all kinds. The Government estimates that "as many as 40 million people use the Internet today, and that figure is expected to grow to 200 million by 1999." This dynamic, multifaceted category of communication includes not only traditional print and news services, but also audio, video, and still images, as well as interactive, real-time dialogue. Through the use of chat rooms, any person with a phone line can become a town crier with a voice that resonates farther than it could from any soapbox. Through the use of Web pages, mail exploders, and newsgroups, the same individual can become a pamphleteer. As the District Court found, "the content on the Internet is as diverse as human thought." We agree with its conclusion that our cases provide no basis for qualifying the level of First Amendment scrutiny that should be applied to this medium.

VI

Regardless of whether the CDA is so vague that it violates the Fifth Amendment, the many ambiguities concerning the scope of its coverage render it problematic for purposes of the First Amendment. For instance, each of the two parts of the CDA uses a different linguistic form. The first uses the word "indecent," while the second speaks of material that "in context, depicts or describes, in terms patently offensive as measured by contemporary community standards, sexual or excretory activities or organs." Given the absence of a definition of either term, this difference in language will provoke uncertainty among speakers about how the two standards relate to each other and just what they mean. Could a speaker confidently assume that a serious discussion about birth control practices, homosexuality, the First Amendment issues raised by the Appendix to our *Pacifica* opinion, or the consequences of prison rape would not violate the CDA? This uncertainty undermines the likelihood that the CDA has been carefully tailored to the congressional goal of protecting minors from potentially harmful materials.

The vagueness of the CDA is a matter of special concern for two reasons. First, the CDA is a content-based regulation of speech. The vagueness of such a regulation raises special First Amendment concerns because of its obvious chilling effect on free speech. *See, e.g., Gentile v. State Bar of Nev.*, 501 U.S. 1030, 1048-1051 (1991). Second, the CDA is a criminal statute. In addition to the opprobrium and stigma of a criminal conviction, the CDA threatens violators with penalties including up to two years in prison for each act of violation. The severity of criminal sanctions may well cause speakers to remain silent rather than communicate even arguably unlawful words, ideas, and images. *See, e.g., Dombrowski v. Pfister*, 380 U.S. 479, 494 (1965). As a practical matter, this increased deterrent effect, coupled with the "risk of discriminatory enforcement" of vague regulations, poses greater First Amendment concerns than those implicated by [civil regulations].

The Government argues that the statute is no more vague than the obscenity standard this Court established in *Miller v. California*, 413 U.S. 15 (1973). But that is not so. In *Miller*, this Court reviewed a criminal conviction against a commercial vendor who mailed brochures containing pictures of sexually explicit activities to individuals who had not requested such materials. Having struggled for some time to establish a definition of obscenity, we set forth in *Miller* the test for obscenity that controls to this day:

> (a) whether the average person, applying contemporary community standards would find that the work, taken as a whole, appeals to the prurient interest; (b) whether the work depicts or describes, in a patently offensive way, sexual conduct specifically defined by the applicable state law; and (c) whether the work, taken as a whole, lacks serious literary, artistic, political, or scientific value.

Id., at 24 (internal quotation marks and citations omitted). Because the CDA's "patently offensive" standard (and, we assume arguendo, its synonymous "indecent" standard) is one part of the three-prong Miller test, the Government reasons, it cannot be unconstitutionally vague.

The Government's assertion is incorrect as a matter of fact. The second prong of the *Miller* test -- the purportedly analogous standard -- contains a critical requirement that is omitted from the CDA: that the proscribed material be "specifically defined by the applicable state law." This requirement reduces the vagueness inherent in the open-ended term "patently offensive" as used in the CDA. Moreover, the *Miller* definition is limited to "sexual conduct," whereas the CDA extends also to include (1) "excretory activities" as well as (2) "organs" of both a sexual and excretory nature.

The Government's reasoning is also flawed. Just because a definition including three limitations is not vague, it does not follow that one of those limitations, standing by itself, is not vague. Each of Miller's additional two prongs – (1) that, taken as a whole, the material appeal to the "prurient" interest, and (2) that it "lack serious literary, artistic, political, or scientific value" – critically limits the uncertain sweep of the obscenity definition. The second requirement is particularly important because, unlike the "patently offensive" and "prurient interest" criteria, it is not judged by contemporary community standards. *See Pope v. Illinois*, 481 U.S. 497, 500 (1987). This "societal value" requirement, absent in the CDA, allows appellate courts to impose some limitations and regularity on the definition by setting, as a matter of law, a national floor for socially redeeming value. The Government's contention that courts will be able to give such legal limitations to the CDA's standards is belied by *Miller's* own rationale for having juries determine whether material is "patently offensive" according to community standards: that such questions are essentially ones of fact.

In contrast to *Miller* and our other previous cases, the CDA thus presents a greater threat of censoring speech that, in fact, falls outside the statute's scope. Given the vague contours of the coverage of the statute, it unquestionably silences some speakers whose messages would be entitled to constitutional protection. That danger provides further reason for insisting that the statute not be overly broad. The CDA's burden on protected speech cannot be justified if it could be avoided by a more carefully drafted statute.

VII

We are persuaded that the CDA lacks the precision that the First Amendment requires when a statute regulates the content of speech. In order to deny minors access to potentially harmful speech, the CDA effectively suppresses a large amount of speech that adults have a constitutional right to receive and to address to one another. That burden on adult speech is unacceptable if less restrictive alternatives would be at least as effective in achieving the legitimate purpose that the statute was enacted to serve.

In evaluating the free speech rights of adults, we have made it perfectly clear that "sexual expression which is indecent but not obscene is protected by the First Amendment." *Sable*, 492 U.S. at 126. . . . Indeed, *Pacifica* itself admonished that "the fact that society may find speech offensive is not a sufficient reason for suppressing it." 438 U.S. at 745.

It is true that we have repeatedly recognized the governmental interest in protecting children from harmful materials. . . . But that interest does not justify an unnecessarily broad suppression of speech addressed to adults. . . . "Regardless of the strength of the government's interest" in protecting children, "the level of discourse reaching a mailbox simply cannot be limited to that which would be suitable for a sandbox." *Bolger v. Youngs Drug Products Corp.*, 463 U.S. 60, 74-75(1983).

In arguing that the CDA does not so diminish adult communication, the Government relies on the incorrect factual premise that prohibiting a transmission whenever it is known that one of its recipients is a minor would not interfere with adult-to-adult communication. The findings of the District Court make clear that this premise is untenable. Given the size of the potential audience for most messages, in the absence of a viable age verification process, the sender must be charged with knowing that one or more minors will likely view it. Knowledge that, for instance, one or more members of a 100-person chat group will be minor – and therefore that it would be a crime to send the group an indecent message – would surely burden communication among adults.

The District Court found that at the time of trial existing technology did not include any effective method for a sender to prevent minors from obtaining access to its communications on the Internet without also denying access to adults. The Court found no effective way to determine the age of a user who is accessing material through e-mail, mail exploders, newsgroups, or chat rooms. As a practical matter, the Court also found that it would be prohibitively expensive for noncommercial – as well as some commercial – speakers who have Web sites to verify that their users are adults. These limitations must inevitably curtail a significant amount of adult communication on the Internet. By contrast, the District Court found that "despite its limitations, currently available user-based software suggests that a reasonably effective method by which parents can prevent their children from accessing sexually explicit and other material which parents may believe is inappropriate for their children will soon be widely available."

The breadth of the CDA's coverage is wholly unprecedented. Unlike the regulations upheld in *Ginsberg* and *Pacifica*, the scope of the CDA is not limited to commercial speech or commercial entities. Its open-ended prohibitions embrace all nonprofit entities and individuals posting indecent messages or displaying them on their own computers in the presence of minors. The general, undefined terms "indecent" and "patently offensive" cover large amounts of nonpornographic material with serious educational or other value. Moreover, the "community standards" criterion as applied to the Internet means that any communication available to a nation-wide audience will be judged by the standards of the community most likely to be offended by the message. The regulated subject matter includes any of the seven "dirty words" used in the *Pacifica* monologue, the use of which the Government's expert acknowledged could constitute a felony. It may also extend to discussions about prison rape or safe sexual practices, artistic images that include nude subjects, and arguably the card catalogue of the Carnegie Library.

For the purposes of our decision, we need neither accept nor reject the Government's submission that the First Amendment does not forbid a blanket prohibition on all "indecent" and "patently offensive" messages communicated to a 17-year old --no matter how much value the message may contain and regardless of parental approval. It is at least clear that the strength of the Government's interest in protecting minors is not equally strong throughout the coverage of this broad statute. Under the CDA, a parent allowing her 17-year-old to use the family computer to obtain information on the Internet that she, in her parental judgment, deems appropriate could face a lengthy prison term. Similarly, a parent who sent his 17-year-old college freshman information on birth control via e-mail could be incarcerated even though neither he, his child, nor anyone in their home community, found the material "indecent" or "patently offensive," if the college town's community thought otherwise.

The breadth of this content-based restriction of speech imposes an especially heavy burden on the Government to explain why a less restrictive provision would not be as effective as the CDA. It has not done so. The arguments in this Court have referred to possible alternatives such as requiring that indecent material be "tagged" in a way that facilitates parental control of material coming into their homes, making exceptions for messages with artistic or educational value, providing some tolerance for parental choice, and regulating some portions of the Internet – such as commercial web sites – differently than others, such as chat rooms. Particularly in the light of the absence of any detailed findings by the Congress, or even hearings addressing the special problems of the CDA, we are persuaded that the CDA is not narrowly tailored if that requirement has any meaning at all.

VIII

In an attempt to curtail the CDA's facial overbreadth, the Government advances three additional arguments for sustaining the Act's affirmative prohibitions: (1) that the CDA is constitutional because it leaves open ample "alternative channels" of communication; (2) that the plain meaning of the Act's "knowledge" and "specific person" requirement significantly restricts its permissible applications; and (3) that the Act's prohibitions are "almost always" limited to material lacking redeeming social value.

The Government first contends that, even though the CDA effectively censors discourse on many of the Internet's modalities – such as chat groups, newsgroups, and mail exploders – it is nonetheless constitutional because it provides a "reasonable opportunity" for speakers to engage in the restricted speech on the World Wide Web. This argument is unpersuasive because the CDA regulates speech on the basis of its content. A "time, place, and manner" analysis is therefore inapplicable. *See Consolidated Edison Co. of N.Y. v. Public Serv. Comm'n of N.Y.*, 447 U.S. 530, 536 (1980). It is thus immaterial whether such speech would be feasible on the Web (which, as the Government's own expert acknowledged, would cost up to $ 10,000 if the speaker's interests were not accommodated by an existing Web site, not including costs for database management and age verification). The Government's position is equivalent to arguing that a statute could ban leaflets on certain subjects as long as individuals are free to publish books. In invalidating a number of laws that banned leafletting on the streets regardless of their content – we explained that "one is not to have the exercise of his liberty of expression in appropriate places abridged on the plea that it may be exercised in some other place." *Schneider v. State (Town of Irvington)*, 308 U.S. 147, 163 (1939).

The Government also asserts that the "knowledge" requirement of both §§ 223(a) and (d), especially when coupled with the "specific child" element found in § 223(d), saves the CDA from overbreadth. Because both sections prohibit the dissemination of indecent messages only to persons known to be under 18, the Government argues, it does not require transmitters to "refrain from communicating indecent material to adults; they need only refrain from disseminating such materials to persons they know to be under 18." This argument ignores the fact that most Internet fora – including chat rooms, newsgroups, mail exploders, and the Web – are open to all comers. The Government's assertion that the knowledge requirement somehow protects the communications of adults is therefore untenable. Even the strongest reading of the "specific person" requirement of § 223(d) cannot save the statute. It would confer broad powers of censorship, in the form of a "heckler's veto," upon any opponent of indecent speech who might simply log on and inform the would-be discoursers that his 17-year-old child – a "specific person . . . under 18 years of age," – would be present.

Finally, we find no textual support for the Government's submission that material having scientific, educational, or other redeeming social value will necessarily fall outside the CDA's "patently offensive" and "indecent" prohibitions.

IX

The Government's three remaining arguments focus on the defenses provided in § 223(e)(5). First, relying on the "good faith, reasonable, effective, and appropriate actions" provision, the Government suggests that "tagging" provides a defense that saves the constitutionality of the Act. The suggestion assumes that transmitters may encode their indecent communications in a way that would indicate their contents, thus permitting recipients to block their reception with appropriate software. It is the requirement that the good faith action must be "effective" that makes this defense illusory. The Government recognizes that its proposed screening software does not currently exist. Even if it did, there is no way to know whether a potential recipient will actually block the encoded material. Without the impossible knowledge that every guardian in America is screening for the "tag," the transmitter could not reasonably rely on its action to be "effective."

For its second and third arguments concerning defenses – which we can consider together – the Government relies on the latter half of § 223(e)(5), which applies when the transmitter has restricted access by requiring use of a verified credit card or adult identification. Such verification is not only technologically available but actually is used by commercial providers of sexually explicit material. These providers, therefore, would be protected by the defense. Under the findings of the District Court, however, it is not economically feasible for most noncommercial speakers to employ such verification. Accordingly, this defense would not significantly narrow the statute's burden on noncommercial speech. Even with respect to the commercial pornographers that would be protected by the defense, the Government failed to adduce any evidence that these verification techniques actually preclude minors from posing as adults. Given that the risk of criminal sanctions "hovers over each content provider, like the proverbial sword of Damocles," the District Court correctly refused to rely on unproven future technology to save the statute. The Government thus failed to prove that the proffered defense would significantly reduce the heavy burden on adult speech produced by the prohibition on offensive displays.

326

X

At oral argument, the Government relied heavily on its ultimate fall-back position: If this Court should conclude that the CDA is insufficiently tailored, it urged, we should save the statute's constitutionality by honoring the severability clause, and construing nonseverable terms narrowly. In only one respect is this argument acceptable.

A severability clause requires textual provisions that can be severed. We will follow § 608's guidance by leaving constitutional textual elements of the statute intact in the one place where they are, in fact, severable. The "indecency" provision, 47 U.S.C. A. § 223(a) (Supp. 1997), applies to "any comment, request, suggestion, proposal, image, or other communication which is obscene or indecent." Appellees do not challenge the application of the statute to obscene speech, which, they acknowledge, can be banned totally because it enjoys no First Amendment protection. As set forth by the statute, the restriction of "obscene" material enjoys a textual manifestation separate from that for "indecent" material, which we have held unconstitutional. Therefore, we will sever the term "or indecent" from the statute, leaving the rest of § 223(a) standing. In no other respect, however, can § [*69] 223(a) or § 223(d) be saved by such a textual surgery.

* * *

XI

In this Court, though not in the District Court, the Government asserts that – in addition to its interest in protecting children – its "equally significant" interest in fostering the growth of the Internet provides an independent basis for upholding the constitutionality of the CDA. The Government apparently assumes that the unregulated availability of "indecent" and "patently offensive" material on the Internet is driving countless citizens away from the medium because of the risk of exposing themselves or their children to harmful material.

We find this argument singularly unpersuasive. The dramatic expansion of this new marketplace of ideas contradicts the factual basis of this contention. The record demonstrates that the growth of the Internet has been and continues to be phenomenal. As a matter of constitutional tradition, in the absence of evidence to the contrary, we presume that governmental regulation of the content of speech is more likely to interfere with the free exchange of ideas than to encourage it. The interest in encouraging freedom of expression in a democratic society outweighs any theoretical but unproven benefit of censorship.

For the foregoing reasons, the judgment of the district court is affirmed.

QUESTIONS

1.   After reading this case, how do you think an appeals court might rule on a jury verdict that a particular edition of a pornographic magazine was "obscene"? What additional information might you need to answer such a question?

2.   Community-based standards govern the determination of what is "obscene." Accordingly, what is obscene in one city or town might not be obscene in another. What are the benefits of community-based standards? The drawbacks? What alternative, if any, would you create to this standard?

3.   Justice O'Connor's opinion, in which she concurred in part and dissented in part with the majority opinion, is not reproduced for you in this text. In it, she emphasized that the state of technology is not yet developed sufficiently to create "adult zones" on the Internet that reliably could exclude minors from accessing those sites, without violating the First Amendment rights of adults. Presuming such technology were developed, Justice O'Connor appears to think something akin to the CDA might be a lawful exercise of congressional power as a "cyber-zoning" law. What do you think of such an argument? Why?

CHAPTER 9
CRIMES AGAINST THE PERSON

A. Assault and Battery

The crimes of assault and battery are often confused. Part of this confusion stems from the fact that a handful of jurisdictions have merged to the definitions of the two crimes. But both at common law and under the Model Penal Code, they are distinct offenses.

Battery is defined as the unlawful application of force to the person of another resulting in either (1) bodily injury; or (2) an unwanted, offensive touching. It is a misdemeanor in most jurisdictions and need not be intentional; reckless conduct will suffice for liability. A simple battery, however, can be raised to an aggravated battery, usually a felony, if a deadly weapon was used, or if serious bodily harm was inflicted on the victim. Some jurisdictions also include the status of the victim – for example, the battery of a child, an elderly person, a judge, or police officer, etc. – in their definitions of what will elevate a simple battery to an aggravated one. Key to the crime of battery, however, is that an actual touching take place.

Simple *assault* is either (1) an attempt to commit a battery; or (2) the intentional creation – other than by mere words – of a reasonable apprehension in the mind of the victim of imminent bodily harm. If there has been an actual touching, the crime is battery, not assault. Like with simple battery, simple assault is usually a misdemeanor, but it can be raised to the felony of aggravated assault if it is perpetrated using a deadly weapon; if is perpetrated against a particular victim (e.g., a police officer in the line of duty); or when the assault is coupled with the specific intent to do another crime, such as assault with intent to kill, assault with intent to rape, or the like.

Often, an assault and battery takes place at the same time. For example, if one creates a reasonable apprehension in the mind of the victim of imminent bodily harm, an assault has been committed. If the person then actually batters his or her victim, a battery has also been committed. But it is possible to commit one without the other. If no actual touching takes place, even if it was one's specific intent to batter another, then only an assault has taken place. In contrast, if one were to sneak up behind his or her victim and hit the victim over the head, a battery has clearly taken place, but since the victim was never placed in reasonable apprehension of imminent bodily harm because the perpetrator snuck up so the victim could not see the batterer approaching, no assault took place.

As stated above, whether dealing with assault or a battery, the use of a "deadly weapon" can raise either crime from their respective simple/misdemeanor forms to their aggravated or felony forms. But what constitutes a deadly weapon? Consider the following case.

UNITED STATES of America, Appellee, v. James Vernell MOORE, Appellant.
846 F.2d 1163 (8th Cir. 1988).

Timbers, Circuit Judge.

Appellant James Vernell Moore appeals from a judgment . . .following Moore's conviction by a jury on June 24, 1987 of two counts of assault with a deadly and dangerous weapon upon federal correctional officers engaged in their official duties

Moore had tested positive for antibodies for the Human Immunodeficiency Virus ("HIV virus") which are considered to be indicative of the presence of Acquired Immune Deficiency Syndrome ("AIDS"). After learning that he had tested positive for the HIV virus, Moore bit two correctional officers during a struggle. The indictment charged that the deadly and dangerous weapon Moore used was his own mouth and teeth. On appeal, Moore claims, first, that the evidence at trial was insufficient to sustain a finding that Moore's mouth and teeth were a deadly and dangerous weapon; and, second, that the district court committed reversible error in refusing to charge the jury in accordance with Moore's proposed Instruction # 12, which would have informed the jury that, if the government failed to prove that AIDS can be transmitted by means of a bite, then it failed to prove that Moore's mouth and teeth were a deadly and dangerous weapon. We hold that the evidence at trial was sufficient to sustain a finding that Moore's mouth and teeth were a deadly and dangerous weapon because that evidence supported a finding that Moore used his teeth in a manner likely to inflict serious bodily harm – even if he had not been infected with the HIV virus. We further hold that the district court correctly refused to charge in accordance with Moore's proposed Instruction # 12. We affirm.

I

At the time of the incident which is the subject of this appeal, Moore was an inmate at the Federal Medical Center ("FMC") in Rochester, Minnesota. On November 25 and December 3, 1986, Dr. Clifford Gastineau had Moore tested for the HIV virus because his long time heroin addiction placed him in a risk category for AIDS. In mid-December, Dr. Gastineau advised Moore that the tests were positive and that the disease could be fatal. He told Moore that the disease could be transmitted by way of blood or semen and counseled him to avoid unprotected intercourse and not to share needles, razor blades or toothbrushes.

On January 7, 1987, Lieutenant Ronald E. McCullough, a correctional officer at the FMC, called Moore to his office as part of his investigation of a report that Moore had been smoking in a non-smoking area in the FMC's medical surgical unit. Moore refused to answer questions. When McCullough told Moore he would have to be placed in seclusion and administrative detention, Moore refused to move. McCullough called for assistance. Correctional officer Timothy Voigt arrived. He told Moore to stand so that he could be handcuffed. Moore said "I won't be cuffed." McCullough called two additional correctional officers who arrived and attempted to lift Moore from his chair. Moore reacted violently.

In the ensuing struggle, Moore kneed McCullough in the groin twice, attempted to bite him on the hand, and did bite him on the left knee and hip without breaking the skin. Moore held his mouth over the bite on the leg for several seconds. He also bit Voigt on the right leg, holding his mouth against the bite from five to seven seconds. Dr. Gastineau testified that during the struggle a mild abrasion appeared at the point on Voigt's thigh where Moore had bitten him. This abrasion apparently resulted from friction with the fabric of Voigt's pants. The abrasion may have come into contact with a wet patch on Voigt's pants which possibly was made by Moore's saliva. During the struggle, Moore threatened to kill the officers.

On January 10, 1987, Moore told Debra Alberts, a nurse at the FMC, that he had "wanted to hurt them bad, wanted to kill the bastards." He also said that he "hopes the wounds that he inflicted on the officers when he bit them were bad enough that they get the disease that he has." On April 9, 1987, Moore was indicted. The indictment charged that Moore willfully had assaulted McCullough and Voigt, federal correctional officers engaged in their official duties, by means of a deadly and dangerous weapon, i.e., Moore's mouth and teeth. The indictment specifically charged that Moore was "a person then having been tested positively for the [HIV] antibody." Although Moore also had tested positive for hepatitis, the indictment did not refer to this disease. At trial, Dr. Gastineau testified that the medical profession knew of no "well-proven instances in which a human bite has resulted in transmission of the [HIV] virus to the bitten person." He agreed with a medical manual that stated there is no evidence that AIDS can be transmitted through any contact that does not involve the exchange of bodily fluids and that, while the virus has appeared in minute amounts in saliva, it has never been shown to have been spread through contact with saliva. He said that theoretically "one cannot exclude the possibility" of transmission through biting. Later he added, however, "it seems that in medicine everything is conceivable or possible." He testified about a case of a person who had been bitten deeply by a person with AIDS and had tested negative 18 months later.

Dr. Gastineau also testified that, apart from the matter of AIDS, a human bite can be dangerous. He said that when a human bite is of a more damaging nature than the ones inflicted by Moore and "where the skin is really broken to greater depths", it can be "much more dangerous than a dog bite." He also said that "there are probably 30 to 50 variet[ies] of germs in the human mouth that together, all of them acting in concert, could cause serious infection." He characterized a human bite as "a very dangerous form of aggression" and "one of the most dangerous of all forms of bites."

On June 24, 1987, the jury found Moore guilty on both counts of the indictment. The jury had been instructed on the lesser included offense of assaulting a federal officer. The court declined to instruct the jury that the government was required to prove that AIDS could be transmitted by way of a bite in order to prove that Moore's mouth and teeth were a deadly and dangerous weapon. Moore was sentenced to concurrent five-year prison terms, which were to run consecutively to the seven-year federal prison sentence he was serving at the time of the incident.

II

In reviewing the sufficiency of the evidence to determine whether it supports the conviction, we must view the evidence in the light most favorable to the government, grant the government the benefit of all inferences that reasonably may be drawn from the evidence, and uphold the conviction if there is substantial evidence to support it. *United States v. Gatewood*, 786 F.2d 821, 824 (8th Cir. 1986).

The question of what constitutes a "deadly and dangerous weapon" is a question of fact for the jury. *United States v. Czeck*, 671 F.2d 1195, 1197 (8th Cir. 1982). We previously have defined a "deadly and dangerous weapon" as an object "used in a manner likely to endanger life or inflict serious bodily harm." *United States v. Hollow*, 747 F.2d 481, 482 (8th Cir. 1984). "Serious bodily harm" has been defined as something more than minor injury, but not necessarily injury creating a substantial likelihood of death. *See United States v. Webster*, 620 F.2d 640, 641-42 (7th Cir. 1980); *United States v. Johnson*, 324 F.2d 264, 267 (4th Cir. 1963). . . .

As a practical matter, it often is difficult to determine whether a particular object is a deadly and dangerous weapon. Almost any weapon, as used or attempted to be used, may endanger life or inflict great bodily harm; as such, in appropriate circumstances, it may be a dangerous and deadly weapon. *United States v. Davis*, 429 F.2d 552, 556 (8th Cir. 1970). Moreover, the object need not be inherently dangerous, or a "weapon" by definition, such as a gun or a knife, to be found to be a dangerous and deadly weapon. Courts frequently have considered various kinds of objects to be deadly and dangerous, including such normally innocuous objects as (1) a chair, *Johnson*, 324 F.2d at 266; (2) a walking stick, *United States v. Loman*, 551 F.2d 164, 169 (7th Cir. 1977), *cert. denied*, 433 U.S. 912 (1978); (3) a broken beer bottle and pool cue, *United States v. Guilbert*, 692 F.2d 1340, 1343 (11th Cir. 1982), *cert. denied*, 460 U.S. 1016 (1983); (4) an automobile, *United States v. Williamson*, 482 F.2d 508, 513 (5th Cir. 1973); and (5) mop handles, *United States v. Bey*, 667 F.2d 7, 11 (5th Cir. 1982). In short, "what constitutes a dangerous weapon depends not on the nature of the object itself but on its capacity, given the manner of its use, to 'endanger life or inflict great bodily harm.'" *Id.*

As a corollary, it is not necessary that the object, as used by a defendant, actually cause great bodily harm, as long as it has the capacity to inflict such harm in the way it was used. *Id.* In *Johnson*, the defendant caused only a minor injury when he struck the victim with a chair; but, since he wielded the chair in a way that could have endangered the victim's eye or caused a serious head wound, the court held that the chair was a dangerous weapon.

Courts also have held that in appropriate circumstances a part of the body may be a dangerous weapon. *United States v. Parman*, 461 F.2d 1203, 1204 (D.C. Cir. 1971) . . .; *State v. Born*, 280 Minn. 306, 159 N.W.2d 283 (1968) (fists or feet in certain circumstances may be dangerous weapons when used to inflict injury).

III

In light of the law on what may be considered a deadly and dangerous weapon, we conclude that the evidence in the instant case was sufficient to support the jury's finding that Moore used his mouth and teeth as a deadly and dangerous weapon. As stated above, Dr. Gastineau testified that a human bite is potentially "more dangerous than a dog bite"; that it is capable of causing "serious infection"; and that it can be "a very dangerous form of aggression". We reaffirm that this potential for "serious infection" is a form of "serious bodily harm" . . . . We therefore hold that Dr. Gastineau's testimony, viewed in the light most favorable to the government, was substantial evidence supporting the jury's finding that Moore used his mouth and teeth in a manner likely to inflict serious bodily harm.

It is true that Dr. Gastineau testified that he was describing a bite "more damaging" than those actually inflicted by Moore. As stated above, however, it is the capacity for harm in the weapon and its use that is significant, not the actual harm inflicted. *Bey*, 667 F.2d at 11; *Johnson*, 324 F.2d at 266. It may be that Moore did not transmit any of the "30 to 50" varieties of germs he might have transmitted to the officers. He nevertheless used his mouth and teeth in a way that could have transmitted disease. It was only a fortuity that he did not do so. The instant case is similar to *Johnson*, where it was only fortuity which prevented the defendant from causing serious bodily injury when he struck the victim in the head with a chair. Since a human bite has the capacity to inflict serious bodily harm, we hold that the human mouth and teeth are a deadly and dangerous weapon in circumstances like those in the instant case, even if the harm actually inflicted was not severe.

The gravamen of Moore's claim is that on the evidence the only way the government could establish that his mouth and teeth were used as a deadly and dangerous weapon was for it to establish that AIDS can be transmitted by biting. As Moore points out, Dr. Gastineau's testimony, which was the only evidence on the transmissibility of the HIV virus, established only a remote or theoretical possibility that the virus could be transmitted through biting. He asserts that the government did not try the case on the theory that any human bite – regardless of the presence of the HIV virus – was a deadly and dangerous weapon. His assertion rests on the facts that the indictment charged that Moore, "a person then having been tested positively for the [HIV] antibody, did willfully and forcibly assault" the two officers "by means of a deadly and dangerous weapon, namely, his mouth and teeth"; that the indictment failed to make any similar charge with respect to his hepatitis infection; and that the government introduced a substantial amount of evidence at trial concerning the transmissibility of AIDS by way of biting.

We reject Moore's massive emphasis on the AIDS aspect of this case. As stated above, the record, viewed in the light most favorable to the government, contained sufficient evidence to allow the jury to find that Moore's mouth and teeth were used as a deadly and dangerous weapon, even if Moore was not infected with AIDS. As the district court correctly held, moreover, the reference to AIDS in the indictment was mere surplusage and did not limit the government to one theory of the case at trial.

QUESTIONS

1.   The court ruled that one's teeth, when used to inflict a bite, can constitute a "deadly weapon." Do you agree? Why or why not? What other instrumentalities are not necessarily inherently dangerous, but can nonetheless be used as deadly weapons?

2.   The court did not focus on the defendant being HIV-positive. Since the time this case was decided, however, we have learned much more about HIV and AIDS. Do you think that people who are HIV-positive are "deadly weapons" in and of themselves? Why? What crimes, if any, do you think might be committed if blood is exchanged during the course of a "routine" physical fight not involving the use of any weapons between someone who is HIV-positive and another who is HIV-negative? Explain your response.

B. Child Abuse and Neglect and their Relationship to Other Crimes

1. Child Abuse

The crimes of assault and battery are often ill-suited the prosecution of a parent or guardian when they assault or batter their children. The reason for that is simple. Parents are given a privilege to use a reasonable amount of physical force to discipline their children. Accordingly, a parent intentionally putting a child in reasonable apprehension of imminent bodily harm is generally not a criminal assault; a parent spanking their child is generally not a criminal battery. But the *parental privilege* to use corporal punishment is limited. When a parent exceeds the scope of the privilege, criminal liability for child abuse may be imposed.

Child abuse may be treated as any number of crimes: assault; battery; assault with a dangerous or deadly weapon; aggravated battery of a child; and homicide if death results. Other jurisdictions have a separate offense of child abuse that is graded as a more serious offense, and therefore carries a more severe sentence, than other types of assaults and/or batteries. The following case illustrates the application of a child abuse law along with the doctrine of parental privilege.

STATE of Maryland v. James W. TAYLOR
701 A.2d 389 (Md. 1997).

Chasanow, J., delivered the opinion of the court.

James W. Taylor, the Respondent, was charged in five separate indictments with child abuse in violation of Maryland Code (1957, 1992 Repl. Vol.), Article 27, § 35A, and the lesser-included, common-law offenses of assault and of battery. The indictments were consolidated for trial on July 29, 1994, despite Taylor's motion to sever the charges. The State entered a nolle prosequi on the assault charges and, on February 15, 1995, the jury returned a verdict of guilty on two counts of child abuse and the corresponding battery charges. The battery convictions were merged into the child abuse convictions, and Taylor was thereafter sentenced to a term of fifteen years of incarceration on each child abuse count, to run concurrently. In an unreported opinion, the Court of Special Appeals reversed and remanded, holding that the trial court erred in denying Taylor's motion to sever. We granted certiorari to decide whether severance was mandated as a matter of law. We conclude that separate trials were not required and shall reverse the judgment of the intermediate appellate court.

The charges lodged against Taylor arose from the physical abuse, in separate incidents, of Taylor's fourteen-year-old stepson, Keith C., during a two and one-half month period in 1994. The first incident occurred between March 1 and March 31, 1994. Keith claimed that Taylor, whom Keith referred to as his "dad," punched him in the jaw with his fist, leaving a bruise that was visible "for maybe a week, maybe two weeks." Keith could not recall the predicate for Taylor's display of anger. The second instance of abuse took place sometime between April 17 and April 31, 1994. Keith testified that, for a reason unknown to the child, Taylor used an electric cord to whip him across the shoulders. This left "two scars on each side of [his] shoulders." The third episode, in which Taylor is alleged to have poked Keith in the chest with the sharpened end of a stick, occurred on May 11, 1994, while the two were laying carpet in the bathroom. Keith could not recall the cause of Taylor's actions. The incident left a scar on Keith's chest. The fourth count of battery and child abuse arose out of events that occurred on May 13, 1994. During dinner that evening, while preparing the family's plates, Keith picked up a piece of chicken with his hand and Taylor "got . . . angry and stabbed [him] with a fork on the top of [his] head." According to Keith, the blow caused his head to bleed. The last offense allegedly committed by Taylor took place two days later, on May 15, 1994. Keith stated that while he and Taylor were straightening up a storage closet in the house, Taylor punched him in the mouth with his fist. Apparently, Keith had "made some sort of mistake," although he could not recall the precise nature thereof.

Later that same day, police officers came to the Taylor residence to execute an arrest warrant on Taylor for an unrelated matter. Following Taylor's arrest, Keith and his mother, Mary Taylor, spoke to Corporal David Suggs of the Howard County Police department and recounted to him the events giving rise to the indictments. Suggs observed that Keith's mouth was swollen. The detective also photographed the scars on Keith's shoulders and a scar from a pointed object on Keith's chest.

The five cases were consolidated for trial on motion of the State after the trial judge determined that even if Taylor were tried separately for each child abuse charge, all of the other alleged acts of child abuse would be admissible in each trial to prove Taylor's intent, malice, and absence of mistake. The charges Taylor was convicted of were the two charges of child abuse and the corresponding two charges of battery for the April 17-April 30 beating with the electrical cord and the May 15 punching. Taylor was acquitted of all other charges.

The State challenges the Court of Special Appeals' reversal of the trial court's decision to consolidate Taylor's indictments. It claims that the evidence as to each of the five acts charged "was not offered to show that Taylor was generally a bad person, but to establish Taylor's intent and the absence of mistake in striking his stepson." In other words, it argues that the evidence as to each of the five acts of child abuse was mutually admissible in separate trials of the other under the malice, intent, and mistake exceptions to the other crimes evidence rule. This being the case, the State asserts that joinder was not prejudicial. It further avers that the prejudice resulting from the admission of the evidence relative to each of the five acts, if any, is outweighed by the interest in judicial economy served by conducting a joint trial on all of the charges.

Taylor complains that the defense was prejudiced by the joinder and, thus, by the admission of the other crimes evidence, "which under the circumstances, showed nothing more than propensity, allowing the jury to conclude that [he] was a '"bad person" and should therefore be convicted, or deserves punishment for other bad conduct and so may be convicted even though the evidence is lacking.'" (quoting *Harris v. State*, 597 A.2d 956, 961 (Md. 1991)).

The Test For Consolidation

This Court recently discussed the test for joinder of offenses in Conyers v. State, 693 A.2d 781 (Md. 1997). We used a two part test. First, is the evidence concerning each of the charged offenses mutually admissible; and second, does the interest in judicial economy outweigh the arguments favoring separate trials. The second part of the test should not be in dispute in the instant case. A paramount interest of our criminal justice system should be avoiding unnecessary trials and the accompanying trauma to young victims of multiple acts of child abuse. These children should not have to testify at multiple trials if the evidence would be the same at each trial and all of the acts of alleged abuse would be mutually admissible at each trial.

Admissibility of Other Assaults or Child Abuse by The Same Defendant on The Same Victim

The admissibility of other crimes evidence is governed by Maryland Rule 5-404(b) which provides:

> (b) Other Crimes, Wrongs, or Acts. – Evidence of other crimes, wrongs, or acts is not admissible to prove the character of a person in order to show action in conformity therewith. It may, however, be admissible for other purposes, such as proof of motive, opportunity, intent, preparation, common scheme or plan, knowledge, identity, or absence of mistake or accident.

Evidence of other crimes or other bad acts committed by the accused is not admissible unless it has special relevance, i.e., it is substantially relevant to some contested issue and is not offered simply to prove criminal character. . . . [T]he evidence must ordinarily tend to prove motive, intent, absence of mistake or accident, a common scheme, or identity embracing the commission of two or more crimes to escape exclusion by the general rule.

Underlying this rule is the concern that the jury will use the other crimes evidence to convict and punish the defendant for having a criminal disposition or to infer that he is more likely to have committed the crime for which he is on trial. . . . With these principles in mind we also note that several of our prior cases construing the child abuse statute have recognized the relevance of intent and malice in child abuse cases. Intent and malice can be critical in distinguishing permissible parental corporal punishment from criminal child abuse.

333

Abuse is defined in the child abuse statute as:

(i) The sustaining of physical injury by a child as a result of cruel or inhumane treatment or as a result of a malicious act by any parent or other person who has permanent or temporary care or custody or responsibility for supervision of a child, or by any household or family member, under circumstances that indicate that the child's health or welfare is harmed or threatened thereby; or

(ii) Sexual abuse of a child, whether physical injuries are sustained or not.

This Court fully explained the mental state required for child abuse in *Bowers v. State*, 389 A.2d 341, 348-49 (Md. 1978). In *Bowers* the defendant challenged the child abuse statute as being void for vagueness and not specifying the difference between permissible corporal punishment and child abuse. We gave a lengthy explanation of the difference between non-criminal corporal punishment and child abuse:

Long before the advent of contemporary child abuse legislation, it was a well-recognized precept of Anglo-American jurisprudence that the parent of a minor child or one standing in loco parentis was justified in using a reasonable amount of force upon a child for the purpose of safeguarding or promoting the child's welfare. So long as the chastisement was moderate and reasonable, in light of the age, condition and disposition of the child, and other surrounding circumstances, the parent or custodian would not incur criminal liability for assault and battery or a similar offense.

On the other hand, where corporal punishment was inflicted with "a malicious desire to cause pain" or where it amounted to "cruel and outrageous" treatment of the child, the chastisement was deemed unreasonable, thus defeating the parental privilege and subjecting the parent to penal sanctions in those circumstances where criminal liability would have existed absent the parent-child relationship. Put another way, a parent was not permitted under the common law to resort to punishment which would exceed "that properly required for disciplinary purposes" or which would extend beyond the bounds of moderation. "Excessive or cruel" conduct was universally prohibited.

In amending the child abuse statute in 1973 so as to include for the first time a definition of abuse, the General Assembly was well aware of the common law limitations on the parental privilege to impose discipline. Indeed, we have repeatedly held that the Legislature is presumed to have had full knowledge and information as to prior and existing law on the subject of a statute it has enacted. By electing to restrict the criminal liability of parents under the statute only to those cases where the parent or custodian causes his child or ward to sustain physical injury as a result of cruel or inhumane treatment or as a result of other acts of malice, the Legislature apparently intended the definition of abuse to correspond to that type of conduct which would have sufficed to destroy the privilege to discipline at common law.

Thus, the terminology employed in Article 27, § 35A(b)(7)(A) appears to be nothing but a codification of the common law principles concerning the limits of permissible parental chastisement. Since the contours of the common law privilege have been subject for centuries to definition and refinement through careful and constant judicial decision-making, terms like "cruel or inhumane" and "malicious" have acquired a relatively widely accepted connotation in the law. The use of such phraseology in the child abuse statute would, therefore, not render the law constitutionally infirm.

For these reasons, the Maryland child abuse law is sufficiently explicit to survive even strict scrutiny under the Due Process Clause. First, it meets the requirement of notice, such that persons of common intelligence need not guess at its meaning or speculate as to its application. If the underlying rationale of the fair notice requirement is that a conviction should not result from conduct which cannot reasonably be understood as proscribed, that danger has been avoided here. Parents of ordinary intelligence are made aware that they do not subject themselves to the statute by merely engaging in corporal discipline for the purpose of punishment or correction. Only when the line is crossed and physical injury is intentionally and maliciously or cruelly inflicted does criminal responsibility attach. In short, the statute provides fair warning; it sets no trap for the unwary or innocent parent.

Lack of intent or malice was a contention of the defense in the instant case. Proof of other brutality against Keith by his stepfather was admissible to prove the Taylor's intent and malice. In addition, where a primary issue is the culpable state of mind of the defendant, any chance of prejudice by virtue of the admission of prior bad acts is less than if the primary issue is identity of the perpetrator. Taylor chose not to take the stand. The defense strategy was to rely on the plea of not guilty and to require the State to prove each element of the crimes beyond a reasonable doubt. Defense counsel did, however, acknowledge that identity was really not in dispute. At the hearing on the motion for separate trials, the defense counsel stated: "There is no suggestion here that there's a problem with identification. I would suggest that identification is not an issue here." The contention was that either Keith was fabricating his claims of child abuse or Taylor was acting in the role of Keith's father, and these were permissible disciplinary acts, not child abuse or battery. Because Keith bore visible evidence of the two acts of abuse for which Taylor was convicted and the blows could not be imaginary, the central issue in the case seemed to be whether the blows exceeded permissible parental discipline.

Intent to cause physical injury and malice were important elements of the State's case. Sexual child abuse and physical child abuse are both crimes under the same statute. This Court has expressly permitted prior acts of sexual child abuse perpetrated by the defendant against the same victim to be admissible in sexual child abuse cases even though malice and intent are irrelevant in such cases, and accident is almost never a defense. *See, e.g., Vogel v. State*, 554 A.2d 1231 (Md. 1989), a sexual child abuse case where this Court sustained the admission of evidence of other sex acts perpetrated by the defendant against the same fourteen-year-old victim. . . . The justification for admitting other acts of abuse is even greater in physical child abuse cases than in sexual child abuse cases, for there is rarely any claim that sexual child abuse is "accidental" or is proper parental discipline.

A case relevant to the issue in the instant case is *Duckworth v. State*, 594 A.2d 109 (Md. 1991). In *Duckworth*, the defendant was convicted of child abuse and battery of a three-year-old girl left in his charge. The evidence was that the defendant was holding a handgun loaded with birdshot that discharged and injured the child. Over objection, the State was permitted to introduce testimony that, on a prior occasion, the defendant injured the same child with a BB pistol. This Court held that the prior shooting incident was admissible on both the battery charge, to prove recklessness, and the child abuse charge. We stated:

> Thus, the State's theory of the case on the battery charge was legally sound, namely, that Duckworth criminally wounded Mandy by recklessly handling a firearm. It follows that the testimony by Mandy's mother concerning an accidental shooting with a BB gun approximately one week prior to the battery was clearly relevant. Mandy was struck by a BB on the earlier occasion – precisely where, we do not know. The jurors might well reason that one in the position of Duckworth would be relieved that the accidental discharge of the BB gun had not blinded Mandy. Certainly, the jury could conclude that the accidental discharge of the BB gun in the earlier incident was a warning to Duckworth that should have reinforced the need for substantial caution when handling firearms. Duckworth's failure, on the occasion of the shooting charged in the indictment, to heed that warning exacerbated the recklessness involved in the crime charged. . . .

Duckworth, 594 A.2d at 114.

A recurring child abuse scenario is one in which an infant is brought to a hospital emergency room with multiple broken bones in various stages of healing. If, in ensuing child abuse prosecutions the multiple, separately occurring injuries are not admissible, then child abuse would be almost impossible to prove. A common defense used by custodians in child abuse cases is that the child's injuries were accidently inflicted, and in many instances the only way the State can rebut this contention is by showing other acts of abuse to prove intent, malice, or that any excessive force could not be an innocent mistake.

* * *

Where a parent uses severe corporal punishment, often the only way to determine whether the punishment is a non-criminal act of discipline that was unintentionally harsh or whether it constitutes the felony of child abuse is to look at the parent's history of disciplining the child. The probative value of recent corporal punishment used on a child in order to determine the parental disciplinarian's malice and intent far exceeds its potential for unfair prejudice. In the instant case, the fact that Taylor was only convicted of acts of violence that left physical evidence of their severity and was acquitted on three other charges of child abuse gives some indication that the jury was not inflamed or prejudiced by the testimony about prior acts of corporal punishment. Victims of child abuse often cannot speak for themselves or are very reluctant to testify unfavorably about a parent, even an abusive parent. A parent's other disciplinary acts can be the most probative evidence of whether his or her disciplinary corporal punishment is imposed maliciously, with an intent to injure, or with a sincere desire to use appropriate corrective measures.

Since each of Taylor's acts of violence against Keith would be admissible in each prosecution for child abuse, there was no reason to require five separate trials and the trial judge did not abuse his discretion in consolidating all cases for trial.

QUESTIONS

1.   Although this case is largely one that pertains to the law of evidence, it illustrates the limits placed on parents when disciplining their children. As discussed in the case, the doctrine of parental privilege shields parents from criminal liability for corporal punishment unless the punishment was inflicted with "a malicious desire to cause pain," or where it amounted to "cruel and outrageous" treatment of the child. What do you think of this doctrine? Why? Are the standards inherently nebulous, or do they allow for reasoned differences of opinion to be discussed by a jury?

2.   Normally, prior bad acts of a defendant are inadmissible in court to show the defendant's propensity to engage in the conduct with which he or she is charged. The court reasoned an exception to this rule was necessary in child abuse cases when the defendant claims the incident was unduly severe by accident or mistake. Acts of prior abuse would go to the defendant's current mens rea. Critique the rule generally barring prior bad acts and the exception as explained in this case.

2. Child Neglect

Parents and other persons responsible for children have a legal duty to provide the children with food, clothing, shelter, medical care, sanitation, education, and a reasonable physical and moral environment in which to live (i.e., supervision). **Child neglect** is the failure to live up to one of the duties. Recall in Chapter 7 the case of *Commonwealth v. Twitchell*, 617 N.E.2d 609 (Mass. 1993), in which parents who failed to reasonably provide for their child's medical needs, even when having failed to do so was based upon the tenets of their religion, were subjected to criminal liability for child neglect.

C. Kidnaping and False Imprisonment

The common law crime of *kidnapping* consisted of the following elements:

a)   the unlawful confinement of a person
b)   for a substantial period of time;
c)   for the purpose of either:
    1)   the commission of another crime; or
    2)   to inflict bodily injury on or terrorize the victim;
d)   where the confinement involved either:
    1)   some movement of the victim; or
    2)   concealment of the victim in a secret place.

Several of the elements above contain terms of art that should be explained. First, the confinement had to be unlawful. Any lawful confinement – such as by police upon arrest, the state upon conviction, or by a shopkeeper who had reasonable grounds to believe someone had stolen from him or her – thus did not count as a "unlawful." Second, there had to be a "substantial" period of time; short detentions never qualified. Third, the mens rea required purpose to either commit another crime while the victim was illegally confined, or to inflict bodily injury or psychic terror on the victim.

Finally, the common law required the forcible movement of a kidnapping victim, or the confinement of the victim in some secret place that made it highly unlikely the victim would ever be found. The movement requirement of the crime had to involve movement of "some distance" or a "substantial distance." Most courts therefore held that forced movement within a structure from one room to another was insufficient to establish a kidnapping. Whenever the movement element was not met – either because there was not movement or concealment in a secret place, or because the movement was not substantial – then no kidnapping could be deemed to have taken place. Instead, the crime would have been one of *false imprisonment*.

Modern kidnapping laws mirror the common law crime. Some jurisdictions have eased the movement requirement. Others have differentiated kidnapping from aggravated kidnapping if the concealment of the victim was for ransom, the commission of another felony, or for some "offensive purpose." Yet others, as the case below indicates, have blurred the lines between kidnapping and the crime of false imprisonment which, at common law, had distinct differences due to the common law requirements of a confinement for a substantial period of time, and some movement of the victim for the crime of kidnapping, but not for false imprisonment. The common law elements for false imprisonment were as follows:

a)   the confinement or restraint on the liberty or freedom of movement of another;
b)   done with the intent to confine;
c)   without the consent of the victim;
d)   where the person so confining or restraining had no legal authority to confine or restrain the victim.

The differences between these crimes of illegal detention are explored in the following case.

STATE of North Carolina v. David Lee FULCHER
243 S.E.2d 338 (N.C. 1978).

Justice Lake delivered the opinion of the North Carolina Supreme Court.

[T]he defendant contends that the alleged two kidnappings were not "true kidnappings" but were merely acts incidental to the commission of the crimes against nature. Consequently, he contends that, as applied to him in the present case, G.S. 14-39(a)(2) violates both the Due Process Clause and the Equal Protection Clause of the Fourteenth Amendment to the Constitution of the United States. If so, the statute would also violate Article I, § 19, of the Constitution of North Carolina.

G.S. 14-39(a), effective 1 July 1975, provides:

(a) Any person who shall unlawfully confine, restrain or remove from one place to another, any other person 16 years of age or over without the consent of such person, or any other person under the age of 16 years without the consent of a parent or legal guardian of such person, shall be guilty of kidnapping if such confinement, restraint, or removal is for the purpose of:
(1) Holding such other person for ransom or as a hostage or using such other person as a shield; or
(2) Facilitating the commission of any felony or facilitating flight of any person following the commission of a felony; or
(3) Doing serious bodily harm to or terrorizing the person so confined, restrained or removed or any other person.

* * *

337

The Court of Appeals . . . [reasoned] the statutory offense of kidnapping is not committed unless the defendant confined or restrained the alleged victim for a substantial period of time or moved the victim a substantial distance. We must, therefore, determine whether G.S. 14-39(a) is reasonably susceptible of such construction.

The cardinal principle of statutory construction is that the intent of the Legislature is controlling. We are not at liberty to give to a statute a construction at variance with such intent, even though such construction appears to us to make the statute more desirable and to free it from constitutional difficulties. As an aid in ascertaining the intent of the Legislature, we must take into account the law prior to the enactment of the statute. Prior to the rewriting of G.S. 14-39 by the Session Laws of 1975, Ch. 843, this statute simply made kidnapping a felony punishable by imprisonment for life and did not define or prescribe the elements of the offense. Consequently, its elements were determined in accordance with the common law of this State. . . .

In *State v. Ingland*, 178 S.E.2d 577 (N.C. 1971), this Court held that "in order to constitute kidnapping there must be not only an unlawful detention by force or fraud but also a carrying away of the victim," the distance the victim is so carried away being immaterial. . . . In *State v. Dix*, 193 S.E.2d 897 (N.C. 1973), . . . we noted that in [our prior precedents], the asportations of the victims by the defendants were substantial, so that there was no necessity in those cases for us to establish the rule that the distance of the victim's removal from his original location was immaterial, and we rejected such rule, saying, "The 62-foot asportation [from one place to another in the same building] was purely incidental to defendant's assault upon the jailer and the rescue or jail delivery which he accomplished," and we held the asportation insufficient to support a conviction of kidnapping.

In *State v. Roberts*, 210 S.E. 2d 396 (N.C. 1974), we set aside a conviction for kidnapping where the defendant had pulled a child a distance of 80 to 90 feet (apparently for the purpose of committing a sexual assault upon her) and said: "Here the entire incident occurred during the seconds it took defendant to pull Kathy a distance of 80 to 90 feet. . . . To constitute the crime of kidnapping the defendant (1) must have falsely imprisoned his victim by acquiring complete dominion and control over him for some appreciable period of time, and (2) must have carried him beyond the immediate vicinity of the place of such false imprisonment. We hold the evidence, when considered in the light most favorable to the State, insufficient to establish either the false imprisonment or the carrying away element of the felony of kidnapping."

The present statutory definition of the crime of kidnapping, enacted in 1975, must be construed in the light of these then recent decisions of this Court. When so considered, it is clear that the Legislature intended to change the law as therein declared. That is, the Legislature rejected our decision in *State v. Ingland* to the effect that there must be both detention and asportation of the victim, the statute plainly stating that confinement, restraint or removal of the victim for any one of the three specified purposes is sufficient to constitute the offense of kidnapping. Thus, no asportation whatever is now required where there is the requisite confinement or restraint.

It is equally clear that the Legislature rejected our determinations . . . to the effect that, where the State relies upon asportation of the victim to establish a kidnapping, the asportation must be for a substantial distance and where the State relies upon "dominion and control," i.e., "confinement" or "restraint," such must continue "for some appreciable period of time." Thus, it was clearly the intent of the Legislature to make resort to a tape measure or a stop watch unnecessary in determining whether the crime of kidnapping has been committed.

It follows that the Court of Appeals erred in its holding that "substantiality" in terms of distance or time is an essential of kidnapping and in its pronouncements that the trial judge must instruct the jury that "confinement" or "restraint," as used in this statute, means confinement or restraint "for a substantial period" and that "removal," as used in this statute, requires a movement "for a substantial distance." We, therefore, cannot approve the instructions proposed by the Court of Appeals upon these points.

We find nothing in G.S. 14-39, as now written, which indicates any legislative intent to change our holding . . . to the effect that the use of fraud, threats, or intimidation is equivalent to the use of force or violence so far as a charge of kidnapping is concerned.

As used in G.S. 14-39, the term "confine" connotes some form of imprisonment within a given area, such as a room, a house or a vehicle. The term "restrain," while broad enough to include a restriction upon freedom of movement by confinement, connotes also such a restriction, by force, threat or fraud, without a confinement. Thus, one who is physically seized and held, or whose hands or feet are bound, or who, by the threatened use of a deadly weapon, is restricted in his freedom of motion, is restrained within the meaning of this statute. Such restraint, however, is not kidnapping unless it is (1) unlawful (i.e., without legal right), (2) without the consent of the person restrained (or of his parent or guardian if he be under 16 years of age), and (3) for one of the purposes specifically enumerated in the statute. One of those purposes is the facilitation of the commission of a felony.

It is self-evident that certain felonies (e.g., forcible rape and armed robbery) cannot be committed without some restraint of the victim. We are of the opinion, and so hold, that G.S. 14-39 was not intended by the Legislature to make a restraint, which is an inherent, inevitable feature of such other felony, also kidnapping so as to permit the conviction and punishment of the defendant for both crimes. To hold otherwise would violate the constitutional prohibition against double jeopardy. Pursuant to the above mentioned principle of statutory construction, we construe the word "restrain," as used in G.S. 14-39, to connote a restraint separate and apart from that which is inherent in the commission of the other felony.

On the other hand, it is well established that two or more criminal offenses may grow out of the same course of action, as where one offense is committed with the intent thereafter to commit the other and is actually followed by the commission of the other (e.g., a breaking and entering, with intent to commit larceny, which is followed by the actual commission of such larceny). In such a case, the perpetrator may be convicted of and punished for both crimes. Thus, there is no constitutional barrier to the conviction of a defendant for kidnapping, by restraining his victim, and also of another felony to facilitate which such restraint was committed, provided the restraint, which constitutes the kidnapping, is a separate, complete act, independent of and apart from the other felony. Such independent and separate restraint need not be, itself, substantial in time, under G.S. 14-39 as now written. Let us suppose, for example, a restraint for the purpose of committing rape followed by a rescue of the victim before the contemplated rape is accomplished. Such a restraint would constitute kidnapping under G.S. 14-39. We need not presently determine whether the perpetrator thereof could also be convicted of and punished for assault with intent to commit rape.

We turn now to the application of these principles to the facts as disclosed by the record in the present case. The evidence for the State is clearly sufficient to support a finding by the jury that the defendant bound the hands of each of the two women, procuring their submission thereto by his threat to use a deadly weapon to inflict serious injury upon them, thus restraining each woman within the meaning of G.S. 14-39, and that his purpose in so doing was to facilitate the commission of the felony of crime against nature. This having been done, the crime of kidnapping was complete, irrespective of whether the then contemplated crime against nature ever occurred.

The restraint of each of the women was separate and apart from, and not an inherent incident of, the commission upon her of the crime against nature, though closely related thereto in time. Each woman was so bound, and thereby restrained, so as to reduce her ability to resist, so as to prevent her escape from the room during the commission of the crime against nature upon the other, and so as to prevent her from going to the assistance of her companion. Thus, the restraint of each was for the purpose of facilitating the commission of the felony of crime against nature. It was also for the purpose of facilitating the flight of the defendant from the room after the perpetration of the two crimes against nature. Either such purpose satisfies the statutory definition of kidnapping.

* * *

It may well be that the Legislature, upon further consideration, may wish to amend G.S. 14-39 so as to restore to the definition of the crime of kidnapping so much of the rule of *State v. Ingland*, as made asportation of the victim an essential element of the offense, leaving confinement or restraint, for the prescribed purpose, without asportation punishable as false imprisonment, but not as kidnapping. It may also wish to consider the advisability of clearly defining "remove from one place to another" so as to require more than a minor asportation, such as is sufficient for larceny at common law. That is, the Legislature may deem it advisable so to word the statute that an assailant who, with knife or gun, forces his victim from the living room of her home into the bedroom where he rapes her, or forces a merchant from the public part of his store into his office and there compels him to open his safe, will not be punishable for kidnapping in addition to the offense of rape or the offense of armed robbery.

QUESTIONS

1.   The court determined that a man who bound his two female victims and forced them to perform oral sex on him committed both the crimes of forcible sodomy and kidnapping. Do you agree with the outcome of this case? Why or why not?

2.   As the court explains, kidnapping required both confinement for a substantial period of time and a movement (an "asportation") of some distance for conviction at common law. The legislature was deemed to have abolished those requirements, clearing the way for kidnapping convictions when short illegal confinements without any substantial movements were involved. How does such a definition of kidnapping differ from false imprisonment? Which approach do you think is the better one? Why?

CHAPTER 10
CRIMES AGAINST PROPERTY AND HABITATION

A. Larceny and Embezzlement

Under modern law, many offenses involving the taking of property that does not rightfully belong to oneself are covered by broad theft statues. But at common law, there were dozens of different types of thefts. A brief study of two of these common law theft crime – larceny and embezzlement – should illustrate why the law has collapsed many of the common law theft offenses into broad, general theft laws.

The common law crime of *larceny* required proof of the following elements:

1) the taking (obtaining control);
2) and asportation (a "carrying away" or "movement");
3) of tangible personal property;
4) of another who had lawful possession of the property;
5) by trespass (i.e., without consent)
6) with *animus furandi* — the specific intent or purpose to steal.

These six elements required proof of some very specific things. For example, if one obtained control, but did not actually carry away the property of another, then no larceny would be deemed to have occurred. Similarly, the requirement of the property being "personal property" excluded realty, services, and intangibles. And the taking had to be accomplished by trespass, meaning without the owner's consent. If consent was given, but it was induced by fraud, then the crime was "larceny by trick," a different theft crime at common law from regular larceny.

As the fourth element states, the property must be taken from someone in *lawful possession* of the property. Thus, if the defendant himself or herself had lawful possession at the time of a taking, there is no larceny, but rather an embezzlement (discussed later). Similarly, if the person from whom the personal property was taken and carried away did not have lawful possession of it to begin with (say, for example, that he or she had stolen it from its rightful owner), then no larceny would be deemed to have taken place either since the element of lawful possession was missing.

Lawful possession is a term of art under the law. Contrary to the common meaning of the term possession, it does not have anything to do with physically possessing property. Rather, lawful possession involves having a great scope of authority to deal with property – such as owning it outright. In contrast, someone who does not have broad authority to deal with property would be deemed to have mere *custody* over that property, not lawful possession.

Ordinarily, a low-level employee only has custody of an employer's property, and can therefore commit a larceny of such property. A high-level employee, like a bank manager, on the other hand, typically has greater authority over property entrusted to his or her care and would therefore not be guilty of larceny for taking such property, but rather would be guilty of embezzlement.

The mens rea requirement in the sixth element required proof that the defendant intended to permanently deprive the rightful owner of his or her interest in the property. In lieu of such permanent intent to deprive, an intent to create a substantial risk of loss or an intent to sell or pledge the goods to the owner is sufficient to constitute animus furandi. Any intent that did not meet these criteria was insufficient to establish animus furandi. For example, if the defendant mistakenly believed he or she took his or her own property, there was no larceny. Also, where the defendant only intended to borrow the personal property of another and then return it later to the person in lawful possession of it, there was no larceny. Similarly, if someone took property under some claim of right, such as to keep the person property of another as repayment for a debt, then there was no larceny, as there was no animus furandi.

As with most crimes, there must be a union of actus reus and mens rea. The timing of the mens rea requirement, therefore, was critical, as it had to exist at the time the actus reus occurred. In other words, animus furandi had to exist *at the time of the taking* for a larceny to have taken place. Thus, if one took and carried away the person property of another in lawful possession of that property without his or her consent, but did not develop permanent intent to deprive the owner of the property until some later period of time, no larceny took place under the common law.

Modern law has eliminated many of these common law technicalities. The Model Penal Code, for example, eliminated the need for an actual asportation and, in its place, substituted "exercise unlawful control." Modern statutory definitions have expanded the requirement of tangible personal property to include services and intangibles, such as stock and goodwill. And many jurisdictions have abolished the distinction between a theft "by trespass" (i.e., without consent) and one "by trick" in which consent was fraudulently obtained.

The distinction between lawful possession and custody, however, has been largely maintained, although the definitions have been modernized in some jurisdictions. The essence of the distinction, however, continues to differentiate larceny-type thefts from embezzlements in many jurisdictions. The common law crime of *embezzlement* required proof of the following elements:

1)   the fraudulent conversion;
2)   of personal property;
3)   of another;
4)   by a person in lawful possession of that property.

The first element required that the state prove the defendant had dealt with property in a manner inconsistent with the arrangement by which the defendant had possession of it; that is the definition of "conversion." But the conversion had to be fraudulent. Thus, as with larceny, embezzlement was not committed if the property was taken pursuant to some claim of right.

Recall that property taken with intent to borrow was not larceny, as borrowing connotes an intent to return the property, thus negating animus furandi. Animus furandi is not an element of embezzlement, though. The element of fraudulent conversion is avoided in the "borrowing" situation only if the defendant intended to restore the *exact* property in the *exact* same condition. If the intent was to restore similar or substantially identical property in only a similar condition, an embezzlement has taken place. See, for example, that if $100 of money was taken and $100 was intended to be returned and was, in fact, returned, an embezzlement has nonetheless occurred unless the same bills with the exact serial numbers were returned.

Modern embezzlement statutes, although still distinguishing between levels of authority over property, have eased the formal distinctions between lawful possession and custody. Consider the following case.

Veronica Lois GWALTNEY v. COMMONWEALTH of Virginia
452 S.E.2d 687 (Va. Ct. App. 1995).

Opinion by Judge Lawrence L. Koontz, Jr.

Veronica Lois Gwaltney appeals her conviction for embezzlement in violation of Code § 18.2-111. Gwaltney . . . contends the evidence was insufficient to prove the entrustment relationship necessary for embezzlement. For the reasons that follow, we affirm Gwaltney's conviction.

The charge of embezzlement arose out of the disappearance of one thousand dollars from a teller's cash drawer at the bank where Gwaltney was employed.

* * *

Gwaltney further contends the evidence was insufficient to show that an entrustment relationship existed between her and her employer with respect to money kept in another teller's cash drawer and that without such evidence her crime would be merely larceny. While we agree that the specific charge of embezzlement requires proof of elements different from those of common law larceny, we reject Gwaltney's assertion that the evidence presented was insufficient to establish those elements. Gwaltney's challenge to the sufficiency of the evidence in effect asserts that the Commonwealth was required to prove the crime charged in the indictment. We agree that the discretion in selection of charges afforded the Commonwealth is a two-edged sword. Once an indictment is brought and jeopardy has attached, the Commonwealth must prove that charge or a lesser-included offense in order to obtain a conviction. *See Martin v. Commonwealth*, 414 S.E.2d 401, 403 (Va. 1992). Discretion implies a thoughtful, informed choice, and here, the designation of embezzlement as the specific form of larceny to be proved was not mere caprice. Code § 18.2-111, as in effect at the time of Gwaltney's trial, required the Commonwealth to state with specificity the larceny statute it would rely on if requested to do so. By stating the statute in the indictment, the Commonwealth avoided confusion and delay that might otherwise result. Accordingly, we assume the Commonwealth understood its duty and undertook to satisfy the burden it had imposed on itself.

Embezzlement, a statutory crime, was devised by legislatures to address an inadequacy in the common law of larceny. Originally, embezzlement was distinguished from common law larceny by the manner in which the property was first obtained. Whereas larceny required a contemporaneous unlawful possession and conversion by caption and asportation, an unlawful taking by trespass, a "black letter" embezzlement statute requires proof of a lawful possession prior to or contemporaneous with an intentional conversion by misappropriation. . . . "One who has mere custody of property, as distinguished from legal possession, and feloniously appropriates the property to his own use is guilty of larceny . . . . The distinction between embezzlement and larceny may exist where the accused was given considerable control over the property." 26 AM. JUR. 2d Embezzlement § 5 (1966); *see also State v. Ward*, 562 A.2d 1040, 1042 (Vt. 1989) (a store clerk had "custody" rather than "possession" of the money which he took from his till, and so was guilty of larceny, not embezzlement). Thus, Gwaltney's assertion that her crime . . . was common law larceny rather than larceny by embezzlement has potential merit if the statutory definition of embezzlement in this Commonwealth parallels the traditional definition of that crime.

Even with the enactment of embezzlement statutes, a deficiency remained in the law with respect to the conversion of property that was neither wholly in the possession of another nor lawfully in the possession of the malefactor. In some instances, legislatures have addressed these "gray areas" of theft by creating additional statutory crimes deemed to be larceny. *See, e.g., State v. Kornegay*, 326 S.E.2d 881, 896-97 (N.C. 1985) (discussing the origin of North Carolina's "Malfeasance of a Corporate Agent" statute). In this Commonwealth, our legislature has addressed the problem by adopting a broad definition of embezzlement, deeming it to be punishable as larceny and defining an array of activities which fall within its ambit.

In pertinent part, Code § 18.2-111 defines embezzlement as the wrongful and fraudulent taking of "any money . . . which [the accused] shall have received . . . by virtue of his office, trust, or employment . . . ." We recognize that "the plain, obvious, and rational meaning of a statute is always preferred to any curious, narrow or strained construction." *Branch v. Commonwealth*, 419 S.E.2d 422, 424 (Va. 1992). Nonetheless, "although penal laws are to be construed strictly [against the Commonwealth], they 'ought not to be construed so strictly as to defeat the obvious intention of the legislature.'" *Willis v. Commonwealth*, 393 S.E.2d 405, 411 (Va. 1990). . . .

The definition of embezzlement in Code § 18.2-111 does not parallel the traditional definition of that crime; rather, it proscribes a broad category of theft offenses, including embezzlement, which fall outside the common law definition of larceny. It is neither a curious nor strained construction of the statute to conclude that the legislature intended to proscribe conversions of property accomplished by virtue of the position of trust given any employee.

This Court has said that "to establish the statutory crime of embezzlement under Code § 18.2-111, it is necessary to prove that the accused wrongfully appropriated to her use or benefit, with the intent to deprive the owner thereof of the property entrusted to her by virtue of her employment." *Waymack v. Commonwealth*, 358 S.E.2d 765, 766 (Va. 1987). Gwaltney was placed in a position of trust by her employer. While she was directly responsible for accounting only for the receipt and disbursement of funds to and from the cash drawer assigned to her, Gwaltney's position of trust extended beyond the confines of her station to the entire teller line and other areas of the bank where her duties would bring her into proximity of her employer's property. The entrustment was inherent in her employment rather than in the daily act of receiving into her possession and dispersing funds from a specific cash drawer. But for the trust placed in her by her employer, Gwaltney would not have been able to accomplish the conversion of cash from another teller's cash drawer to her own use. Accordingly, the Commonwealth established the wrongful taking of money received "by virtue of [her] office, trust or employment" in violation of Code § 18.2-111. For these reasons we affirm Gwaltney's conviction.

QUESTIONS

1.   This case illustrates how some jurisdictions have broadened the scope of their theft laws to eliminate the technicalities that once were required to prove embezzlement. In such jurisdictions, the level of authority exercised by the defendant over the property is no longer determinative. Rather, misappropriation of property entrusted to an employee is all that is necessary. Which approach – this one as used in *Gwaltney*, or the common law approach – do you think is the better approach from a public policy standpoint? Why?

2.   If Virginia had followed the common law approach to the distinction between larceny and embezzlement, of which crime would Ms. Gwaltney have been guilty? Why? *Larceny*

She was an employee → lawful possession

B. Burglary, Criminal Trespass, and Robbery

Upon returning from a vacation to find one's home has been broken into and one's personal possessions have been stolen, people often exclaim "I've been robbed." But under the criminal law, a burglary has taken place, not a robbery. A **burglary** is a crime against property or habitation in which a defendant illegally enters a dwelling with the purpose of committing a felony once inside. The common law elements of burglary were as follows:

1)   a breaking
2)   and entering
3)   of a dwelling
4)   of another
5)   at nighttime
6)   with the intent to commit a felony in the structure

Each one of these elements had special definitions at common law. A "breaking" was defined as the creation or enlargement of an opening. Moreover, the creation or enlargement of such an opening had to be accomplished by at least minimal force, fraud, or intimidation. Accordingly, if a person obtained the owner's consent to enter the premise, the entry was not a breaking. Similarly, if one walked through a wide-open door or crawled through a wide-open window, there was no breaking. And without such a breaking, there was no burglary at common law.

"Entering" was defined as placing any portion of the body into the place being burgled. Alternatively, an entering could be accomplished by using some instrument that was used to commit a crime once inside the dwelling.

A "dwelling" was defined as a structure regularly used for sleeping purposes. Even if such a structure was also regularly used for other purposes, so long as it was regularly used for sleeping purposes, it constituted a dwelling for the purposes of the crime of burglary.

At common law, one could not burglarize one's own dwelling. Actually, ownership was irrelevant. So long as the dwelling was occupied by someone other than the defendant, the dwelling would be deemed that "of another."

The common law crime of burglary could only be committed at night. Night was defined as an hour before sunset to an hour after sunrise. Even if all of the other elements of the crime were met, if they occurred during the day, no burglary could be deemed to have occurred at common law.

Finally, the person breaking and entering the dwelling of another at night had to have the intent to commit a felony once inside at the time he or she entered the dwelling. If there was no such intent, (e.g., one simply wanted to look around and then leave), then no burglary could be deemed to have occurred at common law. Nor would any intent formed *after* entering the dwelling suffice since the intent to commit a felony had to exist at the time of the breaking and entering. It should also be noted that the intended felony did need not need to be carried out. The intent to commit the felony alone was sufficient under the common law.

Modern burglary laws have eliminated many of these arcane technicalities. Most modern burglary statutes no longer require an actual breaking; illegal entry or remaining unlawfully on premises will suffice. No longer must the structure be a dwelling; warehouses and office buildings can thus be burglarized under modern laws. The nighttime requirement has been abolished so that time of day is normally irrelevant to the definition of the crime. And, finally, the intent requirement has been modified in many jurisdictions so that the intent to commit any crime – felony or misdemeanor – will suffice.

Under both the common law and modern burglary statutes, the actor's intent is key to the definition of the crime. Without the intent to commit a crime once inside the structure, there is no burglary. There is, however, the crime of *criminal trespass.*

Robbery, in contrast to burglary and criminal trespass which are crimes against property, is also a crime against a person. It is basically a larceny committed by force or threat of force against the person in lawful possession of the property being stolen. The common law elements of robbery were:

1)   a taking;
2)   of the personal property of another;
3)   from the other's person or in that person's presence;
4)   by force or threats of force to the victim or some person in the victim's presence;
5)   with the intent to permanently deprive the victim of the property.

The type of force contemplated to effectuate a robbery involves a threat of immediate death or physical injury. The classic example of a robbery is when an armed person holds a gun or a knife up to a victim and says, "Your money or your life." Larceny, a crime against property, is a lesser included offense of robbery. Neither, however, are lesser included offenses of burglary, as illustrated by the following case.

===

Johnny Lee KINSEY, Appellant, v. STATE of Arkansas, Appellee.
716 S.W.2d 188 (Ark. 1986).

Holt, Chief Justice.

Mrs. Elaine Paul was the primary witness in the trial of the appellant [Johnny Kinsey]. [Kinsey] came to her door holding the prescription drugs she had ordered for her husband, Dr. Edgar Paul. She opened the door and [Kinsey] came toward her with a gun, backed her to the wall, and told her to hold out her fingers. He inspected her jewelry, commenting that it was "cheap." When Dr. Paul entered the room and told [Kinsey] to get out, the [Kinsey] shot Dr. Paul in the right shoulder. Dr. Paul fell to the floor, and Mrs. Paul ran to the back of the house where she pushed an alarm button and called the police. When she returned [Kinsey] had fled, taking only the medicine.

[Kinsey] appellant contends that the evidence was insufficient to prove that he had the intent or purpose to commit theft as required by the aggravated robbery statutes. . . . Intent or purpose to commit a crime is a state of mind which is not ordinarily capable of proof by direct evidence, so it must be inferred from the circumstances. The jury is allowed to draw upon their common knowledge and experience in reaching a verdict from the facts directly proved . . . . The motives of [Kinsey] in holding Mrs. Paul at gunpoint while he inspected her jewelry were clear and the jury justifiably concluded that appellant intended to commit theft. It follows that Mrs. Paul's testimony was also sufficient to convict the appellant of burglary for unlawfully entering her home with the purpose of committing an offense punishable by imprisonment.

The appellant next argues that the double jeopardy clause prohibit[s] his conviction of attempted first degree murder because it was established by proof of the same or less than all the elements required to establish the aggravated robbery. In some instances this argument would have merit, in that one form of aggravated robbery includes the element that the defendant "inflicts or attempts to inflict death or serious injury upon another person" with the purpose of committing a theft. In this case, however, the aggravated robbery and the attempted first degree murder were two different criminal actions with separate victims. The aggravated robbery had already been fully performed when the appellant held Mrs. Paul at gunpoint and examined her jewelry with the purpose of committing a theft. The attempted first degree murder occurred separately when the appellant shot Dr. Paul. Although crimes are committed in the same escapade, they are not part of the same conduct when committed against different persons.

Neither is aggravated robbery a lesser included offense of burglary. Aggravated robbery requires some type of serious force or threat of force used with the purpose of committing a theft, none of which is required to commit burglary. Burglary requires only that the defendant enters or remains unlawfully in an occupiable structure with the purpose of committing any offense punishable by imprisonment. Although aggravated robbery was the punishable offense which the appellant had the purpose of committing, a defendant may be convicted of the burglary for entering the home and the subsequent offense he commits after the entry. The unlawful entry is an independent and substantive offense with the result that cumulative penalties may be imposed for entering with intent to steal and for stealing. Affirmed.

QUESTIONS

1.   This case demonstrates the difference between burglary and robbery – a distinction that is frequently confused. Neither one requires the other to occur; neither one is a lessor included offense of the other; but both may occur during the same factual series of events. Which do you think is the more dangerous crime deserving a more severe criminal punishment? Why?

2.   As you well know by this point in your study of criminal law, inferring intent from the totality of the circumstances is often the only way the law can decide if the defendant entertained the requisite mens rea for a crime. From what objective facts did the court infer Mr. Kinsey's intent that satisfied the mens rea requirement for burglary? For robbery? Do you agree with the court's reasoning on either count? Explain.

C. Arson

Common law *arson* was defined by the following four elements:

1)   the malicious (i.e., intentional or with reckless disregard of an obvious risk);
2)   burning;
3)   of the dwelling;
4)   of another.

"Burning" was a term of art at common law. It required some damage to the dwelling by fire, as opposed to smoke or water damage. But there was never any requirement that the dwelling be destroyed or even significantly damaged. A "mere charring" was sufficient to impose arson liability.

The use of the term "dwelling" had the same meaning for the crime of arson as it had for the crime of burglary: a place regularly used for sleeping. Interestingly, though, one could not commit an arson of one's own home at common law since the dwelling had to be that of another to qualify as a true arson. When one burned one's own house, it was the common law crime of house burning. Modern arson statutes eliminate the technicalities of a dwelling and the requirement that the structure be that of another. Thus, one can now commit an arson of one's own home, office, or warehouse.

Malice was the common law mens rea for the crime. Accordingly, while specific intent to burn the dwelling of another clearly would have satisfied the above elements, such specific intent was not required. Acting with a reckless disregard of a substantial and unjustifiable risk of fire would suffice. Modern laws have modified the mens rea for arson. Some states differentiate arson in the first degree (or aggravated arson) when it is done with specific intent (i.e., purpose or knowledge), from arson the second degree (or simple arson), which is an arson accomplished via reckless conduct. Other jurisdictions differentiate the levels of arson based on the type of structure, with an occupied dwelling being the most serious type of arson. But as the following case illustrates, neat categories of mens rea are not always easily applied to arson.

=====

Kimberly LAWRENCE v. The STATE of Georgia
453 S.E.2d 733 (Ga. 1995).

Hunt, Chief Justice.

Kimberly Lawrence was found guilty of involuntary manslaughter, arson, aggravated battery, felony murder and cruelty to children. . . . Lawrence argues that the evidence was insufficient to support the arson conviction. We disagree.

In this case, a jury was authorized to find that on the night of November 25, 1991, Kimberly Lawrence awoke when she heard her daughter Tyesha crying for her. Entering the bedroom, she found her four-year-old son Taiwan lying bloody and motionless in his bed. Suspecting that her seven-year-old son had stabbed his brother and thinking that she could cover up the cause of the wounds by starting a fire, she turned on the burners on her stove, ignited newspapers and placed the burning papers under a couch. She then left the room, with the fire burning, and went back to bed. She got up again only to see why the fire alarm had not gone off; at this time the fire was out of control and the apartment was engulfed in flames. Her son Taiwan was killed, her daughter Tyesha suffered third degree burns, lacerations and a punctured lung, and ten units in the apartment complex were destroyed in the fire.

Under § 16-7-60, a person commits first degree arson when she knowingly damages a dwelling under such circumstances that it is reasonably foreseeable that human life might be endangered. Here, the evidence clearly authorized a jury to find Lawrence guilty of arson.

Lawrence argues that she did not intend to endanger a life. Even if she did not specifically intend to endanger a life, she did, as she admitted, set the fire, and damage apartments in the complex, under circumstances that endangered human life, and "that is all that the statute requires be proved." *Sweet v. State*, 382 S.E.2d 376 (Ga. 1989). Lawrence argues further that under *Reinhardt v. State*, 428 S.E.2d 333 (Ga. 1993), arson requires an intent not only to set a fire but also to damage a building, and that there was insufficient evidence of her intent to damage the building. This argument is meritless. There was evidence from which a jury could determine that Lawrence set the fire to cover up the stabbing of her younger son, an act which necessarily involved damage to the building. Indeed, reviewing the evidence in a light most favorable to the jury's determination of guilt, we conclude that a rational trier of fact could have found Lawrence guilty of all of the crimes for which she was convicted.

* * *

Judgment affirmed.

QUESTIONS

1.   Does the arson statute at issue in *Lawrence* require a higher or lower degree of mens rea than the common law crime of arson required?

2.   The court concluded there was sufficient evidence from which to infer Mrs. Lawrence's intent to both endanger human life and to damage a building. Do you agree? Why or why not?

3.   If you represented Mrs. Lawrence at trial, what defenses might you offer on her behalf? Evaluate the likelihood of success of each of the defenses you might offer.

4.   If you were the sentencing judge and had unlimited discretion to sentence the defendant to anything ranging from "time served" to probation to a maximum of 25 years in prison, what sentence would you impose? Why?

INDEX

Abandonment 99
Accessory after the Fact 113
Accomplice 104
Actus Reus 40
Administrative Law 1
Adultery 305
Affirmative Defense 32
Aiding and Abetting 104
Arson 346
Assault 328
Attempt 86
Attendant Circumstances 40
Battered Women's Syndrome 233
Battery 328
Bentham, Jeremy 6, 14
Beyond a Reasonable Doubt 33
Burden of Persuasion 32
Burden of Production 32
Burglary 344
Causation 80
Child Abuse 331
Child Molestation 310
Child Neglect 336
Common Law 1
Competency to Stand Trial 162
Complicity Theory 103
Conspiracy 119
Constitutional Law 1
Crime Control Model 119
Criminal Trespass 345
Culpability 5
Custody 341
Defense of Others 218
Defense of Property 221
Derivative Liability 110
Devlin, Lord Patrick 14
Diminished Capacity 202
Due Process Model 119
Embezzlement 342
Euthanasia 279
Evidence 30
Facilitation 103
False Imprisonment 337
Fornication 305
General Deterrence 5
Hart, H.L.A. 14
Homicide 252
    Corpus Delicti 255
    Criminally Negligent Homicide 274
    Depraved Heart Murder 263
    Felony Murder 265
    Involuntary Manslaughter 273
    Malice Aforethought 259
    Merger Rule 269
    Murder in the First Degree 259
    Murder in the Second Degree 263
    Unlawful Act Manslaughter 279
    Vehicular Manslaughter 274
    Voluntary Manslaughter 270
Imperfect Self Defense 210
Impossibility 93
Incest 310
Inchoate Offenses 86
Infancy 159
Inferences 32

Insanity 174
    ALI/MPC Affective Test 177
    Durham Rule 177
    Guilty But Mentally Ill 180
    Guilty Except Insane 181
    Insanity Defense Reform Act of 1984 179
    Irresistible Impulse Test 178
    M'Naghten Test 176
    Mens Rea Approach 194
Involuntary Intoxication 157
Judicial Notice 31
Kidnapping 336
Larceny 341
Law Enforcement and the Use of Force 224
Learned Helplessness 233
Legality, Principle of 2, 5
Lewd and Lascivious Conduct 310
Megan's Law 311
Mens Rea 40, 49
    General Intent 50
    Knowledge 55
    Malice 54
    Negligence 57
    Purpose 54
    Recklessness 57
    Specific Intent 50
    Strict Liability 64
Mill, John Stuart 14
Mistake of Fact 144
Mistake of Law 146
Mistaken Intervener Rule 219
Necessity 149
Obscenity 317
Omissions (as actus reus) 44
Overt Act (for conspiracy) 134
Packer, Herbert 119
Parental Privilege 332
Penal Codes 2
Pinkerton Rule 140
Possession 341
Precedent 1
Presumption 30
Proportionality, Principle of 6
Prostitution 311
Punishment, Theories of 4-6
Rape 294
Rape Shield Laws 300
Result 40
Robbery 345
Self-defense 210
    Castle Doctrine 212
    Deadly Force 211
Sexual Assault/sexual Battery 303
Sexually Dangerous Person Laws 311
Sodomy 14, 304
Solicitation 101
Specific Deterrence 5
Statutory Law 1
Statutory Rape 305
Suicide 279
Transferred Intent 77
Vicarious Liability 69
Voluntary Intoxication 154
Wharton Rule 122